DATE DUE

FE 20 '97			
MR 13 '97			
RENEW			
MR 11 '99			
RENEW			
AP 1 '99			
MY 4 '99			
DE 29 '99			
AP 18 '05			
MY 9 '05			
MY 31 '05			

DEMCO 38-296

The Cultural Landscape

An Introduction to Human Geography

Third Edition

The Cultural Landscape
An Introduction to Human Geography

James M. Rubenstein

Miami University, Oxford, Ohio

Macmillan Publishing Company
New York

Maxwell Macmillan Canada
Toronto

Maxwell Macmillan International
New York   Oxford   Singapore   Sydney

Cover photo: Uighur family, Western China,
© Galen Rowell 1989

Editor: Paul F. Corey
Production Editor: Mary Harlan
Art Coordinator: Mark D. Garrett
Photo Researcher: Anne Vega
Text Designer: Cynthia Brunk
Production Buyer: Patricia A. Tonneman

This book was set in Garamond by the Clarinda
Company and was printed and bound by R. R. Donnelley
and Sons Company. The cover was printed by Lehigh
Press, Inc.

Macmillan Publishing Company
866 Third Avenue
New York, New York 10022

Macmillan Publishing Company is part of the
Maxwell Communication Group of Companies.

Maxwell Macmillan Canada, Inc.
1200 Eglington Avenue East, Suite 200
Don Mills, Ontario M3C 3N1

Library of Congress Cataloging-in-Publication Data
Rubenstein, James M.
      The cultural landscape : an introduction to human
geography /
      James M. Rubenstein.—3rd ed.
          p.   cm.
      Includes bibliographical references and index.
      ISBN 0-02-404535-7
      1. Human geography.   I. Title.
GF41.R82   1991   91-19600
304.2—dc20   CIP

Printing: 1 2 3 4 5 6 7 8 9 Year: 2 3 4 5

The Goode's Homolosine Equal-Area Projection base
maps in this text are used by permission of the
University of Chicago Committee on Geographical
Studies. Goode Base Map Series copyright © The
University of Chicago.

Preface

What is geography? Geography is the study of where things are located on the earth's surface and the reasons for the location. The word *geography,* invented by the ancient Greek scholar Eratosthenes, is based on two Greek words. *Geo* means "the earth," and *graphy* means "to write." Geographers ask two simple questions: where and why. Where are people and activities located on the earth's surface? Why are they located in particular places?

Geography as a Social Science

Recent world events lend a sense of urgency to geographic inquiry. Geography's spatial perspective helps relate political unrest in Eastern Europe, the Middle East, and other regions to the spatial distributions of cultural characteristics such as languages and religions, demographic patterns such as population growth and migration, and natural resources such as energy and minerals.

Does the world face an overpopulation crisis? Geographers study population problems by comparing the arrangements of human organizations and natural resources across the earth's surface. Given these spatial distributions, geographers conclude that some locations may have more people

than can be provided for, while other places may be underpopulated.

Similarly, geographers examine the energy crisis by relating the spatial distributions of energy sources and consumption. Geographers find that users of energy are located in places with different social, economic, and political institutions than the producers of energy. Geographers seek first to describe the distribution of activities, such as the production and consumption of energy, and then to explain the relationships between these distributions and other human and physical phenomena.

The main purpose of this book is to introduce students to the study of geography as a social science by emphasizing the relevance of geographic concepts to human problems. It is intended for use in college-level introductory human or cultural geography courses. The book is written for students who have not previously taken a college-level geography course and have had little, if any, geography in high school.

Divisions within Geography

Because geography is a broad subject, some specialization is inevitable. At the same time, one of geography's strengths is its diversity of approaches. Rather than being forced to adhere rigorously to established disciplinary laws, geographers can combine a variety of methods and approaches. This tradition stimulates innovative thinking, although students who are looking for a series of ironclad laws may be disappointed.

Human versus physical geography. Geography is both a physical and a social science. When geography concentrates on the distribution of physical features, such as climate, soil, and vegetation, it is a natural science. When it studies cultural characteristics, such as language, social customs, and industries, geography is a social science. This division is reflected in some colleges, where physical geography courses may carry natural science credit and human geography courses social science credit.

While this book is concerned with geography from a social science perspective, one of the distinctive characteristics of geography is its use of physical science concepts to help explain spatial patterns. The distinction between physical and human geography reflects differences in emphasis, not an absolute separation.

Topical versus regional approach. Geographers face a choice between a topical and a regional approach. The topical approach, which is used in this book, starts by identifying a set of important cultural issues to be studied, such as population distribution, migration patterns, and political disputes. Geographers using the topical approach examine the location of different aspects of the topic and the reasons for the distribution.

The alternative approach is regional. Regional geographers start by selecting a portion of the earth and studying the environment, people, and activities within the area. The regional geography approach is used in courses on Europe, Africa, Asia, or other areas of the earth. Although this book is organized by topics, geography students should be aware of the location of places in the world. A separate index section locates the book's maps. One indispensable aid in the study of regions is an atlas, which can also be used to find unfamiliar places that may pop up in the news.

Descriptive versus systematic method. Whether using a topical or a regional approach, geographers can select either a descriptive or a systematic method. Again, the distinction is one of emphasis, not an absolute separation. The descriptive method emphasizes the collection of a variety of details about a particular location. This method has been used primarily by regional geographers to illustrate the uniqueness of a particular location on the earth's surface. The systematic method emphasizes the identification of several basic theories or techniques developed by geographers to explain the distribution of activities.

This book uses both the descriptive and systematic methods because total dependence on either approach is unsatisfactory. An entirely descriptive book would contain a large collection of individual examples not organized into a unified structure. A completely systematic approach suffers because some of the theories and techniques are so abstract that they lack meaning for the student. Geographers who depend only on the systematic approach may have difficulty explaining important contemporary issues.

Features

This book is sensitive to the study needs of students. Each chapter is clearly structured to help students understand the material and effectively review from the book.

Outline. The book discusses the following main topics:

- **What basic concepts do geographers use?** Chapter 1 provides an introduction to basic geographic concepts, as well as a brief summary of the development of the science of geography. Geographers employ several concepts to describe the distribution of people and activities across the cultural landscape and to explain reasons underlying the observed distribution.
- **Where are people located in the world?** Chapters 2 and 3 examine the distribution and growth of the world's population, as well as the movement of people from one place to another. Why do some places on the earth's surface contain a large number of people or attract newcomers while other places are sparsely inhabited?
- **How are different cultural characteristics distributed?** Chapters 4 through 7 analyze the

distribution of different cultural traits and beliefs and the problems that result from those spatial patterns. Important cultural characteristics include political systems, language, religion, and daily customs, such as the choice of food, clothing, shelter, and leisure activities. Geographers look for similarities and differences in the cultural characteristics at different places, as well as reasons for their distribution.

◆ **How do people earn a living in different parts of the world?** Human survival is dependent on the acquisition of an adequate food supply. One of the most significant distinctions in the cultural landscape is whether people produce the food they need directly from the land or obtain it from wealth earned by performing other types of work. Chapters 8 through 10 look at these ways of earning a living. These chapters describe the economic activities people undertake in different regions and the factors that account for the distribution of agricultural and industrial activities.

◆ **How do people organize the earth's surface?** Few people undertake cultural and economic activities in complete isolation from others; instead, nearly everyone lives in some sort of settlement. Chapters 11 and 12 examine the distribution of settlements across the earth's surface, the reasons for their origin and growth, and problems faced by people living in urban settlements.

◆ **What problems result from using the earth's resources?** The final chapter is devoted to a study of three issues related to the use of the earth's resources: energy, pollution, and food supply. Geographers recognize that cultural problems result from the depletion, destruction, and inefficient use of the world's resources.

Chapter organization. To help the student use the material in this book, each chapter is organized with these study aids:

◆ **Case Study.** Each chapter opens with a case study that illustrates some of the key concepts presented in the text. The case studies are generally drawn from news events or from daily experiences familiar to residents of North America.

◆ **Key Issues.** Each chapter contains a set of three or four key issues around which the chapter material is organized. These questions reappear as major headings within the chapter.

Among the careers that geographers pursue is cartography, the science of making maps.

◆ **Key Terms.** The key terms in each chapter are indicated in bold type when they are first introduced. These terms are also defined at the end of each chapter.

◆ **Summary.** The key issues are repeated at the end of the chapter with a brief review of the important concepts covered in detail in the text.

◆ **Case Study Revisited.** Additional information related to the chapter's case study may be used to reinforce some of the main points.

◆ **Thinking Geographically.** A new feature in this edition, this section offers five questions based on concepts and material covered in the chapter. The questions help students apply geographic concepts to explore issues more intensively.

◆ **Further Readings.** At the end of each chapter, a list of books and articles is provided for students who wish to study the subject further.

Appendix. A special appendix on scale and map projections enhances the text discussion of the subject. We are grateful to Phillip Muehrcke, Professor of Geography at the University of Wisconsin–Madison, and former president of the American Cartographic Association, for his clear explanation of the subject.

Ancillaries. Material has been prepared to help instructors use this text. The Instructor's Manual includes a review of each chapter's objectives, test questions related to the text, projects and exercises for students to do at home or in a laboratory environment, and blank base maps. A computerized test bank and transparencies of selected maps and illustrations are also available.

Suggestions for Use

The Cultural Landscape can be used in an introductory human or cultural geography course that extends over one semester, one quarter, or two quarters. An instructor in a one-semester course could devote one week to each of the chapters, leaving time for examinations.

In a one-quarter course, the instructor might need to omit some of the book's material. A course with more of a cultural orientation could include Chapters 1 through 8, plus Chapter 13. If the course has more of an economic orientation, then the appropriate chapters would be 1 through 3 and 7 through 12 or, if time permits, 13.

A two-quarter course could be organized around the culturally oriented Chapters 1 through 7 during the first quarter and the more economically oriented Chapters 8 through 13 during the second quarter. Topics of particular interest to the instructor or students could be discussed for more than one week. The Instructor's Manual includes topics for further discussion in each chapter.

Changes

Readers familiar with the second edition will see some change in content. The explanation of human geography's two fundamental analytic traditions—human-environment and regional studies—has been restructured in Chapter 1 to emphasize such concepts as integration, diffusion, and interaction, as well as physical processes that directly relate to human geography issues. Chapter 1 also provides an expanded section on the historical development of geographic thought.

The economic geography sections have received additional information concerning the role of transnational corporations, the international division of labor, and gender-related development issues. New introductory case studies have been added concerning the role of women in economic development in Bangladesh and relocating industrial work from the United States to Mexico.

Recent changes in Eastern Europe and the Soviet Union receive added attention in this edition. Sections have been added concerning the impact of political changes, including the breakup of the Warsaw Pact, German unification, and the political restructuring from unitary to federal systems. Demographic, cultural, and economic differences among regions within the Soviet Union and such Eastern European states as Czechoslovakia and Yugoslavia are discussed. Also addressed are problems related to industrial restructuring and pollution.

Problems in the Middle East and southwestern Asia are addressed in light of the 1991 Gulf war and unrest in the Caucasus. With the end of the Cold War, conflicts such as those in the Middle East that involve the lack of correspondence between the boundaries of states and of nationalities acquire added importance as organizing elements in global political geography.

The number of maps and photographs has increased by more than twenty-five percent. U.S. maps depict such subjects as AIDS, population change during the 1980s, Japanese-owned automobile plants, acid rain, and golf courses. New world maps include dependency on nuclear power, female attendance at school, female literacy rates, and purchasing power. Maps have been added for several cities, including Paris, Glasgow, Rio de Janeiro, ancient Ur, and Dayton, Ohio. Boundary changes in central Europe, income differences within the Soviet Union, and areas eligible for European Community assistance are among the new maps of Europe and the Soviet Union.

Acknowledgments

The successful completion of a book like this requires the contributions of many people. I would like to gratefully acknowledge the help I received.

A number of people reviewed portions of the manuscript at various stages in the revision process and offered excellent suggestions. These reviewers included:

- Brock Brown, University of Colorado
- Christine Drake, Old Dominion University
- Charles Farmer, Frostburg State University
- George Lewis, Boston University
- Robert Martin, Kutztown University
- David James Nemeth, University of Toledo
- Leland Pederson, University of Arizona

- Roger M. Selya, University of Cincinnati
- Roger Stump, State University of New York at Albany
- Wilbur Zelinsky, Pennsylvania State University

The dedicated production team at Macmillan continues to set exceptionally high standards of professionalism. Textbook writing is a pleasure when the production process is headed by a well-organized and experienced group. I especially wish to thank Cindy Brunk, Paul F. Corey, Mark Garrett, Mary Harlan, Bruce Johnson, and Anne Vega.

Finally, I thank my entire family for all of their support, and I would like to dedicate this book to my wife, Bernadette Unger.

Contents

1
Basic Concepts 1

2
Population 47

3
Migration 85

4
Language 129

5
Religion 171

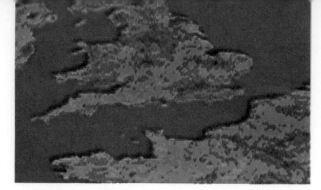

6
Social Customs on the Landscape 215

7
Political Geography 249

8
Economic Development 299

9
Agriculture 347

10
Industry 385

11
Settlements 429

12
Urban Patterns 469

13
Resource Problems 507

The world map at right reveals one of the most significant elements of the cultural landscape—the political boundaries that separate its five billion inhabitants. The numerous states range in size from the USSR, which occupies one-sixth of the world's land area, to microstates such as Singapore, Malta, or Grenada. The names of these states evoke images of different environments, peoples, cultures, and levels of well-being. However, the political boundaries are only one of the many patterns that geographers observe across the earth's surface. Geographers study the distribution of a wide variety of cultural and environmental features—social customs, agricultural patterns, the use of resources—many of which transcend political boundaries. As scientists, geographers also try to explain why we can observe these patterns on the landscape. The facing map and chapters that follow are intended to begin the student on a journey toward understanding our exciting and complex world.

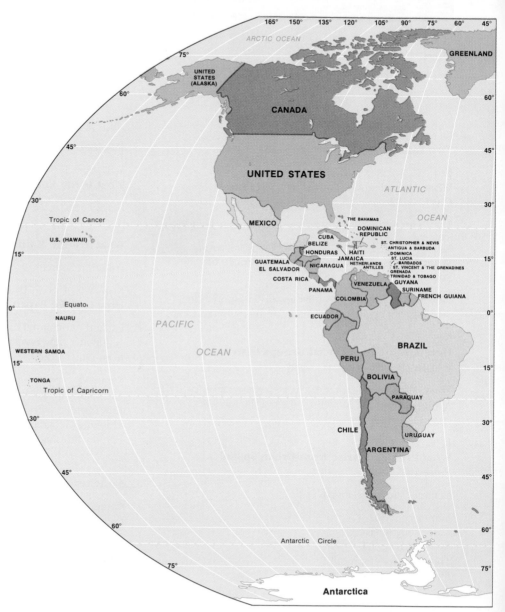

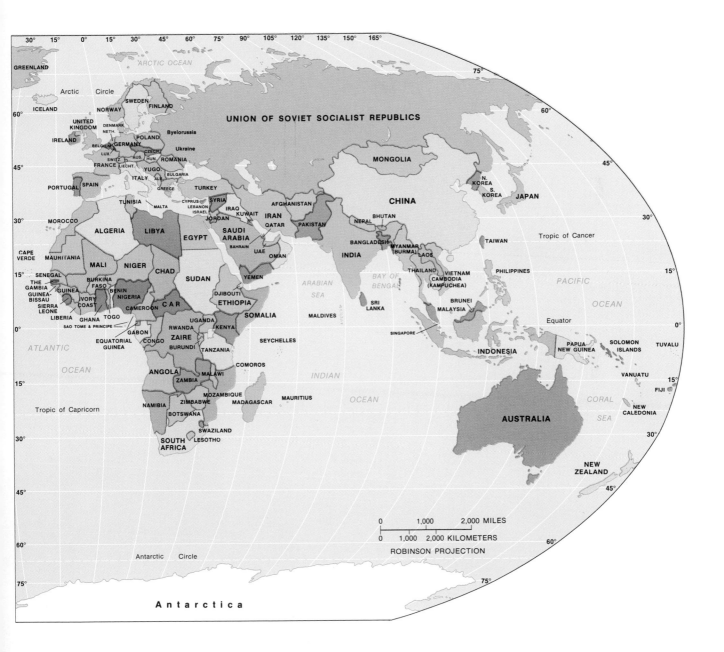

The Cultural Landscape

An Introduction to Human Geography

1
Basic Concepts

What do you expect from a geography textbook? You may think that geography involves memorization of lists of countries and capitals. Perhaps you associate geography with photographic essays of exotic places in popular magazines.

Geography is fundamentally a science. It is the scientific study of the location of people and activities across the earth's surface and the reasons for their distribution. Geographers ask "where" and "why" questions.

Like other sciences, the study of geography requires understanding some basic concepts. The definition of geography in the previous paragraph, for example, included the words *location* and *distribution*. We use these words commonly in daily speech, but geographers give them precise meanings. Other important geographic terms may be less familiar. This first chapter introduces you to some of the basic concepts in geography.

Where Is Miami?

Consider the following conversation between two students during winter vacation:

First student: Where do you go to school?

Second student: Miami University.

First student: I'll bet you enjoy the warm weather and nearby ocean.

Second student: No way. I don't go to school in Florida. We have snow and hills.

First student: Then where is your Miami?

Second student: In Oxford, Ohio.

First student: Where is Oxford, Ohio?

Second student: About thirty-five miles northwest of Cincinnati and two miles from the Indiana border.

First student: [overwhelmed] Oh.

First student: [conversation gets less realistic] Not only that, Miami, Ohio, is located at 39°30′ north latitude and 84°45′ west longitude, in township T5N R1E.

The conversation between two students presents a key question that geographers ask: Where is something located? Geographers study the arrangement of people and activities across the earth's surface. But geography is much more than a description of place names. It is a scientific study of reasons why people and activities are arranged in a particular way. Like other scientists, geographers try to solve problems, in this case those that arise from the location of people and activities.

Geography's most fundamental principle is that location is important: the location of people, activities, and environments can help to explain human behavior and can help to solve human problems. Just as historians study the logical sequence of human activities in time, so do geographers study the logical arrangement of human activities in space.

Geography can explain daily behavior, such as the distribution of students in a classroom. Some students sit in the front of the room to maximize interaction with the instructor. Students near the front can more easily read the blackboard, hear what the instructor and students say during lectures and discussions, and make eye contact with the instructor. Other students choose a location in the rear of the room to avoid interaction with the instructor. Perhaps they have not done the assignment or they wish to spend class time doing other things. Whether in the front or rear, students quickly acquire a sense of place in the classroom: having selected seats at the beginning of the term, they tend to sit in or near the same location every day, even if the instructor does not require it.

Geography is also a way of thinking about more urgent problems than where to sit in a classroom. Geographers document the locations and reasons for human characteristics, such as population growth in Africa, depletion of energy resources in the United States, and disputes among followers of different religions in Asia. Geographers, however, recognize that characteristics in various places are interrelated. For example, to explain the problem of hunger in Ethiopia and neighboring countries in Africa, geographers examine the interrelationship among population growth, environmental degradation, and political unrest, among other characteristics. Geographers explain unrest in the Middle East through such characteristics as the distribution of energy resources, differences in religious beliefs, and alternative strategies for modernizing economies.

This chapter discusses several basic concepts that help geographers both to describe where people and activities are found in the world and to explain why they are arranged in a particular way. The basic "where" and "why" concepts are fundamental to the study of various topics in human geography. Subjects found in subsequent chapters, such as demographic, cultural, political, and economic patterns, make use of the basic concepts presented here.

How Did Geography Develop Historically?

Geography is one of the oldest fields of study. The earliest geographer was probably the first person to cross a river or climb a hill, observe what was on the other side, and return home to tell about it. Over thousands of years, humans have been able to describe more and more of the earth's surface.

Historical Development of Geography

Geography in the ancient world. The first person to use the word *geography* was the Greek Eratosthenes, in the third century B.C. For nearly half a century he served as head of the library in Alexandria, Egypt, the most prestigious in the ancient world.

Eratosthenes not only accepted the concept that the earth was round but also calculated its circumference to within 0.5 percent accuracy. In one of the first geography books, Eratosthenes described the known areas of the world and divided the earth into five climate regions—a torrid zone across the center, two frigid zones at the extreme north and south, and two bands of temperate climate between the torrid zone and each of the frigid zones. He also prepared one of the earliest maps of the known world.

In the next century, Hipparchus, one of the great astronomers of the ancient world, continued the study of geography. Hipparchus' most important contribution was to draw imaginary lines on the earth's surface in order to describe the location of places. We still depend on the concept of meridians and parallels he developed.

The Greeks were concerned with geography for hundreds of years before Eratosthenes invented the term. In the sixth century B.C., Thales of Miletus applied geometric principles to the measurement of land areas. His disciple Anaximander argued that the world was shaped like a cylinder, and he made a map of the world based on information from sailors in Miletus. Aristotle (384–322 B.C.) was the first Greek philosopher to demonstrate that the earth was a sphere. He noted that all matter tended to fall together towards a common center, that during an eclipse the earth's shadow on the moon was circular, and that the configuration of stars changed as one travelled to the north or south.

The best-known geographer in ancient Rome was Strabo (63 B.C.?–?A.D. 24). His seventeen-volume *Geography* was an exhaustive description of the known world, including two introductory volumes, plus eight volumes on Europe, six on Asia, and one on Africa. Strabo regarded the earth as a sphere at the center of a spherical universe.

Ptolemy (A.D. 100?–?170), who lived and worked in Alexandria, represents the culmination of progress in the development of geographic concepts in the ancient world. In the second century A.D., the Roman Empire controlled an extensive area of the known world, including much of Europe, northern Africa, and western Asia. Taking advantage of information collected by Roman merchants and soldiers, Ptolemy wrote an eight-volume *Guide to Geography*. He also prepared a number of maps, which were not exceeded in quality for more than a thousand years.

Geography in the Middle Ages. After Ptolemy, little progress in geographic thought was made in the ancient world, and following the collapse of the Roman Empire in the fifth century, the word *geography* virtually disappeared from European vocabulary. During the Middle Ages, geographic inquiry continued outside of Europe.

Beginning in the seventh century, Muslim armies swept across much of northern Africa and southern Europe, eventually reaching as far east as present-day Indonesia in Southeast Asia. Muslim writers such as Edrisi (1099?–1154), ibn-Batuta (1304?–1378), and ibn-Khaldun (1332–1406) gathered accurate knowledge about the location of coastlines, rivers, and mountain ranges in the conquered areas. Geography also developed in China independently of European and Muslim studies. The oldest Chinese geographical writing, from the fifth century B.C., describes the economic resources of the country's different provinces. Phei Hsiu, known as the father of Chinese cartography, produced an elaborate map of the country in A.D. 267.

Revival of geography in Europe. Geographic thought enjoyed a resurgence in Europe in the seventeenth century, inspired by exploits of European explorers to establish trading routes and gain control of resources elsewhere in the world. *Geographia Generalis,* written by the German Bernhardus Varenius (1622–1650), stood for more than a century as the standard treatise on systematic geography. Varenius also wrote a description of Japan, but he died before he could complete a more comprehensive work on regional geography.

The German philospher Immanuel Kant (1724–1804) placed geography within an overall framework of scientific knowledge. Kant argued that all knowledge can be placed in either a logical classification or a physical classification. A logical classification organizes plants and animals into species, genera, and other systematic frameworks regardless of where they exist. A physical classification identifies plants and animals that occur together in particular times and places. Descriptions according to time comprise history, while descriptions according to place comprise geography. History studies phenomena that follow one another chronologically, while geography studies phenomena that are located beside one another.

Development of Geography as a Science

Until the nineteenth century, geography essentially comprised descriptive studies of people and environments in various places. No longer satisfied with amassing information about exotic places, geographers now develop scientific principles about the earth's surface that enable them to understand and more fully explain the "where" and "why" questions.

A world map, 1571, by Flemish cartographer Abraham Ortelius (1527–1598). The relative accuracy of the east coasts of North and South America as compared with the west coasts, or the relative accuracy of the coastlines of Africa as compared with the South Pacific, indicates the knowledge of the time, based on the extent of exploration of the earth's surface.

The human-environment tradition. The modern academic study of geography begins with two nineteenth-century German geographers, Alexander von Humboldt (1769–1859) and Carl Ritter (1779–1859). Before their work, geographers would describe the physical and social characteristics of places in great detail, with little attempt at explaining their obervations systematically. Humboldt and Ritter argued that geography should move beyond describing the earth's surface to explaining the reasons for the presence or absence of certain phenomena. This is the origin of our "where" and "why" approach.

Humboldt and Ritter urged human geographers to adopt the same method of scientific inquiry used by natural scientists. They argued that the scientific study of social processes and natural processes is fundamentally the same, albeit natural scientists had made more progress in formulating general laws than social scientists. One of the tasks of human geographers, therefore, should be to discover relevant general laws.

These German geographers believed that human geographers could find their general laws in the natural sciences by studying the relationship between the physical environment and human actions.

This geographic approach to the "why" question is sometimes known as cultural ecology and in the past was insensitively called the "man-land" tradition. According to Humboldt and Ritter, geographers should study human-environment relationships by concentrating on how the physical environment causes social development. This perspective became known as **environmental determinism.**

Other influential geographers adopted environmental determinism in the late nineteenth and early twentieth centuries. Friedrich Ratzel (1844–1904) and his American student, Ellen Churchill Semple (1863–1932), claimed that geography was the study of the influences of the natural environment on people. Another early American geographer, Ellsworth Huntington (1876–1947), argued that climate was a major determinant of civilization. For instance, the temperate climate of maritime northwestern Europe, according to Huntington, produced greater human efficiency, as measured by better health conditions, lower death rates, and higher standards of living.

Geographers no longer regard environmental determinism as a legitimate approach to explaining the "why" part of the relationship between human activities and the physical environment. The concept of possibilism is widely accepted instead (as discussed later in the chapter).

Regional studies approach. A second school of geographic thought, the regional studies approach, developed in nineteenth-century France. The regional studies approach—sometimes called the cultural landscape approach—was developed by Paul Vidal de la Blache (1845–1918) and Jean Brunhes (1869–1930) and was later adopted by several American geographers, including Carl Sauer (1889–1975) and Robert Platt (1880–1950).

These geographers rejected the idea that physical factors determine human actions. Instead, they argued that geographers should closely observe the various physical and social characteristics of a particular place, since each place has its own distinctive cultural landscape based on a unique combination of social relationships and physical processes. The science of human geography, according to this approach, involves sorting out the relationships among different social and physical phenomena in a particular study area. All objects in the landscape are interrelated, but physical factors do not necessarily cause human actions, as argued by environmental determinists.

Modern geographers have rejected the extreme position of the environmental determinists that the physical environment causes human actions and have considerably modified the regional studies approach. However, the two traditions of human-environment relationship and regional studies remain fundamental to the scientific study of geography.

KEY ISSUE

How Do Geographers Answer the "Where" Question?

Geographic inquiry, like other sciences, involves two steps. First, geographers address the "where" question by describing the arrangement of peoples and activities across the earth's surface. Second, to explain the "why" questions they look for explanations underlying the observed patterns. To describe where various peoples and activities are found, geographers use three basic concepts: location, maps, and distribution.

Location

The most important concept in geography is **location,** which is the position on the earth's surface an object occupies. Geographers identify the location of something in four ways—name, site, situation, and mathematics.

The chapter-opening dialogue illustrated the use of each method. The student's first response to the "where" question was by the name "Miami." When this response failed to clarify the location of Miami, the student then referred to the characteristics of the site, such as vegetation, topography, and climate. The third response drew on Miami's situation, in the city of Oxford and the state of Ohio and near the city of Cincinnati and the state of Indiana. Finally, the student gave two examples of Miami's mathematical location.

Name. The simplest way to describe a particular location is by referring to its name, because inhabited places on the earth's surface have been named. Geographers call the name given to a portion of the earth's surface the **toponym,** or nominal location, of a place.

The name of a place may give us a clue about its community's founders, physical setting, social customs, or political changes. Some communities take the name of an otherwise obscure founder or early leader, such as Muncie, Indiana, or Dayton, Ohio. Others adopt the name of a famous person who had no connection with the community. George Washington's name has been selected for one state, counties in 30 other states, and dozens of cities, including the national capital. Most states also contain a place named after James Madison.

Places may be named after important leaders or historical events. One of the clearest examples is found in England. The final victory in the Norman conquest of England in 1066 was at the Battle of Hastings. The actual battle site, 10 kilometers (6 miles) from the town of Hastings, is now simply known as "Battle." Another example is that after John F. Kennedy's assassination in 1963, communities throughout the world renamed streets, parks, and other places after him.

Some place names come from features of the physical environment. Trees, valleys, bodies of water, and other natural features appear in the place names of most languages. The capital of the Netherlands, 's Gravenhage (more commonly called The Hague), means "the prince's forest." Aberystwyth, in Wales, means "mouth of the river Ystwyth." Some 22 kilometers (13 miles) upstream lies the tiny village of Cwmystwyth, which means "valley of the Ystwyth." Ystwyth, the river's name, comes from the Welsh word for "meandering."

The community with perhaps the longest name in one word is a town in Wales called Llanfairpwllgwyngyllgogerychwyrndrobwllllantysiliogogogoch. The name means "the church of St. Mary's in the grove of the white hazelnut tree near the rapid whirlpool and the Church of St. Tisilio near the red cave." The town's name originally encompassed only the first twenty letters, but when the railway came through in the nineteenth century the townspeople lengthened it. They decided that signs with the longer name in the railway station would attract attention, bringing more business and visitors to the town.

Pioneers lured to the American west by the prospect of finding gold or silver fixed many picturesque names on the landscape. Place names in Nevada selected by successful miners include Eureka, Lucky Boy Pass, Gold Point, and Empire. Unsuccessful Nevada pioneers sadly or bitterly named other places Battle, Massacre Lake, and Paradise Valley. After gambling was legalized in Nevada, a town at the Idaho state border was named Jackpot.

The name of a place can tell a lot about the social customs of the early inhabitants. Some settlers select place names associated with their religion, such as the name of a saint. Other names indicate the settlers' interest in ancient history such as Athens, Attica, and Rome. A place name may also indicate the origin of the settlers. British place names are common in North America and Australia, Portuguese names are common in Brazil, Spanish names are common elsewhere in Latin America, and Dutch names are common in South Africa.

Repeated use of the same name can cause confusion, as in the case of the two Miamis. Hundreds of streets in London, England, are called High Street, a relic of medieval times when each neighborhood was an independent town. The most important shopping street in each town was known as the High Street.

Confusion may also arise if local residents commonly employ names other than the official ones. New York City has an abundance of unofficial names. The Avenue of the Americas is almost universally known by its former name, Sixth Avenue, and the Queensboro Bridge is generally called the 59th Street Bridge.

Places can change names. The City of Cincinnati was originally named Losantiville. The name was derived as follows: *L* is for Licking River, *os* is Latin for "mouth," *anti* is Latin for "opposite," *ville* is Latin for "town"—hence, "town opposite the mouth of the Licking River." The name was changed to Cincinnati in honor of a society of Revolutionary War heroes named after Cincinnatus, an ancient Roman general.

The Board of Geographical Names, operated by the U.S. Geological Survey, was established in the late nineteenth century to be the final arbiter of names placed on maps produced in the United States. In recent years, the board has been especially concerned with removing offensive place names, such as those signifying racial or ethnic slurs.

Names can also change as a result of political upheavals. For example, following World War II, Poland gained control over territory that was formerly part of Germany and changed many of the place names from German to Polish. Among the larger cities, Danzig became Gdańsk, Breslau became Wrocław, and Stettin became Szczecin.

Someone unfamiliar with foreign languages might have difficulty in identifying the English name for these European countries: Civitas Helvetia, Österreich, Magyarország, and Suomi. These are the official names for Switzerland, Austria, Hungary, and Finland, respectively.

Site. The second way to indicate location is by **site,** which is the physical character of the location. Important site characteristics include climate, water sources, topography, soil, and vegetation. The combination of physical characteristics gives each location a unique character.

Site factors have been historically important in the selection of a location for a settlement, though various peoples differed on the attributes of a good site. Some preferred a hilltop site that could easily be defended from attack. Others preferred settlements near easy river crossings to accommodate trade and communications with people living on the other side.

An island sometimes combined the attributes of both hilltop and riverside locations, when the site provided both good defense and transportation links. The site of the country of Singapore, for example, is a small swampy island approximately one kilometer off the southern tip of the Malay peninsula at the eastern end of the Strait of Malacca. The city of Singapore comprises nearly 20 percent of the island.

In general, the characteristics of a site do not change over time, though human preferences can. The relatively warm, humid climate of the southeastern United States traditionally retarded population growth, but in recent years it has become an attraction. People increasingly prefer the climate in the Southeast because they can participate in outdoor recreational activities throughout the year and don't have to shovel snow in the winter. At the same time, technological change, especially the invention of air conditioning, has increased the Southeast's attractiveness by enabling people to escape the high heat and humidity.

Human actions sometimes modify the characteristics of a site. For instance, the southern portion of Manhattan is twice as large today as it was in 1626, when Peter Minuit bought the island from the Indians for $24. The additional land came from filling in portions of the East and Hudson rivers. In the eighteenth century, landfills were created by sinking old ships and dumping refuse on top of them.

Because of poor health conditions, the city decided in 1797 to cover all of the landfills with earth and gravel and lay out a new street, called South Street, that would block further dumping in the river. Yet today South Street is two blocks inland. More recently, New York City permitted construction of Battery Park City at the southern end of Manhattan, a 57-hectare (142-acre) site designed to house more than 20,000 residents and 30,000 office workers (Figure 1–1). The central areas of Boston and Tokyo have also been substantially expanded through centuries of filling in nearby bays.

Situation. The relative location of a place compared with other places is its **situation.** For two reasons, the situation of a place is an important way to indicate location. First, situation helps identify the location of an unfamiliar place through comparison with another familiar place. We give directions to people who are lost by referring to the situation of a place. We identify important buildings, streets, and other landmarks to direct people to a desired location.

For example, even long-time residents of Paris might have difficulty finding the Marmottan Museum, which contains one of the world's largest collections of paintings by Claude Monet. Its address is 2 rue Louis-Boilly, a street that is only one-block long. The museum can be found by referring to its situation, one block east of the city's largest park (the Bois de Boulogne) and close to the nearest stop on the metro (subway), Muette.

Second, situation helps us understand the importance of a particular location. Many locations are important because they are accessible to other places. For example, because of its location, Singapore has become a center for the trading and distribution of goods for much of Southeast Asia. Singapore stands near the Strait of Malacca, the major passageway for ships travelling between the China seas and the Indian Ocean (Figure 1–2).

Mathematical location. If needed, the absolute location on the earth's surface can be described according to a unique set of numbers, known as latitudes and longitudes. The universally accepted numbering system of latitudes and longitudes derives from two series of imaginary lines—more precisely, arcs—drawn on the globe. These arcs are known as parallels and meridians.

A **meridian** is an arc drawn on the earth's surface between the North and South Poles. Every meridian has the same length and the same beginning and end points. We identify the location of each meridian on the earth's surface according to a numbering system known as **longitude.** One meridian, called the **prime meridian,** which passes through the Royal Observatory at Greenwich, England, has been designated as 0 degrees [°] longitude.

The meridian on the opposite side of the globe from the prime meridian is 180° longitude. All other meridians have numbers between 0° and 180° and are either east or west of the prime meridian. New York City is located at 74° west longitude, while Lahore, Pakistan, is at 74° east longitude. San Diego is

FIGURE 1–1

Much of the lower part of New York City's Manhattan Island was built on landfill. Several times in the past 200 years, the waterfront has been extended into the Hudson and East rivers to provide more land for offices, homes, parks, warehouses, and docks (right). In the photo, Battery Park (foreground), as well as the 110-story World Trade Center and Battery Park City (left side) were built on landfill in the Hudson River. The office buildings on the right were built on landfill in the East River.

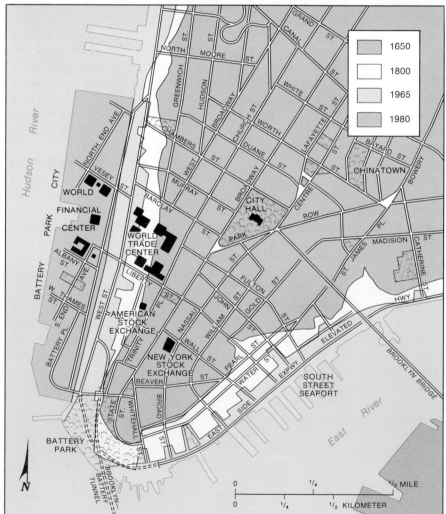

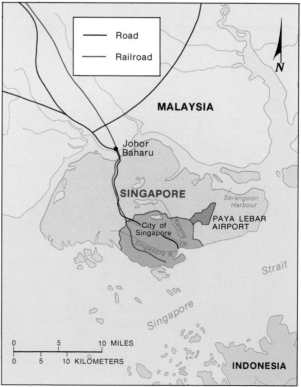

FIGURE 1–2

The small country of Singapore, less than one-fifth the size of Rhode Island, has an important situation for international trade. The country is situated at the confluence of several straits that serve as major passageways for shipping between the South China Sea and the Indian Ocean. Downtown Singapore is situated near where the Singapore River flows into the Singapore Strait. The dome in the right foreground is the National Museum; the spire to its left is St. Andrew's Cathedral.

11

located at 117° west longitude, while Tianjin, China, is at 117° east.

The second set of imaginary arcs drawn on the earth's surface are **parallels,** circles parallel to the equator at right angles to the meridians. The numbering system used to indicate the location of parallels is called **latitude.** The equator is 0° latitude, the North Pole 90° north, and the South Pole 90° south.

New York City is located at 41° north latitude, while Wellington, New Zealand, is at 41° south. San Diego is located at 33° north latitude, while Santiago, Chile, is at 33° south (Figure 1–3).

We can determine the mathematical location of a place more precisely if necessary. Each degree is divided into 60 minutes (′), and each minute in turn is divided into 60 seconds (″). For example, the of-

FIGURE 1–3
Meridians are arcs that connect the North and South Poles. The meridian running through Greenwich, a suburb of London, England, is the prime meridian or 0° longitude. Parallels are circles drawn around the globe parallel to the equator. The equator is 0° latitude, while the North Pole is 90° north latitude.

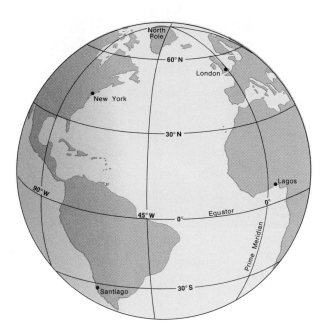

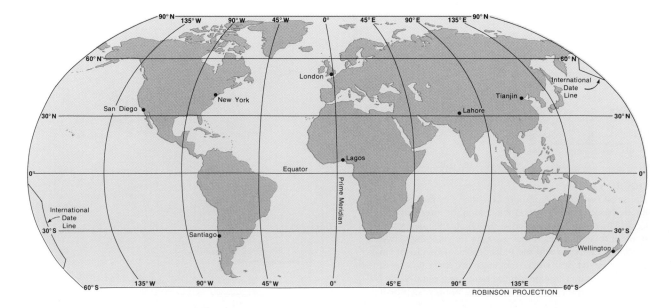

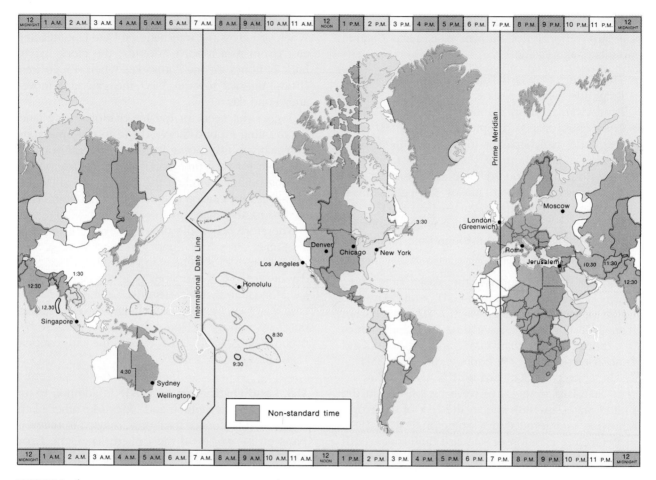

FIGURE 1–4
The world is divided into twenty-four standard time zones, each of which represents 15° of longitude. Greenwich Mean Time (GMT) is the time near the prime meridian, or 0° longitude. The Pacific Standard Time Zone, which encompasses the western parts of the United States and Canada, is eight hours behind GMT because it is situated near 120° west longitude.

ficial mathematical location of Denver, Colorado, is 39°44' north latitude and 104°59' west longitude. The State Capitol building in Denver is located at 39°42'52" north latitude and 104°59'04" west longitude.

Time zones. Longitude plays an important role in calculating time. The earth makes a complete rotation every 24 hours and as a sphere is divided into 360° of longitude, including from 0 to 180° west and 0 to 180° east longitude. Therefore, the earth turns 15° each hour, or 360° divided by 24 hours.

The time at the prime meridian (0° longitude) is designated **Greenwich Mean Time (GMT).** A traveler advances the clock ahead one hour from GMT for each 15° traveled east from the prime meridian. For each 15° traveled west from the prime meridian, the traveler sets the clock one hour earlier than GMT. The eastern part of the United States, which is located near 75° west longitude, is therefore 5 hours earlier than Greenwich Mean Time (75 ÷ 15 = 5). When the time is 11 A.M. GMT, the time in the eastern United States is therefore 5 hours earlier, or 6 A.M. (Figure 1–4).

The 48 contiguous states and Canada share four standard time zones, known as Eastern, Central, Mountain, and Pacific:

♦ The Eastern Standard Time Zone is near 75° west longitude, which passes close to Philadelphia, Pennsylvania, and is 5 hours earlier than GMT.
♦ The Central Standard Time Zone is near 90° west longitude, which passes through Memphis, Tennessee, and is 6 hours earlier than GMT.
♦ The Mountain Standard Time Zone is near 105° west longitude, which passes through Denver, Colorado, and is 7 hours earlier than GMT.
♦ The Pacific Standard Time Zone is near 120° west longitude, which passes through Lake Tahoe, and is 8 hours earlier than GMT.

Most of Alaska comprises the Alaska Time Zone, which is 9 hours earlier than GMT, while Hawaii is in the Hawaii Time Zone, which is 10 hours earlier than GMT. Canada has an Atlantic Time Zone, which is 4 hours earlier than GMT, and Newfoundland Time Zone, which is 3½ hours earlier than GMT.

The concept of standard time zones is rather recent. Standard time zones were established in the United States in 1883 and in the rest of the world following a conference in Washington, D.C., in 1884.

Before the creation of standard time zones, each locality set its own time, usually that of a leading local jeweler. Each railroad company kept its own time, normally that of the largest city served. Train timetables listed two sets of arrival and departure times, one for local time and one for railroad company time. Stations had one clock for local time and a separate clock for each of the railroad companies using the station.

At noon on November 18, 1883, time stood still in the United States so that each locality could adjust to the new standard time zones. In New York City, for example, time stopped for 3 minutes and 58 seconds to adjust to the new Eastern Standard Time. For many years Chicago, resisting the change, continued to be 17 minutes ahead of Central Standard Time.

International Date Line. The role of the International Date Line is the trickiest part of understanding time zones. The **International Date Line** for the most part follows 180° longitude, though it deviates in several places to avoid dividing land areas. When you cross the International Date Line heading east (from Asia toward America) the clock moves back 24 hours, or one entire day. When you go west (from America toward Asia) the calendar moves ahead one day.

To see the need for the International Date Line, try counting around the world from the time zone in which you live. Going from west to east, you add one hour for each time zone. As you return to your starting point by circling the globe, you will reach the absurd conclusion that the time is 24 hours later in your locality than it is in reality.

Therefore, when the time in New York City is 2 P.M. Sunday, it is 7 P.M. Sunday in London, 8 P.M. Sunday in Rome, 9 P.M. Sunday in Jerusalem, 10 P.M. Sunday in Moscow, 3 A.M. Monday in Singapore, and 5 A.M. Monday in Sydney, Australia. Continuing farther east, it is 7 A.M. Monday in Wellington, New Zealand, but 9 A.M. Sunday in Honolulu, Hawaii, because between New Zealand and Hawaii is the International Date Line.

U.S. Land Ordinance of 1785. In addition to the global system of latitude and longitude, other mathematical indicators of locations are used in different parts of the world. In the United States, the **Land Ordinance of 1785** divided much of the country into a system of townships to facilitate the sale of land to settlers in the West.

A **township** is a square, 6 miles long and 6 miles wide. Some of the north-south lines separating townships are called **principal meridians,** and some east-west lines are designated **base lines.** Each township has a number corresponding to how far north or south of a particular base line the township is located (Figure 1–5). The first townships north of a base line are called T1N; the second north, T2N; the first south, T1S; and so on. Each township has a second number, known as the range, corresponding to its location east or west of a principal meridian. The first townships east of a principal meridian are R1E. Camden, Ohio, for example, is in township T6N R2E, north of the Great Miami River base line and east of the principal meridian along the Ohio-Indiana state line.

A township is divided into 36 **sections,** each of which is 1 mile by 1 mile. Sections are numbered in

FIGURE 1–5
To facilitate the numbering of townships, the U.S. Land Ordinance of 1785 designated several north-south lines as principal meridians and several east-west lines as base lines.

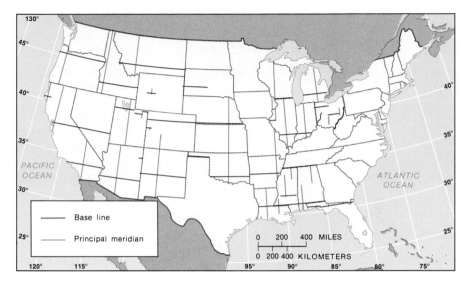

a consistent order, from 1 in the northeast to 36 in the southeast. Each section is divided into four areas, designated as the northeast, northwest, southeast, and southwest quarters of a particular section (Figure 1–6). Each quarter-section is 0.5 mile by 0.5 mile, or 160 acres. The quarter-section was the amount of land many western pioneers bought as a homestead.

Maps

Once the location of a place has been determined, geographers create maps to display information about the location. A **map** is a two-dimensional (flat) representation of the earth's surface or a portion of it. Maps can be visually appealing and intellectually stimulating to both professional geographers and casual users.

The science of making maps is called **cartography.** To communicate geographic concepts effectively through maps, cartographers must create them properly and assure that users know how to read them. Several decisions must be made in creating an accurate map (*see* Appendix).

Scale. The first decision a cartographer faces is how much of the earth's surface is to be presented in the map. A world map conveys information about every country or several places scattered around the

world but omits many details. Another map may cover only a small portion of the earth's surface but provide considerable detail about a particular place.

The level of detail and the amount of area covered on a map depends on its scale. **Scale** is the relationship between the length of an object on a map and the length of the same feature on the earth's surface. Cartographers usually present scale in one of three ways: a fractional scale (or ratio), a written scale, or a graphic scale.

A fractional scale shows the numerical ratio between distances on the map and the earth's surface. A scale of 1:24,000 means that 1 inch or 1 centimeter on the map represents 24,000 inches or 24,000 centimeters on the ground. The unit of distance could also be expressed in feet, millimeters, or some other measure of distance, but the units of measure on each side of the ratio must always be the same. The 1 on the left side of the ratio always refers to a unit of distance on the map, while the number on the right always refers to the same unit of distance on the earth's surface.

The written scale describes the relationshp between map and earth distances in words. For example, the written statement "1 inch to 1 mile" on a map means that one inch on the map represents one mile on the earth's surface. Again, the first number always refers to map distance, and the second to distance on the earth's surface.

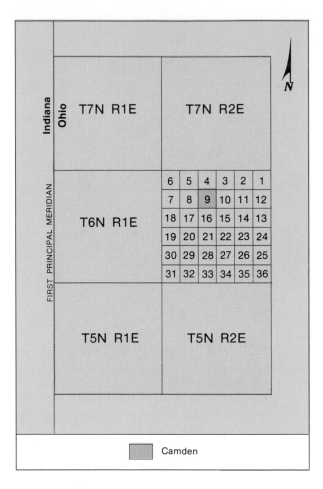

FIGURE 1–6
Townships were typically 6 miles by 6 miles, though physical features such as rivers resulted in some irregularly shaped ones. Camden, Ohio, for example, is located in the sixth township north of the Great Miami River base line and the second range east of the principal meridian along the Indiana-Ohio state line. Townships are divided into 36 sections, each 1 square mile. Sections are further divided into four quarters. Camden, Ohio, is located within section 9, T6N R2E.

A graphic scale usually consists of a bar line drawn on the map. The line is marked to show distance on the earth's surface. To use a bar line, first determine with a ruler the distance on the map in inches or centimeters. Then hold the ruler against the bar line and read the number on the bar line opposite the map distance on the ruler. The number on the bar line is the distance on the earth's surface (Figure 1–7).

When comparing map scales, remember that the smaller the scale the larger the area represented, and the larger the scale the smaller the area covered. A world map uses a smaller scale than a city map because it covers a larger area. A large-scale map is suitable for detailed information about a small area.

Projections. The earth, approximately the shape of a sphere, is accurately represented in the form of a globe. But, a globe is an extremely limited tool to communicate information about the earth's surface. A small globe doesn't have enough space to display detailed information, while a large globe is too bulky and cumbersome to use.

Every cartographer faces the problem that some distortion always results when a portion of a spherical object (such as a globe) is transferred to a flat piece of paper (such as a map). The system used to transfer locations on the earth's surface to locations on a map is called the **projection.** Cartographers have invented hundreds of projections, but none is free of some distortion.

The problem of distortion is especially severe for world and other small-scale maps. Three types of distortions can result. First, the shape of an area can be distorted, so that it appears more elongated or squat than in reality. Second, the relative size of different areas may be altered. One area may appear larger than another on a map but in reality be smaller. Third, the direction from one place to another may be distorted.

Most of the world maps in this book (such as Figure 1–10), are shown on equal-area projections. The primary benefit of this type of projection is that the relative size of the land masses on the map are the same as in reality. The projection also minimizes distortion in the shape of most land masses, although some relatively sparsely inhabited areas, such as Greenland and Australia, are a bit distorted.

To minimize the divergence from reality in the size and shape of land masses, the map displays other distortions. First, the two hemispheres are separated into two pieces, a characteristic known as interruption. Second, the meridians do not all meet at the North and South Poles and are not at right angles to the parallels. In contrast, uninterrupted projections helped in displaying information on Figures 1–3 and 1–4; the Robinson projection was used for Figure 1–3, while Figure 1–4 utilizes the Mercator projection (all discussed in the Appendix).

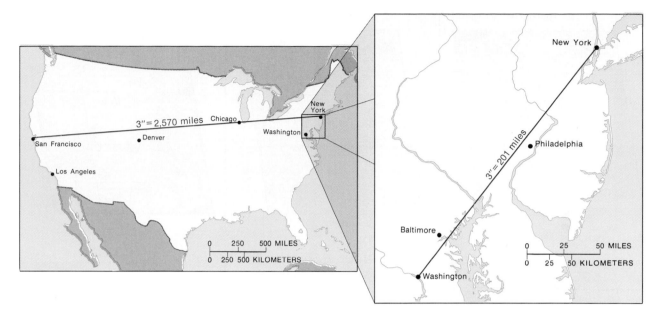

FIGURE 1–7
The distance between the two points, as measured in inches with a ruler, is the same on the
large U.S. map and on the detail at right, but the two maps use different scales. The map on
the left has a fractional scale of 1 : 54,278,400; expressed as a writen statement, the scale is
"1 inch on the map equals approximately 857 miles on the ground." The fractional scale of
the detail map on the right is approximately 1 : 4,245,120; the scale in written form is "1 inch
on the map equals approximately 67 miles on the ground."

Distribution

The arrangement of a phenomenon across the
earth's surface is known as the **spatial distribution.** Many objects are not just distributed randomly
across the earth's surface. Geographers try to find
regularities in the spatial distribution of people and
activities, measure what is found and place that information on a map. Spatial distribution has three
important properties: density, concentration, and
pattern.

Density. Density is the frequency that something
occurs within a given unit of area. The phenomenon being measured could be people, buildings,
dwelling units, cars, or virtually any other object.
Examples of units of area include square miles,
acres, and hectares (Figure 1–8).

Geographers frequently calculate the arithmetic
density, which is the total number of objects, such
as people, in an area. The arithmetic density of the
United Kingdom, for example, is 235 persons per
square kilometer (609 persons per square mile), or
the total population of 58 million people divided by
the total area of 244,833 square kilometers (94,530
square miles). Arithmetic density is a useful measure of living conditions in different places.

Remember that high density is a different concept from crowding. Arithmetic density involves two
measures: the number of people and the area. The
most populous country in the world, China, with approximately 1.2 billion inhabitants, is by no means
the densest. The arithmetic density of China is approximately 120 persons per square kilometer (311
persons per square mile), only one-half as high as
in the United Kingdom. Although China has about
twenty times more inhabitants than the United Kingdom, it also has nearly forty times more land.

High population density is also unrelated to poverty. The Netherlands, one of the world's wealthiest
countries, has an arithmetic density of approximately 403 persons per square kilometer (1,044
persons per square mile). One of the poorest countries, Mali, has an arithmetic density of 7 persons
per square kilometer (17 persons per square mile).

Density	Concentration	Pattern

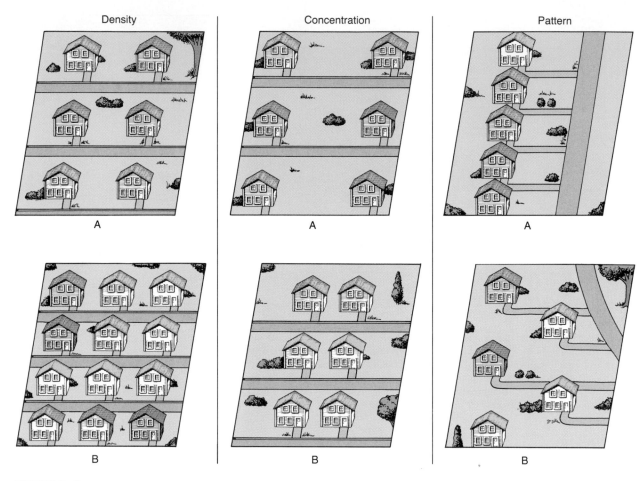

FIGURE 1–8

Spatial distribution is represented in three ways: density, concentration, and pattern. Assume that the area in all figures represents 1 acre. The density (left) is six houses per acre in A and twelve houses per acre in B. The houses (center) are dispersed in A and clustered in B. Note that while the concentration changes, the density is the same in both figures. Five houses (right) are arranged in a linear pattern in A (right) and form an irregular arrangement in B.

Geographers measure density in other ways, depending on the subject being studied. Geographers concerned with the relationship between population growth and food supply often calculate the physiological density and agricultural density. Physiological density is the number of persons per area suitable for agriculture, while agricultural density is the number of farmers per area of farmland. Urban geographers frequently use housing density, which is the number of dwelling units per area (see Chapter 2).

Concentration. The extent of the spread of something over a given study area is called **concentra-tion.** If the objects in a given area are close together, they are considered clustered. If they are relatively far apart, they are considered dispersed. To compare the level of concentration clearly, two study areas should have the same number of objects and the same size area.

Geographers use the concept of concentration in a number of ways. For example, one of the major changes in the distribution of the U.S. population is increasing dispersion. The total number of people living in the United States is growing slowly— less than 1 percent per year—and the total land area is not changing at all. Yet the distribution of population is changing from relatively clustered in the

Northeast to more evenly dispersed across the country.

Concentration is not the same as density. One study area with relatively high density could have a dispersed population, while another study area with the same density could have a clustered population.

We can illustrate the difference between density and concentration by the change in the distribution of major league baseball teams in North America. In 1900, the major leagues had sixteen teams. Both the density and the concentration of teams remained unchanged for more than half a century. Beginning in 1953, the following six of the sixteen teams moved to other cities:

◆ Braves—Boston to Milwaukee in 1953, then to Atlanta in 1966
◆ Browns—St. Louis to Baltimore (Orioles) in 1954
◆ Athletics—Philadelphia to Kansas City in 1955, then to Oakland in 1968
◆ Dodgers—Brooklyn to Los Angeles in 1957
◆ Giants—New York to San Francisco in 1957
◆ Senators—Washington to Minnesota (Twins) in 1960

These moves resulted in a more dispersed distribution, that is, in a change in concentration. Before the moves, seven teams were clustered in the three northeastern cities of Philadelphia, New York, and Boston, compared to only three teams after the moves. In 1953, no team was located south or west of St. Louis, but after the moves teams were located on the West Coast and the Southeast for the first time.

In addition to the shifts by established teams, the major leagues expanded between 1960 and 1977 from sixteen to twenty-six teams. The new teams selected the following locations:

◆ Angels—Los Angeles in 1961, then to Anaheim in 1966
◆ Senators—Washington in 1961, then to Texas (Rangers) in 1972
◆ Mets—New York in 1962
◆ Astros—Houston in 1962
◆ Royals—Kansas City in 1969
◆ Padres—San Diego in 1969
◆ Expos—Montreal in 1969

◆ Pilots—Seattle in 1969, then to Milwaukee (Brewers) in 1970
◆ Blue Jays—Toronto in 1977
◆ Mariners—Seattle in 1977

The addition of Denver and Miami brings the total to 28 as of 1993. Thus, the density of major league teams in North America increases from 16 to 28 at the same time the distribution becomes more dispersed (Figure 1–9).

Pattern. The third property of distribution is the **pattern,** which is the geometric arrangement of objects. Some phenomena are organized in a regular, or geometric, pattern, while others are distributed randomly. Geographers observe that many objects form a linear distribution, such as the arrangement of houses along a street or stations along a subway line.

Objects are frequently arranged in a square or rectangular pattern. Many American cities contain a regular pattern of streets intersecting at right angles at uniform intervals to form square or rectangular blocks. This arrangement of streets is known as a grid pattern. The system of townships and township sections established by the Land Ordinance of 1785 is another example of a square or grid pattern.

Geographers find the hexagon (a six-sided geometric shape) to be useful in describing spatial patterns, because it represents a compromise between a circle and square. All points along the circumference of a circle are the same distance from the center, but a collection of circles will not nestle together without leaving gaps. Squares fit together without any gaps, but the distance from the center to the edge varies. Geographers use hexagons, for example, to represent the theoretical market area of a good or service (see Chapter 11).

The distribution of baseball teams also follows a regular pattern. With a few exceptions, the teams are located in North America's largest cities. The four largest urban areas—New York, Los Angeles, Chicago, and San Francisco-Oakland Bay Area—each have two. The other twenty-two teams are in the next largest urban areas, with a few exceptions. Cincinnati, Milwaukee, Denver, and Kansas City, Missouri, have major league baseball teams, instead of three larger urban areas—Washington, D.C., Tampa, Florida, and Phoenix.

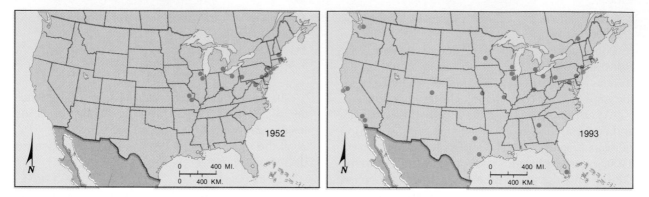

FIGURE 1–9

The changing distribution of North American baseball teams illustrates the difference between density and concentration. The figures show that density of baseball teams in North America has increased from 16 in 1952 to 28 in 1993. At the same time, the distribution has changed from a clustered arrangement in the northeastern part of the United States to a more dispersed arrangement across the United States and southern Canada.

Not all objects are distributed in a regular pattern. The streets in the older part of European cities, for instance, are arranged in a random pattern, following centuries of haphazard development.

How Does the Human-Environment Approach Help to Answer the "Why" Question?

Geographers use the three basic concepts of location, maps, and distribution to describe where objects are placed on the earth's surface. Geographers also wish to know why objects are located in particular places rather than distributed randomly. Two geographic approaches help to explain the reasons underlying spatial patterns—the human-environment approach and the regional studies approach.

Geographers approach the "why" question by assuming the existence of **spatial association,** the concept that the distribution of one object across the landscape is scientifically related to the location of another object. For example, the distribution of livestock in Africa's Sahel desert results from the distribution of watering holes. To determine the spatial association among peoples, activities, and environments, geographers rely on modern versions of the two scientific approaches developed in the nineteenth century—human-environment and regional studies.

Possibilism

The fundamental premise of the human-environment approach to geographic explanation is that human activities and the physical environment are associated with each other. Nineteenth-century environmental determinists believed that the physical environment caused human actions. Modern geographers reject environmental determinism in favor of an approach to the human-environment relationship known as **possibilism.** According to possibilism, the physical environment may limit some human actions, but humans have the ability to adjust to the physical environment. A person can choose a course of action from many alternatives in the physical environment.

Modern geographers utilize the human-environment approach to explain many global issues. For example, world population growth is a problem if the number of people exceeds the capacity of the physical environment to produce food. The possibility exists, though, that people can adjust to the capacity of the physical environment by adopting new technology, consuming different foods, migrating to new locations, and other actions.

Regular patterns, which characterize much of the human landscape, may appear clearly from the air. The houses at Sun City, Arizona, a retirement community near Phoenix, are distributed in a circular pattern.

Physical Processes

Human geographers need some familiarity with global environmental processes to understand the distribution of human activities, such as where people live, how they earn a living, and other human activities. Important physical processes include climate, vegetation, soil, and landforms.

Climate. Climate is the long-term average weather condition at a particular location. Geographers frequently classify climates according to a system developed by Köppen. The modified Köppen system divides the world into five main climate regions (Figure 1–10). These regions are identified by the letters A through E, as well as by names:

A   Tropical Climates
B   Dry Climates
C   Warm Temperate Climates
D   Snow Climates
E   Ice Climates

The modified Köppen system subdivides the five main climate regions into several subregional types.

For all but the B climate, the basis for the subdivision is the amount of precipitation and the season in which it occurs. For the B climate, subdivision is on the basis of temperature and precipitation.

Humans traditionally have a limited tolerance of extreme temperature and precipitation levels and thus avoid living in places that are too hot, too cold, too wet, or too dry. Compare the map of global climate to the distribution of population (*see* Figure 2–1). Relatively large numbers of people live in the C climate region or the lower latitudes of the D climate region. The dry climate region is less intensively settled.

The climate of a particular location influences human activities, especially production of the food needed to survive. From one generation to the next, people learn that different crops thrive in different climates. Rice, for example, requires a good deal of moisture, whereas wheat survives on a limited amount and grows poorly in very wet environments. On the other hand, wheat is more likely than rice to be grown successfully in colder climates.

People in parts of the A climate region, especially southwestern India, Bangladesh, and the Burma coast, anxiously await the monsoon rain, which is

FIGURE 1–10
Geographers frequently classify global climate according to a system developed by Köppen. The modified Köppen system divides the world into five main climate regions, indicated on the map by letters A, B, C, D, and E. These five letters correspond to the following climate regions:

A—Tropical climates: the average temperature of the coldest month exceeds 18°C (64.4°F). Some A climate locations receive heavy precipitation throughout the year, while others have sharp seasonal variations.

B—Dry climates: the amount of evaporation equals or exceeds precipitation. B climate regions are classified as desert if they receive less than 4 centimeters (1.6 inches) of precipitation per year and steppe if they receive more than 4 centimeters.

C—Warm temperature climates: the average temperature of the coldest month is between 0°C (32°F) and 18°C (64.4°F); in addition, the average monthly temperature exceeds 10° (50°F) at least eight months of the year.

D—Snow climates: the coldest month averages below 0°C (32°F) while four of the months have an average temperature above 10°C (50°F). Precipitation is generally lower in D climates than in C climates.

E—Ice climates: the average temperature of every month is less than 10°C (50°F).

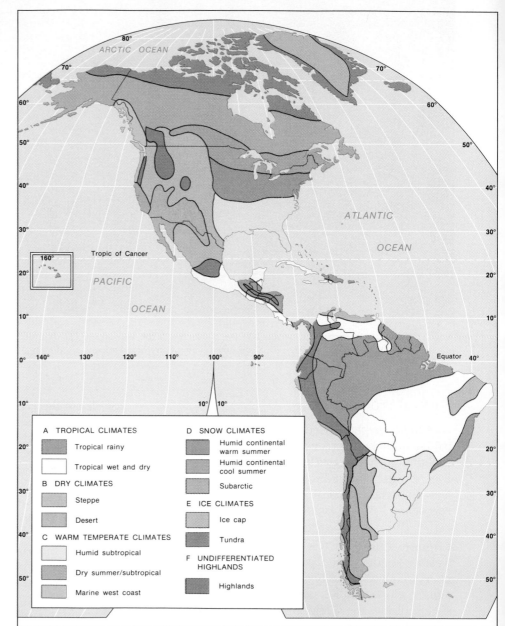

PERCENT OF WORLD
POPULATION
BY CLIMATE REGION

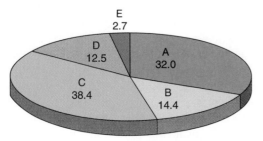

essential for successful agriculture and provides nearly 90 percent of India's water supply. For most of the year, the region receives dry, somewhat cool air from the northeast. In June, the wind direction suddenly shifts, bringing moist, warm southwesterly air from the Indian Ocean, known as the monsoon. The monsoon rain lasts until September.

In years when the monsoon rain is delayed or fails to arrive—in recent decades, at least a quarter

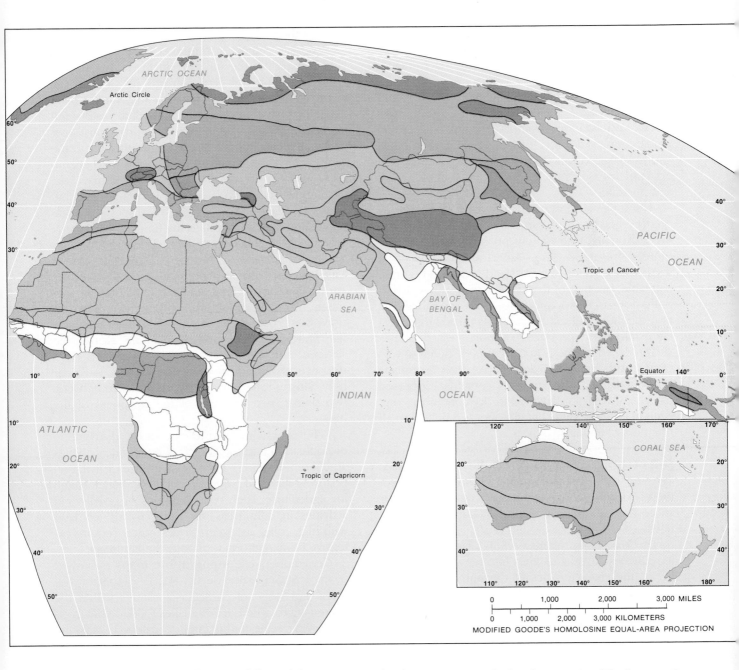

MODIFIED GOODE'S HOMOLOSINE EQUAL-AREA PROJECTION

of the time—agricultural output falls and famine is threatened in the countries of South Asia, where nearly twenty percent of the world's people live. The monsoon rain is so important in India that the words for "year," "rain," and "rainy season" are identical in many local languages.

Vegetation. Nearly the entire land surface of the earth supports some kind of vegetation. The earth's land vegetation includes four major life forms of plants, called **biomes.** Their location and extent are influenced by both climate and human activities. Vegetation and soil, in turn, influence the types of agriculture that people practice in a particular region.

The four main biomes are forest, savanna, grassland, and desert. In the forest biome, trees form a continuous canopy over the ground. Although trees are the dominant vegetation, grasses and shrubs may grow beneath the cover. The forest biome covers a large percentage of the earth's surface, including much of North America, Europe, and Asia, as well as tropical areas of South America, Africa, and Southeast Asia.

The savanna biome comprises a mix of trees and grasses. Trees do not form a continuous canopy, and lack of shade allows grass to grow. Savanna covers large areas of Africa, south Asia, South America, and Australia.

As the name implies, the grassland biome is covered by grass rather than trees. Few trees grow in the region because of low precipitation. Early explorers regarded the American prairies—the world's most extensive grassland area—to be uninhabitable, because of the lack of trees with which to build houses, barns, and fences. But careful cultivation of wheat and other crops has turned the grasslands into a very productive region.

The desert biome is not completely bereft of vegetation. Although many desert areas have essentially no vegetation, the region contains dispersed patches of vegtation adapted to dry conditions. Vegetation is often sufficient for the survival of small numbers of animals.

Soil. The material formed on the earth's surface between the air and the rocks is **soil.** Soil is not merely dirt but contains the nutrients necessary for successful cultivation of plants for human consumption.

The U.S. Comprehensive Soil Classification System divides global soil types into ten orders according to the characteristics of the immediate surface soil layers and the subsoil. The orders are subdivided into suborders, great groups, subgroups, families, and series. More than 12,000 soil series have been identified just in the United States.

Human geographers are concerned with the destruction of the soil through a combination of physical processes and human actions. Two basic problems contribute to the destruction of soil: erosion and depletion. The first problem occurs when the soil washes away in the rain or blows away in the wind. Erosion can be minimized by the periodic planting of crops that help bind the soil. The second problem is depletion of nutrients. Each type of plant withdraws certain nutrients from the soil and re-

stores others. Repeated harvesting of the same type of crop can remove too much of certain nutrients and thus reduce the soil's productivity.

To minimize the depletion problem, farmers in relatively developed countries sometimes plant crops that have no economic return but restore nutrients to the soil, keeping the land productive over the long term. Farmers also restore nutrients to the soil through the application of appropriate chemicals. Farmers in developing countries may face greater problems with depletion of nutrients because they lack the knowledge of proper soil management practices as well as the funds to pay for the restoration of nutrients to the soil.

Landforms. Geomorphology is the study of the earth's landforms. Geographers find that certain elements of geomorphology help explain human actions. Some parts of the earth's surface are relatively flat, while other areas are mountainous. **Relief,** the difference in elevation between two points, is a measure of the extent to which an area is flat or hilly. **Slope,** relief divided by the distance between two points, is a measure of the steepness of the hills.

Relief and slope help to explain the distribution of population and the choice of economic activities at different locations. People usually prefer living on relatively flat land, which generally is better suited for agriculture. High concentrations of people and activities in hilly areas—in other words, on land with high relief and steep slopes—may require extensive human efforts to modify the landscape.

Geographers use **topographic maps** published by the U.S. Geological Survey (U.S.G.S.) to study the relief and slope of particular localities within the United States. The U.S.G.S. makes topographic maps at various scales. The largest scale—1:24,000—covers an area of approximately 150 square kilometers (60 square miles), while the smallest scale—1:1,000,000—represents an area of approximately 250,000 square kilometers (100,000 square miles).

Topographic maps represent a variety of cultural features, such as buildings, roads, parks, farms, and dams. They also indicate the location of forests, bodies of water, and other physical features. Topographic maps also show **contour lines,** imaginary lines on the ground connecting points of equal elevation above sea level. Contour lines are closer together in areas that have higher relief and slope and further apart in flatter areas.

Human Modification of the Environment

Modern technology has altered the historic relationship between people and the environment. Humans can modify the physical environment to a greater extent than in the past. For example, air conditioning has increased the attraction of living in warmer climates, while more elaborate insulation has permitted survival in colder climates.

Geographers are concerned that people do not always employ modern technology to modify the environment sensitively. Human actions can deplete scarce environmental resources, destroy irreplaceable environmental resources, and utilize environmental resources inefficiently. The refrigerants in air conditioners that have increased the comfort of residents of warmer climates have also increased the amount of chlorofluorocarbons in the atmosphere, damaging the ozone and contributing to global warming. We explore the consequences of such use, abuse, and misuse of the environment in more detail in Chapter 13.

Sensitive environmental modification in the Netherlands. Few lands have been as thoroughly modified by humans as has the Netherlands. Because more than half of the Netherlands lies below sea level, most of the country today would be under water if not for massive projects to modify the environment. The Dutch have a saying that "God made the earth, but the Dutch made the Netherlands." The Dutch have modified their environment through two distinctive types of construction projects: with polders and dikes.

A **polder** is a piece of land created by draining water from an area. Polders, first used in the thirteenth century, were constructed in the sixteenth and seventeenth centuries primarily by private developers and by the government during the past 200 years. Altogether, the Netherlands has 6,500 square kilometers (2,600 square miles) of polders, constituting 18 percent of the country's land area.

The first step in making a polder is to build a wall encircling the site, which is still under water. Then the water inside the walled area is pumped from the site into either nearby canals or the remaining portion of the original body of water. Before the invention of modern engines, windmills performed the pumping operation. Many of these windmills remain as a picturesque element of the Dutch landscape, although they were originally built for a practical purpose (Figure 1–11).

Once dry, the site—now known as a polder—can be prepared for human activities. The Dutch government reserves most of the polders for agriculture in order to reduce the country's dependency on imported food, though some of the polders are used for housing. Schiphol, one of the largest airports in Europe, was built on a polder.

The second distinctive modification, massive dikes, prevents the North Sea from flooding much of the country. The Dutch have built dikes in two major locations, the Zuider Zee project in the north and the Delta Plan project in the southwest.

The North Sea once protruded into the heart of the Netherlands as an arm called the Zuider Zee. For centuries, the Dutch unsuccessfully attempted to prevent the Zuider Zee from flooding much of the country. Then in the late nineteenth century, a Dutch engineer named Lely proposed an ambitious project to seal off the Zuider Zee permanently from the North Sea, the ultimate source of the flood waters.

In accordance with Lely's plan, a dike 32 kilometers (20 miles) long was built across the mouth of the Zuider Zee to block the flow of North Sea water. When completed in 1932, the dike caused the Zuider Zee to change from a saltwater sea to a freshwater lake. The newly created body of water was named the IJsselmeer, or Lake IJssel, after the IJssel River, which empties into the lake. Some of the IJsselmeer has been drained to create several polders, encompassing an area of 1,600 square kilometers (620 square miles).

A second ambitious project is the Delta Plan in the western part of the Netherlands. Several important rivers flow through the country, including the Rhine (Europe's busiest river), the Maas (known as the Meuse in France), and the Scheldt (known as the Schelde in Belgium). As these rivers flow into the North Sea they split into many branches and form a low-lying delta area that is vulnerable to flooding (Figure 1–12).

After a devastating flood in January 1953, the Delta Plan called for the construction of several

FIGURE 1–11
(top) The flat land in the foreground is a polder, land that was
once under water. The water was
pumped into a canal on the other
side of the wall in the background.
Because polder land lies below sea
level, the ship in the background is
at a higher level than the house.
(bottom) To create a polder from
land covered by the sea or a lake
(A), a dike is constructed (B)
around the area to be drained, and
the water is pumped into canals
that flow to the North Sea (C). Historically, windmills played a key
role in pumping out the water. The
drained land (D) can then be used
for farming, housing, or other activities.

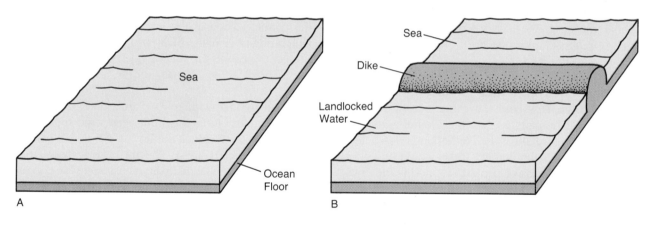

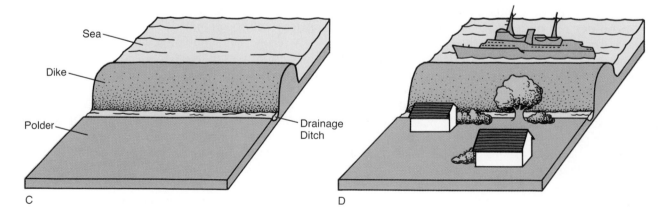

FIGURE 1−12
The Dutch people have considerably altered the site of the Netherlands through the creation of polders and dikes. Since the thirteenth century, the Dutch have reclaimed more than 1,800 square miles (4,500 square kilometers) of polders, more than three-fourths of which have been reclaimed in the past 200 years. The Zuider Zee and Delta Plan have altered the coastline of the Netherlands and enabled the Dutch to reduce the level of destruction caused by flooding.

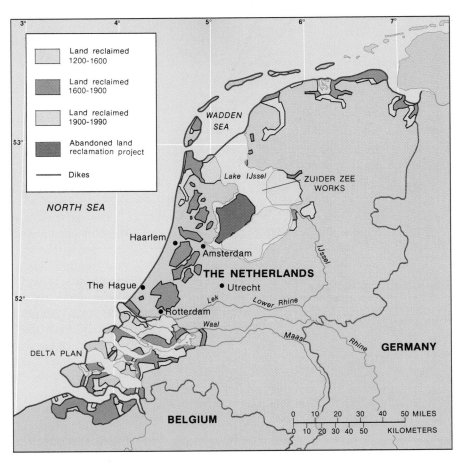

dams to close off most of the waterways from the North Sea. Together these dams shorten the coastline of the Netherlands by approximately 700 kilometers (435 miles). Because Rotterdam, Europe's largest port, is located nearby, some of the waterways were kept open. The project took 30 years and was completed in the mid-1980s.

With these two dike projects finished, attitudes towards modifying the environment have changed in the Netherlands. The Dutch have scrapped plans to build additional polders in the IJsselmeer in order to preserve the lake's value for recreation.

Problems with modifying Florida's environment. Humans do not always modify the environment as sensitively as did the Dutch. The rechannelling of the Kissimmee River and construction on barrier islands demonstrate negative consequences resulting from ill-conceived human actions to modify Florida's environment.

In 1961 the state of Florida asked the U.S. Army Corps of Engineers to straighten the course of the Kissimmee River, which meandered for 160 kilometers (98 miles) from near Orlando to Lake Okeechobee (Figure 1−13). In years with heavy rains, the river flooded 18,000 hectares (45,000 acres) of nearby land, creating an obstacle to cattle grazing and construction of buildings in areas with the potential for rapid population growth. The Corps channelled the river into a 90-meter-wide (300-foot-wide), 9-meter-deep (30-foot-deep) canal, which ran in a straight line for 84 kilometers (52 miles).

The opening of the canal in 1971 changed the region's environment. Tens of thousands of gallons of polluted water, mainly from cattle grazing along the banks, entered the canal as runoff and eventually flowed into Lake Okeechobee, the source of fresh water for half of Florida's population. Fish in the lake began to die from the high levels of mercury,

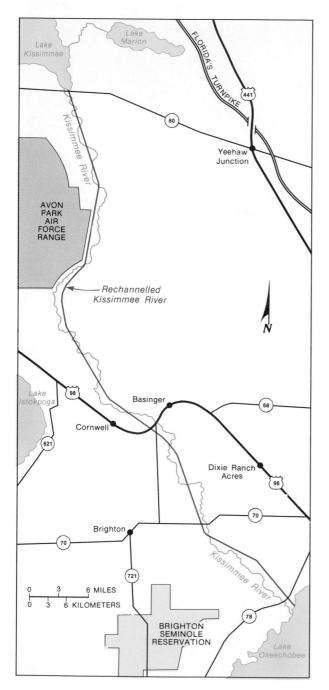

FIGURE 1–13

The U.S. Army Corps of Engineers straightened the course of the Kissimmee River to control flooding in central Florida. After the canal, known as C-38, opened in 1971, millions of gallons of polluted water—mainly runoff from cattle grazing—began pouring into Lake Okeechobee, which is the major source of fresh water for about half of Florida's people. Now the state wants the corps to return the river to its original course.

phosphorous, and other contaminants. The polluted water then continued to flow south, from Lake Okeechobee to the Everglades, where wildlife habitats were also disturbed.

The Corps is now spending hundreds of millions of dollars to restore the Kissimmee River back to its meandering course and to buy the nearby grazing land that will again be subject to flooding. In an ironic reminder of the old Dutch saying, Floridians say that God made the world in six days, and the Army Corps of Engineers has been tinkering with it ever since.

The rechannelling of the Kissimmee River is not the only example of insensitive environmental management in Florida. Barrier islands extend for several hundred kilometers along Florida's east and west coasts, as well as along the rest of the Atlantic Ocean and Gulf of Mexico coasts between Maine and Texas. These barrier islands are in essence large sandbars that serve as buffers to protect the mainland from flooding and storm damage. The force of storms and the pounding surf constantly erodes and shifts the sands, and after a major storm large sections can be washed away and disappear.

Despite the fragile condition of the barrier islands, hundreds of thousands of people live on them. They are increasingly attractive locations for constructing homes and recreational facilities to take advantage of proximity to the seashore. Two-thirds of the barrier islands are linked to the mainland by bridge, causeway, ferry service, or airplane flights.

To fight erosion along the barrier islands, communities build jetties and sea walls, but ironically these projects result in more damage than protection. For example, a sea wall extends out into the sea in order to prevent sand from drifting away. But while the wall traps sand along the up-current side, it also causes erosion on the barrier islands on the down-current side.

KEY ISSUE

How Does the Regional Studies Approach Help to Answer the "Why" Question?

The second model that geographers employ to understand why people and activities are arranged as they are across the earth's surface derives from the regional studies tradition. In the past, writers who utilized the regional studies approach identified an area of the earth's surface and described in careful detail as many of its characteristics as they could uncover. When Julius Caesar wrote that Gaul was divided into three parts, he gave an example of the traditional regional studies approach to geographic explanation.

Today, the regional studies approach to geographic explanation may start by identifying an important characteristic, such as growth of population, level of wealth, or consumption of energy. Then, geographers search for reasons to explain why that characteristic is greater or more intense in one area and lower or less intense elsewhere. Geographers recognize that the distinctive distribution of a characteristic results from a process of movement of people and activities across the earth's surface.

In building a model of explanation, geographers may undertake these tasks:

- Identify areas, known as *regions,* that are distinguished by one or more unique characteristics.
- Document characteristics that are *integrated* and interrelated within and among regions.
- Demonstrate how the integration of characteristics across the earth's surface results from a process of *diffusion.*
- Explain that diffusion results in integration because of *interaction* among people and ideas across space.

We can explore in more detail the importance of each of these concepts to geographic explanation.

Region

Geographers employ the concept of **region** to generalize about what is distinctive among various areas of the earth's surface. The people, activities, and environment within a region can display similarities and regularities. On the other hand, one region's cultural, economic, and physical characteristics will differ in some way from those of other regions. Geographers identify three types of regions: formal, functional, and vernacular. These three types of regions are suitable for explaining the distribution of characteristics.

Formal region. A **formal region**—also known as a uniform or homogeneous region—is an area in which the selected characteristic is present throughout. The people, activities, and environment found in the region share one or more identifiable characteristics.

Geographers typically employ formal or uniform regions to explain broad global or national patterns. A formal region may display a distinctive cultural characteristic, such as a language, religion, or social custom, or an economic characteristic, such as level of development, predominant type of agriculture practiced, or average income. The selected characteristic used to distinguish the formal region may be quantifiable, but it is often designed to illustrate a general concept rather than a precise mathematical distribution.

Some formal regions, such as countries or local government units within countries, may be easy to identify. Montana is an example of a formal region, characterized by a government that passes laws, collects taxes, and issues license plates, among other actions, with equal intensity throughout the state. We have no difficulty identifying the formal region of Montana, because it has clearly drawn and legally recognized boundaries.

Not everyone in a formal region possesses identical characteristics. Not every farmer living in the U.S. or Canadian wheat belt grows wheat, nor does every farmer living in the U.S. ranching area raise cattle. But we can still distinguish the wheat belt as a region in which the predominant agricultural activity is growing wheat. Similarly, we can distinguish formal regions within the United States characterized by the fact that the people tend to vote for Republican candidates. Yet Republicans do not get all 100 percent of the votes in these regions, nor do Republicans always win.

The last examples show one danger in identifying a formal region: the need to recognize cultural, economic, and environmental diversity even while making a generalization. Problems may arise because a minority of people in a region speak a language, practice a religion, or possess resources different from that of the majority. People in a region may play distinctive roles in the economy and hold different positions in society based on gender or ethnicity.

Functional region. A **functional region**—also known as a nodal region—is an area in which a characteristic activity has a focal point. The activity dominates at a central node and diffuses towards the outer boundary with diminishing importance. Geographers often use functional regions to display information about economic characteristics. The region's node may be a shop or service, and the boundaries of the region mark the limits of the trading area of the activity.

An example of a functional region is the circulation area of a newspaper. A newspaper dominates circulation figures in the city in which it is published. Farther away from the city, the percentage of people who choose that newspaper declines while the percentage of people who read a newspaper published in another city increases. At some point, the circulation of the newspaper from the second city matches the circulation of the original newspaper. That point is the boundary between the nodal regions of the two newspapers.

A more contemporary example of a functional region in the United States and Canada is the area served by a television station. Every television market has an area of dominant influence (ADI), the region in which the preponderance of viewers are tuned to that market's stations. The United States is divided into several hundred functional regions, according to the distribution of the ADIs. The culture disseminated by television stations diffuses to the surrounding region.

An ADI is a good example of a functional region, because the characteristic—people viewing a particular station—is dominant at the center and diffuses towards the periphery. For example, in 1991 everyone in Des Moines, Iowa, who wished to watch a program on NBC tuned to channel 13. In Omaha, Nebraska, 225 kilometers (140 miles) to the west, everyone watching NBC was tuned to channel 6. With increasing distance eastward from Omaha, channel 6's signal became weaker and channel 13's became stronger. The percentage of people watching NBC declined for channel 6 and increased for channel 13.

The boundary between the Omaha and Des Moines ADIs was the point where more people watched channel 13 than channel 6, near the Cass/Adair county line. Other functional regions in Iowa defined by NBC affiliation included Sioux City's channel 4 in the northwest, Davenport's channel 6 in the east, Waterloo's channel 7 in the northeast, and Rochester, Minnesota's, channel 10 in the north (Figure 1–14).

FIGURE 1–14
The map shows the regions of dominance for different television stations within Iowa. These areas are known as areas of dominant influence (ADIs). In several cases, the node of the functional region—the location of the television station—is in an adjacent state. Functional regions frequently overlap state or national boundaries.

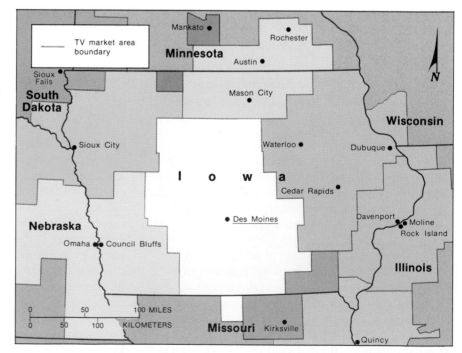

The sunbelt and frostbelt are vernacular regions distinguished by a number of characteristics such as differences in winter climate. In a frostbelt city like Chicago, average winter temperatures are generally 40°F (22°C) lower than in a sunbelt city like Boca Raton, Florida, and snow typically covers the ground for several weeks each winter.

Vernacular region. A **vernacular region,** or perceptual region, is one that people believe to exist, as part of their cultural identity. These regions emerge from concepts that people use informally in daily life, rather than from scientific models developed through geographic thought.

As an example of vernacular regions, Americans frequently use the terms *sunbelt* and either *frostbelt* or *rustbelt* to distinguish two regions in the country. A number of important characteristics distinguish the sunbelt from the frostbelt, including more temperate climate and higher levels of population and economic growth. *Sunbelt* refers to the southern and western parts of the United States, while *frostbelt* or *rustbelt* refers to the northern and eastern parts.

Analysts have difficulty fixing the precise boundary between the two regions. At a conference called "The Sunbelt: A Region and Regionalism in the Making?" participants were given blank outline maps of the United States and asked to delineate the sunbelt. Respondents most frequently cited southern California, from Los Angeles to San Diego, as part of the sunbelt. Other areas of the United States that most participants considered part of the sunbelt included southern Texas, southern Florida, and central Arizona. A few considered the sunbelt to reach as far north as Oregon or Virginia (Figure 1–15).

Perceptual regions can play a critical role in organizing daily life. For example, students at one university were shown a map of the campus divided into squares and asked to indicate in which squares they felt safe walking alone at 10:30 P.M. When combined, the responses portrayed a campus divided into regions that were widely regarded as safe and regions those that were widely regarded as dangerous. Such studies can also determine if perceptions of safety are uniform among groups of students or vary by age, gender, and ethnicity.

Integration

A region gains uniqueness from possessing a distinctive combination of human characteristics. Not content with merely identifying these characteristics, geographers search for relationships among them. Geographers recognize that characteristics are integrated with one another; as a result, the distribution of one characteristic is responsible for the distribution of another.

Integration of cultural characteristics. The variety of human characteristics in the landscape that geographers examine is embodied in the concept of culture. Webster's *Third New International Dictionary* offers a useful definition of **culture:** "the body

FIGURE 1–15
Geographers at a recent conference disagreed on the definition of the sunbelt. Respondents most frequently mentioned southwestern California between Los Angeles and San Diego, followed by south Florida and south central Arizona between Phoenix and Tucson. Some geographers cited areas as far north as Oregon and Virginia.

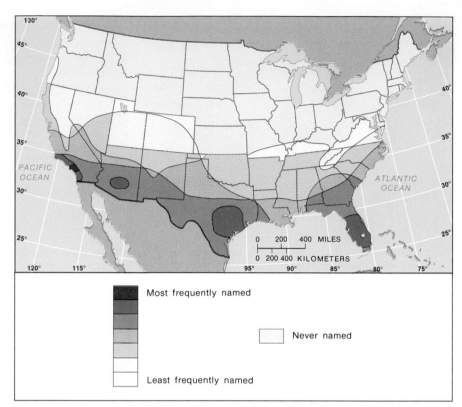

Most frequently named

Never named

Least frequently named

of customary beliefs, social forms, and material traits constituting a distinct complex of tradition of a racial, religious, or social group." To get a manageable grasp on the concept of culture we can examine more closely the three elements that constitute Webster's definition: customary beliefs, social forms, and material traits.

A distinctive landscape results in part from a people's distinctive customary beliefs. The cultural landscape is our unwitting biographer, because it reflects in a tangible, visible form our tastes, values, aspirations, and fears. Customary beliefs are particularly strong in the realm of food. Why do we like to eat the meat of cattle and chickens but not of horses and rats? People living in similar physical environments may prefer to consume specific foods and avoid consuming others because of particular beliefs. Some of these food preferences and avoidances are presented in Chapter 6.

Groups of people create specific social forms and institutions to transform the landscape in accordance with their cultural preferences. Farms, settlements, and other structures are placed on the land-

scape in accordance with the customs of a particular organization. These social forms constitute a second important element defining a people's distinctive culture.

A third important element of culture is the production of a society's material expressions. Technical knowledge limits the capacity of a culture to transform its landscape. Some societies have the capacity to transform the natural environment to a considerable extent whereas others do not. The regional studies approach assesses the technical potential of human communities for using and modifying their landscape. Chapter 8 presents information concerning the ability of different societies to provide for their material needs.

Geographers examine the integration of various cultural characteristics within regions. For example, geographers divide the world into formal regions that are relatively developed economically and those that are developing. The relatively developed regions, such as Europe, North America, the Soviet Union, and Japan, are located primarily in the northern latitudes, while the regions of developing countries—sometimes called less-developed countries (LDCs)—are concentrated in the southern latitudes. This north-south regional split underlies many of the world's social and economic problems.

A variety of characteristics—such as per capita income, literacy rates, televisions per capita, and hospital beds per capita—distinguish relatively developed from developing regions. Geographers demonstrate that the distribution of one characteristic of development is associated with the others.

It is the geographer's job to sort out the associations among various social characteristics, each of which is uniquely distributed across the earth's surface. For example, geographers conclude that political unrest in the Middle East, Eastern Europe, and other areas derives in large measure from the fact that the spatial distributions of important cultural and physical characteristics, such as language, religion, and resources, do not match the political boundaries of individual countries.

In some cases, geographers can build models to prove that the distribution of one characteristic causes the distribution of another. For example, we shall see in Chapter 2 that differences among regions in population growth rates are caused primarily by differences among regions in the crude birth rates. However, geographers often hedge their bets: they recognize that one characteristic must be associated across the earth's surface with others, even if the relationship cannot be modelled precisely. Geographers may have difficulty in constructing exact models of cause and effect, because they must integrate many cultural and physical characteristics to explain a region's distinctiveness.

Integrating information about cancer. Recognizing that the distributions of various cultural and physical characteristics are integrated helps us to understand important social problems. For example, the percentage of people who die each year from cancer differs among regions within the United States. The mid-Atlantic region has the highest levels, with Maryland ranked first among the fifty states, followed by Delaware; the rate in Washington, D.C., which is adjacent to Maryland, is higher than in any state.

Why does Maryland have the highest cancer rate among the fifty states? Mapping the distribution of cancer among Maryland's major subdivisions (twenty-three counties plus an independent city of Baltimore), as well as the District of Columbia, shows sharp internal variations. The cancer rate in Baltimore City is more than 50 percent higher than in Garrett County (Figure 1–16).

The map of cancer rates by county in Maryland does not communicate useful information to someone who knows little about the distribution of people, activities, and environments within the state. By integrating other spatial information, we can begin to see factors that may possibly be associated with regional differences in cancer.

We can divide the state into counties that comprise part of the regions' two large metropolitan areas, Baltimore and Washington, and the counties that are not included in a metropolitan area (*see* Chapter 11 for details on how counties are classified as metropolitan or nonmetropolitan). Thus far, this division does not appear to be very helpful in explaining the distribution of cancer, because we can find high and low rates among both metropolitan and nonmetropolitan counties. However, within the metropolitan areas a pattern emerges: the highest cancer rates are in the cities of Baltimore and Washington, while the suburban counties surrounding the two cities have lower rates.

Once we recognize that the cities have higher cancer rates than the suburbs, we can integrate that information with a variety of other characteristics. People in Baltimore and Washington are more likely than suburbanites to have low incomes and low levels of education. As a result of these characteristics, people living in the cities may be less aware of the risks associated with activities such as smoking and consuming alcohol and less able to afford medical care to minimize the risk of a cancer-related fatality.

Among nonmetropolitan counties, Maryland shows a sharp division between the west, where rates are relatively low, and the east, where rates are relatively high. Income and education do not explain the difference, because levels are lower in most of the nonmetropolitan counties when compared to the levels in the metropolitan areas. Instead, we must attempt to integrate other economic and environmental factors into our explanation.

People on the Eastern Shore may be especially exposed to cancer-causing chemicals, because relatively high percentages are engaged in fishing and

FIGURE 1–16
Maryland has the highest incidence of cancer in the United States, although the rate varies widely within the state (top). The highest rates are in areas where incomes are relatively low, including the large cities and rural Eastern Shore counties (bottom).

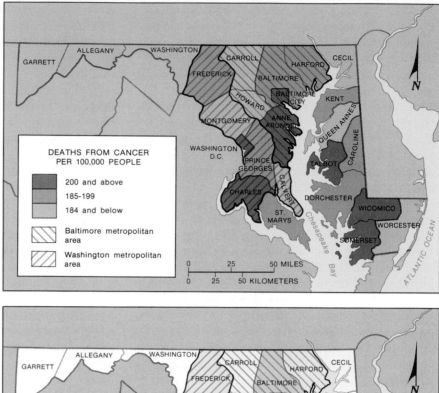

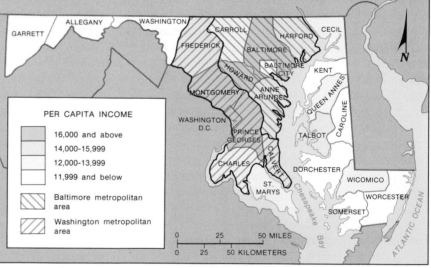

farming compared to people living in the mountainous western counties. The nearby Chesapeake Bay is one of the nation's principal sources of shellfish, and many Eastern Shore residents work in seafood-processing industries. But the Chesapeake Bay also suffers from runoffs of chemicals from Eastern Shore farms, which make heavy use of pesticides, as well as discharges of waste from factories, for the most part located in the metropolitan counties on the western side of the Bay. Prevailing winds also carry pollutants eastward from industries in the metropolitan areas.

Diffusion

Geographers employ the concept of diffusion to help explain the integration of people and activities in regions. **Diffusion** is the process of spread of a characteristic across the landscape. A characteristic originates at a hearth or node and diffuses from there to other locations. Geographers document the location of a node and the process by which diffusion carries the characteristic elsewhere.

Hearths. The region from which an innovation originates is called a **hearth.** How does a hearth emerge? A cultural group must have the willingness to try something new and the ability to allocate resources to nurture the innovation. To develop a hearth, a group of people must also have both the technical ability to achieve the desired idea and the economic structures (such as financial institutions) to facilitate implementation of the innovation.

As discussed in later chapters, geographers can trace the dominant languages, religions, economic systems, political institutions, and other important elements of the modern U.S. and Canadian landscape back to hearths in Europe and the Middle East. But geographers recognize that other areas of the world also contain important hearths. In some cases an idea, such as an agricultural practice, may originate independently in more than one hearth. In other cases hearths may emerge in two regions because two cultural groups modify a shared concept in two different ways.

Types of diffusion. Once a new idea appears in a region it may diffuse to other locations. Geographers observe two basic types of diffusion: relocation and expansion. **Relocation diffusion** is the spread of ideas through movement of people from one region to another. We shall see in Chapter 3 that people migrate for a variety of political, economic, and environmental reasons. When they move, they carry with them their cultural characteristics, such as language, religion, and social customs. The most commonly spoken languages in North and South America are Spanish, English, French, and Portuguese, primarily because several hundred years ago, Europeans who spoke those languages comprised the largest number of migrants. We shall examine the diffusion of languages, religions, and other social customs in Chapters 4 through 6.

Expansion diffusion is the spread of a characteristic among people within a region. This expansion may result from **hierarchical diffusion,** which is the spread of an idea that originates at a node of innovation within a region. That node of innovation may consist of a particular place in the region, such as a large urban center. Ideas generated in a large city may not diffuse to more isolated rural areas until much later. Hierarchical diffusion may also result from the spread of ideas from political leaders or socially elite people to others in the community.

Characteristics may diffuse through two other forms of expansion diffusion: contagious and stimulus diffusion. **Contagious diffusion** is the widespread diffusion of a characteristic throughout the population. As the term implies, this form of diffusion is analogous to the spread of a contagious disease, such as influenza. **Stimulus diffusion** is the spread of an underlying principle, even though a characteristic apparently fails to diffuse.

Whether important cultural concepts diffuse through relocation or expansion diffusion is a critical contemporary issue for many countries. How should today's relatively poor countries promote economic development? One alternative—the approach that emphasizes international trade—assumes that a country's economy develops as a result of the diffusion of economic practices from relatively developed to developing countries. A second alternative—the approach that emphasizes self-sufficiency—assumes that economic development is achieved through a process of innovation inside a country. The health and welfare of a people are vitally affected by the ability of a country's leaders to judge which alternative best suits its region. These alternatives are discussed in more detail in Chapter 8.

Diffusion of AIDS. The process of diffusion helps us to understand the distribution of acquired immunodeficiency syndrome (AIDS) within the United States. During the early 1980s, New York, California, and Florida were the nodes of origin for the disease within the United States. Half of the fifty states had no reported cases, while New York City, with 3 percent of the nation's population, contained more than one-fourth of the AIDS cases. In the neighboring state of New Jersey, AIDS cases dropped with increasing distance from New York City. By the late 1980s, the disease had spread to every state, although California and the New York City area remained the focal points (Figure 1–17).

FIGURE 1–17
Acquired immunodeficiency syndrome (AIDS) has diffused across the United States from nodes in New York, California, and Florida.

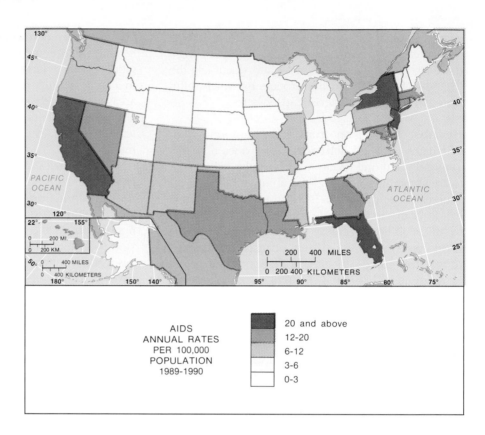

AIDS
ANNUAL RATES
PER 100,000
POPULATION
1989-1990

	20 and above
	12-20
	6-12
	3-6
	0-3

Even within cities, such as New York, the distribution of AIDS cases varied sharply among neighborhoods. An expert on AIDS in New York City, Dr. Ernest Drucker, an epidemiologist at Albert Einstein College of Medicine, was quoted as saying that "in this epidemic, geography is destiny." He meant that the neighborhood in New York City where a person lived was the best predictor of a person's chances of getting AIDS.

Interaction

The diffusion of ideas and characteristics fosters cultural integration because people in different regions interact with each other. To achieve interaction, one group must be accessible to the other; interaction fails to occur when the two groups are isolated from each other. The movement of people, goods, and ideas within and among regions is called **spatial interaction.**

Interaction takes place through networks, which are chains of communication that connect places.

Modern communications and transportation inventions permit ideas that originate in one area to diffuse rapidly to people in other areas. As a result of rapid diffusion, interaction in the contemporary world can be a complex process. People in more than one region may improve and modify an idea at the same time but in different ways.

One well-known example in the United States is a television network, such as ABC, CBS, or NBC, which comprises a chain of stations around the country simultaneously broadcasting the same program, such as a football game. Transportation systems also form networks that connect places to each other. Airlines in the United States, for example, have adopted distinctive networks known as "hub-and-spokes." Under the hub-and-spokes system, airlines fly planes from a large number of places into one hub airport within a short period of time and then a short time later send the planes to another set of places. In principle, travellers originating in relatively small towns can reach a wide variety of destinations by changing planes at the hub airport.

To illustrate the extent of the AIDS epidemic in the United States, a quilt has been sewn with each square representing a different victim. This exhibition took place on the Mall in Washington, D.C., with the U. S. Capitol in the background.

Local differences in farming, clothing, settlements, language, and religion arise through centuries of isolation from inhabitants of other regions. Typically, the farther away one group is from another the less likely the two groups are to interact. Contact diminishes with increasing distance and eventually disappears. This tailing-off phenomenon is called **distance decay.**

Interaction among groups can be retarded by barriers, either physical, such as oceans and deserts, or cultural, such as language and legal systems. We regard the landscape as part of our inheritance from the past. As a result, we may be reluctant to modify the landscape unless under heavy pressure to do so.

A major change in the landscape may reflect an upheaval in a people's culture.

Acculturation. When two groups interact, the more dynamic and powerful culture is likely to dominate the weaker one. The modification of a culture as a result of contact with a more powerful culture is called **acculturation.**

One of two things may happen to the weaker culture through acculturation. First, the weaker culture may be obliterated. For example, most immigrants to the United States traditionally have lost touch rapidly with most of the cultural characteristics of the former home and have adopted the cultural traits of the new community. Second, the weaker culture may be transformed into a new culture, in which a new set of cultural characteristics may coexist with older ones. New patterns emerge through the integration of the two cultures, but elements of the older culture remain.

Cargo cult. The diffusion of cultural elements from Europe and North America may transform rather than destroy local cultural beliefs. For example, people on the Pacific island of Tana, part of the country of Vanuatu, worship Prince Philip, the husband of Britain's Queen Elizabeth, as a god. According to local customary belief, Prince Philip is a messiah who grew up on Tana Island and Queen Elizabeth broke with her great council of chiefs to marry him. Prince Philip was added to the collection of local gods a few years ago when he visited the country, formerly the British colony of New Hebrides. His advance man apparently distributed photographs, which the people regard as holy icons.

The introduction of Prince Philip as a god in Vanuatu was part of a cargo cult. A **cargo cult** is a belief that the arrival of a ship or airplane in a locality has spiritual meaning. Several hundred years ago, some Native Americans regarded Europeans who arrived on ships as gods.

Belief in a cargo cult persists in Papua New Guinea and some other Pacific islands because American ships and airplanes brought new technology and equipment during World War II. Some residents believe that if they remain faithful, the planes will return with vast wealth. Some people in Papua New Guinea have prepared large wooden planes as female "sirens" to lure male planes and their cargo from the sky.

Summary

Here again are the key issues for Chapter 1:

1. **How did geography develop historically?** Traditionally, geographers explored the earth's surface and described the arrangement of things in different locations. During the past century, geographers have tried to explain the reasons underlying the arrangement of people and activities across the earth's surface. Two explanatory models were developed, now known as the human-environment and regional studies approaches.

2. **How do geographers answer the "where" question?** Geographers use the basic concepts of location, maps, and distribution to describe where different phenomena are placed on the earth's surface. Location is the position on the earth's surface occupied by an object. Once geographers fix the locations of different things, they determine the regularities in their arrangement. They then use maps to display the location of these objects across the earth's surface.

3. **How does the human-environment approach help to answer the "why" question?** According to the human-environment, or cultural ecology, approach, the physical environment imposes limits on human actions, though humans have the ability to adjust to the physical environment. Among the environmental processes that influence human actions are climate, vegetation, soil, and landforms.

4. **How does the regional studies approach help to answer the "why" question?** Geographers identify regions and explain the interrelationships among characteristics within and between regions. The diffusion of people and ideas across the earth's surface produces interaction and integration among characteristics within and among regions.

Why Is More Than One Location Named Miami?

CASE STUDY
REVISITED

The chapter-opening dialogue explored some of the differences between two places, Miami, Ohio, and Miami, Florida. After noting such differences, geographers attempt to explain the reasons underlying the observed pattern, such as the repeated use of the name Miami. Geographic processes, such as diffusion and interaction, help in the explanation.

The name originates with the Miami Indians, a Native American tribe belonging to the Algonquin language family. When European explorers first encountered them, the Miami Indians lived in what is now northeastern Wisconsin's Door County peninsula, near Sturgeon Bay. The word *Miami* means "people on the peninsula," a reference to the tribe's homeland.

In the late seventeenth century, the Miamis migrated south from the peninsula and settled primarily along the St. Joseph River (in southwestern Michigan) and the Wabash River (in northeastern Indiana). Pushed out of the southern Lake Michigan area by other tribes, the Miamis then migrated east to present-day Ohio, where they were living when the territory became part of the United States. Early nineteenth-century European settlers retained the name Miami on the landscape to identify rivers, towns, and a university. The Maumee, a river in northern Ohio, is a variant spelling of Miami.

Settlements called Miami were established in several other states by migrants from Ohio or members of the Miami tribe. For example, most of the Miamis were pushed from Ohio to eastern Kansas between 1832 and 1840. The present-day town of Miami, Kansas, is located near the land the government gave to the tribe. In 1867, the tribe relocated with the Illinois Indians further west to Oklahoma, then known as Indian Territory. In 1891, Miami chief Thomas P. Richardville and Colonel W. C. Lykins established a town in the northeastern corner of Oklahoma that they named Miami. In the late nineteenth century, settlers from Ohio established a settlement in Gila County, Arizona, also named Miami. Settlements called Miami were likewise established in Missouri, New Mexico, Texas, and West Virginia.

In Florida, the name Miami apparently derived from a completely independent source. The first recorded European to reside near present-day Miami, Florida, was a Spaniard, Hernando d'Escalante Fontaneda. Following a shipwreck, he became a prisoner of the Tequesta Indians, a branch of the Calusas, between 1545 and 1562. In his memoirs (1575) Fontaneda used the a Calusa Indian word *mayaimi* to describe Lake Okeechobee, as well as a river which flowed from the lake to the Atlantic Ocean. He translated the word *mayaimi* as "very large."

Around 1830 Richard R. Fitzgerald established a plantation at the future site of the city of Miami. He named the plantation Miami, the first time that the Ohio spelling rather than the Spanish/Calusa version was used in Florida. Born in Columbia, South Carolina, Fitzgerald may once have encountered the Ohio spelling of Miami, though he had no known connection with the Ohio Miami.

The army took over the Miami plantation from the late 1830s until the early 1850s, renaming it Fort Dallas. After being abandoned as a fort, the site was only sparsely inhabited until the 1890s. Henry M. Flagler started to build shops and hotels on the site in March, 1896, and extended his Florida East Coast Railroad to the settlement one month later. By July, 1896, the new settlement had 1,500 inhabitants and was incorporated as a city. Given a choice in naming the new settlement, the voters selected the former plantation name Miami, instead of Flagler or Fort Dallas. The choice may have been influenced in part by the presence of several former Ohio residents in the new settlement.

Thus, the name Miami originated with a Native American tribe in what is now Wisconsin and diffused to other locations in the United States as a result of the tribe's migration. The name originated in Florida independently, the sort of coincidence that occurs when groups of people live in isolation from each other. When south Florida became part of the United States, the process of spatial interaction produced a modified spelling in conformance with the name of the northern tribe.

Key Terms

Acculturation The modification of a culture as a result of contact with a more powerful culture.

Base line An east-west line designated in the Land Ordinance of 1785 to facilitate the numbering of townships.

Biome A large collection of the earth's land vegetation.

Cargo cult A belief that the arrival of a ship or airplane in a locality has spiritual meaning.

Cartography The science of making maps.

Climate The long-term average weather conditions at a particular location.

Concentration The extent of spread of a phenomenon over a given area.

Contagious diffusion The widespread diffusion of a characteristic throughout a population.

Contour lines Imaginary lines on the ground connecting points of equal elevation above sea level.

Culture The body of customary beliefs, social forms, and material traits constituting a distinct complex of tradition of a racial, religious, or social group.

Density The frequency that something occurs within a given unit of area.

Diffusion The process of spread of something across the landscape.

Distance decay The diminishing in importance and eventual disappearance of a phenomenon with increasing distance from a node.

Environmental determinism A nineteenth and early twentieth-century approach to the study of geography that argued that the general laws sought by human geographers could be found in the physical sciences. Geography was therefore the study of how the physical environment caused human activities.

Expansion diffusion The spread of a characteristic among people within a region.

Formal region (or uniform or homogeneous region) An area in which the selected characteristic is present throughout at the same degree of intensity.

Functional region (or nodal region) An area in which an activity has a focal point. The characteristic dominates at a central node, diffuses towards the outer part of the region, diminishes in importance, and eventually disappears.

Greenwich Mean Time The time in the time zone which encompasses the prime meridian or 0° longitude.

Hearth The region from which innovative ideas originate.

Hierarchical diffusion The spread of an idea that originates at a node of innovation within a region.

International Date Line An arc running for the most part along 180° longitude, though it deviates in several places to avoid dividing land areas. When you cross the International Date Line heading east (toward America) the clock moves back twenty-four hours, or one entire day. When you go west (toward Asia) the calendar moves ahead one day.

Land Ordinance of 1785 A law that divided much of the United States into a system of townships to facilitate the sale of land to settlers.

Latitude The numbering system used to indicate the location of parallels drawn on a globe.

Location The position on the earth's surface that an object occupies.

Longitude The numbering system used to indicate the location of meridians drawn on a globe.

Map A two-dimensional, or flat, representation of the earth's surface or a portion of it.

Meridian An imaginary arc drawn on the earth's surface between the North and South poles.

Parallel An imaginary circle drawn around the globe parallel to the equator and at right angles to the meridians.

Pattern The geometric arrangement of something in a study area.

Polder A piece of land created by the Dutch by draining water from an area.

Possibilism A theory that the physical environment may set limits on human actions, but people have the ability to adjust to the physical environment and choose a course of action from many alternatives.

Prime Meridian The meridian, designated as 0° longitude, which passes through the Royal Observatory at Greenwich, England.

Principal meridian A north-south line designated in the Land Ordinance of 1785 to facilitate the numbering of townships.

Projection The system used to transfer locations from a globe to a map.

Region An area distinguished by one or more distinctive characteristics.

Relief The difference in elevation between two points in an area; relief measures the extent to which an area is flat or hilly.

Relocation diffusion The spread of an idea through movement of people from one region to another.

Scale The relationship between the length of an object on a map and the same feature on the earth's surface.

Section A square normally one mile long and one mile wide. According to the Land Ordinance of 1785 townships were normally divided into thirty-six sections.

Site The physical character of a location.

Situation The location of a place relative to other places.

Slope Relief divided by the distance between two points; slope measures the steepness of the hills.

Soil The material that lies on the earth's surface between the air and rocks.

Spatial association The distribution of one object across a landscape is scientifically related to the location of another object.

Spatial distribution The arrangement of a phenomenon across the earth's surface.

Spatial interaction The movement of people, goods, and ideas within and among regions.

Stimulus diffusion The spread of an underlying principle, even though a characteristic fails to diffuse.

Topographic maps Maps published by the U.S. Geological Survey which display a variety of physical features, such as relief and slope, as well as cultural features, such as buildings and roads.

Toponym The name given to a portion of the earth's surface.

Township A square normally six miles long and six miles wide. The Land Ordinance of 1785 divided much of the United States into a series of townships.

Vernacular region (or perceptual region) An area that people believe to exist, as part of their cultural identity.

Thinking Geographically

1. Cartography is not simply a technical exercise in penmanship and coloring; nor are decisions confined to scale and projection. Mapping is a politically sensitive undertaking. Look at how maps in this book distinguish between the territories of Israel and its neighbors, the locations of borders in South Asia and the Arabian peninsula, the relationship of China and Taiwan, and the status of the Baltic Republics. Are there other logical ways to draw boundaries and distinguish among territories in these regions?

2. Imagine that a transportation device (perhaps the one in Star Trek) would enable all humans to travel instantaneously to any location on the earth's surface. What impact would that invention have on the distribution of peoples and activities across the earth's surface?

3. When earthquakes, hurricanes, or other environmental disasters strike, humans tend to "blame" nature and see themselves as innocent victims of a harsh and cruel nature. To what extent do environmental hazards stem from unpredictable nature, and to what extent do they originate from human actions? Should victims blame nature, other humans, or themselves for the disaster?

4. The construction of dams is a particularly prominent example of human-environment interaction in regions throughout the world. Turkey is building the Ataturk Dam on the Euphrates River, a move opposed by Syria and Iraq, the two downstream countries. Egypt, which operates the Aswan Dam on the Nile River, has blocked loans to Ethiopia which could be used to divert the source of the Nile. Some Russians oppose construction of the Gorskaya dam in the Gulf of Finland near Leningrad. Similarly, the Balbina dam on the Uatruma River, a tributary of the Amazon, has generated considerable opposition in Brazil. Why do governments push the construction of dams so forcefully, and why do others oppose their construction so passionately?

5. Geographic concepts, such as the human-environment and regional studies traditions, are supposed to help explain contemporary issues. Are there any stories in your newspaper to which geographic concepts can be applied to help understand the issues?

Further Readings

Bennett, John W. *The Ecological Transition: Cultural Anthropology and Human Adaptation.* Oxford: Pergamon Press, 1976.

Blaut, J. M. "Diffusionism: A Uniformitarian Critique." *Annals of the Association of American Geographers* 77 (March 1987): 48–62.

Brown, Lawrence A. *Innovation Diffusion: A New Perspective.* London: Methuen, 1981.

Brunn, Stanley D. "Sunbelt USA." *Focus* 36 (Spring 1986): 34–35.

Claval, Paul. "The Region as a Geographical, Economic and Cultural Concept." *International Social Science Journal* 39 (May 1987): 159–172.

Constandse, A. K. *Planning and Creation of an Environment.* Lelystad, The Netherlands: Rijksdienst voor de IJsselmeerpolders, 1976.

Entrikin, J. Nicholas, and Stanley D. Brunn, eds. *Reflections on Richard Hartshorne's "The Nature of Geography."* Washington, D.C.: Association of American Geographers, 1989.

Espenshade, Edward B., Jr., ed. *Goode's World Atlas.* 18th ed. Chicago: Rand McNally, 1990.

Forman, R. T. T., and M. Godron. *Landscape Ecology.* New York: Wiley, 1986.

Freeman, Donald B. "The Importance of Being First: Preemption by Early Adopters of Farming Innovations in Kenya." *Annals of the Association of American Geographers* 75 (March 1985): 1–16.

Gaile, Gary L., and Cort J. Willmott, eds. *Geography in America.* Columbus, OH: Merrill, 1989.

Gardner, Lytt I., Jr., et al. "Spatial Diffusion of the Human Immunodeficiency Virus Infection Epidemic in the United States, 1985–87." *Annals of the Association of American Geographers* 79 (March 1989): 25–43.

Goliber, Thomas J. *Sub-Saharan Africa: Population Pressures on Development.* World Population in Transition. *Population Bulletin* 40 (no. 1). Washington, D.C.: Population Reference Bureau, 1985.

Gould, Peter R. *The Geographer at Work.* Boston: Routledge and Kegan Paul, 1985.

Gritzner, Charles F., Jr. "The Scope of Cultural Geography." *Journal of Geography* 65 (January 1966): 4–11.

Gross, Jonathan L., and Steve Rayner. *Measuring Culture.* New York: Columbia University Press, 1985.

Hägerstrand, Torsten. *Innovation Diffusion as a Spatial Process.* Chicago: University of Chicago Press, 1967.

Hamm, Bernd, and Martin Lutsch. "Sunbelt v. Frostbelt: A Case for Convergence Theory?" *International Social Science Journal* 39 (May 1987): 199–214.

Hartshorne, Richard. *The Nature of Geography.* Lancaster, PA: Association of American Geographers, 1939.

Jackson, John Brinckerhoff. *American Space.* New York: W. W. Norton, 1972.

James, Preston E. *All Possible Worlds: A History of Geographical Ideas.* New York: Bobbs-Merrill, 1972.

Johnson, Hildegard B. *Order upon the Land.* New York: Oxford University Press, 1976.

Johnston, R. J. *Philosophy and Human Geography.* 2d ed. London: Edward Arnold, 1986.

———, ed. *The Dictionary of Human Geography.* 2d ed. Oxford: Basil Blackwell, 1985.

Leighly, John, ed. *Land and Life: A Selection from the Writings of Carl Ortwin Sauer.* Berkeley: University of California Press, 1963.

Macgill, Sally M. "Environmental Questions and Human Geography." *International Social Science Journal* 38 (no. 3, 1986): 357–376.

Meinig, D. W., ed. *The Interpretation of Ordinary Landscapes.* New York: Oxford University Press, 1979.

Mikesell, Marvin W. "Tradition and Innovation in Cultural Geography." *Annals of the Association of American Geographers* 68 (March 1978): 1–16.

Norton, William. *Explorations in the Understanding of Landscape: A Cultural Geography.* Westport, CT: Greenwood Press, 1989.

Peet, Richard. "The Social Origins of Environmental Determinism." *Annals of the Association of American Geographers* 75 (September 1985): 309–333.

Penning-Rowsell, Edmund C., and David and Lowenthal, eds. *Landscape, Meanings and Values.* London: Allen and Unwin, 1986.

Reed, Michael, ed. *Discovering Past Landscapes.* London: Croom Helm, 1986.

Rice, Bradley R. "Searching for the Sunbelt." *American Demographics* 3 (March 1981): 22–23.

Rowntree, Lester B., and Margaret W. Conkey. "Symbolism and the Cultural Landscape." *Annals of the Association of American Geographers* 70 (December 1980): 459–474.

Salter, Christopher L. *The Cultural Landscape.* Belmont, CA: Duxbury Press, 1971.

———. "What Can I Do With Geography?" *Professional Geographer* 35 (August 1983): 266–273.

Santos, Milton. "Geography in the Late Twentieth Century: New Roles for a Theoretical Discipline." *International Social Science Journal* 36 (no. 4, 1984): 657–672.

Sauer, Carl O. "Morphology of Landscape." *University of California Publications in Geography* 2 (1925): 19–54.

Sawers, Larry, and William K. Tabb, eds. *Sunbelt/Snowbelt: Urban Development and Regional Restructuring.* New York: Oxford University Press, 1984.

Shannon, Gary W., and Gerlad F. Pyle. "The Origin and Diffusion of AIDS: A View from Medical Geography." *Annals of the Association of American Geographers* 79 (March 1989): 1–24.

Shortridge, James R. *The Middle West: Its Meaning in American Culture.* Lawrence: University of Kansas, 1989.

Solot, Michael. "Carl Sauer and Cultural Evolution." *Annals of the Association of American Geographers* 76 (December 1986): 508–520.

Tuan, Yi-Fu. "Cultural Pluralism and Technology." *Geographical Review* 79 (July 1989): 269–279.

Wagner, Philip L., and Marvin W. Mikesell. *Readings in Cultural Geography.* Chicago: University of Chicago Press, 1962.

Also consult the following journals: *Annals of the Association of American Geographers; Canadian Geography (Géographie canadien); Focus; Geographical Analysis; Geographical Review; Geography; Journal of Geography; Professional Geographer; Progress in Human Geography; Transactions of the Institute of British Geographers*

2
Population

How many brothers and sisters do you have? How many brothers and sisters did your parents and grandparents have? Did your parents and grandparents have more, fewer, or the same number of siblings as you? How many children do you have or intend to have in the future? Is that figure larger, smaller, or the same number as your parents and grandparents had?

The typical family in relatively developed countries today contains fewer people than in the past, and the number of children is declining. In much of North America and Europe, a majority of people have the same number or fewer siblings than their parents and grandparents. The answer to the last question on average appears to be "smaller," though only the future can tell what people will actually do in this matter.

In other regions of the world the number of children per household tends to be much higher than in the relatively developed countries. The ability of developing countries to provide food, clothing, and shelter to their people is severely hampered by continued rapid growth in the population.

A study of population is the basis for understanding a wide variety of issues in human geography, as well as other disciplines. To study problems such as increasing the food supply, reducing pollution, and encouraging economic growth, geographers must know the size and distribution of a region's population. Therefore, our study of the cultural landscape begins with a study of population problems.

Population Growth in India

The Phatak family lives in a village of 600 inhabitants in India. At age forty, Indira Phatak has been pregnant five times. Four of her children have survived; they are aged five to eighteen.

When the two Phatak daughters marry a few years from now, how many children will each of them bear? The Indian government hopes that they will choose to have fewer children than their mother. India's population is growing by more than 18 million per year and is projected to exceed 1 billion in the year 1998. Unless attitudes and behavior drastically change in the next few years, India's population will exceed 6 billion a century from now.

Three-fourths of Indians live in rural settlements that have fewer than 5,000 inhabitants. For many of these people, children are an economic asset, because they help perform chores on the farm and are expected to provide for their parents in their old age. The high percentage of children who will die before they reach working age encourages large families. Nearly one out of every ten infants in India dies within one year of birth.

India has made significant progress in recent years in the diffusion of modern agricultural practices, construction of new industry, and development of natural resources. But, in a country with a rapidly expanding population, much of the newly created wealth must be used to provide food, housing, and other services for the additional people. With more than one-third of the population under the age of fifteen, the government must build schools, hospitals, and day-care centers. Will there be jobs for these 300 million children when they are old enough to work?

Geographers and other social scientists study the population problems of countries like India from a variety of viewpoints. The scientific study of population characteristics is known as **demography.**

The study of population is critically important because of three facts:

- More people are alive at this time than at any point in the past.
- The world's population has been increasing at a more rapid rate since the end of World War II than ever before in history.
- Virtually all of the global population growth is concentrated in the poor, developing countries.

These facts lend an urgency to the task of understanding the diversity of population problems in the world today.

Some demographers worry that the world may contain too many people in the future. Will the world's population exceed the capacity of the earth to support people without large-scale starvation, poverty, and revolution? Geographers cannot offer a simple yes or no answer to the question of global overpopulation. But, geographic concepts help explain the nature of the global population problem and the solutions that are possible.

Using the human-environment approach, geographers argue that the so-called **overpopulation** problem is not simply a matter of the total number of people in the world but a matter of the relationship between the number of people and the availability of resources. Problems result when the number of people in an area exceeds the capacity of the environment to support life at a decent standard of living.

Using the regional studies approach, geographers find that overpopulation is a threat in some regions of the world but not in others. The capacity of the earth as a whole to support human life may be high, but some regions have a favorable balance between people and available resources while others do not. Contrary to a common assumption, the regions with the most people are not the same as the regions with an unfavorable balance between population and resources.

This chapter examines the distribution and growth of world population. Subsequent chapters look at the other side of the overpopulation equation—availability of resources.

How Is the World's Population Distributed?

Human beings are not distributed uniformly across the earth's surface. We can understand how population is distributed by using two basic properties of distribution: concentration and density. Geographers identify the regions of the earth's surface where population is clustered and the regions where the population is sparse. Geographers also construct a variety of density measures to help explain the relationship between the number of people and available resources.

Population Concentrations

We can divide the world into regions occupied by large numbers of people and regions that are sparsely inhabited. Approximately three-fourths of the world's population live on 5 percent of the earth's surface; the balance of the earth's surface consists of oceans and less intensively inhabited land. The portion of the earth's surface occupied by permanent human settlement is called the **ecumene.**

The world's population is clustered in five regions: East Asia, South Asia, Southeast Asia, Western Europe, and Eastern North America (Figure 2–1). These five regions display some similarities. Most people live near an ocean or near a river with easy access to an ocean rather than in the interior of major land masses. In fact, approximately two-thirds of the world's population lives within 500 kilometers (300 miles)—and 80 percent within 800 kilometers (500 miles)—of an ocean.

The five population clusters occupy generally low-lying areas, with fertile soil and temperate climate. With the exception of part of the Southeast Asia concentration, the regions are located in the northern hemisphere, between 10° and 55° north latitude. Despite these similarities, we can see significant differences in the pattern of occupancy of the land in the five concentrations.

East Asia. Approximately one-fourth of the world's people live in East Asia, the largest cluster of inhabitants. This region, which borders the Pacific Ocean, includes the eastern part of China, the islands of Japan, the Korean peninsula, and the island of Taiwan.

Five-sixths of the people in this concentration live in the People's Republic of China, the world's most populous country. China is the world's third largest country in land area, but much of the interior of the country consists of sparsely inhabited mountains and deserts. In fact, the Chinese population is clustered near the Pacific coast and several fertile river valleys that extend inland, such as the Huang and the Yangtze. Although China has eight cities with more than two million inhabitants, three-fourths of the people live in rural areas where they work as farmers.

Population is not distributed uniformly within Japan either. More than one-fourth of the people live in two large metropolitan areas—Tokyo and Osaka—that comprise less than 3 percent of the country's land area. Overall, more than three-fourths of the Japanese live in urban areas and work at industrial or service jobs.

South Asia. The second largest concentration of people is in South Asia, which includes India, Pakistan, Bangladesh, and Sri Lanka. More than 20 percent of the world's inhabitants live in South Asia. India, the world's second most populous country, contains more than three-fourths of the people in the South Asia population concentration.

The most important concentration of people within South Asia lives along a 1,500-kilometer (900 mile) corridor from Lahore, Pakistan, through India and Bangladesh to the Bay of Bengal. Much of this area's population is concentrated along the plains of the Indus and Ganges rivers. Population is also heavily concentrated near India's two long coast-lines—the Arabian Sea to the west and the Bay of Bengal to the east.

Like the Chinese, most people in South Asia are farmers living in rural areas. The region contains ten cities with more than two million inhabitants, but only one-fourth of the total population lives in an urban area.

Southeast Asia. A third important Asian population cluster, and the world's fourth largest, is in Southeast Asia. Nearly 500 million people live in Southeast Asia, mostly on a series of islands that lie between the Indian and Pacific oceans. The largest population concentration is on the Indonesian is-

land of Java, inhabited by more than 100 million people. Indonesia, which consists of several thousand islands, is the world's fifth most populous country. Several islands that belong to the Philippines contain high population concentrations, and population is also clustered along several river valleys and deltas at the southeastern tip of the Asian mainland, known as Indochina. Like China and South Asia, the Southeast Asia concentration is characterized by a high percentage of people working as farmers in rural areas.

The three Asian population concentrations together comprise over half of the world's total population, living on less than 10 percent of the world's land area. The same held true 2,000 years ago, when approximately half of the world's population was found in these same regions.

Europe. The world's third largest population cluster encompasses much of Europe, from the United Kingdom to the central part of the Soviet Union. Approximately 15 percent of the world's people live in this cluster. The region includes 23 countries, ranging from Liechtenstein, with 157 square kilometers (62 square miles) and a population of 30,000, to part of the Soviet Union, the world's largest country in land area when its Asian part is included.

In contrast with the three Asian concentrations, three-fourths of Europe's inhabitants live in cities, while less than 20 percent are farmers. A dense network of road and rail lines links the settlements together. The highest concentrations in Europe are near coalfields, historically the major source of power for industry.

Although the region's temperate climate permits the cultivation of a variety of crops, Europeans do not produce enough food for themselves to survive. Instead, they import needed resources from elsewhere in the world. The search for additional resources has been a major incentive for Europeans to explore and colonize other parts of the world during the past six centuries. They now turn many of these resources into manufactured products.

North America. The largest concentration of population in the Western Hemisphere is in the northeastern United States and southeastern Canada. The population cluster extends along the Atlantic coast from Boston, Massachusetts, to Newport News, Virginia, and west along the Great Lakes to Chicago, Il-

FIGURE 2–1

People are not distributed uniformly across the earth's surface. This map illustrates the use of both density and concentration to describe regularities in the distribution of people across the earth's surface.

In Chapter 1, we defined density as the frequency of occurrence of a phenomenon within a given unit of area. In this map, the phenomenon is people and the unit of area is either square kilometers or square miles. The map shows that the density of population in much of Asia and Europe exceeds 50 persons per square kilometer or 125 persons per square mile. In contrast, the density in most of the Western Hemisphere is fewer than 30 persons per square kilometer or 75 persons per square mile.

Concentration is the extent of spread of a phenomenon, such as people, over a given area. More than three-fourths of the world's population is clustered in these five regions, which are listed according to size: (1) East Asia—eastern China, southern Korea, and Japan; (2) South Asia—India, Pakistan, and Bangladesh; (3) Central Europe—from southern United Kingdom to central Soviet Union; (4) Southeast Asia—especially the island of Java, Indonesia; and (5) Northeastern United States/Southeastern Canada.

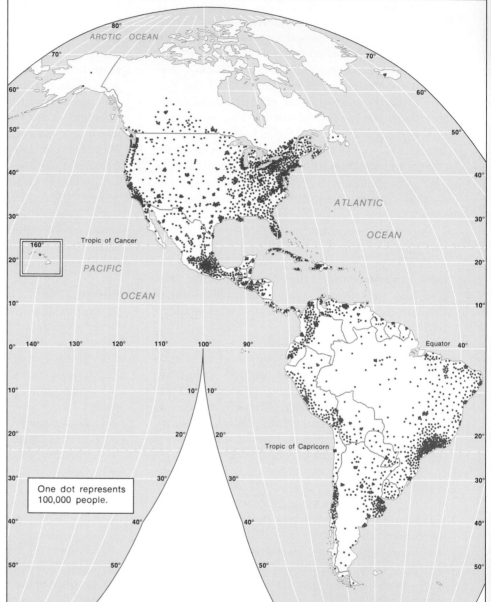

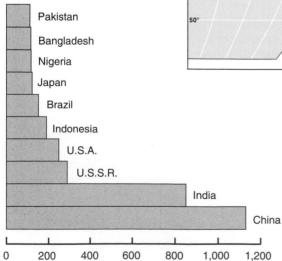

POPULATION (in millions)

linois. Approximately 150 million people live in the area. Like the Europeans, most Americans are urban dwellers; less than 5 percent are farmers.

Sparse Concentrations

Human beings avoid clustering in certain physical environments. Relatively few people live in regions

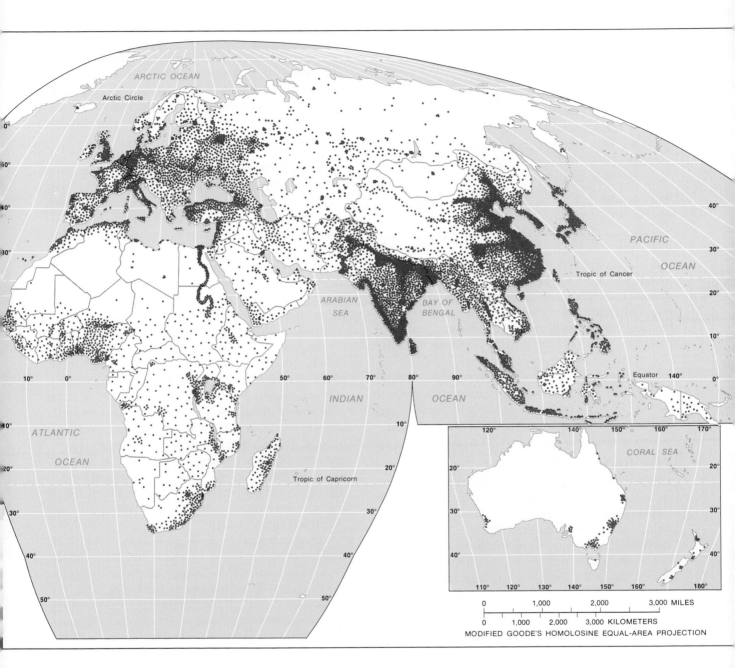

MODIFIED GOODE'S HOMOLOSINE EQUAL-AREA PROJECTION

that are too dry, too wet, too cold, or too mountainous for activities such as agriculture.

Dry lands. Areas too dry for farming cover approximately 20 percent of the earth's land surface. Two large desert regions exist in the world, mostly between 15° and 50° north latitude and between 20° and 50° south latitude. The largest desert region, extending from North Africa to Southwest and Central Asia, is known by several names, including the Sahara, Arabian, Thar, Takla Makan, and Gobi. The smaller desert region in the Southern Hemisphere comprises much of Australia.

The deserts generally lack sufficient water to grow crops that could feed a large population, though some people survive in the deserts by raising animals, such as camels, that are adapted to the climate. By constructing irrigation systems, people can grow crops in some parts of the desert. While dry lands are generally inhospitable to intensive agriculture, they may contain natural resources useful to people—notably, much of the world's oil reserves. The increasing demand for these resources has led to a growth in settlements in or near deserts.

Wet lands. Lands that receive very high levels of precipitation may also be inhospitable for human occupation. These lands are located primarily near the equator between 20° north and south latitudes in the interiors of South America, Central Africa, and Southeast Asia. Rainfall averages more than 1.25 meters (50 inches) per year, with most areas receiving more than 2.25 meters (90 inches) per year. The combination of rain and heat hinders agriculture, because nutrients are rapidly depleted from the soil.

Precipitation may be concentrated in specific times of the year or spread throughout the year. In seasonally wet lands, such as Southeast Asia, enough food can be grown to support a large population.

Cold lands. Few human beings live in very cold climates. Territory near the North and South poles is not suitable for planting crops, and few animals can survive the extremely cold climate. Much of the land is perpetually covered by an ice cap, and—perhaps surprisingly, considering the extensive ice caps—the polar regions receive less precipitation than some of the Central Asian deserts.

High lands. Finally, relatively few people live at high elevations. The highest mountains in the world are sparsely settled. For example, approximately half of Switzerland's land is more than 1,000 meters (3,300 feet) above sea level, but only 5 percent of the country's people live there. There are some significant exceptions to this rule, especially in Latin America and Africa. People may prefer to occupy higher lands if temperatures and precipitation are uncomfortably high at lower elevations. In fact, Mexico City, the world's largest city by some measures, is located at an elevation of 2,243 meters (7,360 feet).

Density

The concept of density helps geographers measure the relationship between population and available resources. Density, which is the number of people within an area of land, can be computed in several ways, including arithmetic density, physiological density, and agricultural density.

Arithmetic density. Geographers most frequently use the **arithmetic density** (or population density), which is the total number of people divided by total land area. Geographers rely on the arithmetic density to compare conditions in different countries because the two pieces of information needed to calculate the measure—total population and total land area—are easy to obtain.

For example, to compute the arithmetic or population density for the United States, we can divide the population (approximately 255 million people) by the land area (approximately 9.4 million square kilometers or 3.6 million square miles). The result shows that the United States has an arithmetic density of 27 persons per square kilometer (71 persons per square mile). By comparison, the arithmetic density is much higher in South Asia—approximately 810 persons per square kilometer (2,097 persons per square mile) in Bangladesh and 261 (677) in India. On the other hand, the arithmetic density is only 3 persons per square kilometer (7 persons per square mile) in Canada and 2 (6) in Australia (Figure 2–2).

Arithmetic density varies even more within individual countries. In the United States, for example, New York County (Manhattan Island) has a population density of approximately 26,000 persons per square kilometer (67,000 persons per square mile), whereas Esmeralda County, Nevada, has a population density of approximately 0.08 (0.22). In Egypt, the arithmetic density is nearly 2,000 persons per square kilometer (5,000 persons per square mile) in the delta and valley of the Nile River, compared to 3 persons per square kilometer (8 persons per square mile) in the rest of the country.

Arithmetic density enables geographers to make approximate comparisons of the number of people trying to live on a given piece of land in different regions of the world. But, other density measures more fully explain why people are not uniformly distributed across the earth's surface.

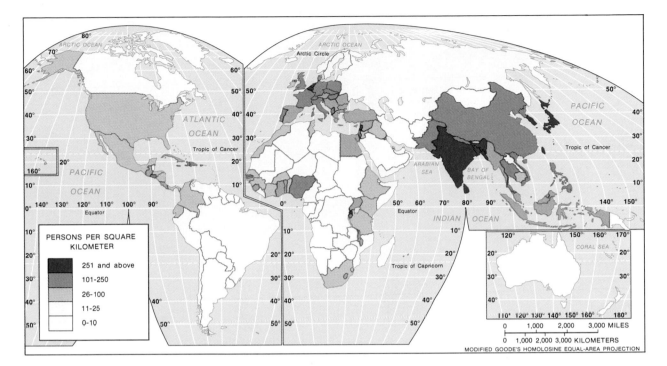

FIGURE 2–2

Arithmetic or population density is the total number of people divided by the total land area. The highest population densities are found in Asia, Europe, and Central America, while the lowest are in North and South America.

High population density is not the same thing as overcrowding, nor is it a measure of the well-being of a society. European countries rank among the highest in most measures of well-being, such as income per person, whereas most Asian countries have relatively low ranks. Conversely, low population densities are found in both North America, one of the world's wealthiest regions, and Africa, one of the world's poorest regions.

Physiological density. Both physiological density and agricultural density provide insights into the relationship between the size of a population and the availability of resources to support life in a region. **Physiological density** is the number of people per unit area of arable land, which is land suitable for agriculture. The higher the physiological density, the greater the potential pressure people may place on the land to produce enough food.

For example, in the United States the physiological density is 134 persons per square kilometer (346 persons per square mile) of land suitable for agriculture, compared to more than 2,000 (5,200) in Egypt. The large difference in physiological densities demonstrates that crops grown on a given unit of land in Egypt must feed more people than in the United States (Figure 2–3).

Comparing physiological and arithmetic densities helps geographers understand the capacity of the land in different countries to yield enough food for the needs of the people. If the physiological density is much larger than the arithmetic density—as in Egypt—most of the country's land area may be unsuitable for intensive agriculture. In fact, all but 5 percent of the Egyptian people live in the Nile River valley and delta because it is the only area in the country that receives enough moisture to allow intensive cultivation of crops (Table 2–1).

Agricultural density. Two countries with similar physiological densities may produce significantly different amounts of food because of different economic conditions. **Agricultural density,** the ratio of the number of farmers to the total amount of land suitable for agriculture, helps to account for these economic differences. Relatively developed societies have lower agricultural densities because a few people are able to farm an extensive area of

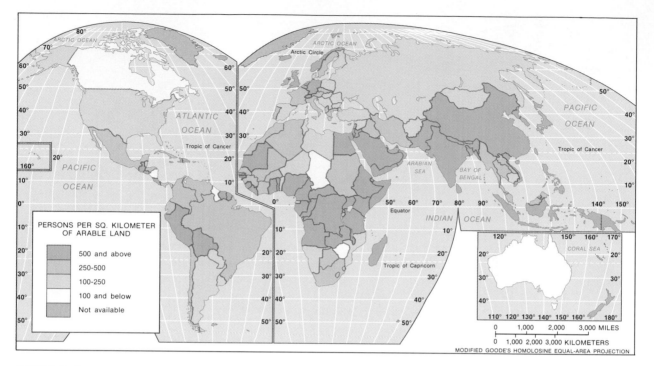

FIGURE 2–3
Physiological density is the number of people per unit area of arable land, which is land suitable for agriculture. Physiological density is a better measure than population density of the relationship between population and the availability of resources in a society.

land and feed a large number of people. Most people are therefore free to work in factories, offices, or shops rather than in the fields.

To develop a picture of the relationship between population and resources in a country, geographers examine its physiological and agricultural densities in combination. As Table 2–1 shows, the physiolog-

ical densities of both Egypt and Japan are high, but the Japanese have a much lower agricultural density than the Egyptians. Geographers conclude that both the Japanese and Egyptians put heavy pressure on the land to produce food, but the more efficient Japanese agricultural system requires a much smaller number of farmers than the Egyptian system.

TABLE 2–1
Measures of density in selected countries, expressed as population per square kilometer

	Arithmetic Density	Physiological Density	Agricultural Density	Percent Farmers	Percent Arable*
Canada	3	64	3	5	4
United States	27	134	4	3	20
Egypt	55	2,003	855	43	3
India	261	544	341	63	48
Japan	332	2,424	194	8	14
Netherlands	403	1,612	73	5	25
Bangladesh	810	1,420	803	57	56
United Kingdom	235	820	17	2	29

*Refers to land utilized for crops or fallow, as measured by the United Nations Food and Agricultural Organization.

Source: Population Reference Bureau, "1991 World Population Data Sheet," and *Encyclopaedia Britannica, 1990 Yearbook.*

Similarly, the Netherlands has a higher physiological density than India but a lower agricultural density. This difference demonstrates that compared to India, the Dutch have an extremely limited amount of arable land to meet the needs of the population. However, the highly efficient Dutch farmers can generate a large food supply from a limited resource.

How Has the World's Population Increased?

The most important source of knowledge about the growth and composition of a country's population is the **census.** A simultaneous global census has never been held, but individual countries generally undertake a census on a regular basis. In the course of counting inhabitants, governments normally require a member of every household to answer questions about the family and its dwelling. Important information includes when people were born, where they live and work, and with whom they live. In some countries, people must answer more detailed questions concerning the characteristics of the dwelling and the people living in it.

Taking the Census

The first comprehensive census of any country took place in Sweden in 1745. Many countries in Africa and Asia have taken their first census only in the twentieth century. We must therefore estimate the past population of the world from fragmentary information, such as reports compiled in ancient Rome and China and parish church records of baptisms, marriages, and burials.

Many countries take a census every ten years. In the United States the census occurs in years ending in zero, such as 1990 and 2000. Canada, the United Kingdom, and a number of other countries once ruled by the British take the census in years ending in the numeral one. The French average seven years between each census, but the government decrees exactly when each should be done.

Successfully counting a country's population frequently depends on the cleverness and resourcefulness of census takers. In some countries, census tak-

ers must communicate with people who live in isolated locations that lack modern services, such as electricity, telephones, and mail delivery. Surveyors in such countries as India must count millions of people who have no permanent address and live on sidewalks. A census worker in Rio de Janeiro, Brazil, opened an icebox in a butcher shop and discovered that it provided access to an otherwise unknown street where people lived.

Securing a complete count of a country's population is difficult. Turkey declares an all-day curfew on census day for the entire population, including foreigners and travelers. Everyone is required to remain indoors between 7:00 A.M. and 5:00 P.M., and no one is allowed in the streets without government permission.

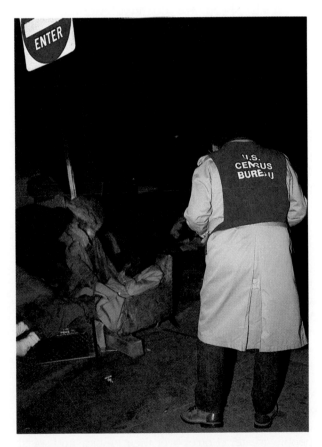

As part of the 1990 census, the U.S. Bureau of the Census made a determined effort to count people who were homeless and sleeping in shelters or outside. Critics charged that census takers found only a small percentage of the homeless people.

Many people do not participate in the census because they are unable to read the forms. Even in the United States, with its relatively high degree of literacy and few isolated communities, not all people are counted. Many undocumented aliens fail to complete a census form because they fear that the government will find them. Other people simply ignore the census, despite noncompliance being illegal.

Hostility to the census was so great in the Federal Republic of Germany that the government cancelled the one scheduled for 1981. German courts ruled that the census was unnecessarily intrusive and ordered the government to rewrite many of the questions. Despite continuing opposition by many Germans, the government finally ran a census in 1987, six years late. Opponents of the census distributed posters that declared "No, thanks" and pamphlets titled "Only Sheep Are Counted." Germans were urged to boycott the census or fill in false answers. After police broke into the office of a Berlin boycott leader, hundreds of people were injured and arrested in rioting.

Despite the hazards and uncertainties, a person-by-person count is the most accurate method of obtaining information about a population. Unless we take a census periodically, our understanding of people is based on speculation rather than on facts. The census is also a prominent symbol that most people do not live in complete isolation but must be counted as part of a global society.

Population Increases

Geographers estimate that for most of human history the size of the world's population was virtually unchanged, at perhaps one-half million. The species multiplied in some regions and declined in others, while remaining small throughout the world. During this period people lived as nomadic hunters and gatherers of food.

The global rate of population growth sharply increased during three periods—around 8000 B.C., A.D. 1750, and 1950. Each population spurt was accompanied by technological advances that gave people greater control over their physical and social environments. In turn, these technological improvements increased the capacity of the earth to support human population.

First period. For several hundred thousand years prior to approximately 8000 B.C., global population had increased very modestly, at an average of only a couple of dozen people per year. Then around that year, the annual growth rate surged to fifty times higher than in the past, and world population grew by several thousand per year. Between 8000 B.C. and A.D. 1750, global population increased from approximately 5 million to 800 million (Table 2–2).

What caused the burst of population growth around 8000 B.C.? Scientists point to the **agricultural revolution,** which is the time when human beings first domesticated plants and animals and no longer relied entirely on hunting and gathering. By growing plants and raising animals, human beings created larger and more predictable sources of food, and more people could survive.

The agricultural revolution involved a series of accidents and experiments over a period of several hundred years. Plant and animal domestication apparently originated independently in several locations, but major advances in agriculture occurred in the Fertile Crescent, an area that extends from the eastern edge of the Mediterranean Sea to present-day Iran (*see* Chapter 9).

Second period. For nearly 10,000 years after the agricultural revolution, the world population grew at a fairly steady pace. After about A.D. 1750, the world's population suddenly began to grow ten times faster than in the past. The average annual increase jumped from several thousand in the early eighteenth century to several hundred thousand in the late eighteenth century. Global population rose from approximately 800 million in 1750 to 2.5 billion in 1950, an average annual increase of 0.6 percent per year.

The second spurt in the rate of population increase resulted from the **industrial revolution,** which began in England in the late eighteenth century and spread to the European continent and North America during the nineteenth century. The industrial revolution involved a series of improvements in industrial technology that transformed the process of manufacturing goods. The result of this industrial transformation was the production of unprecedented levels of wealth, some of which was used to make the community a healthier place to live.

TABLE 2–2
World population and growth rates

Date	Estimated Population (millions)	Percent Average Yearly Growth in Prior Period	Number of Years in Which Population Doubles at Current Growth Rate
400,000 B.C.	0.5	—	—
8000 B.C.	5	0.001	59,007
1 A.D.	300	0.05	1,354
1750	791	0.06	1,250
1800	978	0.43	163
1850	1,262	0.51	136
1900	1,650	0.54	129
1950	2,517	0.85	82
1991	5,384	1.85	40

Source: John D. Durand, "The Modern Expansion of World Population," *Proceedings of the American Philosophical Society,* 39 (June 1967): 137; and Population Reference Bureau, "1991 World Population Data Sheet."

New machines helped farmers increase agricultural production and feed the rapidly growing population. More efficient agriculture freed people to work in factories producing other goods and generated enough food for the industrial workers.

The wealth produced by the industrial revolution was also used to improve sanitation and personal hygiene. Sewer systems were installed in cities, and food and water supplies were protected. As a result of these public improvements, people were healthier and lived longer (*see* Chapter 10).

Third period. The third dramatic increase in global population began after World War II in about 1950. The average annual population increase jumped from approximately 0.5 percent early in the twentieth century to nearly 2 percent by the middle of the twentieth century. Instead of adding a few million people per year, as was the case at the beginning of the twentieth century, the world has grown by more than 70 million per year since the late 1940s. During the 1990s, world population is increasing by nearly 100 million people per year.

The recent era of population growth has been caused by the **medical revolution.** Medical technology invented in Europe and North America has diffused to the poorer countries of Latin America, Asia, and Africa. Improved medical practices have eliminated many of the traditional causes of death in poorer countries and enabled more people to have longer and healthier lives. Penicillin, vaccines, and such insecticides as DDT effectively and inexpensively controlled many infectious diseases, such as malaria, smallpox, and tuberculosis. Current mortality rates are 60 to 80 percent lower in Africa, Asia, and Latin America than in the late 1940s.

Components of Population Change

The two factors that influence the world's rate of population growth are fertility and mortality. At the scale of individual countries, a third factor—migration—also affects population growth. The population of a country rises because of births and inmigration of people from elsewhere in the world, while the population declines as a result of deaths and outmigration of people. Migration is discussed in detail in Chapter 3.

Natural increase. The rate of **natural increase,** the percentage by which a population grows in a year, is computed by subtracting the crude death rate from the crude birth rate. The term *natural* means that a country's growth rate excludes migration.

During the past decade, the rate of natural increase was 1.8 percent, meaning that world population grew in one year by 1.8 percent. For many things in life—such as an examination grade—the difference between 1 percent and 2 percent is not important. But for population studies the difference is critical.

The rate of natural increase affects the **doubling time,** which is the number of years needed to double a population, assuming a constant rate of natural

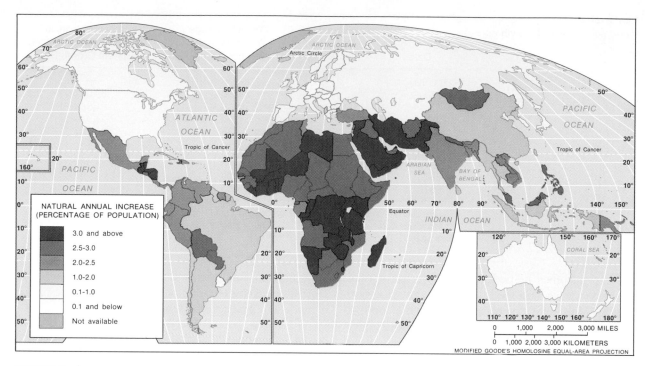

FIGURE 2–4

The natural increase rate is the percentage by which a population of a country grows in a particular year. World average in recent years has been approximately 1.8 percent per year. The countries with the highest natural increase rates are concentrated in Africa. Africa's overall natural increase rate is approximately 2.8 percent per year, but the rate exceeds 3.0 in nearly half of the countries in the region. On the other hand, the natural increase in Europe as a whole is only 0.3 percent per year, and several countries have declining rates.

increase. At the current rate of natural increase the population of the world will double in approximately 40 years. Should the natural increase rate decline to 1.0 percent, global population will double in approximately 70 years. People in the twenty-first century will notice the difference between these two rates of natural increase. The current rate would place global population in the year 2100 at 34 billion, but if the natural increase rate during the next century declines to 1.0 percent, the world's population would be less than 20 billion in 2100.

Very small changes in the rate of natural increase dramatically affect the size of the world's population, because the base used to derive the percentage is so high. When we multiply the natural increase rate of 1.8 percent by the current global population base of more than 5 billion, the result is an annual increase of more than 90 million people. If the rate of natural increase immediately dropped

to 1.0 percent, then the annual population increase would decline to approximately 55 million. As the base continues to grow in the twenty-first century, a change of 0.1 percent will produce very large swings in population growth.

The distribution of rates of natural increase shows significant regional differences (Figure 2–4). The rate of natural increase exceeds 3.0 percent in much of Africa and southwestern Asia. At the other extreme, the United States, Canada, and every European country with the exception of Albania and possibly Iceland have natural increase rates below 1.0 percent. Japan, Australia, New Zealand, and a handful of smaller countries also have crude birth rates below 1.0 percent. Several European countries have negative rates of natural increase, meaning that population is declining.

Not only is world population increasing faster than ever before, but virtually all of the growth is also concentrated in poorer countries. This year, about 66 percent of the world's population growth is in Asia, 20 percent in Africa, and 10 percent in Latin America. Europe and North America account for less than 5 percent of global population growth. Regional differences in rates of natural increase mean that virtually all of the world's additional people live in countries that are the least able to handle the increase.

Why is global population growth not distributed uniformly? Geographers point to regional differences in fertility and mortality rates.

Fertility. To study the number of births at the national or global scale, geographers most frequently refer to the **crude birth rate (CBR),** which is the total number of live births in a year for every 1,000 people alive in the society. A crude birth rate of 20, for example, means that for every 1,000 people in a country, 20 babies are born over a one-year period. The word *crude* in this context means that we are

concerned with society as a whole, rather than particular individuals or groups. In communities with an unusually large number of people of a certain age—such as a college town—a geographer may study separate birth rates for women of each age. These numbers are age-specific rather than crude birth rates.

Geographers also use the **total fertility rate (TFR)** to measure the number of births in a society. The total fertility rate is the average number of children a woman will have throughout her child-bearing years (roughly ages fifteen through forty-nine). To compute the TFR, scientists must assume that as a woman reaches a particular age in the future, she will be just as likely to have a child as are women of that age today. The crude birth rate provides a picture of a society as a whole in a given year, while the total fertility rate attempts to predict the future behavior of individual women.

The world map of crude birth rates mirrors the distribution of natural increase rates (Figure 2–5).

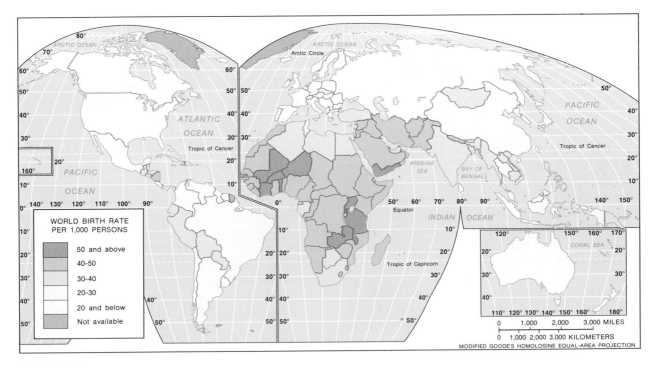

FIGURE 2–5
Crude birth rate is the total number of live births in a year for every 1,000 people alive in the society. The global distribution of crude birth rates parallels that of natural increase rates. Like the natural increase rates, the highest crude birth rates are found in Africa, while the lowest are in Europe.

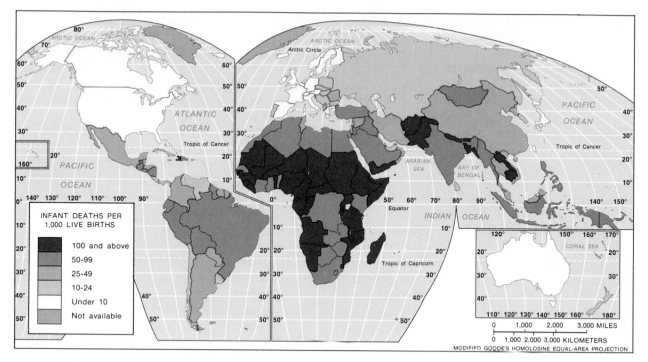

FIGURE 2–6

The infant mortality rate is the number of deaths of infants under one year old per 1,000 live births in a year. World infant mortality rate is approximately 80 per 1,000. The global distribution of infant mortality rates is similar to those for natural increase and crude birth rates. As was the case with natural increase and crude birth rates, the highest infant mortality rates are found in Africa, while the lowest are in Europe.

As was the case with natural increase rates, the highest crude birth rates are in Africa and the lowest are in Europe and North America. Most African countries have a crude birth rate over 40, and some exceed 50. Crude birth rates over 30 are common in Asia and Central America. On the other hand, the United States, Canada, and every European country with the exception of Albania have crude birth rates below 20. Japan, Australia, New Zealand, and a handful of smaller countries also have crude birth rates below 20.

Mortality. The **crude death rate** compares the total number of deaths and the total number of people living in a country in one year. Comparable to the crude birth rate, the crude death rate is expressed as the annual number of deaths per 1,000 population. Geographers also compute different death rates for specific age groups or for males and females.

Another useful measure of mortality is the **infant mortality rate,** which is the annual number of

deaths of infants under age one year compared to the total number of live births. The infant mortality rate is usually expressed as the number of deaths during the first year of life per 1,000 live births.

The global distribution of infant mortality rates follows the familiar pattern. The highest rates are in the poorer countries of Africa and Asia, while the lowest rates are in Europe, North America, and other wealthier societies. Infant mortality rates exceed 100 in many African and Asian countries, meaning that over 10 percent of all babies die before reaching their first birthday. Infant mortality rates are less than 10 in most European countries, Canada, Japan, and Australia (Figure 2–6).

In general, the infant mortality rate reflects a country's health care system. We find lower infant mortality rates in countries with well-trained doctors and nurses and large supplies of hospitals and medicine. Although the United States is well-endowed with medical facilities, it suffers from somewhat higher infant mortality rates than Canada and many European countries. Blacks and other minorities in the United States have infant mortality rates twice as high as the national average. Many health experts explain this high rate by noting that many poor people in the United States, especially minorities, cannot afford good health care for their infants.

Life expectancy at birth measures the average number of years a newborn infant can expect to live under current mortality levels. Like the infant mortality, crude birth, and natural increase rates, life expectancy varies sharply among different regions. Babies born today can expect to live into their early 50s if they are African and into their middle 70s if they are European or North American (Figure 2–7).

The global distribution of crude death rates does not follow the pattern set by the other mortality and fertility variables. Consistent with the other demographic characteristics, the highest crude death rates are in Africa. But perhaps unexpectedly, the lowest crude death rates are in Latin America and Asia, rather than in the wealthy countries of North America and Europe (Figure 2–8).

Furthermore, the spread among different countries between the highest and lowest crude death rates is relatively low. Crude birth rates for individual countries range from about 10 to 50, a spread of over 40. But the highest crude death rate is only in the 20s, and the difference between the highest and lowest rates is around 20.

Why does Sweden, one of the world's wealthiest countries, have a crude death rate higher than Thailand, one of the poorest? Why does the United States, with its extensive system of hospitals and physicians, have a higher crude death rate than Costa Rica or Panama? The answer is that the populations of different countries are at various stages in a process known as the demographic transition, which is discussed in the next section.

K E Y   I S S U E

Why Is Population Increasing at Different Rates in Different Countries?

Every country has experienced changes over time in its natural increase rate, fertility rate, and mortality rate. Historically, these demographic changes have followed similar patterns in different countries,

though the changes have not happened at the same time and at the same speed everywhere.

Demographic Transition

The process of change in a society's population is called the **demographic transition.** The demographic transition is a process with several stages, and every country is in one of the stages. The process has a beginning, middle, and end, and—barring a catastrophe such as a nuclear war—it is irreversible. Once a country moves from one stage of the process to the next it does not revert to an earlier stage (Figure 2–9).

Stage 1. In Stage 1 of the demographic transition the crude birth and death rates are both generally high. These rates may vary considerably from one year to the next but over the long term are roughly comparable. As a result, the rate of natural increase is very low.

Survival is unpredictable in a Stage 1 society. The population may depend on hunting and gathering for food. When food is easily obtained, the population increases; in times of shortage, the population decreases. People who practice settled farming prosper during abundant harvests and suffer when unfavorable climatic conditions result in low output. Wars and diseases also take their toll on the death rate in a Stage 1 society.

Most of human history was spent in Stage 1 of the demographic transition, but today no such society remains. Every country has moved on to at least Stage 2 of the demographic transition and with that transition has experienced profound changes.

Stage 2. In Stage 2 of the demographic transition the crude death rate suddenly plummets, while the crude birth rate remains roughly the same as in Stage 1. Because the difference between the crude birth rate and crude death rate is very high, the rate of natural increase is also very high.

Some demographers divide Stage 2 of the demographic transition into two parts. The first part is the period of accelerating population growth. The second part is when the growth rate begins to slow, though the gap between births and deaths remains high.

Countries in Europe and North America entered Stage 2 of the demographic transition in the late

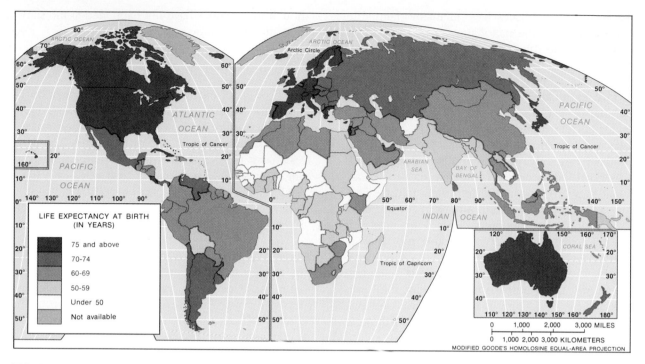

FIGURE 2–7
Babies born this year are expected on average to live until their early sixties. Life expectancy for babies, however, ranges from the mid-thirties in several African countries to the late seventies in much of Europe and North America.

eighteenth or nineteenth century. The change has come in the twentieth century for countries in Africa, Asia, and Latin America. What accounts for the rapid decline in the crude death rate? New technology permits increases in the permanent food supply and control of diseases.

Stage 3. A country moves from Stage 2 to Stage 3 of the demographic transition when the crude birth rate begins to drop sharply. The crude death rate continues to fall in Stage 3 but at a much slower rate than in Stage 2. The population continues to grow because the crude birth rate is still higher than the crude death rate. But the rate of natural increase is more modest in Stage 3 countries than in Stage 2 because the gap between the crude birth and death rates narrows.

European and North American countries generally moved from Stage 2 to Stage 3 of the demographic transition during the first half of the twentieth century. Some countries in Africa, Asia, and Latin America have moved to Stage 3 in recent years, but others remain in Stage 2.

The sudden drop in the crude birth rate during Stage 3 occurs for different reasons than the rapid decline of the crude death rate during Stage 2. The crude death rate declines in Stage 2 following introduction of new technology into the society, but the crude birth rate declines in Stage 3 because of changes in social customs.

A society enters Stage 3 of the demographic transition when people choose to have fewer children. The decision is partly a delayed reaction to a decline in mortality, especially the infant mortality rate. In Stage 1 societies, the survival of any one infant cannot be confidently predicted, and families typically have a large number of babies to improve the chances of some living to adulthood. Medical practices introduced in Stage 2 societies greatly improve the probability of an infant surviving, but many years elapse before families react by conceiving fewer babies.

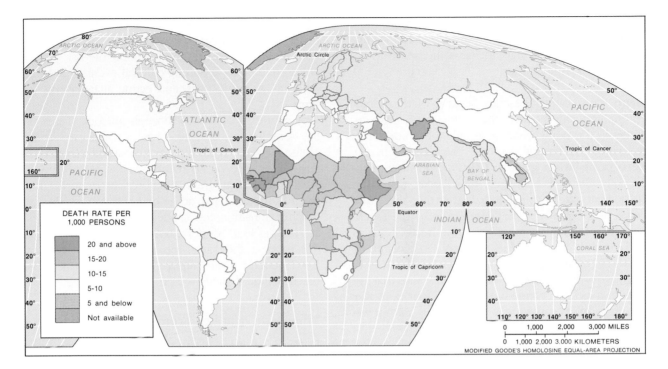

FIGURE 2–8
Crude death rate is the total number of deaths in a year for every 1,000 people alive in the society. The global pattern of crude death rates varies from those for the other demographic variables already mapped in this chapter. First, while Europe has the lowest natural increase, crude birth, and infant mortality rates, it has relatively high crude death rates. Second, the variance between the highest and lowest crude death rates is much lower than was the case for the crude birth rates.

Economic changes in Stage 3 societies also induce people to have fewer babies. People in Stage 3 societies are more likely to live in cities rather than the countryside and work in offices, shops, or facto-ries rather than on farms. Farmers often consider a large family an asset because children can do some of the chores. In contrast, children living in cities are generally not economic assets to their parents

FIGURE 2–9
The demographic transition consists of four stages: *Stage 1*—very high birth and death rates produce virtually no long-term natural increase. *Stage 2*—rapidly declining death rates combined with very high birth rates produce very high population growth rates. *Stage 3*—birth rates rapidly decline, while death rates continue to decline; natural increase rates begin to moderate. *Stage 4*—very low birth and death rates produce virtually no long-term natural increase.

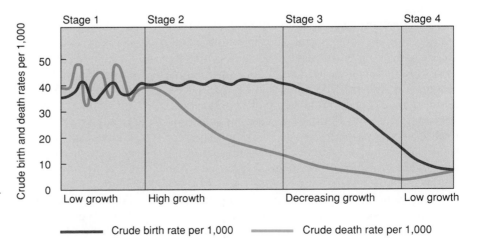

because they are prohibited from working in most types of urban jobs. In addition, urban homes are relatively small and may not have the space to accommodate large families.

Stage 4. A country reaches Stage 4 of the demographic transition when the crude birth rate declines to the point where it equals the crude death rate, and the natural increase rate approaches 0. **Zero population growth (ZPG),** a term often applied to Stage 4 countries, may occur when the crude birth rate is still slightly higher than the crude death rate, because some females die before reaching child-bearing years and the number of females in their child-bearing years can vary. To account for these discrepancies, zero population growth is frequently expressed as the total fertility rate that results in a lack of change in the total population over a long term. At this time, a total fertility rate of approximately 2.1 usually produces ZPG. However, a country experiencing a high level of immigration may need a lower total fertility rate to achieve ZPG.

Several countries in Western and Northern Europe have reached Stage 4 of the demographic transition, including Sweden, Germany, and the United Kingdom. The United States has not completely moved into Stage 4 because birth rates remain higher among some groups, such as recent immigrants from Latin America. In several European countries, including Denmark, Germany, and Hungary, the crude birth rate slips below the crude death rate in some years. However, total population has not been declining, at least not in Denmark and Germany, because people have been immigrating from other countries.

Social customs again explain the movement from one stage of the demographic transition to the next. Increasingly, women in Stage 4 societies enter the labor force rather than remain at home as full-time mothers. Where most families live on farms, economic activities and child-rearing are conducted at the same place, but in urban societies most parents must leave the home to work in an office, shop, or factory. An employed parent must arrange for someone to take care of preschool children during working hours.

Changes in lifestyle also encourage smaller families. People who have access to a wider variety of birth-control methods are more likely to use some of them. With increased income and leisure time, more people participate in entertainment and recreation activities that may not be suitable for young children, such as attending cultural events, traveling overseas, going to bars, and eating at fancy restaurants.

A country that passes through all four stages of the demographic transition has in some ways completed a cycle—from little or no natural increase in Stage 1 to little or no natural increase in Stage 4. Two crucial demographic differences underlie this process, though. First, at the beginning of the demographic transition the crude birth and death rates are high—35 to 40 per 1,000—while at the end of the process the rates are approximately 10 per 1,000. Second, the total population of the country is much higher in Stage 4 than in Stage 1.

The Demographic Transition in England

England, a portion of the United Kingdom, provides a good example of the long-term impact of the demographic transition, because the country has reached Stage 4. At least fragmentary evidence concerning the population in England is available for a period of 1,000 years. Unlike the United States and many other countries, England has not changed its boundaries nor has it been affected by large-scale migration.

Stage 1. In 1066, when the Normans invaded England, the country's population was approximately 1 million. Seven hundred years later the population was only 6 million, and the country was still in Stage 1 of the demographic transition (Figure 2–10).

During that 700-year period, population rose some years and fell in others. Crude birth and death rates averaged more than 35 per 1,000 but varied considerably from one year to the next. For example, England's population declined from 4 million in 1250 to 2 million a century later, after the Black Death (bubonic plague) and famines swept the country. As recently as the 1740s, the crude death rate skyrocketed following a series of bad harvests.

Stage 2. In 1750 the crude birth and death rates in England were both 40 per 1,000. In 1800, the crude birth rate was still very high, at 34, but the crude death rate had plummeted to 20. This 50-year pe-

FIGURE 2–10
Demographic transition for England. Demographers must estimate birth and death rates prior to 1750, because precise records are not available. Church parish records of births, baptisms, marriages, and burials help in making estimates.

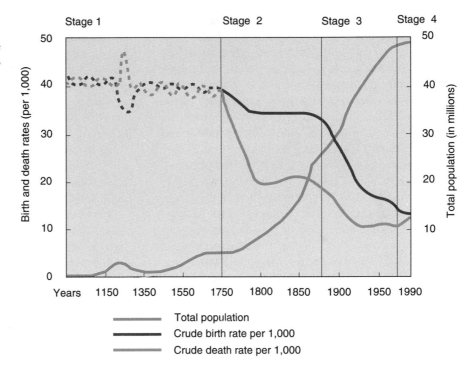

riod marked the start of the industrial revolution in England. New production techniques increased the nation's food supply and generated money that was spent on improvements in public health.

England remained in Stage 2 of the demographic transition for about 125 years. During that period the population rose from 6 million to 30 million, an average annual natural increase rate of 1.4 percent.

Stage 3. Crude birth and death rates changed little in England during most of the nineteenth century. In 1880, the crude birth rate was 33 per 1,000 and the crude death rate 19, in both cases only 1 per 1,000 lower than in 1800. After 1880, England entered Stage 3 of the demographic transition. The crude death rate continued to fall somewhat over the next century, from 19 per 1,000 in 1880 to 12 in 1970. However, the crude birth rate declined sharply, from 33 per 1,000 in 1880 to 18 by 1930 and 15 in 1970. The population increased between 1880 and 1970 from 26 to 49 million, about 0.7 percent per year.

Stage 4. Since the early 1970s, England has been in Stage 4 of the demographic transition. The population has increased only 1 million since 1970, an av-

erage natural increase rate of 0.1 percent. The crude death rate has consistently rested at 12 per 1,000 since the 1970s, while the crude birth rate has varied between 12 and 14. The crude birth rate increases slightly some years because the number of women of child-bearing age is greater, not because of decisions by women to have more children.

When England began to move through the demographic transition in about 1750, the country had 6 million people, crude birth and death rates of 40 per 1,000, and a record of little population growth over the previous 700 years. Today England has entered another period of little population growth. The difference is that the crude birth and death rates are around 12 rather than 40, and the country has 50 million inhabitants instead of 6 million.

Population Pyramids

Countries have distinctive population structures, depending on their stage in the demographic transition. The population of countries varies in two ways: (1) the percentage of people in each age group and (2) the distribution between males and females.

We can display the distribution by gender and age groups of a country's population on a bar graph called a **population pyramid.** A population pyramid normally shows the percentage of the total population in each five-year age group, with the youngest group (zero to four years old) at the base of the pyramid and the oldest group at the top. The length of the bar represents the percentage of the total population contained in that group. Males are usually shown on the left side of the pyramid and females on the right (Figure 2–11).

The shape of a pyramid is determined primarily by the crude birth rate in the country. A country with a high crude birth rate has a relatively large number of young children. Consequently, the base of the population pyramid is broad. On the other hand, if the country has a relatively large number of older people, the top of the pyramid is wider, and the graph looks more like a rectangle than a pyramid.

Age distribution. The age structure of the population is extremely important in understanding similarities and differences among different countries in the world. The most important factor is the **dependency rate,** which is the percentage of people who are either too young or too old to work. The larger the percentage of dependents, the greater the financial burden on those who are working to support those who cannot.

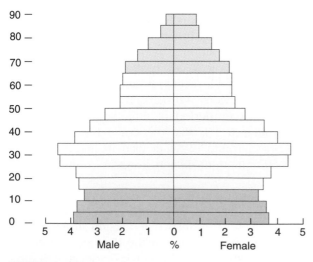

FIGURE 2–11
Population pyramid for the United States, 1990. The graph is not precisely in the shape of a pyramid. The indentation at the base shows that crude birth rate has declined sharply in the United States since the mid-1960s.

To compare the dependency rates of different countries we can divide the population into three age groups: zero to fourteen, fifteen to sixty-four, and sixty-five and over. Geographers generally classify people under fifteen and over sixty-four as dependents. Approximately one-half of all people living in countries in Stage 2 of the demographic transition are dependents, compared to only one-third in Stage 4 countries. Young dependents outnumber elderly ones by ten to one in Stage 2 countries, but the ratio between young and elderly dependents is roughly equal in Stage 4 countries.

In nearly every African country and in many Asian and Latin American countries more than 40 percent of the people are under age fifteen. This high percentage follows from the high crude birth rates in these regions. In contrast, the percentage of children under fifteen is around 20 percent in the European and North American countries at or near Stage 4 of the demographic transition (Figure 2–12). A large percentage of children strains the ability of a poorer country to provide needed services, such as schools, hospitals, and day-care centers. When the children reach the age of leaving school, jobs must be found for them, but the government must continue to allocate scarce resources to meeting the needs of the still-growing number of young people.

As countries pass through the stages of the demographic transition, the percentage of older people increases. The higher percentage partly reflects the lower percentage of young people produced by declining crude birth rates. Older people also benefit in Stage 4 countries from improved medical care and higher incomes. People ages sixty-five and over exceed 15 percent of the population in several European countries, such as Denmark, Sweden, the United Kingdom, and Germany, compared to less than 5 percent in most African countries.

Older people must receive adequate levels of income and medical care after they retire from their jobs. The "graying" of the population places a burden on European and North American governments to meet these needs. More than one-fourth of all government expenditures in the United States, Canada, Japan, and many European countries go to social security, health care, and other programs for the older population. Because of the larger percentage of older people, countries in Stage 3 or 4 of the

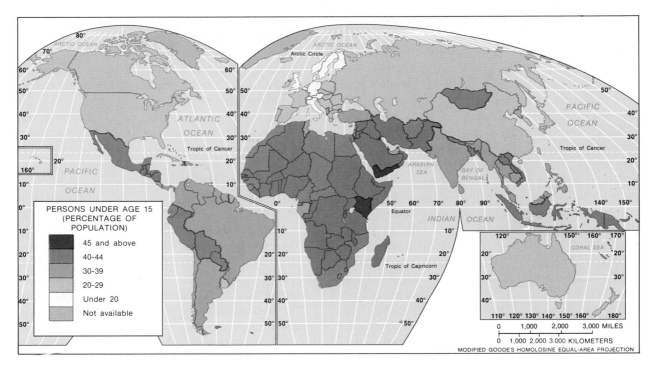

FIGURE 2–12
Percent under age 15. Approximately one-third of the world's inhabitants are under age 15.
But the percentage of young people varies from nearly one-half in much of Africa and Asia to
less than one-fifth in many European countries.

demographic transition—such as the United States and Sweden—have higher crude death rates than Stage 2 countries.

Sex ratio. The number of males per 100 females in the population—the **sex ratio**—varies among countries depending on the particular birth and death rates. In general, slightly more males than females are born, but males have higher death rates. The ratio of men to women is about 95:100 (that is, 95 men for each 100 women) in Europe and North America, compared to 102:100 in the rest of the world.

In the United States, males under fifteen exceed females by a ratio of 105 to 100. Women first outnumber men at about age thirty and comprise 60 percent of the population age sixty-five and above. High mortality rates during childbirth partly explains the lower percentage of women in poorer countries. The difference also relates to the age structure because poorer countries have a larger percentage of young people—where males generally outnumber females—and a lower percentage of older people—where females are much more numerous.

Societies with a high rate of immigration typically have more males than females because males are more likely to undertake long-distance migration. Frontier areas and boom towns typically have more men than women. The rapidly growing state of Alaska, for example, has 113 men for every 100 women.

Countries in Different Stages of the Demographic Transition

Countries display distinctive population characteristics depending on their stage in the demographic transition. No country today remains in Stage 1 of the demographic transition, but we can compare countries in each of the other three stages.

Cape Verde. Stage 1 countries experience wide fluctuations in the crude birth and death rates from one year to the next, depending on economic and environmental conditions. Cape Verde, a collection of twelve small islands in the Atlantic Ocean off the coast of West Africa, recently moved from Stage 1 to Stage 2. A Portuguese colony until 1975, Cape Verde kept unusually good demographic records when it was still in Stage 1.

The crude birth rate in Cape Verde most years ranged between 40 and 45 per 1,000, while the crude death rate was generally between 20 and 30. Although the population increased most years, Cape Verde remained in Stage 1 of the demographic transition until the late 1940s. Between 1900 and 1949 the population of Cape Verde actually declined, from 147,000 to 137,000. Although births exceeded deaths most years, the country was hit several times by severe famines that dramatically disrupted the typical pattern. As a result of famine, the crude death rate skyrocketed to 74 per 1,000 in 1941 and 101 in 1942. Because fewer babies were conceived at the height of the 1942 famine, the crude birth rate fell in 1943 to only 22. Population also declined during periods of famine because survivors migrated to other countries.

The long-term pattern of demographic uncertainty suddenly ended in the late 1940s, when an antimalaria campaign was launched. The crude death rate dropped between 1949 and 1950 by more than one-third, from 27 to 17 per 1,000, and further declined during the 1950s and 1960s to around 10 per 1,000. Since the 1970s, the crude death rate has remained just under 10 for most years, although a drought in 1971 and a famine in 1986 temporarily lifted the rate above 10 (Figure 2–13).

Meanwhile, the crude birth rate increased in the early 1950s to a maximum of 53 per 1,000 in 1954. The crude birth rate declined during the 1960s and dipped below 30 in the 1970s; a major contributing factor was the smaller number of women in child-bearing years, as a result of the low birth rates during the 1940s. But the crude birth rate has increased again and has averaged over 35 since the mid-1980s.

Since entering Stage 2 of the demographic transition in about 1950, the population of Cape Verde has nearly tripled to approximately 400,000. Natural increase has averaged nearly 3.0 per year since 1950. Recent increases in the natural increase and crude birth rates show that Cape Verde remains in Stage 2 of the demographic transition.

Chile. Chile provides an example of a country outside of Europe and North America that has reached Stage 3 of the demographic transition but is likely to take some time before continuing to Stage 4. Chile has changed from a predominantly rural society based on agriculture to an urban society, in which

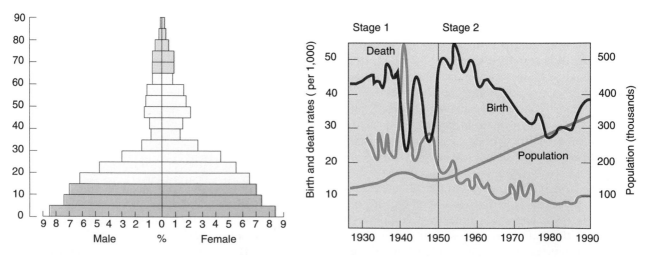

FIGURE 2–13
Demographic transition and population pyramid for Cape Verde. Cape Verde entered Stage 2 of the demographic transition approximately in 1950, as indicated by the large gap between birth and death rates since then. As is typical of countries in Stage 2 of the demographic transition, Cape Verde has a population pyramid with a very wide base.

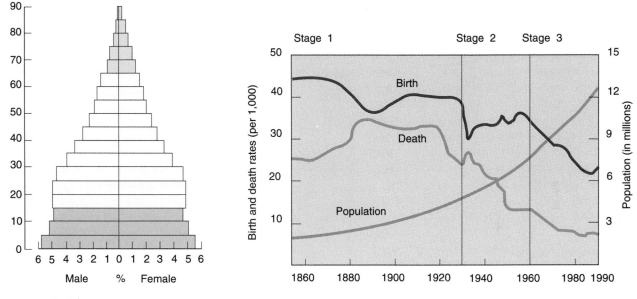

FIGURE 2–14
Demographic transition and population pyramid for Chile. Chile entered Stage 2 of the demographic transition in the 1930s, when death rates declined sharply, and Stage 3 in the 1960s, when birth rates declined sharply. During the 1980s, however, birth rates no longer declined, and Chile's natural increase rate remained over 1.5.

most people work in factories, offices, and shops. Many Chileans, however, still prefer to have large families.

Like most countries outside Europe and North America, Chile entered the twentieth century still in Stage 1 of the demographic transition. Population had grown modestly during the nineteenth century, at a natural increase rate of less than 1 percent per year. But much of Chile's population growth—like other countries in the Western Hemisphere—resulted from European immigration.

Chile's crude death rate declined sharply in the 1930s, moving the country into Stage 2 of the demographic transition. As in other Latin American countries Chile's crude death rate was lowered by the infusion of medical technology from relatively developed countries such as the United States in order to control smallpox, malaria, dysentery, and other diseases. During the 1940s and 1950s Chile's rate of natural increase exceeded 2 percent per year, and the crude death rate dropped from the mid-30s to less than 15 (Figure 2–14).

Chile has been in Stage 3 of the demographic transition since about 1960. The crude death rate declined further during the 1960s and 1970s to less than 10, while the crude birth rate dropped sharply from about 35 in the early 1960s to about 20 by the late 1970s. Recently, though, Chile has failed to make further progress in reducing the gap between births and deaths. The rate of natural increase has remained at about 1.5 percent per year since the 1960s.

Chile moved into Stage 3 of the demographic transition primarily because of a vigorous government family planning policy, initiated in 1966. Reduced income and high unemployment at that time also induced couples to postpone marriage and delay childbearing.

While Chile's natural increase rate is lower today than in the 1950s, the country is unlikely to move into Stage 4 of the demographic transition in the near future. By 1979, Chile's government had reversed its policy and renounced support for family planning. The government policy was that population growth could help promote national security and economic development. Further reduction in the crude birth rate is also hindered by most Chileans belonging to the Roman Catholic church, which opposes the use of what it calls nonnatural birth control techniques.

Denmark. Denmark, like several other northern and western European countries, has reached Stage 4 of the demographic transition. Denmark's history is similar to that of England. The country entered Stage 2 of the demographic transition in the nineteenth century, when the crude death rate began its sustained decline. The crude birth rate dropped in the late nineteenth century, and the country moved into Stage 3 (Figure 2–15).

Since the 1970s, the crude birth and the crude death rates have been roughly equal, at 11 or 12 per 1,000. The country has reached zero population growth, and the population is unlikely to increase from the current level of just over 5 million.

Denmark's population pyramid shows the impact of the demographic transition. Instead of a classic pyramid shape, Denmark has a column. The percentages of young and elderly people are nearly the same in Denmark, but with further medical advances the number of older people may exceed the number of young people by the end of the century. Denmark's crude death rate is unlikely to decline further unless another medical revoluton, such as a cure for cancer, keeps older people alive much longer.

The Demographic Transition and Population Growth

Global population is increasing rapidly at this time because few countries are in the two stages of the demographic transition associated with low population growth. No country remains in Stage 1, and few have reached Stage 4. The overwhelming majority of countries are either in Stage 2 or Stage 3 of the demographic transition—the stages with rapid population growth—and only a few are likely to reach Stage 4 in the near future.

The demographic transition involves two big breaks with the past: (1) the sudden drop in the death rate and (2) the sudden drop in the birth rate. The first break, which comes from technological innovation, has been accomplished throughout the

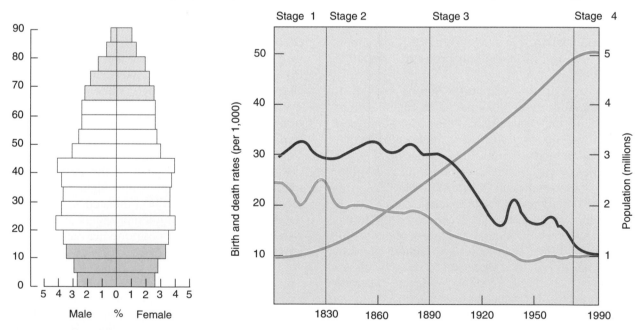

FIGURE 2–15
Demographic transition and population pyramid for Denmark. Denmark has been in Stage 4 of the demographic transition and has experienced virtually no change in total population since the 1970s. The population pyramid is much straighter than those of Cape Verde and Chile, a reflection of the relatively large percentage of elderly people and small percentage of children.

world. The second break, which comes from changing social customs, has not yet been achieved in most countries. If most countries in Europe and North America can reach—or at least approach—Stage 4 of the demographic transition, why cannot countries elsewhere in the world? Fundamental differences prevent other countries from replicating the experience in Europe and North America.

The first demographic change—the sudden decline in the crude death rate—occurred for different reasons in the past. The nineteenth century decline in the crude death rate in Europe and North America took place in conjunction with the industrial revolution. The unprecedented level of wealth generated by the industrial revolution was used in part to stimulate research by European and North American scientists into the causes and cures for diseases. These studies ultimately led to such medical advances as pasteurization, X rays, penicillin, and insecticides.

In contrast, the sudden drop in the crude death rate in Africa, Asia, and Latin America in the twentieth century has been accomplished with less effort by local citizens. For example, the crude death rate in Sri Lanka (then known as Ceylon) plummeted 43 percent between 1946 and 1947. The most important reason for the sharp drop was the use of DDT to control malaria.

European and North American countries were responsible for manufacturing the DDT and training the experts to supervise its use. Furthermore, the houses of the Sri Lankans were sprayed for the residents. The spraying process and other medical services, which cost only $2 per person per year, was paid for primarily by international organizations.

Thus, Sri Lanka's crude death rate was reduced by nearly one-half in a single year with no change in the country's economy or social system. Medical technology was injected from Europe and North America instead of arising within the country as part of an economic revolution. This pattern has been repeated in dozens of countries in Africa, Asia, and Latin America.

Having caused the first break with the past through diffusion of medical technology, European and North American countries now urge countries elsewhere in the world to complete the second break with the past, the reduction of the birth rate. But reducing the crude birth rate is more difficult. A decline in the crude death rate can be induced through introduction of new technology by outsiders, but the crude birth rate will drop only when people decide for themselves to have fewer children.

While many people in Africa, Asia, and Latin America may not be prepared for the second break with the past, they are being urged to move through the demographic transition rapidly. In Europe and North America, Stage 2 of the demographic transition lasted for approximately 100 years. During that time, global population increased by around 1 billion. If Stage 2 of the demographic revolution in Africa, Asia, and Latin America also lasts for 100 years—from about 1950 to 2050—15 billion people will be added to the world in the interim.

KEY ISSUE

Does the World Face an Overpopulation Problem?

In view of the current size and natural increase rate of the world's population, many wonder whether there will soon be too many people on earth. Will continued population growth lead to global starvation, war, and lower quality of life?

The English economist Thomas Malthus was one of the first to argue that the world's rate of population increase was far outrunning the development of food supplies. In his *Essay on Population* (1797) Malthus claimed that population was growing much more rapidly than the earth's food supply, because population increased geometrically while food supply increased arithmetically. According to Malthus, these growth rates would produce the following relationships between people and food in the future:

Today:	1 person, 1 unit of food
25 years from now:	2 persons, 2 units of food
50 years from now:	4 persons, 3 units of food
75 years from now:	8 persons, 4 units of food
100 years from now:	16 persons, 5 units of food

Malthus was writing during the second era of global population increase, which had begun around 1750 in association with the industrial revolution. He concluded that population growth would press against available resources in every country, unless either moral restraint produced lower crude birth rates or disease, famine, war, or some other disaster produced higher crude death rates.

In Malthus's time, only a few relatively wealthy countries had entered Stage 2 of the demographic transition, which is characterized by rapid population increase. Malthus did not foresee critical social, economic, and technological changes that would induce relatively wealthy societies to move into Stages 3 and 4 of the demographic transition. He also failed to anticipate that relatively poor countries would have the most rapid population growth, because of the transfer of medical technology but not wealth from relatively developed countries. Nonetheless, Malthus's view that overpopulation represents an imbalance between people and resources contributes to contemporary geograhpic analysis of population problems.

Debate over Solutions

Experts sharply disagree on appropriate solutions to avoid global overpopulation at some point in the future. Overpopulation results when an area's population exceeds its physical, social, and economic resources. From this definition of overpopulation two types of solutions emerge: either reduce the size of the population or increase the level of an area's resources. The debate is about giving priority either to the population or to the resources side of the relationship.

Proponents of avoiding overpopulation by increasing resources argue that the world can accommodate additional people through further economic development. Those who favor the solution of reduced population growth argue that global resources are limited and must be conserved.

Increasing resources. One approach to meeting the threat of overpopulation emphasizes economic development. Economic growth can generate sufficient resources to eliminate global hunger and poverty, according to this argument. The world can support further population growth as long as the economy continues to expand. The world's resource base is not fixed and limited but is constantly being increased by scientific inventions. New manufacturing processes, agricultural practices, energy sources, and communications systems all help

to expand the world's resources. Can we not expect further technological improvements in the future?

Some analysts carry the argument one step further, claiming that the population problem results from the unequal distribution of resources under capitalism. According to this argument, the world possesses sufficient resources to eliminate global hunger and poverty, if only these resources are shared equally.

The biggest flaw in this argument is that in recent years many developing countries have expanded their economies significantly and yet have more poor people than ever before. For example, income in East African countries rose during the past decade by approximately 2 percent per year above inflation, but the population grew by approximately 3 percent per year. Because population growth outpaced economic development, all of the economic growth was absorbed simply in accommodating the additional population. Economic growth notwithstanding, the average resident of East Africa is worse off today than a decade ago.

Reducing population growth. Proponents of this solution argue that humanity can avoid mass starvation primarily by a drastic reduction in the current rate of population increase. Only two approaches could reduce the current natural increase rate: increase the crude death rate or decrease the crude birth rate.

An increase in the crude death rate may halt the growth of the human population. For example, if the population increases faster than the expansion of the food supply, widespread famine could result. Some argue that sending food to starving Africans is a mistake because a higher death rate now may prevent mass starvation in the future. Other possibilities for increasing the crude death rate include millions dying in wars, especially in an era of nuclear weapons, or from a natural disaster, such as a major earthquake.

The crude death rate may also rise as a result of the spread of diseases. One-third of all children in developing countries other than China die from diarrhea. Another one-third die from one of six infectious diseases: polio, measles, diphtheria, tetanus, whooping cough, and tuberculosis. These diseases have been virtually eliminated in relatively developed countries through improved nutrition and hygiene. But only a minority of children in developing countries have been immunized against these diseases, and water supplies remain unsafe in many places. Even where programs have been implemented to fight these preventable diseases, they have sometimes been unsuccessful because of a lack of qualified medical staff.

The diffusion of acquired immunodeficiency syndrome (AIDS) in both relatively developed and developing countries could produce a rise in the crude death rate. The distribution of AIDS within the United States was discussed in Chapter 1 (*see*

Figure 1–17). Although information is not as easy to obtain, the incidence of AIDS may be more extensive in Africa than in relatively developed countries, and its diffusion across that continent has not been stopped.

Birth control. Few people wish to see population growth curbed through an increase in the death rate, but the only demographic alternative is to reduce the birth rate. A variety of reliable contraceptive devices can help people limit the size of a family. Many governments have undertaken extensive

These people are gathering firewood in Mali. A region can be sparsely inhabited yet overpopulated if the number of people exceeeds the region's resources, as is the case in Mali.

The government in Mexico, as in many developing countries, recognizes that the most effective way to curb population growth is by lowering the crude birth rate. Because people may lack knowledge about alternative methods of family planning, the government must launch massive educational campaigns.

programs to educate citizens about the benefits and risks of the various methods of birth control.

Some people oppose birth control programs for religious and political reasons. Adherents of several faiths, including Roman Catholics, fundamentalist Protestants, Muslims, and Hindus, may consider that their religious convictions prevent them from using some birth control devices. Opposition is strong within the United States to terminating pregnancies through abortions, and the U.S. government has withheld aid to countries and family-planning organizations that counsel abortions, even when such counselling is only a small part of overall activities.

Some countries, especially in Africa, oppose reducing the birth rate for political reasons. Government officials encourage large families in order to increase the supply of young men who could serve in the armed forces. Other leaders of developing countries see birth control as a move by relatively developed countries to prevent further expansion in the percentage of the world's population living in poorer countries.

Many advocates of giving priority to reducing population growth also recognize the importance of expanding economic resources. But people who are opposed to birth control techniques frequently argue exclusively for the economic growth solution. Compromise between the two positions is therefore difficult.

Summary

Overpopulation—more people than the available level of resources—has already hit regions of Africa and threatens other countries in Asia and Latin America. The world as a whole does not immediately face overpopulation, but current trends must be reversed to prevent a future crisis.

Geographers caution that the number of people living in a region is not by itself an indication of overpopulation. Some densely populated regions are not overpopulated, while some sparsely inhabited areas are. Instead, overpopulation is a relationship between the size of the population and a region's level of resources. The capacity of the land to support life derives partly from characteristics of the natural environment and partly from human actions to modify the environment through agriculture, industry, and exploitation of raw materials.

We cannot completely explain the overpopulation problem until we present more information concerning how people in different regions earn a living and modify the environment. However, we can reach some conclusions by briefly reviewing the key issues raised at the beginning of this chapter.

1. **How is the world's population distributed?** Global population is concentrated in a few places. Humans tend to avoid those parts of the earth's surface considered too wet, too dry, too cold, or too mountainous. The capacity of the earth to support a much larger population depends heavily on people's ability to utilize sparsely settled lands more effectively.

2. **How has the world's population increased?** The natural increase rate of the world's population rose dramatically at three points in history: the agricultural revolution around 8000 B.C., the industrial revolution around A.D. 1750, and the medical revolution around 1950. On each occasion significant changes in technology enabled more people to survive.

Today, virtually all of the world's population increase is concentrated in the relatively poor countries of Africa, Asia, and Latin America. Many of these countries do not have the resources to meet the needs of their rapidly growing populations. In contrast, most European and North American countries now have low population growth rates, and some countries are now experiencing population declines.

3. **Why is population increasing at different rates in different countries?** The demographic transition is a change in a country's population. A country moves from a condition of high birth and high death rates and little growth in the size of the population to a condition of low birth and low death rates and low population growth. During the process the total number of people increases enormously, because the death rate starts to decline some years before the birth rate.

The relatively developed countries of Europe and North America have reached or neared the end of the demographic transition. African, Asian, and Latin American countries are at the stages of the demographic transition characterized by rapid population growth. Death rates have declined sharply, but birth rates remain relatively high.

4. **Does the world face an overpopulation problem?** The rate at which global population has been growing in the last three decades is unprecedented in history. A dramatic decline in the death rate has produced the increase. With death rates controlled, for the first time in history the most critical factor determining the size of the world's population is the birth rate. Scientists agree that the current rate of natural increase must be reduced, but they disagree on the appropriate methods for achieving the goal.

India vs. China

The world's two most populous countries, China and India, will heavily influence future prospects for global overpopulation. These two countries—together encompassing more than one-third of the world's population—have adopted different policies to control population growth. In the absence of strong family-planning programs, India adds about 2 million more people each year than China. At current rates of natural increase, India would surpass China as the world's most populous country by the middle of the twenty-first century.

India's population policies. India, like most other countries in Africa, Asia, and Latin America, remained in Stage 1 of the demographic transition until the late 1940s. During the first half of the twentieth century, population increased modestly—less than 1 percent per year—but decreased in some years because of malaria, famines, plagues, and cholera epidemics. For example, more than 16 million Indians—approximately 5 percent of the population—died of influenza in 1918 and 1919, and the population at the 1921 census was lower than ten years earlier.

Immediately following independence in 1947, India's death rate declined sharply, to 20 per 1,000 by 1951, while the crude birth rate remained at about 40. Consequently, the rate of natural increase jumped to 2 percent per year. The demographic pattern has not changed much in India during the past 40 years. Birth and death rates have both drifted a few points lower since the 1950s, but the rate of natural increase has consistently remained around 2 percent per year. In the half-century since independence, India's population has grown by more than one-half billion.

The government of India has launched various programs to encourage family planning, but none have been very successful. In 1952, India became the first country to embark on a national family-planning program. The government has established clinics and distributes educational information about alternative methods of birth control. Birth control devices are distributed free of charge or at subsidized prices. Abortions, legalized in 1972, have been performed at a rate of several million per year. Altogether, the government spends several hundred million dollars per year on various family-planning programs.

India's most controversial family-planning program was the establishment of camps in 1971 to perform sterilizations, surgical procedures by which people were made incapable of reproduction. A sterilized person was entitled to a payment, which has been adjusted several times but generally has been equivalent to the average monthly income in India. At the height of the program, in 1976, 8.3 million sterilizations were performed during a six-month period.

The birth control drive has declined in India since 1976. Widespread opposition to the sterilization program grew in the country because people feared that they would be forcibly sterilized. The prime minister, Indira Gandhi, was defeated in 1977, and the new government emphasized the voluntary nature of birth control programs. The term "family planning," which the Indian people associated with the forced sterilization policy, was replaced by "family welfare" to indicate that compulsory birth control programs had been terminated. Although Mrs. Gandhi again served as prime minister from 1980 until being assassinated in 1984, she did not emphasize family planning because of the opposition during her previous administration.

A government-sponsored family-planning program continues, but with emphasis on education, including advertisements on national radio and television networks and informational material distributed through local health centers. Given the cultural diversity of the Indian people, a national campaign has had only limited success. The dominant form of birth control continues to be sterilization of women, many of whom have already borne several children. Effective methods have not been devised to induce recently married couples to have fewer children.

China's population policies. In contrast with India, China has made substantial progress in reducing its rate of natural increase. Growth declined from approximately 2.0 percent per year in the 1950s to 1.2 percent during the mid-1980s.

The government of China has acted strongly to reduce the number of births. The core of the government's policy is limiting families to one child. Couples receive financial subsidies, a long maternity leave, better housing, and in rural areas more land if they agree to have just one child. The government prohibits marriage for men until they are twenty-seven and women until they are twenty-five. To further discourage births, people receive free contraceptives, abortions, and sterilizations. A family with more than one child must pay a fine, amounting to 5 or 10 percent of its income for ten years, and job promotions may be denied. Some officials in rural villages maintain records of women's menstrual cycles to assure that no unplanned babies are born.

China's crude birth rate has increased somewhat since the mid-1980s. The increase has resulted partly from looser enforcement of the "one-child" rules, especially in rural villages, where families may receive permission to have a second child. Recent changes in China's government have reduced national control over remote rural areas, particularly those inhabited by restive ethnic minorities. The Chinese government has also relaxed enforcement because of international criticism that the one-child policy encouraged the killing of baby girls. If they are limited to one child, most Chinese families prefer to have a boy, in part because of cultural tradition and in part because a boy is regarded as stronger and better able to take care of aging parents.

The crude birth rate has also been rising in China because of greater wealth. The average Chinese family increasingly can afford the fine for the opportunity of having a second child. While small changes in the crude birth rate may not be significant in other countries, in China an increase of 0.1 percent translates into 1 million additional babies per year. To bring the crude birth rate below 20 again, the Chinese government may enforce strict rules more vigorously again.

The government of China has strongly encouraged families to have only one child. This policy has lowered China's natural increase rate, but in recent years, the rate has increased again because increasingly affluent families are willing to pay the fine for having additional children.

Despite recent increases, China is likely to maintain a much lower rate of natural increase than India into the twenty-first century. Following years of intensive educational programs—as well as coercion—the Chinese people have accepted to a greater degree than the Indian people the benefits of family planning. As China moves closer to a market economy, especially in rural areas, women increasingly recognize that having fewer children opens greater opportunities to obtain a job and earn more money.

Should the current rate of natural increase continue for several decades, global population would far exceed even the most optimistic estimates of world food and energy capacities. In another thousand years there would be less than 1 square foot of land per person in the world, including deserts, mountains, and ice caps.

These projections are not intended as predictions. They illustrate the significance of current growth rates and demonstrate the need to modify current trends. The challenge is to lower the current rate of population growth before the negative consequences of a large population pose insoluble social and economic problems.

Key Terms

Agricultural density The ratio of the number of farmers to the total amount of land suitable for agriculture.

Agricultural revolution The time when human beings first domesticated plants and animals and no longer relied entirely on hunting and gathering. *See* Chapter 9.

Arithmetic density The total number of people divided by the total land area.

Census A complete enumeration of a population.

Crude birth rate (CBR) The total number of live births in a year for every 1,000 people alive in the society.

Crude death rate The total number of deaths in a year for every 1,000 people alive in the society.

Demographic transition The process of change in a society's population from a condition of high crude birth and death rates and low rate of natural increase to a condition of low crude birth and death rates, low rate of natural increase, and a higher total population.

Demography The scientific study of population characteristics.

Dependency rate The percentage of people under the age of fifteen and over age sixty-four, most of them supported by people active in the labor force.

Doubling time The number of years needed to double a population, assuming a constant rate of natural increase.

Ecumene The portion of the earth's surface occupied by permanent human settlement.

Industrial revolution A series of improvements in industrial technology that transformed the process of manufacturing goods. *See* Chapter 10.

Infant mortality rate The total number of deaths in a year of infants under one year for every 1,000 births in a society.

Life expectancy The average number of years a person can be expected to live, given current social, economic, and medical conditions. Life expectancy at birth is the average number of years a newborn infant can expect to live.

Medical revolution Diffusion of medical technology invented in Europe and North America to the poorer countries of Latin America, Asia, and Africa. Improved medical practices have eliminated many of the traditional causes of death in poorer countries and enabled more people to live longer and healthier lives.

Natural increase The percentage growth of a population in a year, computed as the crude birth rate minus the crude death rate.

Overpopulation The number of people in an area exceeds the capacity of the environment to support life at a decent standard of living.

Physiological density The number of people per unit of area of arable land, which is land suitable for agriculture.

Population pyramid A bar graph representing the distribution of population by age and sex.

Sex ratio The number of males per 100 females in the population.

Total fertility rate (TFR) The average number of children a woman will have throughout her child-bearing years.

Zero population growth (ZPG) The total fertility rate declines to the point where the natural increase rate equals zero.

Thinking Geographically

1. The current method of counting a country's population by requiring every household to fill out a form once every ten years has been severely criticized as inaccurate. The census allegedly fails to count people who cannot read the form or who do not wish to be found. This undercounting produces a geographic bias, because people who are missed are more likely to live in inner cities, remote rural areas, or communities that attract a relatively high number of recent immigrants. Given the availability of reliable statistical tests, should the current method of trying to count 100 percent of the population be replaced by a survey of a carefully drawn sample of the population, as is done with political polling and consumer preferences?

2. Scientists disagree concerning the effects of high density on human behavior. Some laboratory tests have shown that rats display evidence of increased aggressiveness, competition, and violence when very large numbers of them are placed in a box. Is there any evidence that very high density causes humans to behave especially aggressively or violently?

3. Paul and Anne Ehrlich argue in *The Population Explosion* that a baby born in a relatively developed country such as the United States poses a graver threat to global overpopulation than a baby born in a developing country. The reason is that people in relatively developed countries place much higher demands on the world's supply of energy, food, and other limited resources. Do you agree with this view?

4. In what stage of the demographic transition was Iraq prior to the outbreak of the war in the Persian Gulf in 1991? What might be the impact of the war on Iraq's future natural increase, crude birth, crude death, and other demographic rates?

5. What policies should governments in relatively developed countries pursue with regard to reducing global population growth? If a relatively developed country provides funds and advice to promote family planning, does it gain the right to tell developing countries how to spend the funds and utilize the expertise?

Further Readings

Beaujeu-Garnier, Jacqueline. *Geography of Population,* 2d ed. London: Longman, 1978.

Bennett, D. Gordon. *World Population Problems: An Introduction to Population Geography.* Champaign, IL: Park Press, 1984.

Brown, Lester R., and Jodi L. Jacobson. "Our Demographically Divided World." Worldwatch Paper 74. Washington, D.C.: Worldwatch Institute, December 1986.

Carr-Saunders, A. B. *World Population: Past Growth and Present Trends.* New York: Oxford University Press, 1936.

Clarke, John I. *Population Geography.* 2d ed. Oxford and New York: Pergamon Press, 1972.

————. *Geography and Population: Approaches and Applications.* Oxford and New York: Pergamon Press, 1984.

Coleman, David, and Roger Schofield, eds. *The State of Population Theory: Forward from Malthus.* Oxford and New York: Basil Blackwell, 1986.

Demko, George, George Schnell, and Harold Rose. *Population Geography: A Reader.* New York: McGraw-Hill, 1970.

Donaldson, Peter J., and Amy Ong Tsui. "The International Family Planning Movement." Population Bulletin 45. Washington, D.C.: Population Reference Bureau, November 1990.

Ehrlich, Paul, and Anne Ehrlich. *The Population Explosion.* New York: Simon and Schuster, 1990.

Freedman, Ronald. "Family Planning Programs in the Third World." *The Annals of the American Academy of Political and Social Science* 510 (July 1990): 33–43.

Goliber, Thomas J. "Africa's Expanding Population: Old Problems, New Policies." Population Bulletin 44. Washington, D.C.: Population Reference Bureau, 1989.

Gould, W. T. S., and R. Lawton, eds. *Planning for Population Change.* Totowa, NJ: Barnes and Noble Books, 1986.

Jacobsen, Judith. "Promoting Population Stabilization: Incentives for Small Families." Worldwatch Paper 54. Washington, D.C.: Worldwatch Institute, June 1983.

Malthus, Thomas. *An Essay on the Principles of Population.* Reprint, 1978. London: Royal Economic Society, 1926.

Menken, Jane, ed. *World Population and U.S. Policy.* New York: Norton, 1986.

Merrick, Thomas W. "World Population in Transition." Population Bulletin 41. Washington, D.C.: Population Reference Bureau, April 1986.

Peters, Gary L., and Robert P. Larkin. *Population Geography: Problems, Concepts, and Prospects.* 3d ed. Dubuque, IA: Kendall-Hunt, 1989.

Robert, Godfrey. *Population Policy, Contemporary Issues.* New York: Praeger, 1990.

Scientific American. *The Human Population.* San Francisco: Freeman, 1974.

Thompson, Warren S. *Population Problems.* 4th ed. New York: McGraw-Hill, 1953.

Tien, H. Yuan. "China: Demographic Billionaire." Population Bulletin 38. Washington, D.C.: Population Reference Bureau, 1983.

Trewartha, Glenn T. *A Geography of Population.* New York: Wiley, 1969.

———. *The Less Developed Realm: A Geography of Its Population.* New York: Wiley, 1972.

United Nations. *Demographic Yearbook.* New York: United Nations, published annually.

———. *Statistical Yearbook.* New York: United Nations, published annually.

United States Department of Commerce, Bureau of the Census. *Statistical Abstract of the United States.* Washington, D.C.: Government Printing Office, published annually.

Van der Kaa, Dirk J. "Europe's Second Demographic Transition." Population Bulletin 42. Washington, D.C: Population Reference Bureau, 1987.

Visaria, Pravin, and Leela Visaria. "India's Population: Second and Growing." Population Bulletin 36. Washington, D.C.: Population Reference Bureau, 1981.

Weeks, John R. *Population: An Introduction to Concepts and Issues.* 4th ed. Belmont, CA: Wadsworth, 1989.

World Bank. *World Bank Development Report.* New York: Oxford University Press, published annually.

Wrigley, E. A. *Population and History.* New York: World University Library, 1969.

Zelinsky, Wilbur. "A Bibliographic Guide to Population Geography." Research Paper Number 80. Chicago: University of Chicago Department of Geography, 1962.

———. *A Prologue to Population Geography.* Englewood Cliffs, NJ: Prentice-Hall, 1966.

Zelinsky, Wilbur, Leszek A. Kosinski, and R. Mansell Prothero, eds. *Geography and a Crowding World.* New York: Oxford University Press, 1970.

Also consult the following journals: *American Demographics; Demography; Intercom; Population; Population and Development Review; Population Bulletin; Population Studies.* In addition, the Population Reference Bureau publishes a World Population Data Sheet every year.

3
Migration

KEY ISSUES

- Why do people migrate?

- Why are people forced to emigrate from a country?

- Why do people voluntarily immigrate to another country?

- Why do people migrate within a country?

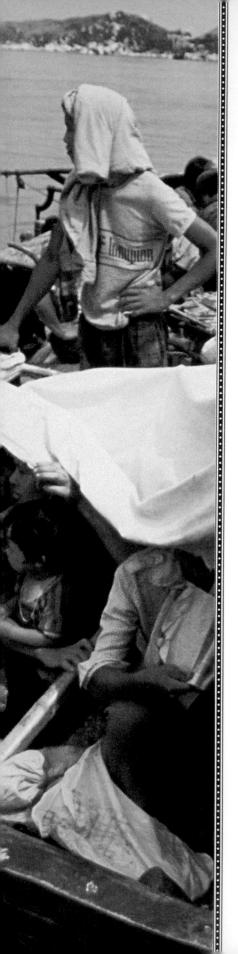

Do you remember when your family last moved? In the United States, the average family moves once every five years. Was your last move traumatic or exciting? The loss of old friends and familiar settings can hurt, but the experiences awaiting you at a new location can be stimulating. Think about the multitude of Americans who migrated from other countries. As difficult as your move may have been, imagine their feelings on arriving in a new land without jobs, friends, or—for many—the ability to speak English.

Why would people make such a perilous journey across the Atlantic or Pacific ocean? And what about the pioneers who crossed the Great Plains, the Rocky Mountains, or the Mojave Desert to reach locations in the American West? Most people migrate in search of three things: economic opportunity, political freedom, and environmental comfort. The hazards many migrants faced are a measure of the strong lure of new locations and the desperate conditions of the old ones. This chapter studies the reasons people migrate.

Migrating to Canada

Early on a Sunday morning during the summer of 1987, 174 Sikhs waded ashore at a rocky cove near the small fishing village of Charlesville, on the southern coast of Nova Scotia, Canada. Each had paid between $1,300 and $2,000 for a passage across the Atlantic Ocean.

Why did these Sikhs migrate from India to Canada? They said they were forced to leave India after losing a fight for religious freedom and political power against the Hindus, the majority of the Indian population. Canada was a logical destination because of its relatively generous laws allowing political refugees to stay pending official review of their cases, which could take many years. In recent years, thousands have migrated from Latin America and Asia in hope of qualifying for permanent residence in Canada as refugees.

Some Canadians contended the Sikhs may actually have migrated for economic opportunity. For example, though the Sikhs claimed to have fled their homeland, Canadian officials found evidence that the group had really migrated from Germany, not directly from India. One refugee scrambled from the sea carrying an attaché case and asked the first Canadian he encountered where he could hire a taxi to take him to Toronto, 1,900 kilometers (1,200 miles) away.

For the United States and Canada, the process of migration is particularly significant because the majority of the inhabitants of these countries are descended from people who migrated to the continent relatively recently—within the past 150 years in the overwhelming number of cases. For example, one-sixth of the current residents of Canada were born in another country, and most migrated for reasons similar to those expressed by the Sikhs—political freedom and economic opportunity.

Human beings have very high **mobility,** which is the ability to move from one location to another. People display their mobility in a variety of ways, such as by journeying every weekday to places of work or education and once a week to shops or recreation areas. These are examples of periodic or cyclical movements—journeys that recur on a regular basis, such as daily, monthly, or annually. College students often display another form of mobility—seasonal mobility—by moving to a college dormitory each fall and returning home the following spring.

The subject of this chapter is a specific type of mobility called **migration,** a permanent move to a new location. Migrants permanently change their place of their residence—where they sleep, store their possessions, and receive legal documents. Migration occurs much less frequently than other forms of mobility but produces far more profound changes for individuals and entire societies.

Migration has two forms, emigration and immigration. **Emigration** is migration *from* a location, whereas **immigration** is migration *to* a location. Given two locations, A and B, some emigrate from A to B while at the same time others immigrate to A from B. The difference between the number of immigrants and the number of emigrants is the **net migration.** If the number of immigrants exceeds the number of emigrants, the net migration is positive and the region has net inmigration. If the number of emigrants exceeds the number of immigrants, the region has net outmigration.

KEY ISSUE

Why Do People Migrate?

If a series of global population distribution maps similar to Figure 2–1 were created for several points in time and shown one after another like frames in a movie film, the pattern would change constantly. Some regions would suddenly increase in population, while other regions would decline. In part, these changes follow from regional differences in crude birth and death rates. Most of the changes, however, result from migration.

Individuals migrate for a variety of reasons, but we can classify them into push factors and pull factors. **Push factors** induce people to move away from old residences, whereas **pull factors** attract people to a particular new location. In reality, most people migrate for a variety of reasons, influenced by a combination of different push and pull factors. Frequently, though, one push or pull factor emerges as the most important, if not the sole, reason for the migration.

Push Factors

We can identify three major kinds of push factors—political, economic, and environmental. Each involves a different type of decision on the part of the migrant.

Political push factors. People forced to migrate from a particular country for political reasons are known as **refugees.** The United Nations defines political refugees as people who have fled their home country and cannot return for fear of persecution because of their race, religion, nationality, membership in a social group, or political opinion. Such people have no home until another country allows them to enter. In 1989, the U.S. Committee for Refugees estimated that there were more than 15 million refugees in the world. The figure increased in 1991, partially as a result of the war in the Persian Gulf.

The largest number of refugees can be found in Southwestern Asia, where some 6 million fled from Afghanistan following the Soviet invasion in 1979. By 1990, more than 3 million Afghan refugees lived in tents or mud huts in Pakistan, mostly near the town of Peshāwar, in the northern part of the country. Peshāwar stands near the eastern end of the Khyber Pass, the major land route through the mountains between Afghanistan and Pakistan. Other Afghan refugees had settled in camps in Pakistan's Baluchistan and Punjab provinces. More than 2 million Afghan refugees had migrated west to Iran, pri-

FIGURE 3–1

Afghan refugees. Nearly one-third of the population of Afghanistan was forced to migrate following the Soviet invasion in 1979, mostly to Pakistan and Iran. Afghan rebels, known as Mujahedeen, took advantage of the country's rugged terrain to offset the Soviet advantage in number of troops and sophisticated equipment. Most of the Afghan refugees have been reluctant to return home because fighting has continued even after Soviet troops left.

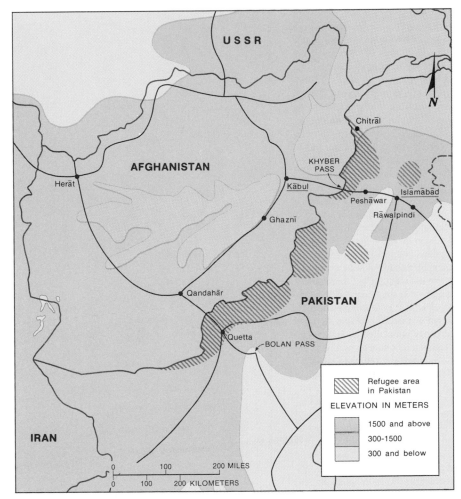

marily to the border cities of Mashhad, Birjand, and Zāhedān, as well as to the capital, Tehrān (Figure 3–1). Altogether, one-third of the Afghan population had migrated during the 1980s to Pakistan or Iran. Although the Soviet Union withdrew its troops in 1989, few refugees returned because of continued fighting in Afghanistan.

In addition to those who left Afghanistan, the largest groups of recent refugees have been generated because of wars involving Ethiopia and Mozambique (discussed later in this chapter), as well as the Middle East (*see* Chapter 5). In the early 1990s, the wars in these four regions were together responsible for three-fourths of the world's refugees (Figure 3–2).

Economic push factors. Economic reasons frequently push people out of their homelands. For

example, several million Irish were pushed out of their country in the 1840s because of poor agricultural conditions. A blight destroyed most of the potato crop, the people's major food source, and produced mass starvation. English landlords, who owned most of the arable land, did little to alleviate the disastrous economic conditions on the island. Millions of Irish died during the famine, and many of the survivors left in search of better economic conditions elsewhere.

Economic factors are again pushing hundreds of thousands of Irish out of their country. During the 1980s, one-fourth of the labor force—10 percent of the total population—emigrated from Ireland. Most of the emigrants were young and well-educated. In a country where one-third of the young people are unemployed, a high school or college diploma is a ticket out of Ireland.

FIGURE 3–2

A refugee is a person who is forced to migrate from a country because of political reasons. The U.S. Committee for Refugees estimated that in 1989 there were nearly 15 million refugees in the world, though the organization warns that the figure is difficult to determine because many refugees are not documented. This figure did not include refugees caused by the 1991 war in the Persian Gulf.

More than two-thirds of the refugees were generated in three locations: Afghanistan, Ethiopia, and the Middle East. Following the Soviet invasion in 1979, nearly 5 million Afghans fled to neighboring countries, primarily Pakistan and Iran. More than 1 million Ethiopian refugees live in the Sudan or Somalia. More than 2 million Palestinians living in Jordan, Lebanon, Syria, or territory controlled by Israel are classified as refugees by the U.S. Committee for Refugees, though determining how many Palestinians are refugees is especially difficult and controversial, as discussed in Chapter 5.

In addition to Ethiopia, several other African countries are generating or receiving large numbers of refugees, especially as a result of tribal wars. Wars in Southeast Asia and Central America are also responsible for generating large numbers of refugees.

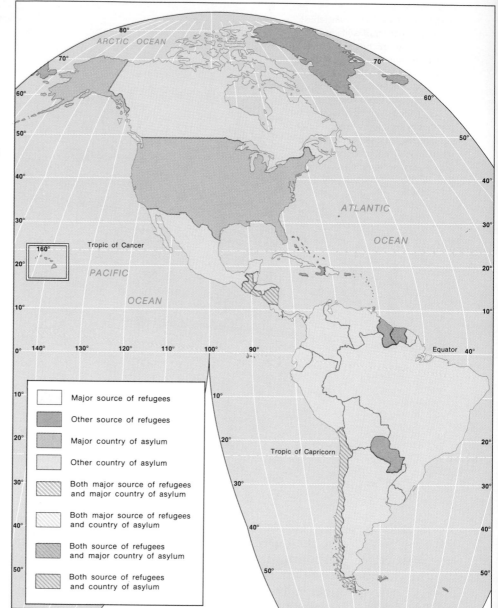

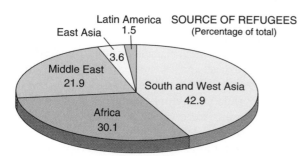

SOURCE OF REFUGEES
(Percentage of total)

Latin America 1.5
East Asia 3.6
Middle East 21.9
Africa 30.1
South and West Asia 42.9

Environmental push factors. People are also pushed from their homes by adverse conditions in the physical environment. Water—either too much or too little—poses the most common environmental threat. People are forced to move when floods or storms destroy homes and farmland. According to a study by Burton, Kates, and White, 40 percent of the world's natural disasters are flood-related and 20 percent storm-related.

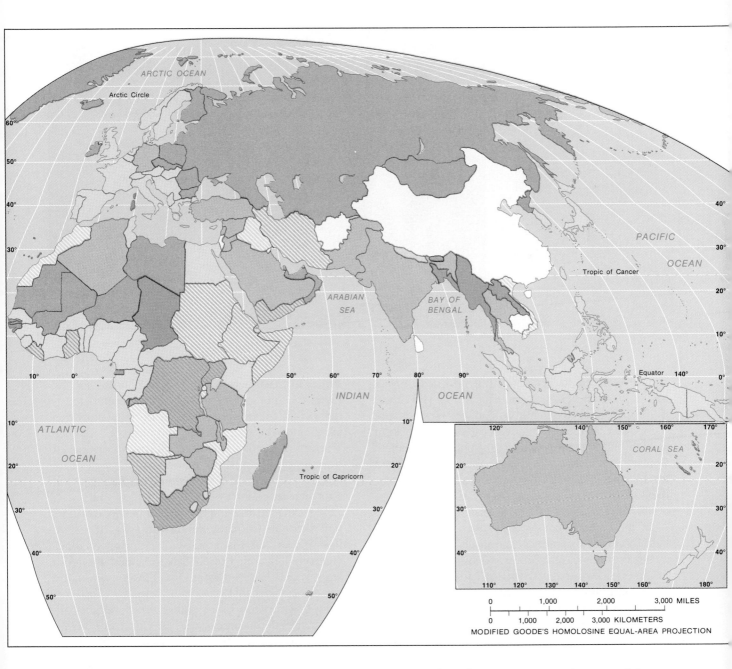

MODIFIED GOODE'S HOMOLOSINE EQUAL-AREA PROJECTION

Many people are forced to move by water-related disasters because they insist on living in a vulnerable area, such as a flood plain. The **flood plain** of a river is the area subject to flooding during a given number of years according to historical trends. People living in the 100-year flood plain, for example, can expect flooding on average once every 100 years. Many people are unaware that they live in a flood plain, and even people who do know often choose to live there anyway. In the United States, families living in flood plains may not be eligible for government insurance to help rebuild after flood damage.

A lack of water pushes others from their land. Hundreds of thousands have been forced to move from the Sahel region of North Africa because of drought conditions. The people of the Sahel have traditionally been pastoral nomads, a form of agri-

Refugees from Afghanistan live in tents in Pakistan and Iran. One-third of Afghanistan's population was forced to migrate after the Soviet invasion in 1979.

culture adapted to dry lands but effective only at low population densities (*see* Chapter 9). The capacity of the Sahel to sustain human life—never very high—has declined recently because of population growth and several years of unusually low rainfall. Consequently, many of these nomads have been forced to move into cities and rural camps, where they survive on food donated by the government and by international relief organizations.

In the United States, people were pushed from land by severe drought conditions as recently as the 1930s. Portions of Oklahoma and surrounding states became known as the Dust Bowl following several years of limited rainfall. Strong, dry winds blew across the plains and buried farms under several feet of dust. Thousands of families abandoned their farms and migrated to California, where they were derisively called Okies. The plight of the Okies was graphically portrayed by John Steinbeck in his novel *The Grapes of Wrath* (1939).

Pull Factors

The attractive features of a new location may lure migrants there. As with push factors, we can identify three types of pull factors: political, economic, and environmental.

Political pull factors. The major political pull factor is the lure of freedom. People are attracted to democratic countries that encourage individual choices in education, career, and place of residence. This pull factor is particularly difficult to distinguish from a political push factor because the pull of democracy is normally accompanied by the push from a totalitarian country.

We can see the importance of democracy as a pull factor in Germany. After World War II, the Allies divided Germany into four occupied zones, controlled by the United States, United Kingdom, France, and Soviet Union. The Soviet portion became the German Democratic Republic (East Germany), while the other three zones became the German Federal Republic (West Germany). People caught in the portion controlled by the Soviet Union, as well as those in other countries of Soviet-dominated Eastern Europe, fled to the West by the hundreds of thousands until this migration was ended by force.

Large-scale migration from Eastern Europe to Western Europe resumed briefly in the late 1980s during the transition from communist-dominated to multiparty systems in several Eastern European countries. In 1989, Hungary became the first communist-controlled country to permit unrestricted travel to a bordering democratic state, Austria. By opening its borders first, Hungary sparked a large-scale, circuitous migration pattern within Europe that lasted for several weeks. People in East Germany realized that the opening of the Hungary-Austria border gave them their first opportunity in thirty-five years to migrate to West Germany. Fearful that the "hole" in the Iron Curtain would be closed quickly, thousands of East Germans traveled across Czechoslovakia to Hungary, crossed the border from Hungary to Austria, and passed through Austria to reach West Germany—a 1,500-kilometer (900-mile) journey. Once Eastern Europeans were able to visit Western countries whenever they wished, the level of migration declined.

Economic pull factors. The most important pull of the United States and Canada for people elsewhere in the world is economic rather than political. Many Europeans were pulled to North America in the nineteenth century because they thought the streets were paved with gold. While not literally so gilded, the United States and Canada did offer prospects for economic advancement. A similar perception now lures people from Latin America and Asia.

People migrate to places where they think jobs are available. Because of changing economic opportunities, job prospects often vary from one country to another and within regions of the same country. A region that has valuable natural resources, such as petroleum or uranium, may attract miners and engineers. A new industry in a region may lure factory workers, technicians, and scientists. Construction workers, restaurant employees, and public-service officials may move to regions where rapid population growth stimulates demand for additional services and facilities.

Economic pull factors have historically been important reasons for migration in West Africa. When most of the region was part of the French or British empire, groups migrated in search of economic opportunities. Sierra Leoneans migrated to other regions to work as craftspeople, Dahomeyans and Beninese became assistants to the French administrators in the region, and Hausa and Yoruba people traded in the markets of a number of cities.

Since West Africa was carved into a collection of independent states during the 1950s and 1960s, millions of people have migrated for economic reasons from one country in the region to another. Laborers from Burkina Faso, Niger, and Mali work in the Ivory Coast and Ghana. Ghanaians, Nigerians, Togolese, Beninese, and Cameroonians migrated to Nigeria during the 1970s, lured by the rapid expansion of the Nigerian economy as a result of increasing revenues from the sale of petroleum.

In the case of Nigeria, an economic pull factor turned to a push factor in February, 1983, when the Nigerian government ordered a large number of foreign workers to leave the country. The Nigerian economy had been jolted by a drastic decline in the world price of petroleum, and unrest was widespread among Nigerians dissatisfied with cutbacks in government services. In order to reduce competition for jobs, the Nigerian government expelled more than 1 million foreigners, primarily Ghanaians.

The relative attractiveness of a region can change as a result of fluctuating economic conditions. After decades of net outmigration, northeastern Scotland has attracted migrants in recent years. Following the discovery of petroleum in the North Sea off the coast of Scotland, thousands of people were lured to jobs in the drilling or refining of petroleum or in supporting businesses.

Environmental pull factors. Environmental conditions also attract migrants. When surveyed, most Americans express a preference for living in a small town. In an age of improved communications and transportation systems, people can live in relatively remote locations of the United States and still not feel too isolated from employment, shopping, and entertainment opportunities.

Mountains also attract an increasing number of migrants. Proximity to the Rocky Mountains lures Americans to the state of Colorado, and the Alps pull French people to eastern France. Some migrants are shocked to find polluted air and congestion in these areas.

Regions with relatively temperate climates—such as the south coast of England, the Mediterranean coast of France and Spain, and the Southwest of the United States—attract migrants from harsher climates. Retired people are especially attracted to climates with a mild winter; one-third of all elderly people who move from one state to another in the United States select Florida as their destination.

Thousands of people with bronchitis, asthma, tuberculosis, and allergies have been lured to Arizona by its dry desert climate. But so many people have migrated to the state that environmental conditions have been modified. The pollen count in Tucson has increased 3,500 percent since the 1940s, and the percentage of people with allergies is twice the national average. Local experts attribute two-thirds of the pollen count to three types of vegetation imported by migrants to Arizona: the mulberry tree, the olive tree, and Bermuda grass. Some communities have banned these three species. The mulberry tree dies after thirty years, but the olive tree—an attractive species in Arizona because it is drought-resistant—can live for 500 years. Bermuda grass sinks deep roots and is difficult to eradicate. Arizona's recent experience shows that migration may no longer be the answer for people with allergies.

Intervening obstacles. Migrants who are attracted to a new location do not always reach their desired destination. Instead they may be blocked by an **intervening obstacle,** an environmental or cultural feature that hinders migration.

Historically, intervening obstacles have primarily been environmental. Before the invention of modern transportation systems, such as railroads and motor vehicles, people migrated across land masses either by horse or on foot. Migration across land masses was frequently difficult because of hostile features in the physical environment such as mountains and deserts. For example, many migrants lured to California during the nineteenth century failed to reach their destination because of an inability to cross such intervening obstacles as the Great Plains, the Rocky Mountains, or one of the deserts.

Bodies of water have traditionally served as important intervening obstacles. The Atlantic Ocean proved a particularly significant intervening obstacle for most European immigrants to North America. Tens of millions of Europeans spent their life savings for the right to cross the rough and dangerous Atlantic in the hold of a ship with hundreds of other immigrants.

Some Eastern Europeans who booked passage on ships to North America never actually crossed the Atlantic. An unscrupulous ship owner would sail the boat through the Baltic and North seas and land

at Liverpool or some other British port, announcing that they had reached America. The passengers—few of whom could speak English—paid for a 13,000-kilometer trans-Atlantic journey but received a 3,000-kilometer trip instead.

Water remains a formidable intervening obstacle for emigrants from Vietnam. Since the late 1970s, 1.5 million people have fled Vietnam; owing to the country's situation—along the South China Sea—most emigrants leave by sea and consequently are called boat people.

The first wave of boat people emigrated from Vietnam during the late 1970s, following the end of the Vietnam war. After North Vietnam captured the capital of South Vietnam, Saigon (since renamed Ho Chi Minh City), the United States, which had supported the government of South Vietnam, evacuated several thousand people who had been closely identified with the American position during the war. Later, many more refugees attempted to emigrate by boat.

The Vietnamese boat people drifted into the open sea, hoping they would be saved by the U.S. Navy. If they were taken on board, the boat people would technically be on U.S. territory and could file for admission to the United States as refugees. U.S. naval officers on the scene wished to save the boat people, but once rescued these Vietnamese would then jump to the head of a long line of people seeking admission to the United States as refugees. Consequently, some boat people were not allowed to board U.S. vessels.

A second surge of Vietnamese boat people began in the late 1980s. The most popular destination was Malaysia, followed by Hong Kong and Thailand; smaller numbers of boat people sought asylum in Indonesia, the Philippines, and Singapore (Figure 3–3). Memories of the Vietnam War had begun to fade, though, and officials in these so-called countries of first asylum were less sympathetic to the boat people. Thailand, in particular, forced the Vietnamese boats back out to sea, even though some of them capsized. Other countries placed the Vietnamese in detention camps surrounded by barbed wire and patrolled by armed soldiers. The more recent boat people have no longer been considered refugees, except for a handful who could prove they had been victims of specific incidents of political persecution.

According to an international agreement, most of the Vietnamese boat people judged to be refugees have been transferred to other places from the Asian countries of first asylum. During the past two decades, some 50 percent have come to the United States, while another 20 percent have emigrated to Canada, Australia, and France. But boat people not considered to be political refugees have languished in camps or been sent back to Vietnam.

These small, crowded boats, not always seaworthy, make inviting targets for pirates. Many Vietnamese have perished during the journey, when the boats capsize or become disabled in the open sea. The hardships the boat people have been willing to endure reflect the intensity of the continuing political and economic problems in Vietnam.

Although modern improvements in transportation, such as motor vehicles and airplanes, have

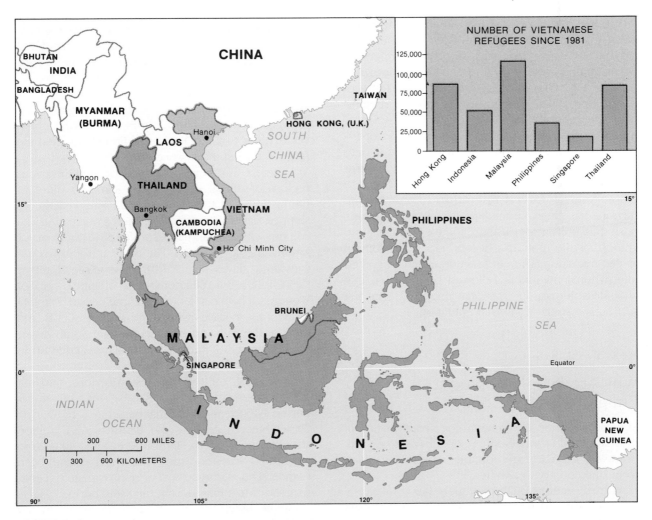

FIGURE 3–3
Destinations of Vietnamese boat people. At first, Vietnamese boat people were regarded as political refugees following the end of a long war. But by the late 1980s, neighboring countries had severely restricted the number of Vietnamese permitted to stay. Other countries have argued that the boat people can no longer make legitimate claims to be refugees from a war that ended back in 1975.

somewhat diminished the importance of environmental features as intervening obstacles, today's migrants need passports, visas, and other legal papers if they are to reach their desired destinations successfully. Migrants often face two kinds of legal obstacles—permission to leave their current home and permission to enter their desired home.

International and Internal Migration

People migrate for a combination of political, economic, and environmental push and pull factors. Such migrations fall into two general categories: international and internal. **International migration** refers to permanent movement from one country to another, whereas **internal migration** refers to permanent movement within a country. Normally, people undertake international migration for economic or political but not environmental reasons, while people undertake internal migration for economic or environmental but not political reasons.

International migration is further divided into two types: forced and voluntary. **Voluntary migration** means that the migrant has made a choice to move, whereas **forced migration** means that the migrant has been compelled to move. Economic push and pull factors usually induce voluntary migration, while political factors normally compel forced migration. The next section examines forced international migration, followed by a section that looks at voluntary international migration. The last section is a study of internal migration.

KEY ISSUE

Why Are People Forced to Emigrate from a Country?

Most people choose to migrate for a combination of push and pull factors. Some people have no choice, however, for they are forcibly moved by others from one country to another.

Forced international migration has historically occurred for two main reasons. First, some people have been shipped to other countries to become slaves. Second, people have been forced to migrate because of the political instability that results from wars, boundary changes following independence of colonies, or government ideology.

Forced International Migration Due to Slavery

African slaves. Millions of Africans were uprooted from their homes by European traders and sent to the Western Hemisphere for sale as slaves. This large-scale slave trade was a response to a shortage of labor in the sparsely inhabited New World. Europeans who owned large plantations in the Americas turned to African slaves as a cheap and abundant source of labor.

The forced migration began when groups of people living along the east and west coasts of Africa, taking advantage of their superior weapons, captured members of groups living further inland and sold the captives to Europeans. Europeans in turn shipped the captured Africans to the New World, selling them as slaves either on consignment or through auctions. The Spanish and Portuguese first participated in the slave trade in the early sixteenth century; the British, Dutch, and French adopted the practice during the next century.

Different European countries operated in various regions of Africa, each sending slaves to different destinations in the New World. The Portuguese shipped slaves primarily from their principal African colonies, Angola and Mozambique, to their major American colony, Brazil. The other European countries took slaves primarily from a 4,000-kilometer (2,500-mile) by 160-kilometer (100-mile) strip of West Africa between Liberia and the Congo. The majority of these slaves went to Caribbean islands, and most of the remainder to Central and South America. Fewer than 5 percent of the slaves ended up in the United States (Figure 3–4).

At least 10 million Africans were forced to migrate to the New World as slaves, about two-thirds during a 100-year period that began in 1710. During the eighteenth century, the British sent 2 million slaves to the Western Hemisphere, some 400,000 to the United States and most of the rest to Caribbean islands. The Portuguese sent approximately 2 million slaves to Brazil during the same period.

At the height of the demand for slaves in the eighteenth century, a number of European countries adopted a system known as the **triangular slave trade.** Under the triangular trading pattern, ships transported slaves as well as gold from Africa to the Western Hemisphere, primarily to the Carib-

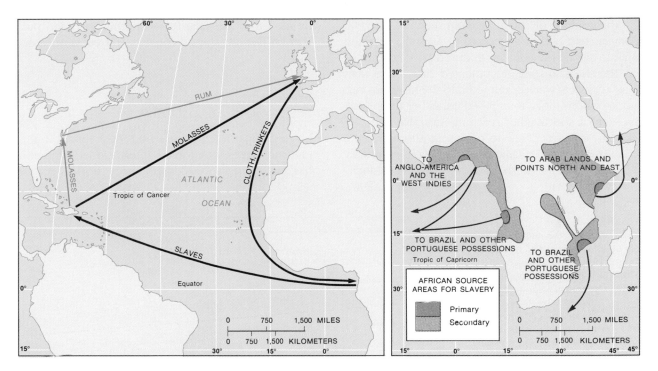

FIGURE 3–4

The British initiated a triangular slave-trading pattern (left). Cloth, trinkets, iron bars, and other goods were carried by ship from Britain to Africa to buy slaves. The same ships then transported slaves from Africa to the Caribbean islands. The ships then completed the triangle by returning to Britain with molasses to make rum. Sometimes the ships formed a rectangular pattern by carrying the molasses from the Caribbean islands to the North American colonies, where the rum was distilled and shipped to Britain.

   The British and other European powers obtained the slaves primarily from a narrow strip along the west coast of Africa, from Liberia to Angola (right). In the early days of colonization, Europeans secured territory along the Atlantic coast and rarely ventured more than 160 kilometers (100 miles) into the interior of the continent.

bean islands. The same ships then carried sugar and molasses from the Caribbean to Europe. Completing the triangle, the ships returned to Africa with cloth, trinkets, and other trade goods. Some ships added a step, making a rectangular trading pattern, in which molasses was carried from the Caribbean to the North American colonies and rum from North America back to Europe.

   The large-scale forced migration of Africans caused considerable hardship to them. The slave trade resulted in the separation of families and the destruction of villages. Traders generally seized the stronger and younger villagers, who could be sold as slaves for the highest price, and left the older and weaker behind. The Africans were packed onto ships at extremely high densities, kept in chains, and provided with only minimal food and sanitary facilities. About a quarter of the captives died crossing the Atlantic.

Australian convicts. The first Europeans to settle in Australia were primarily forced migrants, for the most part convicts deported from England. During the late eighteenth and early nineteenth centuries, British judges sentenced many people convicted of serious crimes to be deported to Australia.

   Australia's first penal colony was located in present-day New South Wales, in the southeastern part of the country. The colony began in 1786 and received its first shipload of convicts two years later.

By the middle of the nineteenth century, 165,000 convicts had been transported to Australia. Like the African slaves, the convicts endured poor conditions on the ships. In one documented case, more than 1,000 convicts were crammed into the hold of a vessel, of whom more than 300 died, either during the passage or shortly after reaching Australia.

Many convicts chose to remain in Australia at the conclusion of their sentences. They were eventually joined by other English colonists who had voluntarily moved to Australia for economic push and pull factors. The last ship of convicts arrived in Australia in 1849.

Forced International Migration Due to Political Instability

Large groups of people are no longer forced to migrate as slaves, but forced international migration has increased in the contemporary world because

FIGURE 3–5
The map shows the number of people in millions forced to migrate as a result of territorial changes after World War II. The largest number were Poles forced to move from territory occupied by the Soviet Union, Germans forced to migrate from territory taken over by Poland and the Soviet Union, and Russians forced to return to the Soviet Union from Western Europe.

MAJOR FORCED MIGRATIONS
(POPULATION MOVEMENT IN THE MILLIONS)

Germans
Baltic peoples
Russians
Poles
Czechs
Settled by International Refugee Organization
Added to USSR
Added to Poland

of political instability. Three types of political instability produce forced international migration: war, independence of former colonies, and government ideology.

War. Global conflicts have twice engulfed the planet during the twentieth century, each time producing a large number of refugees. Approximately 6 million people were forced to migrate as a result of World War I. That figure, however, pales in comparison to the upheaval caused by World War II.

About 45 million people were forced to migrate as a result of events leading up to World War II, the war itself, and postwar adjustments. Forced migration was caused primarily by the German and Japanese military expansions of the 1930s and early 1940s and then by the Allies' counterattack that began in 1942. Between 1939 and 1947 some 27 million people were forced to move in Europe, and several million more died in concentration camps (Figure 3–5).

In recent years, people have been forced to migrate because of wars in other areas of the world. Particularly disruptive wars have been waged in two regions of eastern Africa: the Horn of Africa in the northeast and Mozambique in the southeast.

Civil wars in three countries in the Horn of Africa—Ethiopia, Somalia, and the Sudan—have forced more than 3 million people to migrate. In Ethiopia, the province of Eritrea has been fighting for independence since 1961. Eritrea, with a coast on the Red Sea, was established as an Italian colony in 1890. Ethiopia, an independent country for over 2,000 years, was captured by Mussolini's Italian army during the 1930s. After Italy's side lost in World War II, the British administered Eritrea until 1952, when the United Nations awarded it to Ethiopia, which had regained its independence. Under the U.N. agreement, Eritrea was entitled to maintain a high degree of control over its territory. But after Ethiopia dissolved the Eritrean legislature and banned the use of Tigrinya (the most important local language) Eritreans began a fight for independence that has lasted for more than three decades.

Since the start of the civil war in 1961, 665,000 Eritrean refugees have fled to the neighboring country of the Sudan, especially north to the coastal city of Būr Sūdān (Port Sudan) and west to the Sudanese capital of Khartoum, as well as to the

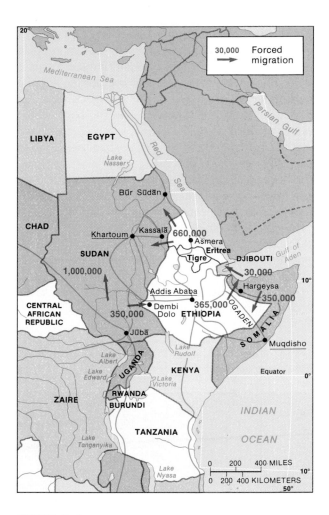

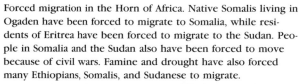

FIGURE 3–6
Forced migration in the Horn of Africa. Native Somalis living in Ogaden have been forced to migrate to Somalia, while residents of Eritrea have been forced to migrate to the Sudan. People in Somalia and the Sudan also have been forced to move because of civil wars. Famine and drought have also forced many Ethiopians, Somalis, and Sudanese to migrate.

smaller border town of Kassalā. Since the 1970s, Tigre, another Ethiopian province south of Eritrea, has also fought for greater autonomy from Ethiopia (Figure 3-6).

In recent decades, Ethiopia has also suffered a war in its eastern province of Ogaden, a desert area also claimed by Somalia, Ethiopia's neighbor to the southeast. The Ethiopian army uprooted several million ethnic Somalis living in the Ogaden who preferred that the province be part of Somalia. According to international refugee organizations, approximately 365,000 Ethiopians have fled to Somalia, though Somali officials argue that more than 800,000 have actually arrived. Half of these refugees were established in camps near the border, and the remainder have wandered from village to village in Somalia. Meanwhile, a civil war in the north of Somalia has forced 350,000 Somalis to flee to Ethiopia and another 30,000 to go to the small neighboring state of Djibouti.

A civil war has also raged since the late 1960s in the Sudan between largely Christian rebels in the southern provinces and the Muslim-dominated government forces in the north. More than 1 million Sudanese have been forced to migrate from the south to the north, and another 350,000 have fled to Ethiopia.

Farther south along the coast of East Africa, Mozambique has been the scene of a civil war be-tween the rebel Mozambique National Resistance force (also known as Renamo) and the Frelimo party, which controls the country's government. This civil war, which began in 1976, has generated 1.3 million refugees. More than 50 percent of those refugees have fled to neighboring Malawi, another 30 percent have gone to South Africa or Zimbabwe, and the remainder have left for Tanzania, Swaziland, or Zambia. In addition, several million people have been forced to migrate within Mozambique as a result of the civil war.

In Africa, drought, famine, and other environmental push factors have also caused forced international migration. In countries like Ethiopia, political refugees are not always clearly distinguished from forced migrants seeking food and water.

The physical condition of the refugees has often been shocking to Western observers. Many refugees

Refugees at a camp near Hargeysa, Somalia. Millions of people have been forced to migrate as a result of several wars in the Horn of Africa. Rapid population growth and limited food supplies add to the misery in the region.

are emaciated and deformed because of inadequate food and water. They have virtually no possessions, in many cases not even one complete set of clothes to wear. To reach another country, they may be forced to walk several hundred kilometers across the desert. Prospects for economic self-sufficiency are grim for most of these refugees. Even if they were given fertile land they would not be healthy enough to farm the land; nor could they obtain machinery and materials needed for farming.

Independence. Forced migration can also result when colonies are carved up into several independent states. In many cases, the boundaries of newly independent states have been drawn to try to match the boundaries of languages, religions, or other cultural characteristics. Yet boundary lines can rarely be fixed to completely segregate two cultural groups. Members of one cultural group caught on the "wrong" side of the boundary line may be forced to migrate to the other side.

South Asia provides a vivid example of large-scale forced migration as a result of independence. When the British ended their colonial rule in 1947, they divided the colony into two irregularly shaped countries, India and Pakistan. Pakistan comprised two noncontiguous areas, West Pakistan and East Pakistan—1,600 kilometers (1,000 miles) apart, separated by India. East Pakistan later became the independent country of Bangladesh. An eastern section of India was also practically cut off from the rest of the country, attached only by a narrow corridor north of Bangladesh that is less than 13 kilometers (8 miles) wide in some places.

The basis for the separation of West and East Pakistan from India was primarily religious. The people living in the two areas of Pakistan were predominantly Muslim, while those in India were predominantly Hindu. Antagonism between the two religious groups was so great that the British decided to place the Hindus and Muslims in separate states.

The partition of South Asia into two countries resulted in a high level of forced migration, because the national boundaries did not correspond precisely to the territory inhabited by the two religious groups. In the late 1940s, approximately 17 million people caught on the wrong side of a boundary were forced to migrate (Figure 3–7). Some 6 mil-

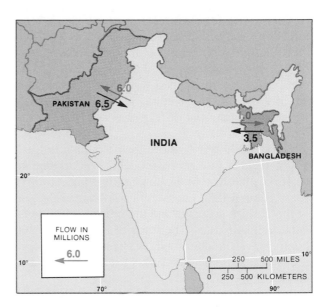

FIGURE 3–7
Forced migration in South Asia. The 1947 partition of British India into two independent nations, India and Pakistan, resulted in the forced migration of an estimated 17 million. The creation of Pakistan as two territories nearly 1600 kilometers (1,000 miles) apart proved unstable, and in 1971 East Pakistan became the independent country of Bangladesh.

lion Muslims moved from India to West Pakistan, and about 1 million moved from India to East Pakistan. Hindus forced to migrate to India included about 6 million from West Pakistan and 3.5 million from East Pakistan.

This large-scale forced migration caused considerable hardship on the population. Hindus in Pakistan as well as Muslims in India were killed attempting to reach the other side of the new border by people from the rival religion. Extremists attacked small groups of refugees travelling by road and halted trains in order to massacre the passengers.

Disputes concerning the correct location of the boundary between India and Pakistan have arisen periodically over the years since independence. The subcontinent's northernmost region—known as Jammu and Kashmir—contains a Muslim majority, yet two-thirds of it was given to India. Many of the Muslims living in India's portion of Jammu and Kashmir have long sought independence or a union with Pakistan. Pakistan has denied charges by India that it is helping to stir up unrest in Jammu and Kashmir (*see* Figure 5–14).

Government ideology. Many people have been forced to migrate because of disagreement with their country's government. In some countries, a person who disagrees with the government may be persecuted and threatened with harm. Members of a minority religious or ethnic group may feel compelled to migrate out of fear of persecution by the majority.

Since World War II, more than 1 million Bulgarians of Turkish ancestry have been forced to migrate to Turkey because of a campaign in Bulgaria to repress cultural differences. Bulgaria banned the use of the Turkish language and the practice of some Islamic religious rites. The town of Bursa, about 100 kilometers (60 miles) south of Istanbul, has become the largest settlement of Turkish refugees from Bulgaria.

In the early 1980s, a flood of political refugees reached the United States from Cuba. In April, 1980, Cuban leader Fidel Castro reversed long-standing policy by suddenly permitting anyone to leave the country who wanted to go. In what became known as the Mariel boatlift (after the Cuban port of Mariel), more than 125,000 Cubans left within a few weeks to seek political asylum in the United States. To reach the United States, most crossed the 200-kilometer (125-mile) Straits of Florida in small boats (many of which were unseaworthy and capsized). In addition, many ethnic Cubans already living in Florida sailed from the United States to Cuba, found their relatives, and brought them back to Florida.

U.S. officials were unprepared for the sudden influx of Cuban refugees. Most of the Cubans were processed at Key West, Florida, and then transferred to camps. Officials identified families or social service agencies willing to be sponsors for the refugees. These sponsors provided food and shelter and also helped secure jobs for those they sponsored.

Most but not all refugees quickly found sponsors. Through the summer of 1980 several thousand Cuban refugees who did not have sponsors lived in army camps and various temporary settlements. About a thousand people lived at Miami's Orange Bowl stadium until the start of the football season, when they were transferred to tents pitched under Interstate 95 in downtown Miami.

Shortly after the Cuban migration, several thousand refugees from Haiti also sailed in small boats for the United States. Their experience provides an interesting contrast to that of the Cuban refugees. At first, the U.S. officials were unwilling to let the Haitians remain in the country because they had migrated for economic rather than political reasons. But a group of Haitians brought a lawsuit against the U.S. government, arguing that if the Cubans were admitted they should be, too. The government settled the case by agreeing to admit the Haitians.

The experience of the Haitians shows that we cannot always distinguish easily between economic and political push factors. While many people have been compelled to migrate because of political reasons, most people move from one country to another at least in part for economic push and pull factors.

Why Do People Voluntarily Immigrate to Another Country?

Most people choose to migrate from one country to another because they hope for economic advancement. In general, people emigrate from countries where they have limited prospects for earning a living, and they migrate to countries where they believe that economic opportunities await them.

European Emigration

Historically, the largest stream of voluntary migration for economic reasons has been from Europe. In the 500 years since Columbus sailed from Spain to the Western Hemisphere, approximately 60 million Europeans have migrated to other continents. Why have so many Europeans chosen to migrate to other parts of the world? As indicated earlier, the reasons include both push and pull economic factors.

Rapid population growth in Europe fueled the push factor, especially after 1800. Application of new technology spawned by the industrial revolution—such as public health, medicine, and food—produced a rapid decline in the death rate and pushed much of Europe into Stage 2 of the demographic transition.

As the population increased, many Europeans found opportunities for economic advancement to be limited. Family farms, for example, often had to be divided among a great number of relatives, and the average farm was becoming too small to be profitable. To promote more efficient agriculture, some European governments forced the consolidation of several small farms into larger units. In England the consolidation policy was known as the enclosure movement. The enclosure movement forced millions to migrate away from rural areas. Displaced farmers could choose between working in factories in the large cities and migrating to another part of the world where farmland was plentiful.

Many of these Europeans were pulled to other continents by the prospect of economic improvement. European migrants were most attracted to the temperate climates of North America, Australia, New Zealand, southern Africa, and southern South America, where farming methods used in Europe could most easily be transplanted.

In more tropical climates, especially in Latin America and Asia, European migrants often established plantations that grew such crops as cotton, rice, sugar, and tobacco for sale back in Europe. Europeans owned most of these plantations, though relatively few literally worked the land. Instead, most of the workers either were native Asians or Latin Americans or were slaves forcibly brought from Africa.

European Immigration to the United States

Historically, the most popular destination for European emigrants has been the United States. Of the 60 million who have migrated from Europe since 1500, 37 million have migrated to the United States. Germany has sent the largest number of migrants, 7.1 million, followed by Italy with 5.4 million, Great Britain with 5.1 million, Ireland with 4.7 million, Austria-Hungary with 4.3 million, and Russia (or the Soviet Union) with 3.4 million. The frequent boundary changes of Europe's history make precise counts impossible. For example, because most ethnic Poles migrated to the United States at a time when Poland did not exist as an independent country, they may be counted as immigrants from Germany, Russia, or Austria-Hungary.

To most European migrants, the United States offered the greatest opportunities for economic suc-cess. Early migrants extolled the virtues of the United States to friends and relatives back in Europe and encouraged still others to come.

The lure of the United States was summarized in the following popular nineteenth-century song, which industrialist and philanthropist Andrew Carnegie once remarked had inspired his father to come to America:

> To the west, to the west, to the land of the free
> Where mighty Missouri rolls down to the sea;
> Where a man is a man if he's willing to toil,
> And the humblest may gather the fruits of the soil.
> Where children are blessings and he who hath most
> Has aid for his fortune and riches to boast.
> Where the young may exult and the aged may rest,
> Away, far away, to the land of the west.
> Away, far away, let us hope for the best
> And build up a home in the land of the west.

The total flow of European migration to the United States and the number of migrants from individual countries have varied from one year to the next. Yet there have been peaks and valleys in the level of migration from individual European countries as well as from the continent as a whole.

From 1607, when the first permanent English settlers landed at Jamestown, Virginia, until 1840, a steady stream of Europeans migrated to the American colonies and then to the newly independent United States. Although early migrants to America included some Dutch, Swedes, French, Spanish, and Portuguese, 90 percent of the immigrants to the United States prior to 1840 came from Great Britain. Perhaps 1 million Europeans migrated to the American colonies prior to independence, and another 1 million migrated from the late 1700s until 1840.

First peak. During the 1840s and 1850s, the level of immigration to the United States surged (Table 3–1). More than 4 million people migrated to the United States during those two decades, more than twice as many as in the previous 250 years combined. Immigration jumped from approximately 20,000 per year during the first fifty years of independence to over 250,000 in the peak immigration years of the 1840s and 1850s.

Over 90 percent of all immigrants to the United States during the 1840s and 1850s came from northern and western Europe, including 40 percent from

TABLE 3–1
Immigration to the United States by decade and region

	Total Immigration (× 1000)	Northern and Western Europe (%)	Southern and Eastern Europe (%)	Canada (%)	Latin America (%)	Asia (%)	Africa (%)
1821—1830	152	88	2	2	6	a	a
1831—1840	599	92	1	2	3	a	a
1841—1850	1,713	93	a	2	1	a	a
1851—1860	2,598	94	1	2	1	2	a
1861—1870	2,315	88	1	7	1	3	a
1871—1880	2,812	76	5	14	1	4	a
1881—1890	5,247	79	12	8	1	1	a
1891—1900	3,688	61	36	a	1	2	a
1901—1910	8,795	46	46	2	2	4	a
1911—1920	5,736	25	50	13	7	4	a
1921—1930	4,107	33	27	23	14	3	a
1931—1940	528	39	27	21	10	3	a
1941—1950	1,035	50	10	17	15	3	1
1951—1960	2,515	40	13	15	22	6	1
1961—1970	3,322	17	16	12	39	13	1
1971—1980	4,493	6	11	4	41	35	2
1981—1989	5,323	5	6	2	38	46	3

NOTE: Percentage figures are rounded and may not add to 100 for any given decade.
a = less than 0.5%

Ireland and another 33 percent from Germany. At first, desperate economic push factors impelled the Irish and Germans to cross the Atlantic. When the potato crop was devastated by blight, Ireland was thrown into a severe famine, a condition made worse by the pattern of absentee land ownership. By the end of the famine, Ireland's population was reduced by one-half through mortality and emigration. During the same period, Germans faced both poor economic conditions and political unrest.

Second peak. Immigration declined somewhat during the 1860s as a result of the Civil War but began to climb again in the 1870s. A second peak occurred during the 1880s, when more than one-half million people per year immigrated to the United States.

More than three-fourths of the immigrants during the late 1800s again came from northern and western Europe. Germans accounted for one-third of all immigrants to the United States, and the Irish still constituted a large number. But other countries in northern and western Europe sent increasing numbers of migrants, especially the Scandinavian countries of Norway and Sweden.

Third peak. Economic problems in the United States discouraged immigration during the early 1890s, but by the end of the decade the level had reached a third peak. About 1 million people per year migrated to the United States during the first fifteen years of the twentieth century. The record single year was 1907, when 1.3 million immigrants arrived.

More than 90 percent of the immigrants during the third peak came from Europe, but they came from different European countries than in the past. Instead of Great Britain, Ireland, and Germany, most immigrants came from countries that had not previously sent many people to the United States. Nearly 25 percent each came from Italy, Russia, and Austria-Hungary (which encompassed portions of present-day Austria, Czechoslovakia, Hungary, Italy, Poland, Romania, Yugoslavia, and the Soviet Union).

Immigrants came from southern and eastern Europe in the early twentieth century for the same reason that northern and western Europeans had migrated in the previous century. The shift in the primary source of immigrants coincided with the diffusion of the industrial revolution from northern and western Europe to southern and eastern European countries. The population of these countries grew rapidly as a result of improved technology and health care. For many, the option of migrating to the United States proved irresistible.

According to the 1910 U.S. census—taken at the peak of immigration—12.9 million U.S. residents (excluding blacks) were either born in a foreign country or had at least one foreign-born parent. This amounted to 13.9 percent of the country's total population of 92.2 million. These recent immigrants comprised more than 20 percent of the population in states in the Northeast, across a northern tier between Michigan and Montana, and along the Pacific coast.

Impact of European migration. The emigration of 60 million Europeans has profoundly changed the world's cultural landscape. As they migrated, Europeans brought elements of their cultural heritage to their new homes. Because of migration, European languages are spoken by half of the world's people, and Europe's most prevalent religion, Christianity, has the world's largest number of adherents. European art, music, literature, philosophy, and ethics have also diffused throughout the world.

Regions that were sparsely inhabited before European immigration, such as North America and Australia, have become closely integrated into Europe's cultural traditions. Distinctive European political structures and economic systems have been diffused to these regions.

Europeans also caused conflict by migrating to regions with large indigenous populations, especially in Africa and Asia. Europeans frequently imposed political domination on indigenous populations and injected their cultural values with little regard for local traditions. Economies in Africa and Asia became based on extracting resources for export to Europe rather than on using those resources to build up local industries. Many of today's conflicts in former European colonies are the result of past practices by European immigrants, such as drawing arbitrary boundary lines and discriminating among different local ethnic groups.

U.S. Immigration Laws

The era of massive European migration to the United States ended with the start of World War I in 1914, and the level has steadily declined since then. Europeans accounted for a third of all immigrants to the United States in the 1960s and only a ninth since 1980.

For several hundred years the United States served as Europe's safety valve. When the population began to increase rapidly because of the industrial revolution, migration to the United States drained off some of the growth. As a result, those remaining in Europe enjoyed more of the economic and social benefits from the industrial revolution.

Most European countries now have a low population growth and an economy capable of meeting the needs of the people. Countries such as Germany, Italy, and Ireland, which once sent several hundred thousand people per year to the United States, now send only a few thousand. The safety valve is no longer needed.

The number of Europeans coming to the United States has also decreased because of changing attitudes towards immigrants. Americans have always regarded new arrivals with suspicion but tempered their dislike during the nineteenth century because immigrants helped to settle the frontier and extend control across the continent. European immigrants converted the forests and prairies of the vast North American interior into productive farms.

By the early twentieth century, though, most Americans believed that the frontier had closed. With the admission of Arizona and New Mexico as the forty-seventh and forty-eighth states in 1912, the United States, for the first time in its history, possessed no contiguous territory that had not been made a state (other than the District of Columbia). This symbolic closing of the frontier meant to many Americans that the country no longer had the space to accommodate an unlimited number of immigrants.

Opposition to immigration also intensified in the United States when the majority of immigrants no longer came from northern and western Europe. German and Irish immigrants in the nineteenth century suffered some prejudice from so-called native Americans, many of whom had in reality arrived only a few years earlier from Britain. But Italians, Russians, Poles, and other southern and eastern Europeans who poured into the United States around 1900 faced much more hostility. A government study in 1911 reflected popular attitudes when it concluded that immigrants from southern and eastern Europe were racially inferior, "inclined toward violent crime," resisted assimilation, and "drove old-stock citizens out of some lines of work."

At about the time immigration from southern and eastern Europe was peaking, a handful of immigrants from China and Japan began to arrive in the United States. Although Asians never accounted for more than 5 percent of immigrants during the late nineteenth and early twentieth centuries, many Americans nevertheless were alarmed at the prospect of millions of Asians flooding into the country, especially to states along the Pacific coast.

The era of unrestricted immigration to the United States ended when the Congress passed the Quota Act of 1921 and the National Origins Act of 1924. These laws established **quotas,** or maximum limits, on the number of people who could immigrate to the United States from each country during a one-year period. The quota for each country was 2 percent of the number of people born in that country who were residing in the United States according to the 1910 census. The number of immigrants from the Eastern Hemisphere was limited to 150,000 per year, virtually all of whom had to be from Europe. The system continued with minor modifications until the 1960s.

The result of the quota laws was to perpetuate the nineteenth-century mix of immigrants to the United States but at a sharply reduced level. The Depression of the 1930s and World War II in the 1940s further reduced immigration to the United States to the lowest level since the early nineteenth century.

Quotas for individual countries were eliminated in 1968, following passage of the Immigration Act of 1965, and replaced with quotas for each hemisphere. The annual number of immigrants was restricted to 170,000 from the Eastern Hemisphere and 120,000 from the Western Hemisphere. In 1978, hemisphere quotas were replaced by a global quota of 290,000, including a maximum of 20,000 per country.

Because the number of applicants for admission to the United States far exceeds the quotas, Congress has set a preference system. Approximately 80 percent of the immigrants are spouses, adult children, and other relatives of U.S. citizens. Priority for the remaining slots is reserved for skilled workers and exceptionally talented professionals. Under the

1980 Refugee Act, refugees do not count against the quota and are admitted separately.

Since the abolition of quotas for individual countries in the late 1960s the national origin of immigrants to the United States has changed sharply. Today, over 80 percent of all immigrants come from Asia and Latin America (Figure 3–8). The surge from Latin America came a bit earlier. By the 1960s, 40 percent of all immigrants came from Latin America, and over the past two decades nearly twice as many immigrants have been admitted from Mexico than from any other country. Immigration has also increased in recent years from the West Indies.

Asia was the leading source of immigrants between the late 1970s and late 1980s until supplanted again by Latin America in 1988. The largest numbers of Asians have come from the Philippines and South Korea, followed by China, India, and Vietnam. Asians have made good use of the priorities set by the U.S. quota laws. Many well-educated Asians enter the United States under the preference given for skilled workers. Once admitted, they can bring in relatives under the family-reunification provisions of the quota. Eventually, these relatives can bring in a wider range of other relatives from Asia, a process known as **chain migration.**

Asians also comprise more than 40 percent of Canadian immigrants, though compared to the United States, Canada receives a much higher percentage of Europeans and a lower percentage of Latin Americans. Canada, however, takes in 50 percent more immigrants per capita than does the United States.

Many immigrants to the United States and Canada are poor people pushed from their homes by economic desperation, but others are young, well-educated people who are lured to economically growing countries. Scientists, researchers, doctors, and other professionals migrate to countries where they can make better use of their abilities. Large-scale emigration by talented people is known as a **brain drain.** Other countries fear that U.S. immigration policy now contributes to a brain drain by giving preference to skilled professionals.

Why has the pattern of immigration to the United States changed? In part, the reason for immigration remains the same—people are pushed by poor conditions at home and lured by good prospects for economic opportunity and social advancement in the United States. Europeans came in the nineteenth

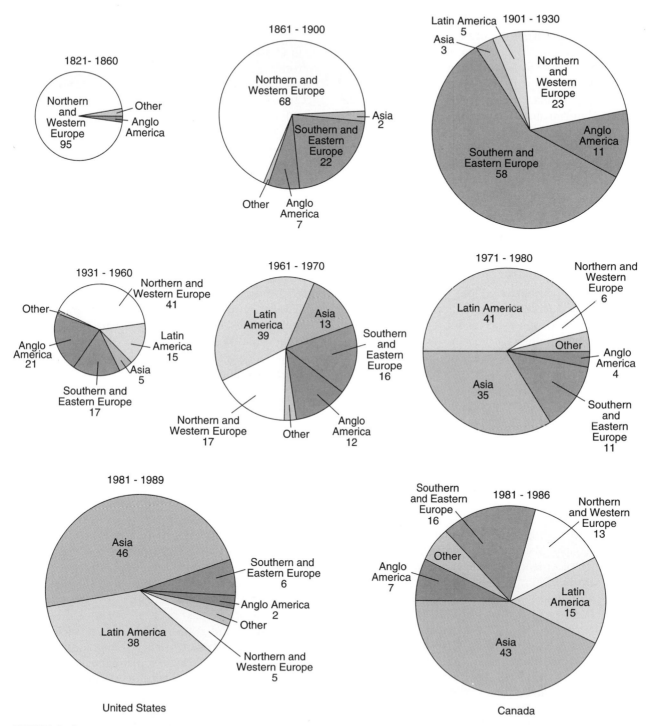

FIGURE 3-8
Europeans comprised more than 90 percent of the immigrants to the United States during the nineteenth century and even as recently as the early 1960s continued to account for more than 50 percent. Latin America replaced Europe as the most important source of immigrants to the United States in the 1960s, while Asia became the largest source in the 1980s. The area of the circles is proportioned to the relative number of immigrants during each period.

century because they saw the United States as a place to escape from the pressures of land shortage and rapid population increase. Similar motives exist today for people in Asia and Latin America.

While the motives for moving to the United States are similar, the country has changed over time. Unfortunately for the people in developing countries, the United States is no longer a sparsely settled, economically booming country with a large supply of unclaimed land. When the U.S. frontier closed, the gates to the country partially closed as well.

Illegal Immigration to the United States

Although legal immigration to the United States has reached the highest level since the early twentieth century, the number of people who wish to migrate to the United States is much higher than the quotas permit. Many people who cannot legally get into the United States immigrate illegally.

No one knows how many people immigrate to the United States illegally—that is, without proper documents—but the U.S. Immigration and Naturalization Service, which apprehends more than 1 million persons per year trying to cross the border, estimates that for every person caught at least two are successful. More than half of the illegal immigrants—sometimes called undocumented immigrants—are thought to be Mexicans, and another one-fourth are thought to be from other Latin American countries.

Why do people enter or remain in the United States illegally? Many wish to immigrate to the country for employment, but only a relative handful can get a visa that permits them to work in the United States. Foreigners who fail to receive work visas have two choices if they still wish to work in the United States: about half of the illegal residents legally enter the country on a temporary student or tourist visa and then remain after the visa has expired; the others cross the border without a visa. Once in the United States, illegal immigrants can purchase for as little as $25 various forged documents, such as a birth certificate, an alien registration card, and a social security number.

Characteristics of illegal immigrants. Although no one knows how many undocumented residents

live in the United States, U.S. and Mexican government reports contain information about those who do come. More than three-fourths of the emigrants from Mexico lived in rural areas and over half come from the four Mexican states of Guanajuato, Jalisco, Chihuahua, and Zacatecas. The destination of choice within the United States is California for more than half, Texas for another fifth, and other southwestern states for most of the remainder.

The overwhelming majority of illegal immigrants from Mexico are young males. People between the ages of 15 and 34 account for more than 70 percent of the undocumented Mexican immigrants, while females comprise less than 15 percent of the total. Most of the young men are married but leave their families in Mexico. The typical illegal immigrant has attended school for four years, one year more than the average for all Mexicans.

Most of the undocumented immigrants from Mexico have jobs in their home village but migrate to the United States to earn more money. The largest number work in agriculture, picking fruits and vegetables, although some work in clothing factories. Even those who work long hours for a few dollars a day as farm laborers or factory workers prefer to earn relatively low wages by American standards than to live in poverty at home.

Most undocumented residents have no difficulty finding jobs in the United States. Many employers like to hire immigrants who do not have visas permitting them to work in the United States, because the employers can pay lower wages and do not have to provide health care, retirement plans, and other benefits. Unsatisfactory or troublesome workers can be fired and threatened with deportation.

Because farm work is seasonal, the flow of immigrants varies throughout the year. The greatest number of Mexicans head north to the United States in the autumn and return home in the spring. The money brought back by seasonal migrants is the primary source of income for many Mexican villages. Shops give credit to the villagers through the winter until the men return in the spring with dollars. During the winter, these villages may be inhabited almost entirely by women and children.

What happens to the minority of illegal immigrants who are caught? To save time and money, the U.S. Immigration and Naturalization Service escorts most of them back to Mexico, but the overwhelming

Undocumented immigrants have little difficulty in entering the United States from Mexico because the boundary between the two countries generally runs through sparsely inhabited land, such as Organ Pipe National Monument in Arizona. The U.S. Immigration and Naturalization Service is able to apprehend only a small percentage of the people crossing the border.

majority simply retrace their steps and recross the border.

Crossing the border. The border itself is not difficult to cross illegally. Guards heavily patrol the official border crossings, most of which are located in such urban areas as El Paso and San Diego or along highways. Yet most of the 3,600-kilometer (2,000-mile) border between the United States and Mexico runs through sparsely inhabited regions and is guarded by only a handful of agents. A barbed wire fence runs along the border itself but is broken in many places.

The typical illegal immigrant from Mexico may have more difficulty reaching the U.S. border than actually crossing it. In one documented case, the route of a group of illegal immigrants to the United States began in Ahuacatlán, a village of a thousand inhabitants in the state of Querétaro. The group first took a local bus from the village to the state capital of Querétaro city, followed by another bus for a 1,800-kilometer (1,100-mile) trip to Sonoita, a town near the U.S. border. At Sonoita, the Mexicans hired a driver to transport them to a deserted border location, where they crossed on foot to Pia Oik, Arizona (Figure 3–9).

Once inside the United States, the group of Mexicans contacted a smuggler, known as a coyote or sometimes a *pollero,* from the Spanish word for someone who sells chickens for a living. The smuggler took them by car to Phoenix, some 160 kilometers (100 miles) away. A U.S. Border Patrol agent ar-

FIGURE 3–9

The documented route of one group of illegal immigrants from Mexico to the United States began in Ahuacatlán (1), a village of 1,000 inhabitants in Querétaro State. The immigrants took buses to Querétaro (2) and Sonoita (3), hired a driver to take them to a remote location, crossed the United States border on foot near Pia Oik, Arizona (4), and paid a driver to take them to Phoenix (5). Arrested in Phoenix by the Border Patrol, they were driven to Tucson (6) and then to the Mexican border at Nogales (7), where they took buses to Santa Ana (8) and Sonoita and repeated the same route back to Phoenix (9).

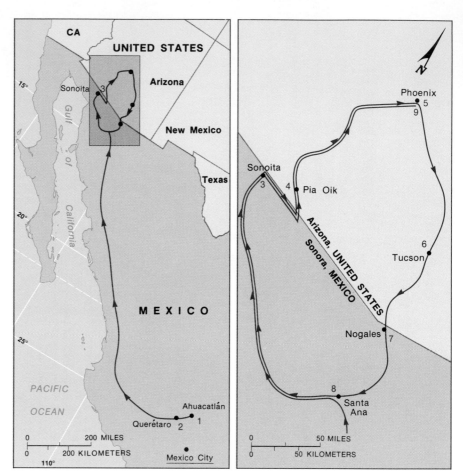

rested them in Phoenix and took them first to Tucson for processing and then across the international border to Nogales. From Nogales, the Mexicans took a bus 110 kilometers (70 miles) to Santa Ana and a second one 260 kilometers (160 miles) to Sonoita. They used the same method as before to cross the border at Pia Oik, Arizona, and eventually reached Phoenix once more. The entire journey cost several hundred dollars.

The United States faces a dilemma in dealing with illegal immigrants. On the one hand, allowing them to stay in the United States could encourage more to come, possibly raising the country's unemployment rate. On the other hand, most undocumented residents take very low-paying jobs that most Americans will not accept.

The 1986 Immigration Reform and Control Act tried to reduce the further flow of illegal immigrants to the United States. Under the law, aliens who proved that they had lived illegally in the United States continuously between 1982 and 1987 could become permanent resident aliens and apply for U.S. citizenship after five years. Seasonal agricultural workers could also qualify for permanent residence and citizenship. But only 1.3 million agricultural workers and 1.8 million others applied for permanent residence, far fewer than government officials estimated would take advantage of the program. Other undocumented residents apparently feared that if their applications were rejected they would be deported.

At the same time, the law attempted to discourage additional illegal immigration to the United States by making it harder for recently arrived immigrants to get a job without proper documentation. An employer must verify that a newly hired worker can legally work in the United States and may be fined or imprisoned for hiring an undocumented worker.

Other countries experience illegal immigration as well. Estimates of the number of illegal foreign workers in Taiwan range from 20,000 to 70,000. Most illegal immigrants to Taiwan are Filipinos, Thais, and Malaysians who are attracted by employment opportunities in textile manufacturing, construction, and other industries. These immigrants accept half the pay demanded by Taiwanese, though that is much higher than what they are likely to get at home if they could find a job.

Immigration to Great Britain. The British also severely restrict the ability of foreigners to obtain work permits. British policy, however, is complicated by the legacy of the country's former empire. When some of the United Kingdom's former colonies were granted independence, local residents could choose between remaining British citizens and becoming citizens of the new country. Millions of residents in such former colonies as Ireland, the West Indies, India, and Pakistan retained their British citizenship and eventually moved to the United Kingdom. But spouses and other family members who are citizens of the new countries do not have the right to come to Britain.

Guest Workers in Europe and the Middle East

Millions of people have migrated to countries in Western Europe and the Middle East in search of economic advancement. Foreigners who work in these countries are known as **guest workers.**

Guest workers provide a useful role in Western European and Middle Eastern countries because they take low-status and low-skilled jobs that local residents will not accept. In cities such as Zurich, Berlin, Brussels, and Paris, guest workers provide essential services, such as driving buses, collecting garbage, repairing streets, and washing dishes. While relatively low paid by European standards, guest workers earn far more than they would at home. Unlike most undocumented workers in the United States, European guest workers are protected by minimum wage laws and labor-union contracts.

The economy of the guest worker's native country also gains from the arrangement. By letting people work elsewhere, poorer countries reduce their own unemployment problem. Guest workers also help their native countries by sending a large percentage of their earnings back home to their families. The injection of foreign currency then stimulates the local economy.

Foreign guest workers perform many of the strenuous and dangerous jobs in northern and western European cities. In Berlin, for example, Turkish guest workers repair the streets.

Origin and destination of guest workers. Guest workers comprise approximately 15 percent of the population in Switzerland and 5 percent in other Western European countries, such as Germany, Denmark, and France. Two-thirds of the workers in such Middle Eastern petroleum-exporting states as Qatar, Saudi Arabia, and United Arab Emirates are foreign.

Most of the guest workers in Europe come from Southern Europe, northern Africa, the Middle East, and Asia. Distinctive migration routes have emerged among different exporting and importing countries. Italy, Turkey, and Yugoslavia send the largest number of guest workers to Western Europe. Italians and Turks flock to Germany as a result of government agreements. Most guest workers in France come from Algeria, Morocco and Tunisia, which are former French colonies in North Africa. Switzerland attracts a large number of Greeks and Yugoslavs, while Luxembourg receives primarily Portuguese (Figure 3–10).

The petroleum-exporting countries of the Middle East attract guest workers primarily from poorer Middle Eastern countries and from Asia. One-fourth of the labor force in Jordan, Lebanon, Syria, and Yemen migrate to petroleum-exporting states to seek employment. India, Pakistan, Thailand, and South Korea also send several million guest workers to the Middle East (Figure 3–11).

Problems with guest workers. Many guest workers suffer from poor social conditions. The guest

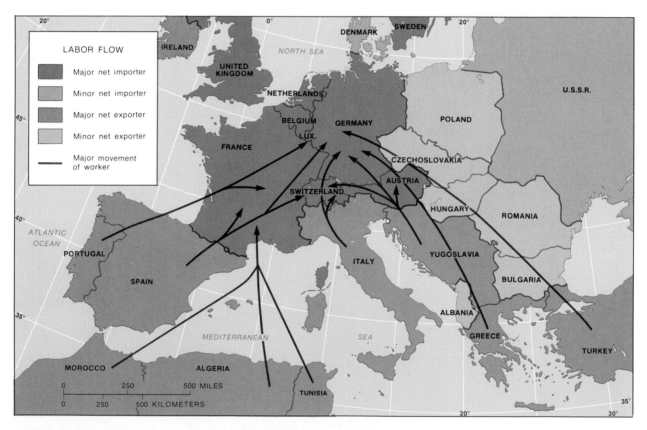

FIGURE 3–10
Guest workers emigrate primarily from southern Europe and northern Africa to work in the relatively developed countries of northern and western Europe. Guest workers follow distinctive migration routes. The selected country may be a former colonial ruler, have a similar language, or have an agreement with the exporting country. (From *The New State of the World Atlas* by M. Kidron and R. Segal. Copyright © 1984 by Pluto Press, Ltd. Reprinted by permission of Simon & Schuster, Inc.)

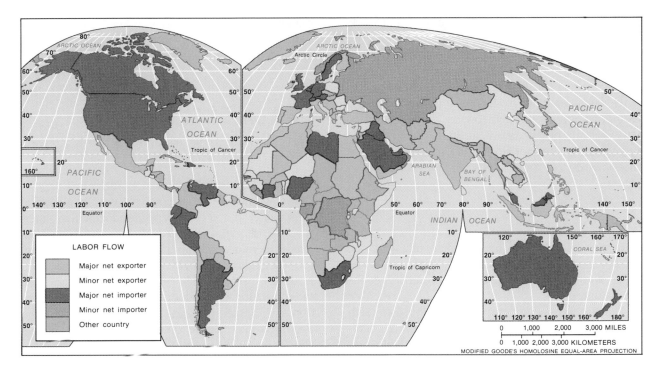

FIGURE 3–11

Migrants are on the move throughout the world in search of work. Major migrations of workers include those going to Argentina from neighboring South American countries, to Saudi Arabia and other petroleum-rich Middle eastern states from Africa and Asia, to Singapore and Malaysia from Indonesia, and to the United States and Canada from Latin America. (From *The New State of the World Atlas* by M. Kidron and R. Segal. Copyright © 1984 by Pluto Press, Ltd. Reprinted by permission of Simon & Schuster, Inc.)

worker is typically a young man who arrives alone in a city. He has little money for food, housing, or entertainment because the primary objective is to send home as much money as possible. Any surplus money is likely to be used to buy a rail ticket home for the weekend.

Far from his family and friends, the guest worker can lead a lonely life. His isolation may be heightened by unfamiliarity with the host country's language and distinctive cultural activities. Many guest workers pass their leisure time at the local railway station. There they can buy native-language newspapers, mingle with other guest workers, and meet people who have just arrived by train from home.

Both guest workers and the host countries regard the arrangement as temporary. In reality, many guest workers remain indefinitely, especially if they are joined by other family members. Some guest workers apply their savings to starting a grocery

store, restaurant, or some other type of small shop. These businesses can fill a need in European cities by being open on weekends and evenings when most locally owned establishments are closed.

Officials in the petroleum-exporting countries of the Middle East fear that the increasing numbers of guest workers in those countries will spark political unrest and abandonment of traditional Islamic customs. To minimize long-term stays, host countries in the Middle East force migrants to return home if they wish to marry and prevent them from returning once they have wives and children.

As a result of lower economic growth rates, Middle Eastern and Western European countries have reduced the number of guest workers in recent years. Several Western European governments now pay guest workers to return home, but countries with their own unemployment problems sometimes refuse to take them back.

Many Western Europeans dislike the guest workers and oppose government programs to improve the workers' living conditions. An incident in France illustrates the tensions between guest workers and local citizens. The French government moved 300 black guest workers from Mali out of condemned dwellings into a publicly owned building in the Paris suburb of Vitry-sur-Seine. On Christmas Eve, fifty townspeople vandalized the project, cut electric lines, sawed off water pipes, and ripped out telephones.

Migration in Asia

Examples of voluntary international migration are found elsewhere in the world. But lack of opportunities and government restrictions tend to reduce the volume.

During the late nineteenth and early twentieth centuries, millions of Asians migrated to other countries for economic advancement. A large proportion of the voluntary migrants comprised so-called time-contract laborers, recruited for a fixed period of time to work in mines or on plantations. When their contracts expired, many laborers settled permanently in the new country. Indians went as time-contract laborers to Burma, Malaysia, British Guiana (present-day Guyana), eastern and southern Africa, Fiji, Mauritius, and Trinidad. Japanese and Filipinos went to Hawaii, and Japanese also went to Brazil. Chinese worked on the U.S. West Coast, helping to build the first transcontinental railroad.

More than 20 million ethnic Chinese live permanently in other Asian countries, according to the most recent evidence, a twenty-five-year-old study. Chinese comprise about 17 percent of the population in Thailand and Vietnam, about 33 percent in Malaysia and Cambodia, and more than 90 percent in Singapore.

Migration by Asians nearly a century ago is producing contemporary problems in several countries. For example, between 1879 and 1920, the British brought Indians as indentured laborers to the Pacific island of Fiji. Today, Fiji includes slightly more Indians than native Fijians. For many decades, Fiji was a model of how two culturally diverse groups could live together peacefully under a democratically elected government. Indians controlled most of the country's businesses, while Fijians dominated the government and army. But after an In-

dian party won the elections in 1987, rioting broke out between the two groups, and Fijian army officers seized temporary control of the government.

Why Do People Migrate within a Country?

Internal migration is a permanent move to a new location within the same country. Most people find migration within a country less traumatic than international migration because they find familiar language, literature, music, and other social customs after they move. Moves within a country also generally involve much shorter distances than those in international migration, though internal migration can result in long-distance moves in large countries, such as the United States and the Soviet Union.

We can divide internal migration into two types. **Interregional migration** is movement from one region of a country to another, while **intraregional migration** is movement within one region. Motives for the two types of moves may not be the same.

Interregional Migration in the United States

In the United States, interregional moves were more important in the past, when most people were farmers. Lack of farmland pushed many people from the more densely settled regions of the country and lured them to the frontier, where land was abundant. Today, most people move to a new region for a better job, though many also move for noneconomic reasons.

The most famous example of large-scale internal migration is probably the opening of the American West. Two hundred years ago, the United States consisted of a collection of settlements concentrated on the Atlantic Coast. Through massive levels of migration, the interior of the continent was settled and developed.

Changing center of population. The U.S. Census Bureau computes the country's population center at the time of each census. The population center is the average location of everyone in the country—the center of population "gravity." If the United States were a flat plain placed on top of a pin and each individual weighed the same, the population center would be the point where the population distribution causes the flat plain to balance on the pin. The changing distribution of the population center graphically demonstrates the march of the American people across the North American continent over the past 200 years (Figure 3–12).

When the first U.S. census was taken in 1790 the population center was located in the Chesapeake Bay, 37 kilometers (23 miles) east of Baltimore, Maryland. Throughout the colonial period, the population center had probably been at about the same place. This location reflects the fact that virtually all settlements were near the Atlantic Coast.

Few colonists ventured far from coastal locations because they depended on shipping with Europe to receive products and export raw materials. Settlement in the interior was also hindered by an intervening obstacle, the Appalachian Mountains. The Appalachians blocked western development because of their steep slopes, thick forests, and lack of gaps. Hostile Indians also retarded western settlements.

Early settlement in the interior. Settlement of the interior began after 1790. By 1830 the center of population had moved to a spot 30 kilometers (19

miles) west of Moorefield, West Virginia (Virginia, until 1863). Encouraged by the opportunity to obtain a large amount of land at a low price, people moved into river valleys and fertile level lowlands as far west as the Mississippi River.

Improvements in transportation, especially construction of canals, encouraged the opening of the interior in the early nineteenth century. The most important canal was the Erie Canal, which enabled people to travel inexpensively by boat between New York City and the Great Lakes. When the Erie Canal opened in 1825, the fare from New York to Detroit was only $10, yet traffic was so heavy on the canal that tolls paid for construction costs within nine years. Between 1816 and 1840, 5,352 kilometers (3,326 miles) of canals were dug in the United States. Steamboats further speeded water travel.

After 1830, the U.S. population center moved west more rapidly and by 1880 reached a location in Kentucky, 13 kilometers (8 miles) west of Cincinnati, Ohio. The center of population moved 11 kilometers (7 miles) per year during that period, compared to 7 kilometers (4 miles) per year during the previous 40 years.

What accounts for the more rapid westward shift between 1830 and 1880? The primary reason was that most western pioneers at the time passed through the interior of the country and headed for California. The continuous westward advance of set-

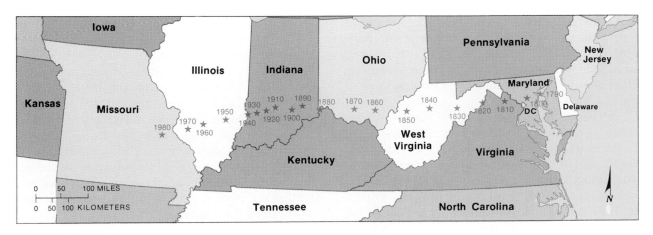

FIGURE 3–12
The Bureau of the Census calculates the center of population in the United States every decade. The center has consistently shifted toward the west, though the rate of movement has varied in different eras. In 1980, the center of population was west of the Mississippi River for the first time. By 1990, the center had reached south-central Missouri.

tlement stopped at the 98th meridian for nearly forty years, as migrants jumped directly to California.

One reason large numbers of migrants passed over the interior was because they were pulled to California, especially by the Gold Rush that began in the late 1840s. Another reason was that the interior of the country confronted early settlers with a physical environment not suitable for familiar agricultural practices.

Early nineteenth-century Americans preferred to start farms in forested areas. They cut down the trees and used the wood to build homes, barns, and fences. When they crossed west of the 98th meridian, pioneers could not find many trees. Instead, they saw a vast expanse of rolling grasslands, an area that receives on average less than 8 centimeters (20 inches) of precipitation per year.

Lacking the technology to overcome the dry climate, lack of trees, and thick grassland sod, early explorers such as Zebulon Pike declared the region unfit for farming. Maps at the time labelled the region from the Dakotas through Nebraska, Kansas, and Oklahoma to Texas as the "Great American Desert." Today, the region west of the 98th meridian and east of the Rocky Mountains, which we call the Great Plains, is one of the nation's most important farming areas.

Settlement of the Great Plains. After 1880, the U.S. center of population continued to move west at a much slower pace. Between 1880 and 1950, the center moved west approximately 5 kilometers (3 miles) per year, less than half the rate of the previous half century. The rate slowed in part because large-scale migration to the East Coast from Europe offset some of the migration from the East Coast to the U.S. West.

The westward movement of the U.S. population center also slowed after 1880 because people began to fill in the area between the 98th meridian and California that was bypassed by earlier generations. The Dakota territory, for example, grew from 14,000 inhabitants in 1870 to 135,000 in 1880 and 539,000 by 1890. Advances in agricultural technology in the late nineteenth century enabled people to cultivate dry lands such as the Great Plains. Farmers used barbed wire to reduce dependence on wood, the steel plow to cut through the thick sod, and windmills and well-drilling equipment to pump more water.

Beginning in the 1840s, the expansion of the railroads encouraged western settlement. By the 1880s, an extensive rail network permitted settlers in the Great Plains to transport their products to the large concentrations of customers in East Coast cities. The railroad companies also promoted western settlement by selling land to farmers. Companies that built the railroad lines received large land grants from the federal government, not just narrow right-of-way strips to lay tracks. The railroad companies in turn financed construction of their lines by selling small parcels of the adjacent land to farmers. Offices were established by the railroad companies in major East Coast and European cities to sell land.

Recent growth of the South. Since 1950, the center of population has moved west at a more rapid rate, 10 kilometers (6 miles) per year. In 1980, the center was located near DeSoto, Missouri, 60 kilometers (40 miles) southwest of St. Louis. The site was significant: for the first time in the nation's history the center of population had moved west of the Mississippi River.

The recent movement of the population center also shows a second trend, movement to the south. In 1790 the center was at 39°16′ north latitude. By 1920, the center had moved only slightly, to 39°10′ north latitude. Beginning in the 1920s, the center moved south, at first slowly but since 1950 at a rate of 4 kilometers (2 miles) per year. In 1980, the center had reached 38°10′ north latitude.

The population center has drifted south because of net migration into southern and western states. The states with the highest levels of net inmigration during the 1980s were located in the South and West; nearly half of the recent population growth in the United States has been concentrated in just three states: California, Texas, and Florida (Figure 3–13). On the other hand, virtually all of the states with the highest net outmigration were located in the North; West Virginia, Wyoming, and Iowa recorded the highest percentages of population decline during the 1980s.

Reasons for migration to the South and West. Why are Americans moving from the North and East to the South and West? More than half of the people

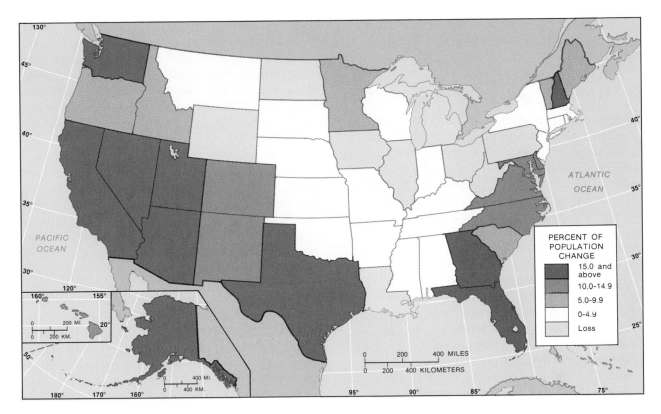

FIGURE 3–13
The fastest-growing states in the United States during the 1980s were located in the South and West, while the slowest-growing states were all located in the North and East. California, Florida, and Texas accounted for nearly half of the country's total population growth during the decade, although some less populous states grew at more rapid rates.

move primarily because of job opportunities. The number of new jobs created each year since 1960 has increased by about 3 percent in the United States, 5 percent in the South and West, and only 1 percent in the North and East.

People also migrate to the South and West for environmental reasons. Americans commonly refer to the South and West as the sunbelt because of the more temperate climate, while the North and East are called the rustbelt because of the dependency on declining steel and other manufacturing industries. As people gain more leisure time they are lured to the sunbelt by the greater opportunities to engage in outdoor activities throughout the year.

The growth in population and employment in the South and West and the decline of the North and East have aggravated regional antagonisms.

Some people in the North and East believe that southern and western states have stolen industries from them. Although some industries relocate from the North and East, most industrial growth in the South and West comprises newly established companies rather than relocated ones.

To some extent, the regional difference in economic growth reduces a historical imbalance, because traditionally people in the Northeast have enjoyed higher incomes than those in the South. If the average income of a U.S. family is arbitrarily designated as 100, then the average income is 115 for people in the Northeast and 90 for people in the South. In comparison, as recently as 1929, average income was 239 in the Northeast and only 52 in the South. But the gap between the Northeast and South has widened since 1970, when the average was 107 in the Northeast and 90 in the South; the increase results from recent problems faced by industries in the South (*see* Chapter 10).

Interregional Migration in Other Countries

Soviet Union. As in the United States, long-distance interregional migration is an important means in the Soviet Union to open up new regions for economic development. Soviet officials have been especially eager to develop the country's Far North, which includes much of Siberia, because it is rich in such natural resources as fossil fuels, minerals, and forests. The Far North encompasses 45 percent of the country's land area but contains less than 2 percent of the total population.

Earlier this century, the Soviet government forced citizens to migrate to locations in the Far North where labor was needed to construct and operate steel mills, hydroelectric power stations, mines, and other enterprises. In recent years, the government has reduced the use of forced migration and instead has provided incentives, including higher wages, more paid holidays, and earlier retirement, to induce voluntary migration to the Far North.

The incentives have not pulled as many migrants to the Far North as Soviet officials desire. People are reluctant to move to the region because of its harsh climate and its remoteness from population centers. Each year, as many as half of the people in the Far North emigrate to other regions of the country and are replaced by other immigrants, especially young males willing to work in the region for a short period of time. One method the government uses to overcome the labor shortage in the Far North is to send a brigade of young volunteers, known as *Komsomol,* during school vacations to help with the construction of projects such as the Baykal-Amur Railroad.

Brazil. Another large country, Brazil, has encouraged interregional migration. Most Brazilians live in a string of large cities near the Atlantic Coast, including Recife, Salvador, Rio de Janeiro, São Paulo, and Pôrto Alegre. São Paulo and Rio de Janeiro have become two of the world's largest cities. In contrast, Brazil's tropical interior is very sparsely inhabited.

To increase the attractiveness of the interior, in 1960 the government of Brazil moved the capital from Rio to a newly built city called Brasília, situated 1,000 kilometers (600 miles) from the Atlantic Coast. From above, Brasília's design resembles an airplane, with government buildings located at the center of the city, and housing arranged along the "wings."

At first, Brasilia's population grew slowly, because government workers and foreign embassy officials resented the forced move from Rio, one of the world's most animated cities. In recent years, thousands of people have migrated to Brasília in search of jobs. Many of these workers could not afford housing in Brasília, living instead in hastily erected shacks on the outskirts.

Europe. Even countries that occupy relatively small land areas have important interregional migration trends. People in Italy migrate from the south, known as the *Mezzogiorno,* to the north in search of job opportunities. Compared to the *Mezzogiorno,* Italy's north benefits from relatively rich agricultural land and a strong industrial base. The *Mezzogiorno* comprises 40 percent of Italy's land area and contains 35 percent of the population but only 24 percent of the national income. Per capita income is nearly twice as high in the north than in the south, and unemployment rates are less than 5 percent in the north, compared to more than 20 percent in the south (Figure 3–14).

Similarly, people in the United Kingdom are migrating because of regional differences in job opportunities, although the pattern is opposite of Italy's: economic growth is in the south, while the north is declining. The northern regions of the United Kingdom were the first in the world to enter the industrial revolution in the eighteenth century. Today, many of the region's industries are no longer competitive in the global economy. On the other hand, industries in the south and east—especially the region around London—are relatively healthy. The pattern of interregional migration is reflected in differences in per capita income in different regions. The regions with net immigration are also the ones with the highest per capita incomes.

Regional differences in economic conditions within European countries may become greater with increased integration of the continent's economy. Regions closer to European markets, such as the south of Britain and the north of Italy, may hold a competitive advantage over more peripheral regions.

India. A number of governments limit the freedom of people to migrate from one region of the country to another. For example, Indians require a permit to migrate to—or even visit—the state of Assam, in the northeast of the country. The restrictions, which date from the British colonial era, are designed to protect the ethnic identity of Assamese by limiting the ability of outsiders to compete for jobs and purchase land. Because Assam is situated on the border with Bangladesh, the restrictions also limit international migration.

Intraregional Migration

While interregional migration attracts considerable attention, far more people move within the same region. Since 1800, the most prominent type of intraregional migration in the world has been from rural to urban areas. Less than 5 percent of the world's people lived in urban areas in 1800, compared to nearly half today.

Migration from rural to urban areas. The process of urbanization began in the 1800s in the countries of Europe and North America that were undergoing rapid industrial development. The percentage of people living in urban areas in the United States, for example, increased from 5 percent in 1800 to 50 percent in 1920. Today, approximately 75 percent of

FIGURE 3–14
Per capita income for regions in Italy. Sharp regional differences exist, with the south or *Mezzogiorno* much less prosperous than the north. Because people tend to migrate to relatively prosperous regions where job opportunities are better, this map closely resembles one for net migration.

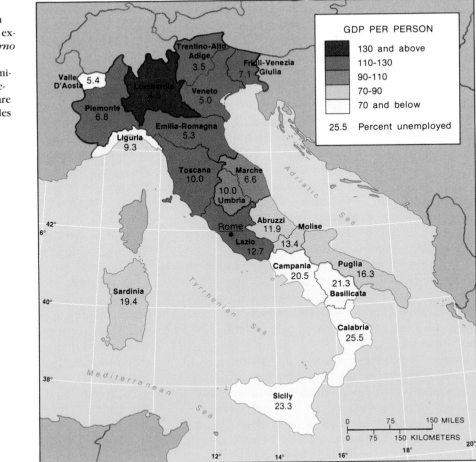

the people in the U.S. and other relatively developed countries live in urban areas.

Migration from rural to urban areas has skyrocketed in recent years in the developing countries of Africa, Asia, and Latin America. Studies conducted in a variety of developing countries show that migration from rural areas accounts for nearly half of the population increase in urban areas, while the natural increase (excess of births over deaths) accounts for the remainder. Geographers estimate that worldwide more than 20 million people migrate each year from rural to urban areas.

Migration to one of the world's largest cities, São Paulo, Brazil, has reached 300,000 people per year. Many of these migrants cannot find housing in the city and must live in squatter settlements, known in Brazil as *favellas*. The *favellas* may lack electricity, running water, and paved streets.

Like interregional migrants, most people who move from rural to urban areas seek economic advancement. They are pushed from rural areas by declining opportunities in agriculture and are pulled to the cities by the prospect of work in factories or services.

Migration from urban to suburban areas. In relatively developed countries, the major form of intraregional migration is from the central cities to the suburbs. Annual net migration from cities to suburbs exceeds 1 million people in the United States. Similar patterns are evident in Canada, the United Kingdom, and other Western European countries. The population of most central cities has declined in North America and Western Europe, while suburbs have grown rapidly.

The major reason for the large-scale migration to the suburbs is not related to employment, as was the case with other forms of migration. For most people, migration to suburbs does not coincide with changing jobs. Instead, people are pulled by a suburban lifestyle.

Suburbs offer the opportunity to live in a detached house rather than an apartment, surrounded by a private yard where children can play safely. A garage or driveway on the property guarantees space to park automobiles at no charge. Suburban schools tend to be more modern, better-equipped, and safer than those in the cities. Automobiles and trains enable people to live in suburbs yet have access to jobs, shops, and recreation facilities throughout the urban area (*see* Chapter 12).

As a result of suburbanization, the territory occupied by urban areas has rapidly expanded (*see* Chapter 11). To accommodate suburban growth, farms on the periphery of urban areas are converted to housing developments, where new roads, sewers, and other services must be built.

Migration from metropolitan to nonmetropolitan areas. During the 1970s, the relatively developed countries of North America and Western Europe witnessed a new trend. For the first time in U.S. history, rural areas grew more rapidly than urban areas. Canada, the United Kingdom, and several other European countries displayed similar patterns. Net migration from urban to rural areas is called counterurbanization.

Counterurbanization results in part from very rapid expansion of suburbs. No one can define precisely where suburbs end and the countryside begins. But most counterurbanization represents genuine migration from cities and suburbs to small towns and rural communities.

Like suburbanization, people move from urban to rural areas for lifestyle reasons. People are lured to rural areas by the prospect of swapping the "rat race" of urban life for the opportunity to live on a farm where they can own horses or grow vegetables. Most people who move to farms, however, do not earn their living from agriculture. Instead, they work in nearby factories or small-town shops and services.

With modern communications and transportation systems, no location in relatively developed countries is truly isolated, either economically or socially. Computers enable us to work anywhere and still have access to an international network. We can obtain money at any time from a conveniently located electronic transfer machine rather than going to a bank building. We can select clothing from a mail-order catalogue, place the order by telephone, pay by credit card, and have the desired items delivered to our home within a few days. We can follow the fortunes of our favorite teams on television anywhere in the country, thanks to satellite dishes.

Many migrants from urban to rural areas are retired people who are attracted by access to leisure activities, such as fishing and hiking. Retirement communities—in reality, small towns restricted to older people—appeal to retired people who like to participate in recreation activities. In France, some elderly people migrate from Paris to the rural village where they were born, while others are attracted to the mild climate in the south of the country along the Mediterranean coast.

Counterurbanization has stopped in the United States since the early 1980s because job opportunities have declined in rural areas. Many factories that located in rural areas a few years ago have become less competitive in a rapidly changing global economy. Industries that located in rural areas to take advantage of the lower costs of doing business have been undersold by Asian competitors who have even lower production costs. Surviving industries in rural parts of the United States and other relatively developed countries have had to become more efficient, often by eliminating jobs.

The rural economy has also been hurt by poor agricultural conditions. The price of farm products has declined, and many farmers have gone bankrupt. Although farmers constitute a small percentage of the labor force, they play an important role in the economy of rural areas. For example, the typical farmer borrows large sums of money from local banks and buys expensive equipment from local farm-implement stores.

No one can predict future migration trends in relatively developed countries because future economic conditions are uncertain. Have these countries reached long-term equilibrium, in which approximately three-fourths of the people live in urban areas and one-fourth in rural areas? Will counterurbanization resume in the future, because people prefer to live in rural areas? Is the decline of the rural economy reversible?

Summary

Here again are the key issues we have raised about migration:

1. **Why do people migrate?** We can group the reasons into push and pull factors. People feel compelled to move from a location for a variety of political, economic, and environmental reasons. Similarly, people are induced to migrate because of the political, economic, or environmental attraction of a new location. We can distinguish between international and internal migration, and within international migration, between forced and voluntary migration.

2. **Why are people forced to emigrate from a country?** Forced international migration usually results from political push factors beyond the control of the migrants. In the past, people were forced to move to become slaves. Today, other political factors produce forced international migration, including wars, boundary changes, and ideology.

3. **Why do people voluntarily immigrate to another country?** Most people voluntarily migrate to another country for economic reasons. They face a combination of limited job opportunities at home and brighter prospects for advancement at another location. In the past, the most important example of voluntary international migration was from Europe to North America. Today, an increasing number of Asians and Latin Americans wish to migrate to the United States for economic opportunities, but immigration laws restrict the number of legal immigrants. As a result, millions of people immigrate illegally to the United States.

4. **Why do people migrate within a country?** We can distinguish between interregional and intraregional migration within the same country. Historically, interregional migration was especially important in settling the frontier of large countries such as the United States, the Soviet Union, and Brazil. Today, interregional migration persists because of different economic conditions in different regions of a country. Some people are attracted to new regions because of climate or other environmental factors. The most important intraregional migration trend in developing countries is from rural to urban areas and from cities to suburbs in relatively developed countries.

Family History

Migration has altered the landscape of the United States and Canada. When people migrate, they bring their language, religion, and other social customs with them to their new home, as discussed in the next three chapters.

Although global trends are important, migration is also significant at a personal scale, because the overwhelming majority of all Canadians and Americans are immigrants or descendents of immigrants, and migration to North America constitutes the most important event in the history of many families.

Suppose that you were asked to trace the migration record for the ancestors of one of your parents. You could use family photo albums, old letters, birth and death certificates, genealogies, and entries in a family Bible to verify the recollections of relatives. What kind of geographical story would unfold? A study like this by geography students at the University of California at San Diego included the following history:

The student's grandmother was born in Yokohama, Japan, in 1885 and emigrated to San Francisco in 1902 as a "picture bride," a young Oriental woman who became engaged to a man who had already emigrated to the United States after he was shown her photograph. The student's grandfather and picture-bride grandmother moved in 1913 to Carmel, California, and four years later to Watsonville, California, where the student's mother was born.

In 1942, during World War II, the U.S. government forced the family to migrate to Poston, Arizona. Japanese-Americans were forced to move because the government feared that the Japanese might invade the West Coast and Japanese-Americans living there might have divided loyalties. After the war, the student's grandmother moved to Santa Cruz, California, while the mother went to Cleveland, Ohio. In 1948, the mother returned to California, first to San Francisco and later to Santa Cruz, where the student was born (Figure 3–15).

Give Me Your Tired

The most famous symbol of migration in the world is surely the Statue of Liberty. The inscription on it, written by Emma Lazarus, begins, "Give me your tired, your poor, your huddled masses yearning to breathe free." The statue stands at the mouth of New York Harbor, near Ellis Island, which was for many years the initial landing and processing point for tens of millions of immigrants.

Residents of the United States in the nineteenth and early twentieth centuries did not greet immigrants with open arms. But immigrants were given the opportunity to enter the country and make new lives, some of them successful. Even recently arrived undocumented immigrants stand a good chance of economic success if given the chance. For example, in August 1986, 155 Tamils from Sri Lanka were found drifting in two lifeboats off Newfoundland. All of them found work, most within one month of their

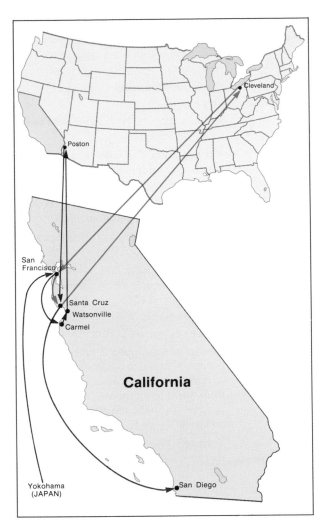

FIGURE 3–15
A student at the University of California at San Diego traced her family's migration history back to her maternal grandmother, who emigrated from Yokohama, Japan, to San Francisco in 1902 and subsequently moved to Carmel, Watsonville, Poston, and Santa Cruz. The student's mother was born in Watsonville and migrated to Poston, Santa Cruz, Cleveland, San Francisco, and back to Santa Cruz. The student moved from Santa Cruz to San Diego.

Ellis Island was the place where the largest number of immigrants entered the United States. This Italian woman immigrated with her three children around 1900.

arrival. Several found two jobs, working 80 hours per week. These Tamils came to have higher salaries than the national average.

But for many Tamils, Sikhs, Mexicans, and other people, the only way to enter the United States or Canada is illegally. In the latter part of the twentieth century, the tradition of universal ability to migrate to these countries no longer exists. Paradoxically, in an era when human beings have invented easy means of long-distance transport, the right of free migration has been replaced by human barriers.

Key Terms

Brain drain Large-scale emigration by talented people.

Chain migration Process by which people are given preference for migrating to the United States because a relative was previously admitted.

Emigration Migration *from* a location.

Flood plain The area subject to flooding during a given number of years according to historical trends.

Forced migration Permanent movement compelled by political factors.

Guest workers Workers who migrate to the relatively developed countries of northern and western Europe, usually from southern Europe or northern Africa, in search of relatively high-paying jobs.

Immigration Migration *to* a new location.

Internal migration Permanent movement within a particular country.

International migration Permanent movement from one country to another.

Interregional migration Permanent movement from one region of a country to another.

Intervening obstacle An environmental or cultural feature of the landscape that hinders migration.

Intraregional migration Permanent movement within one region of a country.

Migration Permanent move to a new location.

Mobility The ability to move from one location to another.

Net migration The difference between the number of immigrants and the number of emigrants.

Pull factors Factors that induce people to move to a new location.

Push factors Factors that induce people to leave old residences.

Quota A maximum limit, often on the number of people who can immigrate to a country.

Refugees People forced to migrate from a country for political reasons.

Triangular slave trade A practice, primarily during the eighteenth century, of European ships transporting slaves from Africa to Caribbean islands, molasses from the Caribbean to Europe, and trade goods from Europe to Africa.

Voluntary migration Permanent movement undertaken by choice.

Thinking Geographically

1. Should preference for immigrating to the United States and Canada be given to individuals with special job skills, or should priority be given to reunification of family members? Should quotas be raised to meet increasing demand for both types of immigrants?
2. What is the impact of large-scale emigration on the places from which migrants depart? On balance, do these places suffer because of the loss of young, upwardly mobile workers, or do these places benefit from the draining away of surplus labor? In the communities from which migrants depart, is the quality of life on balance improved through reduced pressures on local resources or damaged through the deterioration of social structures and institutions?
3. According to the concept of chain migration, current migrants tend to follow the paths of relatives and friends who have moved earlier. Can you find evidence of chain migration in your community? Does chain migration apply primarily to the

relocation of people from one community in a developing country to one community in a relatively developed country, or is chain migration more applicable to movement within a relatively developed country?

4. Three regions account for the largest numbers of refugees—the Horn of Africa, Afghanistan, and the Middle East. What demographic characteristics—such as rates of natural increase, crude birth, and crude death—prevail in the major refugee regions? Is large-scale forced migration alleviating or exacerbating population growth in the various regions?

5. At the same time that some people are migrating from developing to relatively developed countries in search of employment transnational corporations have relocated some low-skilled jobs to developing countries to take advantage of low wage rates. Should developing countries care whether their surplus workers emigrate or remain as employees of foreign companies?

Further Readings

Bennett, D. Gordon, and Ole Fade. *Geographic Perspectives on Migration Behavior: A Bibliographic Survey.* University of North Carolina Studies in Geography, no. 12. Chapel Hill: University of North Carolina Press, 1979.

Berry, Brian J. L., and Lester Silverman, eds. *Population Redistribution and Public Policy.* Washington, D.C.: National Academy of Sciences, 1978.

Bigger, Jeanne C. "The Sunning of America: Migration to the Sunbelt." *Population Bulletin* 34 (3). Washington, D.C.: Population Reference Bureau, 1979.

Bouvier, Leon F. *Immigration and Its Impact on U.S. Population Size.* Washington, D.C.: Population Reference Bureau, 1981.

Bouvier, Leon F., and Robert W. Gardner. "Immigration to the U.S.: The Unfinished Story." *Population Bulletin* 41 (4). Washington, D.C.: Population Reference Bureau, 1986.

Brown, Lawrence A., and Victoria A. Lawson. "Migration in Third World Settings, Uneven Development, and Conventional Modeling: A Case Study of Costa Rica." *Annals of the Association of American Geographers* 75 (March 1985): 29–47.

Brown, Larry A., and R. L. Sanders. "Toward a Development Paradigm of Migration: With Particular Reference To Third World Settings." In *Migration Decision Making: Multidisciplinary Approaches to Micro-level Studies in Developed and Developing Countries,* edited by G. F. DeJong and R. W. Gardner. New York: Pergamon Press, 1981.

Burton, Ian, Robert W. Kates, and Gilbert F. White. *The Environment as Hazard.* New York: Oxford University Press, 1978.

Champion, A. G., ed. *Counterurbanization: The Changing Pace and Nature of Population Deconcentration.* London: Edward Arnold, 1989.

Clark, Gordon L. *Interregional Migration, National Policy and Social Justice.* Totowa, NJ: Rowman and Allanheld, 1983.

Clark, W. A. V. *Human Migration.* Beverly Hills: Sage Publications, 1986.

Clark, W. A. V., and James E. Burt. "The Impact of Workplace on Residential Relocation." *Annals of the Association of American Geographers* 70 (March 1980): 59–67.

Clark, W. A. V., and Eric G. Moore, eds. *Residential Mobility and Public Policy.* Beverly Hills: Sage Publications, 1980.

Davis, Cary, Carl Haub, and JoAnne Willette. "U.S. Hispanics: Changing the Face of America." *Population Bulletin* 38 (3). Washington, D.C.: Population Reference Bureau, 1983.

du Toit, Brian M. and Helen I. Safa, eds. *Migration and Development.* The Hague, Netherlands: Mouton, 1975.

Fredrich, Barbara E. "Family Migration History: A Project in Introductory Cultural Geography." *Journal of Geography (November 1977).*

Frey, William H. "Migration and Metropolitan Decline in Developed Countries: A Comparative Study." *Population and Development Review* 14 (December 1988): 599–628.

Jackson, J. D., ed. *Migration.* London: Cambridge University Press, 1969.

Jensen, Leif. *The New Immigration: Implications for Poverty.* Westport, CT: Greenwood Press, 1989.

Jones, Huw, Nicholas Ford, James Caird, and William Berry. "Counter-urbanization in Societal Context: Long-Distance Migration to the Highlands and Islands of Scotland." *Professional Geographer* 36 (November 1984): 437–43.

Jones, Richard C. "Undocumented Migration from Mexico: Some Geographical Questions." *Annals of the Association of American Geographers* 72 (March 1982): 77–78.

Kidron, Michael, and Ronald Segal. *The New State of the World Atlas.* New York: Simon and Schuster, 1984.

Kontuly, Thomas, and Roland Vogelsang. "Explanations for the Intensification of Counterurbanization in the Federal Republic of Germany." *Professional Geographer,* 40 (February 1988): 42–53.

Kosinski, Leszek A., and R. Mansell Prothero. *People on the Move.* London: Methuen, 1975.

Kritz, Mary M., Charles B. Keely, and Silvano M. Tomasi. *Global Trends in Migrations: Theory and Research on International Population Movements.* New York: Center for Migration Studies, 1981.

Lee, Everett. "A Theory of Migration." *Demography* 3 (no. 1, 1966): 47–57.

McNeill, William, and Ruth S. Adams. *Human Migration: Patterns and Policies.* Bloomington: Indiana University Press, 1978.

Morrison, Peter A. *Population Movements: Their Form and Functions in Urbanization and Development.* Liège, Belgium: Ordina Editions for International Union for the Scientific Study of Population, 1983.

Nam, Charles B., William J. Serow, and David F. Sly. *International Handbook on Internal Migration.* Westport, CT: Greenwood Press, 1990.

Newland, Kathleen. *International Migration: The Search for Work.* Worldwatch Paper 33. Washington, D.C.: Worldwatch Institute, November 1979.

———. Refugees: The New International Politics of Displacement. Worldwatch Paper 43. Washington, D.C.: Worldwatch Institute, March 1981.

Papademetrion, Demetrios G. "International Migration in a Changing World." *International Social Science Journal* 36 (no. 3, 1984): 409–424.

Ravenstein, Ernest George. "The Laws of Migration." *Journal of the Royal Statistical Society* 52 (1889): 241–305.

Rogerson, Peter A. "Changes in U.S. National Mobility Levels." *Professional Geographer* 39 (no. (August, 1987): 344–50.

Rogge, John R., ed. *Refugees: A Third World Dilemma.* Totowa, NJ: Rowman and Littlefield, 1987.

Roseman, Curtis C. *Changing Migration Patterns within the United States.* Washington, D.C.: Association of American Geographers, 1977.

———. "Migration as a Spatial and Temporal Process." Annals of the Association of American Geographers 61 (September 1971): 589–98.

Sanders, Alvin J., and Larry Long. "New Sunbelt Migration Patterns." *American Demographics* 9 (January 1987): 38–41.

Simon, Rita J., and Caroline B. Brettell, eds. *International Migration: The Female Experience.* Totowa, NJ: Rowman and Allanheld, 1986.

Stephenson, George M. *A History of American Immigration.* New York: Russell and Russell, 1964.

Svart, Larry M. "Environmental Preference Migration: A Review." *Geographical Review* 66 (1976): 314–30.

Tabbarah, Riad. "Prospects of International Migration." *International Social Science Journal* 36 (no. 3, 1984): 425–40.

White, Paul E., and Robert I. Woods, eds. *The Geographic Impact on Migration.* London and New York: Longman, 1980.

Williams, James D., and Andrew J. Sofranko. "Why People Move." *American Demographics* 3 (July-August 1981): 30–31.

Wolpert, Julian. "Behavioral Aspects of the Decision to Migrate." *Papers, Regional Science Association* 15 (1965): 159–69.

Zelinsky, Wilbur. "The hypothesis of the mobility transition." *Geographical Review* 61 (July 1971): 219–49.

4
Language

How many languages do you speak? If you are Dutch, you likely speak at least four languages. All school children in the Netherlands are required to learn at least Dutch, English, German, and one other language, usually French or Russian.

For those of you who don't happen to be Dutch, the number is probably a bit lower. In fact, most people in the United States know only English. Less than 15 percent of U.S. high school students are currently taking a foreign language.

Geographers study the spatial distribution of languages across the earth's surface because language is one of the basic elements of a society's culture. Geographic processes such as migration, diffusion, and interaction help explain the similarities and differences in the languages spoken by people in different parts of the world. Geographers also observe that differences in languages—like other cultural characteristics—can lead to disputes among cultural groups.

French and Spanish in the United States and Canada

The Tremblay family lives in a suburb of Montreal, Québec. The parents and two young children speak French at home, work, school, and shops. The Lopez family—also two parents and two children—live in San Antonio, Texas, and speak Spanish in their household.

The Tremblay and Lopez families share a common condition: they live in countries with an English-speaking majority, but English is not their native language. The French-speaking inhabitants of Canada and the Spanish-speaking residents of the United States continue to speak their languages, though English dominates the political, economic, and cultural life of their countries. The two families use languages other than English because they feel that language is an important element in retaining and enhancing their cultural heritage. On the other hand, both families realize that knowledge of English is essential for career advancement and economic success.

The examples of the French-speaking residents of Canada and the Spanish-speaking residents of the United States illustrate the two main functions of language that concern geographers. First, geographers look at the similarities and differences among languages to understand the diffusion and interaction of people around the world. Language is like a piece of luggage: people carry it with them when they move from place to place. They add new words to their own language when they reach new places and contribute words brought with them to the existing stock of language at the new location.

Second, geographers also study language because it is a major characteristic of a region. Language is a source of pride to a people, a symbol of cultural unity. It is both the cause and the consequence of the development of a unique culture. Studying the distribution of languages across the earth's surface helps geographers identify the regions that various cultural groups occupy.

hy does everyone in the world not speak the same language? The diversity of languages in the world is a cultural characteristic largely taken for granted. The heterogeneous collection of languages spoken in the world is one of the clearest and most obvious characteristics of cultural diversity. Geographers use language to identify important regional differences in the cultural landscape.

Language is a system of communication through the use of speech, a collection of sounds that are understood by a group of people to have the same meaning. Many languages also have a **literary tradition,** or a system of communication through writing, though, hundreds of spoken languages do not have a literary tradition.

A **language family** is a collection of individual languages related to each other by virtue of having a common ancestor. Though several thousand languages are spoken around the world, they can be grouped into a small number of language families. Just as languages evolve from a common ancestor, so can several dialects derive from one language. A

dialect is a form of a language spoken in a local area. One dialect of a language is normally recognized as the **standard language,** which is the form used for official government business, education, and mass communications.

This chapter looks at the origin and spatial distribution of languages. Attention will be directed towards English—increasingly the world's most important language for business and culture and obviously a language understood by readers of this book.

KEY ISSUE

How Did the English Language Originate and Diffuse?

The cultural processes influencing the current distribution of English across the landscape can serve as a case study for understanding other languages. Therefore, we will first examine the diffusion of the English language.

FIGURE 4–1

The first speakers of the language that became known as English were tribes that lived in present-day Germany and Denmark before invading England in the fifth century. The Jutes settled primarily in southeastern England, the Saxons in the south and west, and the Angles in the north. From this original spatial separation, the first major regional dialect differences developed in England, as Figure 4–13 shows. (From Albert C. Baugh and Thomas Cable, *A History of the English Language,* 3rd ed., © 1978, p. 47. Reprinted by permission of Prentice-Hall, Inc., Englewood Cliffs, N.J.)

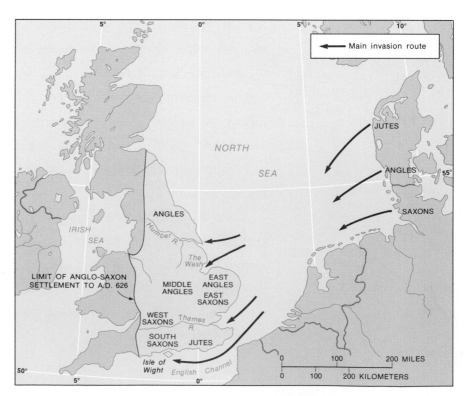

Development of English

The language called English derives primarily from languages spoken in England for only around 1,500 years. The land now known as England was invaded by several tribes, known as the Angles, Jutes, and Saxons. The name *England* is derived from *Angles' land,* and the English language derives primarily from a combination of the dialects spoken by these three tribes.

The Angles, Jutes, and Saxons were all Germanic tribes (Figure 4–1). The Angles lived in the southern part of present-day Denmark, the Jutes in the northern part of Denmark, and the Saxons in the northwestern part of present-day Germany. Other tribes in northern Europe spoke similar languages. English is thus a Germanic language and shares many structural similarities with other Germanic languages.

Before the conquest of England by the Angles, Jutes, and Saxons, the country was inhabited primarily by various tribes who spoke Celtic languages. The languages spoken in the British Isles before the arrival of Celtic tribes around 2000 B.C. are unknown. In the wake of the Germanic invasions, the Celts fled to the remote northern and western parts of Britain, including Cornwall and the highlands of Scotland and Wales.

Other peoples have invaded England and brought their languages with them as well. Vikings from present-day Norway landed on the northeast coast of England in the tenth century. Although ultimately defeated in their bid to control England, many Vikings remained in the country and added new words to the language.

The English language changed considerably as a result of the Norman conquest in 1066. The Normans spoke French, which they established as England's official language for the next 150 years. Although the royal family, nobles, judges, and clergy spoke French, the masses continued to speak English. By the thirteenth century, English again became the country's dominant language. In 1204, during the reign of King John, England lost control of Normandy and entered a long period of conflict with France. As a result, fewer people in England wished to speak French. Given that nearly everyone in England spoke English, Parliament enacted the Statute of Pleading in 1362 to change the official language of court business from French to English. English therefore regained its position as the official language for the inhabitants of England, though with the addition of many French words.

The people of England diffused their language around the world through the establishment of colonies. The first English colonies were built in North America, beginning with Jamestown, Virginia, in 1607, and Plymouth, Massachusetts, in 1620. The English also established colonies in Africa, Asia, and many islands of the Atlantic, Indian, and Pacific oceans.

As recently as the 1950s, one-fourth of the world's people lived in a country where English was the **official language,** that is, the language adopted for use by the government, even in colonies where only a small percentage of people actually spoke English. After independence, leaders of most former British colonies selected an indigenous language as the official one but continued to use English for international communication.

Other Germanic Languages

The groups that brought the English language to England came from present-day Denmark and Germany, where they shared a language similar to that of the other people of the area. At some time in history, all the Germanic people spoke the same language, but that time predates written records. Linguists can reconstruct the common origin of English with other Germanic languages by analyzing differences in the languages that emerged after groups of Germanic people moved to separate territories and lived in isolation from each other. Because English shares a common ancestry with other Germanic languages, it is classified as part of the Germanic language branch. A **language branch** is a collection of languages that share a common origin but that have evolved into individual languages.

West Germanic group. Some language branches are divided into **language groups.** The Germanic language branch consists of three groups: West Germanic, North Germanic, and East Germanic. West Germanic is of particular interest to English speakers because it is the group to which English belongs. West Germanic is further divided into two subgroups: High and Low Germanic. High Germanic—spoken in the southern, mountainous part of present-day Germany—became the basis for the modern standard German language. The people who lived in the northern lowlands, including the Angles, Jutes, and Saxons, spoke Low Germanic. Because the people who migrated to England came from the lowlands, English is classified as one of the Low Germanic languages within the West Germanic group (Figure 4–2).

The other languages of Low Germanic are Old Saxon, Old Low Franconian, and Old Frisian. Old Saxon—spoken by the Saxons who did not migrate to England—has become the major component of Low German, a dialect of modern German spoken

FIGURE 4–2

Germanic languages predominate in northern and western Europe. The most frequently used West Germanic languages are English and German, while Dutch (Netherlandish) is spoken in the Netherlands and northern Belgium. The main North Germanic languages include Swedish, Danish, Norwegian, and Icelandic. Two rarely used Germanic languages are Faeroese, spoken by inhabitants of the Faeroe Islands (part of Denmark), and Frisian, spoken by inhabitants of the northeastern part of the Netherlands.

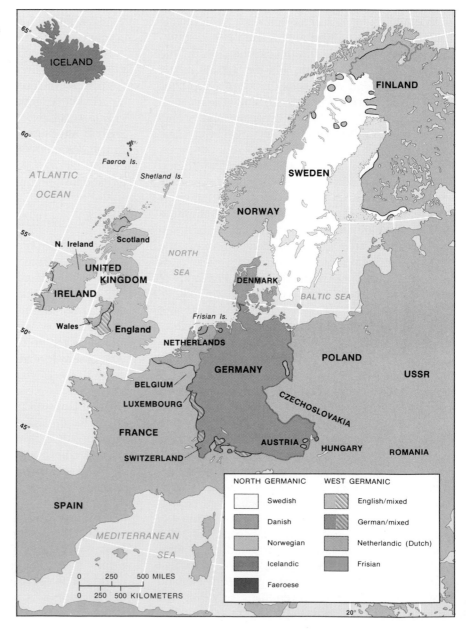

in the northern lowlands. Old Franconian forms the basis for modern Dutch and Flemish, spoken in the Netherlands and northern Belgium. Old Frisian gave rise to modern Frisian, which is spoken by a few residents of the northeastern part of the Netherlands.

North Germanic group. The Germanic language branch also includes North Germanic languages, which are spoken in Scandinavia. The four Scandinavian languages—Swedish, Danish, Norwegian, and Icelandic—all derive from Old Norse, which was the only language spoken in Scandinavia before around A.D. 1000. Four distinct languages emerged after that time because of migration and the political organization of the region into four independent and isolated countries.

For geographers, the most interesting Scandinavian language is Icelandic. The island of Iceland was colonized in A.D. 874 by Norwegian settlers, who soon developed a literary tradition. Because of the relative isolation of Iceland, its language has changed less than any other in the Germanic branch.

Icelandic helps geographers understand the movement of language across the landscape. Groups of people speak different languages because they live in isolation from one another. When members of a group migrate to other locations, they take their language with them. But after centuries of living in isolation from others of the same group, the migrants may speak a different language. The language spoken by most migrants—such as the Germanic invaders of England—changes in part through contact with speakers of other languages. Because the Germanic people who migrated to Iceland had less contact with speakers of other languages, they had less opportunity to learn new words.

East Germanic group. East Germanic languages also existed in the past, but they are now **extinct languages**—that is, they are no longer spoken or read in daily activities by anyone in the world. Thousands of languages once used, some of them in the recent past, no longer exist. The main East Germanic language was Gothic, spoken by people who lived in much of eastern and northern Europe in the third century A.D. The last speaker of Gothic lived in the Crimea in Russia in the sixteenth century. The language died because the descendents of the Goths were converted to other languages through political dominance as well as preference. For example, many Gothic people switched to Latin after their conversion to Christianity.

This review of the origin and diffusion of English and other Germanic languages demonstrates that the spatial distribution of a language is a measure of the fate of a distinctive cultural group. English has been diffused around the world from a small island in northwestern Europe because of England's cultural and political dominance over other territory on the earth's surface. On the other hand, Icelandic has remained a little-used language because of the isolation of the Icelandic people. Just as differences arise because of migration and geographic isolation among speakers of a particular language branch, so can differences arise between speakers of different branches within the same language family.

KEY ISSUE

How Is English Related to Languages Spoken Elsewhere in the World?

The Germanic languages, including English, constitute one branch of a language family known as Indo-European. Nearly half of the people in the world speak an Indo-European language. The Indo-European family includes languages with important artistic and literary traditions and four of the six official languages of the United Nations. This section examines the spatial distribution of the Indo-European language family and presents evidence concerning the common origin of the Indo-European languages.

People use Indo-European languages on every continent of the world. Spoken since the dawn of recorded history in nearly all of Europe and much of Asia, the Indo-European language family has been carried in modern times by colonists to Africa, Australia, and the Western Hemisphere.

The Indo-European language family includes eight branches. More than 400 million people each speak the languages of four of its branches—Ger-

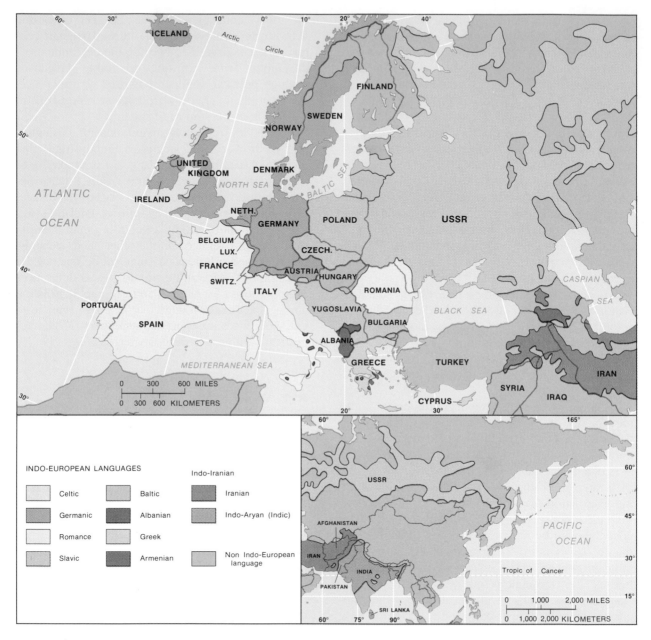

FIGURE 4–3
Most Europeans speak languages of the Indo-European language family. The three most important branches of the family in Europe are Germanic in the north and west, Romance in the south and west, and Slavic in the east. Indo-Iranian, the fourth important branch of Indo-European, is found in southern and western Asia.

manic, Romance, Balto-Slavic, and Indo-Iranian. The four language branches within the Indo-European family less extensively used include Albanian, Armenian, Celtic, and Greek (Figure 4–3).

Romance Languages

The Romance branch of the Indo-European language family may be most familiar to English-speaking people. The Romance languages are those that developed from the Latin spoken by the ancient Romans, hence the name of the branch.

Latin. The rise in importance of the city of Rome was paralleled by the diffusion of the Latin language. At its height in the second century A.D., the Roman Empire extended from the Atlantic Ocean on the west to the Black Sea on the east and encompassed all of the lands bordering the Mediterranean Sea. As the conquering Roman armies occupied the provinces of the vast empire, they brought the Latin language with them. In the process, the languages spoken by the natives of the provinces were either extinguished or suppressed in favor of the language of the conquerors.

After the collapse of the Roman Empire in the fifth century, Latin persisted only in parts of the former colonies. People in some areas of the empire returned to former languages, while others adopted the languages of conquering Germanic- and Slavic-speaking groups from the north and east.

Even during the period of the Roman Empire, however, Latin varied to some extent from one province to another. The empire grew over a period of several hundred years, and the Latin used in each province was based on that spoken by the Roman army at the time of occupation. The Latin spoken in each province also became modified by inclusion of borrowed words from the language formerly spoken in the area.

The Latin learned in the provinces was not the standard literary form but a spoken form, known as **Vulgar Latin,** from the Latin word for masses. Vulgar Latin became the language of the provinces because it was the language spoken by the soldiers stationed throughout the empire. For example, the literary term for horse was *equus,* from which English has derived such words as *equine* and *equestrian.* The Vulgar term, however, used by the common people, was *caballus,* from which are derived the modern terms for horse in Italian *(cavallor),* Spanish *(caballo),* Portuguese *(cavalo),* French *(cheval),* and Romanian *(cal).* Following the collapse of the Roman Empire in the fifth century, communications among the former provinces were reduced, resulting in still greater regional variation in spoken Latin. By the eighth century, regions of the former empire were so isolated from one another that their peoples had begun to speak distinct languages.

Modern Romance languages. The five most widely used contemporary Romance languages are Spanish, Portuguese, French, Italian, and Romanian. The European regions in which these five languages are spoken correspond rather closely to the boundaries of the modern states of Spain, Portugal, France, Italy, and Romania. Romania is separated from the other Romance-speaking European countries by Slavic-speaking people, while rugged mountains serve as boundaries among the other four countries. France is separated from Italy by the Alps and from Spain by the Pyrenees, while a series of mountain ranges marks the border between Spain and Portugal. Physical boundaries such as mountains serve as strong barriers to communications between people living on opposite sides (Figure 4–4).

The distinct Romance languages did not suddenly appear; as with other languages, they evolved over time. Numerous dialects arose within each province, many of which still exist today. The creation of standard national languages, such as French and Spanish, was relatively recent.

Dialects in France. The dialect of the Ile-de-France region, known as *Francien,* became the standard form of French because the region included Paris, which became the capital and largest city of the country. *Francien* French became the country's official language in the sixteenth century, and local dialects tended to disappear as a result of the capital's long-time dominance over French political, economic, and social life.

The most important surviving linguistic difference within France is between the north and south. The northern dialect is known as "langue d'oil" and the southern as "langue d'oc." These terms derive from different ways in which the word for *yes* was said. One Roman term for *yes* was *hoc illud est,* meaning "that is so." In the south, the phrase was shortened to *hoc,* or *oc,* because the /h/ sound was generally dropped. Northerners shortened the phrase to *o-il* after the first sound in the first two words of the phrase, again with the initial /h/ suppressed. If the two syllables of *o-il* are spoken very rapidly, they are combined into a sound like the English word *wheel.* Eventually, the final consonant was eliminated (as in many French words), giving a sound for *yes* like the English *we,* spelled in French *oui.* A province where the southern dialect is spoken in southwestern France is known as Languedoc.

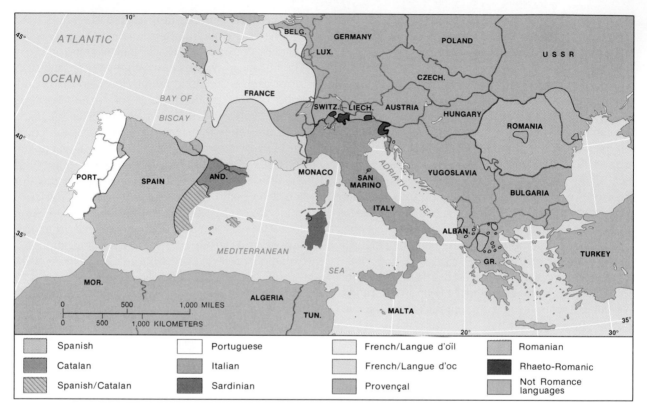

FIGURE 4–4

The Romance language branch of the Indo-European family includes five languages used by a relatively large number of speakers (Spanish, French, Italian, Portuguese, and Romanian), although not all speakers of these languages live in Europe. Catalan is a dialect of Spanish and the official language of Andorra, while Provençal is a dialect of French. Rhaeto-Romanic languages include Romansh, Ladin, and Friulian. The map also shows the boundary between the two main dialects of France, langue d'oïl and langue d'oc.

The southern French dialect itself is now sometimes called Occitan, derived from the French region of Aquitaine, which in French has a similar pronunciation to Occitan. People in southeastern France speak a form of Occitan or *langue d'oc* known as Provençal.

Worldwide diffusion of Spanish and Portuguese. Spain, like France, contained many dialects during the Middle Ages. One dialect, known as Castilian, arose during the ninth century in Old Castile, located in the north-central part of the country. The dialect spread southward over the next several hundred years as independent kingdoms were unified into one large country. Spain grew to approximately its present boundaries in the fifteenth century, when the Kingdom of Castile and Leon merged with the Kingdom of Aragon. At that time, Castilian became the official language for the entire country. Regional dialects—such as Aragon, Navarre, Leon, Asturias, and Santander—survived only in secluded rural areas. The official language of Spain is now called Spanish, though the term *Castilian* is still used in Latin America.

Spanish and Portuguese have achieved worldwide importance because of the colonial activities of their European speakers. Approximately 90 percent of the speakers of these two languages live outside Europe, mainly in Central and South America. Spanish is the official language of eighteen Latin American countries, while Portuguese is spoken in Brazil, which has as many people as all the other

South American countries combined and fifteen times more than Portugal itself.

These two Romance languages were brought to the Americas by Spanish and Portuguese explorers. The division of Central and South America into Portuguese- and Spanish-speaking regions is the result of a decision in 1493 by Pope Alexander VI to give the western portion of the New World to Spain and the eastern part to Portugal. The Treaty of Tordesillas, signed one year later, carried out the papal decision.

The Portuguese and Spanish languages spoken in the Western Hemisphere differ somewhat from the European versions, as is the case with English. The Brazilians and Portuguese are attempting to standardize their common language through a joint language committee.

How many Romance languages exist?. The spatial distribution of Romance branch languages shows the difficulty in trying to establish the number of distinct languages in the world. In addition to the five important languages—Spanish, Portuguese, French, Italian, and Romanian—linguists can identify several other Romance languages. If official languages are counted, two must be added to the list: Romansh and Catalan. Romansh is one of four official languages of Switzerland, though it is spoken by only 25,000 people. Catalan, a dialect of Spanish, is the official language of Andorra, a tiny country of approximately 50,000 inhabitants situated in the Pyrenees Mountains between Spain and France. Catalan is also spoken by another 9 million people, mostly around the city of Barcelona. Sardinian—a mixture of Italian, Spanish, and Arabic—used to be but is no longer the official language of the Mediterranean island of Sardinia.

In addition to those seven or eight official languages, several other Romance languages have separate literary traditions. Ladin is spoken by 20,000 people living in the South Tyrol, while Friulian is spoken by 500,000 in northeast Italy. These two languages, plus Romansh, are dialects of Rhaeto-Romanic. Ladino—a mixture of Spanish, Greek, Turkish, and Hebrew—is spoken by 140,000 Sephardic Jews, most of whom now live in Israel. Provençal is a dialect of French. None of these languages has an official status in any country, though all are used in literature.

The Romance languages spoken in some former colonies could also be classified as separate languages because they differ substantially from the languages originally introduced by the European rulers. These include French Creole in Haiti, Papiamento (Creolized Spanish) in Netherland Antilles, and Portuguese Creole in the Cape Verde Islands.

In other cases, difficulties arise in determining whether two languages are distinct or merely two dialects of the same language. Galician, spoken in northwest Spain, is generally classified as a dialect of Portuguese, and Flemish, spoken in northern Belgium, is generally considered a dialect of Dutch. Many residents of those two regions, however view their languages as distinct. The task of identifying individual languages and dialects is even more difficult in societies where the language is primarily spoken rather than written.

Language conflicts. Few states in the world peacefully embrace nationalities that speak different languages. Switzerland succeeds by having a very decentralized form of government. Local authorities hold most of the power, and decisions are frequently made by special voter referenda. Switzerland has four official languages—German (used by 65 percent of the population), French (18 percent), Italian (12 percent), and Romansh (1 percent). Swiss voters made Romansh an official language in a 1938 referendum, despite the small percentage who use the language (Figure 4–5).

Belgium is another small European country that contains more than one nationality divided by language. But Belgium has had more difficulty than Switzerland in reconciling the interests of the two cultural groups. The residents of the north speak Flemish, a dialect of Dutch, whereas the southerners (known as Walloons) speak French. The language boundary sharply divides the country into two regions. Antagonism between the Flemings and the Walloons is aggravated by economic and political differences. Historically, the Walloons dominated Belgium's economy and political structure, and French was the official state language.

In response to pressure from Flemish speakers, Belgium has been divided into two regions, Flanders and Wallonia, that have considerable autonomy. Each has an elected assembly that controls cultural affairs, public health, road construction, and

FIGURE 4–5
Switzerland has four official languages, including Romansh, used by only 1 percent of the population. Although the country can be divided into four main linguistic regions, people living in individual communities—especially in the mountains—may generally use a language other than the one predominating in that part of the country. The Swiss, relatively tolerant of speakers of other languages, have institutionalized cultural diversity by creating a form of government that places considerable powers in small communities.

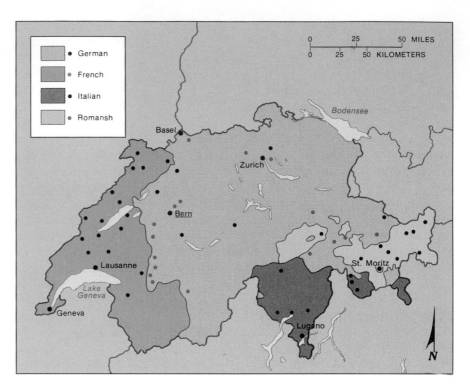

urban development in the region. The national government turns over approximately 15 percent of its tax revenues to pay for the regional governments (Figure 4–6).

Motorists in Belgium can see the clear language boundary when they drive on expressways. Heading north, the highway signs suddenly change from French to Flemish at the boundary between Wallonia and Flanders. Brussels, the capital city, is an exception to the rule. Although located in Flanders, Brussels is officially a bilingual enclave, and signs there are posted in both French and Flemish.

Belgium has difficulty in fixing the precise boundary between Flemish and French speakers, because people living near the boundary may actually use the language spoken on the other side of the line. In the 1980s, such a problem resulted in the jailing of the mayor of the town of Voeren and the collapse of the national government. Jose Happart, the mayor of Voeren, refused to speak Flemish, as required by national law, because the town was located in Flanders. The mayor had been elected to office on a platform of returning Fourons, as the town is known in French, to Wallonia, from which it

had been transferred in 1963, when the national government tried to clear up the language boundary. After refusing to be tested on his knowledge of Dutch, Happart (who in fact knew Dutch) was jailed and removed from office. In protest, French-speaking members quit the coalition governing the country, forcing the prime minister to resign.

Indo-Iranian Languages

The branch of the Indo-European language family with the most speakers is the Indo-Iranian branch, which includes more than 100 individual languages, spoken by more than 1 billion people. The branch can be divided into an eastern group (Indic) and a western group (Iranian).

Indic languages. Most residents of Bangladesh, India, and Pakistan speak an Indic language. The principal language of Pakistan is Urdu, whereas about one-third of Indians, mostly those in the north, speak Hindi. Urdu and Hindi are sometimes considered one language, called Hindustani. Urdu uses the Arabic alphabet, while Hindi has its own alphabet, known as Devanagari. If considered one language, Hindustani constitutes the third-most frequently used language in the world. Bengali is the most important language of Bangladesh, the other populous country of South Asia. Other important Indo-European languages in South Asia include Punjabi, Marathi, and Gujarati. In general, India's most important language families are Indo-European in the north, Dravidian in the south, Sino-Tibetan in the northeast, and Southeast Asian in the central and eastern highlands (Figure 4–7).

One of the main cultural distinctions among the nearly 1 billion residents of India is language. After India became independent in 1947, Hindi was proposed as the official language, but Dravidian speakers from the south strongly objected. Therefore, India's 1950 constitution recognized fourteen official languages, including ten Indo-European languages (Assamese, Bengali, Gujarati, Hindi, Kashmiri, Marathi, Oriya, Punjabi, Sanskrit, and Urdu) and four Dravidian languages (Kannada, Malayalam, Tamil, and Telugu). More than 90 percent of the popula-

tion speak at least one of these fourteen languages, but as many as 10 million Indians use other languages. As the language of the former colonial rulers, English has an "associate" status, even though only 1 percent of the Indian population can speak it. But speakers of two different Indian languages who wish to communicate with each other sometimes are forced to turn to English as a common language.

Iranian languages. Indo-Iranian languages are also used in Iran and neighboring countries in southwestern Asia. The major languages include Persian (sometimes called Farsi) in Iran, Pashto in eastern Afghanistan and western Pakistan, and Kurdish, used by the Kurds living in western Iran, northern Iraq, and eastern Turkey. These languages are written in the Arabic alphabet.

Balto-Slavic Languages

The other Indo-European language branch with large numbers of speakers is Balto-Slavic. Slavic was

FIGURE 4–6
Slightly smaller than Switzerland, Belgium is also multilingual, but in contrast with the Swiss, the Belgians remain sharply divided by language differences. The Flemings, who live in the north and speak a dialect of Dutch, and the Walloons, who live in the south and speak French, have had difficulty sharing national power. As a result, considerable power has been transferred to two regional assemblies, one each for Flanders and Wallonia.

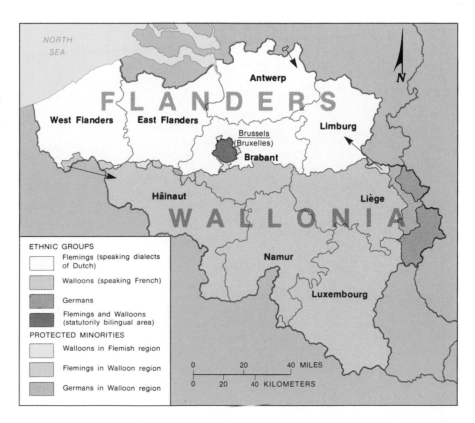

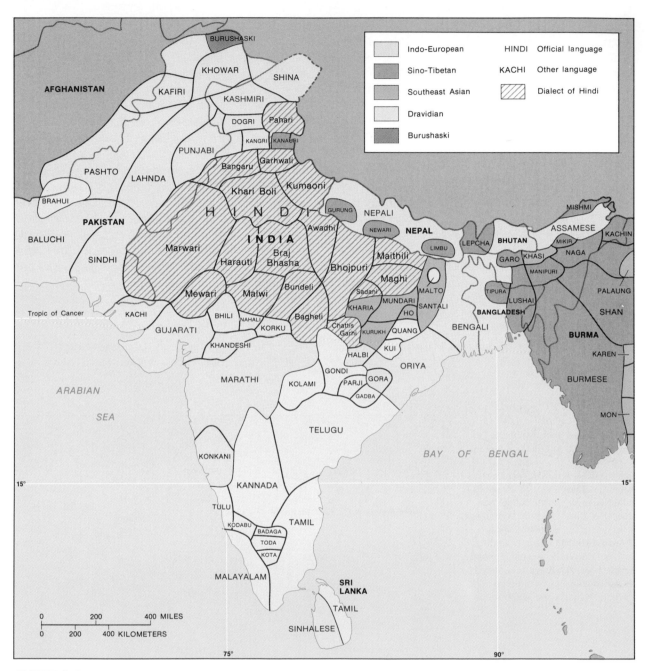

FIGURE 4–7
The languages and dialects of South Asia number several hundred, though there are four main language families—Indo-European, Dravidian, Sino-Tibetan, and Southeast Asian. India recognizes fourteen official languages; more than 90 percent of its population speak at least one of these. The boundaries shown are imprecise; speakers of some languages are dispersed rather than concentrated.

once a single language, but differences developed when, in the seventh century, several groups of Slavs migrated from Asia to different areas of eastern Europe and thereafter lived in isolation from one another. As a result, this branch can be divided into East, West, and South Slavic groups as well as a Baltic group.

East Slavic. The most widely used Slavic languages are the eastern ones—primarily Russian, which is spoken by about 80 percent of the population of the Soviet Union. The importance of Russian has increased since World War II with the rise in power of the Soviet Union. Russian, one of the six official languages of the United Nations, is taught as a sec-

ond language in many countries that have been allied with the Soviet Union.

Approximately 20 percent of the Soviet Union's people speak a language other than Russian, although they may be forced to learn Russian in school. The two most important languages of the Soviet Union, in addition to Russian, are Ukrainian and Byelorussian, or White Russian. The presence of so many non-Russian speakers is a measure of the cultural diversity of the Soviet Union.

West and South Slavic. The most frequently used West Slavic language is Polish, followed by Czech and Slovak. The latter two, both official languages of Czechoslovakia, are quite similar, and speakers of

Lithuanians demonstrate for independence from the Soviet Union in Vilnius, the capital of Lithuania. The sign immediately to the right of the flag is written in Lithuanian, a Baltic language, while the sign in the right foreground is written in Russian, which uses the Cyrillic alphabet. English is increasingly the preferred language for signs in large political demonstrations, so that television viewers in the west can read the message.

one can understand the other. But the 5 million Slovaks, who occupy the eastern portion of the country, fear domination by the majority Czechs. The Slovaks have sought to split the country into two highly autonomous regions—as occurred in Belgium—and to change the name to the Federation of Czecho-Slovakia. As a compromise, Czechs proposed changing the name to the Czech and Slovak Federative Republic.

The most important South Slavic languages include Bulgarian and three languages in Yugoslavia: Serbo-Croatian, Slovene, and Macedonian. Yugoslavs consider Serbo-Croatian to be two distinct languages rather than one, but the main difference between the two is the alphabet: Serbian uses the Cyrillic alphabet and Croatian uses the Latin.

In general, distinguishing between distinct Slavic languages and dialects of the same language is difficult, because differences among all Slavic languages are relatively small. Someone who understands one Slavic language can understand much of what is said or written in another Slavic language. But because language is a major element in a people's cultural identity, relatively small differences among Slavic as well as other languages are being preserved and even accentuated.

Other Indo-European Languages

A relatively small number of people speak one of the languages of the other four Indo-European language branches: Albanian, Armenian, Celtic, and Greek. Celtic is of particular interest to English-speaking people, because it was the most important language in the British Isles before the invasion of Germanic-speaking tribes. At the time of Christ, Celtic languages were spoken in much of present-day Germany, France, and northern Italy, as well as in the British Isles. Today, Celtic languages survive in Ireland and the more remote parts of the British Isles, including in Scotland, Wales, and Cornwall, as well as in the region of Brittany in France.

Celtic languages are divided into Goidelic and Britannic. Goidelic—frequently called Gaelic—is one of the Republic of Ireland's two official languages (along with English), but only 50,000 speak Irish Gaelic exclusively. Fewer than 80,000, or 2 percent, of the people of Scotland speak Scottish Gaelic, the other surviving Gaelic language. An ex-

tensive body of literature exists in the Gaelic languages, including the Robert Burns poem "Auld Lang Syne," the basis for the popular New Year's Eve song.

Over time, speakers of Britannic—also known as Cymric—fled west to Wales, southwest to Cornwall, or south across the English Channel to Brittany, now part of France. Wales—the name derived from the Germanic invaders' word for "foreign"—was conquered by the English in 1283, but Welsh remained the predominant language of the area until the nineteenth century, when many English-speaking workers migrated there to work in coal mines and factories. An estimated 20 percent of the people in Wales still use Welsh as their primary language, though all but a handful know English as well. In some isolated communities in the northwest, especially in the county of Gwynedd, as many as 80 percent of the people speak Welsh.

Cornish became extinct in 1777 with the death of the language's last native speaker, Dolly Pentreath, who lived in Mousehole (pronounced "muzzle"). Before Pentreath died, an English historian recorded as much of her speech as possible, so that future generations could study the Cornish language. One of her last utterances was later translated as "I will not speak English . . . you ugly, black toad."

In Brittany—like Cornwall, an isolated peninsula which juts out into the Atlantic Ocean—300,000 people still speak Breton. Breton differs from the other Celtic languages in that it has more French words.

Preservation of Celtic languages may depend on the political and military strength of its speakers. The Celtic languages declined in importance because the Celts lost most of the territory they once controlled to speakers of other languages. Few Celtic speakers remain who do not also know the language of their English or French conquerors.

Recent preservation efforts have prevented the complete disappearance of Celtic languages. In Wales, the *Cymdeithas yr Iaith Gymraeg* (Welsh Language Society) has been instrumental in preserving the language. For example, the government was pressured into refusing permission for a proposed housing development because it would disrupt a small community where most residents spoke Welsh. The British Broadcasting Corporation pro-

This road sign in southeastern Wales shows the impact of the movement to revive the Welsh language. Three towns in Wales once known only by their English names—Skenfrith, Monmouth, and Newport—are indicated by their Welsh names as well—Ynysgynwraidd, Trefynwy, and Casnewydd, respectively. Two towns on the sign—Cwmbrân and Merthyr Tydfil—are known only by their Welsh names. Hereford does not have a Welsh name because it is actually located in England rather than Wales.

duces Welsh-language television and radio programs. Road signs have been posted in Welsh throughout Wales, and the language is taught in some schools.

A couple of hundred people are now fluent in the Cornish language, which was revived in the 1920s. Cornish is taught in grade schools and adult evening courses, and is utilized in some church services; some banks accept checks written in Cornish. But a dispute has erupted over the proper way to spell Cornish words. Some prefer to revive the confusing, illogical medieval spellings, while others—including the Cornish Language Board—advocate spelling words phonetically. When officials in Camborne erected a welcome sign with the name of the town spelled *Kammbronn,* traditionalists were outraged, because the medieval spelling was *Cambron.* Traditionalists argued that *Kammbronn* looked too "German," a harsh insult, because it recalled both the successful invasion by Germanic people 1,500 years ago and the failed attempt by the Nazis in 1940.

The European Community has established the European Bureau of Lesser Used Languages, based in Dublin, Ireland, to provide financial support for the preservation of a couple of dozen languages. But the long-term decline of such languages as Celtic provides an excellent example of the precarious struggle for survival many languages experi-

ence. Faced with the diffusion of alternatives used by people with greater political and economic strength, speakers of Celtic and other languages must make sacrifices to preserve their cultural identity.

Common Ancestry of Indo-European Languages

If different languages are part of the same family, they must ultimately be descended from the same language. Just as all Romance and Germanic languages can be traced back to a common language, so can all Indo-European languages.

Origins of Indo-European. The development of French, Spanish, and other Romance languages from Latin can be clearly documented because the process unfolded within the past 2,000 years. In contrast, the ancestral language of all Indo-European speakers predates the invention of writing or recorded history. Recent discoveries by linguists and archaeologists confirm that all Indo-European languages can be traced to one source, known as Proto-Indo-European.

Evidence concerning the first speakers of Proto-Indo-European comes in part from examining words for physical features in various Indo-European languages. The words for some animals and trees in the individual Indo-European languages have common roots, including *beech, oak, bear, deer, pheasant,* and *bee.* Linguists believe that these common words represent objects and events familiar to the original Indo-European speakers. Other environmental features, such as *elephant, camel, rice,* and *bamboo,* have different roots in the various Indo-European languages. Words that cannot be traced back to Proto-Indo-European must have been added later, after it split into many languages. Individual Indo-European languages share common root words for *winter* and *snow* but not for *ocean.* The original speakers of Proto-Indo-European therefore probably lived in a cold climate but did not come in contact with oceans.

Scholars disagree, however, on where and when the first speakers of Proto-Indo-European lived. An influential theory espoused by a scholar named Marija Gimbutas is that the first speakers of Proto-Indo-European were the Kurgan people, whose homeland was in the steppes near the Volga River north of the Caspian Sea, east of the Don River, north of the Caucasus, and west of the Ural Mountains, in the present-day Soviet Union. The earliest archaeological evidence of the Kurgans dates to around 4300 B.C.

The Kurgans, who lived primarily by herding animals, were among the first people to domesticate the horse and cattle. Migrating in search of grasslands for their animals took the Kurgans west through Europe, east to Siberia, and southeast to Iran and South Asia. Between 3500 and 2500 B.C., Kurgan warriors, using their domesticated horses as effective weapons, conquered much of Europe and South Asia (Figure 4–8).

Other scholars, such as Colin Renfrew, argue that the first speakers of Proto-Indo-European lived 2,000 years before the Kurgans, and that the language originated in eastern Anatolia, part of present-day Turkey. According to this theory, the Indo-European language diffused from Anatolia in the following sequence:

1. From Anatolia west to Greece (the origin of the Greek language).
2. From Greece north towards the Danube River (present-day Yugoslavia, Romania, and Bulgaria).
3. From the Danube west to central Europe.
4. From central Europe east towards the Dnestr River (the origin of the Slavic language).
5. From central Europe north towards the Baltic Sea (the origin of the Germanic language).
6. From Greece west towards Italy, Sicily, Corsica, and the Mediterranean coast of France (the origin of the Romance language).
7. From the Mediterranean coast west towards Spain and Portugal.
8. From the Mediterranean coast north towards central and northern France (contributing to the development of the Celtic language).
9. From northern France to the British Isles (perhaps the origin of the Celtic language).
10. East from the Dnestr River to the Dnepr River (the origin of the Kurgans).

The Indo-Iranian branch of the Indo-European language family originated either directly through migration from Anatolia along the south sides of the Black and Caspian seas by way of Iran and Pakistan or indirectly by way of Russia north of the Black and Caspian seas.

Renfrew argues that the Indo-European language was carried west into Europe and east into South Asia along with the diffusion of farming practices rather than by military conquest. The language triumphed because its speakers became more numerous and prosperous through growing their own food instead of relying on hunting.

Regardless of whether Proto-Indo-European diffused across Europe and South Asia through military conquest or agricultural innovation, communications between different groups of warriors or farmers were poor. After many generations of complete isolation, various groups spoke increasingly distinct languages.

A Language Survivor: Basque

Only one language currently spoken in Europe survives from the period prior to the invasion by Indo-European speakers. That language is Basque, spoken by approximately 1 million people in the Pyrenees Mountains of northern Spain and southwestern France. No attempt to link Basque to the common origin of the other European languages

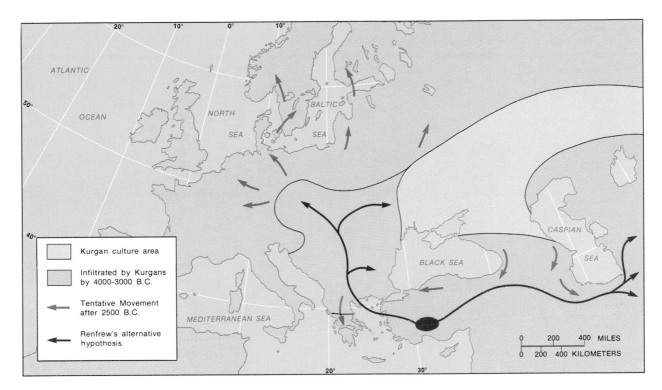

FIGURE 4–8
The first speakers of an Indo-European language, called Proto-Indo-European, may have been the Kurgans, who lived in the steppes north of the Caspian Sea. Beginning approximately 4000 B.C., the Kurgans may have expanded into much of Europe and Southwest Asia. Centuries of isolation and the lingering impact of languages spoken in localities prior to the Kurgan invasion may have led to the separation of Proto-Indo-European into many branches. According to an alternate theory, Proto-Indo-European may have originated in present-day Turkey and diffused along with agricultural innovations.

has been successful. Basque was probably spoken over a wider area prior to the Kurgan invasion but was abandoned where its speakers came in contact with Indo-European.

The uniqueness of the Basque language reflects the isolation of the Basque people in their mountainous homeland. Similarities and differences between languages—our main form of communication—are a measure of the degree of interaction between groups of people. The diffusion of Indo-European languages demonstrates that a common ancestor dominated much of Europe before recorded history. Similarly, the diffusion of Indo-European languages to the Western Hemisphere is a result of conquests by Indo-European speakers in more recent times. On the other hand, the isolation

of the Basques in their mountainous homeland has helped to preserve their language.

KEY ISSUE

What Is the Spatial Distribution of Other Language Families?

Experts disagree on the total number of language families and individual languages in the world. Estimates concerning the total range from 2,000 to 4,000 (Table 4–1). We have already discussed the difficulty in determining the exact number of Romance languages. The problem is more severe with languages in other regions of the world, especially

TABLE 4–1
Languages with more than 5 million speakers (in millions of speakers).

Indo-European Family	**2,838**	**Sino-Tibetan Family**	**1,199**	**Altaic Family**	**117**
Germanic branch	611	Sinitic branch	1,101	Turkish	55
English*	443	Mandarin*	864	Azerbaijani	14
German	118	Cantonese (Yue)	63	Uzbek	13
Netherlandish (Dutch)	21	Wu	62	Kazakh	8
Afrikaans	10	Min	48	Tatar	7
Swedish	9	Hakka (Kejia)	32	Uighur	7
Danish	5	Zhuang	14	Mongolian (Khalkha)	5
		Yi	6	Other	8
Norwegian	5	Miao	5	**Uralic Family**	**22**
Romance branch	739	Other	7	Finnic branch	8
Spanish*	341	Tibeto-Burman branch	98	Finnish	6
Portuguese	173	Thai (& Lao)	52	Other	2
French*	121	Burmese	30	Ugric branch (Magyar)	14
Italian	63	Tibetan	5	**Southeast Asian Family**	**67**
Romanian	25	Sylhetti	5	Vietnamese	57
Catalan	9	Other	6	Khmer	7
Other	7	**Austronesian (Malayo-**		Other	3
		Polynesian) Family	**355**	**Japanese**	**125**
Balto-Slavic branch	446	Malay-Indonesian	142	**Korean**	**71**
Russian*	293	Javanese	58	**Niger-Congo Family**	**261**
Ukrainian	45	Tagalog	36	Benue-Congo branch	161
Polish	43	Sundanese	24	Swahili	43
Serbo-Croatian	20	Cebuano	12	Ruanda	8
Czech	12	Malagasy	11	Shona	7
Byelorussian	10	Madurese	10	Xhosa	7
Bulgarian	9	Ilocano	7	Zulu	7
Slovak	5	Minangkabau	6	Lingala	6
Other	9	Panay-Hilgaynon	6	Luba-Lulue	6
		Santali	5	Rundi	6
Indo-Iranian branch	1,020	Other	38	Kikuyu (Gekoyo)	5
Hindi	352	**Afro-Asiatic (Semito-**		Other	66
Bengali	184	**Hamitic) Family**	**277**	Other branches	100
Urdu	92	Semitic branch	222	Yoruba	18
Punjabi	84	Arabic*	197	Igbo (Ibo)	16
Marathi	64	Amharic	17	Fula (Peulh)	13
Gujarati	38	Other	8	Malinke-Bambara-Dyula	9
Persian	32	Chadic (Hamitic) branch (Hausa)	34	Akan (Twi-Fante)	7
Oriya	30	Cushitic branch	19	Efik (Ibibio)	6
Assamese	22	Oromo (Galla)	10	Wolof	6
Pashto	21	Somali	7	Other	25
Sindhi	16	Other	2	**Nilo-Saharan Family**	**25**
Nepali	13	Other branches	2	**Amerindian Family**	**14**
Sinhalese	13	**Dravidian Family**	**215**	Quechua	8
Kurdish	9	Telugu	68	Other	6
Other	28	Tamil	65	**Other Families**	**4**
Greek	12	Kannada	41	**Total**	**5,590**
Albanian	5	Malayalam	34		
Armenian	5	Other	7		

Source: Adapted from Sidney S. Culbert, "The Principal Languages of the World," *The World Almanac 1991*, pp. 808–809.
*Official language of the United Nations.

in Africa, because documentation concerning the precise distribution of languages is inadequate. Furthermore, people around the world use an unknown number of **isolated languages,** which are unrelated to any other languages and therefore not attached to any language family.

Yet we can group the several thousand languages into a small number of language families. About 50 percent of the world's people speak one of the Indo-European languages, while another 20 percent speak a Sino-Tibetan language. Four other language families—Austronesian (or Malay-Polynesian), Afro-Asiatic (or Semito-Hamitic), Niger-Congo, and Dravidian—account for another 20 percent of the world's speakers. The remaining 10 percent of the world's population speak a wide variety of other languages. Several of the major language families are examined in this section (Figure 4–9).

Sino-Tibetan Languages

Sino-Tibetan is the language family encompassing the languages of the People's Republic of China—the world's most populous state—as well as several smaller countries in Southeast Asia. But no single language is known as Chinese. Rather, the most important language of China is Mandarin. Spoken by approximately three-fourths of the Chinese people, Mandarin is by a wide margin the language spoken by the greatest number of people in the world. Once the language of the emperors in Peking, Mandarin is now the official language of both the People's Republic of China and Taiwan, as well as one of the six official languages of the United Nations.

Four other languages—Cantonese (also known as Yue), Wu, Min, and Hakka (also known as Kejia)—are spoken by tens of millions of people in China, for the most part in the southern and eastern parts of the country. The government of China, however, strongly encourages the use of Mandarin throughout the country. The relatively small number of languages in China, compared to India, for example, is a source of national strength and unity.

Unity is also fostered by the fact that all Chinese languages use the same written form. Although the words are pronounced differently in each language, they are written in the same way.

The construction of the Chinese languages is quite different from Indo-European. The languages are based on a collection of 420 one-syllable words. Because the number of words far exceeds the limited number of possible one-syllable sounds, the Chinese languages use one sound to denote more than one thing. The sound /shi/, for example, may mean "lion," "corpse," "house," "poetry," "ten," "swear," or "die." The sound /jien/ has more than twenty meanings, including "to see." The listener must recognize the meaning by the context in the sentence and the tone of voice the speaker uses. In addition, two one-syllable words can be combined into two syllables, forming a new word. For example, the two-syllable word *Shanghai* is a combination of words that mean "mountain" and "sea." *Kan jien*—a combination of the words for "look" and "see," which is redundant in English—clarifies that "to see" is the intended meaning given to the /jien/ sound.

The other distinctive characteristic of the Chinese languages is the method of writing (Figure 4–10). The Chinese languages are written with a collection of thousands of characters, or pictures. Some of the characters represent sounds pronounced in speaking, as in English. But most are pictures known as **ideograms,** which represent ideas or concepts, not specific pronunciations. The system has developed over 4,000 years.

The main language problem for the Chinese is the difficulty in learning to write because of the large number of characters. A newspaper may contain 6,000 different symbols, but an average ten-year-old has learned only 2,000 symbols and therefore cannot read a paper very well. Only about 20 percent of the Chinese people can read and write the language, a major barrier to their acculturation.

In addition to the Chinese languages, the Sino-Tibetan language family includes a second branch, known as Tibeto-Burman. The two major languages of the Tibeto-Burman branch are Thai—used in Laos, Thailand, and parts of Vietnam—and Burmese, used in Myanmar (Burma). Lao, the dialect of Thai used in Laos, is sometimes classified as a separate language.

Other Asian Language Families

To some Western observers, the languages of the large East Asian population concentrations may be difficult to distinguish because they are written with

FIGURE 4–9
Most people speak a language that can be classified into one of a handful of language families. Languages in the following families are spoken by the largest number of people in the world. *Indo-European:* Spoken by more than 50 percent of the world's people, especially in Europe, the Soviet Union, the Western Hemisphere, and southern and southwestern Asia. *Sino-Tibetan:* Spoken by nearly another 20 percent of the world's people, primarily in East Asia.

Languages belonging to one of these four families are each spoken by approximately 5 percent of the world's people: *Austronesian* (Malayo-Polynesian): Primarily in Southeast Asia. *Afro-Asiatic* (Semito-Hamitic): Primarily in northern Africa and southwestern Asia. *Niger-Congo:* Primarily in central Africa. *Dravidian:* Primarily in southern Asia.

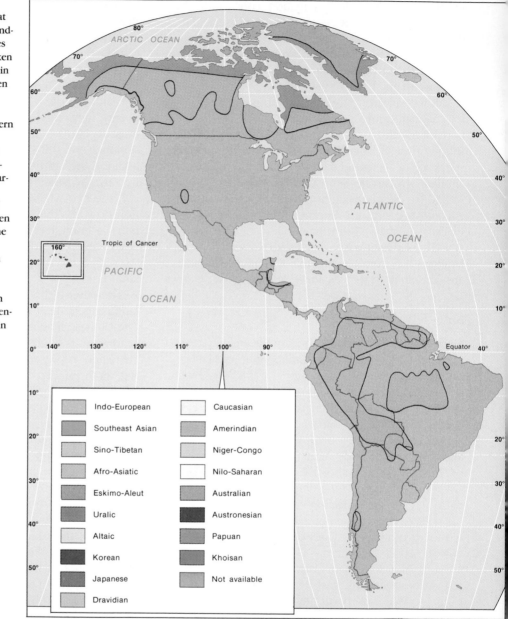

LANGUAGE FAMILIES
(Percentage of people speaking each)

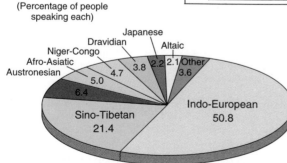

unfamiliar letters. But Japanese belongs to a different language family than the Chinese languages, and Korean forms a third family.

Japanese. Chinese cultural traits have diffused throughout Japanese culture, including the vocabulary of the Japanese language. But the structures of the two languages differ. Japanese is written in part

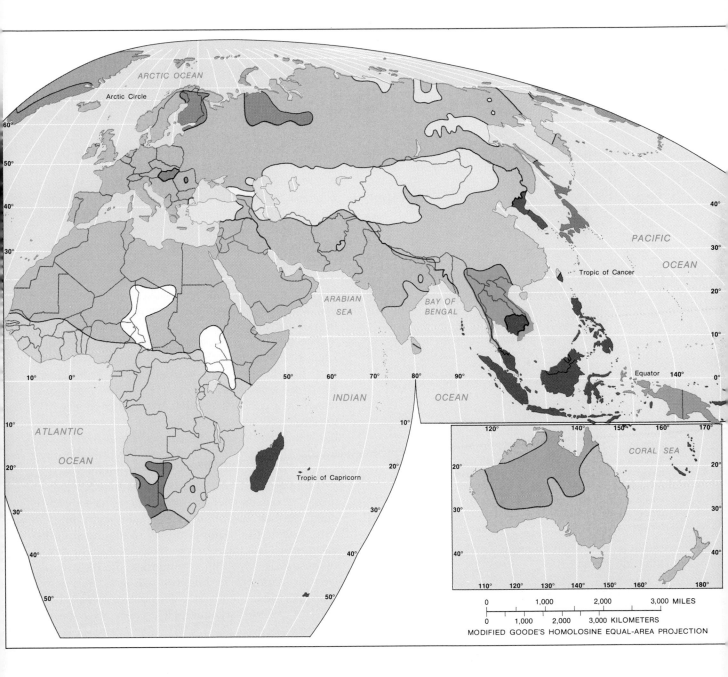

MODIFIED GOODE'S HOMOLOSINE EQUAL-AREA PROJECTION

with Chinese ideograms but also uses phonetic symbols, like Western languages, either instead of the ideograms or alongside them. Foreign terms may be written with another set of symbols.

Korean and Southeast Asian. Korean—a separate East Asian language family—has borrowed many words from the Chinese and Japanese languages, a reflection of Korea's location, situated between the two larger countries. In contrast to Chinese and Japanese, Korean is not written with ideograms. Instead, Korean employs a system known as *hongul,* in which—like Western languages—each letter represents a sound.

Another important language family in Asia is Southeast Asian. Vietnamese, the largest language of

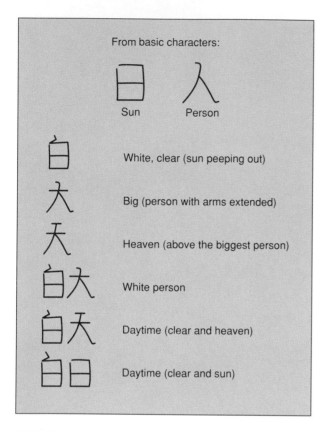

From basic characters:

Sun   Person

White, clear (sun peeping out)

Big (person with arms extended)

Heaven (above the biggest person)

White person

Daytime (clear and heaven)

Daytime (clear and sun)

FIGURE 4–10
The Chinese languages are written with characters known as ideograms, which represent ideas or concepts, not specific pronunciations. There are more than 200 key characters, which may be built into more complex words. These examples of words are built from two basic characters—*sun* and *person*.

the Southeast Asian language family, is written with the Latin alphabet.

Preservation of Obscure Languages

Three language families are spoken but not written by a small number of people in Asia. These are Burushashki, spoken by 20,000 people in the Kashmir; Ainu, spoken by 10,000 people in the north of Japan; and Andamanese, spoken by 400 people on the Andaman Islands in the Bay of Bengal. In addition, six languages with some written records used by a total of 20,000 people in the northeast of Siberia have been assigned to the Paleo-Siberian language family.

These four obscure language families are spoken by small groups of people isolated from the mod-

ern world. They may become extinct soon, for an insufficient number of speakers remains to preserve them. Through increased contact with neighbors, these speakers of isolated languages are exposed to the benefits of communicating by means of a more widely understood language with a literary tradition.

Some obscure languages are being preserved. One example is Dogrib, a language spoken by 2,500 Native Americans in the Northwest Territory of Canada near the Arctic Circle. A man named Herb Zimmerman has spent many years translating the Bible into Dogrib. Some difficulties in the translation are predictable. A language with only 2,500 speakers has no written tradition to serve as a model for the translator, so that grammatical rules are hard to learn. The small number of speakers, a reflection of the historic isolation of the tribe, precludes translation of many documents.

The physical environment inhabited by this isolated tribe influences the language's spoken vocabulary. Dogrib has eight words for *ice* and many words for *white man* but no words for *shepherd* or *camel* or a good many other words that appear in the Bible, because the Indian tribe is nomadic and has no domesticated herds. *Shepherd* has been translated as *baby sitter,* and *horse* is substituted for *camel.*

Although the 2,500 Dogribs live within 300 kilometers of one another, regional dialects have developed, further complicating the translation problems. Adding to the impracticality of the translation effort is that half the tribe can speak English. In view of these facts, why bother to translate the Bible into Dogrib? Zimmerman believes that if only a few more people are integrated into the customary beliefs of Western culture, a benefit has been achieved.

Afro-Asiatic Languages

The Afro-Asiatic language family—also called Semito-Hamitic—includes Arabic and Hebrew, as well as a number of languages found primarily in northern Africa and southwestern Asia. Although one of the world's largest language families, its international significance transcends the number of speakers because its languages were used to write holy books of two of the three major world religions, the Judeo-Christian Bible and the Islamic Koran.

Arabic. Nearly three-fourths of the Afro-Asiatic speakers use Arabic, an official language in approximately two dozen countries of North Africa and Southwest Asia, from Morocco to the Arabian peninsula. Besides the 200 million native speakers of Arabic, a large percentage of the world's Muslims have at least some knowledge of Arabic because the Koran was written in that language in the seventh century. Although a number of dialects exist in Arabic, a standard Arabic has developed because of the influence of the Koran, newspapers, and radio. The United Nations added Arabic as the sixth official language of the General Assembly in 1973 and the Security Council in 1982.

Hebrew. As a native language, Hebrew is spoken by only approximately 4 million people. Even so, it holds considerable interest for two reasons. First, most of the Old Testament was written in Hebrew; a small part of it was written in another Afro-Asiatic language, Aramaic. Second, Hebrew is one of the few dead languages ever to be revived. As a language used in daily activity, Hebrew became extinct in the fourth century B.C. and was thereafter retained only for Jewish religious services. In this way, Hebrew was comparable to Latin, except that there are many more Roman Catholics than Jews in the world. At the time of Christ, the Jews in the Middle East generally spoke Aramaic, which in turn was replaced by Arabic.

When Israel was established in 1948, Hebrew became one of the new country's two official languages, along with Arabic, despite having been dormant for 2,000 years. Hebrew was chosen because the Jewish population of Israel consisted of exiles and migrants from around the world, and no other language could unify the disparate cultural groups in the new country.

The task of reviving Hebrew as a living language was formidable. Words had to be created for thousands of objects and inventions unknown in biblical times, such as telephones, cars, and electricity. The effort was initiated by Eliezer Ben-Yehuda, who lived in Palestine before the creation of the state of Israel and refused to speak any language other than Hebrew. Ben-Yehuda is credited with the invention of 4,000 new Hebrew words—related when possible to ancient ones—and the creation of the first modern Hebrew dictionary.

Uralic and Altaic Language Families

Every European country is dominated by Indo-European speakers with two exceptions: Finland and Hungary. The Finns and Hungarians speak languages that belong to the Uralic family. The Uralic languages can be traced back to a common language, called Proto-Uralic, first used 7,000 years ago by people living in the Ural Mountains of the present-day Soviet Union, near the confluence of the Volga and Kama Rivers, north of the Kurgan homeland.

Like Indo-European, the Uralic languages were carried to Europe by migrants. One branch moved north along the Volga River and then turned either west towards Finland or east into Siberia. The second branch moved overland south and then west to present-day Hungary. These Uralic-speaking migrants carved out homelands for themselves in the midst of Germanic- and Slavic-speaking peoples and retained their language as a major element of cultural identity.

The Altaic languages are spoken over a wide area of Asia, with the largest number in Turkey and the remainder spread across the Soviet Union and Mongolia, from the Ural Mountains to the Pacific Ocean. Among the more widely used Altaic languages in the Asian portion of the Soviet Union are Azerbaijani, Uzbek, Kazakh, and Tatar.

The use of Altaic languages was suppressed for many years in the Soviet Union as part of an attempt to create a homogeneous national culture. One element of the Soviet policy was to force everyone to write with the Cyrillic alphabet, though some of the Altaic languages traditionally employed Arabic letters. Most speakers of Altaic languages in the Soviet Union are Muslims and are thus familiar with Arabic letters, because Islamic holy books are written in Arabic. To placate Tatars who disliked using Cyrillic letters, Soviet officials in 1989 proposed adding three letters to the alphabet to represent Arabic sounds that did not match any existing Cyrillic letters.

Turkish used to be written with Arabic letters, but in 1928 the government of Turkey, led by Kemal

Ataturk, ordered that the language be written with the Latin alphabet instead. Ataturk believed that switching to Latin letters would help modernize the economy and culture of Turkey through increased communications with European countries.

The Altaic language family has traditionally been linked with the Uralic languages because the two families display similar word formation, grammatical endings, and other structural elements. Recent studies, however, point to geographically separate origins of the languages. The Altaic languages are thought to have originated in the steppes bordering the Qilian Shan and Altai Mountains between Tibet and China. Linguists do not know whether one tribe

originally spoke a Proto-Altaic language, as with Proto-Indo-European and Proto-Uralic, or whether the language consisted of a mixture of several others, that merged together through the interaction and integration of different peoples living in the steppes.

African Languages

No one knows the precise number of different languages in Africa, and scholars disagree about the proper classification of the known languages into families. Nearly a thousand distinct languages, as well as several thousand named dialects, have been

FIGURE 4–11

Nearly 1,000 languages have been identified in Africa, and experts have not agreed on how to classify them into families, especially languages in central Africa. The language of the island of Madagascar belongs to a separate branch from all other African languages. Madagascar's Austronesian language comes from a language family spoken across a wide area of the South Pacific. This wide diffusion indicates that early speakers of Austronesian on the island of Madagascar must have migrated long distances.

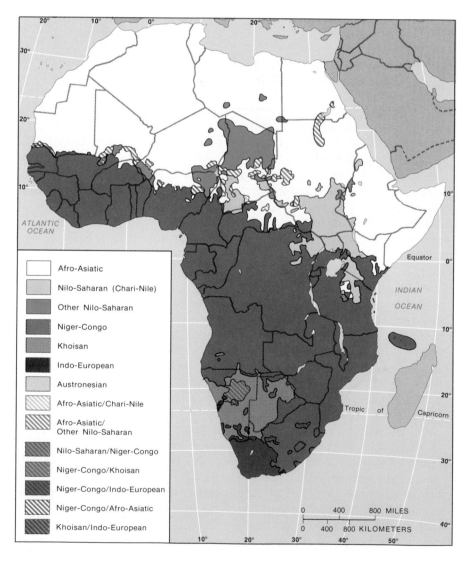

documented in Africa (Figure 4–11). The large number of languages in Africa is a product of more than 5,000 years of minimal interaction among the thousands of groups of people inhabiting the continent. Each group developed its own language, religion, and other cultural traditions in isolation from other groups.

Documenting African languages is a formidable task because most of them do not have a written tradition, and only ten of them are spoken by more than 10 million people. European missionaries and colonial officers in the nineteenth century began to record African languages using the Latin or Arabic alphabet. Twentieth-century researchers continue to add newly discovered languages to the African list and have found no evidence that any have become extinct.

The language pattern is relatively clear in the northern part of Africa, where Afro-Asiatic languages predominate. Arabic is the most widely used, though in a variety of dialects. Other Afro-Asiatic languages spoken by more than 5 million Africans include Amharic, Oromo, and Somali in the Horn of Africa and Hausa in northern Nigeria.

South of the Sahara Desert, the distribution of languages is more complex. More than 95 percent of the people of sub-Saharan Africa use languages belonging to the Niger-Congo family, while most of the remaining population speak a Khoisan or Nilo-Saharan language. But the Niger-Congo family alone includes six branches, and many languages are difficult to classify. In addition, several million people in South Africa speak one of two Indo-European languages, English or Afrikaans, which is a Germanic language similar to Dutch.

Niger-Congo language family. Languages of the Benue-Congo branch account for more than half of the languages in the Niger-Congo family and are used in a wide area, from the Congo (Zaire) River to South Africa. Languages of the other five Niger-Congo branches—Adamawa-Eastern, Gur, Kwa, Mande, and West Atlantic—are spoken in a narrow band that runs east-west across Africa south of the Sahara and north of the Congo River.

The most important language of the Benue-Congo branch is Swahili. Although the official language of only one country, Tanzania, Swahili has become the lingua franca in much of eastern Africa. A

lingua franca is a language mutually understood and commonly used in trade by people who have different native languages. Swahili, originally developed through interaction between various African groups and Arab traders, has strong Arabic influences in its vocabulary and is one of the few African languages with an extensive literature.

Other African language families. The other two African language families are less widely used. Nilo-Saharan languages are spoken by a few million people in north-central Africa, immediately north of the Niger-Congo language region. Divisions within the Nilo-Saharan family exemplify the problem of classifying African languages. Despite the relatively small number of speakers, the Nilo-Saharan family is divided into six branches: Chari-Nile, Fur, Koma, Maba, Saharan, and Songhai. The Chari-Nile branch, which is found in East Africa, from Egypt to Tanzania, can be subdivided into four groups: Berta, Central Sudanic, East Sudanic, and Kunama. The Central Sudanic group in turn comprises ten subgroups, the most important of which are Nilotic and Nubian. The total number of speakers of each individual Nilo-Saharan language is therefore extremely small.

The third important language family of sub-Saharan Africa—Khoisan—is concentrated in the southwest. A distinctive characteristic of the Khoisan languages is the prominent use of clicking sounds. After hearing the clicking sounds, whites in southern Africa derisively named the most important Khoisan language Hottentot.

The map of world languages (Figure 4–9) shows one particularly striking oddity in Africa: Madagascar, the large island situated in the Indian Ocean off the east coast of Africa, is classified as speaking an Austronesian language, even though it is separated by 3,000 kilometers from any other Austronesian-speaking countries, such as Indonesia.

That Malagasy, the language of Madagascar, is classified as an Austronesian language is evidence of long-distance migration. Just as English is the predominant language of North America because of migration from England, so Malagasy, the language of Madagascar, is an Austronesian language because of migration from the South Pacific. Malayo-Polynesian people apparently set sail in small boats and reached Madagascar approximately 2,000 years ago.

Nigeria. Africa's most populous country, Nigeria, suffers from a lack of cultural interaction because it contains many groups of people, each of whom may speak a distinct language (Figure 4–12). Hausa, an Afro-Asiatic language, is spoken by about a quarter of the population, mostly members of the Hausa and Fulani peoples living in the north. In eastern Nigeria, Ibo is the most common language, followed by Efik and Ijaw. Yoruba is the most important language in the west, followed by Edo. More than 200 distinct languages are spoken in Nigeria.

The official language of Nigeria is English, though it is spoken by only 2 percent of the population. Although English is not widely known, the problem for Nigeria is that no indigenous language has widespread use throughout the country. English has the considerable advantage for Nigeria of being intelligible to the governments of other countries.

Groups living in different regions of Nigeria have frequently fought each other. The Ibos attempted to secede from Nigeria during the 1960s, while the northerners have repeatedly claimed they are dis-

FIGURE 4–12
Distribution of Nigeria's main groups of people. These once-isolated groups speak a wide variety of languages. National unity is severely strained by the lack of a language a large percentage of the population can understand.

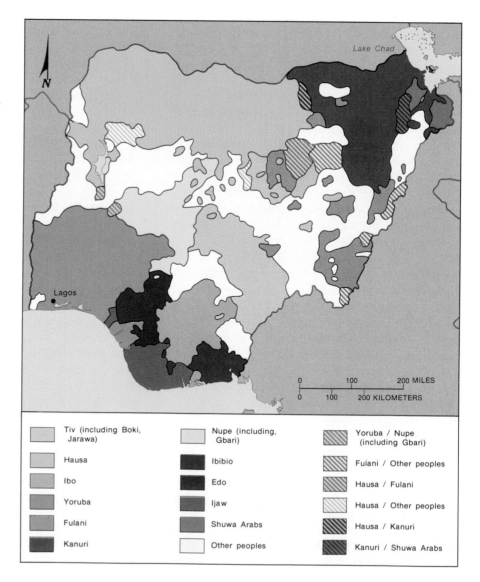

Tiv (including Boki, Jarawa)	Nupe (including, Gbari)	Yoruba / Nupe (including Gbari)
Hausa	Ibibio	Fulani / Other peoples
Ibo	Edo	Hausa / Fulani
Yoruba	Ijaw	Hausa / Other peoples
Fulani	Shuwa Arabs	Hausa / Kanuri
Kanuri	Other peoples	Kanuri / Shuwa Arabs

criminated against by the Yorubas. To reduce regional tensions, the government is moving the capital from Lagos, in the Yoruba-dominated southwest, to Abuja, in the center of Nigeria.

Nigeria's experience reflects some of the problems that arise from cultural diversity in a relatively small region of the earth, as well as the importance of language in identifying distinct cultural groups at a local scale. Yet from a global perspective, the distribution of different language families is reasonably simple, because three-fourths of the world's people speak languages belonging to one of only two families—Indo-European and Sino-Tibetan.

This world-wide scale, however, does not fully display the extent of geographic differences in languages. Speakers of one language within the two large families are unlikely to understand any of the others, while the remaining fourth of the world's population use one of thousands of other languages. The picture of the spatial distribution of language cannot be based solely on the distribution of individual languages, though, because considerable diversity also exists among different speakers of the same language.

KEY ISSUE
Why Do People Living in Different Locations Speak English Differently?

"If you use proper English you're regarded as a freak; why can't the English learn to speak?" asked Professor Henry Higgins in the Broadway musical "My Fair Lady." He was referring to the Cockney Eliza Doolittle, who pronounced *rain* like *rine* and dropped the /h/ sound from the beginning of such words as *happy*. Eliza Doolittle's speech pattern illustrates that English, like other languages, has a wide variety of dialects and that people who speak the same language may use different pronunciations, spellings, and meanings for particular words.

Geographers study dialects in order to understand the relationship between culture and the landscape. Dialects, like language families, acquire distinctive distributions across the landscape through various social processes, such as migration, interaction, and isolation. At the same time, a dialect reflects unique characteristics of the physical environment in which a group of people live, and languages change partially in response to modifications of the landscape. This section examines the spatial distribution of dialects in English, first in England and then in the United States.

Development of Dialects in English

One particular dialect of English, the one associated with upper-class Britons living in the London area, is recognized around the world as the standard form of speech. This speech, known as **British Received Pronunciation (BRP),** is well known to people elsewhere in the world because it is commonly used by politicians, broadcasters, and actors. Why don't Americans or, for that matter, other British people speak that way?

Dialects in England. English, as already shown, originated with the three invading groups from northern Europe: the Angles, Jutes, and Saxons. These three invaders settled in different parts of Britain—the Angles in the north, the Jutes in the southeast, and the Saxons in the south and west. The languages spoken by each formed the basis for the development of distinct regional dialects of Old English (Figure 4–13). The four most important Old English dialects included Kentish in the southeast, West Saxon in the southwest, Mercian in the center of the island, and Northumbrian in the north.

Following the Norman invasion of 1066, French replaced English as the language of the government and aristocracy. By the time English again became the country's dominant language, five major regional dialects had emerged: Northern, East Midland, West Midland, Southwestern, and Southeastern or Kentish. The boundaries of these five regional dialects roughly paralleled the pattern before the Norman invasion (Figure 4–14). But after 150 years of living in isolation in rural settlements under the control of a French-speaking government, people spoke English differently in virtually every county of England.

Out of the large collection of local dialects, one eventually emerged as the standard language for writing and speech throughout England: the dialect used by upper-class residents in the capital city of London and the two important university cities of

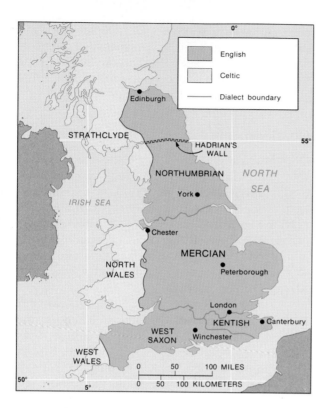

FIGURE 4-13

Dialects of Old English. The Angles, Saxons, and Jutes retained distinctive speech patterns after settling in England. Jutes settled in the southeast and spoke a dialect of German that became known as Kentish. The Saxons settled in the south and west, while the Angles took control of the north of England. The Angles living north of the Humber River spoke a separate dialect from those farther south. (From Albert C. Baugh and Thomas Cable, *A History of the English Language,* 3d ed., © 1978, p. 53. Reprinted by permission of Prentice-Hall, Inc., Englewood Cliffs, N.J.)

Cambridge and Oxford. The diffusion of the dialect spoken in London and the university cities was first encouraged by the introduction of the printing press to England in 1476. Grammar books and dictionaries printed in the eighteenth century established rules for spelling and grammar based on the London dialect. These frequently arbitrary rules were then taught in schools throughout the country.

In other countries, the dialect spoken by the upper-class residents of the capital city also emerged as the standard language. For example, the Paris dialect became the standard form of French, and the Madrid dialect became the standard form of Spanish.

Current dialect differences. Despite the current dominance of British Received Pronunciation, strong regional differences persist in the English dialects spoken in the United Kingdom, especially in rural areas. Although several dozen dialects are identifiable, they can be grouped into three main regions: Northern, Midland, and Southern. Southerners pronounce such words as *grass* and *path* with an /ah/ sound, whereas people in the Midlands and North use a short /a/ as do most people in the United States. People in the Midlands and North pronounce *butter* and *Sunday* with the /oo/ sound of words like *boot.* Northerners pronounce *ground*

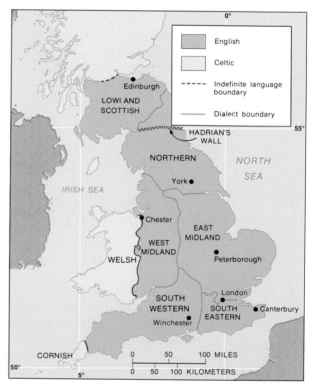

FIGURE 4-14

The regions of important dialects of Middle English corresponded closely to those of Old English. The Northumbrian dialect of Old English became divided into Scottish and Northern dialects, while the Mercian dialect of Old English was split into East and West Midland. The Kentish dialect was considerably extended in area and became known as the South Eastern dialect. West Saxon became known as the South Western dialect. (From Albert C. Baugh and Thomas Cable, *A History of the English Language,* 3d ed., © 1978, p. 190. Reprinted by permission of Prentice-Hall, Inc., Englewood Cliffs, N.J.)

and *pound* like *grund* and *pund,* with the /uh/ sound similar to the word *punt* in U.S. football.

Distinctive southwestern and southeastern accents are found within the Southern dialect. People in the southwest, for example, pronounce *thatch* and *thing* with the /th/ sound of *then* rather than *thin. Fresh* and *eggs* have an /ai/ sound. Southeasterners pronounce the /a/ in *apple* and *cat* like the short /e/ in *bet.* Local dialects can be further distinguished, and some words have distinctive pronunciations and meanings in each county of the United Kingdom.

Some children's words, in particular, show strong regional differences. For example, words used by children in games vary in different regions of the country and in specific communities within particular regions (Figure 4–15).

English in North America

The English language was brought to the North American continent by colonists from England who settled along the Atlantic coast in the seventeenth century. The early colonists naturally spoke the language used in England at the time and established seventeenth-century English as the dominant form of speech used in the United States. Later immigrants to the United States found English already implanted in the country; although migrants from other countries made significant contributions to the development of American English, they were acculturated into an English-speaking society. Therefore, the earliest colonists were most responsible for the dominant language patterns found in the English-speaking part of the Western Hemisphere.

Differences between British and American English. Why is the English language in the United States so different from that in England? The answer is that the United States grew in isolation from England. Separated from each other by the Atlantic Ocean, the United States and England developed their languages in the eighteenth and nineteenth centuries with little influence from each other. The English used in the United States differs from that of England in three significant ways: vocabulary, spelling, and pronunciation.

The vocabulary is different largely because U.S. settlers encountered many unfamiliar objects and

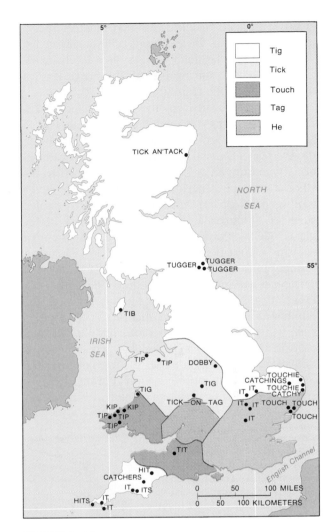

FIGURE 4–15

Regional differences in vocabulary continue to exist in Great Britain, despite the relatively small size of the country and the diffusion of the language through television and other forms of mass media. One example is the word that children use in a game of tag to signal that they have touched another participant. The map also shows that distinctive words to indicate a touch exist in individual communities as well.

experiences. The new continent contained physical features, such as large forests and mountains, that had to be given new names. New animals were encountered, including the moose, raccoon, and chipmunk, all of which were given native American names. Native Americans also provided the English language with the names of objects, such as the canoe, moccasin, and squash. Different names were given in the two countries to such nineteenth-century inventions as the elevator (called a lift in England) and the flashlight (known as a torch in England). Similarly, the British call the hood of a car the bonnet and the trunk the boot.

Spelling diverged from the British standard because of a strong national feeling in the United States for an independent identity. Noah Webster, the creator of the first comprehensive American dictionary and grammar books, was determined to develop a uniquely American dialect of English. He either ignored or was unaware of recently created rules of grammar and spelling developed in England. Webster argued that spelling and grammar reforms would help establish a national language, reduce cultural dependence on England, and inspire national pride. The spelling differences between British and American English, such as the elimination of the *u* from the British spelling of such words as *honour* and *colour* and the substitution of *s* for *c* in *defence,* are due primarily to the diffusion of Webster's ideas inside the United States.

Differences in pronunciation between British and U.S. speakers are immediately recognizable.

Again, geographic concepts help explain the reason for the differences. From the time of their arrival in North America, colonists began to pronounce words differently from the British. Such divergence is normal, since interaction between the two groups was largely confined to exchange of letters and other printed matter rather than by direct speech.

One prominent difference between British and U.S. English is the pronunciation of the letters *a* and *r.* Such words as *fast, path,* and *half,* are pronounced in England like the *a* in *father* rather than the *a* in *man.* The British also eliminate the letter *r* from pronunciation except before vowels. Thus, *lord* in British pronunciation sounds like *laud.* Furthermore, Americans pronounce unaccented syllables with more clarity. The words *secretary* and *necessary* have four syllables in American English but only three in British.

Surprisingly, pronunciation has changed more in England than in the United States. The letters *a* and *r* are pronounced in the United States the way they used to be pronounced in Britain, specifically in the seventeenth century, when the first colonists departed.

When an American boards a red double-decker bus in Piccadilly Circus, London, cultural differences between the two English-speaking countries are apparent. Because the British drive on the left side of the road, passengers board the bus on the left side, while the driver sits on the right side—the opposite of the arrangement in the United States. A sign on the bus advertises a film called "Porridge," a rarely used word in the United States but a common British term for a breakfast cereal like oatmeal. Porridge is also British slang for jail (spelled *gaol* in Britain). The clock behind the statue says 17.01 to indicate 5:01 P.M. The large signs in the background, however, provide evidence of global diffusion of some objects on the cultural landscape.

One of the dialects of Southern English did not emerge as the British national standard until the late eighteenth century, after the American colonies had declared independence and were politically as well as physically isolated from England. Thus, people in the United States do not speak "proper" English because when the colonists left England "proper" English was not what it is today. Furthermore, few colonists were drawn from the English upper classes.

Dialects in the United States

The major dialect differences have originated in the United States because of the differences in dialects among the various groups of original English settlers. The English dialect spoken by the first colonists, who arrived in the seventeenth century, determined the future speech patterns for their communities because later immigrants adopted the language in use in a settlement when they arrived. The language may have been modified somewhat by new arrivals, but the distinctive elements brought over by the original settlers continued to dominate.

Settlement in the East. The original settlements stretched along the Atlantic Coast in thirteen separate colonies. The settlements can be grouped into three areas: New England, Southeastern, and Middle Atlantic. Massachusetts and the other New England colonies were established and inhabited almost entirely by settlers from England. Two-thirds of the New England colonists were Puritans from the East Anglia section of Southeast England, and only a few came from the north of England.

The nucleus of the southeastern colonies was Virginia, where the first permanent settlement by the English in North America was established in Jamestown in 1607. Around half of the southeastern settlers came from Southeast England, though they included a diversity of social class backgrounds, including deported prisoners, indentured servants, and political and religious refugees. The English dialects now spoken in the U.S. Southeast and New England are easily recognizable. Current distinctions result from the establishment of independent and isolated colonies in the seventeenth century.

The immigrants to the Middle Atlantic colonies were more diverse. The early settlers of Pennsylvania were predominantly Quakers from the north of England. Scots and Irish also went to Pennsylvania, as well as to New Jersey and Delaware. In addition, the Middle Atlantic colonies attracted many German, Dutch, and Swedish immigrants who learned their English from the English-speaking settlers in the area. The dialect spoken in the Middle Atlantic colonies thus differed significantly from those spoken further north and south, because most of the settlers came from the north rather than the south of England or from countries other than England.

Current dialect differences in the East. Today, major dialect differences within the United States continue to exist primarily on the East Coast, though some distinctions can be found elsewhere in the country. The different dialects have been documented primarily through the study of particular words. Every word that is not used nationally has some geographic extent within the country and therefore has boundaries. A boundary, known as an **isogloss,** can be constructed for each word. These isoglosses are determined through showing people, especially natives of rural areas, pictures or sentences to be completed with a particular word. While every word has a unique isogloss, boundary lines of different words coalesce in some locations to form regions.

Two important isoglosses separate the eastern United States into three major dialect regions, known as Northern, Midlands, and Southern. The northern boundary runs through Pennsylvania, while the southern one runs through the Blue Ridge Mountains of western Virginia (Figure 4–16).

Words can be found that are commonly used within each of the three major dialect areas but rarely in the other two. In most instances, these words relate to rural life, food, and objects from daily activities. Language differences tend to be greater in rural areas than in cities, because farmers are relatively isolated from interaction with people from other dialect regions.

For example, a container commonly used on farms is known as a *pail* in the North and a *bucket* in the Midlands and South. A small body of water is known as a *brook* in the North, a *run* in the Midlands, and a *branch* in the South. The term *run* was apparently used in the north of England and Scotland, the origin of a large number of settlers in the

FIGURE 4–16
The most comprehensive classification of dialects in the United States was made by Hans Kurath in 1949. He found the greatest diversity of dialects, especially vocabulary used on farms, to be in the eastern part of the country. He divided the eastern United States into three major dialect regions—Northern, Midlands, and Southern—each of which contained a number of important subareas.

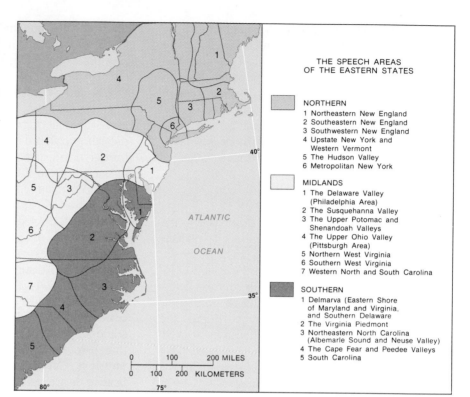

THE SPEECH AREAS
OF THE EASTERN STATES

NORTHERN
1 Northeastern New England
2 Southeastern New England
3 Southwestern New England
4 Upstate New York and
  Western Vermont
5 The Hudson Valley
6 Metropolitan New York

MIDLANDS
1 The Delaware Valley
  (Philadelphia Area)
2 The Susquehanna Valley
3 The Upper Potomac and
  Shenandoah Valleys
4 The Upper Ohio Valley
  (Pittsburgh Area)
5 Northern West Virginia
6 Southern West Virginia
7 Western North and South Carolina

SOUTHERN
1 Delmarva (Eastern Shore
  of Maryland and Virginia,
  and Southern Delaware
2 The Virginia Piedmont
3 Northeastern North Carolina
  (Albemarle Sound and Neuse Valley)
4 The Cape Fear and Peedee Valleys
5 South Carolina

Middle Atlantic colonies but relatively few in New England and the South.

The phrases for some farm activities, such as calling cows from pasture, show particularly sharp differences among the three regional dialects. New England farmers call cows with *boss!* or *bossie!* sometimes preceded by *co* or *come.* In the Midlands, the preferred call is *sook!* or sometimes *sookie!* or *sook cow!* The choice in the South is *cowench!* or its alternative forms, *co-inch!* and *co-ee!*

Many words that were once regionally distinctive are now national in scope. The mass media has influenced the adoption of the same words throughout the country. For example, a *frying pan,* was once commonly called a *spider* in New England and a *skillet* in the Middle Atlantic area.

Pronunciation differences. Differences in pronunciation in the various regions of the United States are more familiar than differences in words, though it is harder to draw precise isoglosses from them. The pronunciations that distinguish the southern dialect include making such words as *half* and

mine into two syllables *(ha-af* and *mi-yen),* pronouncing *poor* as *po-ur,* and pronouncing *Tuesday* and *due* with a /y/ sound.

The New England accent is well known for dropping the /r/ sound, so that *heart* and *lark* are pronounced *hot* and *lock.* Also, *ear* and *care* are pronounced with /ah/ substituted for the /r/ endings. The characteristic of dropping the /r/ sound is shared with speakers from the south of England and reflects the place of origin of most New England colonists. The similarity between the New England and southern England pronunciations also shows the relatively high degree of contact between the two groups. Residents of Boston, New England's main port city, maintained especially close ties to the important ports of southern England such as London, Plymouth, and Bristol. Compared to other colonists, New Englanders received more exposure to changes in pronunciation that occurred in Britain during the eighteenth century.

The New England and southern accents sound odd to most Americans because the standard pronunciation throughout the American West comes from the Middle Atlantic states rather than the New England and Southern regions. This pattern occurred because the Middle Atlantic states provided most of the western settlers.

The diffusion of particular English dialects into the middle and western parts of the United States is a result of the westward movement of colonists from the three dialect regions of the East. The area of the Midwest south of the Ohio River was settled first by colonists from Virginia and the other southern states. The Middle Atlantic colonies sent most of the early settlers north of the Ohio River, though some New Englanders moved to the Great Lakes areas.

As more of the West was opened to settlement during the nineteenth century, though, people migrated from all parts of the East Coast. The California gold rush attracted people from throughout the East, many of whom subsequently moved to other parts of the West. The mobility of Americans has been a major source in the creation of a relatively uniform language through much of the West.

The Future of English

In the twentieth century, English has become the world's most important language of international communication, or lingua franca. When well-educated speakers of two different languages wish to communicate with each other in such countries as India or Nigeria they frequently use English. A Polish airline pilot who flies over France speaks to the traffic controller on the ground in English. The number of people in the world who speak English as a second language is unknown, but it is at least as large as the number who use English as a first language.

English words are increasingly integrated into other languages. The Japanese, for example, refer to *beisboru* (baseball), *naifu* (knife), and *sutoroberi keki* (strawberry cake). *Cowboy, hamburger, jeans,* and *T-shirt* have entered the French language.

The emergence of English as an international language has facilitated the diffusion of popular culture and science and the growth of international trade. But people who forsake their native language must weigh the benefits of using English against the cost of losing a fundamental element of local cultural identity.

Traditionally, language has been a very important source of national pride and identity in France. The French are particularly upset with the increasing worldwide domination of English, especially the invasion of their language by English words and the substitution of English for French as the most important language of international communications.

Since 1635 the French Academy has been the supreme arbiter of the French language. In modern times, it has tried to encourage the use of French terms, such as *stationnement* rather than *parking* and *fin du semaine* rather than *le weekend.* The widespread use of English in the French language is called **franglais,** a combination of *français* and *anglais,* the French words for French and English, respectively.

People in smaller countries of the world need to learn English to participate more fully in a global economy and culture. All children learn English in the schools of countries such as the Netherlands and Sweden in order to aid communication with people of other countries. Obviously, it is more likely that several million Dutch people will learn English than that several hundred million English speakers around the world will learn Dutch.

In view of the global dominance of English, many U.S. citizens do not recognize the importance of learning other languages. But one of the main ways to learn about the beliefs, traits, and other cultural characteristics of a people living in a particular region is to learn the group's language. The lack of effort on the part of Americans to learn other languages is a source of resentment among people elsewhere in the world, especially when Americans visit or work in other countries.

The inability to speak other languages is also a handicap for Americans who try to conduct international business. Successful entry into new overseas markets requires knowledge of local cultural characteristics, and officials who can speak the local language are better able to obtain the needed knowledge. Japanese businesses that wish to expand in the United States send English-speaking officials, but American businesses who wish to sell products to the Japanese are rarely able to find a Japanese-speaking employee.

Summary

Here again are the key issues raised by the geography of languages:

1. **How did the English language originate and diffuse?** English is a Germanic language, related to other languages spoken in northwestern Europe. Germanic tribes invaded England and brought their language with them. From England, the language was diffused around the world through colonization.

2. **How is English related to languages spoken elsewhere in the world?** English is part of the Germanic branch of the Indo-European language family, a collection of languages used by half the world's population. Just as English and other Germanic languages can be traced to a common ancestor, so can all Indo-European languages. Individual languages developed from a single root through the process of migration, followed by the isolation of one people from others who formerly spoke the same language.

3. **What is the spatial distribution of other language families?** The precise number of languages in the world is unknown, but it is probably several thousand. These languages can be grouped into approximately two dozen language families. After Indo-European, the language family with the most speakers is Sino-Tibetan, used by 20 percent of the world's population.

4. **Why do people living in different locations speak English differently?** English speakers use a wide variety of dialects. Differences in vocabulary, spelling, and pronunciation emerge primarily because speakers of one language, especially in rural areas, are isolated from other speakers of the same language. Geographers can document the boundaries that separate different dialect regions within countries, such as those that exist in the United States and the United Kingdom. English has become the most important language for international communication in popular arts, science, and business.

The Future of French and Spanish in the United States and Canada

CASE STUDY REVISITED

The French-speaking people of Canada and the Spanish-speaking people of the United States both live in a continent dominated by English speakers. But future prospects for these two languages in North America are different.

French Canada. In Canada, French is an official language, along with English. French speakers comprise one-fourth of the country's population, most of whom are clustered in Québec, where they comprise more than three-fourths of the province's population (Figure 4–17). Colonized by the French in the sixteenth century, Québec was captured by the British in 1763 and in 1867 became one of the provinces in the Confederation of Canada.

Until recently Québec was one of Canada's poorest and least developed provinces. Its economic and political activities were dominated by an English-speaking minority, and the province suffered from cultural isolation and lack of French-speaking leaders. In recent years, Québec has strengthened links to France, with which it shares a common language. When French President Charles de Gaulle visited Québec in 1967, he encouraged the development of an independent Québec by shouting in his speech, Vive la Québec libre! ("Long live free Québec!").

During the 1970s, the Québec government made the use of French mandatory in many daily activities. Alarmed at the pro-French policies, more than 100,000 English speakers and dozens of major corporations moved from Montreal, Québec's largest city, to Toronto, Ontario. Many Québeçois favored total separation of the province from Canada as the only way to preserve their cultural heritage. In a 1980 referendum, however, a majority of voters in Québec opposed separation.

In recent years, most of Québec's political and business leaders have regarded economic development as a more important issue than language and have increasingly encouraged **bilingualism,** that is, fluency in using two languages—in this case English and French. While most Québeçois support the preservation and enhancement of local cultural traditions, including the use of French as the province's official language, they prefer to be part of Canada because of economic benefits.

Hispanic America. Because of large-scale immigration from Latin America in recent years, Spanish has become an increasingly important language in

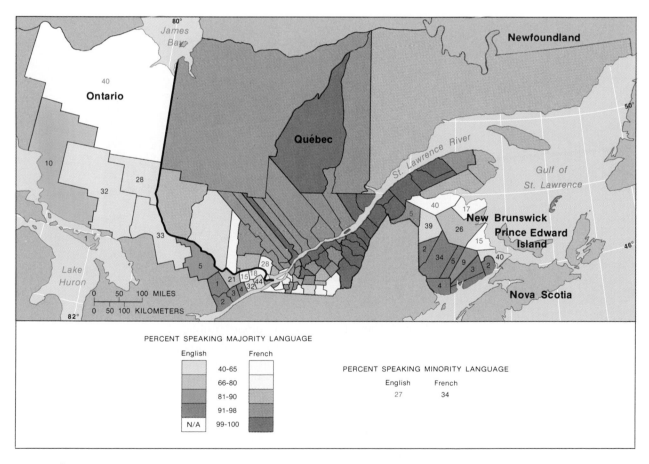

FIGURE 4–17
More than 80 percent of the residents of the province of Québec speak French, compared to approximately 6 percent for the rest of Canada. But the boundary between the French- and English-speaking regions of Canada is not a precise one; two bilingual belts lie on the eastern and western sides of the French-speaking region.

Little Havana, Miami. Most of the people in the neighborhood immigrated from Cuba, especially after Fidel Castro gained power in 1959.

the United States. In some communities, public notices, government documents, and advertisements are printed in Spanish. Several hundred Spanish-language newspapers and radio and television stations operate in the United States, especially in South Florida, California, the Southwest, and large northern cities, where most of the 20 million Spanish-speaking people live.

In a reaction against the increasing use of Spanish in the United States, a number of states and localities have enacted legislation making English the official language. Although some courts have judged laws mandating English as unconstitutional restrictions on free speech, such laws continue to be enacted as symbolic statements concerning the importance of English as the chief cultural bond in the United States, in an otherwise heterogeneous society.

Americans have also debated whether schools should offer bilingual education. Some people want Spanish-speaking children to be educated in Spanish, because they think that children will learn more effectively if taught in their native language. But other English and Spanish speakers argue that learning in Spanish creates a handicap for people in the United States when they look for jobs, virtually all of which require knowledge of English. Bilingual education has also been hampered by the lack of teachers able to speak two languages.

The examples of the French- and Spanish-speaking people of North America illustrate the fact that a shared language is an important element in cultural identity. Yet only a few nationalities in the world have successfully integrated more than one language into their culture.

Key Terms

Bilingualism Ability to use two languages with the fluency characteristic of indigenous speakers.

British Received Pronunciation (BRP) The dialect of English associated with upper-class Britons living in the London area and now considered standard in the United Kingdom.

Dialect A form of a language spoken in a local area.

Extinct language A language that was once used by people in daily activities but is no longer used.

Franglais A term used by the French for English words that have entered the French language, a combination of *français* and *anglais,* the French words for French and English, respectively.

Ideograms The system of writing used in China and other East Asian countries in which each symbol represents an idea or a concept rather than a specific sound, as is the case with letters in English.

Isogloss A boundary that separates regions in which different language usages predominate.

Isolated language A language that is unrelated to any other languages and therefore not attached to any language family.

Language branch A group of languages that share a common origin, but that have evolved into individual languages. The differences are not as extensive or as old as with language families, which may include several branches.

Language family A collection of individual languages related to each other by virtue of having a common ancestor before recorded history.

Language group Several individual languages within a language branch that share a common origin in the relatively recent past and display relatively few differences in grammar and vocabulary.

Lingua franca A language mutually understood and commonly used in trade by people who have different native languages.

Literary tradition A language that is written as well as spoken.

Official language The language adopted for use by the government for the conduct of business and publication of documents.

Standard language The form of a language used for official government business, education, and mass communications.

Vulgar Latin A form of Latin used in daily conversation by ancient Romans, as opposed to the standard dialect, which was used for official documents.

Thinking Geographically

1. At least sixteen U.S. states have passed laws mandating English as the language of all government functions. In 1990, Arizona's law making English the official language was ruled an unconstitutional violation of free speech. Should the use of English be encouraged in the United States to foster cultural integration, or should bilingualism be encouraged to foster cultural diverstiy?
2. Does the province of Québec possess the resources, economy, political institutions, and social structures to be a viable, healthy country? What would be the impact of Québec's independence on the remainder of Canada and on the United States?
3. How is American English different from British English as a result of contributions by African-Americans and immigrants who speak languages other than English?
4. The southern portion of Belgium—Wallonia—suffers from higher rates of unemployment, industrial decline, and other economic problems, compared to Flanders in the north. How do differences in language exacerbate Belgium's regional economic differences?
5. Many countries now receive Cable News Network (CNN) broadcasts that originate in the United States, but even English-speaking viewers in other countries have difficulty understanding some American English. A recent business program on CNN created a stir outside the United States when it reported that McDonalds was a major IRA contributor. Viewers in the United Kingdom thought that the American fast-food chain was financing the purchase of weapons by the Irish Republican Army, which sometimes resorts to violence to achieve the unification of Ireland. However, McDonalds in fact was contributing to Individual Retirement Accounts for its employees. Can you think of other examples in which the use of a word could cause a British-American misunderstanding?

Further Readings

Aitchison, J. W., and H. Carter. "The Welsh Language in Cardiff: A Quiet Revolution." *Transactions of the Institute of British Geographers, New Series* 12 (no. 4, 1987): 482–492.

Allen, Harold B. *The Linguistic Atlas of the Upper Midwest.* 3 vols. Minneapolis: University of Minnesota Press, 1973–76.

Baugh, Albert C., and Thomas Cable. 3rd ed. *A History of the English Language.* Englewood Cliffs, NJ: Prentice-Hall, 1978.

Cardona, George, Henry M. Hoeningswald, and Alfred Senn, eds. *Indo-European and Indo-Europeans.* Philadelphia: University of Pennsylvania Press, 1970.

Delgado de Carvalho, C. M. "The Geography of Languages." In *Readings in Cultural Geography,* edited by Philip L. Wagner and Marvin W. Mikesell. Chicago: University of Chicago Press, 1962.

Dugdale, J. S. *The Linguistic Map of Europe.* London: Hutchinson University Library, 1969.

Gade, Daniel W. "Foreign Languages and American Geography." *Professional Geographer* 35 (August 1983): 261–65.

Greenberg, Johseph H. *Studies in African Language Classification.* Bloomington: Indiana University Press, 1963.

Hughes, Arthur, and Peter Trudgill. *English Accents and Dialects.* Birkenhead: Edward Arnold, 1979.

Hymes, Dell H. *Language in Culture and Society.* New York: Harper and Row, 1964.

Kirk, John M., Stewart Sanderson, J. D. A. Widdowson, eds. *Studies in Linguistic Geography: The Dialects of English in Britain and Ireland.* London: Croom Helm, 1985.

Kurath, Hans. *Word Geography of the Eastern United States.* Ann Arbor: University of Michigan Press, 1949.

Laird, Charlton. *Language in America.* New York and Cleveland: World Publishing, 1970.

Lind, Ivan. "Geography and Place Names." In *Readings in Cultural Geography,* edited by Philip L. Wagner and Marvin W. Mikesell. Chicago: University of Chicago Press, 1962.

Luckmann, Thomas. "Language in Society." *International Social Science Journal* 36 (no. 1, 1984) 5–20.

Meillet, Antoine, and Marcel Cohen. *Les langues du monde.* Paris: Centre National de la Recherche Scientifique, 1952.

Muller, Siegfried H. *The World's Living Languages.* New York: Frederick Ungar, 1964.

Opie, Iona, and Peter Opie. *Children's Games in Street and Playground.* London: Clarendon Press, 1969.

Ramanujan, A. K., and Colin Masica. "A Phonological Typology of the Indian Linguistic Area." In *Current Trends in Linguistics,* edited by Thomas A. Sebeok, vol. 5. The Hague, Netherlands: Mouton, 1969.

Renfrew, Colin. *Archaeology and Language.* Cambridge: Cambridge University Press, 1988.

Sopher, David E., ed. *An Exploration of India: Geographical Perspectives on Society and Culture.* Ithaca, NY: Cornell University Press, 1980.

Thomas, Peter. "Belgium's North-South Divide and the Walloon Regional Problem." *Geography* 75 (no. 1, 1990): 36–50.

Trudgill, Peter. "Linguistic Geography and Geographical Linguistics." *Progress in Geography* 7 (1975) 227–52.

Wagner, Philip L. "Remarks on the Geography of Language." *Geographical Review* 48 (January 1958) 86–97.

Wakelin, Martyn F. *English Dialects.* London: Athlone Press, 1972.

Williams, Colin H., ed. *Language in Geographic Context.* Clevedon, U.K.: Multilingual Matters, 1988.

Wixman, Ronald. *Language Aspects of Ethnic Patterns and Processes in the North Caucasus.* Chicago: University of Chicago Department of Geography, 1980.

Zelinsky, Wilbur. "Generic Terms in the Place Names of the Northeastern United States." In *Readings in Cultural Geography,* edited by Philip L. Wagner and Marvin W. Mikesell. Chicago: University of Chicago Press, 1962.

5
Religion

A nd He shall judge between the nations,
   And shall decide for many peoples;
      And they shall beat their swords into ploughshares,
And their spears into pruning-hooks:
Nation shall not lift up sword against nation,
Neither shall they learn war any more.

Isaiah 2:4

This passage from Isaiah is one of the Bible's most eloquent pleas for peace among the nations of the world. For many religious people, especially in the Western Hemisphere and Europe, Isaiah evokes a highly desirable image of the ideal future landscape.

Islam's holiest book, the Quran (Koran), also evokes powerful images of a peaceful landscape:

He it is who sends down water from the sky, whence ye have drink,
   and whence the trees grow whereby ye feed your flocks.
He makes the corn to grow, and the olives, and the palms, and the
   grapes, and some of every fruit; verily, in that is a sign unto a
   people who reflect.

Sûrah (Chapter) of the Bee XVI.9

Most religious people pray for peace, but religious groups may not share the same vision of how peace will be achieved. Geographers see that the process by which one religion diffuses across the landscape may conflict with the distribution of others. Geographers are concerned with the regional distribution of different religions and the potential for conflict among them that results from the various distributions.

Geographers also observe that religions are derived in part from elements of the physical environment and that religions in turn make a significant contribution to modification of the landscape. Note that the passages from the Bible and the Quran have several agricultural images.

Conflict in the Middle East

Yaakov Zimmerman was killed by terrorists after praying at the tomb of Abraham in the town of Hebron. Five other people were killed, including two American men. Sixteen were wounded, two of whom were American women. The terrorists were Palestinian members of the Palestine Liberation Organization (PLO), devoted to the cause of ridding the territory of all Israelis. Their weapons included Soviet-made Kalashnikov rifles.

Hebron is situated on the West Bank of the Jordan River. At the time of the attack it was controlled by the state of Israel. Until a war in 1967, however, Hebron and the surrounding area belonged to Jordan. The Palestinians believe that, instead of being occupied by Israel, the area should become part of a new state of Palestine. In fact, some Palestinians argue that the entire territory of the state of Israel should be included in a new state of Palestine. To support that cause, some PLO members resort to attacks on Israeli citizens, such as Zimmerman.

One of the alleged terrorists, named Yasir Zeidat, came from the village of Bani Naim, where he was not a hero. Villagers said that he was not especially intelligent and had never helped his father.

In punishment for the act of terrorism, an Israeli demolition squad blew up the house in Bani Naim where Zeidat's father lived. The act stemmed from a British colonial practice: the house of a terrorist who was caught was blown up as a punishment to the individual and as a warning to the entire village.

Yet Zeidat had left his father's house five years earlier. The Israeli retribution missed the mark, punishing the father, not the son. The punishment thus claimed another innocent victim in the fight between Israelis and Palestinians and generated sympathy for the terrorists in a village where few such feelings had previously existed.

eligion, like other cultural characteristics, can be a source of pride and a means of identification with a distinct culture. Indeed, intense identification with one religion can lead supporters into conflicts with followers of other religions. Unrest is especially severe in places like the Middle East where more than one religion has strong historical roots.

We can utilize geographic concepts to understand the religious landscape. As one of the most important characteristics of culture, religion leaves a strong imprint on the physical environment. Viewed from the perspective of a geographic process, each religion has a point of origin, a pattern of diffusion, and a current distribution across the earth's surface.

Geographers also look at the relationship between religion and the physical environment. On the one hand, religious beliefs may be derived from elements in the physical environment. On the other hand, religious ideas may underlie human transformation of the physical environment. In some societies, attempts to modify the environment according to religious principles may conflict with other political and economic values.

KEY ISSUE

How Are Religions Distributed?

Only a few religions can claim the adherence of large numbers of people, and each of these has a distinctive distribution across the earth's surface (Table 5–1 and Figure 5–1). Geographers distinguish two kinds of religions: universalizing and ethnic.

Differences Between Universalizing and Ethnic Religions

Geographers identify the distinctive spatial distributions and diffusion patterns of universalizing and ethnic religions. **Universalizing religions** attempt to appeal to all people, not just to residents of one cultural background or location. In contrast, the religious principles of an **ethnic religion** are more likely to be based on the physical characteristics of a particular location on the earth's surface. Consequently, an ethnic religion carries meaning primarily either for people living in a particular environ-

TABLE 5–1
Estimated membership (in millions) of the principal religions of the world.

	Africa	Europe	Latin America	U.S. and Canada	Oceania	Asia	Soviet Union	All
Christians	294	410	410	235	22	237	105	1712
Roman Catholics	110	260	382	95	8	111	5	972
Protestants	101	106	17	102	13	74	9	422
Orthodox	26	36	1	6	1	3	90	164
Other	56	8	10	32	1	48	a	154
Muslims	263	12	1	5	a	609	34	925
Buddhists	b	a	a	a	b	310	a	311
Hindus	1	1	1	1	a	685	c	689
Confucians	c	c	c	b	d	6	d	6
Shintoists	d	d	c	c	d	3	d	3
Chinese folk	b	b	a	a	b	170	d	170
Jews	a	1	1	7	a	4	3	17
Sikhs	b	a	b	a	b	17	d	18
Animists	66	d	1	b	a	24	0	91
Other	1	1	5	2	a	147	a	158
Nonreligious*	2	71	19	23	4	840	143	1101
Total	628	497	439	274	26	3052	286	5201

a = less than 500,000, b = less than 50,000, c = less than 5,000, d = less than 500
*includes atheists
Note: Because of rounding, the sum of a column may not match "total" and the sum of a row may not match "all."
Source: Encyclopedia Britannica Yearbook, 1990.

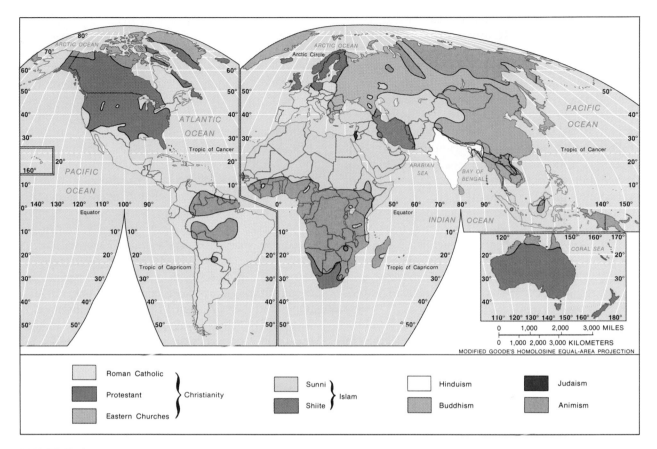

FIGURE 5–1
More than two-thirds of the world's people are adherents of one of these four religions:
Christianity—about 33 percent of the world's people, living especially in Europe, the Soviet
Union, and the Western Hemisphere; Islam—about 18 percent of the world's people, living
especially in northern Africa and Southwest and Southeast Asia; Hinduism—about 13 percent
of the world's people, virtually all living in India; and Buddhism—about 6 percent of the
world's people, living especially in East and Southeast Asia. Hinduism is classified as an ethnic
religion, in part because virtually all Hindus are concentrated in one country, India. The
other three religions, which are considered universalizing religions, have adherents distributed widely across the earth's surface.

ment or for those attracted to a particular environment.

Geographers study the process by which religion, like other cultural characteristics, diffuses
from one location to another, resulting in a distinctive distribution. Regions characterized by adherence of most residents to a particular religion develop through interaction and immigration.
Geographers consider the diffusion of a religion important because religion is a major force in the
spread of cultural values.

The world has three main universalizing religions—Christianity, Islam, and Buddhism. Each began with an individual founder who preached a
message accepted initially only by immediate followers. These followers in turn transmitted the message to people elsewhere on the earth's surface. Today, these three universalizing religions have
hundreds of millions of adherents distributed
across wide areas of the world.

Each of these three religions is divided into different branches, denominations, and sects. A

branch refers to a large and fundamental division within a religion, a **denomination** to divisions within a branch, and a **sect** to a relatively small denominational group that has broken away from an established faith.

An ethnic religion differs from a universalizing religion in that it typically has a more clustered geographic distribution. The ethnic religion with the largest number of followers is Hinduism. Although Hinduism is the world's third largest religion, more than 99 percent of its followers are concentrated in one country, India.

An ethnic religion, because its social forms are rooted in a specific location, is harder to transmit to people elsewhere in the world. Such a religion may change as social, economic, and physical conditions in the homeland change, but the regional extent of the religion's followers is unlikely to expand extensively.

An understanding of the distribution of religions forms the basis for an analysis of the relationship between different religions and the landscape. Since the three main universalizing religions and some ethnic religions have been created during recorded history, their origin, diffusion, and spatial distribution can be documented. This section employs these geographic concepts to examine the three main universalizing religions as well as some representative ethnic religions.

Christianity

The religion most familiar to North Americans is Christianity. Christianity has more than 1.7 billion adherents, far more than any other world religion, and has the most widespread distribution. It is the predominant religion in North America, South America, Europe, and Australia, and countries with a Christian majority exist in Africa and Asia, as well.

Origin and diffusion. How did Christianity become the world's most practiced and most widely distributed religion? Because Christianity's diffusion has been rather clearly recorded since Jesus first set forth its tenets in the Roman province of Palestine, geographers can examine its diffusion by reconstructing patterns of communications, decision making, and migration.

The diffusion of Christianity from its point of origin in Palestine was facilitated by the Roman Empire (Figure 5–2). The followers of Jesus carried the religion to people in other locations along the empire's protected sea routes and excellent network of roads. Thus, people in the commercial and military settlements directly linked by the Roman communications network received the message first. When the Romans adopted Christianity as their official religion during the fourth century, the empire's official administrative organization assured further diffusion of the religion over a larger region.

Migration and missionary activity by Europeans since the year 1500 has extended Christianity to other regions of the world. Through permanent resettlement of Europeans, Christianity became the dominant religion in North and South America, Australia, and New Zealand. Christianity's dominance was further achieved by conversion of the indigenous populations as well as by intermarriage.

Branches. Christianity encompasses three major branches—Roman Catholic, Protestant, and Eastern Orthodox—each with a distinctive spatial distribution. Roman Catholics comprise approximately 57 percent of the world's Christians, Protestants approximately 25 percent, and Eastern Orthodox approximately 10 percent. The remainder includes Catholics other than Roman and followers of isolated African, Asian, and Latin American Christian churches.

Within Europe, Roman Catholicism is the predominant Christian branch in the southwest and east, Protestantism in the northwest, and Eastern Orthodoxy in the southeast and the Soviet Union (Figure 5–3). The regions of Roman Catholic and Protestant majorities frequently have sharp boundaries, which sometimes run through the middle of a country. For example, the Netherlands and Switzerland are divided into approximately equal percentages of Roman Catholics and Protestants, but the Roman Catholic populations are concentrated in the south of these countries and the Protestant populations in the north.

The most troublesome religious boundary within Western Europe is in Ireland. The Republic of Ireland is over 95 percent Roman Catholic, but the six

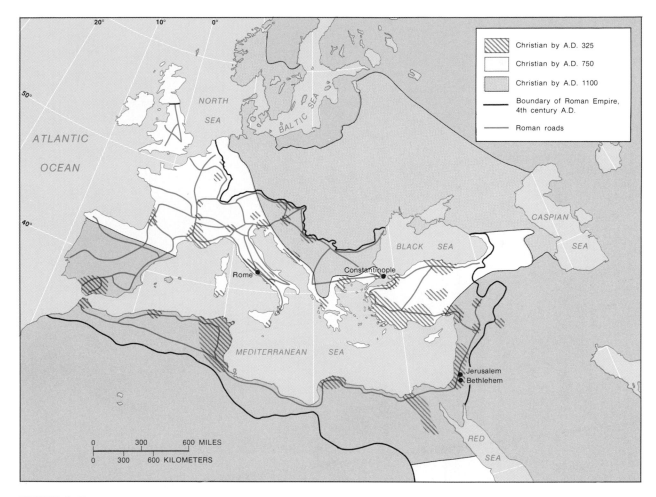

FIGURE 5–2
Christianity diffused from Palestine into Europe. This diffusion began during the Roman Empire but continued after its collapse. Much of southwestern Asia and northern Africa were once predominantly Christian but today are predominantly Muslim. Muslims also controlled portions of the Iberian peninsula (present-day Spain and Portugal) for more than 700 years.

northern counties of the island—part of the United Kingdom rather than the Republic—are divided between Roman Catholic and Protestant.

The entire island of Ireland (Eire) was an English colony for many centuries. The English owned most of the land in Ireland and did little to develop the island's economy. In 1801, Ireland was made part of the United Kingdom, though agitation for independence remained intense among the Irish. Following a series of bloody confrontations, Ireland became a self-governing dominion within the British Empire

in 1921. Complete independence was declared in 1937, and a republic was created in 1949.

Twenty-six of the twenty-nine districts in the Ulster region of Ireland were grouped into six counties and became known as Northern Ireland. The people of Northern Ireland voted to remain in the United Kingdom rather than join the Republic of Ireland because a majority were Protestant—as is the case elsewhere in the United Kingdom—while some 95 percent in the Irish Republic were Roman Catholic (Figure 5–4). Today,

FIGURE 5–3
Europe is divided into three major areas according to predominant Christian denominations. In the United Kingdom, Germany, and the Scandinavian countries, the majority of people adhere to a Protestant denomination, while in the Soviet Union and southeastern Europe, Eastern Orthodoxy is the most important branch of Christianity. Roman Catholicism predominates in southern, central, and southwestern Europe.

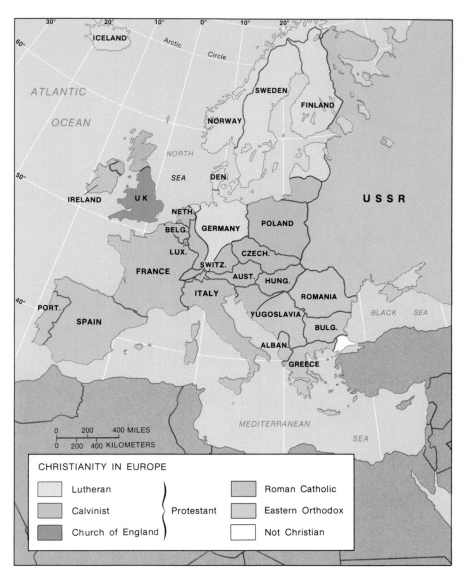

most Protestants in Northern Ireland still wish to remain part of the United Kingdom, while many Roman Catholics in Northern Ireland would prefer the six counties be unified with the Republic of Ireland.

Roman Catholics living in Northern Ireland have been victimized by discriminatory practices, such as exclusion from higher paying jobs and the better schools. A small number of Roman Catholics in both Northern Ireland and the Irish Republic have joined the Irish Republican Army (IRA), a militant organization dedicated to achieving Irish national unity by whatever means available, including violence. Simi-

larly, a scattering of Protestants have created extremist organizations to fight the IRA, including the Ulster Defense Force. While the overwhelming majority of Northern Ireland's citizens prefer peace, the Roman Catholic and Protestant extremists disrupt daily life. As long as some Protestants are firmly committed to remaining in the United Kingdom and some Roman Catholics are equally committed to union with the Republic of Ireland, peaceful settlement appears remote.

Branches in the Western Hemisphere. A fairly sharp boundary divides regions of Roman Catholic

FIGURE 5-4

Distribution of Protestants in Northern Ireland in 1911. Ireland, long a colony of England, became a self-governing dominion within the British Empire in 1921 and a completely independent country in 1937. However, 26 districts in northeastern Ireland were detached from the rest of Ireland and remained part of the United Kingdom. The Republic of Ireland is more than 95 percent Roman Catholic, while Northern Ireland has a Protestant majority. However, the boundary between Roman Catholics and Protestants is not precise, and Northern Ireland includes some communities that are predominantly Roman Catholic.

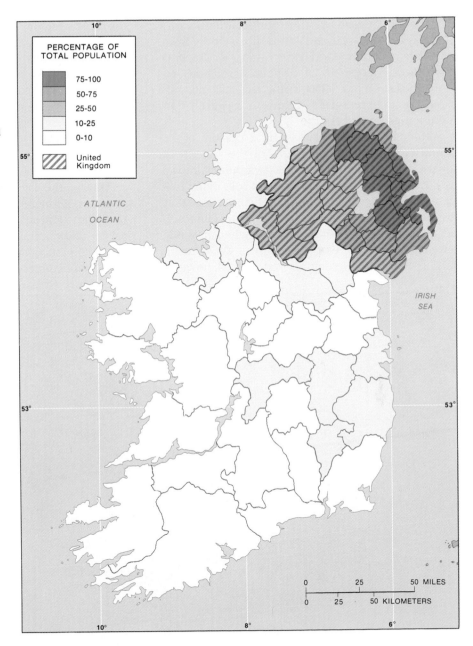

PERCENTAGE OF
TOTAL POPULATION

75-100
50-75
25-50
10-25
0-10

United
Kingdom

ATLANTIC
OCEAN

IRISH
SEA

and Protestant branches in the Western Hemisphere as well. Roman Catholics comprise 87 percent of the population in Latin America, compared to 35 percent in the United States and Canada. Latin America is predominantly Roman Catholic because its territories were colonized by the Spanish and Portuguese, who brought with them to the Western Hemisphere their religion as well as their languages. Canada and the United States have Protes-

tant majorities because their early colonists came primarily from Protestant England.

Different Protestant denominations have distinctive spatial distributions within the United States. The three largest Protestant denominations are Baptist, Methodist, and Lutheran. Baptists constitute over half the population in much of the southeastern United States, from Virginia to Texas. Lutherans are concentrated in the north central states, from

Wisconsin to Montana, and Methodists are primarily in states between 35° and 40° north latitude, from Delaware to Colorado (Figure 5–5). Geographers trace the development of distinctive religious regions in the United States to the fact that migrants came from different parts of Europe, especially during the nineteenth century.

Although constituting less than 2 percent of the country's population, members of the Church of Jesus Christ of Latter-Day Saints—popularly known as the Mormons—play a prominent role in the religious landscape of the United States because they are highly clustered in Utah and several counties in adjacent states. The Mormons' first settlement was at Fayette, New York. After the death of the founder, Joseph Smith, the group moved several times in search of religious freedom. Eventually, under the leadership of Brigham Young, they migrated to the then sparsely inhabited Salt Lake Valley.

Some regions and localities within the United States and Canada are predominantly Roman Catholic because of immigration from Roman Catholic countries. New England and large Midwestern cities such as Cleveland, Chicago, Detroit, and Milwaukee have concentrations of Catholics because of immigration from Ireland, Italy, and Eastern Europe, especially in the late-nineteenth and early-twentieth centuries. Immigration from Mexico and other Latin American countries has produced concentrations of Roman Catholics in the Southwest, while immigration from France has produced a predominantly Roman Catholic Québec.

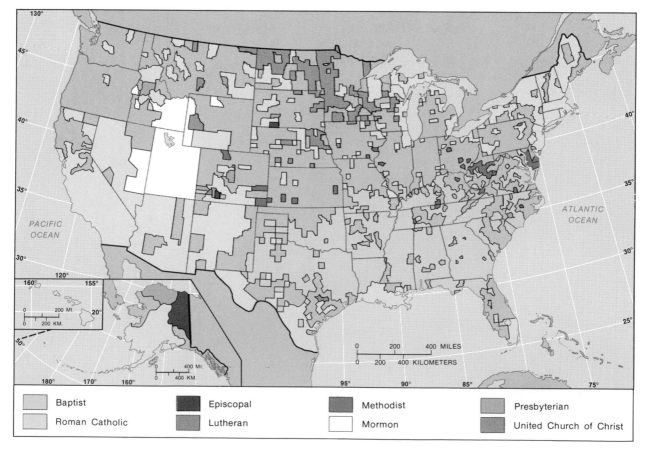

FIGURE 5–5

The shaded areas are counties in which more than 50 percent of church membership is concentrated in either Roman Catholicism or one Protestant denomination. Baptists are concentrated in the Southeast, Lutherans in the Upper Midwest, Mormons in Utah and contiguous states, and Roman Catholics in the Northeast and Southwest.

Eastern Orthodoxy. The Eastern Orthodox branch of Christianity comprises a collection of fourteen self-governing churches in Eastern Europe and the Middle East. Four of these churches—Constantinople, Alexandria, Antioch, and Jerusalem—trace their origins back to ancient times but today have a combined membership of only 4 million, or less than 3 percent of the total. The Russian church, established in the sixteenth century, includes over 40 percent of all Eastern Orthodox Christians. The other nine self-governing churches were established in the nineteenth or twentieth century. The largest of these more-recently established churches—the Romanian church—includes 20 percent of all Eastern Orthodox Christians; the Bulgarian, Greek, and Serbian churches have approximately 10 percent each; and the churches in Albania, Cyprus, Georgia (in the Soviet Union), Poland, and Sinai have a combined membership of fewer than 3 million, or a little more than 2 percent.

Minor branches. Several other Christian churches developed independently of the three main branches. Many of these Christian communities were isolated from others at an early point in the development of Christianity, partly because of differences in doctrine and partly because of Islamic control of intervening territory in Southwest Asia and North Africa. Two small Christian churches survive in Northeast Africa: the Coptic Church of Egypt and the Ethiopian Church. The Ethiopian Church, with perhaps 10 million adherents, split from the Egyptian Coptic Church in 1948, though it traces its roots back to the fourth century, when two shipwrecked Christians taken as slaves ultimately converted the Ethiopian king to Christianity.

The Armenian Church originated in Antioch, Syria, and was important in spreading Christianity to South and East Asia between the seventh and thirteenth centuries. The church's few contemporary adherents are concentrated in Lebanon or between the Black and Caspian seas in northeastern Turkey and the southwestern Soviet Union. Despite the small number of adherents, the Armenian Church, like other small sects, plays a significant role in regional conflicts. For example, Armenian Christians in the Soviet Union have fought with national government officials and with Shiite Muslims concerning control of predominantly Armenian territories within the Armenian and Azerbaijan republics (*see* Chapter 7). The Maronites are another example of a small Christian sect that plays a disproportionately prominent role in political unrest, because they are clustered in Lebanon.

Islam

Islam, the religion of approximately 1 billion people, is practiced predominantly in a region that extends from North Africa to Central Asia, from Morocco to Pakistan. The two most important concentrations of Muslims outside this region are in Bangladesh and Indonesia.

Origin and diffusion. Islam traces its origin from the same narrative as Judaism and Christianity. All three religions consider Adam to have been the first man and Abraham one of his descendents. According to legend, Abraham married Sarah, who did not bear children. Abraham then married Hagar, who bore a son, Ishmael. Sarah then had a child named Isaac, and she prevailed upon Abraham to have Hagar and Ishmael banished. Jews and Christians trace their history through Isaac, Muslims through Ishmael. After their banishment, Ishmael and Hagar wandered through the Arabian desert, eventually reaching Makkah (Mecca). Centuries later, one of Ishmael's descendents, Muhammad (570?–632) became the Prophet of Islam.

Muhammad's successors extended the region of Muslim control over an extensive area of Africa, Asia, and Europe. Within a century of Muhammad's death, armies conquered Palestine, the Persian Empire, and much of India, resulting in the conversion of many non-Arabs to Islam. To the west, the Muslims captured North Africa, crossed the Strait of Gibraltar, and retained part of Western Europe until 1492 (Figure 5–6). During the same century that the Christians regained all of Western Europe, Muslims took control of much of southeastern Europe and Turkey.

Missionaries, those who help diffuse a universalizing religion, carried Islam to portions of sub-Saharan Africa and Southeast Asia. Indonesia, the world's fifth most populous country, is predominantly Muslim, though it is spatially isolated from the Islamic heartland in Southwest Asia. Arab trad-

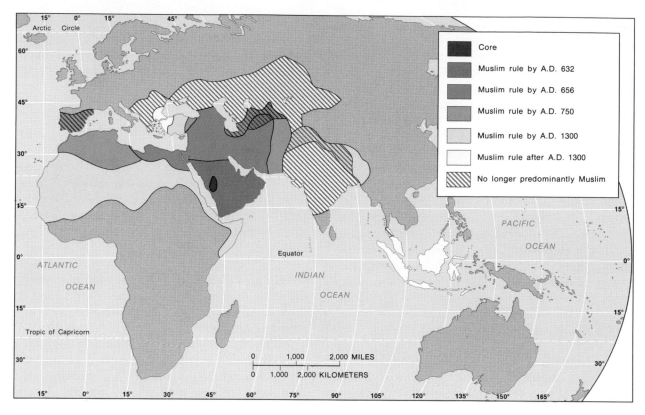

FIGURE 5–6
Islam diffused rapidly from its point of origin in present-day Saudi Arabia. Within 200 years, Islamic armies controlled much of North Africa, southwestern Europe, and southwestern Asia. Subsequently, Islam became the predominant religion as far east as Indonesia.

ers introduced Islam to the islands of Indonesia in the thirteenth century.

Branches. Islam encompasses two important branches: Sunni and Shiite. Sunnis, who comprise 83 percent of Muslims, constitute the largest branch in most Muslim countries. Only 16 percent of Muslims are Shiites, but they constitute the majority in Iran, Bahrain, and Iraq and form important minorities in Afghanistan, Kuwait, Lebanon, the United Arab Emirates, Yemen, and several other Middle Eastern countries.

Differences between Shiites and Sunnis go back to the earliest days of Islam. Muhammad neither had a surviving son nor any followers with the same leadership ability. His successor was Abu Bakr (573–634), an early supporter from Makkah who became known as caliph ("Successor of the Prophet"). The next two caliphs, Umar (634–644)

and Uthman (644–656), expanded the territory under Muslim control to Egypt and Persia.

Uthman was a member of a powerful Makkah clan that had initially opposed Muhammad, before its conversion to Islam. More zealous Muslims criticized Uthman for seeking compromises with Makkah's other formerly pagan families. Uthman's opponents found a leader in Ali (600?–661), a cousin and son-in-law of Muhammad and thus his nearest male heir. After Uthman was murdered in 656, Ali became caliph, but five years later he, too, was assassinated.

Shiites support the claims of Ali's descendants to the leadership of Islam. But Shiites disagree among themselves about the precise line of succession from Ali to modern times. Shiites acknowledge that the chain of leadership was broken, but they dispute the date and events surrounding the disruption. During the 1970s, both the Shah of Iran and the Ayatollah Khomeini claimed to be the divinely appointed interpreter of Islam for the Shiites. The allegiance of the Iranian Shiites switched from the Shah to the Ayatollah largely because the Ayatollah made a more convincing case that he was more faithfully adhering to the laws revealed by Muhammad in the Quran (Koran).

Buddhism

The founder of Buddhism, Siddhartha Gautama, was born in about 563 B.C. in northern India, about 160 kilometers (100 miles) from Vāranāsi (Benares). The son of a lord, he led a privileged existence sheltered from life's hardships. Gautama had a beautiful wife, palaces, and servants.

Origin and diffusion. According to Buddhist legend, Gautama's life changed after a series of four trips. He encountered a decrepit old man on the first trip, a disease-ridden man on the second trip, and a corpse on the third trip. After witnessing these scenes of pain and suffering, Gautama began to feel he could no longer enjoy his life of comfort and security. Then, on a fourth trip, Gautama met a monk who taught him about withdrawal from the world.

At age 29, Gautama left his palace and lived in a forest for the next six years, thinking and experimenting with forms of meditation. Gautama emerged as the Buddha, the awakened or enlightened one, and spent forty-five years preaching his views across India. In the process, he trained monks, established orders, and preached to the public.

Buddhism did not diffuse rapidly from its point of origin in northeastern India. The person most responsible for the spread of Buddhism was Asoka, emperor of the Magadhan Empire from about 273 to 232 B.C. The Magadhan Empire formed the nucleus of several powerful kingdoms in South Asia between the sixth century B.C. and the eighth century A.D. Around 257 B.C., at the height of the Magadhan Empire's power, Asoka became a Buddhist and thereafter attempted to put into practice Buddha's social principles.

A council organized by Asoka at Pataliputra decided to send missionaries to territories neighboring the Magadhan Empire. Emperor Asoka's son,

Mahinda, led a mission to the island of Ceylon (now Sri Lanka), where the king and his subjects were converted to Buddhism. As a result, Sri Lanka is the country that claims the longest continuous tradition of practicing Buddhism. Missions were also sent in the third century B.C. to the Kashmir, Himalayas, Burma (Myanmar), and elsewhere in India.

In the first century A.D., merchants along the trading routes from northeastern India introduced Buddhism to China. Many Chinese were receptive to the ideas brought by Buddhist missionaries, and Buddhist texts were translated into Chinese languages. Chinese rulers allowed their people to become Buddhist monks during the fourth century, and in the following centuries Buddhism turned into a genuinely Chinese religion. Buddhism further diffused from China to Korea in the fourth century and from Korea to Japan two centuries later. During the same era, Buddhism lost its original base of support in India (Figure 5–7).

Branches. Like the other two universalizing religions, Buddhism split into more than one branch, as followers disagreed on interpretation of the founder's statements. The two main branches are Mahayana and Theravada. Mahayana Buddhism predominates in Central and East Asia, including Tibet, Mongolia, China, Japan, and Vietnam, as well as Sri Lanka. Theravada Buddhism is most prevalent in Southeast Asia, especially Burma, Thailand, Laos, and Cambodia.

Theravadists believe that the practice of Buddhism is a full-time occupation. Therefore, to become a good Buddhist, one must renounce worldly goods and become a monk. Theravada means "the way of the elders," which indicates the Theravada Buddhists' belief that they are closer to Buddha's original approach.

Mahayanists claim that their approach to Buddhism can help more people because it is less demanding and all-encompassing. While the Theravadists emphasize Buddha's life of self-help and years of solitary introspection, the Mahayanists emphasize Buddha's later years of teaching and helping others. The Theravadists cite Buddha's wisdom, the Mahayanists his compassion. *Mahayana* is translated as "the bigger ferry" or "raft," and Mahayanists call Theravada Buddhism by the name *Hinayana,* or "the little raft."

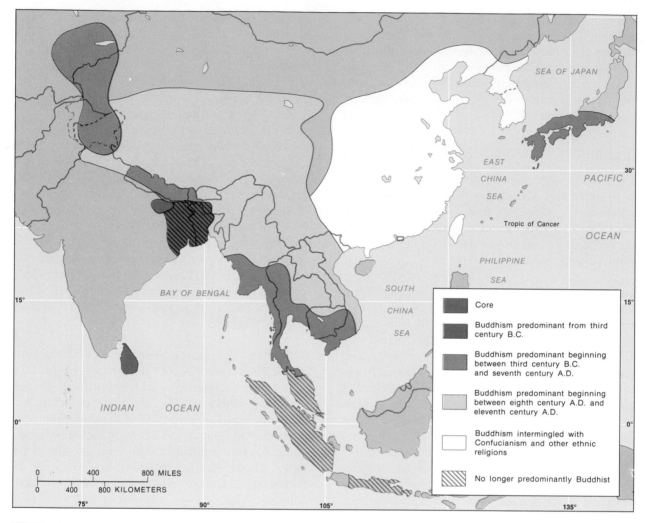

FIGURE 5–7
In contrast with the other large universalizing religions, Buddhism diffused slowly from its core in northeastern India. Buddhism was not well established in China until 800 years after Buddha's death.

Mahayana Buddhism is divided into at least six distinct denominations. Geographers cannot draw a map showing the spatial distribution of Mahayana denominations, such as the one for Protestant denominations within the United States (Figure 5–5), because the different groups do not occupy distinct geographical areas.

Buddhism currently has more than 300 million adherents, though an accurate count is impossible to obtain. Only a few people in Buddhist countries participate in Buddhist institutions, and religious functions are performed primarily by monks rather than by the general public. The number of Buddhists is also difficult to count, because Buddhism, though a universalizing religion, differs in significant respects from the Western concept of a formal religious system. Someone can be both a Buddhist and a believer in other Eastern religions, whereas Christianity and Islam both require exclusive adherence. Most Buddhists in China and Japan, in particular, believe in other religions simultaneously.

Hinduism

Unlike the three universalizing religions, Hinduism did not originate with a specific founder. The word *Hinduism* is simply a term for the religious system of India. The origins of Christianity, Islam, and Buddhism are recorded in the relatively recent past, whereas Hinduism existed prior to recorded history.

The earliest surviving Hindu documents were written in about 1500 B.C., though archaeological explorations have unearthed older objects relating to the religion. Aryan tribes from Central Asia invaded India around 1400 B.C., bringing with them Indo-European languages, as discussed in Chapter 4. In addition to their language, the Aryans brought their religion.

The Aryans first settled in the region now called the Punjab in northwestern India, later migrating east to the Ganges River Valley, as far as Bengal. Centuries of intermingling with the Dravidians already living in the area modified Aryan religious beliefs.

Hinduism adheres to the belief that more than one path exists to reach God. Because people start from different backgrounds and experiences, the appropriate form of worship for any two persons may not be the same. Hinduism neither has a central authority nor a single holy book, so that each believer selects suitable rituals. If one person practices Hinduism in a particular way, other Hindus will not think that the person has made a mistake or strayed from orthodox doctrine.

The type of Hinduism practiced will depend in part on a person's **caste,** which is the class or distinct hereditary order to which a Hindu is assigned according to religious law. A high-caste Brahman may practice a form of Hinduism based on knowledge of relatively obscure historical texts. At the other end of the caste system, an illiterate in a rural village may perform religious rituals without a highly developed set of written explanations for them.

Between these extremes, the average Hindu has allegiance to a particular god or concept within a broad range of possibilities. The three approaches that have the largest number of followers are probably Saivism, Vaishnavism, and Shaktism. Although a variety of deities and approaches are supported throughout India, some geographic concentration exists: Saivism and Shaktism in the north, Shaktism and Vaishnavism in the east, Vaishnavism in the west, and Saivism, along with some Vaishnavism, in the south. Holy places for Saivism and Vaishnavism, however, are dispersed throughout India.

Ethnic Oriental Religions

Important ethnic religions are practiced in East Asia, especially China and Japan. The coexistence of Buddhism with these ethnic religions in East Asia deviates from the Western concept of exclusive religious belief. Confucianism and Taoism are often distinguished as separate ethnic religions in China, but several hundred million Chinese consider themselves both Buddhist and Confucian, Taoist, or some other Chinese ethnic religion.

Confucianism. Both Confucianism and Taoism derive from historical figures. Confucius (551–479 B.C.) was a philosopher and administrator from the ancient Chinese province of Lu. He profoundly influenced the social and intellectual life of China through his sayings, which prescribed a series of ethical principles for the conduct of public life.

Confucius emphasized the importance of following traditions, fulfilling obligations, and treating others with sympathy and respect. The basic moral principle of Confucianism is the maintenance of good relationships with others by treating subordinates as you wish to be treated by your superiors.

Taosim. Lao-tzu (604?–?531 B.C.), a contemporary of Confucius, organized Taoism. He was also an administrator, but Lao-tzu's writings emphasized the mystical and magical aspects of life. According to Taoism, not everything is knowable; myths or legends develop to explain events, and the universe is not ultimately subject to rational analysis. A person's highest goal is to escape from day-to-day cares through adoption of a life of contemplation.

Buddhism, Confucianism, and Taoism (as well as various other ethnic religions) do not in reality compete with one another in China, because many Chinese accept the teachings of all three. Such commingling of diverse philosphies is not totally foreign to Americans. The tenets of Christianity or Judaism, the wisdom of the ancient Greek philosophers, and ideals of the Declaration of Independence can all be held dear without doing grave injustice to any. Different beliefs are applicable to different situations.

Shintoism. Japanese rulers recognized Shintoism as the state religion of Japan until after World War II. One of Shinto's traditional elements was the worship of the Japanese emperor as a god, a practice stopped only after the country's defeat in World War II. Shintoism therefore was as much a political cult as a religion, and in a cultural sense all Japanese are Shintoists. Many Japanese profess adherence to both Shintoism and Buddhism, especially in the rural central part of the country (Figure 5–8).

Judaism

Judaism plays a more substantial role in Western civilization than the number of adherents would suggest. First, two of the three universalizing religions—Christianity and Islam—find at least some roots in Judaism. Second, the spatial distribution of Jews differs from that of other ethnic religions. Third, Jews have been subjected to unique problems in their attempt to occupy a portion of the earth's surface.

Judaism is the oldest surviving religion, with the possible exception of Hinduism. As the first religion to espouse **monotheism,** or the belief in the existence of only one god, Judaism offered a sharp contrast to the practice of neighboring peoples, who worshipped a collection of idols. It developed as a local religion, in the territory of the Middle East called Canaan in the Bible, Palestine by the Romans, and the state of Israel since 1948. Since A.D. 70, most Jews have not lived in this territory but instead were forced to disperse throughout the world, a process known as a diaspora. Unique among ethnic religions, Judaism is practiced in many countries throughout the world as a result of a combination of forced and voluntary migration.

Exiled from the home of their ethnic religion, Jews have lived among other nationalities, retaining their separate religious practices but adopting various cultural characteristics of the host country, such as language. Judaism has remained an ethnic religion because its rituals were drawn from the physical environment of the Middle East. Holidays, for example, derive from the Mediterranean agricultural cycle of planting and harvest, and Jews have always prayed for their return to Jerusalem.

Today, more than two-thirds of the world's Jews live in three countries: about one-third in the United States and about one-sixth each in Israel and the Soviet Union. Jews constitute a majority in Is-

rael, where for the first time since the biblical era an independent state has had a Jewish majority.

In the United States, Jews are integrated into the mainstream, though they are heavily concentrated in the large cities, including one-third of U.S. Jews in the New York area alone. Jews in the Soviet Union, in contrast, are not as integrated and sometimes live in harsher conditions than other Soviets. For many years, their religious practices were strongly discouraged, and few were allowed to emigrate. The number of synagogues in the Soviet Union declined from about 400 in 1960 to 62 by 1975. In recent years, Soviet authorities have allowed more Jews to emigrate to the United States and Israel. But conditions for the remaining Jews have worsened, because some Soviet citizens blame them for the country's economic problems.

Historically, the Jews of many European countries were forced to live in a **ghetto,** originally meaning a neighborhood of a city set up by law to be inhabited only by Jews. The origin of the term *ghetto* is unknown, but it may have originated during the sixteenth century in Venice, Italy, as a reference to the city's foundry or metal-casting district, where Jews were forced to live. Ghettos were frequently surrounded by walls, and the gates were locked at night to prevent escape.

African Religions

Nearly 100 million Africans follow traditional religions, together known as **animism.** Animists believe that such inanimate objects as plants and stones or such natural events as thunderstorms and earthquakes have discrete spirits and conscious life. Relatively little is known about African religions because few holy books or other written documents have come down from ancestors. Religious rituals are passed from one generation to the next by word of mouth.

African traditional religions are often based on monotheistic concepts, though below the supreme god may exist a hierarchy of divinities. These divinities may be assistants to god or personifications of natural phenomena, such as trees or rivers.

The universalizing religions, especially Christianity and Islam, have sent missionaries to regions of Africa traditionally associated with animism. During

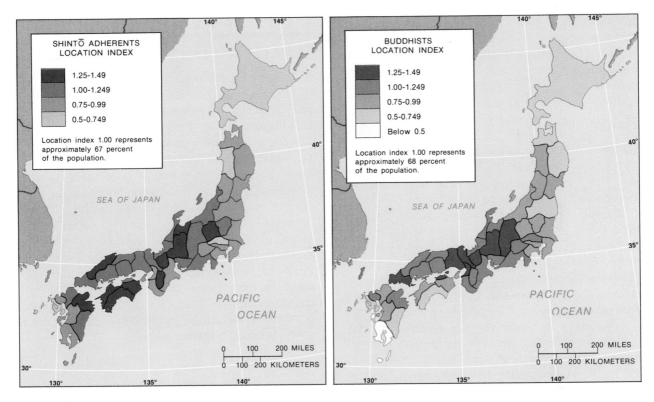

FIGURE 5–8
Adherents of Shintoism and Buddhism, the two most important religions in Japan, are not distributed uniformly throughout the country. For both religions, the percentage of adherents is greater in the southern and central portions of the country than in the north. In a number of areas, more than two-thirds of the people are Buddhists and more than two-thirds are Shintoists; this is possible because many people adhere simultaneously to both religions.

Japanese students have attached notes to a fence outside a Shinto temple. The notes contain prayers prepared by the students in hope of receiving good marks on their examinations.

the 1980s, the number of Africans classified as Christians increased 14 percent per year and the number classified as Muslims increased 9 percent, while the number of animists declined 3 percent per year.

Zoroastrianism

Zoroastrianism is an ethnic religion that has almost completely disappeared. Its decline, therefore, serves as a good example of territorial contraction, the opposite process to spatial diffusion.

The religion's founder, Zoroaster (628?–?551 B.C.), lived in the northeastern part of present-day Iran. The diffusion of Zoroastrianism began after a prince named Cyrus was converted. The prince, later called Cyrus the Great (600?–529 B.C.), was the first ruler to unify the entire territory of present-day Iran into a monarchy, then known as the Persian Empire.

For over a thousand years, Zoroastrianism was the ethnic religion of the Persian Empire. Many of the rituals and teachings were based on events in the empire. In particular, Zoroastrianism helped resolve the conflicts settled farmers experienced with the nomadic customs of their past, such as the sacrifice of useful cattle and the glorification of drinking and robbing. Zoroaster argued that the earth and its inhabitants were created by the forces of good to help fight evil spirits. People control their own destiny and can choose between the forces of good and evil spirits. But at death, people's souls are judged on the basis of performance on earth.

Zoroastrianism completely disappeared from Persia after the Islamic army conquered the country in the seventh century A.D. A few Zoroastrians fled from Persia to China and India, and about a quarter million remain today, for the most part in Bombay, India. Although many of the principles of Zoroastrianism became part of Judaism and Christianity, only a handful of modern religious scholars are aware of that connection.

Thus, we can divide the world into a collection of religious regions, with the predominant religion of each region distinctive. We can also trace the process of diffusion of each religion from a point of origin, for the most part in South and Southwest Asia. The next section demonstrates that the distinctive spatial distribution of religions produces different approaches to organizing the environment.

How Do Religions Organize Space?

Religions are influenced both by natural events and by features of the physical environment. Certain features of the landscape are incorporated into the philosophy and rituals of a religion and interpreted in a way that is consistent with the religion's values. Different religions incorporate environmental features differently; the selection of features is influenced by distinctive physical conditions on the portion of the earth's surface where the religion originated or diffused.

The physical environment influences the organization of religion in three basic ways. First, natural events are incorporated into the structure of the religion. Second, features of the physical environment are designated as holy. Third, religions organize portions of the earth's surface into administrative units to diffuse religious messages.

Incorporation of Natural Features

A variety of natural events may be incorporated into religious principles. These events range from the familiar and predictable to unexpected disasters.

Cosmogony. Individual religions have different concepts of the relationship between human beings and nature. These differences derive from distinctive concepts of **cosmogony,** which is a set of religious beliefs concerning the origin of the universe.

Religions that originated in Southwest Asia, such as Christianity and Islam, consider that God created the universe, including the physical environment and human beings. The earth was given by God to humanity in order to finish the task of creation. To serve God meant to develop nature more fully by cultivating the land, draining wetlands, clearing forests, and building new settlements. Such an attitude has led some people to advocate large-scale development of remaining wilderness in the name of serving God. To those who follow this approach, failure to make full and complete use of the earth's natural resources is considered a violation of biblical teachings.

Practitioners of animist religions do not attempt to transform the environment to the same extent.

For animists, a god's powers are regarded as mystical, and only a few people on earth can harness these powers for medical or other purposes. God can be placated, however, through prayer and sacrifice.

Christians are more likely to consider floods, droughts, and other natural disasters to be preventable and thus may take steps to overcome the problem by modifying the environment. Other religions may accept environmental catastrophes as normal and unavoidable, though even some Christians regard natural disasters as punishment for human sins.

Calendar. The most significant regular event in the natural environment incorporated into many religions is the calendar—the annual cycle of variation in climatic conditions. Knowledge of the calendar is critical to successful agriculture, whether for sedentary crop farmers or nomadic animal herders. The seasonal variations of temperature and precipitation help farmers select the appropriate times for planting and harvesting and make the best choice of crops.

A prominent feature of several religions is celebration of the seasons. Rituals are performed either to pray for favorable environmental conditions in the future or to give thanks for past success. The major religious events of the Bontok people of the Philippines, for example, revolve around the agricultural calendar. Sacred moments, known as *obaya,* include the times when the rice field is initially prepared, the seeds are planted, the seedlings are transplanted, the harvest is begun, and the harvest is complete.

Judaism is classified as an ethnic rather than a universalizing religion in part because the major holidays are generally based on events in the agricultural calendar of the religion's homeland in present-day Israel. In that eastern Mediterranean agricultural region, autumn is the season when grain crops are generally planted in the agricultural cycle and thus is a time of hope and worry over whether the winter's rainfall will be sufficient. The two holiest days in the Jewish calendar, Rosh Hashanah (New Year) and Yom Kippur (Day of Atonement) come in the autumn.

The other three most important holidays in Judaism relate even more closely to the agricultural cycle. Sukkot (Feast of Booths) celebrates the final gathering of fruits for the year, and prayers, especially for rain, are offered to bring success in the upcoming agricultural year. Another holiday, Passover, derived from traditional agricultural practices in which farmers offered God the first fruits of the new spring harvest and herders sacrificed a young animal at the time when sheep began lambing. The holiday also commemorates the biblical exodus from Egypt. The third important agricultural holiday, Shavuot (Feast of Weeks), comes at the end of the grain harvest.

Because universalizing religions are practiced in a variety of locations around the world, the role of the landscape in forming rituals is different than in ethnic religions. The main holidays in the Buddhist and Christian calendars relate to events in the founders' lives. All Buddhists observe Buddha's birth, Enlightenment, and death, though not all of them on the same days. For example, Japanese Buddhists celebrate Buddha's birth on April 8, his Enlightenment on December 8, and his death on February 15; Theravadist Buddhists observe all three events on the same day, usually in April.

Christians may relate Easter to the agricultural cycle, but that relationship differs among Christians, depending on where they live. In southern Europe, Easter is a joyous time of harvest, while in northern Europe it is a time of anxiety over planting new crops, as well as a celebration of spring's arrival after a harsh winter. Christians outside the Mediterranean countries lack a specific harvest holiday—which would be placed in the fall—though Thanksgiving in the United States and Canada has been endowed with Christian prayers to play that role. Holidays are even less related to events in the physical environment for Christians in the Southern Hemisphere, where Easter comes in the fall and Christmas comes in the summer.

Judaism and Islam utilize a lunar rather than a solar calendar. The moon has a mystical quality because of its variation from one day to the next. From its fullest phase, the moon becomes smaller and disappears altogether before reappearing and expanding to a full moon again. The appearance of the new moon marks the new month and is a holiday for both religions.

Because the lunar calendar does not correspond to the agricultural seasons, the Jewish calendar calls for insertion of an additional month every few years. Islam, however, retains a strict lunar calendar of approximately 350 days. As a result, observances arrive in different seasons from generation to generation. For example, during the holy month of Ramadan, Muslims fast during daylight every day and try to make a pilgrimage to the holy city of Mecca. Because Ramadan occurs at different times of the agricultural year in different generations, observances can interfere with critical agricultural activities. On the other hand, as a universalizing religion, Islam is practiced in a wide variety of climates. If holidays were fixed at the same time of the Middle

East's agricultural year, Muslims elsewhere in the world could still be inconvenienced.

A major holiday in some pagan religions was the **solstice,** the time when the sun is furthest from the equator and therefore appears to people on earth to stand still for a day. Stonehenge, a collection of rocks erected in southwestern England, probably by the Druids, is a prominent remnant of a pagan structure apparently aligned in consideration of the solstice.

If you stand at the western facade of the U.S. Capitol in Washington, D.C., at exactly noon on the summer solstice and look down Pennsylvania Ave-

FIGURE 5–9
Hindu holy places can be organized into a hierarchy. Some places are important to Hindus all over India and are visited frequently, while others have importance only to nearby residents. The map also shows that holy places for deities are somewhat clustered in different regions of the country: Shakti in the east, Vishnu in the west, and Siva in the north and south.

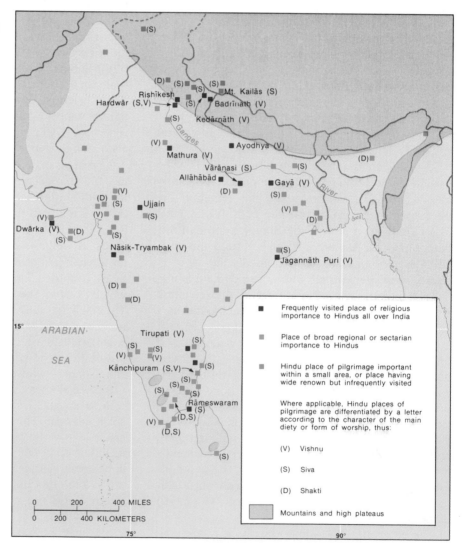

nue, the sun is directly over the center of the avenue. Similarly, at the winter solstice the sun is directly aligned with the view from the Capitol down Maryland Avenue. Will archaeologists of the distant future think we erected the Capitol Building and aligned the streets as a religious ritual? Did the planner of Washington, Pierre L'Enfant, create the pattern accidentally or deliberately but secretly?

Sacred Space

Religions may elevate particular elements in the landscape to a holy position. Two kinds of places may be endowed with holiness: distinctive physical environments, such as mountains, rivers, or stones, and objects on the landscape associated with the religion's origin or diffusion. These holy places are known as shrines and may be incorporated into the rituals of a particular religion.

Holy places in Hinduism. As an ethnic religion of India, Hinduism is closely tied to the Indian landscape. What kind of elements from the physical environment are generally selected as holy places in Hinduism? According to a survey conducted by the geographer Surinder Bhardwaj, the natural features most likely to rank among the holiest shrines in India are riverbanks or coastlines.

Hindus believe that they achieve purification by bathing in holy rivers. The Ganges is the holiest river in India, because it is supposed to spring forth from the hair of Siva, one of the main deities. Indians come from all over the country to Hardwār, the most popular location for bathing in the Ganges.

Hindu holy places are organized into a hierarchy. Some prominent shrines attract pilgrims from the entire country, while other shrines are important to a local community but are seldom visited by people from other regions. Because Hinduism has no central authority, the relative importance of shrines is established by tradition, not by doctrine (Figure 5–9). For example, many Hindus make long-distance pilgrimages to Mt. Kailas, located at the source of the Ganges in the Himalayas, holy because Siva lives there. At the same time, other mountains may attract only local pilgrims. Throughout India, local residents may consider a nearby mountain to be holy if Siva is thought to have visited it at one time.

Buddhist shrines. Several places are holy to Buddhists because they were the locations of important events in Buddha's life. The four most important places are concentrated in a small area of northeastern India (Figure 5–10). Most important is Lumbinī, where Buddha was born, around 563 B.C. Many sanctuaries and monuments were built there, but all are in ruins today.

The second great event in Buddha's life occurred at Bodh Gayā, 250 kilometers (150 miles) southeast of his birthplace, where Buddha reached perfect wisdom. A temple has stood near the site since the third century B.C., and part of the surrounding railing built in the first century A.D. still stands. Because Buddha reached perfect enlightenment while sitting under a bo tree, that tree has become a holy object as well. To honor Buddha, the bo tree has been diffused to other Buddhist countries, such as China and Japan.

The third important location is Deer Park in Sarnath, where Buddha gave his first sermon. The Dhamek pagoda at Sarnath, built in the third century B.C., is probably the oldest surviving structure in India. Nearby is an important library of Buddhist literature, including many works removed from Tibet when the Dalai Lama (Buddhist leader of Tibet) went into exile.

The fourth holy place is Kuśinagara, where Buddha died at age 80 and passed into Nirvana, a state of peaceful extinction. Temples built at the site are currently in ruin.

Four other sites in northeastern India are particularly sacred because they were the locations of Buddha's principal miracles. At Srāvastī, Buddha performed his greatest miracle. Before an assembled audience of competing religious leaders, Buddha created multiple images of himself and visited heaven. Srāvastī became an active center of Buddhism, and one of the most important monasteries was established there.

At the second miracle site, Sāmkāśya, Buddha is said to have ascended to heaven, preached to his mother, and returned to earth. The third site, Rajagrha, is holy because Buddha tamed a wild elephant there, and shortly after Buddha's death, it became the site of the first Buddhist Council. Vaiśālī, the fourth location, is the site of Buddha's announcement of his impending death and the second Bud-

Hindus believe that the Ganges River springs from the hair of Siva, one of the main deities. The river attracts pilgrims from all over India, who achieve purification by bathing in it. Bodies of the dead are washed with water from the Ganges before being cremated.

dhist Council. All four miracle sites are in ruins today, though excavation activity is under way.

Holy places in Islam. The holiest locations in Islam are cities rather than elements of the physical environment. The holiest city for Muslims is Makkah (Mecca), the birthplace of Muhammad. Now a city of more than a half million inhabitants, Makkah contains the holiest object in the Islamic landscape, the Ka'ba, a cubelike structure encased in silk, which

stands at the center of the Great Mosque, al-Haram al-Sharif (Figure 5–11). The Ka'ba, thought to have been built by Ishmael, contains his grave as well as that of his mother, Hagar. According to Muslim tradition, embedded in the Ka'ba is a black stone brought by Adam from the Garden of Eden.

The Ka'ba had been a religious shrine in Makkah for centuries before the origin of Islam. After Muhammad defeated the Makkahans, he captured the Ka'ba, cleared it of idols, and rededicated it to the

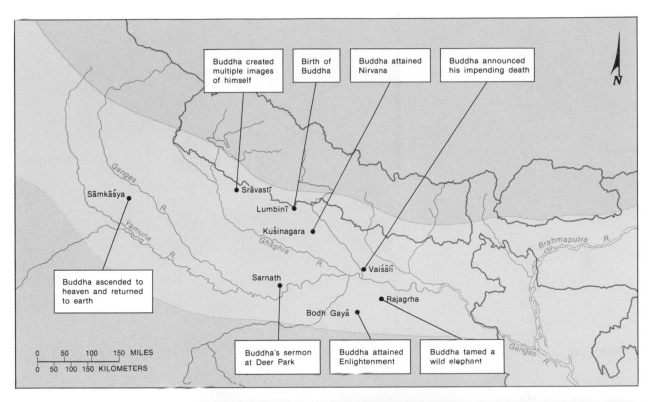

FIGURE 5–10

Holy places in Buddhism are clustered in northeastern India, because they were the locations of important events in Buddha's life. Most of the sites are in ruins today. At right, the Dhamek pagoda at Sarnath, built in the third century B.C., is near where Buddha gave his first sermon two hundred years earlier.

FIGURE 5–11
Makkah (Mecca), in Saudi Arabia, is the holiest city for Muslims, because Muhammad was born there. Thousands of Muslims make a pilgrimage to Makkah each year and gather at al-Haram al-Sharif, a mosque located in the center of the city. The black cubelike structure in the center of the mosque, called the Ka'ba, contains the graves of Ishmael and Hagar.

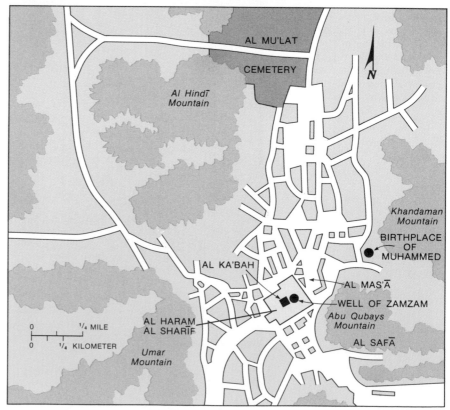

all-powerful Allah (God). The al-Haram mosque also contains the well of Zamzam, considered to have the same water source as that used by Ishmael and Hagar when they were wandering in the desert after their exile from Canaan.

The secondmost holy geographic location in Islam is Madīnah (Medina), approximately 350 kilometers (220 miles) north of Makkah. Muhammad received his first support from the people of Madīnah and became the city's chief administrator. Muhammad's tomb is at Madīnah, inside Islam's first mosque.

Pilgrimages. Religions that have a collection of important holy shrines may also have an organized procedure by which adherents from around the world visit them. Hindus and Muslims are especially encouraged to make **pilgrimages** to visit holy places in accordance with recommended itineraries, and Shintoists are encouraged to visit holy places in Japan. The concept is less important in Christianity and the other East Asian religions.

Every healthy male Muslim who has adequate financial resources is expected to undertake a pilgrimage to Mecca, known as a "hajj." The word *mecca* now has a general meaning in the English language—a place sought as a goal or a center of activity. Regardless of nationality and economic background, all pilgrims dress alike in plain white robes to emphasize common loyalty to Islam and the equality of people in the eyes of Allah. A precise set of rituals is practiced, culminating in a visit to the Ka'ba.

The *hajj* attracts one million Muslims to Makkah from countries other than Saudi Arabia. Roughly 40 percent each come from the Middle East and northern Africa, with the largest numbers from Nigeria, Turkey, and Yemen. Asian countries outside the Middle East are responsible for most of the remaining 20 percent; although Indonesia is the world's most populous Muslim country, it does not send the largest number of pilgrims to Mecca because of the relatively long distance they would have to travel.

Hindus consider a pilgrimage, known as a *tirtha,* to be an act of purification. Although not a substitute for meditation, the pilgrimage is an important act in achieving redemption. Particularly sacred places attract Hindus from all over India, despite the relatively remote locations of some, while less important shrines attract primarily local pilgrims.

The remoteness of holy places from population clusters once meant that making a pilgrimage required major commitments of time and money as well as the possibility of considerable physical hardship. But recent improvements in transportation have increased the accessibility of shrines. Hindus can now reach holy places in the Himalaya Mountains by bus or car, and Muslims from all over the world can reach Makkah by airplane.

Administration of Space

Followers of a particular religion in one location must be connected to adherents living in other communities, though the method of interaction varies among religions. Individual communities within some religions are highly **autonomous,** or self-sufficient, and interaction among communities is confined to little more than loose cooperation and shared ideas. At the other extreme, **hierarchical religions** have a well-defined geographic structure and organize territory into local administrative units. Other religions may combine spatial elements of both self-sufficient and hierarchical administrative systems.

Hierarchical religions. Roman Catholicism provides a good example of a hierarchical religion. Much of the earth's inhabited land is organized into an administrative structure, ultimately accountable to the pope in Rome. The basic unit of geographic organization in the Roman Catholic church is the **diocese.** The Roman Catholic world is divided into several thousand dioceses, each administered by a bishop, whose headquarters, called a see, is typically the largest city in the diocese. A diocese in turn is spatially divided into parishes, each headed by a priest. Several dioceses are grouped into a province headed by one of the bishops in the diocese, who is designated the archbishop. The archbishops are subordinate to the pope, who is also the Bishop of the Diocese of Rome (Figure 5–12).

The area and population of parishes and dioceses vary according to historical factors and the distribution of Roman Catholics across the earth's surface. In parts of southern Europe, population is relatively dense and concentrated, and the over-

FIGURE 5–12
The Roman Catholic church divides the United States into dioceses, each headed by a bishop. Dioceses in turn are combined into provinces, each headed by an archbishop. The archbishop of a province serves at the same time as a bishop of a diocese. The dioceses headed by archbishops are called archdioceses.

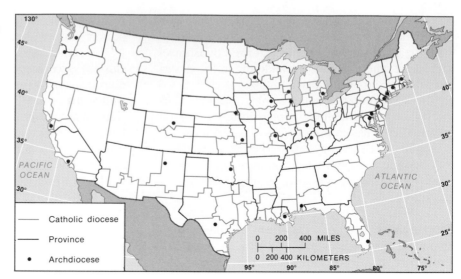

whelming majority of people are Roman Catholics. Consequently, the density of parishes is relatively high. The typical parish may comprise only a few square kilometers and fewer than a thousand people.

At the other extreme, parishes in Latin America may encompass 5,000 people and several hundred square kilometers. The more dispersed distribution in Latin America is attributable partly to a lower population density than in Europe. Because Roman Catholicism is a hierarchical religion, individual parishes must work closely with centrally located officials concerning rituals and procedures. If Latin America followed the European model of small parishes, many would be too remote for the priest to communicate with others in the hierarchy. The less-intensive network of Roman Catholic institutions in Latin America can also be explained in part by colonial traditions, since both the Portuguese and Spanish rulers discouraged development of parishes in Latin America.

The Roman Catholic church faces the need to adjust its territorial organization to coincide more closely with the changing distribution of the Roman Catholic population, which is increasing rapidly in some places, such as the U.S. Southwest and the suburbs of some large North American and European cities. Rapidly growing suburbs in Roman Catholic areas may have a relatively low density of parishes and dioceses compared to the population. New local administrative units can be created, though funds to provide the desired number of

churches, schools, and other religious structures may be scarce. Conversely, the Roman Catholic population is declining in other locations, such as inner cities and rural areas. Maintaining services in these areas is expensive, but the process of combining parishes and closing churches and schools is very difficult.

Among other Christian bodies, Mormons exercise strong organization of the landscape. The territory occupied by Mormons, primarily Utah and portions of surrounding states, is organized into wards, with populations of approximately 750 each. Several wards are combined into a stake of approximately 5,000 population. The highest authority in the church—the board and president—frequently redraws ward and stake boundaries in rapidly growing areas to reflect the ideal population standards.

Locally autonomous religions. Among the three large universalizing religions, Islam provides the most local autonomy. Like other locally autonomous religions, Islam has neither a religious hierarchy nor a formal territorial organization. A mosque is a place for public ceremony and a leader calls the faithful to prayer, but every Muslim male is expected to participate equally in the rituals and is encouraged to pray privately.

In the absence of a hierarchy, the only formal organization of territory in Islam is through the coincidence of religious territory with secular states. Governments in some predominantly Islamic countries include administrators of Islamic institutions as part of the regular bureaucracy. These administrators interpret Islamic law and run welfare programs.

Strong unity within the Islamic world is maintained by a relatively high degree of communications and migration, such as the pilgrimage to Makkah. In addition, uniformity is fostered by Islamic doctrine, which offers more explicit commands than other religions.

Judaism and Hinduism also have no centralized structure of religious control. To conduct a full service, Judaism merely requires the presence of ten adult males. (Females count in some Jewish communities.) Hinduism is even more autonomous, because worship is usually done alone or with others in the household. Hindus share ideas primarily through undertaking pilgrimages and reading traditional writings.

Protestant Christian denominations vary in geographic structure from extremely autonomous to somewhat hierarchical. Extremely autonomous denominations such as Baptists, Quakers, and Unitarians are organized into self-governing congregations. Each congregation establishes the precise form of worship and selects the leadership.

Episcopalians, Lutherans, and most Methodists, have hierarchical structures somewhat comparable to the Roman Catholic church. Presbyterian churches represent an intermediate degree of autonomy: individual churches are united in a presbytery, several of which in turn are governed by a synod, with a general assembly as ultimate authority over all churches. Each Presbyterian church is governed by an elected board of directors with lay members.

Religions adapt to conditions in the physical environment in different ways, organizing space in a manner consistent with the particular doctrine. Religions also modify the landscape, as the next section shows.

KEY ISSUE

What Is the Impact of Religion on the Landscape?

All of the major religions have sacred structures, but the functions of the buildings influence the arrangement of the structures across the landscape. Some religions require a relatively large number of elabo-

rate structures, while others have more modest needs.

Sacred Structures

Christian churches. The Christian landscape is dominated by the high density of churches. The church building plays a more critical role in Christianity than in other religions, in part because the structure is an expression of religious principles, an environment in the image of God. The church is also more prominent in Christianity because, unlike other religions, attendance at a collective service of worship is considered extremely important.

The prominence of churches on the landscape also stems from their style of construction and location. Traditionally, the church was the largest and tallest building in the community and was placed at an important square or other prominent location. Although such characteristics may no longer apply in large cities, they are frequently still true for small towns and neighborhoods within cities.

Underlying the large number and size of Christian churches is their considerable expense. Because of the importance of a place of worship, Christians have contributed much wealth to the construction and maintenance of churches. A wealthier congregation may build an elaborate structure designed by an architect to provide an environment compatible with the religious doctrine and ritual. Over the centuries, the most prominent architects have been commissioned to create religious structures, such as those designed by Christopher Wren in London during the late seventeenth century.

Early churches were modeled after Roman buildings for public assembly, known as basilicas. The basilica was a rectangular building divided by two rows of columns that formed a central nave (hall) and two side aisles. At the western end of the church stood a semicircular apse, in front of which was the altar where the service was conducted by the priest. Later, the apse was placed on the eastern wall. The raised altar, symbolizing the hill of Calvary, facilitated the reenactment at every Roman Catholic service of Christ's sacrifice. The Gothic churches built between the twelfth and fourteenth centuries were designed in the form of the Latin cross.

Because Christianity became the religion with the most adherents and eventually split into many denominations, no single style of church construction dominated. Churches reflect both the cultural values of the denomination and the region's architectural heritage. Eastern Orthodox churches, for example, follow an architectural style that developed in the Byzantine Empire during the fifth century A.D. Byzantine-style Eastern Orthodox churches tend to be highly ornate, topped by prominent domes.

Many Protestant churches in North America, on the other hand, are simple and largely lacking in ornamentation. This austerity is a reflection of the Protestant conception of a church as an assembly hall for the congregation. Availability of building materials also influences church appearance. In the United States, early churches were most frequently of wood in the Northeast, brick in the Southeast, and adobe in the Southwest. Stucco and stone predominated in Latin America. This diversity reflected differences in the most common building materials found by early settlers.

Places of worship in other religions. Other major religions have less of a need than Christianity for a sanctified place of worship. Muslims consider the mosque as a space for community assembly. In contrast to a church, however, a mosque is not viewed as a sanctified place but rather as a location for the community to gather together for worship. Mosques are found primarily in larger cities of the Muslim world. In rural villages simple structures may serve as places of prayer.

The mosque is organized around a central courtyard—traditionally open air, although it may be enclosed in harsher climates. The pulpit is placed at the end of the courtyard facing Makkah, the direction to which all Muslims pray. Surrounding the courtyard is a cloister used for schools and nonreligious activities. A distinctive feature of the mosque is the minaret, a tower where a man known as a muzzan summons people to worship.

Sacred structures for collective worship are relatively unimportant in Oriental religions. Instead, important religious functions are more likely to take place at home within the family. Temples are built to house shrines for particular gods rather than for congregational worship.

The Hindu temple serves as a home to one or more gods, though a particular god may have more than one temple. Wealthy persons or groups usually maintain the local temples. The size and frequency of temples are determined by local preferences and commitment of resources rather than by standards imposed by religious doctrine.

The typical Hindu temple contains a small, dimly lit interior room where a symbolic artifact or some other image of the god rests. The remainder of the temple may be devoted to space for ritual processions. Because congregational worship is not a part of Hinduism, the temple does not need a large closed interior space filled with seats. The site of the temple, usually demarcated by a wall, may also contain a structure for a caretaker and a pool for ritual baths.

The pagoda is a prominent and visually attractive element of the Buddhist and Shintoist landscapes. Frequently elaborate and delicate in appearance, pagodas typically include tall, many-sided towers arranged in a series of tiers, balconies, and slanting roofs.

Pagodas contain relics thought by Buddhists to be a portion of Buddha's body or clothing. After Buddha's death, his followers hastened to obtain these relics. As part of the process of diffusing the religion, Buddhists carried these relics to other countries and built pagodas for them. Pagodas are not designed for congregational worship. Individual prayer or meditation is more likely to be undertaken at an adjacent temple, a remote monastery, or home.

Arrangement of Land

Burial practices. The impact of religion is clearly seen in the arrangement of human activities on the landscape at several scales, from relatively small parcels of land to entire communities. A prominent example of religious arrangement of land at a relatively small scale is burial practices. Differences in practices to shelter the dead may arise because of a combination of environmental characteristics and religious beliefs. Climate and topography may influence the choice, though within a framework of acceptable alternatives established by religious doctrine.

Christians and Muslims usually bury their dead in a specially designated area called a cemetery. The Christian burial practice can be traced to the origin of the religion. Underground passages, known as catacombs, were used to bury early Christians in ancient Rome, as well as to provide protection for the faithful at a time when the religion was still illegal.

After the religion was legalized, Christians buried their dead in the yard around the church. As these burial places became overcrowded, separate burial grounds had to be established outside the city walls. Public health and sanitation considerations in the nineteenth century led to the public management of many cemeteries. Some cemeteries, however, are still operated by religious organizations.

Burial spaces can occupy a significant percentage of land in a community, aggravating the pressures of competing uses for scarce space. In congested urban ares, Christians and Muslims have traditionally used cemeteries as public parks. Before the widespread development of specially designed parks in the nineteenth century, cemeteries were frequently the only green space in rapidly growing cities. Cemeteries are still used as parks in Muslim countries, where the idea faces less opposition than in Christian societies.

Traditional burial practices in China have put pressure on agricultural land. By burying dead relatives on their land, rural residents removed as much as 10 percent of the land from productive agriculture. The government of China has ordered the practice discontinued, even encouraging farmers to plow over old burial mounds.

Hindus generally practice cremation rather than burial. The body is washed with water from the Ganges River and then burned at a slow fire on a funeral pyre. Burial is reserved for children, ascetics, and people with certain diseases. Cremation is considered an act of purification, though it tends to strain India's wood supply.

Zoroastrians expose the body to scavenging birds and animals. Exposure is considered necessary to strip away unclean portions of the body. Tibetan Buddhists also practice exposure for some dead, with cremation reserved for the most exalted priests.

Religious settlements. Religion also has an impact on the landscape at the scale of the entire settlement, not just such individual objects as churches and cemeteries that are located in the community. Although most settlements serve various economic purposes, some are established primarily for religious reasons.

The movement to construct planned religious utopian settlements in the United States began with the founding of Bethlehem, Pennsylvania, in 1741 by the Moravians, who had emigrated from present-day Czechoslovakia. The culmination of the utopian movement in the United States was the construction of Salt Lake City by the Mormons beginning in 1848. The layout of Salt Lake City is based on a plan of the city of Zion given to the church elders in 1833 by the Mormon prophet Joseph Smith. The city has a regular grid pattern, unusually broad boulevards, and church-related buildings situated at strategic points.

While most colonial settlements were not planned primarily for religious purposes, religious principles affected many of the designs. Most of the early New England settlers were members of a Puritan Protestant denomination. The Puritans generally migrated together from England and preferred to live near each other in clustered settlements rather than on dispersed, isolated farms. In recognition of the importance of religion, the New England settlers placed the church at the most prominent location in the center of the settlement, usually adjacent to a public open space, known as a common.

Toponyms. Roman Catholic settlers frequently gave religious names to their settlements in the New World. A relatively high percentage of place names in Québec and the U.S. Southwest have a religious derivation as a result of initial settlement primarily by Roman Catholic immigrants. Québec's boundaries with Ontario and the United States clearly illustrate the difference between toponyms selected by Roman Catholic and Protestant settlers. Religious place names are common in Québec but rare in the two neighbors (Figure 5–13).

The distribution of religious elements on the landscape reflects the importance of religion in people's values. The impact of Christianity on the landscape is particularly profound, for many Christians believe their life on earth ought to be spent in service to God. As the next section demonstrates, however, the attempt by adherents of one religion to organize the earth's surface can conflict with the spatial expression of other religious or nonreligious ideas.

FIGURE 5–13
A map of toponyms near Québec's boundaries with Ontario and New York State shows the impact of religion on the landscape. In Québec, a province with a predominantly Roman Catholic population, a large number of settlements are named for saints whereas relatively few religious toponyms are found in predominantly Protestant Ontario and New York.

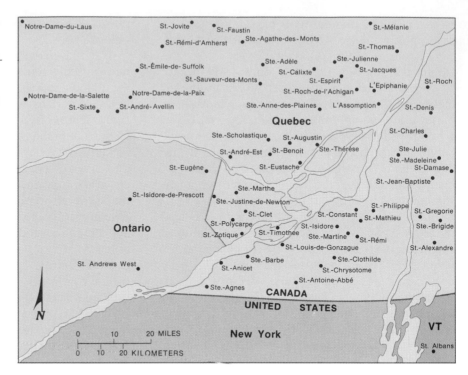

KEY ISSUE

What Territorial Conflicts Arise because of Religion?

People adhering to one religion frequently fight with supporters of other religions for control of the earth's surface. These struggles reflect the importance placed on religious beliefs. A group of people strongly committed to the belief that theirs is the one correct religious view may feel compelled to expand the area of the earth's surface containing supporters of that religion—even at the expense of other religions. In addition, organized religion has been in conflict with nonreligious ideas in the twentieth century. We can cite examples of each type of conflict.

Religion and Social Change

The role of religion in organizing the earth's surface has been reduced in recent years in some societies by political and economic changes. Islam is particularly affected by perceptions of conflicting values between religion and the modernization of the economy. Hinduism has also been forced to react to

new nonreligious ideas from the West. Christianity and Buddhism have both faced challenges from communist governments that reduce the importance of religion in society.

Hinduism and the West. Hinduism has faced a strong challenge since the nineteenth century, when the British colonial administration brought unfamiliar social and moral concepts to India. The most vulnerable aspect of the Hindu religion was its rigid caste system. According to Hinduism, because everyone is different, it is natural that each individual should belong to a particular position in the social order, known as a caste.

The caste system apparently originated around 1500 B.C., when Aryans invaded India. The Aryans were divided into four groups: Brahman, Kshatriya, Vaisya, and Shudra. Considerable differences in social and economic positions developed among these four castes. The Brahmans were the priests and top administrators, the Kshatriyas the warriors, and the Vaisyas the merchants. The Shudras, agricultural workers and artisans, occupied a lower status than the other three castes. Over the centuries, the original castes split into thousands of subcastes.

Below the four castes were the so-called untouchables, or outcasts, who did the work considered too dirty for other castes. The untouchables theoretically were descended from the people living in India prior to the Aryan conquest. Until recently, social relations among the five groups were limited, and the rights of non-Brahmans, especially untouchables, were restricted.

British administrators and Christian missionaries pointed out the shortcomings of the caste system, such as neglect of the untouchables' health and economic problems. The rigid caste system has been considerably relaxed in recent years. The Indian government legally abolished the untouchable caste, and the people formerly in that caste now have equal rights with other Indians.

Although Hinduism suffered attacks by both British values and Islamic fervor in the twentieth century, the religion came to be the greatest source of national unity in India. In the modern state of India, with hundreds of languages and ethnic groups, Hinduism has become the cultural trait shared by the largest percentage of the population.

Religion and Communism

Organized religion has been challenged in the twentieth century by the rise of communism in Eastern Europe and Asia. The two religions most affected are the Eastern Orthodox branch of Christianity and Buddhism.

Eastern Orthodoxy and the Soviet Union. The largest concentration of Eastern Orthodox Christians is in the Soviet Union. In 1721, Czar Peter the Great made the Russian Orthodox Church a part of the Russian government. The patriarch of the Russian Orthodox Church was replaced by a 12-member committee, known as the Holy Synod, nominated by the czar.

After the Russian Revolution in 1917, the government instituted a new policy concerning the Eastern Orthodox Church. The Soviet leaders have generally pursued antireligious programs, though active persecution has not always resulted.

Karl Marx called religion the opiate of the masses (a drug that made them passive), a view shared by Russian revolutionary V. I. Lenin and other early communist leaders. Because Marxism became the

official doctrine of the Soviet Union, religious doctrine became seen as a potential threat to the success of the revolution. Although people's religious beliefs could not be destroyed overnight, the role of organized religion could be reduced.

In 1918, the Soviet government eliminated the official church-state connection created by Peter the Great. All church buildings and property were nationalized and could be used only with permission of the local government. The Orthodox religion continued to have adherents in the Soviet Union, especially among the elderly, but younger people generally had little contact with the church beyond attending a service perhaps once a year. Because religious organizations were prevented from carrying on active social and cultural work, the impact of religion on daily activities became limited.

Yet despite government policies, the Soviet Union recently has witnessed a revival of religious sentiment thought to be irrevocably buried. The multiplicity of religious groups has been one of the elements underlying the unrest in the country (*see* Chapter 7).

Buddhism. The assault by communist governments in Asia against organized religion has crippled Buddhism in several countries. The problem has been particularly acute for Tibet, which has been controlled by the People's Republic of China since 1950.

Daily life in Tibet was traditionally dominated by Buddhist rites. By the 1950s, a quarter of all males were monks, and polygamy was encouraged among other males in order to produce enough children. At the death of the spiritual and political leader, the Dalai Lama, Tibetan Buddhists believe that his spirit enters the body of a child. Traditionally, a group of priests identifies the child who has acquired the spirit of the Dalai Lama and trains him to assume leadership at age eighteen. The fourteenth Dalai Lama was born in 1935 and identified as the future leader when he was only two years old.

After taking control of Tibet in 1950, the Chinese communists sought to reduce the domination of Buddhist monks in the country's daily life. The Chinese closed monasteries and temples and destroyed religious artifacts and scriptures. The government, previously dominated by Buddhist monks, was converted to a Chinese province. Following an unsuccessful rebellion against the Chinese in 1959, tens of thousands of Tibetans were executed or imprisoned and over 100,000 fled the country, including the Dalai Lama, who has lived in exile in India since then.

In recent years, the Chinese have built new roads, power plants, hospitals, and schools to help raise the low standard of living in Tibet. Farmers have been moved to agricultural communes and taught new techniques to increase productivity. Some monasteries have been rebuilt, but no new monks are being trained. When the current generation of priests dies, many Buddhist traditions probably will be lost forever in Tibet.

In Southeast Asia, Buddhists were hurt by the long war between the French and then the Americans on one side and communist organizations on the other. Neither antagonist was particularly sympathetic to the interests of Buddhists. On a number of occasions Buddhist monks set themselves on fire to protest the policy of the government of South Vietnam. United States air bombing in Laos and Cambodia (Kampuchea) destroyed many Buddhist shrines, while others were vandalized by the Vietnamese and the Khmer Rouge (Cambodia communists). The current communist governments in Southeast Asia have discouraged religious activities and permitted monuments to decay, most notably the Angkor Wat complex in Cambodia, considered one of the world's most important and beautiful Buddhist structures.

Wars between Religious Groups

Muslims and Hindus. Muslims have long fought with Hindus for control of territory, especially in South Asia. Mahmud, the Muslim king of Ghazni (modern-day Afghanistan), led raids on the Punjab area of northern India around A.D. 1000, originally to acquire treasure from Hindu temples. But the raids turned into a religious war. The Punjab became part of the Ghazni kingdom, with a governor at Lahore.

The fragmented Hindu kingdoms were unable to stop a second set of invasions by Muslims, who in the thirteenth century seized most of northern India as far east as Bengal. The population consisted primarily of Hindus and Buddhists, but the number of Muslims grew within a few generations as a result of intermarriage and migration from the west.

When the British took over India in the early nineteenth century, a three-way struggle for control

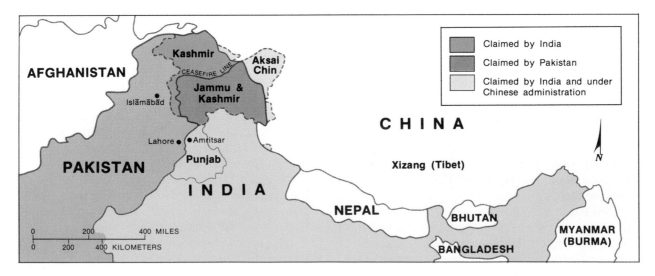

FIGURE 5–14
India and Pakistan dispute the location of their border. India claims the northeastern part of Pakistan, known as the Kashmir. India also accuses Pakistan of encouraging unrest in the Indian state of Jammu and Kashmir, where a majority of the people are Muslims. At the same time, India and China disagree on the location of their border in the Himalaya Mountains.

began, with the Hindus and Muslims fighting each other as well as the British rulers. Muslims believed that the British discriminated more against them than against the Hindus.

After the British granted independence to the region following World War II, Hindus and Muslims fought over the organization of the newly independent region. When Mahatma Gandhi, the leading Hindu advocate of nonviolence and reconciliation with Muslims, was assassinated in 1948, the possibility of creating one country in which Muslims and Hindus lived together peacefully ended. Instead, the predominantly Muslim portions of South Asia became Pakistan and the Hindu portions became India. Millions of Muslims living on the Indian side of the boundaries after partition were forcibly uprooted and marched across the border to Pakistan, with similar movements of Hindus into India.

Pakistan and India never agreed on the location of the boundary line separating the two countries, especially in the northern region, known as Kashmir. The original partition gave India two-thirds of Kashmir even though a majority of the people were Muslims. In recent years, Muslims on the Indian side of Kashmir have begun a guerrilla war to secure independence. India blames Pakistan for the unrest and vows to retain its portion of Kashmir; Pakistan argues that Kashmiris on both sides of the border should choose their own future in a vote, confident that the majority Muslim population would break away from India (Figure 5–14).

India's religious unrest is further complicated by the presence of 15 million Sikhs, whose religion combines elements of Islam and Hinduism. Sikhs have long resented that when India was partitioned, they were not given their own independent country. Although they constitute only 2 percent of India's total population, Sikhs comprise a majority in the Indian state of Punjab, on the border with Pakistan and south of Kashmir. Sikh extremists have fought for more control over the Punjab and even complete independence from India. The Indian army fueled the independence movement in 1984 when it attacked Sikh extremists hiding in the Golden Temple of Amritsar, the religion's holiest shrine.

Hindus and Buddhists. Sri Lanka, an island country in the Indian Ocean, has been torn by fighting between the Sinhalese—Buddhists who speak an

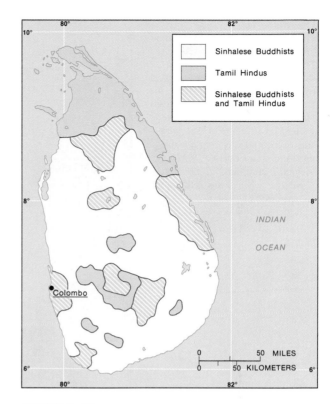

FIGURE 5–15
Sri Lanka is inhabited by two principal groups of people: Tamils and Sinhalese. The Tamils are Hindus who speak a Dravidian language, while the Sinhalese are Buddhists who speak an Indo-European language.

Indo-European language—and the Tamils—Hindus who speak a Dravidian language.

Violence has erupted periodically between the two groups for hundreds of years. The Tamils, who comprise about 20 percent of the island's population, have repeatedly felt that they have been discriminated against by the Sinhalese majority, which controls the government, military, and most of the businesses (Figure 5–15).

India, which is separated from Sri Lanka by only the 80-kilometer (50-mile) Palk Strait, supports the Tamils' position and sent troops to the island for several years during the late 1980s. Indians, like the Tamils, are predominantly Hindus, and the Tamil language is spoken by approximately 60 million Indians. Many of the Tamil-speaking Hindus living in Sri Lanka were born in India and do not enjoy the protection of civil rights in Sri Lanka. Some Indian

FIGURE 5–16
The Old City of Jerusalem contains the holy shrines of three religions. The flattened hill on the eastern side of the Old City is the site of two structures holy to Muslims, the Dome of the Rock and the Al-Aqsa Mosque, built on or near the site of ancient Jewish temples. The west side of the Old City contains the most important Christian shrines, including the Church of the Holy Sepulchre, where Jesus is thought to be buried.

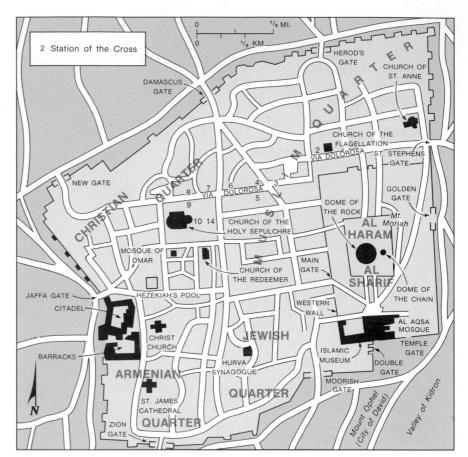

born Tamils, however, have been permitted to become citizens of Sri Lanka.

Religious Wars in the Middle East

Christians and Muslims historically have fought for control of Europe and the Middle East. Why have these two groups fought so intensely to occupy the same portion of the earth's surface, despite both religions tracing their origins to Abraham? To some extent, the hostility between Muslims and Christians stems from the similarity of their heritage. Islam regards Christianity as defective because it violated the principle of strict monotheism by glorifying Jesus. Muhammad accepted moral principles found in the Christian Bible but asserted that more explicit rules of conduct were needed. Christians, on the other hand, have often portrayed Muslims as immoral and backward.

Beginning in the seventh century, Muslim armies captured most of North Africa and Southwest Asia and converted most of the people from Christianity to Islam. Constantinople (present-day Istanbul), the most important city for the Eastern Orthodox Christians, was captured by the Muslims in 1453. Muslims invaded Europe at Gibraltar in 710, crossed the Pyrenees a few years later, and for a time occupied much of present-day France. Their initial advance was halted by a defeat at the hands of the Franks, led by Charles Martel, at Tours and Poitiers, France, in 732. Muslims made further gains in Europe in subsequent years and controlled portions of present-day Spain until 1492, but Martel's victory ensured that Christianity would be Europe's dominant religion.

Battle for the Holy Land. Conflict between Muslims and Christians continued in the Middle East territory known since the time of the Roman Empire as Palestine. Competing claims by religious groups frequently have led to battles for territorial control of Palestine, which is considered holy by Muslims, Christians, and Jews.

As an ethnic religion, Judaism makes a special claim to Palestine. The major events in the Hebrew Bible took place there, and the religion's customs and rituals acquired meaning from the agricultural life of the ancient Hebrew tribe. Jews, however, have often been dispersed from Palestine by conquering nations and restricted or prohibited altogether from visiting holy places.

Muslims captured Palestine and the holy city of Jerusalem in the seventh century and controlled the territory with only minor interruption until 1917.

Muslims regard Jerusalem as their third holiest city, after Makkah and Madīnah. The most important Muslim structure in Jerusalem is the Dome of the Rock, built in 691. The rock to which the name of the mosque refers was thought to be the altar both on which Abraham prepared to sacrifice Isaac and on which Muhammad ascended to heaven. Immediately to the south is the al-Aqsa mosque, built on the site of the two ancient Jewish temples. The only remaining portion of the Jewish Second Temple, which was destroyed by the Romans in A.D. 70, is the Western Wall, called the Wailing Wall by Christians and Muslims, because for many years Jews were allowed to visit the site only once a year to lament the destruction of the temple (Figure 5–16).

Jews pray in front of the Western Wall in Jerusalem. The wall is the only remaining portion of the Second Temple, which was destroyed in A.D. 70. For hundreds of years, Jews were allowed to visit the site only once a year. Jews are still restricted from visiting the rest of the temple site because it is occupied by structures holy to Muslims, including the Dome of the Rock, where Muhammad is thought to have ascended to heaven.

FIGURE 5–17

A—Palestine under British control, between 1922 and 1948. **B**—The 1947 United Nations plan to partition Palestine into Jewish and Arab states. The original boundaries of Israel encompassed the Jewish portion of the U.N. partition. Jerusalem was intended to be an international city, run by the United Nations. **C**—Israel after the 1948–49 war. The day after Israel declared its independence, several neighboring states began a war, which ended in an armistice. Israel's borders were extended to include the western suburbs of Jerusalem. Jordan gained control of east Jerusalem, including the old city. **D**—The Middle East since the 1967 war. Israel captured the Golan Heights from Syria, the West Bank from Jordan, and the Sinai Peninsula and Gaza Strip from Egypt. Israel also gained control of the entire city of Jerusalem. Israel returned the Sinai to Egypt after the two countries signed a peace treaty in 1979 but still controls the other territories.

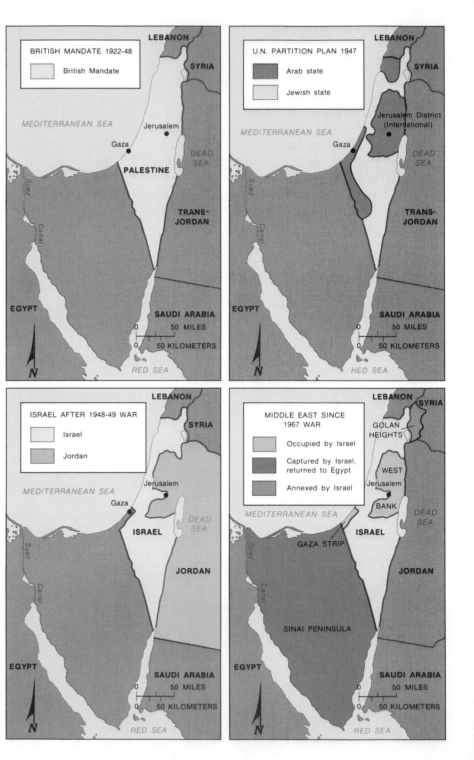

Christians consider Jerusalem and Palestine holy because the major events in Jesus's life were concentrated there. To recapture the Holy Land, European Christians launched a series of battles over a 150-year period known as the Crusades. Crusaders captured Jerusalem from the Muslims in 1099 during the First Crusade, lost it in 1187 (which led to the Third Crusade), regained it in 1229 as part of a peace treaty ending the Sixth Crusade, and lost it again in 1244. Muslims then held Palestine continuously until 1917.

When the Muslim Ottoman Empire, which controlled Palestine for most of the period between 1516 and 1917, was defeated in World War I, Great Britain took over Palestine under a mandate from the League of Nations and, later, the United Nations. For a few years, the British allowed some Jews to return to Palestine, but emigration was restricted again during the 1930s in response to intense pressure by Arabs in the region.

As violence initiated by both Jewish and Arab settlers escalated after World War II, the British announced their intention to withdraw from Palestine. The United Nations voted to partition Palestine into two independent countries, one Jewish and one Arab Muslim. Jerusalem was to be an international city, open to all religions, and run by the United Nations (Figure 5–17).

Recent Arab-Israeli wars. When the British withdrew on May 15, 1948, Jews declared an independent country of Israel in the boundaries prescribed by the U.N. resolution. The next day, its neighboring Arab Muslim states declared war, but after failing to defeat Israel they signed an armistice in 1949. Israel fought three more wars with its neighbors in 1956, 1967, and 1973. Each time, Israel won.

After the 1949 armistice, Jerusalem became a divided city. The Old City of Jerusalem, which contained the famous religious shrines, became part of the Muslim country of Jordan, while the newer western part was in Israel. During the 1967 Six-Day War, Israel captured the entire city and removed the barriers that had prevented Jews from visiting and living in the Old City of Jerusalem. Israel captured four other pieces of territory in that war, including the West Bank from Jordan (the territory west of the Jordan River taken by Jordan in the 1948–49 war),

the Golan Heights from Syria, and the Gaza Strip and Sinai Peninsula from Egypt.

Egypt's President Anwar Sadat and Israel's Prime Minister Menachem Begin signed a peace treaty in 1979, following a series of meetings with U.S. President Jimmy Carter at Camp David, Maryland. In accordance with the treaty, Israel returned the Sinai Peninsula, while Egypt recognized Israel's right to exist. Sadat was assassinated by Egyptian soldiers, who were extremist Muslims opposed to compromising with Israel, but his successor, Hosni Mubarek, carried out the terms of the treaty.

More than a quarter-century after the Six-Day War, the status of the other territories occupied by Israel has not been settled. In 1981, Israel annexed the Golan Heights, a sparsely inhabited, mountainous area where Syria launched attacks against Jewish settlements in the valley. The future of the West Bank and Gaza Strip has been especially difficult to resolve, because—in contrast to the Golan Heights and the Sinai Peninsula—these two areas contain large population concentrations. Israelis are divided between those who wish to retain the occupied territories and those who wish to return most of them in exchange for peace treaties with neighboring states.

Palestinians. Most of the people living in the West Bank, Gaza Strip, and East Jerusalem consider themselves Palestinians, most of whom are Muslim. In general, Palestinians oppose continued Israeli control of the territories. Most Palestinians aspire to establish their own country in the Middle East, but they do not all agree on the appropriate strategy: continue fighting Israel for the entire territory between the Jordan River and the Mediterranean Sea or settle for a Palestinian-controlled country in the occupied territories.

Also complicating the situation, Palestinians include four groups other than those living in the occupied territories:

◆ Non-Jewish citizens of Israel.
◆ People who fled from Israel after the 1948–49 War.
◆ People who fled from the West Bank or Gaza Strip after the 1967 War.

In February 1988, Palestinians in Nablus, one of the largest towns in the West Bank, protested against Israeli occupation by throwing rocks at Israeli soldiers (top). Moments later, Israeli soldiers broke up the demonstration (bottom).

♦ Citizens of other countries, especially Jordan, Lebanon, Syria, Kuwait, and Saudi Arabia, who identify themselves as Palestinians.

The plight of the Palestinians who fled Israel or the occupied territories is especially acute. Many have lived for decades in "temporary" refugee camps in Lebanon, Syria, and Jordan, and they do not enjoy the protection of being citizens of any country.

Civil War in Lebanon

Religious conflict in the Middle East is not confined to Israel. Israel's northern neighbor, Lebanon, contains a number of religious groups (Table 5–2).

They coexisted fairly peacefully from the time of independence in 1943 until the mid-1970s. Since then, the country has been severely damaged by a civil war among the religious factions.

The largest Lebanese Christian sect is Maronite, which split from the Roman church in the seventh century and was ruled by the Patriarch of Antioch. Although some reconciliation has been made with the Roman Catholic church, the liturgy is still performed in ancient Syriac. Approximately one-fifth of Lebanon's total population and one-half of the country's Christians are Maronites.

The second largest Christian sect in Lebanon is Greek Orthodox, one of the Eastern Orthodox churches that split from Roman Catholicism in the eleventh century. Lebanon's Greek Orthodox Christians use a Byzantine liturgy, because Eastern Orthodox Christians were led by the Patriarch of Constantinople from the time of the split with Catholicism in 1054 until the city of Constantinople was captured by Muslims in 1453. Greek Orthodox Christians comprise approximately 5 percent of Lebanon's total population.

Other relatively small and little-known Christian sects in Lebanon include Greek Catholic, Armenian, Syrian Orthodox (Jacobites), and Chaldeans (Assyrian). Greek Catholics split from the Greek Orthodox church and migrated to Lebanon because of persecution elsewhere. Armenians separated from the Roman Catholic church in the fifth century and have a patriarch in the Armenian Soviet Socialist Republic of the Soviet Union.

Approximately 29 percent of the Lebanese belong to one of several Shiite Muslim sects. The largest Shiite sect is called Mitwali, but in recent years, other more militant sects have become more powerful, especially the Party of God—also known as Hezbollah—which has been responsible for holding a number of American and European hostages. The Sunni branch—accepted by about 90 percent of the world's Muslims—is practiced by about 26 percent of Lebanon's total population, including Palestinian refugees.

Lebanon also has religious groups that are neither Christian nor Muslim, the most important of whom is the Druse. The Druse religion combines elements of both Islam and Christianity, but many of the rituals are kept secret from outsiders. Approximately 5 percent of Lebanon's population are estimated to be Druse.

TABLE 5–2
Religious groups in Lebanon

Group	Percentage of Population
Christian	39
Maronite	21
Greek Orthodox	5
Armenian Catholic	3
Other Christian	10
Muslim	56
Shiite	29
Sunni	26
Lebanese	18
Palestinian	8
Druse	5

Lebanon's constitution. To preserve the identity of each religious group, Lebanon's constitution at independence required that each religion be represented in the Chamber of Deputies according to its percentage of Lebanon's overall population in 1932, when the last census had been taken. Accordingly, the 99 members of the Chamber of Deputies comprised 54 Christians, including 30 Maronites, 11 Greek Orthodox, 6 Greek Catholics, 4 Armenian Orthodox, and 3 other Christians; 39 Muslims, including 20 Sunnis and 19 Shiites; and 6 Druses. Thus, the 30 Maronite candidates with the largest vote totals were elected, as were the top vote getters for the other religions.

By unwritten convention, the president of Lebanon was a Maronite Christian, the premier a Sunni Muslim, the speaker of the Chamber of Deputies a Shiite Muslim, and the foreign minister a Greek Orthodox Christian. Other cabinet members and civil servants were similarly apportioned among the religions.

The system survived peacefully until 1975, when fighting among the different religious groups crippled the state. The delicate balance was upset by the arrival of a large number of Palestinian refugees after the 1967 Arab-Israeli War. The Palestine Liberation Organization (P.L.O.) exercised control over much of the southern part of the country, where the refugee camps were clustered, and launched attacks against Israel from southern Lebanon. Lebanon's Muslims were generally sympathetic to the P.L.O.'s cause, while most Lebanese Christians supported Israel.

Lebanon's fundamental problem, however, was how to deal with changing social and economic conditions. When the governmental system was created, Christians constituted a majority and controlled the country's main businesses, but as the Muslims became the majority they demanded political and economic equality.

Lebanon's religious groups have tended to live in different regions of the country. Maronites are concentrated in the west-central part of the country, Sunnis in the northwest, and Shiites in the south and east. Beirut, the capital and largest city, has been divided between an eastern Christian zone and a Muslim western zone. With the breakdown of the national government, each religious group formed a private army or militia to guard its territory. The territory controlled by each militia changes according to results of battles with other religious groups.

Most of Lebanon is now actually controlled by Syria, which has a historical claim over the territory. Syria sent peace-keeping forces into Lebanon in 1976, and most militias support a Syrian-imposed cease-fire. Israel invaded Lebanon in 1982 to clear out the P.L.O.; after the P.L.O. leaders were evacuated to Tunisia, Israel withdrew, but its ally, the Southern Lebanese Army, continued to control southern Lebanon. The United States sent marines to Lebanon in 1982 to supervise the P.L.O.'s evacuation, but they were removed in February 1984, four months after 241 of them died in their barracks from the explosion of a truck wired with a bomb.

Summary

The key issues of this chapter have attempted to demonstrate the importance of religion on the cultural landscape. These again are the key issues for Chapter 5.

1. **How are religions distributed?** Three important universalizing religions can be identified in the world—Christianity, Islam, and Buddhism. Each originated in a particular core area but diffused to other portions of the earth's surface. In addition, several ethnic religions can be identified that are closely rooted to the social customs and physical environment of particular places on the earth's surface.

2. **How do religions organize space?** Elements of the physical environment are organized by different religions in different ways. Some religions incorporate agricultural practices and other environmental processes into their systems of belief and rituals. Religions may identify portions of the earth's surface that are considered holy either because of the spiritual content of the objects or because of their association with human events. Adherents are encouraged to make pilgrimages to these places. Some religions organize the territory occupied by their followers into a rigid administrative structure in order to disseminate religious doctrine, while other religions are locally autonomous.

3. **What is the impact of religion on the landscape?** Some religions establish sacred structures in which adherents gather to pray. In Christianity, such structures play a particularly important role as a space for congregational worship. Other religions emphasize individual or family worship and reserve holy structures for infrequent visits. Religions affect the landscape in other ways: religious communities are built, religious names are placed on the landscape, and extensive tracts of land are reserved for burying the dead.

4. **What territorial conflicts arise because of religion?** With the earth's surface dominated by four large religions, expansion in the territory occupied by adherents of one religion may reduce the territory of another. In addition, religions must compete for control of territory with nonreligious ideas, notably communism and economic modernization.

Conflict in the Middle East

The war in the Persian Gulf brought renewed attention to the conflicting claims that different religions make on the territory in the region of the Middle East. Even before the outbreak of hostilities, Iraq sought to frame the conflict in religious terms. By attacking Israel, Iraq could claim leadership in the fight to expel Israel from the occupied territories and establish a Palestinian state.

With the United States and several European countries representing the principal opposition, Iraq could present itself as the region's leading defender of Islam against the diffusion of western-dominated values. Although the leaders of most Muslim states condemned Iraq's actions, many people in the region sympathized with Iraq in its battle against Christian and Jewish forces. The logic is consistent with an old Middle Eastern expression: the enemy of my enemy is my friend.

Key Terms

Animism Belief that objects, such as plants and stones, or natural events, such as thunderstorms and earthquakes, have discrete spirit and conscious life.

Autonomous religion Religions that do not have a central authority but share ideas and cooperate informally.

Branch A large and fundamental division within a religion.

Caste The class or distinct hereditary order into which a Hindu is assigned according to religious law.

Cosmogony A set of religious beliefs concerning the origin of the universe.

Denomination Divisions within a branch of a religion.

Diocese The basic unit of geographic organization in the Roman Catholic church.

Ethnic religion A religion with a relatively concentrated spatial distribution whose principles are likely to be based on the physical characteristics of the particular location in which its adherents are concentrated.

Ghetto During the Middle Ages, a neighborhood in a city set up by law to be inhabited only by Jews; term now used to denote a section of a city in which members of any minority group live because of social, legal, or economic pressure.

Hierarchical religion A religion in which a central authority excercises a high degree of control.

Missionary A person who helps diffuse a universalizing religion.

Monotheism The doctrine or belief of the existence of only one god.

Pilgrimage A journey to a place considered sacred for religious purposes.

Sect A relatively small denominational group that has broken away from an established church.

Solstice One of the two points in the year when the sun is furthest from the equator.

Universalizing religion A religion that attempts to appeal to all people, not just those living in a particular location.

Thinking Geographically

1. A widespread view outside of the Middle East is that peace between Israel and its neighbors can be achieved by trading land for peace. In other words, Israel would return the occupied territories in exchange for enforceable peace treaties. What are some of the obstacles that make acceptance of this formula unlikely for either side?

2. Sharp differences in demographic characteristics, such as natural increase, crude birth, and migration rates, can be seen among Jews, Christians, and Muslims in the Middle East and between Roman Catholics and Protestants in Northern Ireland. How might demographic differences affect future relationships among the groups in these two regions?

3. People carry their religious beliefs with them when they migrate. How has the distribution of religious groups within the United States been affected by changes over time in both the regions of the world from which most immigrants to the United States originated and the regions within the United States in which they tended to settle?

4. To what extent have increased interest in religion and ability to practice religious rites served as forces for unification in Eastern Europe and the Soviet Union, or has the growing role of religion in the region fostered instability?

5. Why does Islam seem strange and threatening to some people in predominantly Christian countries? To what extent are these attitudes on the part of many Christians towards Islam and Muslims shaped by knowledge of the teachings of Muhammad and the Quran, and to what extent are they based on lack of knowledge of Islam?

Further Readings

Al Faruqi, Isma'il R., and Lois Lamaya' Al Faruqi. *The Cultural Atlas of Islam.* New York: Macmillan, 1986.

Al Faruqi, Isma'il R., and David E. Sopher. *Historical Atlas of the Religions of the World.* New York: Macmillan, 1974.

Archer, John Clark, and Carl E. Purinton. 2d ed. *Faiths Men Live By.* New York: Ronald Press, 1958.

Bapat, P. V., ed. *2500 Years of Buddhism.* Delhi: Government of India Ministry of Information and Broadcasting, 1959.

Barraclough, Geoffrey, ed. *The Times Concise Atlas of World History.* Maplewood, NJ: Hammond, 1982.

Barrett, David B., ed. *World Christian Encyclopedia.* Oxford: Oxford University Press, 1982.

Bhardwaj, Surinder M. *Hindu Places of Pilgrimage in India.* Berkeley: University of California Press, 1973.

Curry-Roper, Janet M. "Contemporary Christian Eschatologies and their Relation to Environmental Stewardship." *Professional Geographer* 42 (May 1990): 157–69.

Fickeler, Paul. "Fundamental Questions in the Geography of Religions," In *Readings in Cultural Geography,* edited by Philip L. Wagner and Marvin W. Mikesell. Chicago: University of Chicago Press, 1962.

Francaviglia, Richard V. *The Mormon Landscape.* New York: AMS Press, 1978.

Gaustad, E. S. *Historical Atlas of Religion in America.* New York: Harper and Row, 1962.

Hardon, John A. *Religions of the World.* 2 vols. Garden City, NY: Image Books, 1968.

Heatwole, Charles A. "Exploring the Geography of America's Religious Denominations: A Presbyterian Example." *Journal of Geography* 76 (March 1977): 99–104.

———. "Sectarian Ideology and Church Architecture." *Geographical Review* 79 (January 1989): 63–78.

Hiller, Carl E. *Caves to Cathedrals: Architecture of the World's Great Religions.* Boston: Little, Brown, 1974.

Jackson, Richard H. "Mormon Perception and Settlement." *Annals of the Association of American Geographers* 68 (September 1978): 317–34.

Jackson, Richard H., and Roger Henrie. "Perception of Sacred Space." *Journal of Cultural Geography* 3 (Spring/Summer 1983): 94–107.

Levine, Gregory J. "On the Geography of Religion." *Transactions of the Institute of British Geographers, New Series* 11 (no. 4, 1987): 428–40.

Ling, Trevor. *A History of Religion East and West.* London: Macmillan, 1968.

Meinig, Donald W. "The Mormon Culture Region: Strategies and Patterns in the Geography of the American West, 1847–1964." *Annals of the Association of American Geographers* 55 (June 1965): 191–220.

Nolan, Mary Lee, and Sidney Nolan. *Christian Pilgrimage in Modern Western Europe.* Chapel Hill, NC: University of North Carolina Press, 1989.

Quinn, Bernard, Herman Anderson, Martin Bradley, Paul Geotting, and Peggy Shriver. *Churches and Church Membership in the U.S.* Atlanta: Glenmary Research Center, 1982.

Short, Ernest. *A History of Religious Architecture.* New York: Norton, 1951.

Shortridge, James R. "Patterns of Religion in the United States." *Geographical Review* 66 (October 1976): 420–34.

Smith, Huston. *The Religions of Man.* New York: Harper and Bros., 1958.

Sopher, David E. *The Geography of Religions.* Englewood Cliffs, NJ: Prentice-Hall, 1967.

———. "Geography and Religions." *Progress in Human Geography* 5 (1981): 510–24.

Thompson, Jan, and Mel Thompson. *The R. E. Atlas: World Religions in Maps and Notes.* London: Edward W. Arnold, 1986.

Topping, Gary. "Religion in the West." *Journal of American Culture* 3 (Summer 1980): 330–50.

Zelinsky, Wilbur. "An Approach to the Religious Geography of the United States: Patterns of Church Membership in 1952." *Annals of the Association of American Geographers* 51 (June 1961): 139–67.

6
Social Customs on the Landscape

W hat did you do today? Presumably, your first activity was to get out of bed—for some of us the most difficult task of the day. Shortly thereafter, you got dressed. What did you wear? That depended on both the weather (shorts or sweater) and the day's activities (suit or T-shirt).

After work or school you returned home (house, apartment, or dorm room). You then ate dinner (roast beef or salad). After studying or finishing some work, you may have the evening free for leisure activities (watching television, listening to music, or playing or watching sports).

This narrative may not precisely describe you, but you can recognize the day of a "typical" North American. But the routine described and the choices mentioned in parentheses may not accurately reflect the practices of people elsewhere in the world. People living in other locations may have extremely different social customs. Geographers are concerned with understanding the reasons for such differences and the relationship between social customs and the cultural landscape.

As you watch television in your single-family dwelling, wearing jeans and munching on a hamburger, consider the impact if someone from rural Botswana or New Guinea were suddenly placed in the room. Despite the significant differences in social customs across the landscape, given recent trends your visitor might be attracted to the same customs within a short period of time.

The Aboriginal Artists of Australia at Lincoln Center

The Aboriginal Artists of Australia, a group of aborigines living in the isolated interior of Australia, visited New York a few years ago and danced at the Lincoln Center for the Performing Arts. Their series of dances, handed down from their ancestors, reflected their customs and local landscape.

The aboriginal dancers represented a challenge to the New York audience to understand the significance of the movements and music. The aborigines considered the dances an essential component of their social customs. The dances were designed to reflect daily experiences and activities, such as the need for rain or the behavior of particular animals living in a specific environment. At best, the New York audience could recognize that the dances were meaningful to the aborigines, but understanding was inevitably limited by the lack of a comparable role for dances in Western customs.

The geographic contrast between the aboriginal dancers and the New York theater audience is heightened by differing attitudes towards the physical environment. The aboriginal dancers represent a response to specific landscape features and environmental conditions of their Australian homeland. In contrast, New York's Lincoln Center is not a product of an isolated and unique set of social customs. Nothing at Lincoln Center is indigenous to the unique conditions of the site—not the arrangement of structures, the building materials, the variety of performances, or the performers' places of origin. Lincoln Center reflects the diffusion of social customs across a large portion of the earth's surface. Through interaction and integration, regional differences in social and physical characteristics become less important in the distribution of cultural activities.

Geographers are interested in two aspects of social customs. First, each social custom has its own spatial distribution, and geographers study the origin, process of diffusion, and integration of different characteristics. Second, geographers study the relationships between social customs and the landscape. Different social groups take particular elements from the physical environment in their culture and in turn leave different impacts on the landscape.

A **custom** is the frequent repetition of an act, to the extent that it becomes characteristic of the group of people performing the act. Custom is a more precise word than culture, one of the hardest words to define in English. Culture, as defined in Chapter 1, is the body of customary beliefs, social forms, and material traits of a group of people. **Habit,** a similar word to custom, is a repetitive act a particular person performs. Unlike custom, habit does not imply that an act has been adopted by most of the society's population. A custom is therefore a habit that a group of people has widely adopted.

Social customs fall into two basic categories: folk and popular. **Folk customs,** also known as vernacular customs, are traditionally practiced primarily by small, homogeneous groups living in rural areas. **Popular customs,** sometimes called international customs, are found in large, heterogeneous societies that share certain habits despite differences in other personal characteristics.

Two kinds of social customs are examined in this chapter. First are customs deriving from necessary activities of daily life: all human beings must have food, clothing, and shelter to survive, but social groups provide these needs in their own ways. Second are customs involving leisure activities, especially the arts and recreation: each social group has its own definition of meaningful art and stimulating recreation.

The most significant geographic characteristic that distinguishes popular from folk customs is the degree of interaction. Differences in folk customs arise because of lack of communication among social groups. Each group develops unique customs as a result of the particular social and physical conditions it experiences. In contrast, popular customs are based on the ease of global interaction through communications and transportation.

Today popular customs are becoming more dominant than ever before, threatening the survival of unique folk customs. These folk customs—along with language and religion—provide a unique identity to a group of people who occupy a specific portion of the earth's surface. The disappearance of local folk customs reduces cultural diversity in the world and the stimulation that arises from differences in background.

The dominance of popular customs can also threaten the quality of the physical environment. Folk customs, derived from distinctive elements of the local landscape, are more likely to be sensitive to the protection and enhancement of a particular landscape. Popular customs are less likely to reflect the diversity of physical landscapes and are more likely to modify local physical environments in accordance with global values.

KEY ISSUE

How Are Social Customs Distributed?

The spatial distribution of each social custom is unique. How can a geographer make generalizations about the world's large collection of individual customs? In general, the spatial distribution is more extensive for popular customs than for folk customs. This section examines processes by which popular customs achieve their relatively wide diffusion across the landscape. Two basic factors can help explain the spatial differences between popular and folk customs: the process of origin and the pattern of diffusion.

Origin of Social Customs

Music. Folk customs most frequently originate from an anonymous source, at an unknown date, through an unidentified originator. An example is folk music. According to a Chinese legend, music was invented in 2697 B.C., when the Emperor Huang Ti sent Ling Lun to cut bamboo poles in order to produce a sound that would match the call of the phoenix bird. In reality, folk songs usually have an anonymous composer and are transmitted orally. A song may be modified from one generation to the next as conditions change, but the content is most often derived from the events in daily life that are familiar to the majority of the people.

Folk customs may have multiple origins as a result of a lack of communication among groups of people living in different places. U.S. country music provides a recent example of the process by which folk customs originate independently at multiple locations. The geographer George Carney identified four major hearths of country music in the southeastern United States during the late-nineteenth and early-twentieth centuries: southern Appalachia, central Tennessee and Kentucky, the Ozark and Ouachita mountains of western Arkansas and eastern Oklahoma, and north-central Texas (Figure 6–1). Carney documented these hearths on the basis of the birthplaces of performers and others active in the field.

In contrast to folk customs, popular customs are most often a product of the economically developed countries, especially in North America, Western Europe, and Japan. They arise from a combination of advances in industrial technology and increases in leisure time. Industrial technology permits the uniform reproduction of objects in large quantities. Many of these objects help people enjoy leisure time, which has increased as a result of the widespread change in the labor force from predominantly agricultural to predominantly service and manufacturing jobs.

Music illustrates the differences between the origins of folk and popular customs. Popular music is written by specific composers for the purpose of being sold to a large number of people. It displays a high degree of technical skill and is frequently capable of being performed only in a studio with electronic equipment.

Popular music as we know it today originated around 1900. The main form of popular music entertainment in the United States and Western Europe at the time was a series of performances in a variety show, called the music hall in the United Kingdom and vaudeville in the United States. To provide songs for vaudeville acts and early Broadway musicals, a music industry developed in New York City near 28th Street and Broadway that became known as Tin Pan Alley (Figure 6–2). Tin Pan Alley housed song writers and music publishers, as well as orchestrators and arrangers for musically illiterate composers. Companies on Tin Pan Alley originally tried to sell as many song sheets as possible, though sales of recordings ultimately became the most important measure of success.

The diffusion of American popular music to other countries began in earnest during World War II, when the Armed Forces radio network broadcast to American soldiers as well as to those of other countries in which the American forces were stationed or fighting. English eventually became the international language for popular music. Today,

FIGURE 6–1
U.S. country music has four major hearths, or regions of origin. These include southern Appalachia, central Tennessee and Kentucky, the Ozark and Ouachita mountains of western Arkansas and eastern Oklahoma, and north-central Texas.

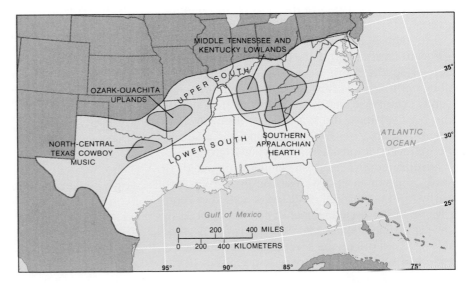

many popular musicians in Japan, Poland, the Soviet Union, and other countries write and perform in English, even though few people in their audiences understand the language.

Diffusion of Folk and Popular Customs

The broadcasting of American popular music on Armed Forces radio helps illustrate the difference between the diffusion of folk customs and popular customs. Popular customs diffuse rapidly and extensively through the use of modern communications and transportation inventions. Folk customs are transmitted from one location to another at a slower pace and on a smaller scale, primarily through migration rather than electronic communications.

The Amish. An example of the diffusion of folk customs by migration is the distribution of Amish customs. The Amish have distinctive religious practices, clothing, farming, and other customs that leave a unique pattern on the landscapes where they settle. Shunning mechanical power, the Amish still travel by horse and buggy and continue to use hand tools for farming.

Although the 1976 Amish population in the United States numbered only about 67,100, a mere 0.03 percent of the total population, Amish folk customs still are visible on the landscape in at least seventeen states. What accounts for the distribution of Amish folk customs across a major portion of the U.S. landscape? The answer is found by examining the process of diffusion of the customs through migration.

The Amish originated in Bern, Switzerland; Alsace, in northeastern France; and the Palatinate region of southwestern Germany. They migrated to other portions of northwestern Europe in the eighteenth century, primarily for religious freedom. In Europe, the Amish did not develop distinctive language, clothing, or farming customs and gradually merged with various Mennonite church groups.

Several hundred Amish families migrated to North America in two waves. The first group, primarily from Bern and the Palatinate, settled in Pennsylvania in the early eighteenth century, enticed by low-priced land offered by William Penn. Because of lower land prices, the second group, from Alsace, settled in Ohio, Illinois, Iowa, and Ontario in the

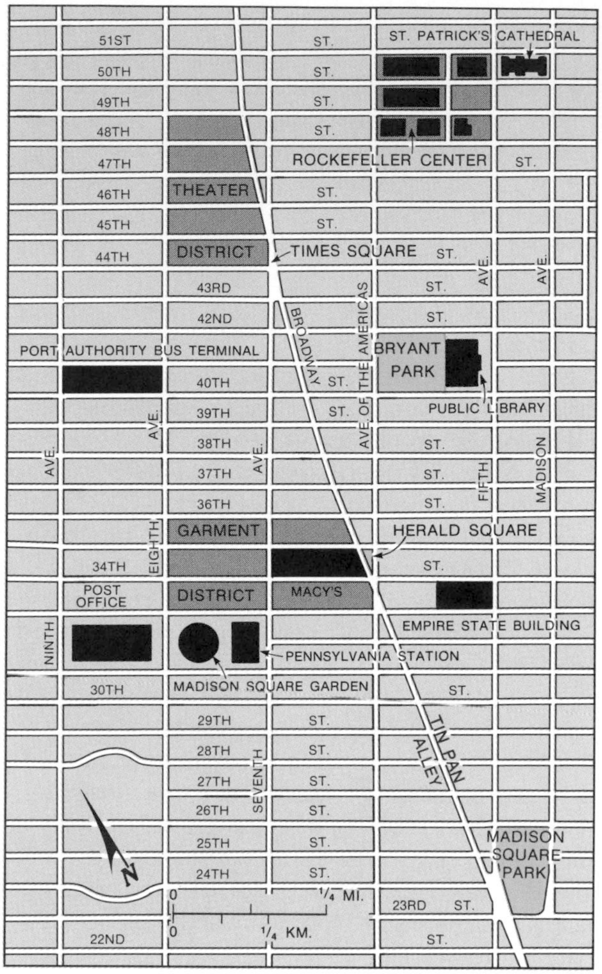

FIGURE 6–2

At the beginning of the twentieth century, most writers and publishers of popular music were clustered in New York City in a few buildings near the corner of 28th Street and Broadway, which became known as Tin Pan Alley. Tin Pan Alley is no longer a center of popular music, but performing arts are still clustered in New York City. The Theater District, near 45th Street and Broadway, contains the country's largest concentration of theaters featuring live plays and shows. Lincoln Center for the Performing Arts, a center for music and theater productions, is located near 63rd Street and Broadway, a few blocks north of this area.

early nineteenth century (Figure 6–3). From these core areas, groups of Amish migrated to other locations where inexpensive land was available.

Living in rural and frontier settlements relatively isolated from other groups, Amish communities retained their traditional customs, even as other Euro-

FIGURE 6–3
Amish settlements are distributed throughout the northeastern United States. According to Crowley, who documented the distribution, the number of church districts within a settlement should be regarded as an indicator of the number of Amish in the community.

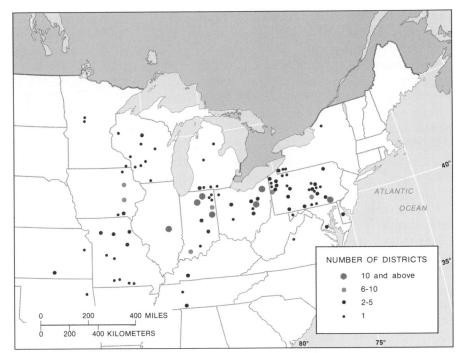

pean immigrants to the United States adopted new ones. We can observe Amish customs on the landscape in such diverse states as southeastern Pennsylvania, northeastern Ohio, and east-central Iowa. These communities are relatively isolated from each other but share cultural traditions distinct from those of other Americans.

Soccer. In contrast with the diffusion of folk customs, organized sports provides an example of the process of diffusion of popular customs. Many sports originated as isolated, unique folk customs, and at one time most sports were diffused like other folk customs through the migration of persons and groups. The contemporary diffusion of or-

An Amish farmer near Lancaster, Pennsylvania, gives his English neighbor a lift in his buggy, while Amish children sell vegetables by the side of the road.

ganized sports, however, displays the characteristics of popular customs, as in the case of the world's most popular sport, soccer.

The origin of soccer (called football in many countries) is obscure, though the earliest documented English contest took place in the eleventh century. According to football historians, after the Danish invasion of England between 1018 and 1042, workers at a building site encountered a Danish soldier's head, which they began to kick. "Kick the Dane's head" was imitated by boys, one of whom got the idea of using an inflated cow bladder.

Early football games resembled mob scenes. A large number of people from two villages would gather to kick the ball. The winning side was the one that kicked the ball into the center of the rival village. In the twelfth century this game—by then commonly called football—was confined to smaller vacant areas, and the rules were standardized. Because football disrupted village life, King Henry II banned the game from England in the late twelfth century, and it was legalized again only in 1603 by King James I. At this point, football was an English folk custom rather than a popular global custom.

The transformation of football from an English folk custom to a global popular custom began in the nineteenth century. Football and other recreation clubs were founded in Britain, frequently by churches, to provide factory workers with organized recreation during leisure hours. Sport became a subject that was taught in school.

Increasing leisure time permitted attendance at sporting events as well as participation in them. And with higher incomes, people were willing to pay to see first-class events. To meet the public demand, football clubs began to hire professional players. Several British football clubs formed an association in 1863 to standardize the rules of the game and organize professional leagues. Organization of the sport into a formal structure in Great Britain marks the beginning of football as a popular custom.

The word *soccer* originated after 1863, when supporters of the game formed an organization called the Football Association. *Association* was shortened to *assoc,* which ultimately became *soccer.* The terms *soccer* or *association football* also helped to distinguish the game from rugby football, which permits both kicking and carrying of the ball. Rugby originated in 1823, when a football player at Rugby College picked up the ball and ran with it.

Beginning in the late-nineteenth century, the British exported association football around the world, first to continental Europe and then to other countries. Football was first played in continental Europe in the late 1870s by Dutch students who had been in Britain. The game spread to other countries after contact with English players. For example, football was introduced to Spain by English engineers working in Bilbao in 1893 and was quickly adopted by local miners. British citizens further diffused the game throughout the extensive territory of the British Empire. In the twentieth century, association football, like other sports, has been further diffused by new communication systems, especially radio and television.

Soccer reached Russia in a curious manner. The English manager of a textile factory near Moscow organized a factory football team in 1887 and advertised in London for workers who could play the game. After the Russian Revolution in 1917, the factory was absorbed into the Soviet Electric Trade Union. The team, renamed the Moscow Dynamo, has become the country's most famous, though the official history of Soviet football does not refer to its English origin.

Soccer was also exported to the United States, but it has never gained the same level of popularity as in Europe and Latin America. The first college football game played in the United States, between Princeton and Rutgers in 1869, was soccer, and officials of several colleges met four years later to adopt football rules consistent with those of British soccer. But Harvard's representatives successfully argued for adoption of rugby rules instead. Rugby was so thoroughly modified by the U.S. colleges that an entirely new game emerged, now known as American football. Similar modifications of football were undertaken in other English-speaking countries, including Canada, Australia, and Ireland.

Other sports. Although soccer is the world's most popular sport, people participate in other sports in different parts of the world. Cricket is popular primarily in former British colonies, whereas ice hockey is found primarily in the colder climates of the northern latitudes, especially in Canada, Northern Europe, and the Soviet Union. The most popular sports in China are the martial arts, known as *wushu,* including archery, fencing, wrestling, and boxing. Baseball, once confined to North America, has become popular in Japan. The game was introduced to the Japanese by American soldiers who occupied the country after World War II.

Despite the diversity in the distribution of sports across the earth's surface and the anonymous origin of some games, organized spectator sports today are part of popular customs. The common element in professional sports is the willingness of people throughout the world to pay for the privilege of viewing—either in person or on television—those sports events played by professional athletes. Competition for the World Cup is clear evidence of the global diffusion of sports. The national soccer teams from countries throughout the world compete every four years, including in Italy in 1990 and the United States in 1994. Thanks to television, more spectators view the final match than any other event in history.

Television. The diffusion of popular customs such as professional sports is facilitated by modern communication systems, especially television. Technicians in a number of countries, including the United States, the United Kingdom, France, Germany, Japan, and the Soviet Union, simultaneously contributed to the invention of television. The U.S. public first saw television in the 1930s, but its diffusion was blocked for a number of years when broadcasting was curtailed or suspended entirely during World War II. In 1945, for example, there were only 10,000 television receivers in the United States. The number rapidly increased to 1 million in 1949, 10 million in 1951, and 50 million in 1959; by the mid-1950s three-fourths of all U.S. homes had a television.

Television diffused from the United States to the rest of the world with remarkable speed. Between 1945 and 1950, only three countries other than the United States had television: Great Britain, France, and the Soviet Union. But since 1950 television has rapidly spread to the rest of the world. Today, only a handful of countries still lack television stations.

While differences exist among countries in the type of programming and the organization of television systems, the primary result of this diffusion has been to promote uniformity in the leisure activities of people in different countries. Nevertheless, distinctive folk customs remain in all parts of the world even despite the diffusion of popular customs through modern communications.

What Is the Relationship between the Landscape and the Development of Unique Folk Regions?

Folk customs are distinguished by their uniqueness in a concentrated area, derived through centuries of relative isolation from the customs of other cultural groups. The study of folk customs is particularly useful to geographers because the physical environment plays a significant role in the development of unique folk customs.

The relationship between folk customs and the landscape can be seen in two ways: the impact of the landscape on human organization of space and the effect of human actions on the landscape. First, specific features of the natural environment, such as climate, topography, and vegetation, can encourage cultural groups to adopt distinctive folk customs. Second, isolated folk societies can create unique cultural expressions on the landscape.

The unique landscape created by folk customs is caused in part by direct observation of the local physical environment and in part by cultural values that may have been derived indirectly from observations of the natural environment. We can examine both types of relationships between the physical environment and folk customs, though in reality a combination of the two types will produce a unique folk culture region.

Response of Folk Customs to the Physical Environment

Unique folk customs originate in part as a response to conditions of the local physical environment. Nature can limit a variety of human actions, but folk societies are often particularly responsive to the physical environment because of the level of technology and the predominant form of economy.

Environmental determinists once theorized that folk customs are caused by elements in the physical environment, but most contemporary geographers reject this notion. There are many examples of different peoples living in similar physical environments who adopt different folk customs and, conversely, of peoples living in different physical environments who adopt similar folk customs. However, geographers generally recognize that people do not ignore their physical environment.

Folk customs such as food, clothing, and shelter customs must in part be influenced by the prevailing climate, soil, and vegetation. For example, residents of arctic climates may wear fur-lined boots, which protect against the cold, and use snowshoes to walk on soft, deep snow without sinking in. On the other hand, people living in warm and humid climates may not need any footwear if the heavy rainfall and time spent in water discourage its use. The custom in the Netherlands of wearing wooden shoes may appear quaint but actually derives from environmental conditions. Dutch farmers wear the wooden shoes to work in the fields, which are likely to be extremely moist in a country where much of the land is below sea level.

Yet folk customs can seem to ignore the physical environment. Not all arctic residents wear snowshoes, nor do all people in moist temperate climates wear wooden shoes. Geographers merely observe that broad differences in social customs generally arise with some consideration of physical conditions, even though those conditions may produce a variety of customs.

Food. Folk food habits derive from the physical environment. According to the nineteenth-century geographer Vidal de la Blache, "Among the connections that tie man to a certain environment, one of the most tenacious is food supply; clothing and weapons are more subject to modification than the dietary regime, which experience has shown to be best suited to human needs in a given climate."

Food is composed for the most part of living things that spring from the soil and water of a region in the form of either plants or animals. Inhabitants of a region must consider the soil, climate, and other characteristics of the physical environment in deciding to produce particular foods.

The spatial distribution of wine production clearly demonstrates the significance of the landscape to folk food customs, because a wine's distinctive character derives from unique properties of the physical environment. Grapes are grown in a wide variety of locations across the earth's surface, but each bottle of wine reflects the characteristics of grapes grown in the unique soil and climate of its origin.

A wine label can convey precise information about the origin of the wine. This wine came from Bernkastel, a town on the Mosel River, part of the Mosel-Saar-Ruwer region of Germany. The wine was produced and bottled (Erzenger-Abfullung) on the estate (Weingut) of Dr. Thanisch, which is located in Bernkastel.

Vineyards are best cultivated in temperate climates of moderately cold, rainy winters and fairly long, hot summers. Hot, sunny weather is necessary in the summer for the fruit to mature properly, while winter is the preferred season for rain, because plant diseases that cause the fruit to rot are more active in hot, humid weather. Vineyards are planted on hillsides, if possible, both to maximize exposure to sunlight and to facilitate drainage. A site near a lake or river is also desirable because water can temper extremes of temperature.

Grapes can be grown in a variety of soils, but the best wine tends to be produced from grapes grown in soil that is coarse-grained and well drained—a soil not necessarily very fertile for other crops. For example, the soil is generally sandy and gravelly in the Bordeaux wine region, chalky in Champagne country, and a slate composition in the Moselle. The distinctive character of each region's wine is especially influenced by the unique combination of trace elements (such as boron, manganese, and zinc) in the rock or soil. In large quantities, these elements could destroy the plants, but in small quantities they lend a unique taste to the grapes.

Because of the unique product created by the distinctive soil and climate characteristics, the world's finest wines are most frequently identified by their place of origin. Wines may be labeled with the region, town, district, or specific estate. A wine expert can determine the precise origin of a wine just by tasting because of the unique taste imparted to the grapes by the specific soil composition of each estate.

The year of the harvest is also indicated on the bottles of finer wines because specific weather conditions each year affect the quality and quantity of the harvest. Wines may also be identified by the kind of the grape used rather than the location of the vineyard. Less expensive wines may be composed of a blend of grapes from a variety of estates and years.

Folk housing. The type of building materials used to construct folk houses is influenced in part by the availability of particular resources in the environment. The two most common building materials in the world are wood and bricks, though stone, grass, sod, and skins are also used. If available, wood is generally preferred for house construction. In the past, pioneers who settled in forested regions could build log cabins for themselves. Today, people in relatively developed societies go to a store and buy wood cut by machine to a variety of shapes. Cut lumber is used to erect a frame, and sheets or strips of wood are attached for the walls, floors, ceilings, and roof. Shingles, stucco or other materials may be placed on the exterior for insulation or decoration.

For people living in regions without access to forests, folk customs point to the use of other building materials. In relatively hot, dry climates—such as the U.S. Southwest, Mexico, North China, and parts of the Middle East—bricks are made by baking wet mud in the sun. Stone is used to build houses in parts of Europe and South America and as decoration on the outside of brick or wood houses in other countries.

Even in areas that share similar climates and available building materials, folk housing types can vary as a result of relatively slight differences in environmental features. For example, R. W. McColl compared house types in four villages situated in the dry lands of northern and western China: Kashgar (Kashi), Turpan, Yinchuan, and Dunhuang (Figure 6–4). All use similar building materials, including adobe and timber from the desert poplar, and

they share a similar objective: protection from the extremes of temperatures, from very hot summer days to below-freezing winter nights.

Despite the similarities in environmental conditions and building materials, the houses in the four Chinese villages have distinctive appearances. The houses in Kashgar have second-floor open-air patios, where the residents can catch evening breezes. Poplar and fruit trees can be planted around the houses, because the village has a river that is constantly flowing rather than seasonal, as is the case in much of China's dry lands. These deciduous trees provide shade in the summer and openings for sunlight in the winter.

Turpan is situated in a deep valley with relatively little open land, because much of the space is allocated to drying raisins. Houses in Turpan have small, open courtyards for social gatherings; second-story patios, which would utilize even less land, are avoided because the village is subject to strong winds. At Yinchuan, houses are built around large, open-air courtyards, which contain tall trees to provide shade. Most of the residents are Muslims, who regard courtyards as private spaces to be screened from outsiders. The adobe bricks are square or cubed-shaped rather than rectangular, as is the case in the other villages, though McColl found no reason for this distinctive custom.

Houses at Dunhuang also are characterized by walled central courtyards, but they are covered by an open-lattice grape arbor. The cover allows for the free movement of air but provides shade from the especially intense direct summer heat and light. Rather than the flat roofs characteristic of dry lands, houses in Dunhuang have sloped roofs, typical of wetter climates, so that rainfall can run off. The practice is apparently influenced by Dunhuang's relative proximity to the population centers of eastern China, where sloped roofs predominate.

Expression of Folk Customs on the Landscape

The distribution of folk customs derives in part from consideration of particular environmental conditions and in part from expressions of unique social values. Distinctive values may arise from either direct observation of nature or through such cultural institutions as religion. These values influence

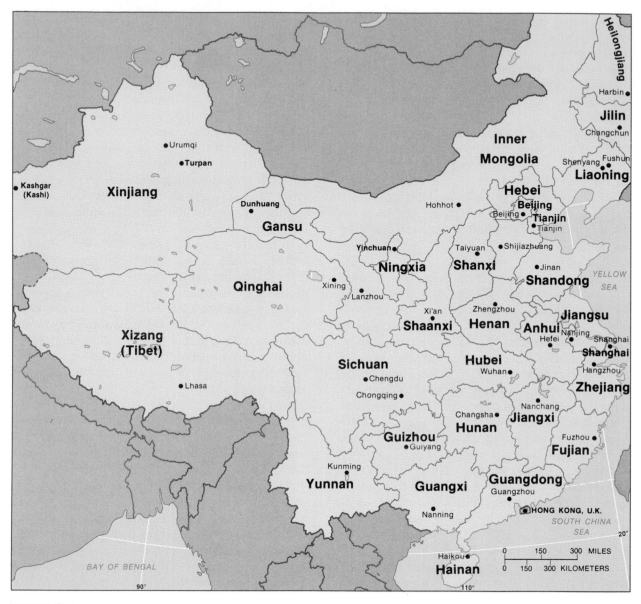

FIGURE 6–4
Houses can vary among communities in the dry lands of northwestern China partly in response to local environmental conditions, such as wind direction and proximity to bodies of water.

the development of folk customs that have particular expressions on the landscape.

Folk music. Folk music provides an example of the development of unique folk customs through observations of distinctive elements in the local environment. Folk songs tell a story or convey information about daily activities such as farming, life-cycle events (birth, death, marriage) or mysterious events such as storms and earthquakes.

In Vietnam, where most people are subsistence farmers, information concerning agricultural technology is conveyed through folk songs. For example, the following folk song provides advice about the difference between seeds planted in the summer and winter:

Ma chiêm ba tháng không già
*Ma mùa tháng rưỡi ắt lakhông non.**

This song can be translated as follows:

While seedlings for the summer crop are not old
   when they are three months of age,
Seedlings for the winter crop are certainly not
   young when they are one-and-a-half months old.

---

* From John Blacking and Joann W. Kealiinohomoku, eds., *The Performing Arts: Music and Dance* (The Hague: Mouton, 1979), 144. Reprinted by permission of the publisher.

The song hardly sounds lyrical to a Western ear. But when American folk songs appear in cold print, similar themes emerge even if the specific information conveyed about the environment differs.

Himalayan art. In a study of artistic customs in the Himalaya Mountains, geographers. P. Karan and Cotton Mather demonstrated the unique expressions on the landscape that can emerge among different groups who live in isolation but near one another. The study area—a narrow, 2,500-kilometer (1,500-mile) corridor in the Himalaya Mountains of Bhutan, Nepal, and northern India—contains four religious groups: Tibetan Buddhists in the north, Hindus in the south, Muslims in the west, and Southeast Asian animists in the east (Figure 6–5). Despite their spatial closeness, limited interaction among the groups produces distinctive folk customs.

The typical subjects selected for paintings by each of the four groups reflect how folk customs mirror distinctive views of the surrounding landscape. The Tibetan Buddhists in the northern region of the study area paint idealized divine figures, such as monks and saints. Some of these figures are depicted in a bizarre or terrifying manner, perhaps as a reflection of an inhospitable physical environment. Hindus in the southern region create scenes from everyday life and familiar local landscapes. Their paintings sometimes portray a god in a do-

FIGURE 6–5
Karan and Mather found four cultural regions in the rugged Himalaya mountains of Bhutan, Nepal, and northern India. Variations among the groups were found in painting, dance, and other folk customs.

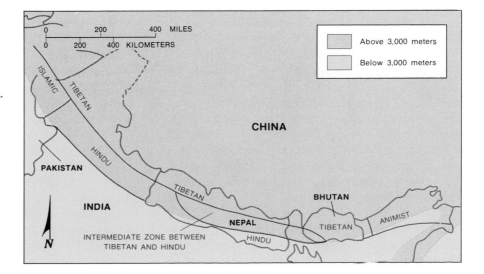

FIGURE 6–6
According to Kniffen, house types in the United States originated in three main source areas and diffused to the west along separate paths. These paths coincided with the predominant routes taken by migrants from the East Coast to the interior of the country.

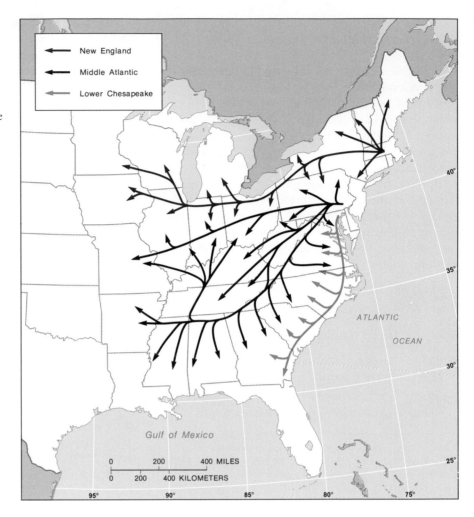

mestic scene and frequently represent the region's violent and extreme climatic conditions.

Paintings in the Islamic western portion of the study area show the region's beautiful plants and flowers, because Muslims are prohibited from displaying humans or animals in art. In contrast with the paintings from the Buddhist and Hindu regions, the Muslims do not depict the harsh weather conditions. Animist groups from Myanmar (Burma) and elsewhere in Southeast Asia, who have migrated to the eastern region of the study area, paint symbols and designs that derive from their religion rather than from the local landscape.

The four groups in the Himalaya study area also display differences in other artistic forms, such as dance, music, architecture, and crafts. Despite close geographic proximity, the four groups have re-

tained their specific traditions and unique views of the landscape.

Folk housing. Although the physical environment is important in determining the choice of building materials for a house, social values are more important in determining the form of folk dwellings. Patterns of colonial settlement along the American East Coast as well as migration into the Midwest during the nineteenth century have been instrumental in creating regional variations in the form of houses within the United States. The geographer Fred Kniffen has shown that many forms of houses in the eastern half of the country can be traced to three source areas on the East Coast, which he calls Northeast, Middle Atlantic, and Lower Chesapeake (Figure 6–6).

When settlers from the Northeast migrated to the west, they took their house type with them. The Northeast house type is found throughout the Great Lakes region as far west as Wisconsin, because this was the area settled by migrants from the Northeast. As the Northeast house changed somewhat over time, the precise form that migrants took to the west depended on when they left the Northeast. Consequently, geographers can observe differences within the Northeast house-type region, based on the date of initial settlement.

The typical Northeast house was two rooms deep, two rooms wide, and two full stories tall. Around 1700, the Northeast house featured a central fireplace. This style is found in the area first settled at that time—Maine, Vermont, and New Hampshire—but not farther west. Around 1750, the style changed to a central hall and two end fireplaces. This style is found in the area first settled by 1750, including northern New England, upstate New York, and Ohio. Northeastern houses built at a later date in Michigan and states farther west reflected other changes in the basic type (Figure 6–7).

The Lower Chesapeake style of house was one or one-and-a-half stories rather than two, with a steeper roof. It was one room deep rather than two, but two rooms wide, and frequently was placed on a one-story foundation. These houses spread from the Chesapeake Bay area to the south.

The most widespread house type was the Middle Atlantic, which originated in eastern Pennsylvania. This house type, called the I-construction, was one room deep, at least two rooms wide, and two full stories tall. Settlers built this type of house in much of the Midwest because most of them were migrants from the Middle Atlantic.

Today, such distinctions are relatively difficult to observe in the United States. The style of housing does not display the same degree of regional distinctiveness because rapid communication and transportation systems provide people throughout the country with knowledge of alternative styles. Furthermore, most people do not build the houses in which they live. Instead, houses are usually mass-produced by construction companies.

Influence of religious values on housing. The form of houses in some societies may reflect religious values. For example, houses may have sacred walls or corners. In Fiji the east wall of a house is considered sacred, and the northwest in parts of China. Sacred walls or corners are also found in parts of the Middle East, India, and Africa.

In Madagascar, religious considerations dictate the use of each part of the house, as well as the arrangement of furniture. The main door is on the west, considered the most important direction, while the northeast corner is the most sacred. The north wall is for honoring ancestors; in addition, important guests enter a room from the north and are seated against the north wall. The bed is placed against the east wall of the house, with the head facing north.

In various parts of the world, the choice of building materials may be influenced by social factors as well as by the physical environment. If the desired material is not locally available, then it must be imported. For example, migrants have sometimes paved streets and built houses in a new location with the stone ballast from the hold of the ship that transported them.

The form of housing is related in part to environmental as well as social conditions. The construction of a pitched roof is important in wet or snowy climates to facilitate runoff. Windows may be aligned to the south in temperate climates to take advantage of the sun's heat and light. In hot climates, on the other hand, window openings may be smaller in order to protect the interior from the full heat of the sun.

Food customs. Similarly, food customs are inevitably affected by the availability of products, but people do not simply eat what is available in their particular environment. Food habits are strongly influenced by cultural traditions derived from events and features of the physical environment. According to many folk customs, everything in nature carries a signature, or distinctive characteristic, based on its appearance and natural properties. Consequently, persons may desire or avoid certain foods in response to perceived beneficial or harmful natural traits.

Certain foods are eaten because their natural properties are perceived to enhance qualities considered desirable by the society, such as strength, fierceness, or love-making ability. The Abipone Indians of Paraguay eat jaguars and bulls to make them

FIGURE 6–7
Kniffen suggests that each of the four house types was popular in southern New England at the indicated dates. As settlers migrated west, they carried memories of familiar house types with them and built similar structures on the frontier. The house types popular during the nineteenth century diffused farther west than those popular during the eighteenth century, because people migrated farther west at a later date.

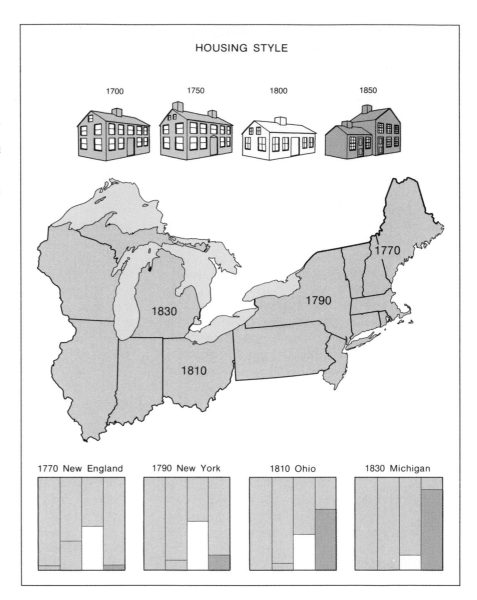

strong, brave, and swift. The mandrake, a plant native to Mediterranean climates, was thought to enhance a person's love-making abilities. The smell of the plant's orange-colored berries is attractive, but the mandrake's association with sexual prowess comes primarily from the appearance of the root, which is thick, fleshy, and forked—suggestive of a man's torso. In parts of Africa and the Middle East, the mandrake's root is administered as a drug. Several references to its powers are found in the Bible.

Food taboos. People refuse to eat particular plants or animals that are thought to embody negative forces in the physical environment. Such a restriction on behavior imposed by social custom is known as a **taboo.** The Ainus in Japan avoid eating otters, because otters are believed to be forgetful animals and consuming them could cause loss of memory. Europeans blamed the potato—the first edible plant they had encountered that grew from tubers rather than seeds—for a variety of problems

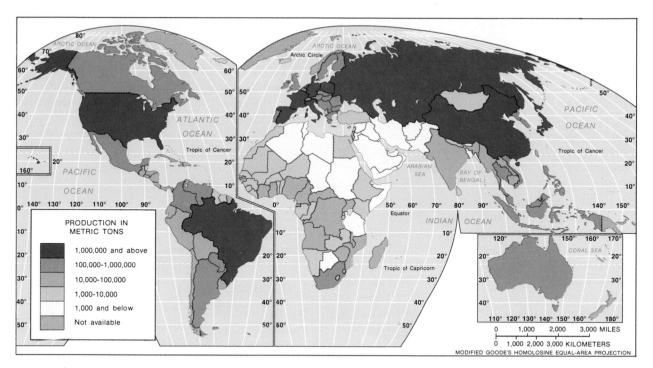

FIGURE 6–8
The amount of pork produced in different parts of the world is influenced to a considerable extent by religious taboos against consuming pork. Pork production is virtually nonexistent in predominantly Muslim regions, such as northern Africa and southwestern Asia, while the level is high in predominantly Buddhist China.

during the seventeenth and eighteenth centuries, including typhoid, scrofula, and famine. Initially, Europeans also resisted eating the potato because it resembled human deformities caused by leprosy.

Some food taboos arise out of concern for the natural environment. These taboos may help to protect endangered animals or conserve scarce natural resources. For example, to preserve scarce animal species, only a few high-ranking people in some tropical regions are permitted to hunt, while the majority of the population cultivate crops. Most food avoidance customs, however, arise from cultural values.

Relatively well-known taboos against consumption of certain foods can be found in the Bible. The ancient Hebrews were prohibited from eating a wide variety of foods, including animals that did not chew a cud or have cloven feet and fish without fins or scales. These taboos arose partially from concern for the physical environment by the Hebrews, who lived as pastoral nomads in lands bordering the eastern Mediterranean. The pig, for example, was prohibited in part because it is more suited to sedentary farming than pastoral nomadism and in part because its meat spoils relatively quickly in hot climates, such as the Mediterranean.

But the taboo against pork among many peoples, including Muslims, Hindus, and Jews, cannot be explained primarily by physical environment factors (Figure 6–8). Social values must influence the choice of diet, since people in similar climates and with similar levels of income consume different foods. One reason biblical food taboos were established was to set the Hebrew people apart from others. That Christians ignore the biblical food injunctions reflects their desire to distinguish themselves from Jews. Furthermore, as a universal religion, Christianity was less tied to taboos that originated in the Middle East.

Although grapes can be grown and wine produced in a wide variety of locations, wine distribution is based principally on cultural values, both historical and contemporary. Wine is made today primarily in locations where people like to drink it and have a tradition of excellence in making it.

The social custom of wine production in much of France and Italy extends back at least to the Roman Empire. Wine consumption declined after the fall of Rome, and many vineyards were destroyed. Monasteries preserved the wine-making tradition in medieval Europe, for both sustenance and rituals. Wine consumption has become extremely popular again in Europe in recent centuries, as well as in the Western Hemisphere, which was colonized by Europeans. Vineyards are again owned by private individuals and corporations rather than by the church.

Wine production is discouraged in regions of the world dominated by religions other than Christianity. Hindus and Muslims in particular avoid alcoholic beverages. Thus, wine production is limited in the Middle East (other than Israel) and South Asia primarily because of cultural values, especially religious values (Figure 6–9).

Food taboos are significant even in countries dominated by popular customs, such as the United States. Americans avoid eating insects despite the nutritional value of such food. In Peru and Ecuador, on the other hand, movie theaters sell toasted ants rather than popcorn, and in Borneo ants are mixed into the rice to add a tangy flavor. The North American dislike of eating insects is amusing because many foods, such as canned mushrooms and tomato paste, contain insects, even though that is not commonly known.

KEY ISSUE

How Are Popular Customs Organized on the Landscape?

Popular customs have a different relationship to events in the physical environment than do folk customs. Popular customs, like folk customs, may orig-

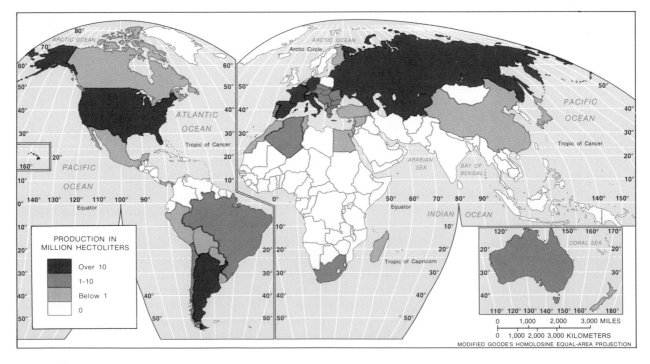

FIGURE 6–9
The distribution of wine production is influenced in part by the physical environment and in part by social customs. Most grapes used for wine production are grown on land near the Mediterranean Sea or in areas elsewhere in the world that share a similar climate. But income, preferences, and other social customs also influence wine production, as seen in the lower production levels of predominantly Muslim countries along the southern Mediterranean.

inate in one location within the context of a particular social and physical environment. But, in contrast to folk customs, popular customs diffuse rapidly across the earth's surface to locations with a variety of physical conditions. The critical factor in the diffusion of popular customs is not the distinctive physical environment of a location but the presence of beliefs, institutions, and material traits conducive to accepting popular customs. In particular, the diffusion of popular customs depends on a people's having sufficient income to acquire the tangible elements or products of popular customs and the leisure time to make use of those elements.

Like folk customs, popular customs have a spatial distribution. But folk customs are more likely to be responsive to the physical environment, whereas popular customs may be organized across the landscape with relatively little regard for physical features. Instead, the spatial organization of popular customs depends more on the distribution of social and economic characteristics. Popular customs can significantly modify or control the landscape, however, and they may appear to be imposed on the landscape rather than springing forth from the local physical environment, as with many folk customs. With changing technology, popular customs acquire an increasingly uniform appearance.

Spatial Organization of Popular Customs

The most critical social characteristic influencing the acceptance of popular customs is the level of economic development. People in a country with a relatively developed economy are likely to have higher incomes, more time, and other material traits that result in greater utilization of popular customs.

Television service. The distribution of television service across the earth's surface is not influenced by the physical environment. Instead, regional differences in television service can be distinguished by cultural characteristics, including the number of television sets available and the method of government control.

Television service falls into four categories. The first category consists of countries in which nearly every household owns a television set. This category includes the relatively developed countries of North America and Europe as well as Australia, New Zealand, and Japan. A second category consists of countries in which television ownership is common but by no means universal. These are primarily Latin American countries and the poorer European countries, such as Turkey and Portugal.

The third category consists of countries in which television exists but has not yet been widely disseminated to the population as a whole because of the high cost of the sets. This category includes the remaining countries of Latin America as well as some in Africa and Asia. Many countries in this category have established television stations both as a matter of national prestige and as a symbol of economic development. Finally, the fourth category consists of approximately 40 countries, most of which are in Africa and Asia, that have very few television sets per capita (Figure 6–10). Some of the countries do not have operating television stations, though programs from neighboring countries may be received with antennas.

The mix of television programming varies among countries. Compared to other countries, television in the United States devotes smaller percentages of time to news and education and more time to entertainment. The U.S. figures are explained in part by the great number of stations and the method of ownership.

Control of television. In the United States, most television stations are owned by private corporations that receive licenses from the government to operate at specific frequencies. The company makes a profit by selling air time for advertisements. Some stations, however, are owned by local governments or other nonprofit organizations and are devoted to educational or noncommercial programs. The U.S. pattern of private stations is found in other countries of the Western Hemisphere but not elsewhere in the world.

Government control of broadcasting is more extensive in other countries. In most Western European countries and Japan, television is operated by a public corporation, whose board of directors is appointed by the government. The British Broadcasting Corporation (BBC), for example, obtains revenue from the sale of licenses, required of all owners of television sets; the fee is higher for color televisions than for black and white sets. The BBC accepts no advertising, a factor that may add to the enjoyment of programs but at the same time re-

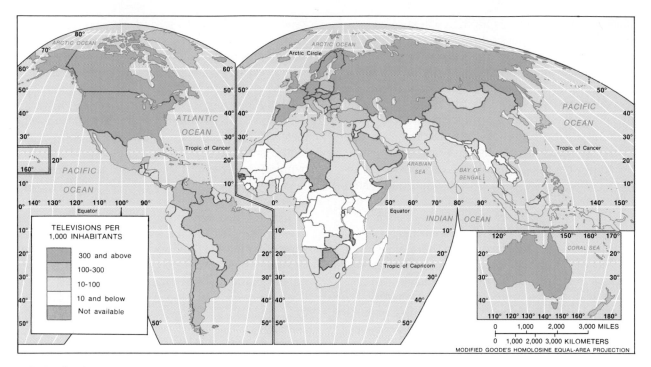

FIGURE 6-10
Television has diffused from North America and Europe to other regions of the world, but the number of television sets per capita still varies considerably among countries. This number is also an important indicator of a society's level of development, as discussed in Chapter 8.

duces the potential of the corporation to generate income. Government-controlled stations in other countries do show advertisements, though typically in extended blocks of time between programs rather than in the midst of programs, as in the United States. However, some European countries, including the United Kingdom and France, have turned over some channels to private companies.

In a third kind of television control, the government directly operates the station. Such a pattern can be found in the Soviet Union, Eastern Europe, and many developing countries. Soviet television, run by the Radio and Television Committee of the Council of Ministers, is financed as a part of the national budget.

From a geographic viewpoint, television plays an important role in enhancing communications and understanding among people around the world. The air waves are free: once a program has been broadcast, it is available to people without regard for cultural barriers. Long before the 1990 unification of East and West Germany, for example, the

principal means of cultural interaction between the two areas was by television. Easterners obtained news, as well as awareness of the higher level of material comfort, from West German television.

The internationalization of broadcasting has been markedly enhanced by the development of satellite technology and home receiving stations. Cable television, available in more than a third of U.S. homes, has diffused to Europe as well. Cable television permits a wider choice of programs, including those from distant and foreign sources. Satellite dishes enable individual owners to select signals from stations anywhere in the world, not just from those in the immediate range or from those chosen by the cable operator. As with the diffusion of early television technology, current changes in American television will soon reach other regions.

Clothing styles. The invention of rapid communication and transportation systems has helped the diffusion of other popular customs, such as clothing styles. Clothing habits reveal how popular customs can be distributed across the landscape with little regard for distinctive physical features. Such habits reflect the availability of income as well as social forms such as job characteristics.

In Western countries, clothing habits generally reflect occupations rather than particular physical environments. A lawyer or business executive, for example, tends to wear a dark suit, light shirt or blouse, and necktie or scarf, whereas a factory worker wears jeans and a workshirt. A lawyer in California is more likely to dress like a lawyer in New York than like a steelworker in California.

A second influence on Western clothing is higher income compared with the rest of the world. Women's clothes, in particular, change in fashion from one year to the next. The color, shape, and design of dresses change to imitate pieces created by cloth-

ing designers. For social purposes, people with sufficient income may update their wardrobe frequently with the latest fashions.

Improved communications have permitted the rapid diffusion of clothing fashions from one part of the earth's surface to another. Original designs for women's dresses created in Paris, Milan, London, or New York are reproduced in large quantities at factories in Asia and sold for relatively low prices at American and European chain stores. Speed is essential in manufacturing copies of designer dresses because fashion tastes change quickly.

Until recently, one year could elapse from the time an original dress was displayed to the time that inexpensive reproductions were available in the stores. Now, the time lag is less than six weeks because of the diffusion of facsimile machines, com-

Watching television has become an important leisure activity and source of information for people in most countries, including South Africa. In developing countries, large crowds may gather to watch television, because rates of ownership are still low.

FIGURE 6–11
States that have a high incidence of consumption of Canadian whiskey are located in the north, along the Canadian border. Preference for Canadian whiskey has apparently diffused south from Canada into the United States. Rum has a higher incidence of consumption in east-coast states, where it is imported into the country.

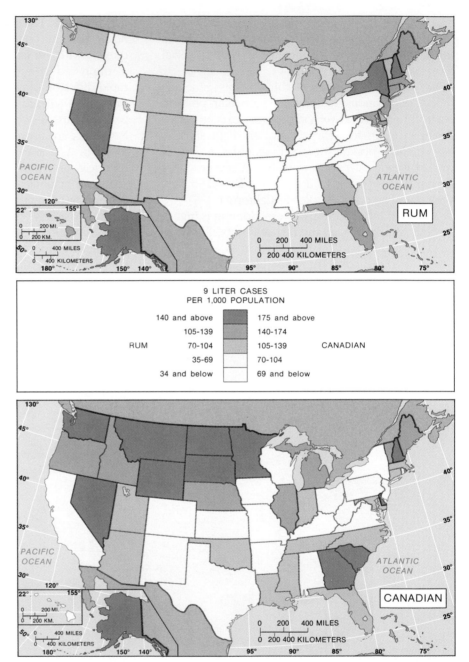

puters, and satellites. Sketches, patterns, and specifications are sent instantly from European fashion centers to American corporate headquarters, and then on to Asian factories. Buyers from the major retail chains can view the fashions on large, high-definition televisions linked by satellite networks.

The internationalization of clothing styles has involved increasing awareness by North Americans and Europeans of the variety of folk costumes around the world. Increased travel and the diffusion of television have exposed Westerners to other forms of dress, just as people in other parts of the world have come into contact with Western dress. The poncho from South America, the dashiki of the Yoruba people of Nigeria, and the Aleut parka have been adopted by people elsewhere in the world. The continued use of folk costumes in some parts of the world may persist not because of distinctive environmental conditions or traditional cultural values but to preserve past memories or to attract tourists.

Jeans. An important symbol of the diffusion of Western fashion customs is jeans, which has become a prized possession for young people throughout the world. In the late 1960s, jeans acquired an image of youthful independence in the United States, as young people adopted a style of clothing previously associated with low-status manual laborers and farmers.

Jeans have since become one of the most highly sought objects in countries throughout the world. In November 1978, Levi Strauss shipped 800,000 pairs of jeans to East Germany for $9 million ($11.25 a pair). The East German government felt compelled to buy the shipment because of strong dissatisfaction with the denim trousers manufactured inside the country. Long lines formed to buy the jeans, and each customer could only buy one pair. Although priced at the equivalent of $74 each, the jeans sold quickly to customers willing to buy them because they were authentic Levi jeans.

A similar situation existed in the Soviet Union, where jeans became an obsession and a status symbol among the young. Gangs would attack people in order to steal their American-made jeans, and authentic jeans would sell for the equivalent of $400 on the black market. Ironically, jeans were brought into the Soviet Union by the elite, including diplomats, bureaucrats, and business executives—essentially, those who were permitted to travel to the West. These citizens obtained scarce products in the West and resold them inside the Soviet Union for a considerable profit.

Problems such as the scarcity of high-quality jeans played a major role in the dismantling of communist governments in Eastern Europe during the late 1980s and early 1990s. Eastern Europeans, who were aware of Western fashions and products— thanks to television—could not obtain them because government-controlled industries were ineffi-

cient and geared to producing steel rather than consumer-oriented goods (*see* Chapter 10).

Popular food customs. Consumption of large quantities of alcoholic beverages and fresh produce are characteristic of the food customs of popular societies. But the amounts of alcohol and produce consumed, as well as the preferences for particular types, vary by region within relatively developed countries, such as the United States.

Americans choose particular beverages, fruits, or vegetables partly on the basis of preference for what is produced, grown, or imported locally. Bourbon consumption in the United States is concentrated in the upper South, where most of it is produced. Rum consumption is heavily concentrated on the East Coast, where it arrives from the Caribbean, while Canadian whiskey is preferred in communities close to Canada (Figure 6–11).

Similarly, Southerners prefer okra, beans, melons, and other warm-weather fruits and vegetables grown in the region, while they consume relatively small quantities of vegetables grown in cooler climates or in California. Supermarkets in the Northeast and on the West Coast stock more varieties of fruits and vegetables compared with those in the South or Midwest, possibly because the clustering of larger percentages of foreign-born residents in the cities of the former areas produces greater diversity in preferences (Figure 6–12).

Californians may consume more fresh produce than other Americans in part because the state grows nearly half the total national output. But cultural backgrounds also affect the amount of alcohol and fresh produce consumed. People in California may be more aware of evidence concerning the health benefits of consuming fresh produce, as evidenced by the relatively high concentration of health food stores in the state.

Alcohol consumption relates partially to religious backgrounds and partially to income and advertising. Baptists and Mormons, for example, drink less than adherents of other denominations. Because Baptists are concentrated in the Southeast and Mormons in Utah, these regions have relatively low consumption rates. Nevada has a high rate because of the heavy concentration of gambling and other resort activities there.

FIGURE 6–12
Preferences for some fruits and vegetables vary among U.S. regions. The items shown are consumed at a rate of at least twice the average in the cities indicated. Variations derive at least somewhat from local growing conditions and from ethnicity of local residents.

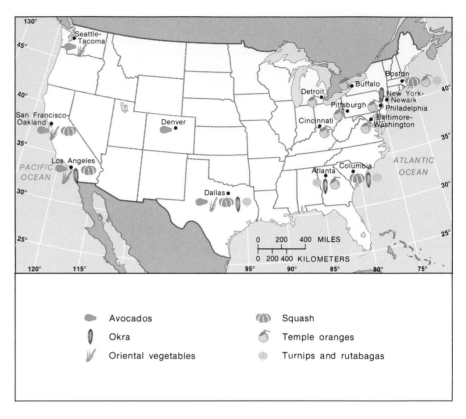

Geographers cannot explain all the regional variations in food preferences. Why do urban dwellers generally prefer Scotch and Easterners consume grapes and Temple oranges? Why is per capita consumption of fresh produce nearly four times higher in Columbia, South Carolina, and Boston than in Washington, D.C., Baltimore, and Chicago? Why does consumption of gin, vodka, lemons, and cauliflower show little spatial variation within the United States?

In general, though, consumption of alcohol and fresh produce is a popular custom that is primarily dependent on two factors—high income and national advertising. Variations within the United States are much less significant than differences between the United States and developing countries of Africa and Asia.

Impact of Popular Customs on the Landscape

For popular customs, landscape is something to be modified to enhance participation in a leisure activity or to promote the sale of a product. Even if the resulting landscape looks "natural," it is actually the deliberate creation of people in pursuit of popular social customs.

Golf courses, because of their large size (80 hectares, or 200 acres), provide a particularly prominent example of the imposition of popular customs on the landscape. A surge of interest in playing golf in the United States has resulted in construction of roughly 200 courses annually since the late 1980s. The geographer John Rooney attributes the increase in participation to increased income and leisure time, especially among recently retired older people and younger people with flexible working hours.

According to Rooney, the provision of golf courses is not uniform across the United States. Although perceived as a warm-weather sport, the number of golf courses per person is actually highest in north central states, from Kansas to North Dakota, as well as the northeastern states abutting the Great Lakes, from Wisconsin to upstate New York (Figure 6–13). People in these regions have a long tradition of playing golf, and social clubs with golf courses are important to the fabric of the regions' popular customs.

In contrast, access to golf courses is more limited in the South and California, as well as in the heavily urbanized Middle Atlantic region between New York City and Washington, D.C. Rapid population growth in the South and West and the lack of buildable land in the Middle Atlantic region have reduced the number of courses per capita. But selected southern and western areas— such as coastal South Carolina, southern Florida, and central Arizona—have high concentrations of golf courses as a result of the arrival of large numbers of golf-play-ing northerners, either as vacationers or permanent residents.

Golf courses are designed partially in response to local environmental conditions. Species of grasses are selected depending on what will thrive in the local climate and still be suitable for the distinctive needs of greens, fairways, and roughs. Existing trees and other vegetation are retained if possible; not too many fairways in Michigan are lined by palm trees. Yet, like other popular customs, golf courses require remaking the landscape: creating or flattening hills, cutting grass or letting it grow tall, carting in or digging up sand for traps, and draining or expanding bodies of water for hazards.

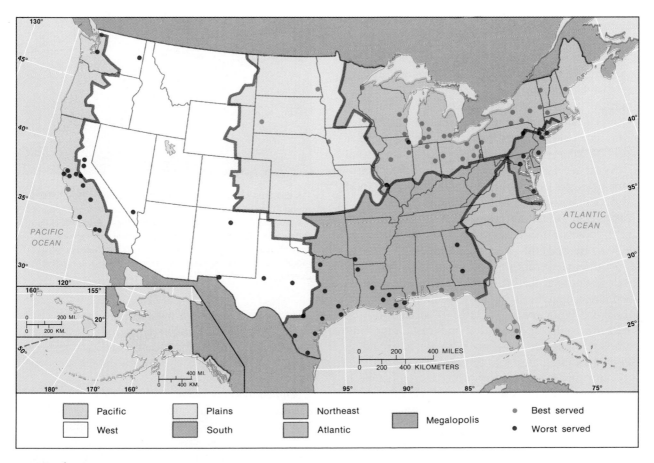

FIGURE 6–13
The 50 best-served and worst-served metropolitan areas in terms of the number of golf holes per capita. In the north central states, people have a long tradition of playing golf, even if it is confined to summer months. The ratio is less favorable for golfers in the large urban areas of the east coast, as well as in the rapidly growing areas of the south and west.

Fast-food restaurants. The distribution of popular customs across the earth's surface tends to produce more uniform landscapes. The spatial expressions of a particular popular custom in one location will be similar to the expressions elsewhere. In fact, the promoters of various popular customs want a uniform impact on the landscape in order to generate higher consumption.

The diffusion of fast-food restaurants provides an example of landscape uniformity. Such restaurants are usually organized as franchises and owned by local operators who have contracts to use a national company's methods, symbols, trademarks, and architectural styles. The buildings are designed to be immediately recognizable as part of a national or multinational company to both local residents and travelers. Prominent display of a uniform sign is one way to promote immediate familiarity.

Much of the attraction of fast-food restaurants comes from the convenience of the product and the use of the building as a socializing location for teenagers or families with young children. At the same time, the success of fast-food restaurants depends on large-scale mobility: people who travel or move to another city immediately recognize a familiar place. Newcomers to a particular place know what to expect in the restaurant, because the establishment does not reflect strange and unfamiliar local customs that could be uncomfortable.

Fast-food restaurants originally developed to attract people who arrived by car. The buildings were likely to be brightly colored and gaudy in order to attract the eye of motorists. More recently built fast-food restaurants feature a more subdued appearance, including brick facades, pseudoantique fixtures, and other stylistic details. To make sure the structure could be reused if the restaurant fails, company signs are now likely to be freestanding rather than integrated into the building design.

Uniformity in the appearance of the landscape is promoted by a wide variety of other popular structures in North America, such as gas stations, supermarkets, and motels. These structures are designed so that both local residents and visitors immediately recognize the purpose of the building, even if not the name of the company.

Global diffusion. Physical expression of uniformity in popular customs has diffused from North America to other parts of the world. American mo-

U.S. fast-food chains have diffused to developing countries, although the price of a bucket of chicken may exceed the average worker's daily wages. The first Kentucky Fried Chicken in the People's Republic of China offers drive-through service, even though the customer in China is likely to arrive by a mode of transportation different from that used in relatively developed societies.

tels and fast-food chains have opened in other countries. These establishments appeal to North American travelers, but most customers are local residents who wish to sample the American customs they have seen on television.

Diffusion of popular customs across the earth's surface is not confined to products that originate in North America. With more rapid communications and transportation, customs from any place on the earth's surface can rapidly diffuse elsewhere. Japanese automobiles and electronics, for example, have diffused in recent years to the rest of the world, including North America. Until the 1970s, automobiles produced in North America, Europe, and Japan differed substantially in appearance and size, but in recent years styling has become more uniform, largely because of consumer preference around the world for Japanese cars. Automakers such as General Motors, Ford, Toyota, and Honda now manufacture similar models in North and South America, Europe, and Asia instead of separately designed models for each continent.

KEY ISSUE

What Problems Result from Worldwide Convergence of Popular Customs?

The international diffusion of popular customs has led to two problems, both of which can be understood in a geographic perspective. First, the diffusion of popular customs may threaten the survival of traditional folk customs in many countries. Second, popular customs may be less responsive to the diversity of local conditions in the physical environment than folk customs and consequently may have adverse environmental impacts.

Threat to Folk Customs

Many developing countries fear the loss of folk customs for two reasons. First, the disappearance of folk customs may be symbolic of the loss of tradi-

tional values in society. Second, the diffusion of popular customs from relatively developed countries can lead to dominance of Western perspectives in developing countries.

Loss of traditional values. One example of the symbolic importance of folk customs is clothing. In African and Asian countries today, there is a contrast between the clothes of rural farm workers and the clothes of urban business and government leaders. Adoption of Western clothing styles is part of a process of imitation and replication of Western symbols of success. Leaders of African and Asian countries have traveled to the West and experienced the sense of social status attached to Western clothes, especially men's business suits. Adoption of Western clothes has become a symbol of authority and leadership at home. The Western business suit has been accepted as the uniform for business executives and bureaucrats around the world.

Western clothes, however, can become a political symbol. In the 1970s, Shiite Muslim fundamentalists in Iran opposed the widespread acceptance of Western customs and attitudes in the country, including adoption of Western clothes, especially by women living in the cities. After fundamentalists gained control of the government in 1979, women were strongly urged to abandon skirts and blouses in favor of the traditional black *chador,* a combination head covering and veil. Today, more moderate lead-

Clothing in a number of African countries demonstrates the diffusion of popular customs from relatively developed societies. Some people prefer to wear traditional robes, while others have adopted Western-style clothes, such as business suits.

ers in Iran tend to wear Western business suits, while extremists tend to wear traditional uncut robes.

The global diffusion of popular customs threatens the subservience of women to men embedded in many folk customs. Women were traditionally relegated to performing household chores, such as cooking, cleaning, and bearing a large number of children. Those in the labor force were likely to perform backbreaking agricultural or industrial work. Advancement was limited by low levels of education and high rates of victimization from violence, often inflicted by husbands. The concepts of legal equality and availability of economic and social opportunities outside the home have become widely accepted concepts in relatively developed countries, even where women in reality continue to suffer from discriminatory practices.

Contact with popular customs, however, has also brought negative impacts for women in developing societies, such as an increase in prostitution. Hundreds of thousands of men from relatively developed countries such as Japan and northern Europe (especially Norway, Germany, and the Netherlands) purchase tours from travel agencies that include airfare, hotels, and the use as they wish of a predetermined number of women. The principal destinations of these "sex tours" include the Philippines, Thailand, South Korea, and to a lesser extent Indonesia and Sri Lanka. International prostitution is encouraged in these countries as a major source of foreign currency. Through this form of global interaction, popular customs may regard women as essentially equal back home but as objects that money can buy in foreign folk societies.

Threat of domination. Developing countries do not fear the incursion of popular customs only for symbolic reasons. Leaders of some developing countries consider the dominance of popular customs from relatively developed countries to be a threat to national independence. The threat is posed primarily by the electronic media, especially news-gathering organizations and television.

Three countries—the United States, the United Kingdom, and Japan—dominate the television industry in developing countries. The Japanese operate primarily in South and East Asia, selling their electronic equipment to other countries. British

companies have invested directly in management and programming for television in Africa. U.S. corporations own or provide technical advice to many Latin American stations. These three countries, along with the Soviet Union, are the major exporters of programs. For example, only 1 percent of all television programs in the United States and 4 percent in Japan are foreign-made, compared to 84 percent in Guatemala and 71 percent in Malaysia.

Leaders of many developing countries view the spread of television as a new method of economic and cultural imperialism on the part of the developed countries, especially the United States. American television, like other media, presents characteristically American beliefs and social forms, such as upward social mobility, relative freedom for women, glorification of youth, and stylized violence. These themes may conflict with and drive out traditional social customs.

Developing countries fear the effects of the news-gathering capability of the media even more than the entertainment function. The diffusion of information to newspapers around the world is dominated by three organizations—Associated Press (AP), United Press International (UPI), and Reuters—all owned by British or American companies. The process of gathering news throughout the world is expensive, and most newspapers and broadcasters are unable to afford their own correspondents. Instead, they buy the right to use the dispatches of one or more of the main news organizations. AP and UPI transmit most news photographs as well and provide radio stations around the world with reports from their correspondents. Similarly, two joint British-American organizations—Visnews and UPITN—supply most of the world's television news film.

The news media in most developing countries are dominated by the government, which typically runs the radio and television service as well as the domestic news-gathering agency. The newspaper may be owned by the government, a political party, or a private individual, but in any event the paper is usually dependent on the government news-gathering organization for information. Sufficient funds are not available to establish a private news service.

Many African and Asian government officials criticize the Western concept of freedom of the press.

They argue that the American news organizations reflect American values and do not provide a balanced, accurate view of other countries. U.S. news-gathering organizations are more interested in covering earthquakes, hurricanes, or other sensational disasters than more meaningful but less visual and dramatic domestic stories, such as family-planning programs, health care innovations, or construction of new roads.

Veteran travelers and journalists invariably pack a portable shortwave radio when they visit other countries. In many regions of the world, the only reliable and unbiased news accounts come from the British Broadcasting Corporation (BBC) World Service shortwave radio newscasts. During the civil war in Iran in 1979, the television news anchor, who was not allowed to report the government's deteriorating position, urged citizens to listen to the BBC World Service to learn the most accurate local news. During the 1991 Gulf War, the BBC World Service again provided the most reliable information to many residents of the Middle East.

In the United States and Canada, native Americans increasingly recognize the importance of retaining traditional folk customs. For example, the sport of lacrosse has fostered cultural identity among the Iroquois Confederation of Six Nations—Cayugas, Mohawks, Oneidas, Onondagas, Senecas, and Tuscaroras—who live in the northeastern United States and southeastern Canada. As early as 1636, European explorers observed the Iroquois playing lacrosse, known in their language as *guhchigwaha,* which means "bump hips." European colonists in Canada picked up the game from the Iroquois and diffused it to a handful of U.S. communities, especially Maryland and upstate and Long Island, New York. The name *lacrosse* derived from the French words, *la crosse,* for a bishop's crosier or staff, which has a shape similar to the lacrosse stick.

In 1990, the International Lacrosse Federation invited the Iroquois nation to participate in the Lacrosse World Championships, held in Perth, Australia, along with teams from Australia, Canada, England, and the United States. Although the Iroquois did not win any games, they had the satisfaction of hearing their national anthem played and seeing their flag fly alongside those of the other participants.

Negative Environmental Impact

The second geographic problem is the adverse impact on environmental quality caused by the diffusion of some popular customs. Environmental problems are of two kinds: depletion of scarce natural resources and pollution of the landscape. To some degree, environmental problems are caused by the form of particular popular customs as well as by the large quantity of objects produced to foster popular customs. These problems are examined more comprehensively in Chapter 13.

Depletion of scarce resources. The first problem caused by the diffusion of some popular customs is increased demand for raw materials. Popular habits may demand a large supply of certain animals, resulting in the extinction of some species and imbalance in other ecological systems. Some animals are killed for their skins, which can be shaped into fashionable clothing and sold to people living thousands of kilometers from the animals' habitat. The skins of the mink, lynx, jaguar, kangaroo, and whale, for example, have been highly valued for various articles of clothing, to the point of endangering the survival of these species. Many folk customs may also encourage the use of animal skins but the need is usually smaller than for popular customs. Folk customs have also resulted in the virtual elimination of some species, such as the buffalo.

Increased demand for consumption of some products can strain the capacity of the environment to support popular customs. Increased consumption of meat, for example, has not resulted in the elimination of cattle and poultry. But animal consumption is a relatively inefficient method for people to acquire needed calories because the animals are normally fed grain, which could otherwise be used to feed people directly. On average, nearly 10 kilograms (20 pounds) of grain are used to produce 1 kilogram of beef sold in the supermarket, and nearly 3 kilograms (6 pounds) of grain are used for every kilogram of chicken. With a large percentage of the world's population undernourished, some people question the use of grain to feed animals for eventual human consumption.

Pollution. Popular customs can also cause adverse environmental impacts through pollution. The physical environment has the capacity to accept some discharges from human activities. Popular customs generate a relatively high amount of residuals—gas, liquid, solids, heat, and noise—which must be disposed of in the environment. With an increasing number of people in the world adopting popular customs, adverse effects are greater.

The physical environment provides five alternatives for the discharge of residuals—air, water, land, heat, and noise—discussed in Chapter 13. While residuals generated by popular customs are discharged in all five forms, the most visible alternative is solid waste, such as cans, bottles, old cars, and plastic products. These products are often discarded on the landscape rather than reused.

Folk customs, like popular customs, can also cause environmental damage, especially when natural processes are ignored. Ironically, relatively developed societies, which produce large quantities of consumer goods essential for the diffusion of popular customs, have developed both the technological capacity for large-scale environmental damage and the knowledge to control or minimize the adverse effects if a commitment of time and money were made to the effort.

Summary

Social customs can be divided into folk and popular. Folk customs are most often found among small, homogeneous groups living in relative isolation at a low level of economic development. Popular customs are characteristic of societies with relatively developed channels of communications, which enable rapid diffusion of uniform concepts. Geographers are concerned with several aspects of folk and popular customs. Here again are the key issues for Chapter 6.

1. **How are social customs distributed?** Because of distinctive processes of origin and diffusion, folk customs have different distribution patterns from popular customs. Folk customs are more likely to have an anonymous origin and to diffuse slowly through migration, whereas popular customs are more likely to be invented and diffused rapidly with the use of modern communications.

2. **What is the relationship between the landscape and the development of unique folk regions?** Geographers examine the impact of the physical environment on social customs and the impact of social customs on the land. A folk custom is more likely than a popular custom to develop in response to natural conditions. On the other hand, a unique folk custom may create a unique landscape.

3. **How are popular customs organized on the landscape?** Popular customs and folk customs have different relationships to the physical environment. On the one hand, popular customs are less likely to derive from physical environment conditions. On the other hand, they are more likely to cause greater uniformity in the landscape.

4. **What problems result from worldwide convergence of popular customs?** Geographers observe two kinds of problems as a result of the diffusion of popular customs across the landscape. First, popular customs—generally originating in Western economically developed countries—may cause elimination of some folk customs. Second, popular customs may adversely affect the physical environment.

The Aboriginal Artists Return to Australia

The Aboriginal Australian Artists and their audience in New York's Lincoln Center represented a clash between folk customs—rooted in the uniqueness of an isolated landscape—and popular customs, which impose uniform standards on the landscape. Will the aboriginal dancers maintain their traditions? Or will they be enticed by the consumer goods characteristic of popular customs, such as televisions and cars? What did they take from the United States back with them to Australia?

By observing the reaction of groups such as these aborigines, geographers can observe the changing distribution of folk and popular customs. Geographers also recognize the relationship between the increasing acceptance of popular customs and the development of modern economies across the earth's surface.

Key Terms

Custom The frequent repetition of an act, to the extent that it becomes characteristic of the group of people performing the act.

Folk custom A custom traditionally practiced by a small, homogeneous, rural group living in relative isolation from other groups; also known as a vernacular custom.

Habit A repetitive act performed by a particular person.

Popular custom A custom found in a large, heterogeneous society that shares certain habits despite differences in other personal characteristics; also known as an international custom.

Taboo A restriction on behavior imposed by social custom.

Thinking Geographically

1. Should geographers regard culture and social customs as meaningful generalizations about a group of people, or should they concentrate instead on understanding how specific individuals interact with the landscape?
2. In what ways might gender affect the impact of social customs on the landscape?
3. Are there examples of groups—either in relatively developed countries or in developing countries—that have successfully resisted the diffusion of popular customs?
4. What elements of the landscape are emphasized in the portrayal of various places on television?
5. What images of social customs do countries depict in campaigns to promote tourism? To what extent do these images reflect local social customs realistically?

Further Readings

Bale, John. *Sport and Place: A Geography of Sport in England, Scotland, and Wales.* Lincoln, NE: University of Nebraska Press, 1983.

Ballas, Donald J., and Margaret J. King. "Cultural Geography and Popular Culture: Proposal for a Creative Merger." *Journal of Cultural Geography* 2 (1981) 154–63.

Bennett, Merrill K. *The World's Foods.* New York: Harper and Bros., 1954.

Bigsby, C. W. E., ed. *Superculture: American Popular Culture and Europe.* Bowling Green, OH: Bowling Green Popular Press, 1975.

Blacking, John, and Joann W. Kealiinohomoku. *The Performing Arts: Music and Dance.* The Hague, Netherlands: Mouton, 1979.

Carlson, Alvar W. "The Contributions of Cultural Geographers to the Study of Popular Culture." *Journal of Popular Culture* 11 (Spring 1978): 830–31.

Carney, George O. "Bluegrass Grows All Around: The Spatial Dimensions of a Country Music Style." *Journal of Geography* 73 (April 1974): 34-55.

———. "From Down Home to Uptown: The Diffusion of Country-Music Radio Stations in the United States." *Journal of Geography* 76 (March 1977): 104-110.

Chakravarti, A. K. "Regional Preference for Foods: Some Aspects of Food Habit Patterns in India." *Canadian Geographer* 18 (Winter 1974): 395–410.

Chubb, Michael, and Holly R. Chubb. *One Third of Our Time?* New York: Wiley, 1981.

Crowley, William K. "Old Order Amish Settlement: Diffusion and Growth." *Annals of the Association of American Geographers* 68 (June 1978): 249–65.

DeBlij, Harm J. *A Geography of Viticulture.* Miami: University of Miami Geographical Society, 1981.

Fusch, Richard, and Larry Ford. "Architecture and the Geography of the American City." *Geographical Review* 73 (July 1983): 324–39.

Jakle, John A. "Roadside Restaurants and Place-Product-Packaging." *Journal of Cultural Geography* 3 (1982): 76–93.

Jakle, John A., and Richard L. Mattson. "The Evolution of a Commercial Strip." *Journal of Cultural Geography* 1 (Spring/Summer 1981): 12–25.

Karan, Pradyumna P., and Cotton Mather. "Art and Geography: Patterns in the Himalayas." *Annals of the Association of American Geographers* 66 (December 1976): 487–515.

Kniffen, Fred B. "Folk-Housing: Key to Diffusion." *Annals of the Association of American Geographers* 55 (December 1965): 549–77.

Lamme, Ary J., III, ed. *North American Culture.* Vol. 1. Stillwater, OK: Society for the North American Cultural Survey, 1984.

Lewis, Pierce F., Yi-Fu Tuan, and David Lowenthal. *Visual Blight in America.* Washington, D. C.: Association of American Geographers, 1973.

Lomax, Alan. *The Folk Songs of North America.* Garden City, NY: Doubleday, 1960.

Lornell, Christopher, and W. Theodore Mealor, Jr. "Traditions and Research Opportunities in Folk Geography." *Professional Geographer* 35 (1983): 51–56.

McColl, Robert W. "By Their Dwellings Shall We Know Them: Home and Setting Among China's Inner Asian Ethnic Groups." *Focus* 39 (no. 4, 1989): 1–56.

Rooney, John F., Jr. *A Geography of American Sport.* Reading, MA: Addison-Wesley, 1974.

Rooney, John F., Jr., and Paul L. Butt. "Beer, Bourbon and Boone's Farm: A Geographical Examination of Alcoholic Drink in the United States." *Journal of Popular Culture* 11 (Spring 1978): 832–56.

Rooney, John F., Jr., Wilbur Zelinsky, and Dean R. Louder, eds. *This Remarkable Continent: An Atlas of United States and Canadian Society and Culture.* College Station, TX: Texas A & M University Press for the Society for the North American Cultural Survey, 1982.

Rubin, Barbara. "A Chronology of Architecture in Los Angeles." *Annals of the Association of American Geographers* 69 (September 1979): 339–61.

Shortridge, Barbara G., and James R. Shortridge. "Consumption of Fresh Produce in the Metropolitan United States." *Geographical Review* 79 (January 1989): 79–98.

Szalai, Alexander, ed. *The Use of Time.* The Hague, Netherlands: Mouton, 1972.

Tunstall, Jeremy. *The Media Are American.* New York: Columbia University Press, 1977.

Van Doren, Carlton S., George B. Priddle, and John E. Lewis. *Land and Leisure: Concepts and Methods in Outdoor Recreation.* 2d ed. Chicago: Maaroufa Press, 1979.

Zelinsky, Wilbur. "North America's Vernacular Regions." *Annals of the Association of American Geographers* 70 (March 1980): 1–16.

Also consult the following journals: *International Folk Music Council Journal; Journal of American Culture; Journal of American Folklore; Journal of American Studies; Journal of Cultural Geography; Journal of Leisure Research; Journal of Popular Culture; Journal of Sport History; Landscape; Leisure Science.*

7
Political
Geography

KEY ISSUES

- What is the difference between a state and a nation?

- How are boundaries drawn between states?

- What problems result from the location of boundaries between states?

- Which geographic elements contribute to national power?

How many countries can you name? The old style of geography sometimes required memorization of countries and their capitals. Today, human geography emphasizes a thematic approach. We are concerned with the location of activities in the world and the reasons for particular spatial distributions. Despite the change in emphasis, you should still know the location of countries. Without such knowledge you are like someone translating an article in a foreign language by looking up each word in a dictionary.

In recent years, Americans have repeatedly seen military conflicts and revolutionary changes in previously obscure places in the world. Political geography can help people understand the various cultural and physical factors that underlie such political unrest.

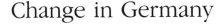

Change in Germany

C A S E   S T U D Y   Helmut Leder lives in Streignitz, a village of 2,500 in the state of Saxony-Anhalt, Germany. Between 1949 and 1990, Streignitz was part of the German Democratic Republic (DDR), created after Germany's defeat in World War II. The victorious allies—the United States, the United Kingdom, France, and the Soviet Union—divided Germany, as well as the capital of Berlin, into four occupation zones. . When sharp political differences between the Soviet Union and the other three made reestablishment of one Germany impossible after World War II, two countries were created: the Democratic Republic (East Germany) in the Soviet occupation zone and the Federal Republic (West Germany) in the territory of the other three occupation zones.

The Leders are farmers, producing grain and vegetables on rich agricultural land. Back in 1958, the East German government forced the Leders, along with everyone else in Streignitz, to turn over control of their small farm to create a large state-run collective. The Ministry of Agriculture gave detailed instructions concerning what to grow, how much to grow, and what prices to charge.

The Leder's son Roland fled to the Federal Republic in September 1989. He was fed up with the poor conditions of daily life: no telephone or color television, a fourteen-year waiting list for an underpowered Trabant automobile. Roland had wanted to live in the East German city of Leipzig but was neither able to find an apartment nor secure government permission to move there.

During the late 1940s and early 1950s, 3.5 million Germans migrated from the DDR to the Federal Republic, one-sixth of the country's population. To prevent further population loss, in 1952 the East Germans sealed the West German border with barbed wire fences and mines. For a while, Easterners could still escape into West Berlin, but that access was closed in 1961, when the DDR constructed the Berlin Wall.

Roland Leder was able to reach West Germany, because in August 1989, Hungary—like East Germany, at the time still a communist country—opened its border with democratic Austria. East Germans could travel through then-communist Czechoslovakia to Hungary, cross into Austria, and reach West Germany. When Roland left, he feared that he would never see his family in Streignitz again. Yet, less than six months later the border between the two Germanys was opened, and within eighteen months the country was reunified.

After the reunification of Germany, the Leder's collective farm was dissolved. The Leders are among the more fortunate members of the former collective: because they owned their farm prior to the forced collectivization, they could regain possession. Other members of the collective face an uncertain future: because Germany's eastern states contain twice as many farmers as needed, many began looking for other jobs. But job opportunities are scarce throughout the eastern states, a threat to the stability of Germany—and, therefore, to all of Europe.

The global political landscape has been altered fundamentally in the 1990s by the end of the so-called Cold War—that is, the polarization of countries into two camps, one allied with the Soviet Union and the other allied with the United States. Geographic concepts help us to understand the changing political organization of the earth's surface. We can also use geographic factors to examine the causes of political change and instability and to anticipate potential trouble spots around the world.

When looking at photographs of the earth transmitted by satellites, we can distinguish land masses from the large bodies of water. We can see mountains and rivers, deserts and fertile agricultural land, urban areas and forests. The photograph of the earth at the beginning of this chapter, taken from a European Space Agency satellite, clearly shows much of Europe, including France, Germany, Ireland, Italy, and the United Kingdom.

What we cannot see in the satellite photograph are boundaries between countries. Boundary lines are not painted on the earth's surface like markings on a football field. Yet the maps in this text show lines separating countries. Aerial photographs do not show individual countries in different colors, but the maps in this text do. Although lines are not painted on the actual surface of the earth, these national divisions are very real and more important than most of the natural features seen so clearly from the air. One of the planet's most fundamental characteristics—and one we take for granted—is the division of the earth's surface into a collection of states.

Political geographers observe two significant global patterns. First, the world is inhabited by peoples who have embraced a variety of languages, religions, and other social customs. The territory occupied by cultural groups does not always coincide with the territory controlled by individual states. Conflicts develop among and within states as a result of the imposition of political boundaries on the cultural and physical landscapes.

Second, states possess different amounts of power as a result of their distinctive geographic characteristics. Between the 1940s and 1980s, two states exercised significantly greater power than all others: the United States and the Soviet Union. In their role as superpowers, these two states became involved with events in all corners of the earth's surface. With the possibility that the United States and Soviet Union will be less dominant in the political landscape of the 1990s, prospects increase for instability in places where cultural groups demand more political control over the territory they inhabit, including the Soviet Union itself.

What Is the Difference between a State and a Nation?

We sometimes confuse two important political geography concepts—state and nation. Before examining issues that arise from the distribution of political units across the earth's surface, we must understand the difference between these two fundamental concepts.

Characteristics of a State

The earth's land surface is divided into a collection of states. A **state** is an area organized into a political unit and ruled by an established government with control over its internal and foreign affairs. It occupies a specific territory on the earth's surface and contains a permanent population. A state has **sovereignty,** that is, independence from control of its internal affairs by other states. Because the entire area of a state has the same national government, laws, army, and leaders, it is a good example of a uniform region. The term *country* is a synonym for *state.*

The term *state,* as used in political geography, should not be confused with local government inside the United States. The fifty states of the United States are subdivisions within one state, the United States of America.

The earth's land surface has been allocated to approximately 170 states (Figure 7–1). Included in the total are 157 sovereign states belonging to the United Nations as of 1991, plus 12 other states that are not in the U.N. (Table 7–1). The number of sovereign states has increased dramatically since 1945, when only approximately 50 existed.

Korea. There is some disagreement about the actual number of sovereign states. Is Korea one sovereign state or two? A colony of Japan for many years, Korea was divided along 38° north latitude into two occupation zones by the United States and the Soviet Union after they defeated Japan in World War II.

The division of these zones became permanent in the late 1940s, when the two superpowers established separate Korean governments and withdrew their armies. The new government of North Korea invaded the South in 1950, touching off a three-year war that ended when an armistice established a cease-fire line again at the 38th parallel. Both Korean governments are committed to reuniting the country into one sovereign state but do not agree on how this can be accomplished.

China. Is the island of Taiwan a sovereign state? According to its government officials, Taiwan is not a separate sovereign state but rather is a part of China. The government of China agrees. Yet most other governments in the world consider China and Taiwan two separate and sovereign states.

This confusing situation arose from a civil war between the Nationalists and the Communists in China during the late 1940s. After losing the civil war to the Communists in 1949, the Nationalist leaders fled to the island of Taiwan, 200 kilometers (120 miles) off the coast of China. The Nationalists proclaimed they were still the legitimate rulers of the entire country of China. Until some future occasion when they would defeat the Communists and recapture all of China, the Nationalists argued, at least they could continue to govern one island of the country.

The question of who constituted the legitimate government of China plagued U.S. officials during the 1950s and 1960s. The United States had supported the Nationalists during the civil war, and many Americans opposed acknowledging that China was firmly under the control of the Communists. Consequently, the United States continued to regard the Nationalists as the official government of China until 1972, when U.S. policy finally changed, and the Communist government was officially recognized. The United States has since withdrawn official recognition of Taiwan as the legitimate government of China but still offers protection to the island in case of invasion.

FIGURE 7–1
When the United Nations was organized in 1945, only forty-nine sovereign states were members. Eight
more states joined in the late
1940s. The United Nations added
twenty-four states during the
1950s, forty-three during the
1960s, twenty-six during the 1970s,
seven during the 1980s, and two
during the 1990s. The United Nations has also lost two members
during the 1990s as a result of unification of the two Germanys and
the two Yemens.

The greatest increase in sovereign states has occurred in Africa.
Only four African states—Egypt,
Ethiopia, Liberia, and South
Africa—were original members of
the United Nations, and only six
more joined during the 1950s. Beginning in 1960, however, a collection of independent states was
carved out of most of the remaining region. In 1960 alone, fifteen
newly independent African states
became members of the United
Nations.

Most of the recently created sovereign states have been groups of
small islands. Among the states that
joined the United Nations since
1980, only Zimbabwe and Namibia
have populations in excess of
200,000.

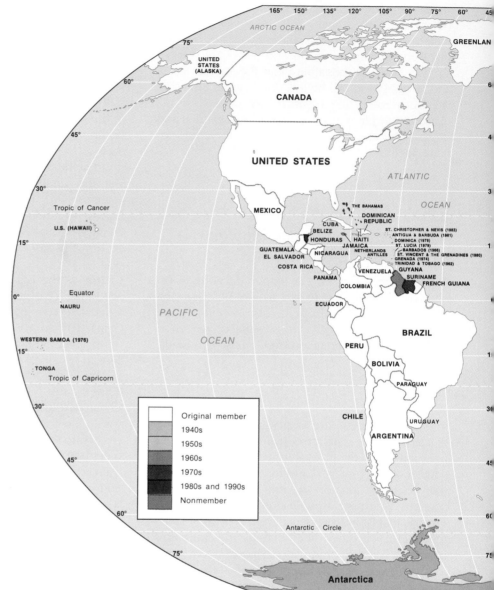

UNITED NATIONS MEMBERS
BY DATE

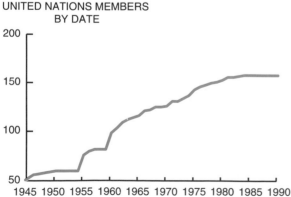

Antarctica. Antarctica is the only large land mass
on the earth's surface not part of a sovereign state.
Several states claim portions of Antarctica, including
Argentina, Australia, Chile, France, New Zealand,
Norway, and the United Kingdom (Figure 7–2). Argentina, Chile, and the United Kingdom make conflicting claims to Antarctica. The United States, the
Soviet Union, and a number of other states do not
recognize the claims of any of these countries. Sev-

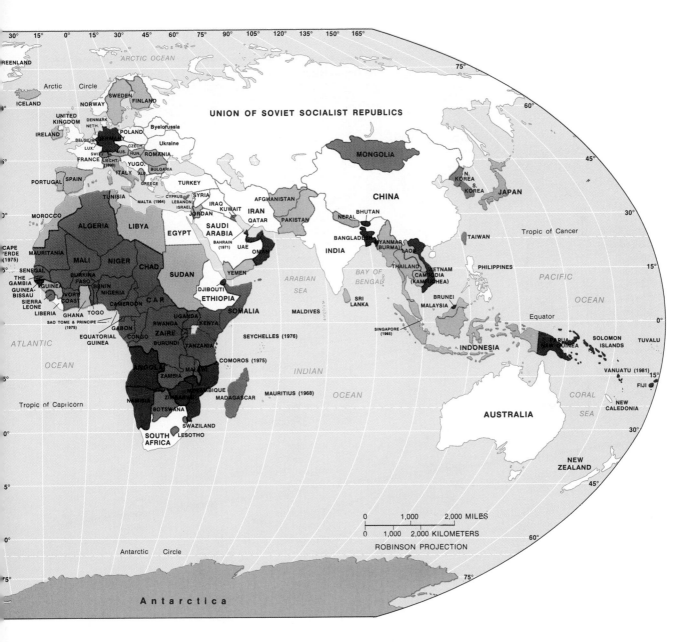

eral states have established stations on Antarctica to conduct scientific experiments and monitoring, but as yet no permanent settlements exist there.

Colonies. A **colony** is a territory that is legally tied to a sovereign state rather than completely independent. A sovereign state in some cases runs only the colony's military and foreign policy, while in other cases it controls the colony's internal affairs as well. At one time, much of the earth's surface comprised colonies, but today only a handful remain (Table 7–2).

The most populous remaining colony is Hong Kong, with nearly 6 million inhabitants. Hong Kong is a British colony situated on several islands and a small portion of the mainland of China. Britain gained control of portions of Hong Kong in a variety of ways. China surrendered Hong Kong Island to

TABLE 7–1
Sovereign states

Members of the United Nations (157)			
Afghanistan	Dominica	Liberia	Saint Vincent and the
Albania	Dominican Republic	Libya	Grenadines
Algeria	Ecuador	Liechtenstein	São Tomé e Príncipe
Angola	Egypt	Luxembourg	Saudi Arabia
Antigua and Barbuda	El Salvador	Madagascar	Senegal
Argentina	Equatorial Guinea	Malawi	Seychelles
Australia	Ethiopia	Malaysia	Sierra Leone
Austria	Fiji	Maldives	Singapore
Bahamas	Finland	Mali	Solomon Islands
Bahrain	France	Malta	Somalia
Bangladesh	Gabon	Mauritania	South Africa
Barbados	Gambia	Mauritius	Spain
Belgium	Germany	Mexico	Sri Lanka
Belize	Ghana	Mongolia	Sudan
Benin	Greece	Morocco	Suriname
Bhutan	Grenada	Mozambique	Swaziland
Bolivia	Guatemala	Myanmar (Burma)	Sweden
Botswana	Guinea	Namibia	Syria
Brazil	Guinea-Bissau	Nepal	Tanzania
Brunei	Guyana	Netherlands	Thailand
Bulgaria	Haiti	New Zealand	Togo
Burkina Faso	Honduras	Nicaragua	Trinidad and Tobago
Burundi	Hungary	Niger	Tunisia
Cambodia (Kampuchea)	Iceland	Nigeria	Turkey
Cameroon	India	Norway	Uganda
Canada	Indonesia	Oman	U.S.S.R.
Cape Verde	Iran	Pakistan	United Arab Emirates
Central African Republic	Iraq	Panama	United Kingdom
Chad	Ireland	Papua New Guinea	United States
Chile	Israel	Paraguay	Uruguay
China	Italy	Peru	Vanuatu
Colombia	Ivory Coast	Philippines	Venezuela
Comoros	Jamaica	Poland	Vietnam
Congo	Japan	Portugal	Western Samoa
Costa Rica	Jordan	Qatar	Yemen
Cuba	Kenya	Romania	Yugoslavia
Cyprus	Kuwait	Rwanda	Zaire
Czechoslovakia	Laos	Saint Christopher-Nevis	Zambia
Denmark	Lebanon	Saint Lucia	Zimbabwe
Djibouti	Lesotho		

Nonstate Members (2)	Nonmembers of the United Nations (12)		
Byelorussian S.S.R.	Andorra	Monaco	Taiwan
Ukrainian S.S.R.	Kiribiti	Nauru	Tonga
	Korea, North	San Marino	Tuvalu
	Korea, South	Switzerland	Vatican

FIGURE 7–2

National claims to Antarctica. Antarctica is the only large land mass in the world not part of a sovereign state. This land mass, which comprises 14 million square kilometers (5.4 million square miles), is 50 percent larger than Canada. Argentina, Australia, Chile, France, New Zealand, Norway, and the United Kingdom claim portions of Antarctica, and the claims of Argentina, Chile, and the United Kingdom are conflicting. In 1959, these seven countries, along with Belgium, Japan, South Africa, the Soviet Union, and the United States, signed a treaty suspending any territorial claims for thirty years. After the treaty expired in 1989, several countries reasserted their claims.

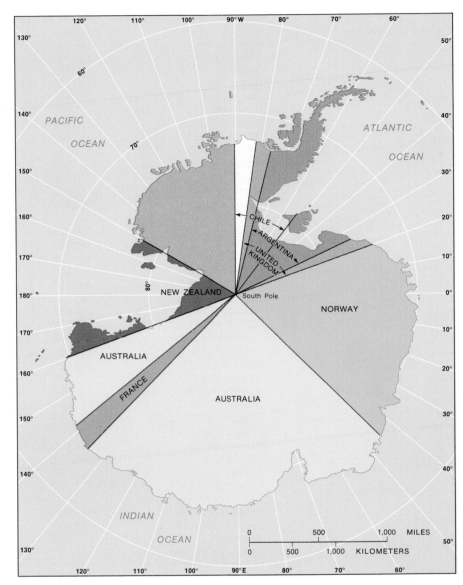

the British in 1841, and then in 1860 Britain annexed Stonecutters Island and the Kowloon Peninsula. In 1898, China leased the New Territories, which are mainly agricultural lands, to Britain for a period of 99 years. The lease expires in 1997 (Figure 7–3).

In anticipation of the end of the lease, China and Britain have reached an agreement whereby the entire Hong Kong colony returns to Chinese sovereignty in 1997. But China agrees that Hong Kong

can continue its status as a free port and its separate social, economic, and legal systems for another 50 years. China also guarantees that the people of Hong Kong can retain their freedoms of speech, religion, and unrestricted travel.

China's impending takeover, however, has provoked concern in Hong Kong that the former colony will continue to enjoy political liberties and unrestricted international trade. Many Hong Kong residents have migrated to Britain as well as to Can-

TABLE 7–2
Colonies of the world

Colony	Population	Status
American Samoa	39,000	U.S. Territory
Anguilla	7,000	British Associated State
Aruba	62,000	Dutch Self-Governing Territory
Ascension	1,000	British Colony
Bermuda	58,000	British Colony
Cayman Islands	23,000	British Colony
Channel Islands	145,000	British Dependency
Christmas Island	2,300	Australian External Territory
Cocos Islands	600	Australian External Territory
Cook Island	18,000	New Zealand Self-Governing Territory
Falkland Islands	1,800	British Colony
French Polynesia	191,000	French Overseas Territory
Gibraltar	29,000	British Colony
Guam	130,000	U.S. Territory
Hong Kong	5,700,000	British Crown Colony
Isle of Man	61,000	British Self-Governing Territory
Johnston Atoll	1,000	U.S. Territory
Macao	432,000	Portuguese Territory
Mayotte	67,000	French Territorial Collectivity
Midway Island	1,500	U.S. Territory
Montserrat	12,000	British Colony
Netherlands Antilles	183,000	Dutch Self-Governing Territory
New Caledonia	151,000	French Overseas Territory
Niue	2,500	New Zealand Self-Governing Territory
Norfolk Island	2,400	Australian Territory
Northern Mariana Island	21,000	U.S. Self-Governing Commonwealth
Palau	14,000	U.S. Self-Governing Republic
Pitcairn	55	British Colony
Puerto Rico	3,360,000	U.S. Self-Governing Commonwealth
St. Helena	8,600	British Colony
Svalbard	3,000	Norwegian Territory
Tokelau	1,700	New Zealand Territory
Tristan da Gunha	300	British Colony
Turks and Caicos Islands	9,000	British Colony
Virgin Islands, British	12,000	British Colony
Virgin Islands, U.S.	113,000	U.S. Territory
Wake Island	300	U.S. Territory
Wallis and Futuna	14,000	French Overseas Territory

ada and the United States, but those who have been denied visas claim that Britain has an obligation to take in anyone who wishes to emigrate from its soon-to-be relinquished colony before the Chinese gain control.

The world's smallest colony is Pitcairn Island, also controlled by the British. This island, in the South Pacific, comprises less than 5 square kilometers (about 2 square miles) and approximately 55 inhabitants. The island was settled in 1790 by British mutineers from the ship *Bounty,* commanded by Captain William Bligh. Today, the islanders survive by selling fish and postage stamps.

Characteristics of a Nation

On what basis has the earth's surface been divided into a collection of states? In the modern world, the most important principle in the creation of a state is that it should encompass the same area occupied by a nation. A nation, or **nationality,** is a collection of people occupying a particular portion of the earth's

FIGURE 7–3
Hong Kong is the most populous remaining colony. The 1,060-square-kilometer (410-square-mile) territory has been controlled by the British under a 99-year lease, which expires in 1997. At that time, Hong Kong will be returned to China and will no longer constitute a colony.

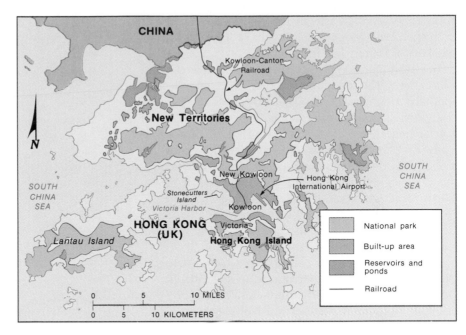

surface who have a strong sense of unity based on a set of shared beliefs and attitudes. The concept of a nation differs from that of a state: *nation* refers to people, whereas *state* refers to a political structure.

There is no precise set of beliefs and attitudes that will distinguish one nation from another, though in general two elements are important. First is a common set of cultural characteristics, such as language and religion. For example, in Europe a strong sense of national unity exists among speakers of Italian.

The second element that will distinguish a nation is a unique set of shared attitudes and emotions. The people of a particular nation may share a common ancestry and take pride in their own historical events. Many different nationalities exist in Latin America, for example, despite the fact that most people are Roman Catholic and speak Spanish. The people of each Latin American country have their own cultural identity, gained in large measure through a unique history, beginning with the series of events leading to national independence.

Shared attitudes also encompass appreciation of distinctive forms of creative arts, such as music, theater, and painting. Being a nation involves being different and being proud of one's differences.

Nation-States

Desire for self-rule is a particularly important shared attitude for many nations. To preserve and enhance distinctive cultural characteristics, most nationalities now increasingly seek the right to govern themselves without interference from other groups. The concept that nationalities have the right to govern themselves is known as **self-determination.**

During the nineteenth and twentieth centuries, world political leaders have generally supported the right of self-determination for many nationalities and have attempted to organize the earth's surface into a collection of nation-states. A **nation-state** is a state whose territory corresponds to that occupied by a particular nation. Yet despite this attempt to create nation-states, there exist only a few instances in which the boundaries of a state correspond precisely to the boundaries of a nation.

Denmark. Denmark is a fairly good example of a nation-state, because the territory occupied by the Danish nation closely matches the state of Denmark. The Danes have a strong sense of unity that derives from shared cultural characteristics and attitudes and a recorded history that extends back more than a thousand years. Nearly all Danes speak the same language, Danish, and nearly all of the world's speakers of Danish live in Denmark.

But even Denmark is not a perfect example of a nation-state. The country's 80-kilometer (50-mile) southern boundary with Germany does not precisely divide Danish and German nationalities. The border region, known as Schleswig-Holstein, historically was part of Denmark. Denmark lost the region to Germany during the nineteenth century, but after the German defeat in World War I the people in North Schleswig voted to rejoin Denmark (Figure 7–4). As a result, some German speakers live in Denmark, while some Danish speakers live in Germany.

To further dilute the concept of a nation-state, Denmark controls two territories in the Atlantic Ocean that do not share Danish cultural characteristics. One of these is the Faeroe Islands, a group of twenty-one islands ruled by Denmark for more than 600 years. The nearly 50,000 inhabitants of the Faeroe Islands speak Faeroese.

Denmark also controls Greenland, the world's largest island, which is fifty times larger than Denmark proper. The nearly 60,000 Greenlanders have received more authority from Denmark in recent years to control their own domestic affairs. One of their decisions has been to change all place names from Danish to the local language. Greenland is now officially known as Kalaallit Nunaat.

FIGURE 7–4
Denmark is a fairly good example of a nation-state. The Danes have a long-established sense of national unity and share distinctive cultural characteristics, such as the Danish language. Yet the boundary between the Danish and German nationalities is not precise, and the two groups intermingle in the region known as Schleswig-Holstein.

Centripetal forces. A state, once established, tries to hold the loyalty of its citizens. Most states find that the most effective means to achieve the support of its citizens is to emphasize shared attitudes that unify the people. Attitudes that tend to unify a people and enhance support for the state are known as **centripetal forces.**

One of the most significant centripetal forces shared by citizens of a state is nationalism. **Nationalism** involves loyalty and devotion to the state that represents a particular nation's distinctive cultural characteristics. People display nationalism by supporting the creation and growth of the state that preserves and enhances the culture and attitudes of their nationality.

For many states, mass communications are the most effective means of fostering nationalism. Most countries regard an independent source of news as

more a risk than a benefit to the stability of the government. Consequently, only a few states permit systems of mass communications to operate without government interference. Nearly all countries control or at least regulate most forms of communications, including mail, telephone, telegraph, television, radio, and satellite transmissions. The government either owns or controls newspapers in many countries.

States also foster nationalism by promoting symbols of the nation-state, such as flags and songs. The symbol of the hammer and sickle on a field of red has long been synonymous with the beliefs of communism. One of the strongest forms of political protest is to burn a state's flag, and laws are widely supported in the United States to make burning the Stars and Stripes illegal. Nationalism is also instilled through the creation of songs extolling the country's virtues. Nearly every state has a national anthem, which usually combines respect for the state with references to the nation's significant historic events or symbols of unity.

Nationalism can have a negative impact. The sense of unity within a nation-state is sometimes achieved through the creation of negative images of other nation-states. A relatively mild method is the proliferation of jokes about members of other nationalities. Travelers find that jokes directed by one nationality against another recur in the same form throughout the world, with only the name of the nationality changed. Such jokes may seem harmless in themselves, but they can reflect a deeper dislike for other nations that leads to conflict.

KEY ISSUE

How Are Boundaries Drawn between States?

The concept of dividing the world into a collection of independent states is recent. Before the seventeenth century, the earth's surface was organized in other ways, such as city-states, empires, tribes, and unorganized territory.

Development of State Concept

The modern movement to divide the earth's surface into states originated in Europe. Yet historians can trace the development of states to the part of the ancient world known as the Fertile Crescent.

Ancient states. The historic Fertile Crescent extended from the Persian Gulf to the Mediterranean Sea, beginning in the east with the area called Mesopotamia, that is, the valley formed by the Tigris and Euphrates rivers, in present-day Iraq. The Fertile Crescent then curved westward over a desert, finally turning south to encompass the Mediterranean coast through present-day Syria, Lebanon, and Israel. Sometimes, the rich Nile River Valley of Egypt is considered an extension of the Fertile Crescent. Situated at the crossroads between Europe, Asia, and Africa, the Fertile Crescent was a center for land and sea communications in ancient times (Figure 7–5).

The first states in Mesopotamia were known as city-states. A **city-state** is a sovereign state that com-

prises a town and the surrounding countryside. Walls clearly delineated the boundaries of the city, and outside the walls the city controlled agricultural land in order to produce food for the urban residents. The countryside also provided the city with an outer line of defense against attack by other city-states. Periodically, one city or tribe in Mesopotamia would gain military dominance over the others and form an empire. Mesopotamia was organized into a succession of empires by the Sumerians, Assyrians, Babylonians, and Persians.

Meanwhile, the state of Egypt emerged as a separate empire at the western end of the Fertile Crescent. Egypt controlled a long, narrow area along the banks of the Nile River, extending from the Nile Delta at the Mediterranean Sea south several hundred kilometers. Egypt's empire lasted from approximately 3000 B.C. until the fourth century B.C.

Political unity in this part of the ancient world reached its height with the establishment of the Roman Empire, which controlled most of Europe, North Africa, and Southwest Asia, from modern-day Spain to Iran and from Egypt to England. At its maximum extent, the empire comprised thirty-eight provinces, each using the same set of laws that were created in Rome. Massive walls helped the Roman army defend many of the empire's frontiers. The Roman Empire collapsed in the fifth century A.D. after a series of attacks by people living on the frontiers of the empire.

The European portion of the empire was fragmented into a large number of estates owned by competing kings, dukes, barons, and other nobles. A victorious noble would seize control of a defeated rival's estate, but after a noble died, others fought to take possession of the land. Meanwhile, the vast majority of people were forced to live on an estate working and fighting for the benefit of the noble.

Nation-states in Europe. By about 1100, a handful of powerful kings controlled large pieces of territory in Europe, especially in England, France, and Spain. Much of central Europe, however, remained fragmented into a large number of estates until the nineteenth century.

By the end of the nineteenth century, most of western Europe comprised nation-states. But these nation-states disagreed with one another about the proper location of their boundaries, and they com-

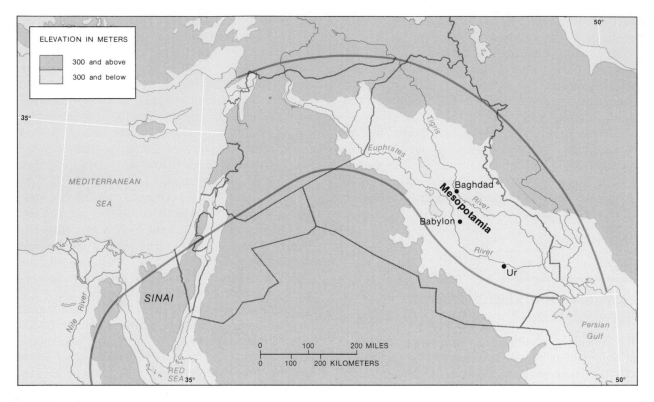

FIGURE 7–5
The Fertile Crescent is a crescent-shaped area of relatively fertile land situated between the
Persian Gulf and the Mediterranean Sea. The Nile Valley of Egypt is sometimes included as an
extension of the Fertile Crescent. Several thousand years ago, the territory was organized into
a succession of empires. As shown in Chapter 9, many important early developments in agriculture also originated in the region.

peted to control territory in Africa and Asia. Eastern
Europe included a mixture of empires and states
that did not match the distribution of nationalities.
In June, 1914, the heir to the throne of Austria-Hungary was assassinated in Sarajevo by a Serb who
sought independence for the empire's province of
Bosnia. The incident ultimately led to World War I.
Following the war, large empires were dismantled,
and many European boundaries were redrawn according to the principle of nation-states.

During the 1930s, the Nazis claimed that all Ger-
man-speaking parts of Europe constituted one nationality and should be unified into one state. The
other European powers did not attempt to stop the
Germans from taking over Austria and the German-
speaking portion of Czechoslovakia known as the
Sudetenland, but when the Germans invaded Poland in 1939, England and France declared war.

Since the end of World War II, the nation-state principle has remained strong in Europe.

Colonialism

European states, while agreeing to the principle of
nation-states in Europe, came to control much of
the rest of the world through a process of colonialism. **Colonialism** is the attempt by one country to
establish settlements and to impose its political,
economic, and cultural principles in another territory.

Colonialsim is different from imperialism. **Imperialism** is control of territory already occupied and
organized by an indigenous society, whereas colonialism is control of previously uninhabited or
sparsely inhabited land. In practice the two terms
are often used interchangeably because imperialism

and colonialism are done for similar reasons and have similar consequences for the occupied territory.

European states established colonies elsewhere in the world for a variety of reasons. First, European missionaries established colonies to promote Christianity. Second, colonies provided resources that helped the economy of European states. Third, European states considered the number of colonies to be an indicator of relative power. In summary, the three motives were God, gold, and glory.

The colonial era began in the fifteenth century, when European explorers sailed west for Asia but settled in the Western Hemisphere instead. The European states eventually lost most of their Western Hemisphere colonies: independence was declared by the United States in 1776 and by most Latin American states between 1800 and 1824. The Europeans then turned their attention to Africa and Asia.

The United Kingdom assembled by far the largest colonial empire. Britain planted colonies on every continent, including much of eastern and southern Africa, South Asia, the Middle East, Australia, and Canada. The British proclaimed that the sun never set on their empire. France had the second-largest amount of overseas territory, though its colonies were concentrated in two locations, West Africa and Southeast Asia. Both the British and the French took control of a large number of islands in the Atlantic, Pacific, and Indian oceans as well.

Portugal, Spain, Germany, Italy, Denmark, the Netherlands, and Belgium all established colonies outside Europe but controlled less territory than the British and French (Figure 7–6). Germany tried to compete with Britain and France by obtaining African colonies that would interfere with communications in the rival European holdings.

Colonial practices. The colonial practices of the European states varied. France attempted to assimilate its colonies into French culture and educate an elite group of local people to provide administrative leadership. After independence, most of these leaders retained close ties with France.

The British created different government structures and policies for various territories of the empire. The decentralized approach helped to protect the diverse cultures, local customs, and educational systems found in the extensive empire. British colo-

nies generally made peaceful transitions to independence, though exceptions can be found in the Middle East and Southern Africa, as well as in Ireland.

Most African and Asian colonies became independent after World War II. Only fifteen African and Asian states were members of the United Nations when it was established in 1945, compared to ninety-six in 1991. The boundaries of the new states frequently but not always coincide with former colonial provinces.

Boundaries

A state is separated from its neighbors by boundaries. A **boundary** is an invisible line marking the extent of a state's territory. Boundaries completely surround an individual state and mark the outer limits of its territorial control.

Boundaries interest us because the process of selecting their location is frequently difficult and can lead to conflict. The boundary line, which by definition must be shared by more than one state, is the only location where direct contact must take place between two neighboring states. Therefore, the boundary has the potential to become the focal point of conflict between neighboring states.

Frontiers. Historically, frontiers rather than boundaries separated two states. A **frontier**—a zone where no state exercises political control—is a geographic area, whereas a boundary is a thin, invisible line. A frontier provides an area of separation, whereas a boundary brings two neighboring states into direct contact, increasing the potential for violent face-to-face meetings. A frontier area is either uninhabited or settled by a few isolated pioneers seeking to live outside organized society.

Almost universally, frontiers between states have been replaced by boundaries. Modern communications systems permit countries to monitor and guard boundaries effectively, even in previously inaccessible locations. Once-remote frontier regions have become more attractive for agriculture and mining.

Other than Antarctica, the only region of the world that still has frontiers rather than boundaries is the Arabian peninsula. Frontiers separate Saudi Arabia from Qatar, the United Arab Emirates, Oman, and Yemen. These frontier areas are inhabited by a

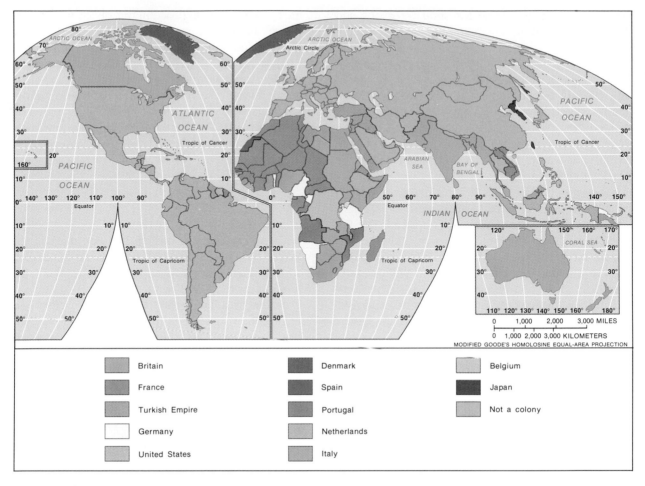

FIGURE 7–6
Colonial possessions. In 1914, at the outbreak of World War I, European states held colonies in much of the world, especially in Africa and Asia. Most of the countries in the Western Hemisphere at one time had been colonized by Europeans but gained their independence in the nineteenth century.

handful of nomads who cross freely with their herds from one country to another. Until recently, part of Saudi Arabia's border with Iraq included an 8,000-square kilometer (3,000 square-mile) frontier marked on maps as a "Neutral Zone" (Figure 7–7). But by stationing troops on either side of an east-west line across the Neutral Zone, Saudi Arabia and Iraq effectively transformed the frontier into a boundary, though not one officially ratified by the governments of the two countries.

Cultural Boundaries

Boundaries are of two types: physical and cultural. Physical boundaries coincide with significant fea-

tures of the natural landscape, whereas cultural boundaries follow the distribution of social customs. Neither type of boundary is better or more natural. The best boundaries are those to which all affected states agree, regardless of the method used to draw the line. Some cultural boundaries between states coincide with such characteristics as language and religion, while other cultural boundaries are drawn according to geometry.

Language. Language is an important cultural characteristic for drawing boundaries, especially in Europe. By global standards, European languages have substantial literary traditions and formal rules of grammar and spelling. Language has long been a significant means of distinguishing distinctive nationalities in Europe.

The French language was a major element in the development of France as a unified state in the seventeenth century. The states of England, Spain, and Portugal also coalesced around distinctive languages. In the nineteenth century, Italy and Germany also emerged as states that unified the speakers of particular languages.

The movement to identify nation-states on the basis of language spread throughout Europe in the twentieth century. After World War I, leaders of the victorious countries met at the Versailles Peace Conference to redraw the map of Europe. One of the chief advisors to U.S. President Woodrow Wilson, the geographer Isaiah Bowman, played a major role in the decisions. Language was the most important criterion the allied leaders used to create new states in Europe and adjust the boundaries of existing ones.

The conference was particularly concerned with the Balkans, an area in southeastern Europe long troubled by political instability and conflict. Bound-aries were drawn around the states of Bulgaria, Hungary, and Romania to conform as closely as possible to the distribution of Bulgarian, Hungarian, and Romanian speakers, while speakers of several South Slavic languages were placed together in the new country of Yugoslavia. The boundaries imposed by the Versailles conference on the basis of language have been somewhat adjusted, especially around World War II, but they have proved to be much more stable and peaceful than previous boundaries (Figure 7–8).

Religion. Religious differences coincide with boundaries for a number of states, but in only a few cases has religion been used to select the actual boundary line. The most notable example was in South Asia, when the British partitioned India into two states on the basis of religion. The predominantly Muslim portions were allocated to Pakistan, while the predominantly Hindu portions became the independent state of India.

Religion was also used to some extent to draw the boundary between two states on the island of

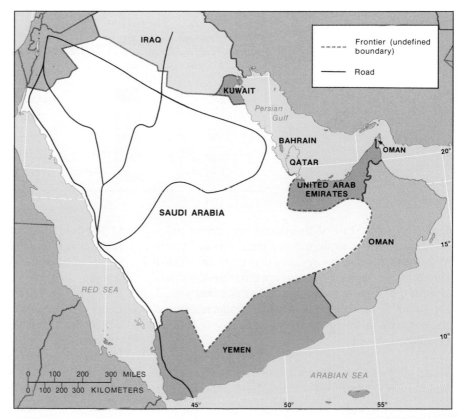

FIGURE 7–7
Several states in the Arabian peninsula are separated from each other by frontiers rather than by precisely drawn boundaries. Historically, the principal occupants of this desert area have been nomads, who have wandered freely through the frontier.

FIGURE 7–8
Language of the Balkans. Southeast Europe, an area commonly called the Balkans, was traditionally politically unstable, partly because of a lack of correspondence between the boundaries of states and of nationalities. After World War I, world leaders created several new states and realigned the boundaries of existing ones, so that the state boundaries matched language boundaries as closely as possible. While not perfectly matched, the state boundaries have proved to be more stable than in the past.

INDO-EUROPEAN FAMILY			
SLAVIC BRANCH		**ROMANCE BRANCH**	
Polish	Russian	Italian	German
Czech	Ukrainian	Romansh	Albanian
Slovak	Slovene	Romanian	**OTHER FAMILIES**
Serb	Bulgarian	**OTHER BRANCHES**	Turkic
Croat	Macedonian	Greek	Hungarian

Eire (Ireland). Most of the island became an independent country, while the northeast—now known as Northern Ireland—remained part of the United Kingdom. Catholics comprise approximately 95 percent of the population in the 26 counties that joined the Republic of Ireland, while Protestants constitute the majority in the six counties of Northern Ireland (*see* Figure 5–4).

Geometry. Other boundaries simply constitute straight lines drawn on a map. The 2,100-kilometer (1,300-mile) boundary between the United States and Canada between 95° west longitude and the Strait of Georgia (near the Pacific Ocean) is a straight line along 49° north latitude. The line (more precisely, an arc) was established in 1846 by treaty between the United States and Great Britain, which still controlled Canada at the time.

Some people in the United States wanted the boundary to be fixed 600 kilometers (400 miles) farther north at 54°40′ north latitude. Before a compromise was reached, U.S. militants proclaimed "fifty-four forty or fight." The United States and Canada share an additional 1,100-kilometer (700-mile) boundary between Alaska and the Yukon Territory along the north-south line of 141° west longitude.

The 1,000-kilometer (600-mile) boundary between Chad and Libya is a straight line drawn across the desert in 1899 by the French and British to set the northern limit of French colonies in Africa. But subsequent actions by European countries created confusion concerning the location of the boundary. In 1912, Italy seized control of Libya from the Turks and demanded that the boundary with French-controlled Chad be changed. In 1935, France agreed to move the boundary 100 kilometers (60 miles) to the south, but the Italian government was not satisfied with the settlement and never ratified the treaty. The land that the French would have ceded is known as the Aozou Strip, named for the only settlement in the 100,000 square-kilometer (36,000 square-mile) area (Figure 7–9).

When Libya and Chad became independent countries, the boundary was set at the original northern location. Libya, claiming that the president of Chad had secretly sold the Aozou Strip to Libya,

seized the territory in 1973, as well as a tiny bit of northeastern Niger that may contain uranium. In 1987, Chad expelled the Libyan army and regained control of the strip.

Physical Boundaries

Important physical features on the earth's surface can make good boundaries because they are easily seen both on a map and on the ground. Three types of physical elements serve as boundaries between states—mountains, deserts, and water.

Mountain boundaries. Mountains can be effective boundaries if they are difficult to cross. Contact between nationalities living on each side may be limited—or even completely impossible if passes are closed by winter storms. Mountains are also useful boundaries because they are permanent as well as usually sparsely inhabited.

Mountains do not always provide for the amicable separation of neighbors. For instance, Argentina and Chile agreed to be divided by the crest of the Andes Mountains but could not decide on the precise location of the crest. Was the crest a line connecting each adjacent mountain peak or a line connecting the continental divide (the point where the rivers flow east or west)? In the nineteenth century the two countries almost fought a war over the boundary line, but finally decided—with the help of the United States—on the line connecting adjacent mountain peaks.

Deserts. A boundary drawn in a desert can also effectively divide two states. Like mountains, deserts are hard to cross and are usually sparsely inhabited. Desert boundaries are common in Africa and Asia. In North Africa, the Sahara has generally proved to be a stable boundary separating Algeria, Libya, Egypt, Mauritania, Mali, Niger, Chad, and the Sudan. The main exception has been the boundary between Chad and Libya, as previously discussed.

Water boundaries. Rivers, lakes, oceans, and other bodies of water are the physical features most commonly used as boundaries. Water boundaries are both readily visible on a map and relatively unchanging. And, of course, no permanent human settlement is found on water.

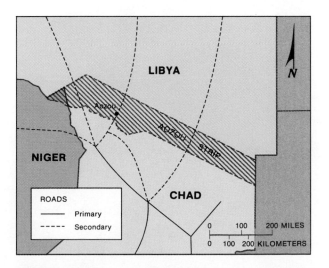

FIGURE 7–9
The boundary between Libya and Chad is a straight line, drawn by European countries early in the twentieth century when the area comprised a series of colonies. Libya, however, claims that the boundary should be located 100 kilometers to the south and that it should have sovereignty over the Aozou Strip.

Water boundaries offer good protection against attack from another state. An invading state must transport its troops by airplane or ship as well as secure a landing spot in or near the country being attacked. The state being invaded can concentrate its defenses at the landing point.

The use of water as boundaries between states can cause difficulties, though. One problem is that the precise location of the water may change over time. Rivers, in particular, can change their course. The Rio Grande, the river separating the United States and Mexico, has frequently meandered from its previous course since it became part of the boundary in 1848. Land that had once been on the U.S. side of the boundary was suddenly on the Mexican side, and vice versa. The United States and Mexico have concluded treaties that restore land affected by the shifting course of the river to the country in control at the time of the original nineteenth-century delineation.

Water boundaries also cause problems because many states claim that the boundary lies not at the coastline but out at sea. Traditionally, most states recognized boundaries extending 3 miles (5 kilometers) from land into the ocean. This distance, known as the territorial limit, initially represented the furthest range of land-based cannons and therefore, in times past, the limit of effective military control. Beyond the territorial limit, most states recognize a so-called contiguous zone where most of the

After Iraq invaded Kuwait in August 1990, thousands of guest workers were forced to leave Kuwait. For people from relatively poor countries in the Middle East and South Asia, the only available route was west across the Iraqi desert to Jordan. After the United States and its coalition partners began air bombardment of Iraq in January 1991, this escape route to Jordan became dangerous.

The Great Wall of China historically served as one of the world's most visible boundaries. Originally built in the third century B.C. during the Qin (Ch'in) dynasty, the wall was extended the following century during the Han dynasty to keep out barbarian horsemen. The wall was partially reconstructed between the fourteenth and sixteenth centuries A.D. during the Ming dynasty.

laws of the state can also be enforced. The United States, for example, recognizes a 12-mile (19-kilometer) contiguous zone.

In recent years, some states have claimed more extensive territorial limits; Chile, Ecuador, and Mexico, for example, claim a 200-mile (320-kilometer) off-shore limit. Some states consider the 12-mile zone to be the territorial limit rather than just the contiguous zone. States may wish to control extensive ocean areas to regulate fishing or lay claim to minerals on or beneath the ocean floor.

Landlocked States

Water boundaries are critical to states because they facilitate international trade. Relatively bulky goods are normally transported long distances by ship, but to send or receive goods by such means a country needs a port, where the goods can be transferred between land and sea. A state that does not have a direct outlet to the sea is called a **landlocked** state. To send and receive goods by sea, a landlocked state must depend on another country's port.

Africa. Landlocked states are most common in Africa, where fourteen of the continent's fifty-four states have no direct access to the ocean. The prevalence of landlocked states in Africa is a remnant of the colonial era, when Britain and France controlled extensive regions. The European powers built railroads, mostly in the early twentieth century, to connect the interior of Africa with seaports. Railroads helped move minerals from the interior and import mining equipment and supplies to the interior. Now that the British and French empires have been divided into a collection of independent states, some

269

of the important railroad lines of the colonial era pass through several countries. Newly created land-locked states must cooperate with neighboring states that have ports (Figure 7–10).

Cooperation between neighboring states in southern Africa is complicated by racial patterns. Botswana, Lesotho, and Swaziland are landlocked states that ship 90 percent of their exports by rail through neighboring South Africa. Zaire, Zambia, and Zimbabwe must also transport most of their imports and exports through South Africa.

The states of southern African have had to balance their economic dependency on South Africa with their dislike of the country's racial policies. Despite constituting more than 80 percent of South Africa's population, blacks are denied a number of civil rights, including the right to vote in elections for the national government. But if neighboring states were to sever ties with South Africa because of its racial policies, they could face economic disaster.

Zimbabwe. Zimbabwe's problem is particularly delicate. When the white minority living in the land-locked British colony of Rhodesia (now Zimbabwe) unilaterally declared itself an independent country in 1965, most other countries reduced or terminated trade with it. The impact of trade sanctions on Rhodesia was limited because its most important ports were located in South Africa, also ruled by a white-minority government. But because Rhodesia's main rail line ran through black-ruled Botswana before reaching South Africa, the Rhodesian government completed a new rail line directly to South Africa in 1974, thereby avoiding Botswana.

In 1979, the white-minority government of Rhodesia agreed to give blacks the right to vote, and blacks were elected to lead the government. The following year, Britain formally recognized the independence of the country, which was renamed Zimbabwe. The government of Zimbabwe, now controlled by the black majority, faced a new set of relationships in southern Africa. Instead of working

FIGURE 7–10

To trade with countries in North America, Europe, or Asia, African states must ship goods through ocean ports. Landlocked African states must import and export goods by land-based modes of transportation, primarily rail lines, to reach ocean ports located in neighboring states. Cooperation with neighboring states is especially difficult in southern Africa, where neighboring states oppose South Africa's policy of apartheid but temper their opposition to keep their trade routes open.

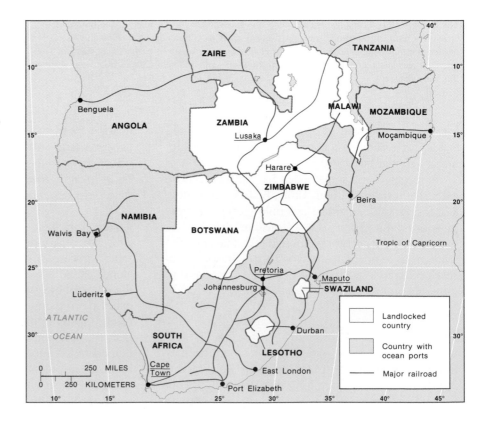

closely with South Africa, Zimbabwe tried to reduce its dependency on the neighboring white-minority government. Most important in Zimbabwe's strategy has been to utilize railroads that connect to ports outside of South Africa.

The closest port to Zimbabwe is Beira, Mozambique, and a railroad known as the Beira corridor runs west from that port to the Zimbabwean capital Harare. But Mozambique has been caught in a devastating civil war since the mid-1970s between its Marxist-oriented government and rebels backed by South Africa. Zimbabwe has had soldiers in Mozambique to keep the 500-kilometer (300-mile) Beira corridor repaired and protected from rebel attack, but the port of Beira itself has not been well-maintained.

More distant ports are not reliable, either. Mozambique's other two major deep-water ports—Nacala in the north and Maputo in the south—have suffered even more than Beira from the civil war. The Benguela railway, which runs east across Angola to Zaire and Zambia, has also been disrupted by a civil war in Angola, which has continued since 1975 between the Marxist-oriented government and the rebels supported by South Africa and the United States.

The Tazara line, which runs from Zambia to Dar es Salaam, Tanzania, has remained open, but service has been unreliable. The equipment, much of it supplied by the Chinese in the 1970s, has frequently broken down, and landslides have periodically closed the line. The line running across Namibia has not been an alternative to shipping through South Africa because the port of Walvis Bay remained under South African control when the rest of Namibia became independent in 1990. As a result of obstacles to using other rail lines, Zimbabwe has had to ship more than half of its freight through the South African port of Durban.

KEY ISSUE

What Problems Result from the Location of Boundaries between States?

As people divide the earth's surface into a collection of states, they try to correlate the boundaries of states with the distribution of nations to create a series of nation-states. In reality, however, few true nation-states have been created.

Many of the problems faced by the states of the world derive from the fact that the boundaries of nations and states do not coincide. This lack of correspondence causes instability in the alignment of state boundaries and unrest among people who are part of many nations.

Problems concerning the boundaries of nations and states generally develop for two reasons. In some cases, the boundaries of a state encompass more than one nationality. In other cases, the population of a nation is split among more than one state.

One State with More Than One Nationality

A state that contains more than one nationality is known as a **multinational state.** Relationships among nationalities vary in different multinational states. In some states, one nationality tries to dominate another, especially if one of the nationalities is much more numerous than the other, while in other states nationalities coexist peacefully. The people of one nation may be assimilated into the cultural characteristics of another nation, but in other cases, the two nationalities remain culturally distinct.

In some multinational states, nationalities coexist only by occupying geographically distinct regions. Cyprus is an example of a multinational country that maintains peace by allocating territory to different nations which formerly mingled. South Africa is a multinational state in which one nationality preserves its dominance over others by allocating a distinct geographical area to each nationality.

Cyprus. Cyprus, the third-largest island in the Mediterranean Sea, is a state that contains two nationalities: Greek and Turkish. Although the island is situated closer to Turkey, Greeks comprise 78 percent of the country's population, while Turks comprise only 18 percent. When Cyprus gained independence from Britain in 1960, its constitution guaranteed the Turkish minority a substantial share of the elected offices and control over its own education, religion, and culture.

Cyprus has never peacefully integrated the Greek and Turkish nationalities. In 1974, several Greek Cypriot military officers who favored unification of Cyprus with Greece seized control of the government. Shortly after the coup, Turkey invaded Cyprus to protect the Turkish Cypriot minority, occupying 40 percent of the island. The Greek coup leaders were removed within a few months and an elected government was restored, but the Turkish army remained on Cyprus.

Traditionally, the Greek and Turkish Cypriots mingled, but since the coup and invasion the two nationalities have become geographically isolated. The northeastern part of the island is now overwhelmingly Turkish, while the southern part is overwhelmingly Greek. Approximately one-third of the island's Greeks were forced to move from the region controlled by the Turkish army, while nearly one-fourth of the Turks moved from the region now known as the Greek side. The percentage of one nationality living in the region dominated by the other nationality is now very low. The Turkish sector declared itself the independent Turkish Republic of Northern Cyprus in 1983, but only Turkey recognizes it as a separate state (Figure 7–11).

A buffer zone patrolled by U.N. soldiers stretches across the entire island to prevent Greek and Turks from reaching the other side. The barrier even runs through the center of the capital, Nicosia. Only one official crossing point has been erected, and cross-ing has been difficult except for top diplomats and U.N. personnel. Nevertheless, some cooperation continues between sectors: the Turks supply the Greek side with water and in return receive electricity.

South Africa. South Africa is a multinational state where the government divides the population into nationalities according to race. The first whites, who arrived in South Africa from Holland in 1652, settled in Cape Town, at the southern tip of the territory. They were known either as Boers, from the Dutch word for farmer, or Afrikaners, from the word *Afrikaans,* the name of their language, which is a dialect of Dutch.

In 1795, the British seized the Dutch colony at Cape Town for military reasons. To escape British administration and the freeing of slaves in 1833, about 12,000 Boers trekked northeast into the interior of South Africa, settling in the regions known as the Transvaal and the Orange Free State. After diamonds and gold were discovered in the Transvaal during the 1860s and 1870s, the British followed the Boers into South Africa's interior. A series of wars between the British and the Boers culminated in a British victory in 1902, and all of South Africa became part of the British Empire.

British descendents continued to control South Africa's government until 1948, when the Afrikaner-dominated Nationalist Party won elections. The Afri-

FIGURE 7–11
Since 1974, Cyprus has been divided into Greek and Turkish portions, with little mingling between the two groups. The Turkish sector has declared itself to be the Turkish Republic of Northern Cyprus, but only Turkey recognizes it as an independent country.

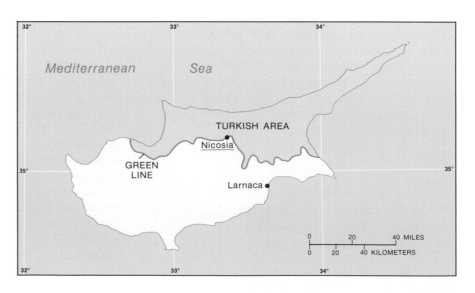

South Africa's apartheid laws were designed to spatially segregate races as much as possible. As part of this segregation, separate public restrooms were provided for whites and nonwhites.

kaners gained power at a time when colonial rule was being replaced in the rest of Africa by a collection of independent states run by the local black population. The Afrikaners vowed to resist pressures to turn over South Africa's government to blacks.

The cornerstone of the Afrikaners' policy was the creation of a legal system called apartheid. **Apartheid** is the physical separation of different races into different geographic areas. In South Africa, a newborn baby has been assigned to one of four races: black, white, colored (mixed white and black), or Asian. Blacks constitute approximately 68 percent of South Africa's population, whites 18 percent, colored 11 percent, and Asians 3 percent.

Each of the four races have had a different legal status in South Africa. The apartheid laws have determined where different races can live, attend school, work, shop, and own land. Blacks have been restricted to certain occupations and paid far lower wages than whites for similar work. The apartheid laws have also disallowed blacks from voting or running for office in national elections. In 1991, the white-controlled government of South Africa declared its intention to dismantle the remaining apartheid laws.

To further assure the geographic isolation of different races, the South African government designated ten so-called homelands for blacks. The government expects every black to become a citizen of one of the homelands and move there. The first four homelands designated by the government were called Bophuthatswana, Ciskei, Transkei, and Venda. Bophuthatswana included six discontinuous areas, Transkei three discontinuous areas, and Venda two discontinuous areas. South Africa declared these four homelands to be independent countries, but no other government in the world recognized the claim. If this government policy would ever be fully implemented, the ten black homelands together would contain approximately 70 percent of South Africa's population on only 13 percent of the land (Figure 7–12).

Most people in the world have opposed the concept of apartheid but have disagreed on how to deal with South Africa. Some opponents of apartheid have argued that world governments should maintain economic sanctions against South Africa and force private corporations to withdraw their investments from the country. Others have claimed that sanctions hurt South Africa's blacks more than whites.

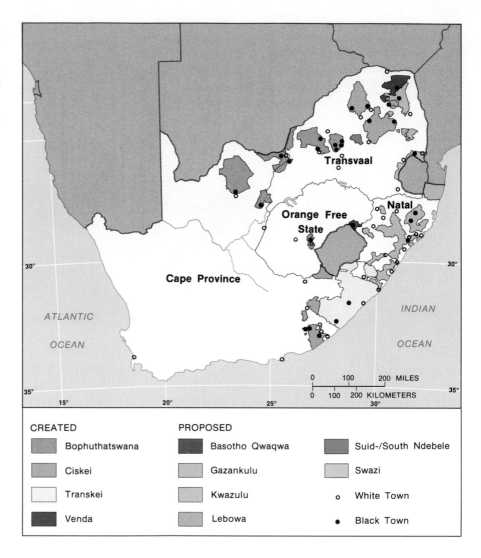

FIGURE 7–12
As part of its apartheid system, the government of South Africa designated ten so-called homelands, expecting that ultimately every black would become a citizen of one of them. South Africa declared some of these homelands to be independent states, but no other country recognized the action.

Underlying the international debate has been South Africa's importance in regional and global economies. An effective boycott would devastate neighboring states, which depend on South Africa to provide jobs for their unemployed people and ports for distribution of their goods. Relatively developed countries also depend on South Africa for the provision of chromium, platinum, manganese, and other minerals that are critical for manufacturing and chemical processes. Once the apartheid laws are dismantled, other countries will be less reluctant to trade with South Africa, even if nonwhites still suffer from other forms of discrimination.

Nations Divided among More Than One State

Conflicts may develop when one nation finds itself divided among more than one state. Some nationalities consider that they have been excluded from the goal of dividing the earth into a collection of nation-states. A nationality split among more than one state—unable to control the government of any state—may seek to carve out a new nation-state from portions of existing ones. Alternatively, a nationality may already dominate one country but wish to expand the country's boundaries to include members of the nationality living in other states.

The division of nationalities among more than one state has proved especially troublesome in the rugged, isolated Caucasus, Zagros, and Taurus mountains of southwestern Asia. The Kurds, Armenians, and Azerbaijanis are all examples of nationalities in the region that have not been able to organize nation-states.

Kurds. The Kurds are a non-Arab group of Sunni Muslims who speak a language similar to Farsi and have distinctive literary, dress, and other cultural

traditions. The Kurdish population is split among five countries, including 10 million in eastern Turkey, 5 million in western Iran, 4 million in northern Iraq, and smaller numbers in northeastern Syria and southwestern Soviet Union. A fifth of the population of Iraq, a sixth of the population of Turkey, and nearly a tenth of the population of Iran are Kurdish (Figure 7–13).

When the allies carved up the Ottoman Empire after World War I, they created an independent state of Kurdistan to the south and west of Van Gölü

FIGURE 7–13
In the Caucasus, Zagros, and Taurus mountains of southwestern Asia, the Kurds, Armenians, and Azerbaijanis are all examples of nationalities whose homelands do not correspond to the boundaries of countries. All three nationalities did constitute nation-states briefly following World War I, but since the 1920s they have been forced to live under the control of such countries as Iran, Iraq, Turkey, and the Soviet Union.

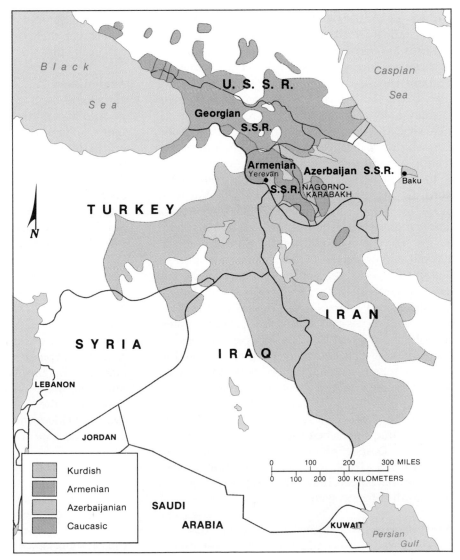

(Lake Van) under the 1920 Treaty of Sevres. Before the treaty was ratified, however, the Turks, under the leadership of Mustafa Kemal (later known as Kemal Atatürk), fought successfully to expand the territory under their control beyond the small area the allies had allocated to them. The Treaty of Lausanne in 1923 established the modern state of Turkey, with boundaries nearly identical to the current ones. Kurdistan became part of Turkey and disappeared as an independent state.

Since then, the Turks have tried repeatedly to suppress Kurdish culture. Use of the Kurdish language is illegal, and Turkey's leading pop singer once was arrested for speaking it during a concert. Kurdish nationalists for their part have waged a long-standing guerilla war against the Turkish army.

Kurds in other countries have fared just as poorly as those in Turkey. Iran's Kurds secured an independent republic in 1946 that lasted less than a year. Iraq's Kurds made two unsuccessful attempts to gain independence, in 1931–32 and again in 1944–45. As a concession to the Kurds, Iraq made Kurdish the official language in the north, yet schools are still required to teach in Arabic.

In recent years, Iraq has destroyed some 4,000 Kurdish villages and forced 1.5 million Kurds to move, including a half million to camps in remote desert regions. For example, on June 1, 1989, Iraqi troops entered Qal'at Diza, a Kurdish city of 100,000, and ordered everyone to pack one suitcase. Within two weeks, the entire population of the city had been deported. The Iraqi government claimed that the forced migration was designed to provide Kurds with access to electricity, running water, schools, and medical facilities. Independent observers suggested that the Iraqi government wanted to create a secure frontier region along the Iranian border, before it turned attention south towards Kuwait.

After the 1991 Gulf War, the Kurds living in northern Iraq intensified their struggle for greater autonomy. Despite widespread international opposition to Iraq's harsh treatment of the Kurds, other countries have been reluctant to support creating a new Kurdish nation-state.

Azerbaijanis. Azerbaijanis trace their roots to Turkish invaders who migrated from central Asia in the eighth and ninth centuries and merged with the existing, mostly Persian, population. They are Shiite Muslims who speak an Altaic language similar to Turkish. A treaty in 1828 allocated the northern portion of the Azerbaijani's territory to Russia and the southern portion to Persia (now Iran). After the Russian Revolution in 1917, the Russian portion briefly operated as an independent state, but it became a republic within the Soviet Union in 1923.

Approximately 6 million Azerbaijanis now live in the Soviet republic, while another 6 million are clustered in northwestern Iran, where they constitute 10 percent of the country's population. Azerbaijanis are well-represented in Iran's government and economy, but Iran restricts teaching of the Azerbaijani language. In the Soviet Union, Azerbaijanis have fought with their neighbors, the Armenians, another nationality divided among more than one state.

Armenians. The Armenian homeland lies generally west of the Azerbaijanis in the Soviet Union and north of the Kurds in northeastern Turkey. In contrast to their Muslim neighbors, Armenians are Eastern Orthodox Christians who speak an Indo-European language. They have lived in the region for thousands of years, and they controlled an independent kingdom before the founding of either Christianity or Islam. In recent centuries, they have lived mostly as an isolated enclave of Christians under the rule of Turkish Muslims.

During the late nineteenth and early twentieth centuries, hundreds of thousands of Armenians were killed in a series of massacres organized by the Turks. Others were forced to migrate to Russia, which had gained possession of the eastern portion of Armenia in 1828. After World War I, the allies created an independent state of Armenia at the same time they established Kurdistan. But Armenia, like Kurdistan, was soon swallowed up by its neighbors: Turkey and the Soviet Union concluded a treaty in 1921 to divide Armenia between the two. The Soviet portion became the Armenian Soviet Socialist Republic.

In addition to fighting for the right to form nation-states, the Armenians and Azerbaijanis, in particular, have fought with each other for control of territory within the Soviet Union. The two groups first fought against each other from 1905 to 1907 in what became known as the Armeno-Tatar conflict. During the brief period of independence after the

People in the Soviet Union's Republic of Azerbaijan demonstrate for more local autonomy. The crescent flags reflect the fact that Azerbaijanis are predominantly Shiite Muslims.

1917 Russian Revolution, the two countries repeatedly clashed over the location of boundaries. When the Soviets took control in 1923, the national government established the current arrangement, by which Azerbaijan comprises two discontinuous pieces to the south and east of Armenia. Armenians and Azerbaijanis have fought bitterly for control of territory in recent years, but since both are republics within the Soviet Union, this problem cannot be considered that of a nationality divided among more than one state.

Nationalities within the Soviet Union. Until recently, Soviet policy strongly discouraged nationalities from expressing their cultural uniqueness. Writers and artists throughout the Soviet Union were pressured to conform to a style known as "socialist realism," which emphasized Soviet economic and political values. Use of the Russian language was promoted, and the role of organized religion was minimized.

After Mikhail Gorbachev became general secretary of the Communist Party in 1985, he began an era he called *glasnost,* which meant "openness" or "candor." Under *glasnost,* nationalities were able to articulate long-simmering grievances. In the case of the Armenians and Azerbaijanis, violence erupted in the late 1980s and early 1990s over the administration of an autonomous region within the Azerbaijan Republic known as Nagorno-Karabakh.

Historically, Nagorno-Karabakh was inhabited mostly by Azerbaijanis, but Armenians overran the area in the early nineteenth century and currently constitute more than three-fourths of the region's population. When the area became part of the Soviet Union in the early 1920s, Nagorno-Karabakh was awarded to Azerbaijan. Under *glasnost,* how-

277

ever, Armenians demanded that the region be turned over to them.

Armenians have claimed that their language, religion, and other cultural characteristics have been suppressed by the predominantly Muslim, Turkish-speaking Azerbaijanis. Nagorno-Karabakh's television programs, rail lines, and other communications networks emanate from Baku, the Azerbaijani capital to the east, while communications to the west, with the Armenian capital of Yerevan, are minimal.

In February 1988, after Armenians killed two Azerbaijanis near Nagorno-Karabakh, thousands of people in the second-largest city in Azerbaijan (Sumgait) went on a rampage, killing several dozen Armenians. In January 1990, after an Armenian attacked two Azerbaijanis with an axe, gangs of Azerbaijanis searched through Baku looking for Armenians to murder. Thirty-four Armenians died in Baku by being burned, beaten with iron bars, or thrown out of windows. Soviet troops entered Azerbaijan to restore peace, and President Gorbachev announced that the existing boundaries would remain.

Soviet officials hoped that beaming Armenian-language television programs into the area would quell the unrest in Nagorno-Karabakh. In the meantime, after centuries of living jumbled together—if not always peacefully—the two groups have been becoming more segregated through migration patterns. During 1988 and 1989, 600,000 Armenians and Azerbaijanis migrated to the other side; many of these homeless refugees are at the forefront of the fighting and the rebirth of militant nationalism in the Caucasus region.

Distinguishing between the two types of boundary problems. In some regions, political disputes stem from lack of agreement concerning which of the two types of boundary problems applies to the situation. One faction may argue that the issue derives from one nation divided among states while the other faction may claim that the problem is accommodating more than one nationality in one state.

In Ireland, for example, many Roman Catholics believe that the Irish nation has been divided into more than one country—Northern Ireland, which is part of the United Kingdom, and the Republic of Ireland. On the other hand, many residents of Northern Ireland—especially Protestants—see Ire-

land's problems as two nationalities—Roman Catholics and Protestants—trying to live together in the United Kingdom (*see* Chapter 5).

Some politicians in the Middle East, such as Iraq's Saddam Hussein, have argued that Arabs should be united into one state. According to this argument, Arabs belong to one nation because most of them speak Arabic, practice the Sunni Muslim religion, and are descendants of people who lived in the Arabian peninsula.

Internal Organization of States

There are two main methods of organizing governments—the unitary system and the federal system. The **unitary state** places most power in the hands of central government officials, whereas the **federal state** allocates strong power to units of local government within the country. A country's cultural and physical characteristics influence the evolution of its governmental system.

In principle, the unitary government system works best in countries that have both relatively few internal cultural differences and a strong sense of national unity. Therefore, states whose boundaries coincide closely with the boundaries of nations are more likely to consider a unitary system of government. In addition, because the unitary system requires effective communications with all regions of the country, smaller states are more likely to adopt it. If the country is very large or has isolated regions, strong national control is difficult.

In reality, multinational states often have unitary systems so that the values of one nationality can be imposed on others. In a number of African and Asian countries, for instance, the mechanism of a unitary state has enabled one ethnic group to extend dominance over weaker groups. In some cases, a minority group is able to impose its values on the majority of the population. When communist parties controlled the governments of Eastern European countries, for example, the unitary systems enabled the imposition of uniform cultural values on otherwise multinational societies.

In a federal state, local governments possess more authority to adopt their own laws. Multinational states usually adopt a federal system of government in order to give power to different nationalities, especially if they live in separate regions of the country. Under a federal system, local government boundaries can be drawn that correspond to the regions inhabited by different nations. The federal system is also more suitable for very large states. The national capitals of very large states may be too remote to provide effective control over isolated regions.

In the late twentieth century, a strong global trend occurred in favor of the federal system of government. Most of the world's largest states were already federal, including the Soviet Union, Canada, the United States, Brazil, and India. During the late 1980s and 1990s, unitary systems have been sharply curtailed in a number of countries and scrapped altogether in others.

France. A good example of a nation-state, France has a long tradition of unitary government in which a very strong national government dominated local government decisions. The basic unit of local government in France is the department. Each of the 100 departments is headed by a powerful prefect appointed by the national government rather than directly elected by the people. Engineers, architects, planners, and other technical experts working in each department are actually employed by ministries of the national government.

A second tier of local government in France is the commune. Each of the 36,000 communes has a locally elected mayor and council, but the mayor can be a member of the national Parliament at the same time. Further, the average commune has only 1,500 inhabitants, too small to govern effectively, with the possible exception of the largest ones, such as in Paris, Lyon, Lille, and Marseille.

During the 1980s, the French government granted additional legal powers to the departments and communes. Local governments could borrow money freely to finance new projects without explicit national government approval, as was required in the past. The national government agreed to turn over a block of funds to localities with no strings attached. In addition, twenty-two regions that previously held minimal authority were converted into full-fledged local government units, with elected councils and the power to levy taxes.

Yugoslavia. An extreme example of a federal system is the one adopted in the 1970s in Yugoslavia, known as workers' self-management. Primary power was given to individual factories and other places of work, each managed by a board of directors that would establish policy for investments, prices, profits, wages, and so on. Each board of directors, elected by the workers, would answer to a workers' council, consisting of all workers in the company.

Representatives selected from the community's different workers' councils would meet together in a local assembly. In this way, the fundamental decisions concerning the community would be made by local workers. The system also included a second branch of the local assembly comprising officials elected by all of the people. The local units of government, known as communes, were grouped into six republics.

An important purpose of this federal system was to protect the rights of its different nationalities. There is a saying in Yugoslavia that roughly translates as follows: Yugoslavia has seven neighbors, six republics, five nationalities, four languages, three religions, two alphabets, and one dinar. Here is an explanation:

- Yugoslavia's seven neighbors include four states governed after World War II by communists (Bulgaria, Hungary, Romania, and Albania) and three by noncommunists (Austria, Greece, and Italy).
- The six republics—Bosnia-Hercegovina, Croatia, Macedonia, Montenegro, Serbia, and Slovenia— have considerable autonomy from the national government to run their own affairs (Figure 7–14).
- The republics generally correspond to the location of the country's five recognized nationalities—Croats, Macedonians, Montenegrens, Serbs, and Slovenes. The republic of Bosnia-Hercegovina comprises primarily Serbs and Croats.
- Yugoslavia's four official languages are Croatian, Macedonian, Serbian, and Slovene (Montenegrens speak Serbian). Most linguists outside of Yugoslavia consider Serbian and Croatian to be the same language except for different alphabets.
- The three major religions include Roman Catholicism in the north, Eastern Orthodoxy in the east, and Islam in the south.
- Two of the four main languages—Croatian and Slovene—are written in the Western alphabet, while Macedonian and Serbian are written in Cyrillic.
- The saying concludes with a reference to Yugoslavia's one dinar—the national unit of cur-

FIGURE 7–14
In the late 1940s, the communist government divided Yugoslavia into six republics. The boundaries of Macedonia, Montenegro, and Slovenia corresponded closely to the territory occupied by the Macedonians, Montenegrins, and Slovenes, respectively. However, Serbs lived in Bosnia-Hercegovina and in Croatia, as well as in Serbia, and Croats lived in both Croatia and Bosnia-Hercegovina. Serbia governs the autonomous provinces of Kosovo, inhabited primarily by Albanians, and Vojvodina, inhabited primarily by Serbs and Magyars (Hungarians).

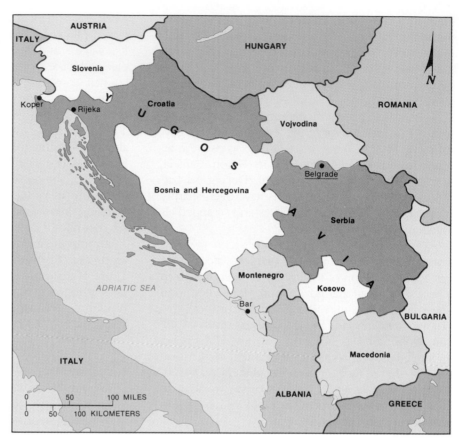

rency. Despite cultural diversity, economic interdependency has kept Yugoslavia's nationalities together.

Yugoslavia's political fragmentation has long been a source of problems. Nationalities other than the five officially recognized claim they are victims of discrimination. For example, 90 percent of the residents of the southern region of Kosovo are Albanians, but Yugoslavia does not recognize Albanian as a distinct nationality. Kosovo's official status is an autonomous region administered by Serbia, but in recent years Serbia has taken over direct rule of the region, under the pretext that the Albanians (who, remember, do not officially exist as a nationality) were threatening to detach Kosovo from Yugoslavia and unite it with the neighboring state of Albania. A similar situation has existed in Vojvodina, another autonomous region administered by Serbia, where ethnic Hungarians lack official recognition as one of Yugoslavia's nationalities.

Another problem for Yugoslavia has been competition among republics for resources, rather than cooperation to develop the country's economy as a whole. For example, from the viewpoint of international competitiveness, Yugoslavia should concentrate its resources to modernize and expand one large port, but each republic has wanted its own port: Rijeka in Croatia, Koper in Slovenia, and Bar in Montenegro. Instead of one large port, Yugoslavia has had several medium-sized ones that are less successful at attracting foreign trade.

Regional cooperation has also been hurt by economic differences among the republics. Slovenia, which borders Austria and Italy and contains only about 8 percent of Yugoslavia's population, has generally produced about 18 percent of the gross national product and 25 percent of the exports. With average incomes twice the national level, Slovenes have estimated that one-fourth of their production goes to subsidizing the economies of the poorer republics in the south.

The future role of communism has also threatened national unity in Yugoslavia. The republics of Croatia and Slovenia have elected noncommunist governments, whereas Serbia—the most powerful republic—has been slower to adopt economic and political reforms. If the Serbian-dominated national government impedes their moves towards democracy and a market economy, Croatia and Slovenia have threatened to secede from Yugoslavia.

To satisfy the demands of Croatia and Slovenia, Yugoslavia may become a **federation** (or confederation)—a form of federal state in which the local governments possess the right to secede. Federations have been adopted or at least considered in other countries that have sharp internal cultural differences. Czechoslovakia has become a federation between the Czechs and Slovaks, and Québec is seeking a federation in Canada (*see* Chapter 4).

Poland. Eastern European countries made far-reaching structural changes in their governmental systems once the communists lost power. Although a fairly good example of a nation-state, Poland switched from a unitary to a federal system after reformers wrested control of the national government from the communists. The federal system was adopted to dismantle legal structures by which the communists had maintained unchallenged power for more than forty years.

Under the communists' unitary system, local governments in Poland held no legal authority. The national government appointed local officials and claimed ownership of public property. This system led to deterioration of buildings, roads, and water systems because the national government did not allocate sufficient funds to maintain property and because no one had clear responsibility for keeping property in good condition.

Poland's 1989 constitution called for creation of 2,400 municipalities to be headed by directly elected officials. The national government turned over ownership of housing, water supplies, transportation systems, and other publicly owned structures to the new municipalities. The local authority decided on a case-by-case basis whether to take over a school, to let the national government continue to run it, or to turn it over to a private group, such as a church. Similarly, businesses owned by the national government, such as travel agencies, were either turned over to the municipalities or turned into private enterprises. Local authorities were allowed for the first time to levy income and property taxes; as in France, the national government also allocated blocks of funds for localities to use as they wanted.

The transition to a federal system of government has proved difficult in Poland, as well as in other Eastern European countries. In May 1990, Poles elected 52,000 municipal councillors; given the absence of local government for a half-century, not one of these officials had experience in governing a community. The first task for many newly elected councillors was to attend a training course in how to govern.

To compound the problem of adopting a federal system, Poland's locally elected officials had to find thousands of qualified people to fill appointed administrative positions, such as directors of education, public works, and planning. Municipalities had the option of hiring some of the 95,000 national government administrators who had previously overseen local affairs under the unitary system. Many of these former officials were rejected by the new local governments because of their close ties to the discredited Communist party. The national government was not allowed to intervene in local decisions concerning whether to retain or replace the former administrators.

KEY ISSUE

Which Geographic Elements Contribute to National Power?

The world has been divided into a collection of sovereign states of widely varying sizes and shapes. And partly because of these geographic differences, not all states hold the same degree of power. For over forty years, beginning in the late 1940s, the United States and Soviet Union exercised more power than other states, but in the 1990s, smaller states have successfully challenged the dominance of the two superpowers.

Size

The land area occupied by the states of the world varies considerably. The largest state is the Soviet

Union, which encompasses 22.4 million square kilometers (8.6 million square miles), 15 percent of the world's entire land area. The distance between the country's western border with Poland and the eastern border at the Pacific Ocean is more than 8,000 kilometers (5,000 miles).

At the other extreme, the smallest state in the United Nations—Liechtenstein—encompasses only 161 square kilometers (62 square miles), about the size of the city of St. Louis, Missouri. Other U.N. member states smaller than 1,000 square kilometers include Antigua and Barbuda, Bahrain, Barbados, Dominica, Grenada, Maldives, Malta, St. Christopher-Nevis, St. Lucia, St. Vincent and the Grenadines, São Tomé e Príncipe, the Seychelles, and Singapore. Nonmembers of the United Nations include the European microstates Andorra, Monaco, San Marino, and the Vatican. These independent microstates range in size from Andorra, at 453 square kilometers (175 square miles), to the Vatican, at 44 hectares (109 acres).

Historically, very large size generally has not been an important element in defining power. In the past, some states even found that very large size was a liability, because a very large state could not effectively guard the entire territory against invasion by neighboring states. People living far from the capital frequently displayed less intense loyalty to the state. Consequently, very large states in the past were compelled to devote energy to defending their own territory. Since World War II, however, very large size has become a clear asset in global power, while small size has become more of a hardship. The two main reasons for large size being an asset are availability of resources and military defense.

Availability of resources. The larger the state, the more likely it can obtain the resources necessary to be self-sufficient. Critical resources include food and raw materials.

A country that can grow enough food for its population has an advantage over one that must import food. The United Kingdom, which imports over two-thirds of its food supply, was threatened during both world wars in the twentieth century by enemy attacks on its supply ships. In contrast, the United States and the Soviet Union are less concerned with safeguarding food imports during wartime. If either country were involved in a major war, the population would probably not starve, though shortages of certain products might cause inconvenience. One of the most important elements of U.S. power is the production of a substantial food surplus. Inability of the Soviet economy to maximize agricultural output has been one of the basic problems leading to unrest in that country.

The production of consumer goods and military equipment requires a large supply of coal, iron ore, and many other raw materials. Although no state is entirely self-sufficient in raw materials, very large states have access to most of the important ones. The Soviet Union is particularly well-endowed with raw materials, ranking among the world's leaders in the mining of a wide variety of them.

Raw materials change in importance over time. In the last century, coal and wood supplies were essential elements of global power. During the twentieth century, however, countries that possess large supplies of petroleum and uranium have become more powerful. States in the Middle East have become more powerful in recent decades because they claim a large percentage of the world's oil reserves. South Africa's reserves of uranium and other minerals are a source of strength that has helped its government to withstand foreign pressures to reform the apartheid system.

Very large states have also become more powerful because of the development of nuclear weapons. Only a very large state can plan for the possibility of surviving a nuclear war. Many observers assert that a nuclear war would inevitably destroy the planet, but leaders in the United States and the Soviet Union plan for the possibility that each side might launch a handful of nuclear weapons (perhaps by accident) and then reach an agreement before completely destroying each other. On the other hand, most European and African states could not recover from even one or two bombs.

Shape

The shape of a state can also affect its power. Countries display a wide variety of shapes, and the shape of a particular state—such as the outline of the United States or Canada—is part of its unique identity. Beyond its symbolic value, the shape of a state can both influence the ease of internal administration and affect social unity. The shape also affects the length of boundaries with other states and

FIGURE 7–15
Shapes of states. Examples are shown of states that are compact (Bulgaria), prorupted (Namibia), elongated (Chile), fragmented (Philippines), and perforated (South Africa). The five states are drawn to the same scale. In general, compactness is an asset, because it fosters good communications and integration among all regions of the country.

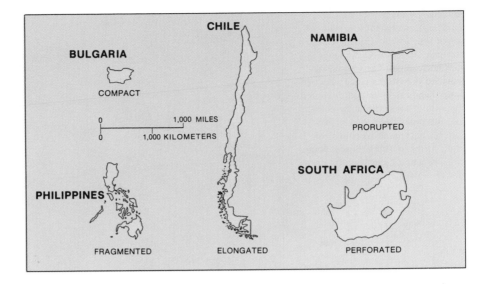

therefore the potential for both communications and conflicts with neighbors.

There are five main types of shapes—compact, prorupted, elongated, fragmented, and perforated (Figure 7–15). Each displays distinctive characteristics and problems.

Compact. In a **compact state,** the distance from the center to any boundary does not vary significantly. Compactness is a beneficial characteristic for most smaller states because good communications can be more easily established to all regions, especially if the capital is located near the center. Examples of compact states include Bulgaria, Hungary, and Poland.

Prorupted. An otherwise compact state with a large projecting extension is a **prorupted state.** There are two main reasons for proruptions. First, proruptions can separate two states that otherwise would share a boundary. When the British ruled the otherwise compact state of Afghanistan, they created a long, narrow proruption to the east, approximately 300 kilometers (200 miles) long and as narrow as 20 kilometers (12 miles) wide. The proruption prevents the Soviet Union from sharing a border with Pakistan.

A proruption can also provide a state with access to a resource, such as water. When the Belgians gained control of the Congo (now Zaire), they carved out a 500-kilometer (300-mile) proruption to the west. The proruption, which followed the

Congo (Zaire) River, gave the colony access to the Atlantic Ocean. The proruption also divided the Portuguese colony (now the independent state) of Angola into two discontinuous fragments 50 kilometers (30 miles) from each other. The northern region, called Cabinda, constitutes less than 1 percent of Angola's total land area (Figure 7–16).

FIGURE 7–16
Zaire is an example of a prorupted state. When the Belgians gained control of the territory, formerly known as the Congo, they created the proruption to assure direct access from the interior of the country to the Atlantic Ocean along the Congo (Zaire) River. The proruption also had the effect of making Angola a fragmented state.

FIGURE 7–17
Namibia, formerly the German colony of South-West Africa, includes a proruption to the east known as the Caprivi Strip. The Caprivi Strip provided the Germans with access to the Zambezi River and disrupted communications within the British colonies of southern Africa. Namibia became independent of South Africa in 1990, though South Africa retained control of the port of Walvis Bay.

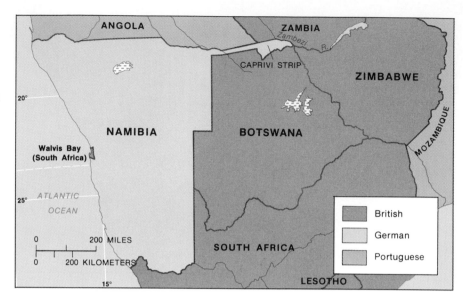

In their colony of South-West Africa (now Namibia), the Germans carved out a 500-kilometer (300 mile) proruption to the east. The proruption, known as the Caprivi Strip, provided the Germans with access to one of Africa's most important rivers, the Zambezi. The Caprivi Strip also disrupted communications within the British colonies of southern Africa. In recent years, South Africa, which controlled Namibia until its independence in 1990, stationed troops in the Caprivi Strip to fight enemies located in Angola, Zambia, and Botswana (Figure 7–17).

Elongated. There are a handful of **elongated states,** or states with a long, narrow shape. The clearest example is Chile, which stretches north-south for more than 4,000 kilometers (2,500 miles) but rarely exceeds an east-west distance of 150 kilometers (90 miles). Chile is wedged between the Pacific coast of South America and the rugged Andes Mountains, which rise more than 6,700 meters (20,000 feet).

Somewhat less extreme examples of elongated states are found elsewhere in the world. Italy extends more than 1,100 kilometers (700 miles) from northwest to southeast but is only approximately 200 kilometers (120 miles) wide in most places. In Africa, Malawi is approximately 850 kilometers (530 miles) north-south but only 100 kilometers (60 miles) east-west.

Elongated states may suffer from poor internal communications. A region located at an extreme end of the elongation may be isolated from the capital, which is usually placed near the center.

Fragmented. A **fragmented state** includes discontinuous pieces of territory. Technically, all states that have offshore islands as part of their territory are fragmented. But fragmentation is particularly significant for some states.

There are two kinds of fragmented states. In one kind, the discontinuous areas are separated by water. For example, Indonesia comprises more than 13,000 islands extending more than 5,000 kilometers (3,000 miles) across the Indian Ocean. Although more than 80 percent of the country's population live on two of the islands—Java and Sumatra—the fragmentation hinders communications and makes integration of people living on remote islands nearly impossible. Japan, the Philippines, and New Zealand are also states that comprise more than one island.

A more difficult type of fragmentation occurs when two pieces of territory are separated by another state. Picture the difficulty of communicating between Alaska and the lower forty-eight states if

Canada were not a friendly neighbor, since all land connections between Alaska and the rest of the United States must pass through Canada. As mentioned above, the division of Angola into two pieces by Zaire's proruption creates a fragmented state.

Panama—otherwise an example of an elongated state, 700 kilometers (450 miles) long and 80 kilometers (50 miles) wide—is fragmented by the Canal Zone, built and owned by the United States. U.S. ownership of the Canal Zone was a source of tension for many years, but the United States and Panama signed a treaty in the late 1970s that transfers the Canal to Panama on December 31, 1999. The treaty guarantees the neutrality of the Canal Zone and permits the United States to use force if necessary to keep the canal operating (Figure 7–18).

Perforated. A state that completely surrounds another one is a **perforated state.** The one good example of a perforated state is South Africa, which completely surrounds the state of Lesotho. Lesotho must depend almost entirely on South Africa for the import and export of goods despite the fact that it is governed by blacks, while South Africa is controlled by a white minority government. If the homelands created by South Africa would ever be recognized as sovereign by other countries, South Africa would be further perforated.

Emergence of Two Superpowers

Following World War II, in the late 1940s, two states emerged as superpowers—the United States and the Soviet Union. Before then, the world as a matter of course contained more than two superpowers. For example, in the early 1800s at the time of the Napoleonic Wars, Europe included eight superpowers— Austria, France, Great Britain, Poland, Prussia, Russia, Spain, and Sweden. At the outbreak of World War I, eight great powers again existed, as Germany, Italy, Japan, and the United States replaced Poland, Prussia, Spain, and Sweden on the list. By the end of World War II, most of the former superpowers had been beaten or battered by the two world wars, and only the United States and the Soviet Union remained as superpowers.

When a large number of states ranked as great powers of approximately equal strength, no single state could dominate the others. Instead, major powers joined together to form temporary alliances. A condition of roughly equal strength between opposing alliances is known as a **balance of power.**

Historically, the addition of one or two states to an alliance could tip the balance of power. The British in particular entered alliances to restore the balance of power and prevent any other state from becoming too powerful. In contrast, the post–World War II balance of power was a bipolar one between the United States and the Soviet Union. Because the power of these two states was so much greater than all others, the world comprised two camps, each under the influence of one of the superpowers.

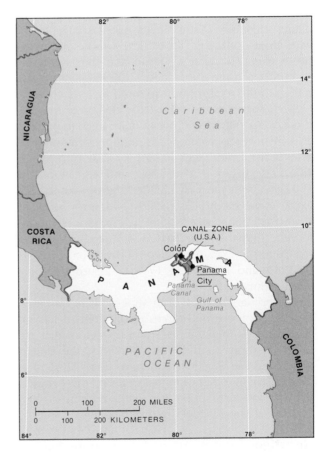

FIGURE 7–18
Panama currently is an example of a fragmented state, because the United States controls the Canal Zone. After the United States completes the process of turning over control of the Canal Zone to Panama in 1999, the country will become a good example of an elongated state.

Other states lost the ability to tip the scales significantly in favor of one or the other superpower. They were relegated to a new role, that of ally or satellite. The two superpowers collected allies like works of art. The acquisition of one state not only added to the value of one superpower's collection but also prevented the other superpower from acquiring it.

An ally could cause trouble for a superpower. Other states could remain in an alliance either as willing and effective partners in pursuing the objectives of the superpower or as balky and unreliable members with limited usefulness. When the United States attacked Libya by air in 1986, the planes took off from England. The direct route went over France, but the French refused to give the U.S. planes clearance. Rather than risk a confrontation with an ally, the U.S. planes flew a more circuitous route over the Atlantic Ocean and the Mediterranean Sea, a route that added 1,200 kilometers (800 miles) to the total round-trip mission.

Both superpowers repeatedly demonstrated that if necessary they would use military force to prevent an ally from becoming too independent-minded. The Soviet Union sent its armies into Hungary in 1956, Czechoslovakia in 1968, and Afghanistan in 1979 to install more sympathetic governments. Because these states were clearly within the orbit of the Soviet Union, the United States chose not to intervene militarily. Similarly, the United States sent troops to the Dominican Republic in 1965, Grenada in 1983, and Panama in 1989 to assure that they would remain allies.

As very large states, both superpowers can fairly quickly deploy armed forces to different regions of the world. To maintain strength in regions that are not contiguous to their own territory, the United States and the Soviet Union have established military bases in other countries. From these bases, ground and air support can enter regions of conflict. Naval fleets patrol the major bodies of water.

Nonaligned states. Many of the more recently independent states in Africa and Asia consider themselves uncommitted to either superpower. The Nonaligned Movement, founded in 1961, has approximately 100 members, including nearly every country in Africa and the Middle East. But the Nonaligned Movement's members are a heterogeneous collec-

tion of states that do not agree on many common policies. Some members of the Nonaligned Movement, such as Cuba and North Korea, have clearly been allied with one of the superpowers.

Neither of the world's two most populous states, China and India, are firmly allied with a superpower. China was a close ally of the Soviet Union following the 1949 communist victory in the civil war, but by the 1960s relations had deteriorated between the two countries. India has not followed the lead of its former colonial ruler, Great Britain, into the U.S. sphere of influence. While China and India may be large enough to avoid formal alliance with a superpower, most of the nonaligned states lack the resources, technological capability, or military strength to remain completely independent.

Regional and International Cooperation

In the 1990s, the era of a bipolar balance of power has ended. Instead, the world has returned to the pattern of more than two superpowers that predominated prior to World War II. The 1990s pattern, however, displays two important differences. First, the most important elements of state power are increasingly economic rather than military. Japan has joined the ranks of superpowers entirely on its economic successes, while the Soviet Union and to a lesser extent the United States have slipped because of economic problems. Second, the leading economic superpower in the 1990s is not a single state, such as the United States or Soviet Union, but a union of European states led by Germany.

After World War II, most European states joined one of two military alliances dominated by the superpowers. The North Atlantic Treaty Organization (NATO) is a military alliance among 16 states, including the United States and Canada, plus fourteen European states. Twelve European states—Belgium, Denmark, Germany, Greece, Iceland, Italy, Luxembourg, the Netherlands, Norway, Portugal, Turkey, and the United Kingdom—participate fully in NATO, while France and Spain are members but do not contribute troops (Figure 7–19). NATO headquarters are in Belgium, and integrated troops are stationed elsewhere in Europe.

The Warsaw Pact was a military agreement among Eastern European countries to defend each other in case of attack. Seven members joined the

Warsaw Pact when it was founded in 1955, including the Soviet Union, Bulgaria, Czechoslovakia, East Germany, Hungary, Poland, and Romania. In 1956, some of Hungary's leaders asked for the help of Warsaw Pact troops to crush an uprising that threatened communist control of the government. Warsaw Pact troops also invaded Czechoslovakia in 1968 to depose a government committed to reforms.

NATO and the Warsaw Pact were designed to maintain a bipolar balance of power in Europe. For NATO allies, the principal objective was to prevent the Soviet Union from overrunning West Germany and other smaller countries. The Warsaw Pact provided the Soviet Union with a buffer of allied states between it and Germany to discourage a third German invasion of the Soviet Union in the twentieth century.

As Eastern Europe states have shed their communist governments, the roles of both NATO and the Warsaw Pact have changed. The Soviet Union no longer has the right—or the financial resources—to station troops in a large number of other Eastern European countries, and the Warsaw Pact was dissolved in 1991. At the same time, NATO members no longer see a Soviet attack on Western Europe as a credible possibility in the coming years. The Soviet military is more likely to respond to restive nationalities within the country than to problems elsewhere in Europe.

With the decline in the military-oriented alliances, European states have increasingly cooperated economically. In 1949, the same seven Eastern European states in the Warsaw Pact formed the Council for Mutual Economic Assistance (COMECON). Cuba, Mongolia, and Vietnam have since joined the alliance, which is designed to promote trade and sharing of natural resources.

Western Europe's most important economic organization is the European Community, frequently known as the Common Market. When it was established in 1958, the European Community included six countries: Belgium, France, West Germany, Italy, Luxembourg, and the Netherlands. Membership was widened to include Denmark, Ireland, and the United Kingdom in 1973, Greece in 1981, and Portugal and Spain in 1986.

The main task of the European Community is to promote development within the member states through economic cooperation. At first, the European Community played a limited role, such as providing subsidies to farmers and to depressed regions like southern Italy. But the organization has taken on more importance in recent years, as members move towards greater integration of their economies. According to an agreement among member states, as of December 31, 1992, all barriers to free trade among the states were to be removed, as were all barriers to the movement of people and capital. A European Parliament is elected by the people in each of the member states simultaneously. The effect of these actions has been to turn Western Europe into the world's wealthiest and most populous market.

Other regional organizations. The Organization of American States (OAS) includes thirty-two of the thirty-three states in the Western Hemisphere, with the exception of Canada. Cuba is a member but was suspended from most OAS activities in 1962. The organization's headquarters, including the permanent council and general assembly, are located in Washington, D.C. The OAS promotes social, cultural, political, and economic links among member states.

A similar organization exists in Africa, known as the Organization for African Unity (OAU). Founded in 1963, OAU includes every African state with the exception of South Africa, which has been excluded because of its apartheid policies. The organization's major issue is the elimination of minority white-ruled governments in southern Africa.

The Commonwealth of Nations includes the United Kingdom and forty-seven states that were once British colonies, including Australia, Bangladesh, Canada, India, and Nigeria. Most of the other members comprise African states or island countries in the Caribbean or Pacific. Commonwealth members seek economic and cultural cooperation.

The United Nations

The most important international organization is the United Nations, created at the end of World War II by the victorious allies. When established in 1945, the United Nations comprised 49 states, but by the early 1990s it had grown to 159 members (*see* Table 7–1). The United Nations includes 157 sovereign states, plus two republics of the Soviet Union (the Byelorussian S.S.R. and the Ukrainian S.S.R.). When

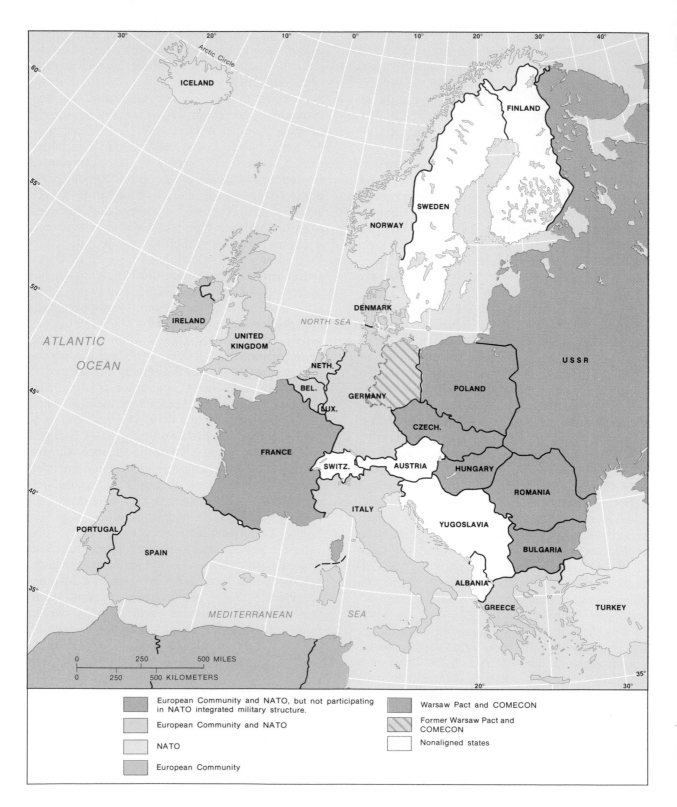

the United Nations was founded in 1945, these two republics were given seats to reduce Soviet fears that they would be outvoted by the Western allies.

Only four populous states are not members of the United Nations: North Korea, South Korea, Switzerland, and Taiwan. Neither North nor South Korea is a member because both regard the division of the Korean nationality into two states to be temporary. Switzerland protects its neutrality by avoiding membership in most international organizations. Taiwan resigned when the United Nations voted to admit the People's Republic of China in 1971, because the government of Taiwan still considered itself the proper ruler of the Chinese mainland. North and South Korea, Monaco, San Marino, Switzerland, and the Vatican maintain nonvoting observer status at the United Nations.

The United Nations replaced another organization known as the League of Nations, established after World War I. The League was never an effective peace-keeping organization. The United States did not join, despite the fact that President Woodrow Wilson initiated the idea, because the U.S. Senate refused to ratify the membership treaty. By the 1930s, Germany, Italy, Japan, and the Soviet Union had all withdrawn, and the League could not stop aggression by these states against neighboring countries.

The United Nations is frequently criticized for failing to keep world peace. Members can vote to establish a peace-keeping force and request states to contribute soldiers, but any one of the five permanent members of the Security Council—China, France, the Soviet Union, the United Kingdom, and the United States—can veto the operation. The United Nations organized a large peace-keeping operation in the early 1950s to repel North Korea's invasion of the south. In a tactical error, the Soviet

Union boycotted the vote instead of vetoing the proposal. More recently, the United Nations has sent soldiers to Lebanon and Cyprus.

The United Nations is also attacked for being one-sided on a number of world issues, such as the Arab-Israeli struggle in the Middle East. For example, the Palestine Liberation Organization (P.L.O.) has been granted an observer status at the United Nations, even though the United States and Israel consider it to be a terrorist organization. For many years, U.S. citizens claimed that the United Nations did not reflect their interests. On the other hand, after the United Nations voted to permit its members to use force to expel Iraq from Kuwait, Iraq and several other states believed that the United States was dominating the organization. Yet, with all its weaknesses, the United Nations still represents a forum where for the first time in history virtually all states of the world can meet and vote on issues.

The United Nations reinforces rather than replaces the concept of a collection of sovereign states. Virtually all U.N. members united to oppose Iraq's attempted annexation of Kuwait in August 1990, because it represented a clear challenge to the principle of dividing the world into a collection of sovereign states. Other countries feared that if international boundaries could be changed by force in the Middle East, they could be changed by force elsewhere in the world as well.

Summary

This is a review of issues raised at the beginning of the chapter.

1. **What is the difference between a state and a nation?** A state is a political unit, with an organized government and sovereignty, whereas a nation is a group of people with a strong sense of cultural unity. Most of the earth's surface is allocated to states, and only a handful of colonies and tracts of unorganized territory remain. In the modern world, states have been created to match the distribution of nations whenever possible.

2. **How are boundaries drawn between states?** The concept of allocating the earth's surface to a collection of states is relatively modern. Prior to recent centuries, most of the earth's surface was organized into a mix of city-states, empires, and

FIGURE 7–19 (opposite)
Ten Western European countries, plus Greece, have joined both the European Community (EC) and the North Atlantic Treaty Organization (NATO). Ireland is a member of the European Community but not NATO, while Iceland, Norway, and Turkey are in NATO but not the EC. Seven Eastern European countries joined an economic alliance, known as COMECON, and a military alliance, known as the Warsaw Pact. Once East Germany ceased to exist and the other Eastern European states adopted noncommunist governments, the economic alliance lost its importance and the military alliance was dismantled.

kingdoms. The modern state system originated in Europe and diffused to other regions of the world. Boundaries separate states from each other and are drawn according to a variety of cultural and physical features.

3. **What problems result from the location of boundaries between states?** Problems arise when the boundaries of states do not coincide with the boundaries of nationalities. In some cases, one state contains more than one nation, while in other cases, one nationality is split among more than one state.

4. **Which geographic elements contribute to national power?** Countries vary widely in size and shape. In the modern world, very large size is an asset, and two very large states—the United States and the Soviet Union—emerged as superpowers after World War II. In the 1990s, however, Japan and Western Europe have gained superpower status through economic rather than military strength. States have joined a variety of regional and international organizations to foster economic cooperation and provide mutual protection.

United Germany

Political changes in Eastern Europe and the Soviet Union have reduced the threat of direct confrontation between two alliances led by superpowers. But a critical consequence of reduced tensions between superpowers is the increased likelihood of unrest in places where the boundaries of states do not match those of nationalities.

Few Germans mourned the extinction of East Germany in 1990. Reunification put an end to many hardships for East Germans, such as the forced separation of families, limitations on civil rights, and harsh economic conditions.

On the surface, a unified Germany is consistent with the nation-state principle that has governed the organization of the earth's surface this century. The arbitrary division of Germany into the Democratic and Federal republics resulted from the German defeat in World War II and the cold war that soon followed. Unification of Germany brought together two groups of people who both spoke German and referred to their country as "Germany."

But Germany is not an especially good example of a nation-state. A state known as Germany was not created until 1871. Before that time, the map of central Europe was a patchwork of small states, more than 300 during the seventeenth century, for example. Under Frederick the Great (1712–86), the previously obscure state of Prussia was able to control a continuous stretch of territory abutting the Baltic Sea from Memel on the east to beyond the Elbe River on the west. Other consolidations reduced the number of states in the area to approximately two dozen by 1815.

In 1871, Prussia's Prime Minister Otto von Bismarck was instrumental in forcing most of the remaining states in the area to join a Prussian-dominated German Empire, which extended west beyond the Rhine River. Bismarck failed to consolidate all German speakers into the empire; Austria, Switzerland, and Bohemia were excluded. The German Empire lasted less than fifty years.

When the Berlin Wall was opened on November 11, 1989, residents of East Berlin poured into the western sector. Within a year, the two parts of Berlin were united, and the German Democratic Republic ceased to exist.

After it lost World War I, Germany lost much of its territory (Figure 7–20). While the boundaries of southern European states were fixed to conform when possible to those of nationalities, Germany's new boundaries were arbitrary. Germany became a fragmented state, with East Prussia separated from the rest of the country by the Danzig Corridor, created to give Poland a port on the Baltic Sea. German takeovers of Austria, Poland, and portions of Czechoslovakia during the 1930s were justified as attempts to reconstruct a true German nation-state.

After Germany's defeat in World War II, boundaries were again shifted. Germany lost its eastern territory to Poland, which in turn gave up its

German speaking territory in 1914

FIGURE 7–20
In 1914, at the outbreak of World War I, Germany extended
1,300 kilometers (800 miles) from Memel (now Klaipeda) on
the east to Strasbourg on the west. After losing World War I,
Germany was divided into two discontinuous areas, separated
by the Danzig Corridor, part of the newly created state of Poland. Germany's boundaries changed again after World War II,
as eastern portions of the country were taken by Poland and
the Soviet Union. When the boundaries were drawn after
World War II, millions of Germans were forced to migrate to
the west; as a result, the eastern boundaries of Germany and
the German language region now correspond fairly closely.
Yet, at no time have the borders of Germany coincided with
the area of German speakers.

eastern territory to the Soviet Union. In the process, millions of Germans—as well as other nationalities—were forced to give up their property. Germany has been pressured by other states to accept the relocated boundary with Poland—along the Oder and Neisse rivers—but some Germans, especially those forced to move in 1945, resent the concession.

Germany's western boundary has been no more stable. France regards the Rhine River as the proper boundary with Germany, but Prussia and more recently Germany have considered the Rhine to be entirely German. The area west of the Rhine, known as Alsace and Lorraine, has passed back and forth between French and German control, depending on who won the latest war. By living on the frontier between two cultures, Alsace (to a greater extent than Lorraine) reflects a mix of French and German language and social customs. Because France was on the winning side in World War II, it now controls the area.

Germany is not likely to repeat its past policy of territorial expansion through military conquest. Instead, as the most populous and economically strongest member of the European Community, Germany will likely take the lead in setting the political agenda for a united Europe. When the European Community was founded, Germany was a quiet member, content to subsidize inefficient French farmers and impoverished southern Italians in exchange for acceptance as a respectable ally and reliable trading partner. In the future, Germany will probably gain through economic competition what previous generations failed to obtain through military means: to be the most powerful state in the midst of the world's largest market. This prospect worries its European neighbors.

The Soviet Union has become the world's most prominent example of a state that faces problems as a result of demands by its many nationalities for increased control over their economic and political affairs, if not complete independence. The Baltic republics of Estonia, Latvia, and Lithuania have been especially eager to achieve independence from the Soviet Union. These republics were independent states between the world wars, but the Soviet Union took control of them in 1939, as part of a deal with Germany to divide Eastern Europe between them. The Baltic republics feel that they have contributed more to the Soviet economy than they have received in benefits. Consequently, they might be better off as independent states free to make economic arrangements with other states.

Meanwhile, the Soviet republics in central Asia, where most people are Muslims, are fighting for more cultural freedom and standards of living comparable to those in the European portion of the Soviet Union. Thus, underlying the unrest in all regions of the Soviet Union are significant differences in the levels of economic development among the nationalities, as we shall see in more detail in the next chapter.

Key Terms

Apartheid Laws in South Africa that physically separate different races into different geographic areas.

Balance of power A condition of roughly equal strength between opposing countries or alliances of countries.

Boundary An invisible line that marks the extent of a state's territory.

Centripetal forces Attitudes that tend to unify a people and enhance support for the state.

City-state A sovereign state that comprises a town and surrounding countryside.

Colonialism The attempt by one country to establish settlements and to impose its political, economic, and cultural principles in another territory.

Colony A territory that is legally tied to a sovereign state rather than completely independent.

Compact state A state in which the distance from the center to any boundary does not vary significantly.

Elongated state A state with a long, narrow shape.

Federal state An internal organization of a state that allocates most powers to units of local government.

Federation A form of federal state in which the local governments possess the right to secede.

Fragmented state A state that includes discontinuous pieces of territory.

Frontier A zone separating two states in which neither state excercises political control.

Imperialism The imposition by one state of its culture and political organization on another inhabited territory.

Landlocked state A state that does not have a direct outlet to the sea.

Multinational state A state that contains more than one nationality.

Nationalism The attitude of the people in a nation in support of the existence and growth of a particular state.

Nationality (or nation) A group of people who occupy a particular area and have a strong sense of unity based on a set of shared beliefs and attitudes.

Nation-state A state whose territory corresponds to that occupied by a particular nation.

Perforated state A state that completely surrounds another one.

Prorupted state An otherwise compact state with a large projecting extension.

Self-determination The concept that nationalities have the right to govern themselves.

Sovereignty The ability of a state to govern with its territory free from control of its internal affairs by other states.

State An area organized into a political unit and ruled by an established government with control over its internal and foreign affairs.

Unitary state An internal organization of a state that places most power in the hands of central government officials.

Thinking Geographically

1. In his book *1984,* George Orwell envisaged the division of the world into three large unified states, held together through technological controls. To what extent has Orwell's vision of a global political arrangement been realized?

2. Regions such as Slovenia, Croatia, Slovakia, and Québec are attempting to create extreme examples of federal states in which virtually all authority is vested in local governments. Are there any elements of authority that must remain in the hands of a national government, or can a country exist in which governments exercise all authority?

3. Given the movement towards increased local government autonomy on the one hand and increased authority for international organizations on the other hand, what is the future of the nation-state?
4. To what extent does national identity derive from economic interests rather than from such cultural characteristics as language and religion?
5. Nearly a century ago, the British geographer Halford J. Mackinder identified a heartland in the interior of Eurasia (Europe and Asia) that was isolated by mountain ranges and the Arctic Sea. Surrounding the heartland was a series of fringe areas, which the geographer Nicholas Spykman later called the rimland, oriented towards the oceans. Mackinder argued that whoever controlled the heartland would control Eurasia and hence the entire world. To what extent has the emergence of the Soviet Union as a superpower validated Mackinder's theory?

Further Readings

Arlinghaus, Sandra L., and John D. Nystuen, "Geometry of Boundary Exchanges." *Geographical Review* 80 (January 1990): 21–31.

Bennett, D. Gordon, ed. *Tension Areas of the World: A Problem Oriented World Regional Geography.* Champaign, IL: Park Press, 1982.

Boal, Frederick W., and J. Neville H. Douglas, eds. *Integration and Division: Geographical Perspectives on the Northern Ireland Problem.* London and New York: Academic Press, 1982.

Brown, Curtis M., Walter G. Robillard, and Donald A. Wilson. *Boundary Control and Legal Principles.* New York: Wiley, 1986.

Burghart, A. F. "The Bases of Territorial Claims." *Geographical Review* 63 (April 1973): 225–45.

Burnett, Alan D., and Peter J. Taylor, eds. *Political Studies from Spatial Perspectives.* Chichester, England: Wiley, 1981.

Busteed, M. A., ed. *Developments in Political Geography.* London: Academic Press, 1983.

Christopher, A. J. *The British Empire at Its Zenith.* London: Croom Helm, 1988.

Cox, Kevin R. *Location and Public Problems: A Political Geography of the Contemporary World.* Chicago: Maaroufa Press, 1979.

Dale, E. H. "Some Geographical Aspects of African Land-Locked States." *Annals of the Association of American Geographers* 58 (September 1968): 485–505.

Dikshit, R. D. "Geography and Federalism." *Annals of the Association of American Geographers* 61 (March 1971): 97–130.

Gottmann, Jean, ed. *Centre and Periphery: Spatial Variation in Politics.* Beverly Hills: Sage, 1980.

Johnston, R. J. *Geography and the State.* New York: St. Martin's Press, 1982.

Kliot, Nurit, and Stanley Waterman, eds. *Pluralism and Political Geography—People, Territory and State.* New York: St. Martin's Press, 1983.

Mathieson, R. S. "Nuclear Power in the Soviet Bloc." *Annals of the Association of American Geographers* 70 (June 1980): 271–79.

Morgenthau, Hans J. *Politics Among Nations.* 4th ed. New York: Knopf, 1967.

Murphy, Alexander B. "Territorial Policies in Multiethnic States," *Geographical Review* 79 (October 1989): 410–421.

Murphy, Alexander B. "Historical Justifications for Territorial Claims," *Annals of the Association of American Geographers* 80 (December 1990): 531–548.

O'Loughlin, John, and Herman van der Wusten. "Political Geography of Panregions," *Geographical Review* 80 (January 1990): 1–20.

O'Sullivan, Patrick. *Geopolitics.* New York: St. Martin's Press, 1986.

O'Sullivan, Patrick, and Jesse W. Miller. *The Geography of Warfare.* London: Croom Helm, 1983.

Ovendale, Ritchie. *The Origins of the Arab-Israeli Wars.* London and New York: Longman, 1984.

Pacione, Michael, ed. *Progress in Political Geography.* London: Croom Helm, 1985.

Parker, W. H. *Mackinder: Geography as an Aid to Statecraft.* Oxford: The Clarendon Press, 1982.

Prescott, J. R. V. *Boundaries and Frontiers.* London: Croom Helm, 1978.

———. *The Geography of State Politics.* Chicago: Aldine, 1968.

———. *Political Geography.* London: Methuen, 1972.

———. *The Political Geography of the Oceans.* Newton Abbot, England: David and Charles, 1975.

Pringle, D. G. *One Island? Two Nations? A Political Geographical Analysis of the National Conflict in Ireland.* Letchworth, England: Research Studies Press, Wiley, 1985.

Richmond, Anthony H. "Ethnic Nationalism: Social Science Paradigm." *International Social Science Journal* 39 (February 1987): 3–18.

Rose, Richard. "National Pride in Cross-National Perspective." *International Social Science Journal* 37 (no. 1, 1985): 85–96.

Soffer, Arnon, and Julian V. Minghi. "Israel's Security Landscapes: The Impact of Military Considerations on Land Uses." *Professional Geographer* 38 (February 1986): 28–41.

Taylor, Peter J., and John W. House, eds. *Political Geography: Recent Advances and Future Directions.* London: Croom Helm, 1984.

Xihu, Ruan. "Races, Classes, Ethnic Groups and Bantustans in South Africa." *International Social Science Journal* 39 (February 1987): 85–96.

Also consult these journals: *American Journal of Political Science; American Political Science Review; Foreign Affairs; International Affairs; International Journal; International Journal of Middle East Studies; Political Geography Quarterly; Soviet Geography.*

8
Economic Development

KEY ISSUES

◆ How do geographers measure economic development?

◆ How do social and demographic characteristics relate to development?

◆ How does the level of development vary among regions?

◆ How can countries promote economic development?

Have you ever traveled to a Caribbean island? Even if not, you have probably seen the travel advertisements featuring a bronzed couple sipping exotic drinks, lying on a deserted beach surrounded by palm trees.

Beyond the hotel is another world, fleetingly glimpsed by tourists traveling between the resort and the airport. The permanent residents of the islands may live in poverty, earning less money in one year than a week's hotel bill. Many are ill fed, ill clothed, and underemployed.

This depressing view of conditions on the islands is, naturally, shielded from the tourists, who do not travel hundreds of kilometers for a vacation in order to encounter misery. Tourists bring money to the islands and in the process help pay for whatever improvements can be made in the squalid living conditions.

At the same time, though, can you imagine the feelings of the local residents? What would you think if a very expensive and exclusive resort were built in your neighborhood, and you and your family, who were economically disadvantaged, were expected to work there (for good wages, perhaps) to serve the needs of the vacationers? You might welcome the money, but would you resent the wealthy tourists?

The world is divided between relatively rich and relatively poor countries. Geographers try to understand the reasons for this division and learn what can be done about it.

Bangladesh's Development Problems

Rabea Rahman lives in the village of Bathoimuri, Bangladesh, with her three children, an eighteen-year-old son and two daughters, ages ten and seven. Rahman's two other children died in infancy, and her husband died of tuberculosis two years ago after a long illness.

When he was alive, Rahman's husband had been a tenant farmer, known as a sharecropper; under this arrangement, a portion of his crops was turned over to the landowner instead of rent. After her husband died, Rahman went to work as a domestic servant and water carrier, from 7 A.M. to 4 P.M. and from 6 P.M. to 11 P.M., seven days a week. Her son sells bread and is responsible for preparing a mid-day meal for his two sisters. Total household income is $16 per month.

Their house has a dirt floor and leaky roof, but the rent is only $2 per month, plus $3 per month for fuel. The remaining $11 a month goes for food; the sum is sufficient to provide each member of the household with 100 grams (about a quarter pound) of rice per day, but little else. The diet is supplemented by leftover food Rahman receives from her employer. After paying for rent, fuel, and food, the family has no extra money for other necessities. Because they can't afford shoes, the family members often go barefoot. Rahman suffers from a gastric ulcer but can't afford treatment.

Underlying the impoverished condition of the Rahman household is the role of women in a predominantly Muslim country like Bangladesh. In rural villages, less than 10 percent of the women can read and write. The typical woman is married as a teenager and bears six babies in her lifetime, although typically one of the six does not survive infancy. A woman like Rahman who is forced to find a job is limited to working as a servant or farm laborer. The condition of women—poor, illiterate, overburdened with children—is one of the most important factors holding back economic development in such South Asian countries as Bangladesh.

In previous chapters, we have examined important global demographic and cultural patterns. We have seen that rates of birth, death, and natural increase vary from one state to another. People in different countries also display different languages, religions, and other social customs. Political problems arise when the distribution of social customs do not match the boundaries between states.

Countries fall into nine major regions according to these demographic and cultural characteristics. In the Western Hemisphere, Anglo-America (Canada and the United States) and Latin America can be distinguished on the basis of predominant languages, religions, and natural increase rates. Although there is considerable diversity within these regions, at a global scale the individual countries within each region display cultural similarities.

Europe falls into two regions: Western and Eastern. Although the two regions share cultural characteristics, recent political experiences differ sharply. The Soviet Union is considered part of Eastern Europe because they have similar political and economic problems.

Asia comprises four major regions: East, South, Southeast, and Southwest. Major cultural, demographic, and political differences distinguish these four regions. Southwest Asia, however, is usually combined with Northern Africa to become a region known as the Middle East, because of similarities in language, religion, and population growth. Africa south of the Sahara Desert comprises the ninth major region.

In addition to those nine major regions, there are three other important areas: Japan, South Africa, and the South Pacific. Japan and South Africa are populous countries with cultural and demographic characteristics that contrast sharply with most of their neighboring states. The South Pacific—primarily Australia and New Zealand—covers an extensive area of the earth's surface but is much less populous than any other region.

The nine major regions also differ from each other in their distinctive types of economic activities, the way people earn their living, how the societies use their wealth, and other economic characteristics. As the world moves towards a global economy, geographers increasingly study the similarities and differences in the economic patterns of the various regions.

The most fundamental economic distinction among world regions is their level of **economic development,** which is a process of improvement in the material conditions of people through diffusion of knowledge and technology. This is not a process with a beginning and end. Rather, economic development is a continuous process involving a never-ending series of actions intended to promote constant improvement in the health and prosperity of the people.

Every country falls at some point on a continuum of economic development. A more-developed or **relatively developed country** has progressed farther along the development continuum. A country at an earlier stage of development is frequently called a less-developed country (LDC) but many analysts prefer to refer to it as **developing.** The term *developing* implies that the country has already made some progress and expects to continue the development process in the future.

Geographers find that countries which have achieved relatively high levels of economic development are clustered in some regions of the world, while developing countries are found in other regions. The regions geographers identify according to prevailing level of economic development correspond closely to the nine regions distinguished according to demographic, cultural, and political characteristics. Three of the nine major cultural regions—Anglo-America, Western Europe, and Eastern Europe/Soviet Union—rank relatively high on the economic-development continuum, while the other six are less developed. Japan, South Africa, and the South Pacific are also relatively developed areas.

The distribution of these relatively developed and developing regions reflects a clear global pattern. From a circle drawn around the world at 30° north latitude, we find that the three major relatively developed regions, plus Japan, are all situated to the north, while every developing region lies predominantly, if not entirely, south of the circle. This division of the world between relatively developed and developing regions is known as the north-south split.

A map of relatively developed and developing regions appears somewhat different on a north polar projection (Figure 8–1). Most of the relatively developed countries form a core region, while devel-

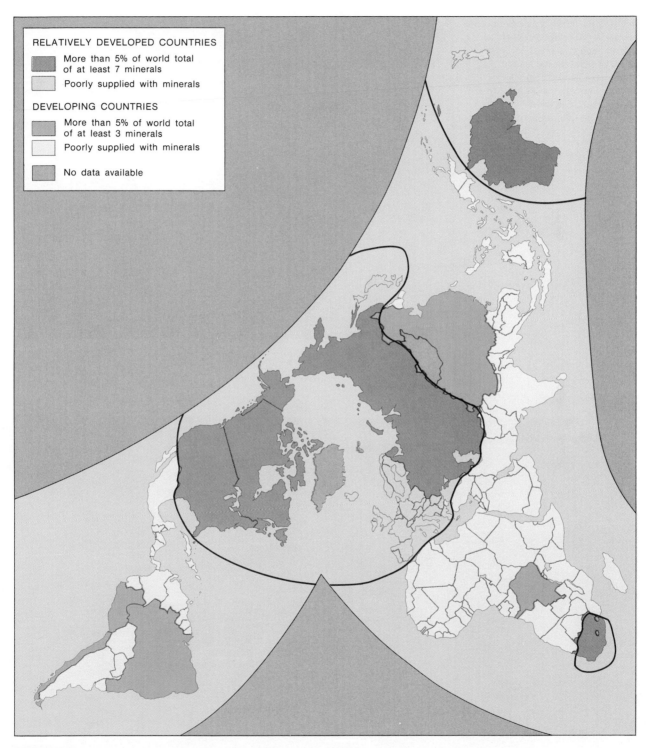

RELATIVELY DEVELOPED COUNTRIES

More than 5% of world total of at least 7 minerals

Poorly supplied with minerals

DEVELOPING COUNTRIES

More than 5% of world total of at least 3 minerals

Poorly supplied with minerals

No data available

FIGURE 8–1

Most of the countries that have achieved relatively high levels of economic development are located north of 30° north latitude. Viewed from a north polar projection, most of the relatively developed countries appear clustered in an inner core, while developing countries generally appear relegated to a peripheral or outer-ring location.

One prominent difference between a relatively developed country and a developing country is access to motor vehicles. In the United States, most people commute to work by car, whereas in Agra, India, the bicycle is widely used, since few people can afford a car.

oping countries occupy peripheral locations. Countries located in the periphery have less access to the world centers of consumption, communications, and political power, which are clustered in the core region.

The task of distinguishing between relatively developed and developing regions is made easier because the gap is increasing between the regions at the relatively high and low ends of the development continuum. The developing regions face considerable difficulties in achieving a level of economic development comparable to the level of countries that currently have relatively developed economies.

KEY   ISSUE

How Do Geographers Measure Economic Development?

Many factors help determine the level of a society's economic development. Geographers measure the level of economic development partly through a number of economic indicators, but social and demographic characteristics are also important considerations.

People in a relatively developed country are generally wealthier than in a developing country because they are more productive. Higher productivity results from taking advantage of modern technology to earn a living in a factory, office, or shop rather than struggling every day to grow food.

The wealth that productive industries generate goes partly to pay for the expensive modern technology required to operate efficient economic enterprises. Factories, offices, and shops also depend both on the creation of expensive communications and transportation networks and on the availability of large supplies of energy and other resources. Consumers in relatively developed countries use part of the wealth generated by economic activities to buy goods and services. Demand for these products in turn increases the number of needed factories, offices, and shops.

Part of the wealth produced in relatively developed countries goes to make people healthier, safer, and better educated. As a result, infants are more likely to survive, and adults are more likely to live longer. Armed with these social benefits, people in relatively developed countries can be more productive.

Three kinds of characteristics distinguish a country's level of development: economic, social, and demographic. Geographers can measure most of these characteristics in dollars or other numerical indicators.

Several indicators measure the economic factors that contribute to a society's level of development. These measures include per capita income, economic structure, worker productivity, access to raw materials, and availability of consumer goods.

Per Capita Income

The average person earns a much higher income in a relatively developed country than in a developing one. The typical worker receives $5–10 per hour in relatively developed countries, compared to less than $0.50 per hour in most developing countries. Relatively developed countries generally mandate a minimum wage of at least several dollars per hour.

Per capita income is a difficult figure to obtain in many countries. Therefore, to get a sense of average incomes in various countries, geographers frequently substitute per capita gross national product, a more readily available indicator. The **gross national product (GNP)** is the value of the total output of goods and services produced in a country in a given time period (normally, one year). Dividing the GNP by total population measures the contribution the average person makes to generating a country's wealth in a year.

Annual per capita GNP exceeds $15,000 in most relatively developed countries but less than $1,000 per year in most developing countries (Figure 8–2). Switzerland has the world's highest per capita GNP at nearly $30,000, while the figure is more than $20,000 in several other Western European countries, Japan, and the United States. As recently as the late 1980s, several oil-rich states bordering the Persian Gulf had the world's highest per capita GNPs, but the figures fell because of wars and declining petroleum prices. The lowest per capita GNPs are found in Sub-Saharan Africa and South and Southeast Asia. Nearly every country in these regions has a per capita GNP of less than $500 per year.

The gap in per capita GNP between relatively developed countries and developing countries has

FIGURE 8–2

The annual gross national product per capita exceeds $10,000 in most relatively developed countries but less than $1,000 in most developing countries, especially in Africa and Asia. Several petroleum-rich countries in southwestern Asia have relatively high GNPs per capita, though by other measures they may rank among the developing countries. The difference in annual GNP per capita between relatively developed and developing countries grew during the 1980s. In 1982, for example, relatively developed countries had an average GNP per capita of approximately $8,000, compared with $700 in developing countries. A decade later, the GNP per capita for developing countries had declined by $40 while increasing nearly $6,000 for relatively developed countries. Most countries in Sub-Saharan Africa had lower per capita GNPs in the early 1990s than a decade earlier.

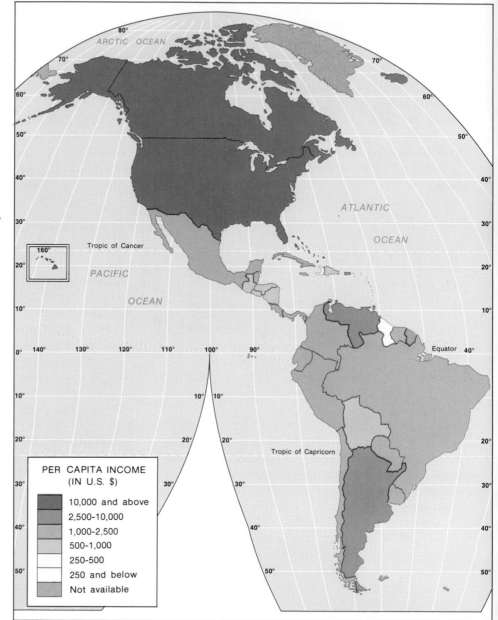

PER CAPITA INCOME
(IN U.S. $)

10,000 and above
2,500-10,000
1,000-2,500
500-1,000
250-500
250 and below
Not available

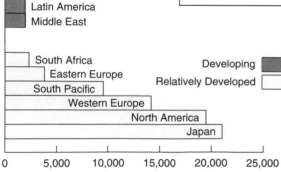

1990 GNP PER CAPITA
(U.S. dollars)

Sub-Saharan Africa
Southeast Asia
East Asia
South Asia
Latin America
Middle East

South Africa
Eastern Europe
South Pacific
Western Europe
North America
Japan

Developing
Relatively Developed

0   5,000   10,000   15,000   20,000   25,000

been increasing. Since the early 1980s, per capita GNP has increased by more than $10,000 in relatively developed, compared with less than $300 in developing countries. Per capita GNP has actually declined over the past decade in many African and Latin American countries.

Per capita GNP—or, for that matter, any other single indicator—does not measure perfectly the

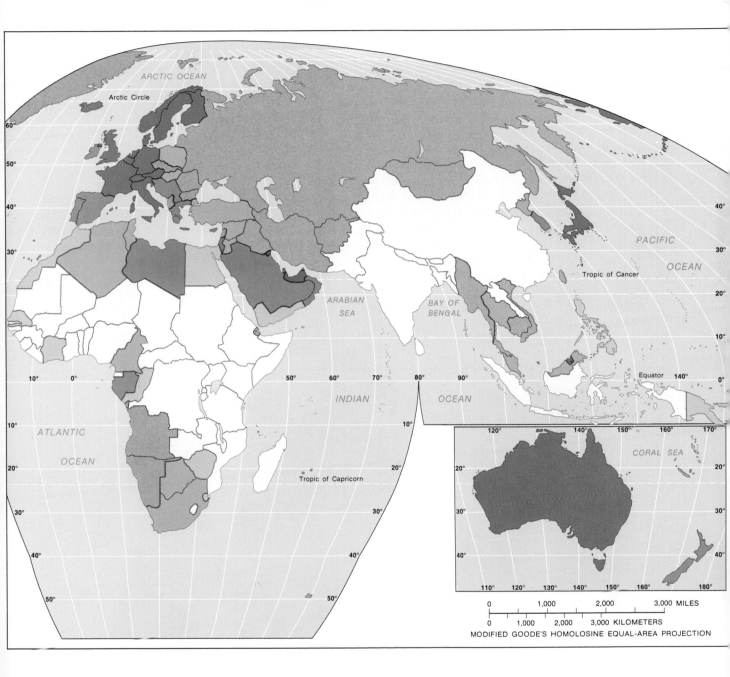

level of a country's economic development. Not everyone is starving in a developing country with a per capita GNP of a few hundred dollars; one-sixth of all people live in poverty in the United States, which has a per capita GNP of more than $20,000. Per capita GNP measures average wealth, not its distribution. If only a few people receive a high percentage of the GNP, then the standard of living for the majority of people may be lower than the average figure implies. On the other hand, the higher the per capita GNP, the greater the potential for ensuring that all citizens enjoy a comfortable life.

Anyone who has traveled abroad knows that prices of products vary widely among countries. To reflect these differences, the United Nations has computed the per capita purchasing power for every country with more than one million inhabitants. A country's per capita purchasing power is the per capita gross domestic product adjusted by the relative cost of purchasing the same set of goods in each country. The gross domestic product is similar to the gross national product, except that it excludes income people earn abroad, such as by a Canadian working in the United States.

The per capita purchasing power exceeds $10,000 in relatively developed countries, compared with less than $1,000 in most of Africa (Figure 8–3). The United States has the highest per capita purchasing power, followed by Canada. The United States and Canada have somewhat lower per capita GNPs than Japan and several European countries, but prices are lower for most consumer goods, from food to automobiles.

A light-hearted measure of consumers' purchasing power in different countries is *The Economist* magazine's McDonald's Index. The magazine reports that McDonald's charges widely varying prices for the identical hamburger, fries, and a milkshake in different countries. Prices are higher outside the United States because the company must spend more for meat, potatoes, milk, rent, and other costs of doing business.

Economic Structure

Average per capita income is higher in relatively developed countries because people typically earn a living by different means than in developing countries. Jobs fall into three categories: primary sector, secondary sector, and tertiary sector. To compare the types of economic activities found in relatively developed and developing countries, we can compute the percentage of people working in each of these three sectors.

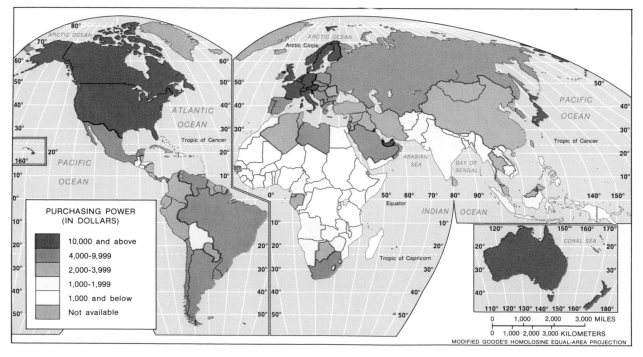

FIGURE 8–3

Per capita purchasing power is a more reliable measure than per capita gross national product in assessing the average person's standard of living in a country. Purchasing power accounts for the fact that products do not cost the same in every country. The United States has a lower per capita gross national product than several European countries, but it has the world's highest per capita purchasing power because of relatively low prices for many consumer products.

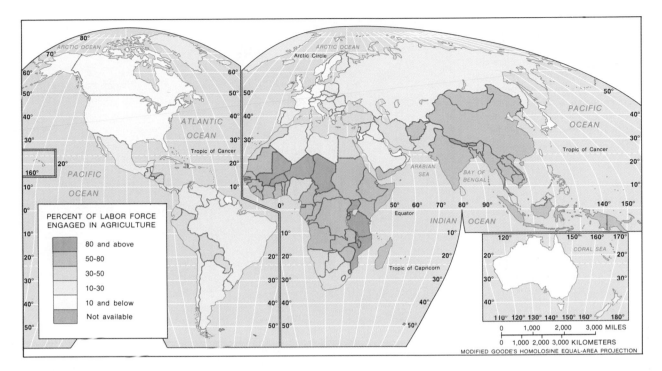

FIGURE 8–4
A priority for all people is to secure the food they need to survive. In developing countries, most people work in agriculture to produce the food they and their families need. This dependency on producing food for survival is reflected in the high percentage of workers engaged in agriculture in developing countries. Approximately 60 percent of all people in the labor force are involved in agricultural work in developing countries, and the figure exceeds 75 percent in a number of African countries. In relatively developed countries few people are farmers, and most people buy food with money earned by working in factories, offices, or other services. Less than five percent of workers in Anglo-America and Western Europe are farmers.

Jobs in the **primary sector** are concerned with the direct extraction of materials from the earth's surface, generally through agriculture, though sometimes by mining, fishing, and forestry. The **secondary sector** includes manufacturers that process, transform, and assemble raw materials into useful products. Other secondary-sector industries take manufactured goods and fabricate them into finished consumer goods. The **tertiary sector** involves the provision of goods and services to people in exchange for payment. Jobs in this sector include offices, shops, physicians, attorneys, entertainment facilities, and universities. Some analysts identify a **quaternary sector,** which involves the processing of information, especially through computer technology.

The distribution of workers among the primary, secondary, and tertiary sectors varies sharply between relatively developed and developing countries. The percentage of people working in agriculture exceeds 75 percent in many developing countries of Africa and Asia, compared with less than 5 percent in Anglo-America and many Western European countries (Figure 8–4).

The first priority for all people is to secure the food needed for survival. A high percentage of agricultural workers indicates that most people in a country must spend their days producing food for their own survival. In contrast, a low percentage of primary-sector workers indicates that a handful of farmers can produce enough food for the rest of society. Freed from the task of growing their own

Workers in developing countries, such as this woman using a wood rake in Rajasthan, India, are less productive than those in relatively developed countries, partly because they must rely on human power to perform much of their work rather than on robots, such as these welders in a Japanese automobile factory.

food, most people in a relatively developed country can contribute to an increase in the national wealth by working in the secondary and tertiary sectors.

Within relatively developed countries, the number of jobs has decreased in the secondary sector and increased in the tertiary sector. The decline in manufacturing jobs reflects greater efficiency inside the factories as well as increased global competition in many industries. At the same time, employment in the tertiary sector continues to expand as a result of increased consumer demand for many goods and services.

Productivity

Workers in relatively developed countries are more productive than in developing countries. **Productivity** is the value of a particular product compared with the amount of labor needed to make it.

Workers in relatively developed countries produce more with less effort because they have access to more machines, tools, and equipment to perform much of the work. On the other hand, production in developing countries must rely more on human and animal power. The larger per capita GNP in relatively developed countries in part pays for the manufacture and purchase of machinery, which in turn makes workers more productive and generates more wealth.

Productivity can be measured by the value added per worker. The **value added** in manufacturing is the gross value of the product minus the costs of raw materials and energy. The value added per worker is thirty times more in relatively developed countries than in developing countries. The average production worker generates a value added of nearly $100,000 in the United States compared with only a few thousand dollars in developing countries.

Raw Materials

Economic development requires access to raw materials that can be fashioned into useful products and provide energy to operate the factories. In the late eighteenth century, Great Britain, the first country to become an economically developed society, had abundant supplies of coal and iron ore, which

were the most important raw materials for industry at the time. During the nineteenth century, other European countries also took advantage of domestic supplies of coal and iron ore to promote industrial development.

European countries in the nineteenth century ran short of many raw materials essential for economic development and began to import them from other regions of the world. To ensure an adequate supply of these materials, European countries established colonies, especially in Africa and Asia. The international flow of raw materials helped sustain economic development in Europe and retard it in Africa and Asia. Although most of the old colonies have become independent states, they still export raw materials to relatively developed countries and import finished goods and services. In the twentieth century, the United States and the Soviet Union have become powerful industrial states, in part because they both possess a wide variety of raw materials essential for economic development.

As certain raw materials become more important, a country's level of economic development can advance. In recent years, developing countries that possess energy resources, especially petroleum, have been able to charge higher prices and use the additional revenues to finance economic development. Prices for other raw materials, such as cotton and copper, have fallen because of excessive global supply and declining industrial demand. Developing countries dependent on the sale of these resources have been less successful in pursuing economic development.

In a global economy, availability of raw materials and energy resources measures a country's development potential rather than the actual level of economic development. A country with abundant raw materials has a better chance of achieving greater development. Yet countries that lack them—such as Japan, Singapore, and South Korea—have developed through world trade.

Consumer Goods

Part of the wealth generated in relatively developed countries goes to purchasing goods and services in addition to the minimal human needs of food, clothing, and shelter. The purchase of these so-called nonessential goods and services promotes

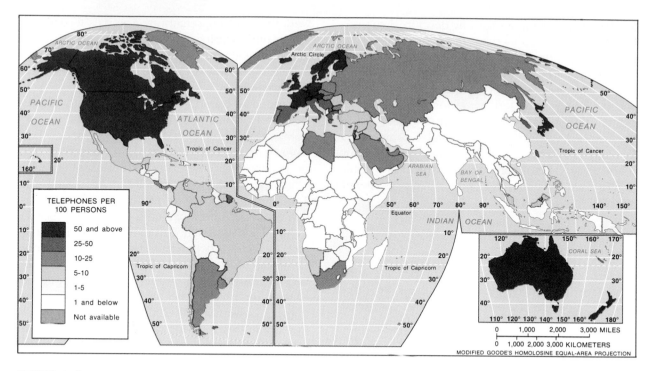

FIGURE 8–5
Relatively developed countries have more than 60 telephones for every 100 inhabitants. In other words, on average, three telephones are shared by fewer than five people. In developing countries, from 10 to more than 300 people must share each telephone.

expansion of manufacturing, which in turn generates additional wealth in society.

The quantity and type of goods and services purchased in a society is a good measure of the level of economic development. Among the thousands of goods that consumers buy, three are particularly good indicators of a society's economic development: motor vehicles, telephones, and televisions.

These products are accessible to virtually all residents in relatively developed countries and are vital to the health of the economy. In relatively developed countries, the ratio of people to motor vehicles, telephones, and televisions is between 1:1 and 4:1. In other words, each motor vehicle, telephone, and television is shared by a handful of people in relatively developed countries.

The motor vehicle, telephone, and television all play important economic roles. Motor vehicles provide individuals with access to jobs and services and permit businesses to distribute their products. Telephones enhance communications with suppliers

and customers of goods and services. Televisions provide exposure to activities in different locations.

In contrast, these products do not play a central role in the daily life for many people in developing countries. Motor vehicles are not essential for those who live in a small village and work all day growing food in nearby fields. Telephones are not essential for those who live in the same village as their friends and relatives. Televisions are not essential for those who have little leisure time.

The ratio of persons to television sets is greater than 100:1 in most of the developing countries, and the ratio of motor vehicles and telephones generally exceeds 300:1 (Figure 8–5). The large difference in the ratios indicates that people have much less access to these products in developing countries than in relatively developed ones.

Most people in developing countries are familiar with these consumer goods even if they cannot afford them. These objects may be desired as symbols of development rather than as essential elements in the functioning of daily life. Because possession of consumer goods is not universal in developing countries, a gap may emerge between the "haves" and the "have-nots." The minority who have these goods may include the rulers, landowners, and other elites, while the majority who are denied access to these goods may incite political unrest.

In many developing countries, the haves are concentrated in urban areas, while the have-nots live in the countryside. Access to consumer goods is more

Relatively developed countries possess more elaborate hospitals and medical technology to diagnose and treat people's illnesses than is the case in developing countries, such as this hospital (below) in Ho Chi Minh City, Vietnam.

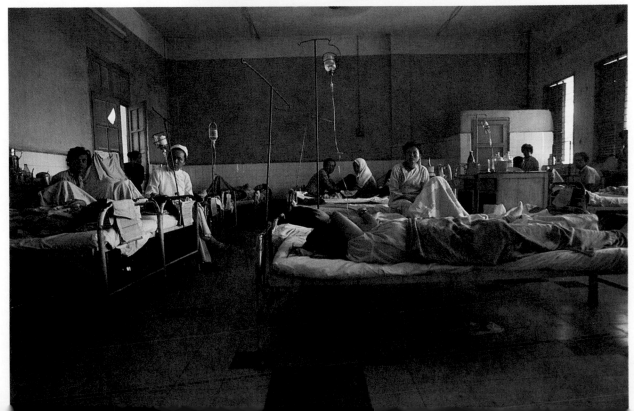

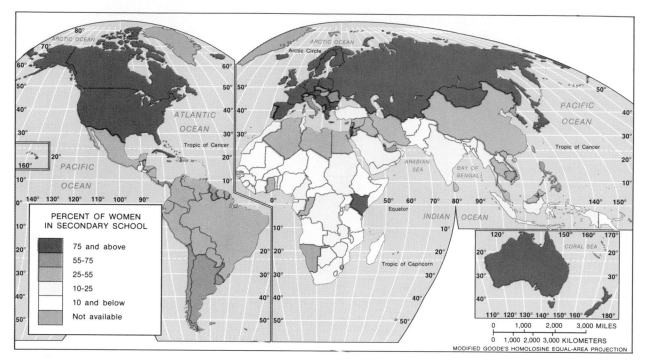

FIGURE 8–6
In developing countries, women are much less likely than men to attend secondary school.
Lower educational levels among women impede prospects for economic development.

important in urban areas because of the dispersion of homes, factories, offices, and shops.

Motor vehicles, telephones, and televisions also contribute to social and cultural elements of development. These consumer goods provide people with access to leisure activities as well as exposure to new ideas. A person can explore new places in a motor vehicle, talk to people in distant locations by telephone, and see what life is like elsewhere by television. As a result of greater exposure to cultural diversity, people in relatively developed countries display different social characteristics from people in developing countries.

KEY ISSUE

How Do Social and Demographic Characteristics Relate to Development?

Relatively developed countries use their greater wealth in part to provide schools, hospitals, and welfare services. As a result, people are better educated, healthier, and better protected from hardships in relatively developed countries than in developing countries. A well-educated, healthy, and secure population is an economically productive population.

Education and Literacy

In general, the higher the level of economic development, the greater are both the quantity and the quality of education. A measure of the quantity of education is the number of years that the average person attends school. The assumption is that no matter how poor the school, the more years pupils attend the more likely they are to learn something. The average pupil attends school for about ten years in relatively developed countries, compared with only about two years in developing countries.

Women are less likely to attend school in developing countries. Globally, 73 women attend secondary schools for every 100 men. The ratio is 99 women for 100 men in relatively developed coun-

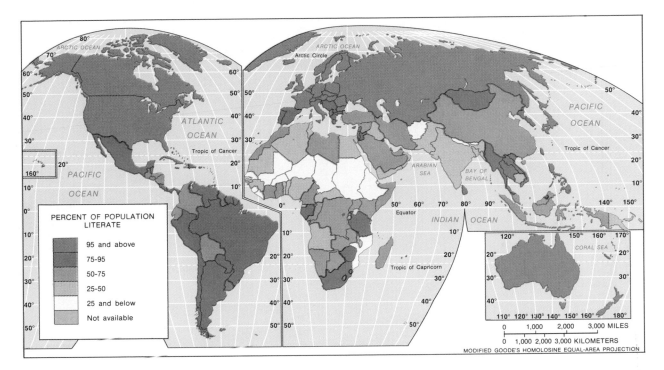

FIGURE 8–7
Literacy rate. In most of the relatively developed countries, at least 95 percent of adults are able to read and write. The percentage ranges from about 50 percent to only 10 percent in most developing countries, especially in Africa and Asia.

tries, compared with only 60 women for 100 men in developing countries. In other words, females constitute less than 40 percent of the secondary school students in developing countries while comprising roughly 50 percent of the total population in that age group. But the ratio in developing countries has improved over the past quarter-century; in 1970, only 45 women attended secondary school for 100 men (Figure 8–6).

The quality of education is measured in two ways. One indicator is the ratio of teachers to pupils. The fewer pupils a teacher has, the more likely each receives instruction. The ratio of teachers to pupils is twice as high in developing countries than in relatively developed ones.

Another measure of the quality of education is the **literacy rate,** which is the percentage of a country's people who can read and write. The literacy rate exceeds 95 percent in relatively developed countries compared with less than 33 percent in many developing countries (Figure 8–7).

The gap between relatively developed and developing countries is greater if literacy rates are compared for women rather than both sexes. In a number of countries in the Middle East and South Asia, literacy rates fall between 25 and 75 percent for both sexes combined but are less than 25 percent for women (Figure 8–8). Elsewhere in Asia and Latin America, gender differences are lower, but in nearly every developing country the literacy rate is higher for men than for women. In contrast, literacy rates for men and women are virtually the same in relatively developed countries.

Because a higher percentage of people can read and write, publishers in relatively developed countries print more books, newspapers, and magazines per person. Relatively developed countries dominate the worldwide distribution of scientific and other nonfiction publications. Students in developing countries must learn technical information by reading books in English, German, Russian, or French.

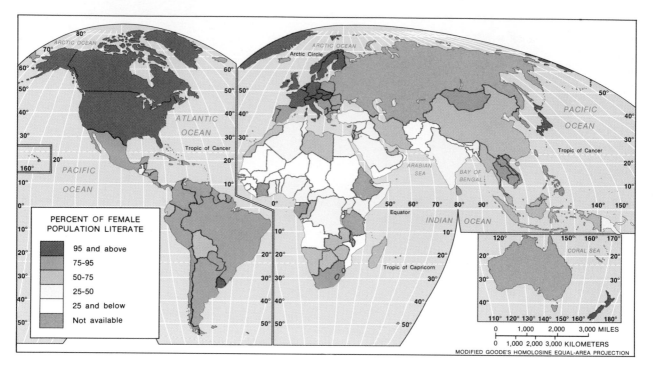

FIGURE 8–8
Female literacy rate. In some developing countries, the percentage of women who can read and write is much lower than that for men. Compare with total literacy (Figure 8–7). The gender gap is relatively high in South Asia and the Middle East.

For many people in developing countries, education is the ticket to better jobs and higher status in society. Improving education is a major goal of many developing countries, but funds are scarce. Education may receive a higher percentage of the GNP in developing countries than in relatively developed countries, but because relatively developed countries have much higher GNPs they far outspend developing countries on a per pupil basis. A low female literacy rate is an obstacle to development.

Health and Welfare

People are healthier in relatively developed countries than in developing ones. The health of a population is influenced by diet. Most people in developing countries of Africa and Asia do not receive the UN recommended daily minimum allowance of calories and proteins (Figure 8–9).

When people get sick, relatively developed countries possess the resources to take care of them. Relatively developed countries have more favorable ratios of people to hospitals, doctors, and nurses (Figure 8–10). In many relatively developed countries, health care is a public service available at little or no cost, though in the United States health care is generally met by private profit-making enterprises.

Relatively developed countries use part of their wealth to protect people who, for various reasons, are unable to work. In relatively developed countries, some financial assistance is offered to those who are sick, elderly, poor, disabled, orphans, war veterans, widows, unemployed, or single parents. Countries in northwestern Europe typically provide the highest level of public-assistance payments.

Relatively developed countries are hard-pressed to maintain the current levels of public assistance. In the past, rapid economic growth permitted relatively developed countries to finance these programs with little hardship. But in recent years, economic growth has slowed, and the percentage of people needing public assistance has increased. Governments have faced a choice between reducing benefits and increasing taxes to pay for them.

Demographic Characteristics of Development

Relatively developed countries display many demographic differences in comparison to developing countries. A number of demographic characteristics were discussed in Chapter 2. The four major demographic characteristics that distinguish relatively developed and developing countries are infant mortality, natural increase, and crude birth rates, and age structure.

Infant mortality rate. The higher levels of health and welfare in relatively developed countries permit more babies to survive infancy. The number of babies that die before reaching one year is fewer than 10 per 1,000 per year in many relatively devel-

oped countries, compared with more than 100 in many developing countries (*see* Figure 2–6).

The infant mortality rate is greater in developing countries for a number of reasons. Babies may die because of malnutrition or the lack of medicine needed to survive illness such as dehydration from diarrhea. They may also die from poor medical practices arising from lack of education. For example, the use of a dirty knife to cut the umbilical cord is a major cause of fatal tetanus in India.

Natural increase rate. The natural increase rate averages more than 2 percent per year in developing countries and less than 1 percent in relatively developed ones. A higher natural increase rate strains the ability of a country to provide hospitals, schools, jobs, and other services that can make peo-

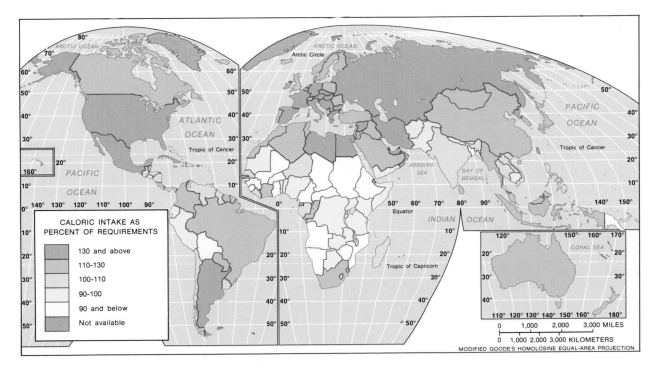

FIGURE 8–9
Daily calories per capita. In order to maintain a moderate level of physical activity, an average person requires at least 2,360 calories per day, according to the United Nations Food and Agricultural Organization (the figure varies somewhat according to age, sex, and other characteristics). In relatively developed countries, the average citizen consumes about one-third more calories than the minimum needed. The typical resident of a developing country receives almost precisely the minimum number of calories needed to maintain moderate physical activity. But remember that the figures represent averages, and a substantial proportion of the population therefore are getting less than the necessary daily minimum.

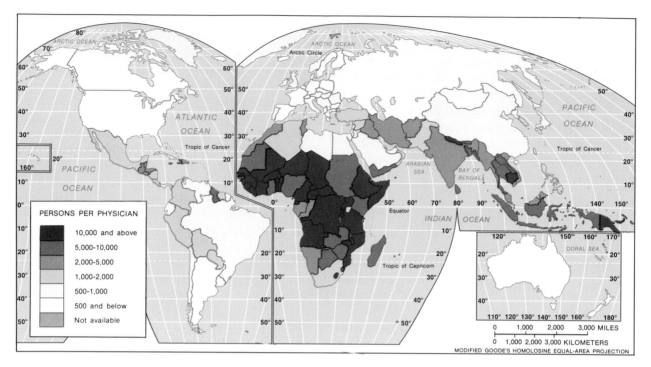

FIGURE 8–10
Relatively developed countries have more access to health care, as shown in the ratios between people and hospital beds, nurses, doctors, and other medical indicators. In relatively developed countries, for example, there is 1 doctor for each 1,000 persons, but in developing countries, thousands of people share each doctor.

ple healthier and more productive. Many developing countries must allocate increasing percentages of their GNPs just to care for the rapidly expanding population rather than to improve the condition of the current population (*see* Figure 2–4).

Crude birth rate. Developing countries have higher natural increase rates because they have higher crude birth rates. The annual crude birth rate exceeds 40 per 1,000 population in many developing countries, compared to approximately 15 in relatively developed countries. Women in relatively developed countries choose to have fewer babies for a variety of economic and social reasons, and they have access to a variety of birth control devices to achieve their goal (*see* Figure 2–5).

The crude death rate is not an indicator of a society's level of economic development. Relatively developed and developing countries both have crude death rates around 10 per 1,000 per year.

There are two reasons for the lack of difference. First, diffusion of medical technology from relatively developed countries has eliminated or sharply reduced the incidence of several diseases in developing countries. Second, relatively developed countries have higher percentages of older people, who have high mortality rates, as well as lower percentages of children, who have low mortality rates once they survive infancy.

For women in childbirth, however, the mortality rate is significantly higher in developing countries. For every 100,000 babies born, less than 10 mothers die giving birth in most relatively developed countries, compared with several hundred in developing countries.

Age structure. The higher crude birth rates in developing countries result in differing age structures compared to relatively developed countries. Developing countries have a higher percentage of children under age 15, who are too young to work and must be supported by employed adults and government programs. Relatively developed countries have a higher percentage of older people who have retired from jobs and also need public support. The overall percentage of young and old dependents is lower in relatively developed countries than in developing ones (*see* Figure 2–12).

Correlation of Development Characteristics

A country's level of economic development is a relative concept, because every country is at some position on a continuous development scale. But many countries fall into one of two extreme positions on the scale. Geographers can justify dividing countries into relatively developed and developing groups because a wide variety of economic, social, and demographic characteristics tend to coincide.

The correlation of economic, social, and demographic indicators of development is clearly demonstrated by comparing the United States and India. By every measure of level of development the United States ranks among the world's leaders, while India falls among the world's lowest ranked countries by most development indicators (Figure 8–11).

Per capita GNP in India is less than 2 percent of the level in the United States, and the gap between the two countries has increased during the past two decades. The lower per capita GNP in India reflects the fact that approximately 75 percent of the people are farmers, compared with less than 5 percent in the United States. The preponderance of non-primary-sector workers in the United States produce a variety of goods and services that increase the country's wealth.

The United States has an abundant supply of many raw materials needed for industrial production and can purchase such remaining resources as copper and petroleum from other countries. India has many raw materials essential for manufacturing but needs a number of other critical resources and lacks the funds to import them.

Consumer goods are scarcer in India. The number of people per motor vehicle, telephone, and television are several hundred times larger in India than in the United States. Because of its much higher GNP, the United States can afford to pay much more for education, social security, and other public-assistance programs. Underlying the social and economic differences are demographic contrasts, discussed in more detail at the end of Chapter 2. The natural increase rate is much higher in India than in the United States, because of a higher crude birth rate. Women in India especially suffer from relatively high rates of illiteracy and mortality.

The same economic, social, and demographic indicators that distinguish the United States and India can be used on a global scale. In that way, geogra-

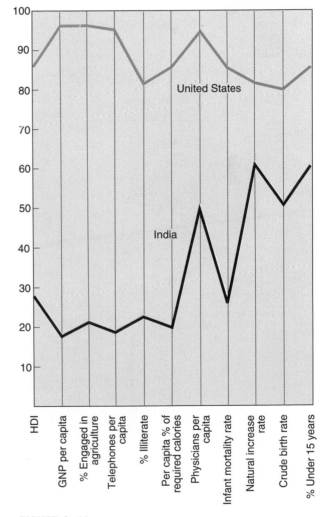

FIGURE 8–11

The graph shows the percentage of all countries that rank below the United States or India according to the particular measure. As a relatively developed country, the United States ranks among the highest percentages in a wide variety of development indicators.

phers can divide the world into a number of regions based on a correlation of the various measures of development.

KEY ISSUE

How Does the Level of Development Vary among Regions?

The United Nations has attempted to measure the level of development for every country with more than 1 million inhabitants. The UN figure, called the Human Development Index (HDI), combines three indicators of development, including one economic (per capita purchasing power), one social (literacy rate), and one demographic (life expectancy). The highest HDI possible is 1.0. Any measure of eco-

nomic development is arbitrary, but the HDI is useful because it includes social and demographic as well as economic indicators (Figure 8–12).

According to the UN study, Japan had the highest HDI, while Niger had the lowest. Japan had a life expectancy of 78 years, a literacy rate of 99 percent, and a per capita purchasing power of $13,135. In contrast, Niger had a life expectancy of 45 years, a literacy rate of 14 percent, and a per capita purchasing power of $452.

As discussed previously, geographers group countries into nine major regions, plus three other areas, according to level of economic development (Figure 8–13). Three of the nine regions are relatively developed, including Western Europe, Anglo-America, and Eastern Europe/Soviet Union. The HDI exceeds .9 in these three regions, as well as in Japan

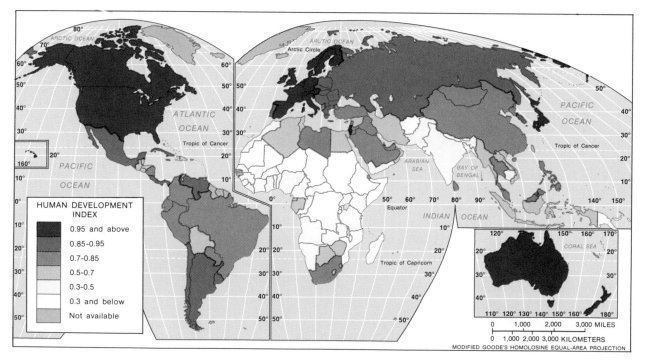

FIGURE 8–12

The Human Development Index, developed by the United Nations, combines three measures of economic development: per capita purchasing power, life expectancy at birth, and literacy rate. Each country received an index for each of the three measures which ranged between minimum and desirable levels. The minimum for each index was set as the lowest level actually observed; for example, the minimum index for literacy was 12 percent, which was Somalia's rate. The desirable levels were 100 percent for literacy and the maximum observed (seventy-eight years) for life expectancy. The desirable level for purchasing power was the official poverty level in nine relatively developed countries.

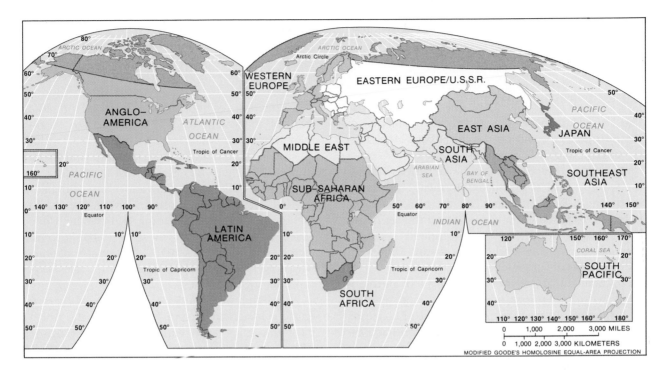

FIGURE 8–13
The six developing regions are the Middle East, Latin America, Sub-Saharan Africa, East Asia, Southeast Asia, and South Asia. Anglo-America, Western Europe, and Eastern Europe/U.S.S.R. rank among the world's relatively developed regions. Japan, the South Pacific, and South Africa, which are surrounded by developing regions, are also relatively developed areas.

and the South Pacific. South Africa, classified as a relatively developed area, has a lower HDI because of the poorer conditions endured by its nonwhite population (Table 8–1).

Six other regions are classified as developing; the HDI is .8 in Latin America, .7 in the Middle East and East Asia, .6 in Southeast Asia, .4 in South Asia, and .3 in Sub-Saharan Africa. The relatively wide varia-

tion in HDI among the developing regions reflects different levels of progress, as well as future potential, in achieving economic development. The nine regions correspond to important differences in cultural characteristics, such as language, religion, and political traditions. The boundaries among regions generally follow major physical features, such as oceans, deserts, and mountains. The following is a

TABLE 8–1
Human Development Index by world regions

Developing Regions		Relatively Developed Regions and Areas	
Latin America	.80	Japan	.99
Middle East	.70	Western Europe	.98
East Asia	.70	South Pacific	.97
Southeast Asia	.60	Anglo-America	.96
South Asia	.40	Eastern Europe/U.S.S.R.	.92
Sub-Saharan Africa	.30	South Africa	.73

Source: Adapted from United Nations Development Programme, *Human Development Report 1990.*

brief description of each of the nine regions, plus several other areas, in descending order of the level of economic development.

Western Europe

The UN's Human Development Index ranks Western Europe as the most economically developed region in the world. The level of development is especially high in the region's core area, which includes the western part of Germany, northeastern France, northern Italy, Switzerland, southern Scandinavia, Belgium, the Netherlands, and Luxembourg. Western Europe's peripheral areas—Ireland, southern Italy, Portugal, Spain, and Greece—rank somewhat lower on the development scale.

To maintain a relatively high level of development Western Europe must import food, energy, and minerals. In past centuries, Western Europeans explored and mapped the rest of the world and established colonies on every continent. These colonies supplied many of the resources that Europeans needed to foster economic development. Colonization also promoted the diffusion of Western European languages, religions, and other social customs throughout the world.

Now that most colonies have been granted independence, Western Europeans must buy raw materials from other countries. To pay for their import, Western Europeans provide high-value goods and services, such as insurance, banking, and such luxury motor vehicles as the Mercedes-Benz and Rolls-Royce.

On a global scale, Western Europe displays cultural unity, because most Western Europeans speak a language from the same family (Indo-European) and practice the same religion (Christianity). In reality, both the large number of individual Christian denominations and sects and the large number of Indo-European languages have been consistent sources of conflict in Western Europe. Competition among Western European states for control of territory has led to many wars, most recently World War II. Since the end of World War II, however, most Western European states have joined multinational organizations that promote economic and military cooperation. The elimination of economic barriers within the European Community as of December 31, 1992, makes Western Europe the world's largest and richest market.

Anglo-America

The United States and Canada, the two large countries in Anglo-America, rank among the world's most developed countries, according to the various economic, social, and demographic characteristics presented earlier. This region has the highest per capita GNP and is well-endowed with most minerals needed for industry. Despite having the world's highest per capita purchasing power, the United States is ranked below most Western European countries on the U.N.'s HDI scale because of somewhat lower life expectancy and literacy rates, especially among minorities.

Although fewer than 5 percent of the workers are engaged in agriculture, Anglo-America is the world's most important food exporter and the only one with a significant amount of idle agricultural land. On the other hand, the region has the world's highest percentage of tertiary-sector employees. Anglo-America is the leading provider of word-processing services, media, computer analysis, and information monitoring. The region also specializes in entertainment, mass media, sports, recreation equipment, and other industries that promote use of leisure time.

Compared with other regions, Anglo-America has relatively homogeneous language and religious patterns. More than 95 percent of the population speak English, and 70 percent are Protestants, though Quebec contains predominantly French-speaking Roman Catholics and the United States has concentrations of Spanish-speaking Roman Catholics. The relative cultural homogeneity of Anglo-America reduces the possibility that a large minority will be excluded from participating in the national economy, though protection of cultural diversity produces some tension.

Economic growth in recent years has been slower in Anglo-America than in other relatively developed areas, especially Japan and Western Europe. Global competition for the region's industrial and agricultural products has increased, while investment has lagged for the development of innovative products and techniques. Prospects for future economic growth in the United States are also clouded by the country's large budget deficit, a result of Americans' reluctance to raise taxes to cover spending for desired social welfare and military programs. To cover the budget deficit, the United States borrows large sums of money, and as a result owes by far more money to foreigners than any other country.

Eastern Europe and the Soviet Union

Winston Churchill declared in a 1946 speech that an "Iron Curtain" had descended across Europe, from the Baltic Sea on the north to the Adriatic Sea on the south. East of 15° east longitude, most of the European states came under communist control in the late 1940s, while to the west most were democratic. This political division was a prominent feature of the European landscape for some forty years.

Eastern Europe comprises seven relatively small countries—Albania, Bulgaria, Czechoslovakia, Hungary, Poland, Romania, and Yugoslavia—plus the Soviet Union, which occupies fifteen percent of the world's land area. Slavic languages predominate in all of these countries, except for Hungary and Romania. Between the late 1940s and early 1990s, most of the smaller states (except for Albania and Yugoslavia) were formally allied, both militarily and economically, with the Soviet Union. Until incorporation into the Federal Republic of Germany in 1990, the German Democratic Republic was also an ally of the Soviet Union.

Under communism, the government actively directed the national economy and sharply reduced the role of private enterprise. The government made decisions concerning investment and wages, as well as how much would be manufactured, by whom, and where. By centrally planning their economies, Eastern European states significantly improved their level of development, according to some measures. Annual per capita GNPs increased from a few hundred to several thousand dollars, and social and demographic indicators in most Eastern European countries became comparable to those in Western Europe. Progress in Eastern Europe was achieved primarily by concentrating scarce resources in the expansion of basic industries, such as steel and energy.

During the late 1980s and early 1990s, the communist parties lost power throughout Eastern Europe, and the national governments began to exercise less control over the economies. Aside from the desire for freedom, the principal reason that Eastern Europeans rejected communism was that central planning proved to be inefficient at running national economies. Scarce funds were used to meet annual production targets rather than invest in long-term improvements in productivity, such as installing more modern equipment and redeploying workers to other tasks. Despite an abundant supply of productive farmland, Eastern Europe had to import food from the West because of inefficient agricultural practices. In the absence of heavy government subsidies and strong controls, Eastern Europe's industries have faced difficulty competing in global markets in the post-communism era.

Orders sent from national government offices hundreds of kilometers away were often not implemented in the factories. Some targets were impossible to achieve, but others were simply ignored: why work hard when your job is guaranteed and your supervisor can't fire you? Factories polluted the air and water, and citizens were unable to pressure their governments into investing in pollution control devices.

For many Eastern Europeans, the most fundamental problem was that by concentrating on production in basic industries the communists neglected consumer-oriented products, such as automobiles, refrigerators, and clothing. Severe shortages of housing forced entire families to live in dwellings the size of a college dormitory room. Although restricted from visiting western countries, many Eastern Europeans could see on television the much higher level of comfort on the other side of the Iron Curtain.

Regional differences within the Soviet Union. Economic development was further hindered in the Soviet Union by sharp regional differences. The country has suffered from a mismatch in the locations of markets, population growth, and resources. The major markets are located in the far western, or European, part of the Soviet Union, where the large cities are clustered (Figure 8–14). Per capita GNP is much higher in the European republics than in the

ARCTIC OCEAN

Estonia

Latvia

RSFSR

Lithuania

Belorussia

Russian Soviet Federated Socialist Republic

Ukraine

Moldavia

Baltic Sea

Black Sea

Kazakhstan

Aral Sea

Caspian Sea

Uzbekistan

Kirgizia

Tajikistan

Georgia

Armenia

Azerbaijan

Turkmenistan

NET MATERIAL PRODUCT
(IN RUBLES PER PERSON)

2,500 and above
2,000-2,500
1,500-2,000
1,000-1,500

0   500 MILES

0   500 KILOMETERS

FIGURE 8–14 (opposite)
Per capita gross national product varies widely among the republics of the Soviet Union. Levels are much higher in the European portion of the country.

rest of the Soviet Union. As the Soviet economy becomes more responsive to the needs of its consumers, the optimal location for many industries will be in the European portion of the country.

But the Soviet Union has long pursued a policy of placing industries near raw materials rather than near consumers. Because the country's most important fields of iron ore, copper, manganese, and other minerals are located in the Ural Mountains, the region has received a disproportionate percentage of national industrial investment. For example, although the Urals contain only 7 percent of the country's population, 25 percent of the national steel production is concentrated in the region.

Because of rapid population growth, Central Asia has the largest surplus of labor in the Soviet Union. The region has 11 percent of the country's total population, but 30 percent of the country's population increase during the 1980s. The annual rate of natural increase during the 1980s was 2.5 percent in Central Asia, compared to 0.7 percent in the rest of the country. The principal cause of more rapid population growth is much higher total fertility rates in Central Asia. Total fertility rates exceed 4 in the Central Asian republics, compared with 2–3 elsewhere in the Soviet Union (Figure 8–15).

As a result of higher fertility rates, the population pyramid for a Central Asian republic, such as Tajik, has a much broader base than one for a European republic, such as the Ukraine (Figure 8–16). Tajik's broader base reflects the fact that the percentage of its population under age fifteen exceeds 40 percent, compared with 20 percent in the Ukraine. As young Central Asians enter the labor force in the next few years, they may be forced to migrate north to find employment.

Compounding the problem, most of the people in the Central Asian republics are Muslims. Because of rapid population growth in this region, Russians—who control the Soviet government and economy—will comprise a smaller percentage of the country's total population.

Other Relatively Developed Areas

Japan, South Africa, and the South Pacific are also relatively developed areas. Japan and South Africa are surrounded by countries with much lower levels of economic development. The South Pacific is a relatively developed area with a much lower population than the other two areas.

South Pacific. More than 90 percent of the population in the South Pacific region is concentrated in two relatively developed countries: Australia and New Zealand. The remaining people of the South Pacific are scattered among a number of sparsely inhabited islands that can generally be classified as developing countries.

Australia and New Zealand, both former British colonies, share many cultural characteristics with the United Kingdom. Over 90 percent of the residents are descendants of nineteenth-century British settlers, though indigenous populations remain.

Much of Australia is desert, but the ratio of people to resources is extremely favorable, because of the small total population. Australia and New Zealand are net exporters of food and other resources and are closely tied economically to Western Europe and Anglo-America.

South Africa. The level of economic development is much higher in South Africa than any other African country. But as a result of the legacy of apartheid laws, the benefits of a relatively developed economy have been enjoyed primarily by the minority of South Africa's people who happen to be white.

Japan. The relatively developed regions and areas already examined share many cultural characteristics. They are dominated by the Indo-European language family and the Christian religion and share similar social customs and political traditions. All either are in Europe or were colonized by European immigrants.

The level of economic development in Japan, the fourthmost populous state in Asia, contrasts sharply with other large Asian countries. Japan ranks among the world's most productive states, while the GNP per capita is generally less than $1,000 per year in the rest of East, South, and Southeast Asia. The

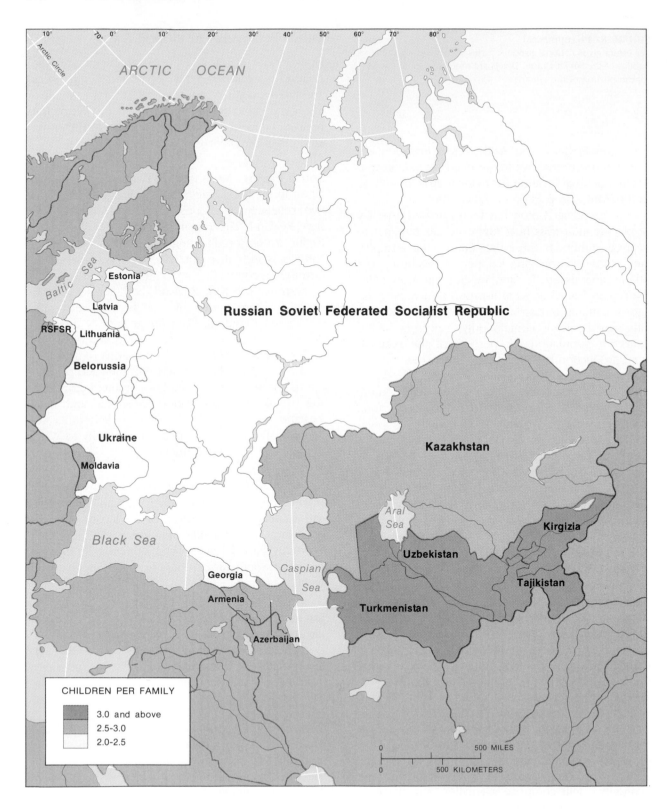

CHILDREN PER FAMILY

- 3.0 and above
- 2.5-3.0
- 2.0-2.5

FIGURE 8–15 (opposite)
Within the Soviet Union, total fertility rates are much higher in the Central Asian republics than in the European ones. The average woman bears twice as many babies in Central Asia as in Europe. As a result, the percentage of the Soviet population living in Central Asia will increase in the future.

United Nations considers Japan to have a higher level of economic development than any other country.

Japan's economic development is especially remarkable because it has an extremely unfavorable ratio of population to resources. The country has some of the world's most intensively farmed land and one of the highest physiological densities (*see* Table 2–1). The Japanese consume relatively little meat and grain but still must import these products. Japan also lacks many of the important raw materi-

als for basic industry. For example, though Japan is the world's leading steel producer, it must import virtually all of the coal and iron ore needed for steel production.

How has Japan become an industrial power? At first, the Japanese economy developed by taking advantage of the country's one asset, an abundant supply of people willing to work hard for low wages. The Japanese government encouraged manufacturers to sell their products in other countries at lower prices than domestic competitors. Having gained a foothold in the global economy by selling low-cost products, Japan then began to specialize in high-quality, high-value products, such as electronics, motor vehicles, and cameras.

Japan's dominance was achieved in part by concentrating resources in rigorous educational systems and training programs to create a skilled labor

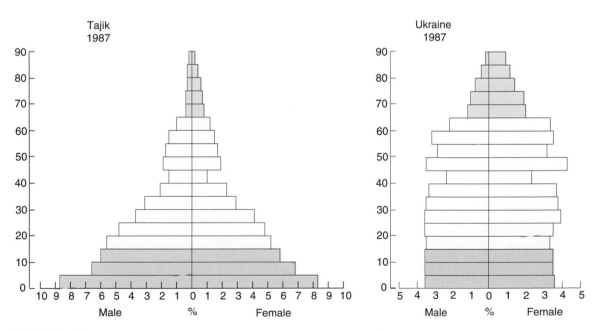

FIGURE 8–16
Although the Soviet Union is a relatively developed country by most measures, the population pyramid for the Tajik Soviet Socialist Republic resembles that of a developing country in Stage 2 of the demographic transition (*see* Figure 2–13). The Ukraine's pyramid shows the lingering impact of World War II in the European portion of the Soviet Union. The top of the pyramid shows a higher percentage of women over seventy than is typical in relatively developed countries, as a result of high mortality rates among male soldiers during the 1940s. Low birth rates during the war years are reflected in the unusually small numbers of people now in their forties.

force. Japanese companies spend 8 percent of their revenues on research and development, twice as high as U.S. firms, and the government provides further assistance to develop new products and manufacturing processes.

The Middle East

Among the developing regions, the Middle East shows the most promise of joining the ranks of the relatively developed regions, even though much of the region consists of deserts that can sustain only sparse concentrations of animal life and most products must be imported. But the Middle East possesses one major economic asset: a large percentage of the world's petroleum reserves.

Because of petroleum exports, the Middle East is the only one of the nine major world regions that enjoys a trade surplus. The value of imports exceeds exports in every other major region, to a considerable extent because they must purchase large quantities of petroleum from Middle East states.

Government officials in many of the Middle East states, such as Saudi Arabia and the United Arab Emirates, use the billions of dollars generated from petroleum sales to finance economic development. The Middle East is the only region where development is not hindered by lack of capital for new construction. To the contrary, many governments in the region have access to more money than they can use to finance development.

On the other hand, not every country in the region has abundant petroleum reserves, because most of the petroleum reserves are concentrated in states that border the Persian Gulf. Development possibilities are limited in Egypt, Jordan, Syria, and other Middle East countries that lack significant petroleum reserves (Figure 8–17).

The large gap in per capita income between the petroleum-rich countries and those that lack resources is a major source of tension in the Middle East. People in the poorer Middle Eastern states held little sympathy for Kuwait after Iraq's invasion in August, 1990. Kuwait was charged with not sharing its petroleum-generated wealth and failing to

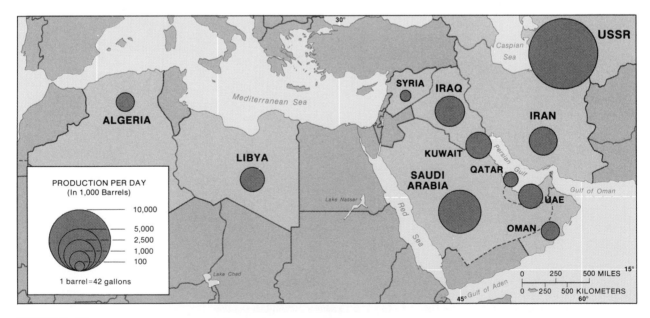

FIGURE 8–17

A large percentage of the world's petroleum comes from the Middle East, but the resource is not distributed uniformly within the region. Because of petroleum production, the per capita GNP of the United Arab Emirates, Qatar, and Bahrain ranks among the highest in the world, whereas for some other countries in the region it ranks among the lowest.

provide good living conditions for guest workers from the poorer Arab countries.

The challenge for many Middle East states is to promote economic development without abandoning traditional cultural values. Many people in the Middle East regard some Western business practices as incompatible with some Islamic religious principles, which are followed by more than 95 percent of the region's population. As a result, many countries in the Middle East sharply restrict the role of women in business and prevent the diffusion of gambling, alcohol consumption, and other leisure activities prohibited by Islam. The low level of literacy among women is the main reason that the United Nations considers the level of economic development among the petroleum-rich states of the Middle East to be lower than the per capita GNP would indicate.

The region also suffers from serious internal cultural disputes, as discussed in Chapter 5. Iraq's long war with Iran and attempted annexation of Kuwait split the Arab world. Countries dominated by Shiite Muslims, especially Iran, have promoted revolutions elsewhere in the region in order to sweep away elements of economic development and social customs they perceive as influenced by Europe or Anglo-America.

Most states in the Middle East—even those who opposed Iraq's invasion of Kuwait—refuse to recognize the existence of Israel, the region's only state controlled by Jews. Israel has successfully repelled several attacks by neighboring states and, since 1967, has occupied territory captured from its adversaries. Palestinians living in the occupied territories prefer to establish an independent state rather than live under Israeli rule. Meanwhile, Lebanon's civil war between Christian and Muslim groups has continued for nearly two decades. Settlement of these disputes is unlikely without resolving the conflicting claims of different cultural groups to control the territory. Money that could be used for economic development is diverted to military funding and rebuilding war-damaged structures.

Latin America

Like the Middle East, individual states in Latin America share many cultural characteristics but differ considerably in level of economic development.

Most Latin Americans speak one of two Romance languages, Spanish or Portuguese, and adhere to Roman Catholicism. These cultural characteristics resulted from the fact that Brazil was a colony of Portugal and most of the remaining states once belonged to Spain. In reality, the region is culturally diverse. A large percentage of the population are descendents of inhabitants living in the region prior to the European conquest, while others trace their ancestors to African slaves.

The level of economic development varies within Latin America. Per capita GNP is relatively high along the South Atlantic coast from Curitiba, Brazil, to Buenos Aires, Argentina. This area enjoys high agricultural productivity and ranks among the world's leaders in production and export of wheat and corn (maize). Venezuela's per capita GNP is higher than the region's average, in part because it is the only South American country with extensive petroleum reserves. The region's lowest per capita GNPs are concentrated in Central America, several Caribbean islands, and the interior of South America.

Latin Americans are more likely to live in urban areas than people in other developing regions. Mexico City is the world's second-largest urban area, while two Brazilian cities, São Paulo and Rio de Janeiro, rank among the ten largest. The region's population is highly concentrated along the Atlantic coast, while population density remains low in most of the region, especially the tropical interior of South America. Large areas of the interior rainforests are being destroyed, either to sell the timber or to clear the land for settled agriculture.

Economic development in Latin America is hindered by inequitable income distribution. In many countries, a handful of wealthy families control much of the land and rent parcels to individual farmers. Many tenant farmers grow coffee, tea, and fruits for export to relatively developed countries rather than food for domestic consumption. Latin American governments encourage redistribution of land to peasants but do not wish to alienate the large property owners, who generate much of the national GNP.

In the 1970s, Latin America achieved the highest growth rate of GNP of any region outside the petroleum-rich Middle East. But since the early 1980s, development has slowed in Latin America. To finance economic development, the region's countries have borrowed large sums from international organizations and banks in relatively developed countries but have been unable to repay some of the loans.

East Asia

China, the largest country in East Asia, ranks among the world's poorest in per capita GNP. But the very low per capita GNP does not accurately portray the region's potential for economic development.

Traditionally, most farmers in China were forced to pay high rents and turn over a percentage of the crops to a property owner. Farmers in a typical year produced enough food to survive but frequently suffered from famines, epidemics, floods, and other disasters. Exploitation of the country's resources by Europe and Japan further retarded China's economic development.

Following its victory in a civil war, the Communist party declared the creation of the People's Republic of China on October 1, 1949. Since then, dramatic changes have been made in the country's economy. To ensure the production and distribution of enough food, China's government took control of much of the agricultural land. In some villages, officials assigned specific tasks to each farmer, distributed food to each family according to individual needs, and sold any remaining food to urban residents. In other cases, farmers rented land from the local government, received orders to grow specific amounts of particular crops, and sold for their own profit any crops above the minimum production targets.

In recent years, strict governmental control of agriculture has been loosened, and individuals again are able to own land and control production. Farmers have an incentive to work hard because the sale of surplus crops is the main source of revenue to buy desired household goods. But agricultural land must be worked intensively in order to produce enough food for China's large population, and farmers in the country's less-fertile areas may not be able to produce a large surplus.

The Chinese people are subject to more government control over daily life than in other countries, and they have difficulty obtaining some goods. Nonetheless, most Chinese recognize that they are better off now than before the revolution, since they have less fear of famines than in the past. Because China has a much lower natural increase rate than other developing regions, more of the country's growing GNP can contribute to increasing the standard of living of the existing population rather than meeting the needs of a rapidly expanding population.

Southeast Asia

The Southeast Asia region comprises five countries situated entirely on the Asian mainland—Cambodia, Laos, Myanmar (Burma), Thailand, and Vietnam—and six others scattered across thousands of islands in the Indian and Pacific oceans. Most of these islands are part of Indonesia or the Philippines.

The region's tropical climate limits intensive cultivation of most grains. The heat is nearly continuous, the rainfall abundant, and the vegetation dense. Soils are generally poor, because the heat and humidity rapidly destroy nutrients when land is cleared for cultivation. Economic development is also limited in Southeast Asia by several mountain ranges, active volcanos, and frequent typhoons.

As a result of the inhospitable environment, population was traditionally low in Southeast Asia. The injection of Western medicine and technology has resulted in one of the most rapid rates of population increase in the world, approximately 2.5 percent per year since the 1940s.

Southeast Asia's most populous country, Indonesia, includes 13,667 islands, but nearly two-thirds of the population live on the island of Java, which has one of the world's highest arithmetic densities. People concentrated on Java in part because the island's soil (derived from volcanic ash) is more fertile than elsewhere in the region and in part because the Dutch established their colonial headquarters on the island.

Rice, the region's most important food, is exported in large quantities from some countries, such as Thailand and Myanmar, but must be imported in large quantities to other countries in the region, such as Malaysia. Because of distinctive vegetation and climate, farmers in Southeast Asia concentrate on harvesting products that are used in manufacturing. The region produces a large per-

Consumers in relatively developed countries are more likely to obtain their food in supermarkets. Farmers in developing countries who have produced a surplus may sell products in
a market, such as the floating one in Bangkok, Thailand.

centage of the world's supply of palm oil and copra (coconut oil), natural rubber, kapok (fibers from the ceiba tree used for insulation and filling), and abaca (fibers from banana leafstalks used in fabrics and ropes).

Southeast Asia contains a large percentage of the world's tin as well as some petroleum reserves. But economic development lags because of an unfavorable ratio of population to most resources essential for manufacturing.

The region has suffered from a half-century of nearly continuous warfare. Japan, the Netherlands, France, and the United Kingdom were all forced to withdraw from colonies they had established in the region. In addition, France and the United States both fought unsuccessfully to prevent communists from controlling Vietnam. Wars have also devastated Laos and Cambodia.

South Asia

South Asia is the region with the second-highest population and the second-lowest per capita GNP. The population density is very high throughout the region, and the rate of natural increase is among the world's highest.

India, the region's largest country, is the world's leading producer of jute (used to make burlap and twine), peanuts, sugar cane, and tea and contains reserves of minerals such as uranium, bauxite, coal, manganese, iron ore, and chromite. Yet the overall ratio of population to resources is unfavorable because of the magnitude of the region's population.

India is one of the world's leading rice and wheat producers, and the region was one of the principal beneficiaries of the Green Revolution, a series of inventions beginning in the 1960s that dramatically increased agricultural productivity. As a result of the Green Revolution, "miracle" rice and wheat seeds were widely diffused through South Asia, as discussed in Chapter 13.

Agricultural productivity in South Asia also depends on climate, however. The region receives nearly all of its precipitation from rain that falls during the monsoon season between May and August. Agricultural output declines sharply when the monsoon rains fail to arrive. In a typical year, farmers in South Asia produce a surplus of grain that is stored for distribution during dry years. But several con-secutive years without monsoon rains produces widespread hardship in South Asia.

Sub-Saharan Africa

Geographers divide Africa into three regions. Countries north of the Sahara Desert share economic and cultural characteristics with the Middle East, while, at the other end of the continent, white-dominated South Africa constitutes a unique situation. Sub-Saharan Africa includes the area between the Sahara Desert and South Africa.

Per capita GNP in Sub-Saharan Africa is comparable to the level in South, East, and Southeast Asia, and population density is lower than in any other developing region. Sub-Saharan Africa contains many resources important for economic development, including bauxite (aluminum ore) in Guinea, cobalt and copper in Zaire and Zambia, iron ore in Liberia, chromite in Zimbabwe, petroleum in Nigeria, and uranium in Gabon and Niger (Figure 8–18).

Despite these assets, Sub-Saharan Africa is the region with the least-favorable prospects for increasing the level of economic development. Some of the region's economic problems are a legacy of the colonial era. Mining companies and other businesses were established to supply European industries with needed raw materials rather than to promote overall economic development in Sub-Saharan Africa. In recent years, African countries have suffered because world prices for their resources have fallen.

Poor leadership has also plagued Sub-Saharan Africa. After independence, leaders of many countries in the region pursued personal economic gain and local wars rather than policies to promote development of the national economy. Frequent wars within and between countries in Sub-Saharan Africa have retarded economic development.

The fundamental problem in many countries of Sub-Saharan Africa, however, is a dramatic imbalance between the number of inhabitants and the capacity of the land to feed the population. Nearly all of the region consists of either tropical or dry climate. These climate regions can support some human life, but not large population concentrations. Yet because Sub-Saharan Africa has by far the world's highest rate of natural increase, the region's

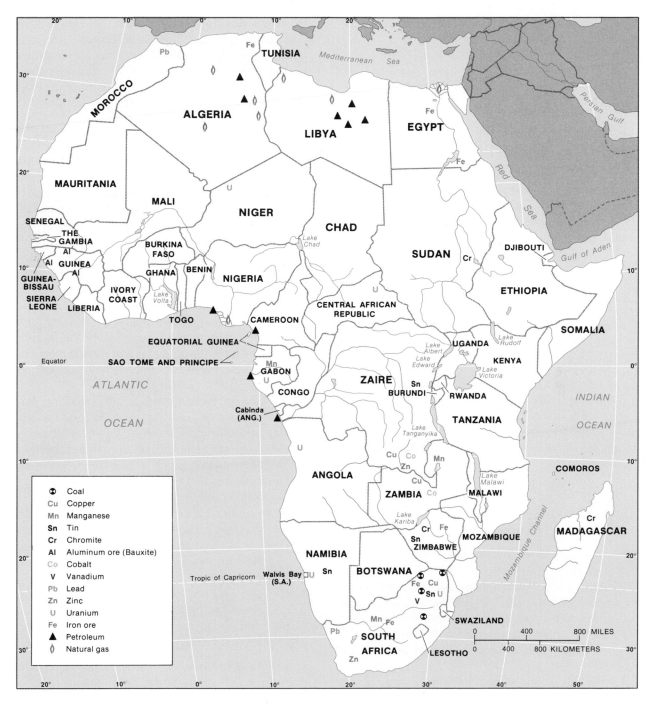

FIGURE 8–18
Several African countries contain minerals important for industrial development. World prices
for many of these minerals, however, have declined or failed to rise at the same rate as the
prices for industrial products, transportation, and energy.

land is more and more overworked, and agricultural output has declined.

KEY ISSUE

How Can Countries Promote Economic Development?

Developing countries in every region share the same priority: to increase the level of economic development. This means increasing the per capita GNP and using the additional funds to improve the social and economic conditions of the people.

Developing countries face two fundamental questions in trying to encourage economic development:

◆ What are the best policies to produce economic development?
◆ How can economic development be financed?

Developing countries must choose one of two approaches in answering the first question. One approach emphasizes international trade, whereas the other advocates self-sufficiency. Each has important advantages and serious problems. There are many examples of countries that have successfully and unsuccessfully used each alternative.

International Trade Approach to Economic Development

The first approach to economic development calls for a country to identify its distinctive or unique economic assets. What animal, vegetable, or mineral resource does the country have in abundance that other countries are willing to buy? What product can the country manufacture and distribute at a higher quality and a lower cost than other countries?

According to the international trade approach, a country can promote economic development by concentrating scarce resources into the expansion of its distinctive local industries. The sale of these products in the world market brings funds into the country that can be used to finance other development projects.

Rostow's development model. A leading advocate of this approach was W. W. Rostow, who proposed a five-stage model of economic development in the 1950s that a number of countries have adopted. According to Rostow, economic development should proceed in the following steps:

1. *The traditional society.* Rostow employed this term to define a country that has not yet started a process of economic development. A traditional society contains a very high percentage of people engaged in agriculture and a high percentage of national wealth allocated to what Rostow calls "nonproductive" activities, such as military and religion.
2. *The preconditions for take-off.* According to Rostow, the process of economic development begins when an elite group of people initiates innovative economic activities. Under the influence of these well-educated leaders, the country starts to invest in new technology and infrastructure, such as water supplies and transportation systems. These projects ultimately will stimulate an increase in productivity.
3. *The take-off.* Rapid growth is generated in a limited number of economic activities, such as textiles or food products. These few take-off industries achieve technical advances and become productive, while other sectors of the economy remain dominated by traditional practices.
4. *The drive to maturity.* Modern technology, previously confined to a few take-off industries, diffuses to a wide variety of industries, which then experience rapid growth comparable to the take-off industries. Workers become more skilled and specialized.
5. *The age of mass consumption.* The economy shifts from production of heavy industry, such as steel and energy, to consumer goods, like motor vehicles and refrigerators.

According to Rostow's model, each country is in one of the five stages of the development process. Relatively developed countries are in stage 4 or 5, while developing countries are in one of the three earlier stages. The model also asserts that today's relatively developed countries have already passed through the early stages. The United States, for example, was in Stage 1 prior to independence, Stage

2 during the first half of the nineteenth century, Stage 3 during the middle of the nineteenth century, and Stage 4 during the late nineteenth century before entering Stage 5 during the early twentieth century.

A country that concentrates on international trade to promote economic development benefits from exposure to consumers in other countries. To remain competitive, the take-off industries must constantly evaluate changes in international consumer preferences, marketing strategies, production engineering, and design technologies. This concern for international competitiveness in the exporting take-off industries will filter through less-advanced economic sectors.

Rostow's optimistic projection for economic development was based on two factors. First, the relatively developed countries of Western Europe and Northern America had been joined by others, notably Japan. If Japan could become more economically developed, why not other countries?

Second, many developing countries contain an abundant supply of raw materials sought by manufacturers and producers in relatively developed countries. In the past, European colonial powers extracted many of these raw materials without compensation. In a global economy, the sale of these raw materials could generate funds for developing countries to promote economic development.

Petroleum-rich Persian Gulf states. A handful of countries have embraced the international trade alternative over the past quarter-century (Figure 8–19). One group of countries oriented towards international trade is located along the Arabian Peninsula near the Persian Gulf. Saudi Arabia is the most prominent member of this group; others include Bahrain, Oman, and the United Arab Emirates.

Until the 1970s, this region was one of the world's least developed, but escalation of petroleum prices transformed these countries overnight into some of the wealthiest per capita. These countries use their petroleum revenues to finance large-scale projects, such as housing, highways, airports, universities, and telecommunications networks. Recently built steel, aluminum, and petrochemical factories compete on world markets with the help of government subsidies.

The landscape has been further changed by the diffusion of consumer goods. Large motor vehicles, color televisions, stereos, and motorcycles are readily available and affordable. Supermarkets are stocked with food imported from Europe and North America. At the height of the petroleum boom, Saudis joked that they traded their cars for newer models as soon as the ash trays were filled.

While the region's economy has changed dramatically in a short period of time, people's social customs have changed more slowly. Daily life is dominated by Islamic religious principles, some of which conflict with Western business practices. Women are excluded from holding most jobs and visiting public places, such as restaurants and swimming pools. They are expected to wear traditional black clothes, a shroud, and a veil. All business halts several times a day when Muslims are called to prayers; shops close their checkout lines and permit people to unwrap their prayer rugs and prostrate themselves on the floor. Many people buy video cassette recorders so that they can watch publicly banned movies and television programs in their homes.

The stationing of several hundred thousand European and Anglo-American troops in Saudi Arabia in 1991 sharpened the contrast and tensions between Middle Eastern and western social customs. In deference to Saudi customs, Western troops did not have access to alcoholic beverages or to entertainment featuring scantily clad women. On the other hand, Saudis were exposed to western women performing tasks prohibited to Saudi women, such as driving motor vehicles and serving in the armed forces.

The four Asian dragons. The other group of countries that has utilized the international trade alternative includes South Korea, Singapore, and Taiwan, as well as the British colony of Hong Kong. These four areas have been given several nicknames, including the "four dragons," the "four little tigers," and "the gang of four."

Singapore (a British colony until 1965) and Hong Kong have virtually no natural resources; both comprise large cities surrounded by very small amounts of rural land. South Korea and Taiwan have traditionally taken their lead from Japan, which occupied both of them until after World War II; Japan's suc-

FIGURE 8–19

The value of exports compared to the total gross national product is a measure of a country's dependence on international trade. A country with a relatively high ratio of exports to GNP has placed a high priority on international trade in order to stimulate economic development. To some extent, the degree of reliance on exports is a function of size, especially among relatively developed countries. Western Europe countries are more dependent than the United States on trade to obtain the goods and services they need.

Substantial differences emerge in the importance of exports in the national economy of developing countries, especially those in Asia. Exports are important for a number of countries in southwestern Asia which stimulate development through the sale of petroleum. International trade is very important for some countries in East and Southeast Asia, such as Singapore, South Korea, and Malaysia. On the other hand, most countries in South Asia have small ratios between the value of exports and the total GNP, reflecting the importance of the self-sufficiency approach in this region.

Below, debt as a percentage of GNP for developing countries with more than 50 million people, excluding Vietnam, Myanmar, and Iran.

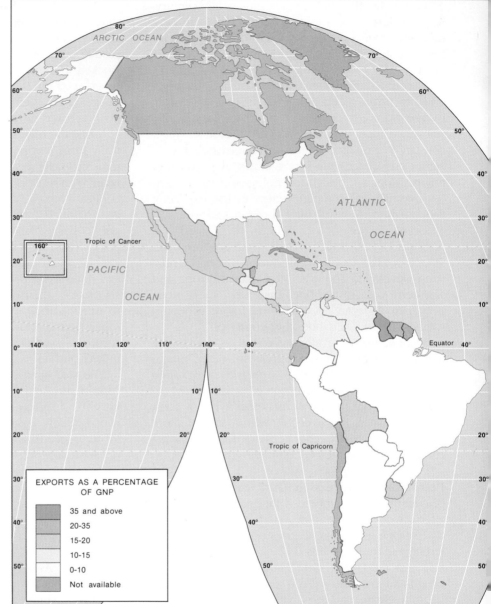

EXPORTS AS A PERCENTAGE OF GNP

- 35 and above
- 20-35
- 15-20
- 10-15
- 0-10
- Not available

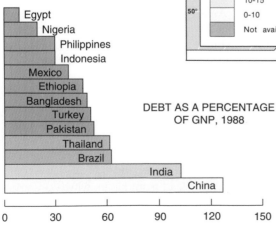

DEBT AS A PERCENTAGE OF GNP, 1988

Egypt
Nigeria
Philippines
Indonesia
Mexico
Ethiopia
Bangladesh
Turkey
Pakistan
Thailand
Brazil
India
China

0   30   60   90   120   150

cess with the international trade approach strongly influenced their adoption of the strategy.

Lacking natural resources, the four dragons have promoted development by concentrating on the production of a handful of manufactured goods, especially clothing and electronics. Low labor costs enable these countries to sell these products inexpensively in relatively developed countries.

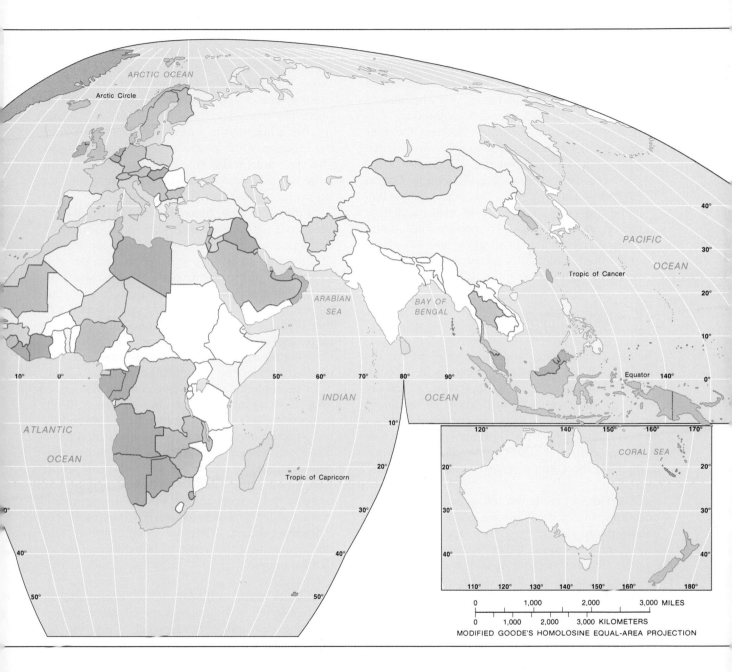

MODIFIED GOODE'S HOMOLOSINE EQUAL-AREA PROJECTION

Problems with international trade approach.
Two problems have hindered countries outside the Persian Gulf and the four Asian dragons from increasing their level of economic development through the international trade approach:

1. *Resource distribution*. Resources are not distributed uniformly among developing countries.

Several Middle East countries have successfully moved to more advanced stages of development because the price of petroleum products skyrocketed during the 1970s. Other countries find that the prices of their commodities have not increased—and in some cases actually decreased—in recent years. Developing countries that depend on the sale of one product have suffered because the price of their leading commodity has not increased as rapidly as the cost of the products they need to buy. For example, Zambia's economy, which depends on the sale of copper, has suffered in recent years because of declining world prices for that commodity.

2. *Market stagnation.* Countries such as the four dragons that depend on selling low-cost manufactured goods find that the world market for many products is expanding less rapidly than in the past. Relatively developed countries have limited growth in population, consumer purchasing power, and market size. To increase sales, developing countries may need to capture sales from established competitors rather than share in an expanding market.

Self-Sufficiency Approach to Economic Development

The second approach to promoting economic development is the self-sufficiency alternative. According to the self-sufficiency approach, a country should spread investment throughout all sectors of the economy rather than concentrate on one or two take-off industries. This approach promotes balanced growth, because people and enterprises throughout the country receive a fair share of resources.

Countries that adopt the self-sufficiency approach encourage businesses to make goods for domestic consumption rather than for export. Economic growth may be modest, but in the long run the country benefits because it is not dependent on changing policies in other countries and fluctuations in the price of commodities.

States promote self-sufficiency by setting barriers that limit the import of goods from other places. These barriers may include setting high taxes on imported goods to make them more expensive than domestically produced goods, fixing quotas to limit the quantity of imported goods, and requiring licenses to restrict the number of legal importers.

India. The two most populous developing countries—China and India—are both strong advocates of the self-sufficiency approach. Businesses are discouraged from exporting goods, and barriers prevent the import of many goods.

India makes heavy use of all three of the main types of barriers to importing. To import goods into India, most foreign companies must secure a license. The process is long and cumbersome, because several dozen government agencies must approve the request for a license. Once a company receives a license, the government severely restricts the quantity of the product they can sell in India. The government also imposes heavy taxes on imported goods, which could double or triple the price to consumers.

At the same time, Indian businesses are discouraged from producing goods for export to relatively developed or other developing countries. Instead, priority goes to making goods for domestic consumption. If private companies cannot make a profit from selling goods only inside India, the government provides subsidies or takes over direct operation of the company. As a result, India produces more steel and motor vehicles per capita than generally found in developing countries, but the products sell at twice the world market price.

In recent years, India's government has moved away from complete adherence to the self-sufficiency approach. The government has lowered the tax on some imported goods and eliminated the license requirement for some importers. Indian companies are encouraged to become more competitive with foreign firms. India's GNP has increased by more than 4 percent per year over the past quarter century, but population has increased by more than 2 percent per year. Therefore, more than half of India's economic growth goes to taking care of the additional people.

Problems with self-sufficiency approach. India's experience illustrates some of the problems with the self-sufficiency approach. First, the approach may encourage inefficient industries. In a global economy, firms increasingly find that the domestic market is too small to make a profit. Unable to make a profit through increased overseas sales, companies may need government subsidies to remain in operation. Companies protected from international competition may not experience pressure to keep abreast with rapid technological changes.

The second problem with the self-sufficiency alternative is the need for a large bureaucracy to administer the controls. A complex administrative system encourages abuse and corruption. Potential entrepreneurs find that struggling to produce goods or services may be less rewarding financially than advising others on how to manipulate the controls. Other potential entrepreneurs may earn more money by illegally importing goods and selling them at inflated prices on the black market.

Financing Economic Development

The most critical obstacle to economic development that most developing countries face is lack of money. To pay for economic development, developing countries generally must obtain funds from relatively developed countries. Developing countries receive some of the money in the form of direct grants but must borrow much of it from financial institutions in relatively developed countries, including commercial banks and international lending organizations, such as the World Bank and the International Monetary Fund.

Developing countries use much of the money to build new hydroelectric dams, electric transmission lines, flood protection systems, water supplies, roads, hotels, and other so-called infrastructure projects. New infrastructure can improve people's living conditions and promote economic growth.

New projects do not always succeed. Tanzania, for example, built a new railroad line in the 1970s to transport copper from neighboring landlocked Zambia to the port of Dar es Salaam. Yet more than a decade later, Tanzanians were still not trained to operate the system, little copper had been hauled out, and the trains ran only with foreign engineers. In Mali, a French-sponsored project to pump water from the Niger River through solar energy functioned for only one month. Even when it worked, the project, which cost over $1 million, produced no more water than could two diesel pumps that together cost $6,000.

In principle, the new economic activities that are attracted to an area will provide the additional revenue needed to repay the loans. But in recent years, many developing countries have been unable to repay the interest on their loans, let alone the principal. Brazil, Mexico, and several other Latin American countries have accumulated the largest debts, though several African countries have very high ratios of debt to GNP.

When countries cannot repay their debts, financial institutions in relatively developed countries refuse to make further loans, and development of needed infrastructure stops. The inability of many developing countries to repay loans also hurts the relatively developed countries, whose financial institutions suffer losses.

The relatively developed and developing countries run the risk of increasing confrontation. Although economically dominant, the relatively developed countries represent a minority of the earth's population and have been pressed by developing countries to share the world's wealth more evenly. Developing countries point out that prices have declined for many of their resources but increased for most of the goods manufactured in relatively developed countries. As a result, developing countries argue that they receive less for exporting their raw materials but must pay more to import manufactured goods. Developing countries also demand an increased role in the decisions to issue loans made by international agencies. A 1974 UN declaration called for creation of a "new international economic order" based on greater equality and economic interpendence between relatively developed and developing countries.

For their part, relatively developed countries are increasingly concerned about their own economic health and are more careful in providing grants or loans to developing states. In exchange for cancelling or refinancing the debts, the international lending agencies—which are dominated by the relatively developed countries—require the governments of developing countries to impose economic austerity programs. Developing countries must raise taxes, reduce government spending, and increase charges for using public services. These programs may prove unpopular with the voters and encourage political unrest.

Summary

In recent years, many countries have failed to make further progress in economic development and have suffered a declining standard of living. The world remains divided between relatively developed regions and developing regions, and the gap between the two is growing wider. These again are the key issues for Chapter 8:

1. **How do geographers measure economic development?** Economic development is the process by which the material conditions of a country's people are improved. A relatively developed country has a higher level of per capita GNP, achieved through a transformation in the structure of the economy from a predominantly agricultural to an industrial and service-providing society.

2. **How do social and demographic characteristics relate to development?** Relatively developed countries use their wealth in part to provide better health, education, and welfare services. Developing countries must use their additional wealth primarily to meet the needs of a rapidly growing population.

3. **How does the level of development vary among regions?** We can identify three relatively developed regions—Western Europe, Anglo-America,

and Eastern Europe/Soviet Union—as well as three other relatively developed areas—South Pacific, Japan, and South Africa. Six developing regions include the Middle East, Latin America, East Asia, Southeast Asia, South Asia, and Sub-Saharan Africa. These developing regions face different prospects for promoting economic development.

4. **How can countries promote economic development?** A developing country must choose between the international trade and the self-sufficiency approaches towards economic development. In either alternative, developing countries may need to borrow considerable sums of money to promote economic development. The inability of many developing countries to pay back these loans is a source of considerable tension between them and relatively developed countries.

 ## Future Prospects for Economic Development

**C A S E S T U D Y
R E V I S I T E D**

Which approach has been more successful at promoting economic development, international trade or self-sufficiency? A few years ago, the World Bank attempted to answer the question by classifying forty-one developing countries into four groups: strongly oriented towards international trade, moderately oriented towards international trade, strongly oriented towards self-sufficiency, and moderately oriented towards self-sufficiency. The World Bank then compared the growth in the per capita GNP achieved by the countries in the four groups for two periods, 1963–73 and 1974–85.

Between 1963 and 1973, the per capita GNP generally increased in all four groups, but the countries strongly oriented towards international trade registered the largest increases (more than 7 percent per year), followed by those moderately oriented towards international trade (nearly 4 percent per year); countries strongly oriented towards self-sufficiency had the lowest increases (less than 2 percent per year).

The rate of change in the GNP per capita was lower among all four groups of countries between 1974 and 1985, a period when higher petroleum prices triggered a worldwide economic slowdown, but the relative performance of the four groups remained the same as during the earlier period. The per capita GNP increased more than 6 percent per year in countries strongly oriented towards international trade, and it declined by more than 1 percent per year in countries strongly oriented towards self-sufficiency (Figure 8–20).

FIGURE 8–20
Countries that have adopted the international trade approach to development have generally enjoyed higher levels of economic growth than those that have adopted the self-sufficiency approach.

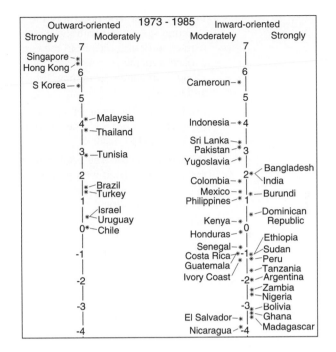

Regardless of the alternative selected, countries still must find the funds to finance economic development. The most effective means to promote economic development may be providing small loans to a large number of individuals rather than concentrating funds in a handful of massive projects.

The Grameen Bank, based in Bangladesh, made over 300,000 loans to people in South Asia in the first decade after its founding in 1977. Three-fourths of the borrowers were women. Only 1 percent of the borrowers have failed to make their weekly loan repayments.

Rabea Rahman borrowed $90 from the Grameen Bank to buy a cow. Earnings from selling the cow's milk enabled her to buy her son an $85 rickshaw bicycle so that he could make a living. The smallest loan the bank has made was $1, to a woman who wanted to sell plastic bangles door-to-door. Other women have borrowed money to make perfume, bind books, and sell matches, mirrors, and bananas.

Key Terms

Developing country Sometimes called a less developed country (LDC), or a country that is at a relatively early stage in the process of economic development.

Economic development A process of improvement in the material conditions of people through diffusion of knowledge and technology.

Gross national product (GNP) The value of the total output of goods and services produced in a country in a given time period (normally, one year).

Literacy rate The percentage of a country's people who can read and write.

Primary sector The portion of the economy concerned with the direct extraction of materials from the earth's surface, generally through agriculture, though sometimes by mining, fishing, and forestry.

Productivity The value of a particular product compared with the amount of labor needed to make it.

Quaternary sector The portion of the economy concerned with processing of information, especially through computer technology.

Relatively developed country A country that has progressed relatively far along a continuum of economic development.

Secondary sector The portion of the economy concerned with manufacturing useful products through processing, transforming, and assembling raw materials.

Tertiary sector The portion of the economy concerned with the provision of goods and services to people in exchange for payment.

Value added The gross value of the product minus the costs of raw materials and energy.

Thinking Geographically

1. Review the major economic, social, and demographic characteristics that contribute to a country's level of development. Which indicators can vary significantly by gender within countries and between countries at various levels of development?
2. Which of the two main alternatives to promoting development—international trade and self-sufficiency—has been used by various Persian Gulf countries to rebuild after the 1991 War? How has the rebuilding been financed? What priority has been given to promoting development in economic sectors other than petroleum production?
3. China has relied on the self-sufficiency approach to promote development, whereas Hong Kong has been a prominent practitioner of the international trade approach. Can these two approaches be reconciled once Hong Kong becomes part of China in 1997?
4. Some developing countries claim that the requirements placed on them by lending organizations such as the World Bank impede rather than promote development. Should developing countries be given a greater role in deciding how much the international organizations should spend, and how such funds should be spent?
5. What obstacles do Eastern European countries face as they try to dismantle forty years of socialism and convert to market economies?

Further Readings

Alexander, John W., and Lay J. Gibson. *Economic Geography.* 2d ed. Englewood Cliffs, NJ: Prentice-Hall, 1979.

Babek, Hans. "The Main Stages in Socioeconomic Evolution from a Geographic Point of View." In *Readings in Cultural Geography,* edited by Philip L. Wagner and Marvin W. Mikesell. Chicago: University of Chicago Press, 1962.

Ballance, R., J. Ansari, and H. Singer. *The International Economy and Industrial Development: Trade and Investment in the Third World.* Totowa, NJ: Allanheld, Osmun, 1982.

Barker, Randolph, and Robert W. Herdt. *The Rice Economy of Asia.* Washington, D.C.: Resources for the Future, 1985.

Bater, James H. *The Soviet Scene: A Geographical Perspective.* New York: Routledge, 1989.

Berry, Brian J. L., Edgar C. Conkling, and D. Michael Ray. *Economic Geography.* Englewood Cliffs, NJ: Prentice-Hall, 1987.

Blakemore, Harold, and Clifford T. Smith, eds. *Latin America: Geographical Perspectives.* 2d ed. London: Methuen, 1983.

Chang, Sen-dou. "Modernization and China's Urban Development." *Annals of the Association of American Geographers* 71 (December 1981): 572–79.

Chisholm, Michael. *Modern World Development: A Geographical Perspective.* Totowa, NJ: Barnes and Noble Books, 1982.

———. "The Wealth of Nations." *Transactions of the Institute of British Geographers* 5 (1980): 255–76.

Cole, John P. *The Development Gap: A Spatial Analysis of World Poverty and Inequality.* New York: Wiley, 1980.

———. *Geography of the Soviet Union.* London: Butterworth, 1984.

Crow, Ben, and Alan Thomas. *Third World Atlas.* Philadelphia: Open University Press, 1985.

Demko, George, ed. *Regional Development: Problems and Policies in Eastern and Western Europe.* New York: St. Martin's Press, 1984.

DeSouza, Anthony R., and Phillip Porter. *The Underdevelopment and Modernization of the Third World.* Washington, D.C.: Association of American Geographers, 1974.

Dickenson, J. P., C. G. Clarke, W. T. S. Gould, R. M. Prothero, D. J. Siddle, C. T. Smith, E. M. Thomas-Hope, and A. G. Hodgkiss. *A Geography of the Third World.* New York: Methuen, 1983.

Dott, Ashok K., ed. *Southeast Asia: Realm of Contrasts.* 3d ed. Boulder, CO: Westview Press, 1985.

Flavin, Christopher. *Electricity for a Developing World: New Directions.* Worldwatch Paper 70. Washington, D.C.: Worldwatch Institute, June 1986.

Forbes, D. K. *The Geography of Underdevelopment: A Critical Survey.* Baltimore: The Johns Hopkins University Press, 1984.

Fryer, Donald D. "The Political Geography of International Lending by Private Banks." *Transactions of the Institute of British Geographers* 12 (no. 4, 1987): 413–32.

Ginsburg, Norton S. *Atlas of Economic Development.* Chicago: University of Chicago Press, 1961.

Ginsburg, Norton S., ed. *Essays on Geography and Economic Development.* Chicago: University of Chicago Press, 1960.

Grossman, Larry. "The Cultural Ecology of Economic Development." *Annals of the Association of American Geographers* 71, (June 1981): 220–36.

Hoffman, George W., ed. *A Geography of Europe: Problems and Prospects.* 5th ed. New York: Wiley, 1983.

James, Preston E. *Latin America.* 4th ed. New York: Odyssey House, 1969.

Jones, D. B., ed. *Oxford Economic Atlas of the World.* 4th ed. London and New York: Oxford University Press, 1972.

Jumper, Sidney R., Thomas L. Bell, and Bruce A. Ralston. *Economic Growth and Disparities: A World View.* Englewood Cliffs, NJ: Prentice-Hall, 1980.

Lydolph, Paul E. "Recent Population Characteristics and Growth in the USSR," *Soviet Geography* 30 (December 1989): 711–729.

Mabogunje, Akinlawon L. *The Development Process: A Spatial Perspective*. London: Hutchinson University Library, 1981.

Momsen, Janet Henshall, and Janet Townsend. *Geography of Gender in the Third World*. Albany: State University of New York Press, 1987.

Myrdal, Gunnar. *Rich Lands and Poor*. New York: Harper, 1957.

O'Connor, A. M. *The Geography of Tropical African Development*. 2d ed. Oxford: Pergamon Press, 1978.

"Panel on Nationalism in the USSR: Environmental and Territorial Aspects," *Soviet Geography* 30 (June 1989): 441–509.

Rostow, Walter W. *The Stages of Economic Growth*. Cambridge, Eng.: Cambridge University Press, 1960.

Seager, Joni, and Ann Olson. *Women in the World: An International Atlas*. New York: Simon & Schuster, 1986.

Smith, David M. *Where the Grass is Greener: Living in an Unequal World*. London: Croom Helm, 1979.

Szentes, Tamas. *The Political Economy of Underdevelopment*. 4th ed. Budapest, Hungary: Akadémiai Kiadó, 1983.

Wheeler, James O., and Peter O. Muller. *Economic Geography*. New York: Wiley, 1981.

Wilbanks, Thomas J. *Location and Well-Being: An Introduction To Economic Geography*. San Francisco: Harper & Row, 1980.

Also consult these journals: *Economic Development and Cultural Change; Economic Geography; International Development Review; International Economic Review; International Journal of Political Economy; Journal of Developing Areas; Netherlands Journal of Economic and Social Geography; Regional Studies.*

9
Agriculture

When you buy food in the supermarket, are you reminded of a farm? Not likely. The meat is sold in pieces wrapped in paper and cellophane. The vegetables are often canned or frozen. The milk and eggs are in cartons.

The provision of food in the United States and Canada is an industry. Only a few people are full-time farmers, and they may have more familiarity with the operation of computers and advanced machinery than does the typical factory or office worker.

The mechanized, highly productive American or Canadian farm contrasts with the subsistence farm found in much of the world. The "typical" human—if there is such a person—is an Asian farmer who grows enough food to survive, with little surplus. This contrast in agricultural practices constitutes one of the most fundamental differences between the relatively developed and developing nations of the world.

Wheat Farmers in Kansas and Pakistan

The Iqbel family grows wheat on their 1-hectare (2.5-acre) plot of land in the Punjab province of Pakistan in a manner similar to that of their ancestors. They perform most tasks by hand or with the help of animals. To irrigate the land, for example, they lift water from a 20-meter (65-foot) well by pushing a water wheel. More prosperous farmers in Pakistan use bullocks to turn the wheel.

The farm produces about 1,500 kilograms (3,300 pounds) of wheat per year, enough to feed the Iqbel family. Some years, they produce a small surplus that can be sold in town for the equivalent of a few dollars. They can then use that money to buy other types of food or household items. In drought years, however, the crop yield is lower, and the Iqbel family must receive food from government and international relief organizations.

The McKinleys are farmers in Kansas. Like the Iqbels, they grow wheat in a climate that receives little rain. Otherwise, the two farm families lead very different lives. The McKinley family's farm is 200 hectares (500 acres), compared to the Iqbel's 1 hectare. The McKinleys derive several hundred times more income from the sale of wheat than do the Iqbels.

The wheat grown on the American farm is not consumed directly by the McKinley family. Instead, it is sold to a processing company and ultimately turned into bread wrapped in cellophane and sold in a supermarket hundreds of kilometers away. In contrast, most of the wheat from the Pakistani farm is consumed in the village where it is grown.

Approximately two-thirds of the people in the world are farmers. The overwhelming majority of them are like the Iqbels, growing enough food to feed themselves, but little more. In most African and Asian countries more than 75 percent of the people are farmers. In contrast, fewer than 5 percent of the people in the United States and Canada are farmers. Yet, these relatively few farmers produce enough food to feed not only the rest of the people in the United States and Canada at a very high standard, but many people elsewhere in the world as well.

Geographers study the distribution of agriculture across the earth's surface and how that distribution relates to cultural and environmental factors. Elements of the physical environment, such as climate, soil, and topography, set broad limits on agricultural practices, but farmers can also observe and modify the environment in a variety of ways.

How farmers deal with the physical environment varies according to customary beliefs, preferences, technological capabilities, and other cultural factors. The farmers of a society possess specific knowledge about environmental conditions and particular technological capabilities for modifying the landscape. Within the limits of technological capability, farmers choose particular agricultural practices based on perceptions of the relative value of various alternatives. These values are partly economic and partly cultural. Farmers generally try to undertake the most profitable type of agriculture, though economic calculations can be altered by government programs that subsidize the production of some products and discourage others. Farmers also select agricultural practices based on cultural perceptions, because a society may hold some foods in high esteem while avoiding others (*see* Chapter 6).

This chapter examines the predominant types of agriculture practiced around the world. While geographers can observe a wide variety of agricultural practices on the landscape, the most important distinction is what happens to the product that has been produced on the farm. As discussed in Chapter 8, geographers divide the world into the economically developing countries and the relatively developed countries. In the former, the output is frequently consumed on or near the farm where it is produced; in the latter, the farmer sells the crops and livestock off the farm.

After examining the origins and diffusion of agriculture, this chapter considers the agricultural practices in developing and relatively developed regions as well as the problems farmers in these two regions face. Although each farm has a unique set of physical conditions and choice of crops, geographers can group the farms within the developing and relatively developed regions into several types on the basis of distinctive environmental and cultural characteristics.

What Were the Origin and Process of Diffusion of Agriculture?

We cannot document the origins of agriculture with certainty, because it began before recorded history. Scholars try to reconstruct a logical sequence of events based on fragments of information about ancient agricultural practices and historical environmental conditions. Improvements in cultivating **crops** and domesticating animals evolved over thousands of years. This section offers one explanation for the process of origin and diffusion of agriculture.

Hunters and Gatherers

Before the invention of agriculture, all humans probably obtained the food they needed for survival through hunting for animals, gathering wild plants, or fishing. Hunters and gatherers lived in small groups, usually fewer than fifty, because a larger number would quickly exhaust the available resources. They survived by collecting food often, perhaps every day. The daily search for food could take only a short amount of time or much of the day, depending on conditions in the particular location. In general, the men went out to hunt wild animals or to fish, and the women collected berries, nuts, and roots.

The group travelled frequently, establishing new home bases or camps. The direction and frequency of migration depended on the movement of wild animals and the growth of seasonal plants at various locations. Groups communicated with each other concerning hunting rights, intermarriages, or other specific subjects. For the most part, though, groups tried to steer clear of each other's territory.

Today, only about 250,000 people, or less than 0.005 percent of the world's population, still survive by hunting and gathering rather than by agriculture. These people live in a number of isolated locations, including Arctic areas and parts of the interiors of Africa, Australia, and South America. Examples include the Bushmen of Namibia and Botswana and the aborigines of Australia.

Contemporary hunting and gathering societies are isolated groups living on the margins of world settlement. But they provide insight into human customs prevailing in prehistoric times, before the invention of agriculture.

Origin of Agriculture

Why did nomadic groups convert from hunting, gathering, and fishing to agriculture? Determining the origin of agriculture first requires a definition of agriculture—not an easy term to define precisely. **Agriculture** involves the deliberate effort to modify a portion of the earth's surface through the cultivation of crops and the rearing of livestock for sustenance or economic gain. Agriculture thus originated when humans domesticated plants and animals for their use.

The cultivation of plants may have originated by accident. In the process of gathering wild vegetation, members of the group may have accidentally cut plants or dropped berries. These hunters would have been surprised to see that after a period of time, damaged or destroyed food sources produced new plants. Eventually, members of the group may have decided to cut plants or drop berries on the ground deliberately to see if they produced new plants. Subsequent generations of the group may have poured water over the site, introduced manure and other soil types, or performed other experiments. Over hundreds or thousands of years, plant cultivation evolved from a series of accidents and deliberate experiments.

Prehistoric people may have originally domesticated animals for noneconomic reasons, such as sacrifices and other religious ceremonies. Other animals probably were domesticated as household pets. These animals would have survived on the group's food scraps.

The earliest form of plant cultivation, according to the prominent cultural geographer Carl Sauer, consisted of vegetative planting. Sauer defined **vegetative planting** as the reproduction of plants by direct cloning from existing plants, such as cutting stems and dividing roots. Plants found growing wild were deliberately divided and transplanted.

Seed agriculture, practiced by most contemporary farmers, came later, according to Sauer. **Seed agriculture** involved the reproduction of plants through the annual introduction of seeds, which result from sexual fertilization.

Location of First Agriculture

Agriculture probably did not originate in one location, but in multiple, independent hearths, or points of origin. From these hearths, agricultural practices diffused to other portions of the earth's surface.

Vegetative planting probably originated in Southeast Asia, according to Sauer. The diversity of climate and topography in the region probably encouraged the growth of a wide variety of plants suitable for dividing and transplanting. Also, because the people obtained food primarily by fishing rather than by hunting and gathering, they may have been able to devote more attention to growing plants. The first plants domesticated in Southeast Asia through vegetative planting probably included roots such as the taro and yam and tree crops such as the banana and palm. The dog, pig, and chicken were probably first domesticated in Southeast Asia.

Early hearths of vegetative planting may have also emerged independently in West Africa and northwestern South America. Vegetative planting may have been based on the oil-palm tree and yam in West Africa and the manioc, sweet potato, and arrowroot in South America. Vegetative planting diffused from the Southeast Asian hearth north and east to China and Japan and west through India to Southwest Asia, tropical Africa, and the Mediterranean lands. The practice spread from northwestern South America to Central America and eastern portions of South America (Figure 9–1).

Seed agriculture also originated in more than one hearth. Sauer identified three hearths in the Eastern Hemisphere: western India, northern China, and Ethiopia. But seed agriculture diffused quickly from western India to Southwest Asia, where important early advances were made. People in Southwest Asia first domesticated wheat and barley, two grains that became particularly important thousands of years later in European and American civilizations (Figure 9–2).

Inhabitants of Southwest Asia also apparently were the first to integrate seed agriculture with the domestication of herd animals such as cattle, sheep,

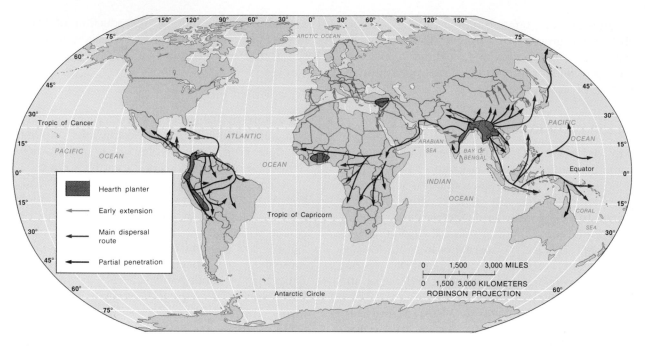

FIGURE 9–1

Origin and diffusion of vegetative planting. Vegetative planting, the reproduction of plants by direct cloning from existing plants, originated primarily in Southeast Asia, according to Carl Sauer. Two other early centers of vegetative planting were in West Africa and northwestern South America. From these hearths, the practice diffused to other regions. (Adapted from Carl O. Sauer, *Agricultural Origins and Dispersals,* with the permission of the American Geographical Society.)

and goats. These animals were used to plow the land before planting seeds and, in turn, were fed part of the harvested crop. Other animal products, such as milk, meat, and skins, were first exploited at a later date, according to Sauer. This integration of plants and animals is a fundamental element of modern agriculture.

Seed agriculture diffused from Southwest Asia to the west across Europe and through North Africa. Greece, Crete, and Cyprus display the earliest evidence of seed agriculture in Europe. From these countries, agriculture may have diffused northwest through the Danube basin, eventually to the Baltic and North seas, and northeast to the Ukraine. Most of the plants and animals domesticated in Southwest Asia spread into Europe, though barley and cattle became more important further north, perhaps because of cooler and moister climatic conditions.

Seed agriculture also diffused east from Southwest Asia to northwestern India and the Indus River plain. Again, a variety of domesticated plants and an-

imals were brought from Southwest Asia, though other plants, such as cotton and rice, arrived in India from different hearths.

From the northern China hearth, millet diffused to South and Southeast Asia. Rice, which ultimately became the most important crop in much of Asia, has an unknown hearth, though some geographers consider Southeast Asia to be the most likely location. Sauer identified a third independent hearth in Ethiopia, where millet and sorghum were domesticated at an early time. Sauer argued, however, that the agricultural advances made in Ethiopia did not diffuse widely to other locations. That Ethiopia is a hearth for seed agriculture is ironic, because rapid population growth, devastating civil wars, and adverse envrionmental conditions have combined to make Ethiopia one of the modern world's centers for starvation.

Two independent hearths for seed agriculture originated in the Western Hemisphere: southern Mexico and northern Peru. The hearth in Southern

Mexico, which extended into Guatemala and Honduras, was the point of origin for squash and maize (popularly known as corn in the United States). Squash, beans, and cotton may have been domesticated in northern Peru. From these two hearths, agricultural practices diffused to other parts of the Western Hemisphere, though agriculture was not widely practiced until European colonists began to arrive some 500 years ago. The only domesticated animals were the llama, alpaca, and turkey; herd animals were unknown until European explorers brought them in the sixteenth century.

Classification of Agricultural Regions

That agriculture had multiple origins means that from the earliest times people have produced food differently in particular regions. This diversity derives from a unique legacy of wild plants, climatic conditions, and cultural preferences in each region. Improved communications in recent centuries have encouraged the diffusion of some plants to a variety of locations in the world. Many plants and animals thrive across a wide portion of the earth's surface, not just in the place of original domestication. Only since A.D. 1500, for example, have wheat, oats, and barley been introduced to the Western Hemisphere and maize to the Eastern Hemisphere.

Despite increased knowledge of alternatives, farmers will still practice forms of agriculture unique to their area of the world. Characteristics of the physical environment continue to influence the type of agriculture, but areas with similar climates often show different agricultural practices because of their unique cultural traits. Many analysts have attempted to classify the world's major types of agriculture into meaningful regions, but—significantly— few of these classifications have included maps.

Many modern geographers accept Derwent Whittlesey's 1936 classification with some modification. Whittlesey identified eleven main agricultural regions, plus an area where agriculture was nonexistent (Figure 9–3). These eleven types of agriculture

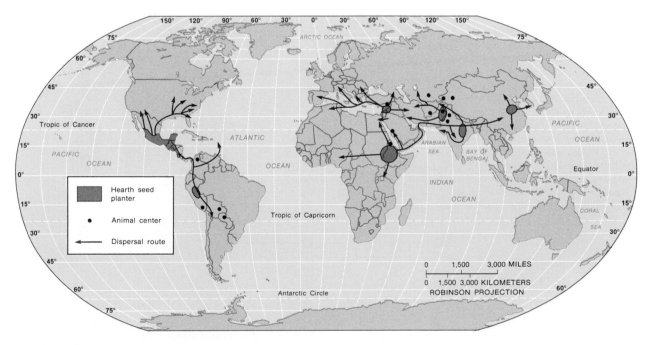

FIGURE 9–2
Origin and diffusion of seed agriculture and livestock herding. Seed agriculture may have originated in several hearths, including western India, northern China, and Ethiopia. Southern Mexico and northwestern South America may have been other early hearths. Early advances were made in southwestern Asia. (Adapted from Carl O. Sauer, *Agricultural Origins and Dispersals,* with the permission of the American Geographical Society.)

FIGURE 9–3

Geographers can divide the major agricultural practices of the world into subsistence and commercial regions. **Subsistence** regions include: *shifting cultivation*—primarily the tropical regions of South America, Africa, and Southeast Asia; *intensive subsistence, wet-rice dominant*—primarily the large population concentrations of East and South Asia; *intensive subsistence, crops other than rice dominant*—primarily the large population concentrations of East and South Asia where growing rice is difficult; *pastoral nomadism*—primarily the dry lands of North Africa and Asia; and *plantation*—primarily the tropical and subtropical regions of Latin America, Africa, and Asia.

Commercial regions include: *mixed crop and livestock*—primarily U.S. Midwest and central Europe; *dairying*—primarily near population clusters in northeastern United States, southeastern Canada, and northwestern Europe; *grain*—primarily north-central United States, south-central Canada, and central Soviet Union; *ranching*—primarily the dry lands of western United States, southeastern South America, southwestern Soviet Union, southern Africa, and Australia; *Mediterranean*—primarily lands surrounding the Mediterranean Sea, western United States, and Chile; and *truck farming* (commercial gardening and fruit farming)—primarily southeastern United States and southeastern Australia.

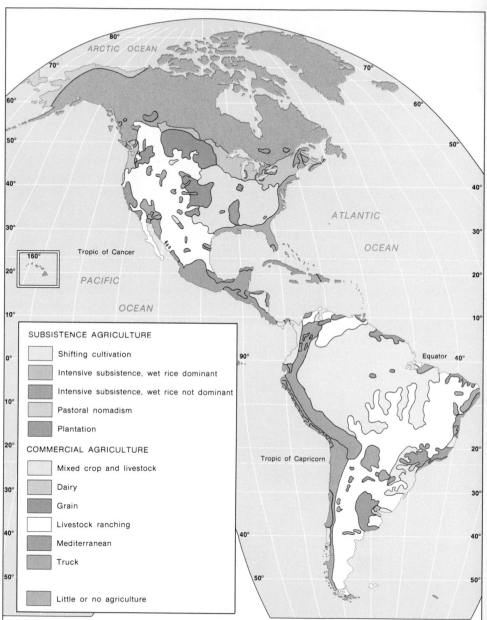

SUBSISTENCE AGRICULTURE

- Shifting cultivation
- Intensive subsistence, wet rice dominant
- Intensive subsistence, wet rice not dominant
- Pastoral nomadism
- Plantation

COMMERCIAL AGRICULTURE

- Mixed crop and livestock
- Dairy
- Grain
- Livestock ranching
- Mediterranean
- Truck

Little or no agriculture

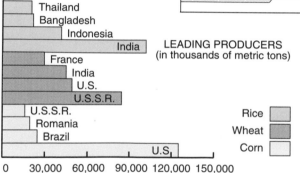

LEADING PRODUCERS
(in thousands of metric tons)

Thailand
Bangladesh
Indonesia
India
France
India
U.S.
U.S.S.R.
U.S.S.R.
Romania
Brazil
U.S.

Rice
Wheat
Corn

0   30,000   60,000   90,000 120,000 150,000

include five that are important in developing countries and six that are important in relatively developed countries. The next section considers four of the five agricultural types characteristic of developing countries: shifting cultivation, two types of intensive subsistence, and pastoral nomadism. The fifth type—plantation—is considered in a subsequent section of this chapter, along with agriculture in relatively developed countries.

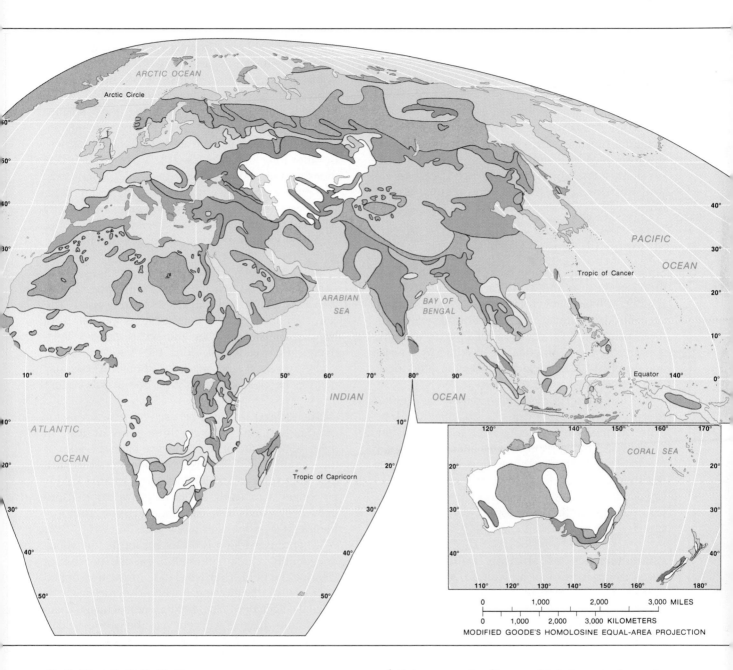

MODIFIED GOODE'S HOMOLOSINE EQUAL-AREA PROJECTION

KEY ISSUE

What Are the Main Types of Agriculture in Developing Countries?

The largest percentage of people in the developing countries, including most people in Asia and Africa and a significant number in Latin America, practice **subsistence agriculture,** which is agriculture designed primarily to provide food for direct consumption by the farmer and the farmer's family. While practices vary from one society to another, subsistence agriculture has several distinguishing characteristics.

First, in regions where subsistence agriculture predominates, most people work in agricultural rather than industrial or service jobs. Second, most people produce food for their own consumption. Some surplus may be sold to the government or to private firms for distribution in cities or foreign markets. But the surplus product is not the farmer's primary purpose and may not be available some years because of poor harvests.

Subsistence farmers employ a wide variety of agricultural practices. This section looks at four types of subsistence agriculture: shifting cultivation, intensive subsistence (both with wet rice dominant and with wet rice not dominant), and pastoral nomadism.

Shifting Cultivation

Shifting cultivation is the main form of agriculture found in much of the world's tropical, or A, climate regions, which have relatively high temperatures and abundant rainfall. Shifting cultivation predominates primarily in three tropical regions: the Amazon area of South America, Central and West Africa, and Southeast Asia, including Indochina, Indonesia, and New Guinea.

We use the term *cultivation* rather than *agriculture* to describe this means of obtaining food, because *agriculture* implies greater use of tools and animals and more sophisticated attempts to modify the landscape. Shifting cultivation bears little relationship to the agriculture of the relatively developed countries of Western Europe and North America or even of other developing countries such as China.

Characteristics of shifting cultivation. Compared to other types of agriculture, **shifting cultivation** has two particularly important characteristics. First, farmers usually clear the land for planting, in part by slashing the vegetation and burning the debris. As a result, shifting cultivation is sometimes known as slash-and-burn agriculture. Second, farmers grow crops on a cleared field for only a few years and then leave it fallow for many years.

People who practice shifting cultivation generally live in a small village and grow food in the surrounding land, which the village controls. Well-recognized boundaries usually separate a village from its neighbors.

Each year, the villagers designate for planting an area surrounding the settlement. Before planting,

they must remove the dense vegetation that typically covers tropical land. The villagers cut down most of the trees with axes, sparing only those that are economically useful. One strategy is to chop down a handful of large trees situated at key junctures; as they fall, the larger trees will bring down smaller ones that may have been weakened by notching.

The undergrowth is cleared away with a machete or other long knife. On a windless day, the debris is then burned under carefully controlled conditions. The rains wash the fresh ashes into the soil, providing needed nutrients. The cleared area is known by a variety of names in different regions of the world, including **swidden,** ladang, milpa, chena, and kaingin.

Before planting, fields are prepared by hand, perhaps with the help of a simple implement such as a hoe; plows and animals are rarely used. The only fertilizer generally available is potash from burning the debris when the site is cleared. Relatively little weeding is done the first year that a cleared patch of land is farmed, though weeds may need to be cleared away with a hoe in subsequent years.

The cleared land can be used to grow crops for only a short time, usually three years or less. In many regions, the most productive harvest comes in the second year after burning. Thereafter, the nutrients in the soil are rapidly depleted, and the land is no longer sufficiently fertile to grow crops. Rapid growth of weeds also contributes to the abandonment of a swidden after a few years.

When the swidden is no longer fertile, the villagers identify a new site and begin the process of clearing the field. They leave the old site uncropped for many years, allowing it to be overrun again by natural vegetation. The field is not actually abandoned: the villagers will return to the site some day, perhaps as few as six years or as many as twenty years later, to begin the process of clearing the land again. In the meantime, they may still care for fruit-bearing trees on the site.

If a cleared area outside a village is too small to provide food for the entire population of a village, then some of the people may establish a new village and practice shifting cultivation there. In some cases, farmers may have to move temporarily to another settlement if the field they are clearing that year is relatively distant from the village.

The particular crops grown by each village vary by local custom and taste. The predominant crops include upland rice in Southeast Asia, maize (corn) and manioc (cassava) in South America, and millet and sorghum in Africa. Yams, sugar cane, plantain, and vegetables may also be grown in some regions. These crops may have been originally associated with one region of shifting cultivation but have diffused to other areas in recent years.

The Kayapo people of Brazil's Amazon tropical rainforest arrange crops in concentric rings. At first, they plant sweet potatoes and yams in the inner area and corn and rice, manioc, and more yams in successive rings. The outermost ring contains papaya, banana, pineapple, mango, cotton, and beans. Plants that require more nutrients are located in the outer ring, where the leafy crowns of the large trees

land when they are cut to clear the field. In subsequent years, the inner area of sweet potatoes and yams expands to replace corn and rice.

Most families grow for their own needs, though some may concentrate on a few crops and trade with villagers who specialize in others. Consequently, one swidden may contain a large variety of intermingled crops, which are harvested individually at the appropriate time. The field in shifting cultivation appears much more chaotic than a farm in a relatively developed country, where one crop, such as corn or wheat, may grow over an extensive area.

Traditionally, land is owned by the village as a whole rather than separately by each resident. The chief or ruling council allocates a patch of land to each family and allows it to retain the output. Individuals may also have the right to own or protect

These shifting cultivation farmers in Guatemala are preparing fields for planting by slashing the vegetation and burning it.

specific trees surrounding the village. This land-tenure system has been replaced by private ownership in some communities, especially in Latin America.

Shifting cultivation occupies approximately one-fourth of the world's land area, a higher percentage than any other type of agriculture. But only 5 percent of the world's population engage in shifting cultivation. The gap between the percentage of people and land area is not surprising, because the practice of moving from one field to another every couple of years requires more land per person than other types of agriculture.

Future of shifting cultivation. The percentage of land devoted to shifting cultivation is declining in the tropics, and its future role in world agriculture is not clear. Shifting cultivation is being replaced by logging, cattle ranching, and cultivation of cash crops.

All of the alternatives to shifting cultivation require cutting down vast expanses of forest. In recent years, tropical rainforests have disappeared at the rate of 10 to 20 million hectares (25 to 50 million acres) per year. The amount of the earth's surface allocated to tropical rainforests has already been reduced to less than 50 percent of its original area, and unless drastic measures are taken, the area will be reduced by another 20 percent within a decade.

Governments in developing countries have supported the destruction of rainforests because they view activities such as selling timber to builders or raising cattle for fast-food restaurants as more effective strategies for promoting economic development than shifting cultivation. Until recent years, the World Bank has provided loans to finance development schemes that require clearing forests. Furthermore, shifting cultivation is regarded as a relatively inefficient approach to growing food in a hungry world. The problem with shifting cultivation compared to other forms of agriculture is that it can support only a low level of population in an area without causing environmental damage.

To its critics, shifting cultivation is at best a preliminary step in the process of economic development for a society. Pioneers use shifting cultivation to clear forests in the tropics and open up land for development where permanent agriculture has never existed. People unable to find agricultural land elsewhere can migrate to the tropical forests and initially practice shifting cultivation. It then should be replaced by other forms of agriculture that produce greater yields per land area.

Defenders of shifting cultivation consider it the most environmentally sound form of agriculture for the tropics. Practices associated with other forms of agriculture, such as introduction of fertilizers and permanent clearing of fields, may damage the soil and upset the ecological balance in the tropics. Destruction of the rainforests may also contribute to global warming. When large numbers of massive trees are cut, they release a significant amount of carbon. The resulting build-up of carbon dioxide acts like a greenhouse to trap solar energy in the atmosphere (*see* Chapter 13).

Elimination of shifting cultivation could upset traditional cultural customs as well. The activities involved in shifting cultivation may be intertwined with other social, religious, and political traditions. A drastic change in the agricultural economy could disrupt other activities of daily life.

In recognition of the importance of tropical rainforests to the global environment, developing countries have been pressured into restricting further destruction of them. In one innovative strategy, Bolivia agreed to set aside 1.5 million hectares (3.7 million acres) in a national reserve in exchange for cancellation of $650,000 of its debt to relatively developed countries.

Intensive Subsistence Agriculture

The greatest number of farmers living in the large population concentrations of East, South, and Southeast Asia practice **intensive subsistence agriculture.** The term *intensive* implies that farmers in this region must expend a relatively large amount of effort to produce the maximum feasible yield from a given parcel of land.

The typical farm in the intensive subsistence agriculture regions of Asia is much smaller than elsewhere in the world. Many Asian farmers own several fragmented plots, frequently a result of dividing individual holdings among several children over a several-hundred-year period.

Because the agricultural density—the ratio of farmers to arable land—is so high in parts of East and South Asia, families must produce enough food for their survival from a very small area of land.

They do this through careful agricultural practices, refined over thousands of years in response to local environmental and cultural patterns. Most of the work is done by hand or with animals rather than with machines, in part because of the abundance of labor but largely because of shortage of funds to buy equipment.

In order to maximize food production, intensive subsistence farmers waste virtually no land. Corners of fields and irregularly shaped pieces of land are planted rather than left idle, while paths and roads are kept as narrow as possible to minimize the loss of arable land. Livestock are rarely permitted to graze on land that could be used to plant crops, and little grain is grown to feed the animals.

Wet rice dominant. Geographers can divide the intensive agriculture region of Asia between areas in which **wet rice** dominates and areas where other crops dominate. Although wet rice occupies a relatively small percentage of the continent's agricul-

tural land, it is the most important source of food in Asia. Intensive wet rice farming is the dominant type of agriculture in Southeast China, East India, and much of Southeast Asia (Figure 9–4).

Successful production of large yields of rice is an elaborate, time-consuming process, done mostly by hand. The people who actually consume the rice perform the work, and each family member, including the children, contributes to the effort.

The process of growing rice involves a number of steps. First, a farmer prepares the field for planting using a plow drawn by water buffalo or oxen. The use of a plow and animal power is one characteristic that distinguishes subsistence agriculture from shifting cultivation.

The next step in the rice-growing process is to flood the plowed land with water collected from either rainfall, river overflow, or irrigation. Too much or too little water can damage the crop—a particular problem for farmers in South Asia who depend on monsoon rains, which do not always arrive at the

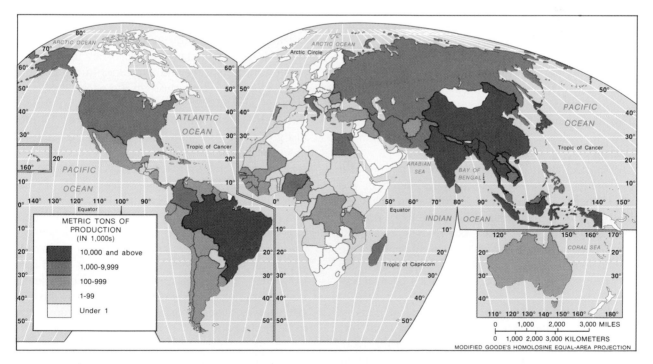

FIGURE 9–4
Rice production. Rice is the most important crop in the large population concentrations of East and South Asia. Asian farmers grow more than 90 percent of the world's rice. The United States—usually the largest producer of rice outside Asia but recently surpassed by Brazil—accounts for only 1 percent of world production.

same time each summer. Before the rice can be planted, dikes and canals must be repaired to assure that the quantity of water in the field is appropriate. The flooded field is called a **sawah** in the Austronesian language widely spoken in Indonesia, including Java. Europeans and North Americans frequently, but incorrectly, call it a **paddy,** the Malay word for wet rice.

Rice is introduced to a field in one of two ways. One is to broadcast dry seeds by scattering them through the field, a method used to some extent in South Asia. The more customary way to introduce the rice is by transplanting seedlings, which are first grown in a nursery. Typically one-tenth of a sawah is devoted to the cultivation of seedlings. After about a month the seedlings are transferred to the rest of the field. Rice plants grow submerged in water for approximately three-fourths of the growing period.

Rice plants are harvested by hand, usually with knives. To separate the husks, known as **chaff,** from the seeds, the heads are **threshed** by beating them on the ground or treading on them barefoot. The threshed rice is placed in a tray, and the lighter chaff is **winnowed,** that is, allowed to be blown away by the wind. If the rice is to be consumed directly by the farmer, the **hull,** or outer covering, is removed by mortar and pestle. Rice that is sold commercially is frequently whitened and polished, a process that removes some nutrients but leaves rice more pleasing in appearance and taste to many consumers.

Wet rice should be grown on flat land, because the plants are submerged in water much of the time. Therefore, most wet-rice cultivation is located in river valleys and deltas. The pressure of population growth in parts of East Asia has resulted in expansion of the land area under rice cultivation. One method of developing additional land suitable for growing rice is to terrace the hillsides of river valleys.

Land is used even more intensively in parts of Asia by obtaining two harvests per year from one field, a process known as **double cropping.** Double cropping is common in places with relatively warm winters, such as South China and Taiwan, but is relatively rare in India, where most areas have dry winters. Normally, double cropping involves alternating between wet rice and a dry crop. Wet rice is grown in the summer, when precipitation is higher, and wheat, barley, or another dry crop is grown in the drier winter season. Crops other than rice may be grown in the wet rice region in the summer on nonirrigated land.

Wet rice not dominant. Climate prevents farmers from growing wet rice in portions of Asia, especially where summer precipitation levels are too low and winters are too harsh. Agriculture in much of interior India and northeast China is devoted to crops other than wet rice.

This region shares most of the characteristics of intensive subsistence agriculture with the wet-rice region. Land is intensively used and worked primarily by human power with the assistance of some hand implements and animals. Wheat is the most important crop, followed by barley. A wide variety of other grains and legumes are grown, including millet, oats, corn, kaoliang, sorghum, and soybeans, as well as some cash crops such as cotton, flax, hemp, and tobacco.

In milder parts of the region where wet rice does not dominate, more than one harvest can be obtained some years through skilled use of crop rotation. In colder climates, wheat or another crop is planted in the spring and harvested in the fall, but no crops can be sown through the winter.

Most agricultural land in China is no longer owned by private individuals. Instead, the communist government of China has organized agricultural producer communes, which typically combine several villages containing several hundred people. Inhabitants may still own small private parcels of land, which they farm after completing the tasks the commune assigns. Combining several small fields into a larger unit has promoted agricultural efficiency, because scarce equipment and animals can be shared, and larger improvement projects, such as flood control, water storage, and terracing, can be completed. Reorganization has been more difficult in the wet rice regions, where existing irrigation systems have to be replaced.

Pastoral Nomadism

Pastoral nomadism is a form of subsistence agriculture based on the herding of domesticated animals. It is adapted to dry climates where intensive

This Egyptian woman is thrashing grain using a norag.

subsistence agriculture is difficult or impossible. Pastoral nomads live primarily in the large belt of arid and semiarid land that includes North Africa, the Middle East, and parts of Central Asia. The Bedouins of Saudi Arabia and North Africa and the Masai of East Africa are examples of nomadic groups. Only approximately 15 million people are pastoral nomads, but they occupy approximately 20 percent of the earth's land area.

In contrast with other subsistence farmers, pastoral nomads depend primarily on animals rather than crops for their survival. They take milk from the animals for food and skins and hairs for clothing and tents. But most pastoral nomads—like other subsistence farmers—consume mostly grain rather than meat. Their animals are commonly not slaughtered for meat, though dead ones may be consumed, because nomads consider the size of their herd to be not only an important measure of power and prestige but also the main element of security in periods of adverse environmental conditions.

Pastoral nomads obtain grain in several ways. Some exchange the animal products with sedentary subsistence farmers for grain. More often, a group combines nomadism with sedentary agriculture. Part of the group—perhaps the women and children—may plant crops at a fixed location while the rest of the group wanders with the herd. Nomads may hire workers to practice sedentary agriculture in return for grain and protection. Other nomads may sow grain in recently flooded areas and return later in the year to harvest the crop. Yet another strategy is to remain in one place and cultivate the land when rainfall is abundant; then, during periods that are too dry to grow crops, the group can increase the size of the herd and migrate in search of food and water.

Nomads select the type and number of animals for the herd according to local cultural and physical characteristics. The choice depends on the relative prestige of animals and the ability of species to adapt to a particular climate and vegetation. The camel is most frequently desired in North Africa and the Middle East, followed by sheep and goats. In Central Asia, the horse is particularly important.

The camel is well suited to arid climates, because it can go long periods without water, carry heavy baggage, and move rapidly. Yet the camel is particularly bothered by flies and sleeping sickness and has a relatively long period—12 months—from conception to birth. Goats need more water than camels but are tough and agile. They can survive on virtually any vegetation, no matter how poor. Sheep are relatively slow-moving and are more affected by variations in weather. They require more water and are more selective in which plants they will consume. The minimum number of animals necessary to support each family adequately varies according to the particular group and animal. The typical nomadic family needs between twenty-five and sixty goats or sheep or between ten and twenty-five camels.

Agricultural experts once regarded pastoral nomadism as a stage in the evolution of agriculture, from the hunters and gatherers who migrated across the earth's surface in search of food to sedentary farmers who cultivated grain in one place. Because they had domesticated animals but not plants, pastoral nomads were considered more advanced than hunters and gatherers but less advanced than settled farmers.

Pastoral nomadism is now generally recognized to be an offshoot of sedentary agriculture, not a primitive precursor of it. It is a practical way of surviving on land that receives too little rain for the cultivation of crops. The domestication of animals— the basis for pastoral nomadism—probably was achieved originally by sedentary farmers, not by no-

Pastoral nomads in the dry lands of Somalia obtain water for their goats by passing buckets up from a deep well.

madic hunters. Pastoral nomads therefore had to be familiar with sedentary farming. Furthermore, many pastoral nomads also practice some sedentary farming.

Pastoral nomads do not wander aimlessly across the landscape but have a strong sense of territoriality. Every group controls a piece of territory and will invade another group's territory only in an emergency or if war is declared. The goal of each group is to control a territory large enough to contain the forage and water needed for survival. The actual amount of land a group controls depends on its wealth and power.

The precise migration patterns evolve from intimate knowledge of the area's physical and cultural characteristics. Groups frequently divide into herding units of five or six families. The choice of routes each herding unit takes depends on individual experience concerning the most likely water sources during the season and varies in unusually wet or dry years. Nomads are also influenced by the condition of their animals and the area's political stability.

Some pastoral nomads practice **transhumance,** which is seasonal migration of livestock between mountains and lowland **pastures.** Sheep or other animals may graze in alpine meadows in the summer and be herded back down into valleys for the winter.

Pastoral nomadism is a declining form of agriculture, a victim in part of modern technology. Before recent transportation and communications inventions, pastoral nomads played an important role as carriers of goods and information across the sparsely inhabited dry lands. Nomads used to be the most powerful inhabitants of the dry lands, but now, with modern weapons, national governments can control the nomadic population more effectively.

Government efforts to resettle nomads have been particularly vigorous in the Soviet Union, China, and several Middle Eastern countries, including Egypt, Israel, Saudi Arabia, and Syria. But because nomads are reluctant to cooperate, these countries have experienced difficulties in trying to force settlement in collectives and cooperatives. Governments force groups to give up pastoral nomadism because they want the land for other uses. Land that can be irrigated can be converted from nomadic to sedentary agriculture. In some instances, the mining and petroleum industries now operate in dry lands formerly occupied by pastoral nomads.

Some nomads are encouraged to try sedentary agriculture or to work for mining or petroleum companies. Others are still allowed to move somewhat but only on ranches with fixed boundaries. In the future, however, pastoral nomadism will be increasingly confined to areas that cannot be irrigated or that lack valuable raw materials.

KEY ISSUE

How Does Agriculture in Developing and Relatively Developed Countries Differ?

Farmers in relatively developed countries—including the United States, Canada, Europe, the Soviet Union, South Africa, Australia, and New Zealand—practice commercial agriculture. **Commercial agriculture** is agriculture undertaken primarily to generate products for sale off the farm.

Characteristics of Commercial Agriculture

Several important characteristics distinguish commercial agriculture from subsistence agriculture, which predominates in the developing countries.

Small percentage of farmers. The first distinctive characteristic of commercial agriculture is the small percentage of farmers in the labor force. The percentage of people who work as farmers is less than 5 percent in relatively developed countries such as the United States, Canada, and the United Kingdom, compared to 60 percent in developing countries. Yet the small percentage of farmers can produce not only enough food for themselves and the rest of the country but also a surplus to help people elsewhere in the world as well.

The number of farmers has declined in relatively developed societies during the twentieth century. Both push and pull migration factors have been responsible: people have moved away from farms because they were no longer needed and, at the same time, have been lured to higher-paying jobs in urban areas. The United States had approximately 2 million farms in 1990, compared with 5.6 million in 1950 and 4 million in 1960.

Although there are fewer farms and farmers, the amount of land devoted to agriculture has remained fairly constant in Western Europe and Anglo-America since 1900. The growth of urban areas has taken away some agricultural land, though the annual loss of farmland in the United States is only 0.01 percent. This loss has been offset by the creation of new agricultural land through irrigation and reclamation. A more serious problem in the United States is the loss of the most productive farm land, known as prime agricultural land, because of the sprawl of urban areas into the surrounding countryside.

Heavy use of machinery. The second distinctive characteristic of commercial farming is the high degree of reliance on technological and scientific improvements. A small number of farmers are able to feed a large number of people in relatively developed societies because commercial farmers rely on machinery rather than people or animals to supply power.

Traditionally, the farmer or local craftsperson made the equipment from wood, but beginning in the late eighteenth century factories produced farm machinery. The first all-iron plow was produced in the 1770s and was followed in the nineteenth and twentieth centuries by a series of inventions designed to make farming less dependent on human or animal power. Tractors, combines, corn pickers, planters, and other factory-made farm machines have replaced or supplemented manual labor.

Transportation improvements also aid commercial farmers. The coming of railroads in the nineteenth century and trucks in the twentieth century have enabled farmers to transport crops and livestock more rapidly. Cattle arrive at the destination heavier and in better condition when transported by truck or train than when driven on foot. Crops reach markets without spoiling.

Commercial farmers also make extensive use of scientific advances to increase productivity. Experiments conducted in the laboratories of universities, industries, and research organizations generate new fertilizers, herbicides, hybrid plants, and animal breeds, which produce higher crop yields and healthier animals. Access to other scientific information has enabled farmers to make more intelligent decisions concerning proper agricultural practices.

Commercial agriculture depends heavily on expensive machinery to efficiently manage large farms. These combine machines are reaping, threshing, and cleaning wheat.

Large farm size. The third distinctive characteristic of commercial agriculture is the relatively large size of the average farm, especially in the United States and Canada. The average U.S. farm is nearly 200 hectares (500 acres).

Despite the large size, most commercial farms in relatively developed countries (other than in parts of Eastern Europe and in the Soviet Union) are family owned and operated. The percentage of farmers who own their land is over 90 percent in the United States and Scandinavia and approximately 50 percent in France and the United Kingdom. But commercial farmers frequently expand their holdings by renting nearby fields.

Large size is partly a consequence of mechanization. Combines, pickers, and other machinery perform most efficiently at very large scales, and their considerable expense would not be justifiable on a small farm. As a result of the large size and the high level of mechanization, commercial agriculture is an expensive business. Farmers must spend hundreds of thousands of dollars to buy or rent land and machinery before beginning operations. This money is frequently borrowed from a bank and repaid after the output is sold.

Output sold to processors. The fourth distinctive characteristic of commercial farming is that the farmers grow crops and raise animals primarily for sale off the farm rather for their own consumption. These agricultural products are not sold directly to consumers but to food processing companies. Large processors, such as General Mills and Ralston Purina, typically sign contracts with commercial farmers to buy their chickens, cattle, and other output. Farmers may have contracts to sell sugar beets to sugar refineries, potatoes to distilleries, and oranges to manufacturers of concentrated juices.

Integration with other businesses. The fifth distinctive characteristic of commercial farming is its close ties to other businesses. The system of commercial farming found in the United States and other relatively developed countries has been called **agribusiness,** because the family farm is not an isolated activity but is integrated into a large food-processing industry. Less than 5 percent of the U.S. labor force are farmers, but more than 20 percent are engaged in other activities related to agribusiness. These activities include processing, packaging, storing, distributing, and retailing food. Agribusiness encompasses such diverse enterprises as tractor manufacturers, fertilizer producers, and seed distributors, as well as restaurants, supermarkets, and pizza delivery services. While most farms are owned by individual families, many other aspects of agribusiness are controlled by large corporations.

How Do Commercial Farmers Choose a Crop to Plant?

The type of agriculture practiced on a commercial farm depends on situation, site, and cultural factors. The situation factor—critical for a commerical farm—is the farm's location in relation to the markets where its products are sold. Important site factors that determine the suitability of the land for particular crops and animals include climate, soil, and slope of the land. A commerical farmer is also influenced by cultural factors, such as the beliefs, traditions, and preferences of consumers.

Von Thünen's model. A model emphasizing the importance of situation factors was first proposed in 1826 by Johann Heinrich von Thünen, a farmer in northern Germany, in a book titled *The Isolated State.* According to von Thünen's model, which was later modified by geographers, a commercial farmer initially considers alternative crops to cultivate and animals to raise on the basis of the location of the market.

In making a choice, a commercial farmer compares two costs: the price of the land and the expense of transporting the products to the market. First, a commercial farmer identifies the crops that can be sold for more than the rent. Assume that a farmer rents land at a cost of $100 per hectare. In this example, a farmer would consider planting wheat if the output from one hectare of land can be

Hens are still needed to lay eggs, but most other steps in the production of poultry foods are highly mechanized. Here food workers process eggs.

sold at the market for more than $100, minus the nonrent expenses. Another crop, such as corn, will also be considered if the yield from one hectare of land can be sold for more than $100.

A farmer may not always plant the crop that sells for the highest price per hectare. The choice also depends on the distance of the land from the central market city. Distance to the market is a critical factor because each crop has a unique transportation cost.

Example of von Thünen model. The following example illustrates the influence of transportation costs on the profitability of growing wheat:

1. Gross profit from sale of wheat grown on one hectare of land *not* including transportation costs:
   a. Wheat can be sold for $0.25 per kilogram
   b. Yield per hectare of wheat is 1,000 kilograms
   c. Gross profit = $0.25 per kilogram × 1,000 kilograms per hectare = $250 per hectare
2. Net profit from sale of wheat grown on one hectare of land *including* transportation costs:
   a. Cost of transporting 1,000 kilograms of wheat to the market is $62.50 per kilometer
   b. Net profit from sale of 1,000 kilograms of wheat grown on a farm located 1 kilometer from the market = $250 − $62.50 = $187.50
   c. Net profit from sale of 1,000 kilograms of wheat grown on a farm located 4 kilometers from the market = $250 − ($62.50 × 4) = 0

The example shows that a farmer would make a profit growing wheat on land located less than 4 kilometers from the market. Beyond 4 kilometers, wheat is not profitable because the cost of transporting it exceeds the gross profit.

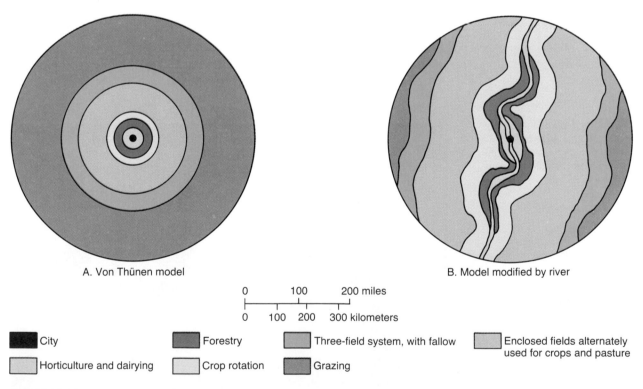

A. Von Thünen model   B. Model modified by river

0   100   200 miles
0   100   200   300 kilometers

■ City   ■ Forestry   ■ Three-field system, with fallow   ■ Enclosed fields alternately used for crops and pasture
■ Horticulture and dairying   ■ Crop rotation   ■ Grazing

FIGURE 9–5
According to the Von Thünen model, in the absence of topographic factors, different types of farming would appear at different distances from a city, depending on the cost of transportation and the value of the product. Von Thünen argued that his model would be modified by distinctive physical features, such as a river. Because a river changes the pattern of relative accessibility of land to the market center, agricultural uses that seek to be highly accessible could locate closer to the river.

The von Thünen model shows that a commercial farmer must combine two sets of monetary values to determine the most profitable crop:

- the value of the yield per hectare
- the cost of transporting the yield per hectare

These calculations demonstrate that farms located closer to the market tend to select crops with higher transportation costs per hectare of output, whereas more distant farms are more likely to select crops that can be transported less expensively.

Application of von Thünen model. Von Thünen based his general model of the spatial arrangement of different crops on his experiences as owner of a large estate in northern Germany during the early nineteenth century (Figure 9–5). He found that specific crops were grown in different rings around the cities in the area. Market-oriented gardens and milk producers were located in the first ring out from the cities. These products are expensive to deliver and must reach the market quickly because they are perishable.

The next ring out from the cities contained wood lots, where timber was cut for construction and fuel. The next rings were used for various crops and for pasture, though the precise choice was rotated from one year to the next. The outermost ring was devoted exclusively to animal grazing.

Von Thünen did not consider site or cultural factors in his model. The model assumed that all land in a study area had similar physical characteristics and was of uniform quality, though he recognized that the model would vary according to topography and other distinctive physical conditions. For example, a river might modify the shape of the rings because transportation costs change when products are shipped by water routes rather than over roads. The model also failed to acknowledge that tradition, taste, and other social customs influence the attractiveness of plants and animals for a commercial farmer.

Although von Thünen developed the model for a small region with a single market center, it also applies to a national or global scale. Farmers in relatively remote locations who wish to sell their output in the major markets of Western Europe and North America, for example, are less likely to grow highly perishable and bulky products.

Von Thünen's model helps to explain the spatial distribution of various types of commercial agriculture. Farmers in one region tend to practice types of agriculture different from farmers in another region, based on a combination of environmental characteristics and access to markets. Some of the most important regions of commercial agriculture are discussed in the next section.

KEY ISSUE

What Are the Main Types of Agriculture in Relatively Developed Countries?

Geographers divide the agriculture practiced in relatively developed countries into six main types: mixed crops and livestock, dairying, livestock ranching, grain farming, gardening and fruit culture, and Mediterranean agriculture. In addition, this section examines plantation farming, a form of commercial agriculture in developing countries.

Mixed Crop and Livestock Farming

The most common form of commercial agriculture is mixed crop and livestock. Mixed commercial farming is found in much of Europe from Ireland to the Soviet Union, North America west of the Appalachians and east of 98° west longitude, South Africa, northeastern Argentina, southeastern Australia, and New Zealand.

Characteristics of mixed crop and livestock farming. The most distinctive characteristic of mixed crop and livestock farming is the integration of crops and livestock. Most of the crops grown on a mixed commercial farm are fed to animals rather than consumed directly by humans. In turn, the livestock can supply manure to improve soil fertility to grow more crops. A typical mixed commercial farm devotes nearly all of the land area to growing crops but derives more than three-fourths of its income from the sale of animal products, such as beef, milk, and eggs. In the United States, pigs are often bred directly on the farms, while cattle may be brought in to be fattened on corn.

Mixed crop and livestock farming permits farmers to distribute the work load more evenly through the year. Fields require less attention in the winter than in the spring, when crops are planted, and in the fall, when they are harvested. Livestock, on the other hand, require attention throughout the year. A mix of crops and livestock also reduces seasonal variations in income; most income from crops comes during the harvest season, but livestock products can be sold throughout the year.

Crop rotation system. A mixed crop and live-stock farmer typically practices crop rotation. The farm is divided into a number of fields, and the crop planted in a particular field differs from one year to the next. Crop rotation enables a farmer to maintain the fertility of a field, because various crops deplete the soil of certain nutrients and re-store others. The practice of crop rotation contrasts with the system used in shifting cultivation, in which nutrients depleted from a field are restored by leav-ing the field uncropped for many years. Because in any given year crops cannot be planted in most of an area's fields, overall production level is much lower in shifting cultivation than in mixed commer-cial farming.

A two-field crop rotation system was developed in Northern Europe as early as the fifth century A.D. A **cereal grain,** such as oats, wheat, rye, or barley, was planted in Field A one year and in Field B the next year. Field B was left fallow the first year, Field A the second year. Beginning in the eighth century, a three-field system was introduced. The first field was planted with a winter cereal, the second was planted with a spring cereal, and the third was left fallow. As a result, each field yielded four harvests every six years, compared with three every six years under the two-field system.

By the eighteenth century, a four-field system was used in Northwest Europe. The first year, the farmer could plant a root in Field A, a cereal in Field B, a rest crop in Field C, and a cereal in Field D. The second year, the farmer might select a cereal for Field A, a rest crop for Field B, a cereal for Field C, and a root for Field D. The rotation would con-tinue for two more years before the cycle would start again. As a result, each field passed through a cycle of four steps—root, cereal, rest crop, and an-other cereal.

Farmers sold cereals such as wheat and barley for flour and beer production, and they kept the straw for animal bedding. Root crops such as tur-nips were fed to the animals during the winter. Clo-ver and other rest crops were used for cattle graz-ing and restoration of nitrogen to the soil.

In the United States, the most important mixed crop and livestock farming region extends from Ohio to the Dakotas, with its center in Iowa. The re-gion is frequently called the Corn Belt, because ap-proximately half of the crop land is planted in corn (maize). Mixed commercial farmers select corn most frequently because of higher yields per area than other crops. Some of the corn is consumed by people either directly or as oil, margarine, and other food products, but most is fed to pigs and cat-tle (Figure 9–6).

Soybeans have become the secondmost impor-tant crop in the United States' mixed commercial farming region. Like corn, soybeans are used some-times to make products consumed directly by peo-ple but mostly to make animal feed. Tofu—made from soybean milk—is a major food source, espe-cially for people in China and Japan. Soybean oil is widely used in U.S. foods, but as a hidden ingredi-ent.

Dairy Farming

Dairy farming is the most important type of com-mercial agriculture practiced on farms outside the large urban areas of the Northeast United States, Southeast Canada, and Northwest Europe. It ac-counts for approximately 20 percent of the total value of agricultural output throughout Western Eu-rope and North America. The Soviet Union, Austra-lia, and New Zealand also have extensive areas de-voted to dairy farming. Nearly 90 percent of the world's supply of milk is produced and consumed in these relatively developed regions (Figure 9–7).

Traditionally, fresh milk was rarely consumed ex-cept directly on the farm or in nearby villages. With the rapid growth of cities in relatively developed countries during the nineteenth century, demand for the sale of milk to urban residents increased. Rising incomes permitted urban residents to buy milk products which were once considered luxu-ries. Average weekly consumption of milk per per-son in England, for example, rose from 0.8 liters (0.2 U.S. gallons) in the 1870s to 2.7 liters (0.7 U.S. gallons) by the 1950s.

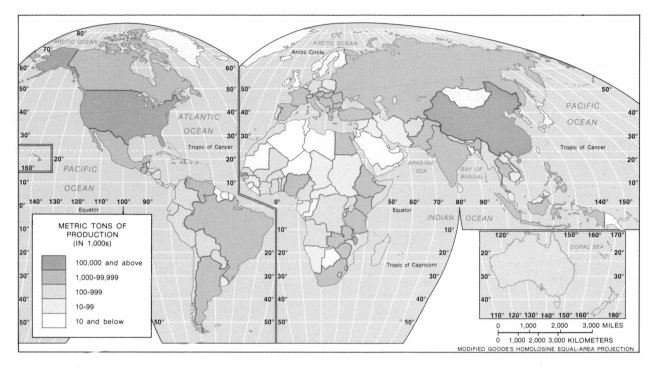

FIGURE 9—6
Corn (maize) production. The United States accounts for more than 30 percent of the world's production of corn, which is known as maize outside of North America. China is the second-leading producer.

Why dairy farms locate near urban areas. Dairying has become the most important type of commercial agriculture in the first ring outside large cities because of transportation factors. Dairy farms need to be located closer to the market than other products because milk is highly perishable and must reach the consumer quickly to prevent spoiling. The ring surrounding a city from which milk can be supplied without spoiling is known as the **milkshed.**

Improvements in transportation have permitted dairying to be undertaken farther away from the market. Until the 1840s, when railroads were first used for transporting dairy products, milksheds rarely extended beyond a radius of more than 50 kilometers (30 miles). In the twentieth century, milk can be driven quickly from the farm to the railroad station, and refrigerated rail cars and trucks enable farmers to ship milk more than 500 kilometers (300 miles). As a result, nearly every farm in the Northeast United States and Northwest Europe is within the milkshed of at least one urban area.

Some dairy farms specialize in products other than milk. Originally, butter and cheese were made directly on the farm, primarily from the excess milk produced in the summer, before modern agricultural methods evened the flow of milk through the year. In the twentieth century, however, dairy farmers have generally chosen to specialize either in milk producton or other products such as butter and cheese.

In general, the farther the farm is from large urban concentrations, the lower the percentage of the output devoted to fresh milk. Farms located farther from consumers are more likely to sell their output to processors who make butter, cheese, or dried, evaporated, and condensed milk. The reason is that butter and cheese keep longer than milk and therefore can be safely shipped from remote farms.

Regional differences. Geographers can see regional differences in the choice of product within the United States depending on whether the farms are within the milkshed of a large urban area. In the

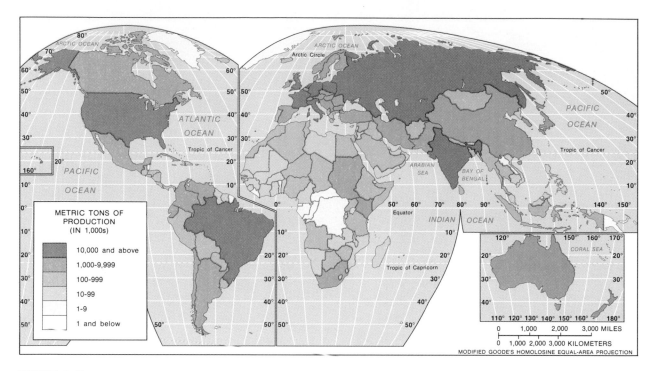

FIGURE 9–7

Milk production. The distribution of milk production closely matches the division of the world into relatively developed and developing countries. Consumers in relatively developed countries have the income to pay for milk products, and farmers in those countries can afford the high cost of establishing dairy farms. Brazil and India rank among the world leaders in total milk production but not in production per capita.

East, virtually all milk is sold in liquid form to consumers living in New York, Philadelphia, Boston, and the other large urban areas, whereas farther west, most of it is processed into cheese and butter. Virtually all of the milk in Wisconsin is processed, for example, compared to only 5 percent in Pennsylvania. The proximity of northeastern farmers to several large markets accounts for these regional differences.

Countries likewise tend to specialize in certain products. New Zealand, the world's largest producer of dairy products, devotes only 8 percent to liquid milk, compared to 68 percent in the United Kingdom. New Zealand farmers do not sell much liquid milk because the country is too far from North America and Northwest Europe, the two largest relatively wealthy population concentrations.

Dairy farmers, like other commercial farmers, usually do not sell their products directly to consumers. Instead, they generally sell milk to wholesalers, who distribute it in turn to retailers. Retailers then sell milk to consumers in shops or at home. Farmers also sell milk to butter and cheese manufacturers.

Distribution of milk to consumers differs between the United States and the United Kingdom. Home delivery of milk has become rare in the United States but is still common in the United Kingdom. Many British families have a small card that looks like a clock with one hand. Before they go to sleep, they set the hand to the number of pints of milk they want delivered the next morning and place the card outside the front door. Early the next morning the milk is delivered, in bottles rather than cartons. The cream usually rises to the top of the bottle and can either be poured off or mixed in. Empty bottles are then set outside and taken away the next morning by the milkman.

Like other commercial farmers, dairy farmers face economic problems because of declining revenues and rising costs. But distinctive features of dairy farming have exacerbated the economic difficulties. First, dairy farming is labor-intensive, because the cows must be milked twice a day, every day. Although the actual milking can be done by machines, dairy farming nonetheless requires constant attention throughout the year.

Dairy farmers also face the expense of feeding the cows in the winter, when they may be unable to graze on grass. In Northwest Europe and New England, farmers generally purchase hay or grain for winter feed. In the western part of the U.S. dairy region, crops are more likely to be grown in the summer and stored for winter feed on the same farm.

Grain Farming

Some form of **grain** is the major crop on most farms. Geographers distinguish between commercial grain agriculture and mixed crop and livestock farming because crops on a grain farm are grown primarily for consumption by humans rather than

by livestock. Although farms in developing countries also grow crops for human consumption, the output is directly consumed by the farmers. Commercial grain farms, on the other hand, sell the output to manufacturers of food products.

Large-scale commercial grain production is found in only five countries: the United States, Canada, the Soviet Union, Argentina, and Australia. Commercial grain farms are generally located in regions that are too dry for mixed crop and livestock agriculture (Figure 9–8).

The most important crop grown is hard wheat, used to make bread flour. Wheat generally can be sold for a higher price than other grains, such as rye, oats, and barley, and has more uses as human food. It can be stored relatively easily without spoiling and can be transported a long distance. Because wheat has a relatively high value per unit weight, it can be shipped profitably from remote farms to markets.

Large-scale grain production is concentrated in three areas of North America. The first is the winter

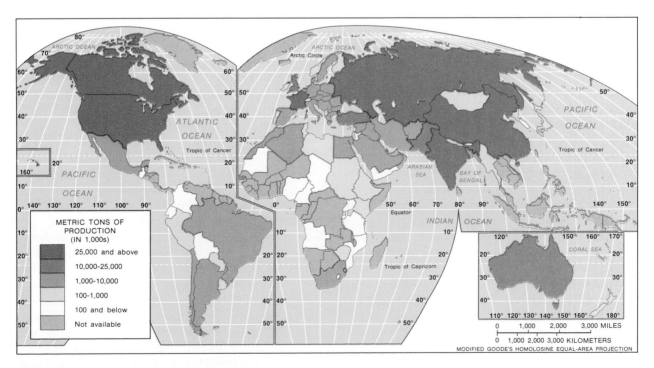

FIGURE 9–8
Wheat production. China is the world's leading wheat producer, followed by the Soviet Union and the United States. But the United States is by far the leading wheat exporter.

wheat belt that extends through Kansas, Colorado, and Oklahoma. In the **winter wheat** area, the crop is planted in the autumn and develops a strong root system before growth stops for the winter. The wheat survives the winter, especially if it is under a snow blanket, and is ripe by the beginning of summer.

The second important grain-producing region in North America is the spring wheat belt of the Dakotas, Montana, and southern Saskatchewan, Canada. Because winters are usually too severe for winter wheat in the Dakotas and Canada, **spring wheat** is planted in the spring and harvested in the late summer. Approximately two-thirds of the wheat grown in the United Staets comes either from the winter or the spring wheat belt. A third important grain-growing region is the Palouse region of Washington state.

Large-scale grain production, like other commercial farming ventures in relatively developed countries, is heavily mechanized, conducted on large farms, and oriented to consumer preferences. The McCormick reaper, invented in the 1830s, first permitted large-scale wheat production. Today, the **combine** machine performs in one operation the three tasks of **reaping,** threshing, and cleaning.

Unlike work on a mixed crop and livestock farm, the effort required to grow wheat is not uniform throughout the year. Some individuals or firms may therefore have two sets of fields, one in the spring-wheat belt and one in the winter-wheat belt. Because the planting and harvesting in the two regions occur at different times of the year, the work load can be distributed throughout the year. In addition, the same machinery can be used in the two regions, thus spreading out the cost of the expensive equipment. Combine companies start working in Oklahoma in early summer and move north.

Wheat's significance extends beyond the amount of land or number of people involved in growing it. Unlike other agricultural products, wheat is grown to a considerable extent for international trade and is the world's leading export crop. Because the United States and Canada account for about half of the world's wheat exports, the North American prairies are accurately labelled the world's "breadbasket." The ability to provide food for many people elsewhere in the world is a major source of eco-

nomic and political strength for the United States and Canada.

Ranching

Ranching, the commercial grazing of livestock over an extensive area, is a form of agriculture adapted to semiarid or arid land. It is practiced in relatively developed countries where the vegetation is too sparse and the soil too dry to support crops. The importance of ranching in the United States extends beyond the number of people who choose this form of commercial farming because of its prominence in popular culture, especially in Hollywood films and television.

Columbus, on his second voyage, first brought cattle to the Americas because the animals were sufficiently hardy to survive the ocean crossing. Living in the wild, the cattle multiplied and thrived on the abundant supply of grazing land on the frontiers of North and South America. Immigrants from Spain and Portugal—the only European countries with a tradition of cattle ranching—began ranching in the Americas. They taught the practice to settlers from Northern Europe and the Eastern United States who moved to Texas and other frontier territories in the nineteenth century.

Transportation of cattle to markets. Cattle ranching in Texas, as glamorized in popular culture, actually dominated commercial agriculture for a short period of time—from 1867 to 1885. This period of cattle ranching began because of increased demand for beef in the eastern United States during the 1860s.

The challenge for ranchers was to transport the cattle to the Eastern markets. Ranchers who could get the cattle to Chicago were paid $30–40 per head, compared to only $3–4 per head in Texas. Once in Chicago, the cattle could be slaughtered and processed by meat-packing companies and sold to consumers in the East.

To reach Chicago, cattle were driven several hundred kilometers over trails from Texas to the nearest rail line and transferred to cattle cars for the rest of the journey. In 1867, the western terminus of the rail line reached Abilene, Kansas. That year, a man named Joseph G. McCoy (on whom the expression "the real McCoy" was based) launched a massive construction effort to provide Abilene with homes, shops, and stockyards. As a result, the number of cattle brought into Abilene increased from 1,000 in 1867 to 35,000 in 1868 and 150,000 in 1869. McCoy became the first mayor of the city of Abilene.

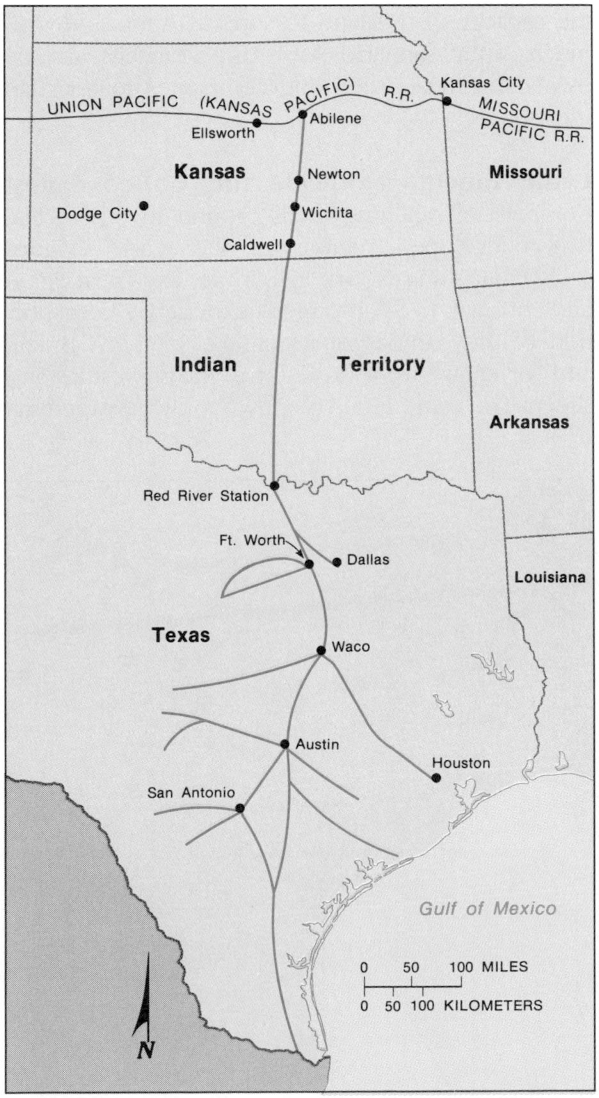

FIGURE 9–9
Chisholm Trail. Although actively used for only a few years, the Chisholm Trail became famous in American folklore as the main route for the movement of cattle from Texas to railheads in Kansas.

Like other frontier towns, Abilene became a haven for cowboys to let off steam. Gunfights, prostitution, gambling, and alcoholism were rampant until McCoy hired James B. "Wild Bill" Hickock as sheriff. After a few years, the terminus of the railroad moved further west. Wichita, Caldwell, Dodge City, and other towns in Kansas took their turn as the main destination for the cattle driven north on trails from Texas. Abilene became a ghost town for awhile. Eventually, though, use of the surrounding land changed from cattle grazing to crop growing, and Abilene became a prosperous market center.

The most famous route from Texas was the Chisholm Trail, which began near Brownsville and extended northward through Texas, Indian Territory (now the state of Oklahoma), and Kansas. The Trail had many branches, but the main line extended through Austin, Waco, Fort Worth, and Caldwell (Figure 9–9). The Western Trail became more important in the 1870s when the railroad terminus moved further west. Today, U.S. Route 81 roughly follows the course of the Chisholm Trail.

Fixed-location ranching. Cattle ranching declined in importance during the 1880s, after it came in conflict with sedentary agriculture. Most early U.S. ranchers adhered to "The Code of the West," though the system had no official legal status. Under the code, ranchers had range rights—that is, their cattle could graze on any open land and had access to scarce water sources and grasslands. The early cattle ranchers in the West owned little land, only cattle.

The U.S. government, which owned most of the land used for open grazing, began to sell it to farmers to grow crops, leaving ranchers with no legal claim to it. For a few years, the ranchers tried to drive out the farmers by cutting fences and then illegally erecting their own fences on public land. The farmers' most potent weapon proved to be barbed wire, first produced commercially in 1873. The farmers eventually won the battle, and ranchers were compelled to buy or lease land to accommodate their cattle. Large cattle ranches were established, primarily on land that was too dry to support crops—though ironically, 60 percent of the cattle grazing done today is on land leased from the U.S. government.

Ranchers were also induced to switch from cattle drives to fixed-location ranching by a change in the predominant breed of cattle. Longhorns, the first cattle used by ranchers were hardy animals, able to survive the long-distance drive along the trails with little weight loss. But longhorns had two fundamental problems. First, they were susceptible to cattle ticks, which carried a fever and were difficult to remove. Second, the meat of longhorns was poor quality.

New cattle breeds introduced from Europe, such as the Hereford, offered superior meat but were not adapted to the old ranching system. The new breeds could not survive the winter by open grazing, as could the longhorns. Instead, crops had to be grown or feed purchased for them. The cattle could not be driven long distances, and they required more water. These breeds thrived once open grazing was replaced by fixed ranching, and long-distance trail drives and rail journeys to Chicago gave way to short rail or truck trips to nearby meat packers.

With the spread of irrigation techniques and hardier crops, land in the United States has been converted from ranching to crop growing. Ranching generates lower income per area of land, though it has lower operating costs. Cattle are still raised on ranches but are frequently sent for fattening to farms or to local feed lots along major railroad and highway routes rather than directly to meat processors. The average size of a ranch is large, because the capacity of the land to support cattle is low in much of the semiarid West. Large ranches may be owned by meat-processing companies rather than individuals.

Cattle ranching outside the United States. Commercial ranching is also found in other relatively developed regions of the world (Figure 9–10). Ranching is rare in Europe, except in Spain and Portugal. In South America, though, a large portion of the pampas of Argentina, southern Brazil, and Uruguay are devoted to grazing cattle and sheep. The cattle industry grew rapidly in Argentina

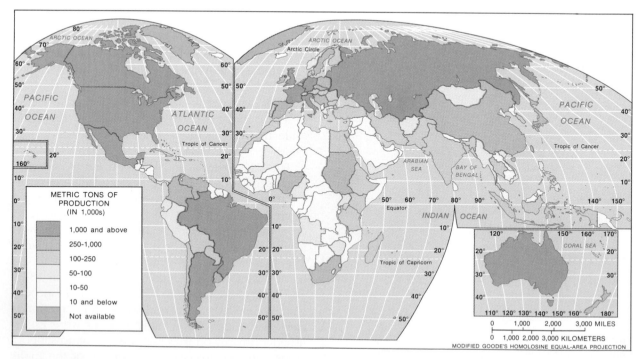

FIGURE 9–10
Beef and veal production. The production of beef, like milk, is clustered in relatively developed countries. People in developing countries consume few meat products, both because of cultural preferences and because of lack of income to pay for them.

in part because the land devoted to ranching was relatively accessible to the ocean, and meat could be transported to overseas markets.

The relatively humid climate on the pampas also stimulated the growth of ranching in South America, because more cattle can graze on a given area of land than in the U.S. West. Land was divided into large holdings in the nineteenth century, in contrast to the U.S. practice of permitting common grazing on public land. Ranching has declined in Argentina, as in the United States, because growing crops is more profitable except on very dry lands.

The interior of Australia was opened for grazing in the nineteenth century, though sheep are more common than cattle. Ranches in the Middle East, New Zealand, and South Africa are also more likely to have sheep. Like the U.S. West, Australia's dry lands went through several land use changes. Until the 1860s, shepherding was practiced on the open range. Then large ranches with fixed boundaries were established, stock was improved, and water facilities were expanded. Eventually, ranching was confined to drier lands, and wheat—which yielded greater profits per hectare than ranching—was planted where precipitation levels permitted.

Thus, ranching has followed similar stages around the world. First was the herding of animals over open ranges, in a seminomadic style. Then, ranching was transformed into fixed farming by dividing the open land into ranches. Many of the farms converted to growing crops, and ranching was confined to the drier lands. To survive, the remaining ranches experimented with new methods of breeding and sources of water and feed. Ranching became part of the meat-processing industry rather than an economic activity carried out on isolated farms. In this way, commercial ranching differs from pastoral nomadism, the form of animal herding practiced in developing regions.

Mediterranean Agriculture

Mediterranean agriculture exists primarily in the lands that border the Mediterranean Sea in southern Europe, northern Africa, and western Asia. Farmers in California, Central Chile, the southwestern part of South Africa, and Southwest Australia practice Mediterranean agriculture as well. The Mediterranean areas share a similar physical envi-

ronment. Every Mediterranean area borders a sea and—with the exception of some of the lands surrounding the Mediterranean Sea—are all located on the west coast of a continent. As a result, prevailing winds from the sea help to provide moisture and mild temperatures during the winter. Summers are hot and dry, but sea breezes provide some relief. The land is very hilly, and mountains frequently plunge directly down to the sea, leaving very narrow strips of flat land along the coast.

Farmers derive a smaller percentage of income from animal products in the Mediterranean region than in the mixed crop and livestock region. Livestock production is hindered during summer by the lack of water and good grazing land. Some farmers living along the Mediterranean Sea traditionally used transhumance to raise animals, though the practice is now less common. Under transhumance, animals—primarily sheep and goats—are kept on the coastal plains in the winter and transferred to the hills in the summer.

Most crops in Mediterranean lands are grown for human consumption rather than for animal feed. Tree crops and horticulture form the commercial base of the Mediterranean farming areas. Most of the world's olives, grapes, and other fruits and vegetables are grown in the Mediterranean agriculture area. A combination of local physical and cultural characteristics determines which crops will be grown in which Mediterranean farming areas. The hilly landscape encourages farmers to plant a variety of crops within one Mediterranean farming area.

In the lands bordering the Mediterranean Sea, the two most important cash crops are olives and grapes. Two-thirds of the world's wine is produced in countries that border the Mediterranean Sea, especially Italy, France, and Spain, while Mediterranean agricultural regions elsewhere in the world produce most of the remaining one-third. The lands near the Mediterranean Sea are also responsible for a large percentage of the world's supply of olives, an important source of cooking oil.

Although olives and grapes are the most important sources of income to commercial farms bordering the Mediterranean Sea, approximately half of the land is devoted to growing cereals, especially wheat for pasta and bread. As in the U.S. winter-wheat belt, the seeds are sown in the fall and harvested in early summer. After cultivation, cash crops are planted on approximately 20 percent of the land, while the remainder is left fallow for a year or two to conserve moisture in the soil.

Cereals occupy a much lower percentage of the cultivated land in California than in other Mediterranean climates. Instead, 30 percent of the California farmland is devoted to fruits and vegetables. California supplies most of the citrus fruits, tree nuts, and deciduous fruits consumed in the United States. Horticulture is practiced in other Mediterranean climates, but not to the extent found in California.

The rapid growth of urban areas in California, especially the Los Angeles area, has resulted in the conversion of high-quality agricultural land to housing developments. Thus far, the loss of farmland has been more than offset by the expansion of agriculture into arid lands. But farming in arid lands requires massive irrigation projects to provide an adequate water supply. In the future, agriculture may face stiffer competition to divert the Southwest's increasingly scarce water supply.

Commercial Gardening and Fruit Farming

Commercial gardening and fruit farming is the predominant type of agriculture in the U.S. southeast. The region has a long growing season and is accessible to the large markets of New York, Philadelphia, Washington, and the other eastern U.S. urban areas. The type of agriculture practiced in this region is frequently called truck farming, because *truck* was a Middle English word meaning bartering or the exchange of commodities.

Truck farms grow many of the fruits and vegetables that consumers demand in relatively developed societies, such as apples, asparagus, cherries, lettuce, mushrooms, and tomatoes. Some of these fruits and vegetables are sold fresh to consumers, but most are sold to large processors for canning or freezing.

Truck farms, highly efficient operations, are often large farms that take full advantage of available machines at every stage of the growing process. Truck farmers are willing to experiment with new varieties, seeds, fertilizers, and other inputs in order to maximize efficiency. Labor costs are kept down by hiring migrant farm workers, some of whom are illegal aliens from Mexico, to work at very low wages. Farms tend to specialize in a few crops, and a handful of farms may dominate national output of some fruits and vegetables.

Plantation Farming

The plantation is a form of commercial agriculture found in the tropics and subtropics, especially in Latin America, Africa, and Asia. Although generally situated in developing countries, plantations are often owned or operated by Europeans or North Americans and grow crops for sale primarily in relatively developed countries.

A **plantation** is a large farm that specializes in the production of one or two crops for sale. Among the most important crops found on plantations are cotton, sugar cane, coffee, rubber, and tobacco. Cocoa, jute, bananas, tea, coconuts, and palm oil are also produced in large quantities. Latin American plantations are more likely to grow coffee, sugar cane, and bananas, while Asian plantations may provide rubber and palm oil.

Because plantations are usually situated in sparsely settled locations, they must import workers and provide them with food, housing, and social services. Plantation managers try to spread the work as evenly as possible throughout the year to make full use of the large labor force. Where the climate permits, more than one crop is planted and harvested during the year. Rubber tree plantations can try to spread the task of tapping the trees through the year. Crops such as tobacco, cotton, and sugar cane, which can be planted only once a year, are less likely to be grown on large plantations today than they were in the past.

Crops are normally processed at the plantation before shipping. Processed goods are less bulky and therefore cheaper to ship long distances to the North American and European markets.

Until the Civil War, plantations were important in the U.S. South. The principal crop was cotton, followed by tobacco and sugar cane. Demand for cotton increased dramatically after the establishment of textile factories in England at the start of the industrial revolution in the late eighteenth century. Cotton production was stimulated by the invention of the cotton gin by Eli Whitney in 1793 and the development of new varieties which were hardier and easier to pick. Slaves brought from Africa performed most of the labor, until the abolition of slavery and the defeat of the South in the Civil War. Thereafter, plantations declined in the United States; they were subdivided and either sold to individual farmers or worked by tenant farmers.

Summary

Although most people in the world are farmers, significant differences exist among the types of farming practiced. A country's agricultural system is one of the best measures of its level of economic development and standard of material comfort. These again are the key questions concerning agricultural geography:

1. **What were the origin and process of diffusion of agriculture?** Prior to the development of agriculture, people survived by hunting animals, gathering wild vegetation, or fishing. Agriculture was not simply invented but was the product of thousands of years of experiments and accidents. Vegetative planting apparently originated primarily in Southeast Asia and diffused to the north and west. Significant advances in settled agriculture, including domestication of wheat and barley and integration of herd animals with crop grazing, originated in Southwest Asia. Agricultural practices probably originated independently in the Western Hemisphere.

2. **What are the main types of agriculture in developing countries?** Most people in the world, especially those in developing countries, are subsistence farmers, growing crops primarily to feed themselves. Geographers can identify several kinds of subsistence agriculture in the world, including shifting cultivation, intensive farming, and pastoral nomadism. Regions where subsistence agriculture is practiced are characterized by a large percentage of the labor force engaged in agriculture, with few mechanical aids.

3. **How does agriculture in developing and relatively developed countries differ?** Few people in the relatively developed countries are farmers. These few farmers are able to produce an abundant supply of food through the use of expensive machinery and scientific techniques. Farmers in relatively developed countries, who grow crops and raise livestock for sale off the farm to processors, are only one part of a large food production industry.

4. **What are the main types of agriculture in relatively developed countries?** The most common type of farm found in relatively developed societies is mixed crop and livestock. Land is generally devoted to growing crops, but income is derived primarily from the sale of animal products, because most of the crops are used to feed animals rather than people. Where mixed crop and livestock farming is not suitable, commercial farmers practice a variety of other types of agriculture, including dairying, commercial grain, and ranching.

Problems for Farmers

Ironically, both subsistence and commercial farmers face a similar problem: farming is not producing a sufficiently high income for the desired standard of living. The underlying cause of low incomes, however, differs significantly between developing and relatively developed countries.

Problems for Subsistence Farmers. The fundamental problem in developing countries is to assure an adequate supply of food for the people. Traditional subsistence farming can continue to produce enough food for people living in rural villages to survive, assuming there is no drought, flood, or other natural disaster. But developing countries must provide enough food for a rapidly increasing population as well as for the growing number of urban residents who cannot grow their own food.

Subsistence farmers lack the land and supplies needed to expand crop production; they need higher-yield seeds, fertilizer, and tools. How can they obtain these aids? To some extent, farmers can secure needed supplies through the barter of food with urban dwellers. For many African and Asian countries, though, agricultural supplies must be obtained primarily by importing from other countries. Yet these countries do not have enough money to buy agricultural equipment and replacement parts from relatively developed countries.

How can developing countries generate the funds they need to buy agricultural equipment? They must produce something they can sell in relatively developed countries. Developing countries try to sell manufactured goods, but most raise funds through the sale of crops in relatively developed countries. Consumers in relatively developed countries are willing to pay high prices for fruits and vegetables that would otherwise be out of season or for crops such as coffee and tea that cannot be grown there because of the climate.

A handful of developing countries, especially in Latin America and Asia, have turned to production of crops that can be converted to drugs (Figure 9–11). Various drugs, such as coca leaf, marijuana, opium, and hashish, have distinctive geographic arrangements. Coca leaf is grown principally in four contiguous countries in northwestern South America. One-half of the supply comes from Peru, more than one-fourth from Bolivia, and most of the remainder from Columbia and Ecuador. Some 80 percent of the processing of cocaine, as well as its distribution to the United States and other relatively developed countries, is based in Colombia.

Mexico grows the overwhelming majority of marijuana that reaches the United States, followed by Colombia, Jamaica, and Belize. Mexico is also responsible for some of the opium, but most originates in Asia. Southeast Asia is the center of opium production, with more than half produced in Myanmar, followed by Laos. Thailand produces some opium, as well, but its main role is to serve as the transportation hub for distribution to relatively developed countries. Farther west in Asia, Afghanistan, Iran, and Pakistan are also major opium producers. Afghanistan and Pakistan are also major producers of hashish, as are Lebanon and Morocco.

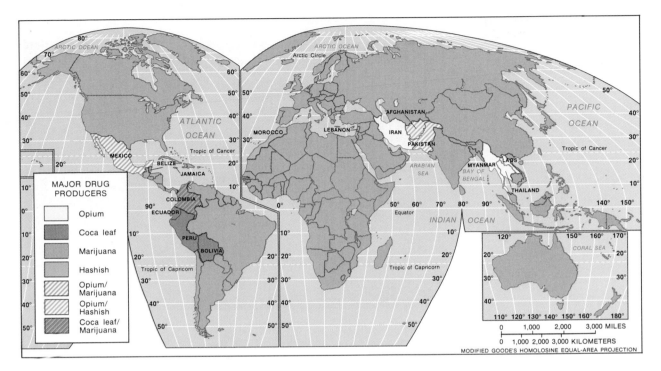

FIGURE 9–11
Sources of drugs. Instead of concentrating on subsistence agriculture, farmers in some developing countries prefer to grow crops that are converted to drugs sold in relatively developed countries.

The sale of export crops brings a developing country foreign currency, a portion of which can be used to buy agricultural supplies. But governments in developing countries face a dilemma: the more land that is devoted to growing export crops, the less is available to growing crops for domestic consumption. Rather than helping to increase productivity, the funds generated through the sale of export crops may be needed to feed the people who switched from subsistence farming to growing export crops.

Problems for Commercial Farmers. Commercial farmers suffer from low incomes because they produce too much rather than too little food. A surplus of food has been produced because of widespread adoption of efficient agricultural practices. The diffusion of new seeds, fertilizers, and pesticides, as well as mechanical equipment, has enabled farmers to obtain greatly increased yields per area of land. Thus, commercial farmers have dramatically increased the capacity of the land to produce food.

While the supply of food has increased in the relatively developed countries, demand has remained constant because the market for most products is already saturated. In relatively developed countries, consumption of a particular commodity may not change significantly if the price changes. Americans, for example, do not switch from wheat to corn products if the price of corn falls more rapidly than wheat. Demand is also stagnant for most agricultural products in relatively developed countries because of low population growth.

Afghanistan is a major producer of opium, produced from dry juice from opium poppies.

The U.S. government has adopted three types of policies to attack the problem of excess productive capacity. First, farmers are encouraged to avoid producing crops that are in excess supply. Because soil erosion is a constant threat, the government encourages planting fallow crops, such as clover, to restore nutrients to the soil. These crops can be used for hay, forage for pigs, or producing seeds for sale.

Second, the government buys surplus food production. The main method by which the policy is carried out is a system of price supports. The government guarantees to buy certain commodities at fixed prices, which are calculated to give the farmer the same price for the commodity today as in the past, when compared with other consumer goods and services.

Third, the government encourages consumption of excess grain by selling or donating it to foreign governments. In addition, low-income Americans receive food stamps in part to stimulate their purchase of additional food.

The United States spent $134 billion during the 1980s on farm subsidies, including $59 billion for feed grains, such as corn and soybeans, $22 billion for wheat, and $16 billion for dairy products. But spending varied annually, from more than $25 billion in 1986 and $22 billion in 1987 to less than $5 billion in 1981 and $10 billion in 1989. Subsidy payments are lower in years when market prices rise and production is down, typically as a result of poor weather conditions in the United States or political problems in other countries.

U.S. policies point out a fundamental irony in worldwide agricultural patterns. In a relatively developed country such as the United States, farmers are encouraged to grow less food, while developing countries struggle to increase food production at the same rate as the growth in population.

Key Terms

Agribusiness Commercial agriculture characterized by integration of different steps in the food-processing industry, usually through ownership by large corporations.

Agriculture The deliberate effort to modify a portion of the earth's surface through the cultivation of crops and the raising of livestock for sustenance or economic gain.

Cereal grain A grass-yielding grain for food.

Chaff Husks of grain separated from the seed by threshing.

Combine A machine that reaps, threshes, and cleans grain while moving over a field.

Commercial agriculture Agriculture undertaken primarily to generate products for sale off the farm.

Crop Grain or fruit gathered from a field as a harvest during a particular season.

Double cropping Harvesting twice a year from the same field.

Grain Seed of a cereal grass.

Hull The outer covering of a seed.

Intensive subsistence agriculture A form of subsistence agriculture in which farmers must expend a relatively large amount of effort to produce the maximum feasible yield from a parcel of land.

Milkshed The area surrounding a city from which milk is supplied.

Paddy Malay word for wet rice, commonly but incorrectly used to describe a sawah.

Pastoral nomadism A form of subsistence agriculture based on herding domesticated animals.

Pasture Grass or other plants grown for feeding grazing animals, as well as land used for grazing.

Plantation A large farm in tropical and subtropical climates that specializes in the production of one or two crops for sale, usually in a relatively developed country.

Ranching A form of commercial agriculture in which livestock graze over an extensive area.

Reaping Process of gathering a harvest by cutting.

Sawah A flooded field for growing rice.

Seed agriculture Reproduction of plants through introduction of seeds, which result from sexual fertilization.

Shifting cultivation A form of subsistence agriculture in which people shift activity from one field to another; each field is used for crops for a relatively few years and left fallow for a relatively long period.

Spring wheat Wheat planted in the spring and harvested in the late summer.

Subsistence agriculture Agriculture designed primarily to provide food for direct consumption by the farmer and the farmer's family.

Swidden A patch of land cleared for planting through slashing and burning.

Thresh To beat out grain from stalks by trampling it.

Transhumance The seasonal migration of livestock between mountains and lowland pastures.

Vegetative planting Reproduction of plants by direct cloning from existing plants.

Wet rice Rice grown for much of its growing period in deliberately flooded fields.

Winnow To remove chaff by allowing it to be blown away by the wind.

Winter wheat Wheat planted in the fall and harvested in the early summer.

Thinking Geographically

1. Assume that the United States constitutes one agricultural market, centered around New York City, the largest metropolitan area. To what extent can the major agricultural regions of the United States be viewed as irregularly shaped rings around the market center, as von Thünen applied to northern Germany?
2. New Zealand once sold nearly all of its dairy products to the British, but since the United Kingdom joined the European Community in 1973, New Zealand has been forced to find other markets. Are there other examples of countries that have restructured their agricultural production in the face of increased global interdependence and regional cooperation?
3. Review the concept of overpopulation (the number of people in an area exceeds the capacity of the environment to support life at a decent standard of living). What agricultural regions have relatively limited capacities to support intensive food production? Which of these regions face rapid population growth?
4. Compare world distributions of corn, wheat, and rice production. To what extent do differences derive from environmental conditions and to what extent from food preferences and other social customs?
5. How might the loss of farmland on the edge of rapidly growing cities alter the choice of crops that other farmers make in a commercial agricultural society?

Further Readings

Babbington, Anthony, and Judith Carney. "Geography in the International Agricultural Research Centers: Theoretical and Practical Concerns," *Annals of the Association of American Geographers* 80 (March 1990): 34–48.

Bascom, Johnathan B. "Border Pastoralism in Eastern Sudan," *Geographical Review* 80 (October 1990): 416–430.

Cochran, Williard W., and Mary E. Ryan. *American Farm Policy 1948–73.* Minneapolis, MN: University of Minnesota Press, 1976.

Cromley, Robert G. "The Von Thünen Model and Environmental Uncertainty." *Annals of the Association of American Geographers* 72 (September 1982): 404–10.

Dahlberg, Kenneth A., ed. *New Directions for Agriculture and Agricultural Research: Neglected Dimensions and Emerging Alternatives.* Totowa, NJ: Rowman and Allanheld, 1986.

Dove, Michael R. *Swidden Agriculture in Indonesia: The Subsistence Strategies of the Kalimantan Kantú.* Amsterdam: Mouton, 1985.

Duckham, A. N., and G. B. Masefield. *Farming Systems of the World.* New York: Praeger, 1970.

Durand, Loyal, Jr. "The Major Milksheds of the Northeastern Quarter of the United States." *Economic Geography* 40 (January 1964): 9–33.

Ebeling, Walter. *The Fruited Plain: The Story of American Agriculture.* Berkeley, CA: University of California Press, 1979.

Furuseth, Owen J., and John T. Pierce. *Agricultural Land in an Urban Society.* Washington, D.C.: Association of American Geographers, 1982.

Grigg, David B. *An Introduction to Agricultural Geography.* London: Hutchinson Education, 1984.

————. *The Agricultural Systems of the World: An Evolutionary Approach.* London: Cambridge University Press, 1974.

Hart, John Fraser. "Change in the Corn Belt." *Geographical Review* 76 (January 1986): 51–73.

Heathcote, R. L. *The Arid Lands: Their Use and Abuse.* London: Longman, 1983.

Hewes, Leslie, and Christian I. Jung, "Early Fencing on the Middle Western Prairie." *Annals of the Association of American Geographers* 71 (June 1981): 177–201.

Ilbery, Brian W. *Agricultural Geography: A Social and Economic Analysis.* New York: Oxford University Press, 1985.

Lewthwaite, G. R. "Wisconsin and the Waikato: A Comparative Study of Dairy Farming in the United States and New Zealand." *Annals of the Association of American Geographers* 54 (March 1974): 59–87.

Pannell, Clifton. "Recent Chinese Agriculture." *Geographical Review* 75 (April 1985): 170–85.

Peters, William J., and Leon F. Neuenschwander. *Slash and Burn: Farming in the Third World Forest.* Moscow, ID: University of Idaho Press, 1988.

Sauer, Carl O. *Agricultural Origins and Dispersals.* 2d ed. Cambridge, MA: M.I.T. Press, 1969.

Smith, Everett G., Jr. "America's Richest Farms and Ranches." *Annals of the Association of American Geographers* 70 (December 1980): 528–41.

Symons, Leslie. *Agricultural Geography.* rev. ed. London: G. Bell, 1979.

Tarrant, John R. *Agricultural Geography.* New York: Wiley, 1974.

Turner, B. L., II, and Stephen B. Brush, eds. *Comparative Farming Systems.* New York: Guilford, 1987.

Von Thünen, Johann Heinrich. *von Thünen's Isolated State: An English Edition of "Der Isolierte Staat."* Translated by Carla M. Wartenberg. Elmsford, NY: Pergamon Press, 1966.

Whittlesey, Derwent. "Major Agricultural Regions of the Earth." *Annals of the Association of American Geographers* 26 (September 1936): 199–240.

10
Industry

Japanese products, including televisions, cars, and cameras, have deluged the United States and Canada in recent years. Although manufactured thousands of kilometers away, these products are often sold in North America at a lower cost than those of domestic competitors and, according to many people, at a higher level of quality. This accomplishment seems even more remarkable when recalling that Japan in 1945 was a defeated and battered enemy.

The recent success of Japan, as well as South Korea, Taiwan, and other Asian countries, represents a change from the historic dominance of world industry by Western countries. The industrial revolution originated in Great Britain in the eighteenth century and diffused to Europe and North America in the nineteenth century. The high standard of living most people in Western Europe and North America enjoy is based on industrial power.

While the success of Asian countries is admirable, their profit may be North America's loss. For every new Toyota sold in the United States and Canada, one fewer Chevrolet may be manufactured. As Asian manufacturers expand their factories, North American companies lay off workers. Thus, the preference of American and Canadian consumers for Japanese motor vehicles hurts the economies of the United States and Canada.

On the other hand, if we truly believe in international cooperation, then consumers should be encouraged to buy products regardless of national origin. If the Japanese or South Koreans can build better cars at lower prices, perhaps that should be a challenge to North American companies.

Maquiladoras in Mexico

Edi Bencomo is a factory worker in Ciudad Juárez, Mexico. Her job is to clip together several color-coded wires for Alambrados y Circuitos Electricos, a factory owned by the Packard Electric Division of General Motors.

Bencomo migrated to Juárez four years ago, at age 16, from Madera, a village in the Sierra Madre Occidental mountains 300 kilometers (200 miles) to the southwest. One of seven children, Bencomo saw no future for herself remaining on her parent's corn farm. Had she remained in Madera, Bencomo would have probably joined the ranks of the unemployed, who comprise 25 percent of the villagers.

In Juárez, Bencomo lives with her husband in a two-room shack located more than one hour away from the plant. They could afford to rent a somewhat better dwelling, but none are available in the rapidly growing city. She leaves their house each weekday at 4 A.M. to battle the crowds of workers trying to get on one of the buses that serve the city's factory area.

Bencomo earns Mexico's minimum wage, about 50 cents an hour. In addition to her wages, she receives two important benefits by working for Packard: a bus pass so she can reach the plant at no cost and two meals in the cafeteria paid for almost entirely by the company. She considers her job to be superior to that of her husband, who makes piñatas; both are paid the minimum wage but he receives no benefits.

Packard's Juárez plant is known as a *maquiladora,* derived from the Spanish verb *maquilar,* which means to take measure or payment for grinding or processing corn; the term originally applied to a tax when Mexico was a colony of Spain. Under U.S. and Mexican laws, companies receive tax breaks if they ship materials from the United States, assemble components at a *maquiladora* plant in Mexico, and import the finished product back to the United States. More than a thousand U.S. companies have established *maquiladoras* in Mexico; General Motors alone has two dozen *maquiladoras* employing more than 25,000 people and is now Mexico's largest employer (other than the Mexican government).

In January 1985, General Motors revealed that it was designing an entirely new car called the Saturn and that it would need a factory somewhere in the United States to build it. The announcement touched off a fierce competition among states and localities to become the home for the Saturn plant. All 1,700 schoolchildren in New Hampton, Iowa, wrote letters to GM executives urging that their town be selected. Thousands of Cleveland residents sent GM "We Want Saturn" coupons clipped from their local newspapers. Seven governors appeared on Phil Donohue's popular daytime television show to explain why their states should be chosen.

Swamped with material from competing communities, General Motors took seven months to select a factory site. The choice was Spring Hill, Tennessee, a village of 1,000 inhabitants, 50 kilometers (30 miles) south of Nashville.

GM's process of selecting a location for its Saturn factory raises several issues that geographers address. First, what factors did General Motors consider in evaluating alternative locations? Geographers recognize that two types of factors are critical in locating factories: where the automobiles will be sold, and what needs to be brought to the factory to produce them.

Second, why did communities throughout the United States compete to get the Saturn factory? Government officials throughout the world recognize the critical role such an industry plays in the economic health of a community. In the global competition to attract new industries—or, in many places, to retain existing ones—a community possesses distinctive locational characteristics. Geographers identify a community's assets that enable it to compete successfully for industries, as well as its locational handicaps that must be overcome to retain older companies.

Third, why did GM feel compelled to build a new plant at all? At approximately the same time that it was building the new factory in Tennessee, GM closed more than a dozen factories elsewhere in the country. Why didn't the corporation choose to modernize one of its closed factories or perhaps construct a new factory on land cleared by demolishing an older one? To succeed in an intensely competitive global market for products such as automobiles, corporations must find the best locations for their factories.

What Were the Origin and Process of Diffusion of Industrialization?

The modern concept of industry—manufacturing goods in a factory—began in Great Britain in the late eighteenth century. The process of change known as the industrial revolution transformed both the way in which goods are produced for a society and the way people obtain food, clothing, and shelter. The industrial revolution has penetrated virtually all economic, social, and political elements of society. This section examines the sequence of changes associated with the industrial revolution and its diffusion from Great Britain to the rest of the world.

The Industrial Revolution

The industrial revolution involved a series of inventions that transformed the way in which goods were manufactured. These improvements in industrial technology created an unprecedented expansion in human productivity, resulting in substantially higher standards of living.

The term *industrial revolution* is somewhat misleading. The industrial revolution resulted in new social, economic, and political inventions, not just industrial ones. The changes involved a gradual diffusion of new ideas and techniques rather than an overnight revolution. Nonetheless, the term is commonly used to define the events of the late eighteenth and early nineteenth centuries in Western Europe and North America.

When and where did the industrial revolution originate? These questions can be answered with some precision: the north of Great Britain around 1750. From there, the industrial revolution diffused to other countries in Europe and North America in the nineteenth century and to the rest of the world in the twentieth.

Before the industrial revolution, industry was geographically dispersed across the landscape. People made household tools and agricultural equipment in their own homes or obtained them in the local village. Home-based manufacturing was known as the **cottage industry** system. One important cottage industry was textile manufacturing. People known as putters-out were hired by merchants to drop off wool at homes, where women and children sorted, cleaned, and spun it. The putters-out then picked up the finished work and paid according to the number of pieces that were completed.

The industrial revolution was characterized by the invention of hundreds of mechanical devices, but the one invention most important for the development of factories was the steam engine. The story of the steam engine begins in 1765, when James Watt, a mathematical instrument maker in Glasgow, Scotland, was asked to repair a broken model of a Newcomen engine. The Newcomen engine worked by the alternating injection and condensation of steam. To prevent the steam from condensing before the piston had completed its upward stroke, the cylinder was heated. The cylinder then had to be cooled in order to condense the steam for the return stroke. The Newcomen engine was fairly inefficient, because most of its generated energy was used to constantly warm and then cool the cylinder.

Watt's steam engine solved the problem. He introduced a separate condenser kept permanently cool while the cylinder could be permanently hot. The cylinder was drilled with precision to provide a tight fit for the piston, using a device patented by James Wilkinson in 1774 for boring the barrel of a cannon. The steam engine could pump water far more efficiently than watermills or the Newcomen engine, let alone human or animal power.

The iron and textile industries were the first to increase production through extensive use of the steam engine and other new inventions. From the needs of these two pioneer industries, new industrial techniques diffused during the nineteenth century.

Diffusion from the Iron Industry

The first industry to benefit from Watt's steam engine was iron. To produce iron, the iron **ore** had to be **smelted** in a **blast furnace** and the molten metal turned into crude, easily transported molds, known as **pigs.** The pig iron could then be remelted to form **cast iron, wrought iron,** or steel.

Although the usefulness of iron and steel had been known for centuries, the scale of production had always been small. The process of constantly heating and cooling the iron was a time-consuming

and skilled operation, because power could not be generated to keep the ovens hot for a sufficiently long time. The Watt steam engine enabled ovens to be heated more economically at a higher temperature.

Henry Cort, a navy agent, established an iron **forge** near Fareham, England, and in 1783 patented two processes known as puddling and rolling. **Puddling** involved reheating pig iron until it was pasty and then stirring it with iron rods until carbon and other impurities were burned off. The **rolling** process involved passing pig iron between iron rollers to remove remaining **dross.** The combination of Watt's engine and Cort's iron purification process resulted in an increase in iron-manufacturing capability.

The needs of the iron industry generated innovations in coal mining, engineering, transportation, and other industries. These inventions, in turn, permitted the modernization of other industrial activities.

Coal. Iron and steel manufacturing required power for both the blast ovens and the engines. Wood, the main source of power before the industrial revolution, became increasingly scarce because it was needed for the construction of ships, buildings, and furniture, as well as for heat. When Abraham Darby of Coalbrookdale in Shropshire, England, produced high-quality iron smelted with purified carbon made from coal—known as **coke**—an abundant source of energy for industry was developed.

To a considerable extent, because of the need for large quantities of coal, the iron industry changed from a dispersed to a clustered pattern. Blast furnaces, forges, and mills that had been scattered in separate small plants were combined into large, integrated factories. These factories clustered at four locations: Staffordshire, South Yorkshire, Clydeside, and South Wales. Each of the four sites was near a large coalfield (Figure 10–1).

Engineering. In 1795, Watt decided to go into business for himself rather than serve as a consultant to industrialists. He and Matthew Boulton established the Soho Foundry at Birmingham, England, and produced hundreds of new machines designed to improve industrial processes still further. The modern engineering and machine-parts industries derived from this operation. Technical expertise

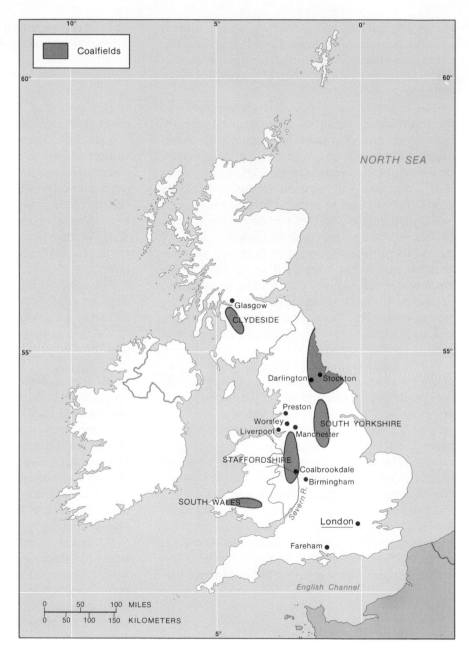

FIGURE 10–1
The industrial revolution originated in northern England and southern Scotland in the late eighteenth century. Factories clustered near large coalfields.

was required to invent new machines, apply existing ones to new situations, and repair broken equipment.

Transportation. The new engineering profession made its biggest impact on transportation, especially canals and railways. Transportation inventions played a critical role in the diffusion of the industrial revolution. New transportation systems enabled factories to attract large numbers of workers, bring in bulky raw materials, and ship finished goods to consumers.

In 1759, Francis Egerton, the second duke of Bridgewater, decided to build a canal between

Worsley and Manchester. He hired James Brindley to direct the project, which took two years to complete. This feat launched a generation of British canal construction that enabled industrial goods and workers to be moved longer distances relatively quickly and inexpensively. An extension of the duke's canal in 1767 permitted ships to travel between the sea and Manchester, 80 kilometers (50 miles) inland.

The canals were soon superseded by the invention of another transportation system, the railway. The iron horse—as the railway was frequently called—more than any other invention symbolized the impact of the new engineering profession on the industrial revolution. The railway was not invented by one person; two separate engineering improvements were required: the locomotive and the iron rail.

A locomotive using Watt's steam engine was invented by William Symington and William Murdoch in 1784, but it was impractical to operate in congested city streets. Meanwhile, in 1767, Richard Reynolds had constructed an iron track to facilitate the movement of horse-drawn wagons from the Coalbrookdale coal mines to the Severn River.

Many people thought that running a steam locomotive on iron rails was impossible because the wheels would slip off the rails. William Hedley demonstrated in 1812, however, that the steam locomotive could run on rails if the wheels had rims. The first public railway was opened between Stockton and Darlington in the north of England in 1825, using a locomotive named the Rocket, designed by George Stephenson. The Rocket firmly established the benefits of steam locomotives when, in 1829, it won a race against a horse on the Liverpool and Manchester Railway and averaged 38 kilometers (24 miles) per hour.

Diffusion from the Textile Industry

At the same time the engineering industries developed, a revolution in **textile** (woven-fabric) manufacturing was underway. A series of inventions between 1760 and 1800 transformed the production of textiles from a dispersed cottage industry to a concentrated factory system.

Richard Arkwright, a Preston barber and wig-maker, produced a **spinning frame** for yarn in 1768 that used **rollers** to untangle the twisted cotton before being wrapped around a **spindle.** Seven years later Arkwright patented a process for **carding** with cylinders to untwist the thread prior to its use in sewing. Because these two operations required more power than human beings could provide, the textile industry joined iron at an early date in adopting Watt's steam engine to generate power.

Like iron, the textile industry changed from a large collection of dispersed home-based enterprises, each performing a separate task, to a small number of large, integrated firms clustered in a few locations. The large supply of steam power produced by Watt's engines induced firms to concentrate all steps in one building attached to the same power source.

The changes in the textile industry so far discussed relate to early stages in the process—the conversion of rough cotton into usable thread followed by **weaving,** which involves lacing together strands of yarn to form cloth. Cotton also had to be bleached and dyed before it was cut into patterns. From the clothing industry's need for new bleaching techniques emerged another industry characteristic of the industrial revolution: chemicals.

Chemicals. The traditional method of **bleaching** cotton involved either exposing the fabric to the sun or boiling it, first in a solution of ashes and then in sour milk. In 1746, John Roebuck and Samuel Garbett established a factory using sulfuric acid, obtained from burning coal, instead of sour milk. Bleaching was further modernized in Glasgow by Charles Tennant, who in 1798 produced a bleaching powder made from chlorine gas and lime, a safer product than sulfuric acid.

Meanwhile, sulfuric acid was also used to dye clothing. When combined with various metals, sulfuric acid produces another acid, called vitriol, that varies in color depending on the metal. Sulfuric acid produced a blue vitriol when combined with copper, green with iron, and white with zinc.

The chemical industry has continued to contribute to textile manufacturing in more recent times. Natural forms of cloth such as cotton and wool have been combined with chemically produced fibers made from petroleum or coal derivatives, such as nylon, dacron, and orlon. The largest textile factories are now owned by chemical companies.

Food processing. Another characteristic new industry that developed from the chemical industry was food processing. An increasing number of urban factory workers, who could not grow their own food or obtain fresh produce, required preserved food. Although such preserving techniques as drying, fermenting, and pickling had been known since ancient times, these had limited application to the needs of nineteenth-century urban residents.

In 1810, a French confectioner, Nicholas Appert, developed a method of preserving food in glass bottles that had been sterilized in boiling water. The process was made more practical by Peter Durand's 1839 invention of the tin can, which was lighter, cheaper, and easier to handle than a glass bottle. The tin can was in reality 98.5 percent steel, with a thin tin coating.

The major obstacle to large-scale canning was the time the cans had to be kept in boiling water. This is where chemical experiments contributed. In 1861, calcium chloride was added to the water, raising the temperature of boiling water from 100° C to 116° C. The time the can needed to be immersed in boiling water to ensure safety was consequently reduced from four or five hours to between twenty-five and forty minutes, depending on the product. Production of canned foods increased tenfold that year.

Diffusion of the Industrial Revolution

One structure in Great Britain, the Crystal Palace, became the most visible symbol of the industrial revolution. The Crystal Palace, a glass and iron building that looked like a very large greenhouse, was erected in London's Hyde Park to house the 1851 World's Fair, more formally known as the Great Exhibition of the Works of Industry of All Nations. The fair featured hundreds of exhibits of modern machinery, virtually all invented within the previous 100 years.

When Queen Victoria opened the Crystal Palace on May 1, 1851, Great Britain was the world's dominant industrial power. The country was responsible for producing more than half of the world's cotton fabric and iron and for mining two-thirds of the coal. The first country to be transformed by the industrial revolution, Britain had a system of production that far outpaced that of the rest of the world.

From Britain, the industrial revolution diffused to other countries in two main directions: to the east through Europe and to the west across the Atlantic Ocean to North America. From these places, industrial development subsequently reached other parts of the world.

Europeans were responsible for many early inventions of the industrial revolution in the late eighteenth century. The Belgians led the way in new coal-mining techniques, the French had the first coal-fired blast furnace for making iron, and the Germans had the first industrial cotton mill. But the industrial revolution did not make a significant impact elsewhere in Europe until the late nineteenth century.

Political instability delayed the diffusion of the industrial revolution in Europe. The French Revolution and Napoleonic Wars disrupted Europe during the late eighteenth and early nineteenth centuries, and Germany did not become a unified country until the 1870s. Other revolutions and wars plagued Europe throughout the nineteenth century.

Political problems in Europe retarded the development of modern transportation systems, especially the railway. Cooperation among small neighboring states was essential to build an efficient rail network and raise the money needed to construct and operate the system. Because such cooperation could not be attained, construction of railways in some parts of Europe did not occur until fifty years after their first appearance in Britain (Figure 10–2).

The industrial revolution reached Italy, the Netherlands, Russia, and Sweden in the late nineteenth century, though industrial development in these countries did not match the level in Belgium, France, and Germany until the twentieth century. Other Southern and Eastern European countries joined the industrial revolution during the twentieth century.

Industry arrived a bit later in the United States than in such Western European countries as France and Belgium, but it grew at a much more rapid rate. At the time of independence, the United States was a predominantly agricultural society, dependent on the import of manufactured goods from Great Britain. Manufacturing was more expensive in the United States than in Great Britain, because of a scarcity of labor and capital and the high cost of shipping to European markets.

The Crystal Palace, designed by Sir Joseph Paxton, was erected in London's Hyde Park to house the Great Exhibition of 1851. The glass and iron building was longer than six football fields and enclosed two giant elm trees. After the fair closed, the structure was rebuilt in a south London park. It burned in 1936.

The first U.S. textile mill was built in 1791 at Pawtucket, Rhode Island, by Samuel Slater, a former worker at Arkwright's factory in England. The textile industry grew rapidly after 1808, when the U.S. government imposed an embargo on European trade in order to avoid entanglement in the Napoleonic Wars. The textile industry grew from 8,000 spindles in 1808 to 31,000 in 1809 and 80,000 in 1811.

By 1860, the United States had become a major industrial nation, second only to Great Britain. With the exception of textiles, however, the leading industries at the time in the United States did not make widespread use of the new industrial processes. Instead, many engaged in processing North America's abundant food and lumber resources. Industries such as iron and steel did not apply new manufacturing techniques on a large scale in the

United States until the final third of the nineteenth century.

In the twentieth century industry has diffused to other parts of the world, including Japan, Eastern Europe, and many former British colonies, such as Canada, Australia, New Zealand, South Africa, and India. Although industrial development has diffused across the earth's surface, much of the world's industry is concentrated in four regions.

KEY ISSUE

How Is Industry Distributed?

Approximately three-fourths of the world's industrial production is concentrated in four regions—

FIGURE 10–2
The diffusion of the railway from Great Britain to the European continent reflects the diffusion of the industrial revolution. More than fifty years passed between the construction of the first railways in Britain and the first ones in some Eastern European countries.

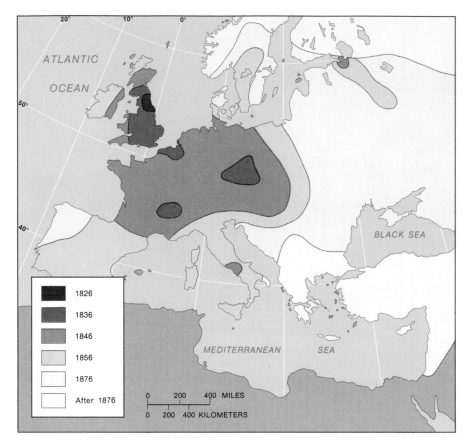

eastern North America, northwestern Europe, the west-central Soviet Union, and Japan (Figure 10–3).

The distribution of industry differs from that of agriculture. Agriculture occupies 25 percent of the earth's land area and covers extensive areas throughout the inhabited areas of the world. In contrast, less than 1 percent of the earth's land is devoted to industry. We will examine in this section each of the four industrial regions, as well as important industrial subareas within each region.

North America

Manufacturing in North America is concentrated in the northeastern portion of the United States and in southeastern Canada. The region comprises only 5 percent of the land area of these countries but contains one-third of the population and nearly two-thirds of the manufacturing output.

This manufacturing belt has achieved its dominance through a combination of historical and envi-

ronmental factors. As the first area of settlement, the East Coast of the United States was tied to European markets and industries during the first half of the nineteenth century. The early date of settlement gave the eastern cities an advantage in creating the infrastructure needed to become the country's dominant industrial center.

The northeast U.S. and southeast Canadian region became the manufacturing center of North America in part because of the availability of essential raw materials, such as iron and coal. Good transportation facilitated the movement of raw materials to the factories and manufactured goods to markets. The Great Lakes and the Mississippi, Ohio, St. Lawrence, and other rivers were supplemented in the nineteenth century by canals, railways, and highways, which helped to connect the frontier with the manufacturing centers.

New England. Within the North American manufacturing belt several subareas have emerged (Figure 10–4). The oldest industrial area in North America is southern New England. The area developed as an industrial center in the early nineteenth century, beginning with cotton textiles. Cotton was imported from southern states, and finished products were shipped to Europe. European immigrants provided an abundant supply of inexpensive labor throughout the nineteenth century. Today, New England is known for relatively skilled but expensive labor.

Middle Atlantic. The Middle Atlantic region, which includes New York City and several other important urban areas, is the United States' largest market and has long attracted industries that need proximity to a large number of consumers. Many in-

dustries that depend on foreign markets or sources of raw materials have selected a location near one of the region's main ports, including New York City (the largest U.S. port), Baltimore, Philadelphia, and Wilmington, Delaware. Other firms seek locations near the financial, communications, and entertainment industries, which are highly concentrated in New York.

Mohawk Valley. A linear industrial belt developed in upper New York state along the Hudson River and Erie Canal, the only water route between New York City and the Great Lakes. Buffalo, near the confluence of the Erie Canal and Lake Erie, is the region's most important industrial center, especially for steel and food processing. Inexpensive, abun-

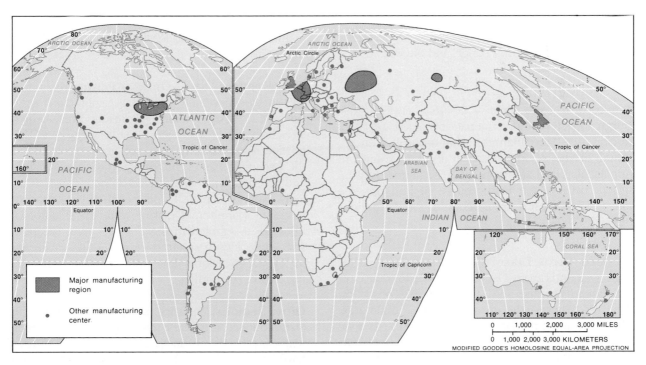

FIGURE 10–3

Distribution of industry. Manufacturing is clustered in four main regions: *Northeastern United States–Southeastern Canada*—primarily along the East Coast of the United States from Boston to Baltimore and along the Great Lakes from Toronto and Buffalo west to Chicago and Milwaukee. *Western Europe*—primarily near the Rhine and Ruhr rivers in Germany, France, Belgium, the Netherlands, and Luxembourg; southern Great Britain and northern Italy also form part of the industrial cluster. *Soviet Union*—primarily in the western or European part of the country, though more recent industrial activities have been located in the Asian part of the country, east of the Ural Mountains. *Japan*—primarily in the southern part of that country, though industrial growth has also occurred elsewhere in East Asia, especially South Korea, Taiwan, and China.

FIGURE 10-4
Manufacturing is highly clustered in several regions within the northeastern United States and southeastern Canada, though important manufacturing centers exist elsewhere in the two countries.

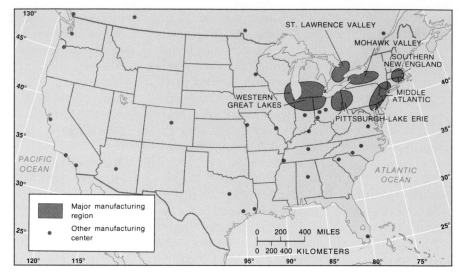

dant electricity, generated at nearby Niagara Falls, has attracted aluminum, paper, and electrochemical industries to the region.

Pittsburgh–Lake Erie. The area between Pittsburgh and Cleveland is the nation's oldest steel-producing area. Steel manufacturing originally concentrated in the region because of its proximity to Appalachian coal and iron ore. When northern Minnesota became the main source of iron ore, the Pittsburgh–Lake Erie region could bring in the ore through the Great Lakes.

Western Great Lakes. The western Great Lakes region extends from Detroit and Toledo, Ohio, on the east to Chicago and Milwaukee, Wisconsin, on the west. Chicago, the third largest U.S. urban area, is the dominant market center between the Atlantic and Pacific coasts and the hub of the U.S. transportation network. Because road, rail, air, and sea routes converge on Chicago, the city has become a transfer point between transportation systems or between routes within the same type of transportation system. Automobile manufacturers and other industries with a national market locate in the western Great Lakes region to take advantage of the convergence of transportation routes. The region's industries are also the main suppliers of machine tools, transportation equipment, clothing, furniture, agri-

cultural machinery, and food products to people living in the interior of the United States.

St. Lawrence Valley–Ontario Peninsula. Canada's most important industrial region is the St. Lawrence Valley–Ontario Peninsula area, which stretches across southern Canada along the U.S. border. The region has several assets: centrality to the Canadian market, proximity to the Great Lakes, and access to inexpensive electric power at Niagara Falls. Most of Canada's steel production is concentrated in Hamilton, Ontario, while most automobiles are assembled in the Toronto area. Inexpensive electricity has attracted aluminum manufacturing, paper making, flour mills, textile manufacturing, and sugar refining.

Other regions. Industry has grown in the United States outside the main manufacturing belt. Steel, textiles, tobacco products, and furniture industries have been dispersed through smaller communities in the South. The Gulf Coast is becoming an important industrial area because of access to oil and natural gas. Oil refining, petrochemical manufacturing, food processing, and aerospace product manufacturing are located along the Gulf coast.

Los Angeles is the largest industrial area on the West Coast for aircraft, electronics, oil refining, and sportswear. Other important West coast industrial concentrations include the aerospace industry in Seattle, food processing in the San Francisco Bay area, and naval services in San Diego.

Europe

The principal industrial region of Europe is situated in the northwest and encompasses a portion of several countries. Like the North American manufacturing belt, the European industrial region appears to be one region on a world map. In reality, several distinct districts have emerged, primarily because European countries have competed with each other to develop their own industrial areas.

The four major industrial areas within the European region are: Rhine-Ruhr Valley, mid-Rhine, Great Britain, and northern Italy. Each of these areas in turn is divided into subareas (Figure 10–5). These four areas became important for industry because of their proximity to both raw materials, such as coal and iron ore, and to large concentrations of wealthy European consumers.

Rhine-Ruhr Valley. Europe's most important industrial area is the Rhine-Ruhr Valley. The region lies for the most part in northwestern Germany but also extends into nearby areas of Belgium, France, and the Netherlands. Because of political differences, each country established its own industrial complexes.

At the heart of the region lie two rivers: the Rhine, which flows north through Germany and west through the Netherlands, and the Ruhr, which flows west across Germany into the Rhine. Within the region, industry is dispersed rather than concentrated in one or two cities. Although more than 20 million people live in the region, no individual city has more than 1 million inhabitants. Larger cities in the German portion of the region include Dortmund, Düsseldorf, and Essen. The city of Duisburg is located near where the Ruhr flows into the Rhine.

The Rhine divides into a number of branches as it passes through the Netherlands. The city of Rotterdam is located near where several of the more important branches flow into the North Sea. Because it is located at the mouth of Europe's most important river, Rotterdam has become the world's largest port.

FIGURE 10–5
A large percentage of manufacturing in Western Europe extends in a belt from the United Kingdom on the north to Italy on the south. At the core of the European manufacturing region lie Germany, France, and the Benelux countries of Belgium, the Netherlands, and Luxembourg.

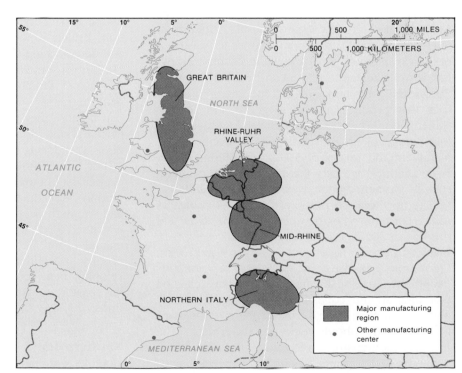

Iron and steel manufacturing has concentrated in the Rhine-Ruhr Valley because of proximity to large coalfields. Access to iron and steel production stimulated the location of other industries that made heavy use of the metals, such as locomotives, machinery, and armaments.

Mid-Rhine. The secondmost important industrial region in Europe includes southwestern Germany, northeastern France, and the small country of Luxembourg. In contrast to the Rhine-Ruhr region, the German portion of the Mid-Rhine region lacks an abundant supply of raw materials. When Germany was split into two countries after World War II, however, the Mid-Rhine region became a major industrial center. The region's primary asset was proximity to the population center of the newly created West Germany, Europe's most important market for consumer goods. Although the Mid-Rhine region is once again on the periphery of a reunified Germany, it is the most centrally located industrial area within the European Community.

The three largest cities in the German portion of the region are Frankfurt, Stuttgart, and Mannheim. Frankfurt became West Germany's most important financial and commercial center and the hub of its road, rail, and air networks As a result, Frankfurt attracted industries that produce goods for distribution to consumers throughout the country. Frankfurt is well-situated to play a comparable role in the European Community. Stuttgart specializes in industries that produce high-value goods and require skilled labor. The Mercedes-Benz and Audi automobiles rank among the city's best-known products. Mannheim, an inland port along the Rhine, has a large chemical industry that manufactures products such as synthetic fibers, dyes, and pharmaceuticals.

The northeastern portion of France—known as Alsace-Lorraine—lies between the Rhine River and the Vosges Mountains. For hundreds of years, Germany and France have fought to control the region for reasons linked to physical as well as economic geography. Historically, the Germans have claimed that they should control the Rhine River entirely and, therefore, the west bank of the river—Alsace and Lorraine—should belong to Germany. The French traditionally have argued that the Rhine formed a logical physical boundary between France and Germany.

The two countries have fought for control of Alsace and Lorraine because of economic reasons as well, since the region included Europe's largest iron ore field. Now part of France, the region produces two-thirds of that country's steel. The tiny country of Luxembourg is also one of the world's leading steel producers, because the Lorraine iron ore field extends into the southern part of the country.

Great Britain. The industrial revolution originated in the Midlands and North of England and southern Scotland, as described earlier in this chapter. Through the nineteenth century, this region dominated world production of iron and steel, textiles, and coal.

In the twentieth century, the region lost its preeminent global position. British industries are now more likely to locate in southern England, near the country's largest concentrations of population and wealth. International competition has hurt the British industrial region even more, because the world suffers from an oversupply of steel and textiles, the industries traditionally associated with the area.

British industries have faced an especially difficult challenge in regaining global competitiveness. As the first country to enter the industrial revolution, Britain is saddled with relatively outmoded and deteriorating factories and supporting services. The British sometimes refer ironically to their "misfortune" of winning World War II. The losers, Germany and Japan, have become industrial powers in part because they received American financial assistance to build modern factories in place of the ones devastated during the war.

But the problems of British industries run deeper than outmoded factories. The industrial revolution began in the northern regions of England and southern Scotland in part because those areas contained a remarkable concentration of innovative engineers and mechanics during the late eighteenth century. In the twentieth century, leadership in developing new products and industrial techniques has passed to American, German, and Japanese firms.

Northern Italy. A fourth European industrial region of some importance is found in the Po Basin of northern Italy. The region contains about one-fifth of Italy's land area but approximately half of the country's population and two-thirds of its industries.

Modern industrial development in the Po Basin began with the establishment of textile manufacturing during the nineteenth century. The Po Basin has attracted textile manufacturers and other industries because the region possesses two principal assets compared with Europe's other industrial regions. First, the region has a large supply of people willing to work for lower wages than in northern Europe. Second, the nearby Alps provide the region with inexpensive hyrdroelectricity. Industries that have concentrated in the region include processors of raw materials and assemblers of mechanical parts.

The Soviet Union

The Soviet Union has five major industrial regions: two established in the nineteenth century and three established after the 1917 revolution that brought the Communist party to power. The two prerevolutionary regions—the central industrial district and the Ukraine—are located in the western portion of the country, relatively close to other European states. The three more recently established regions—the Volga, the Urals, and Kuznetsk—are closer to the center of the country (Figure 10–6).

Central industrial district. The oldest industrial region of the Soviet Union is centered in Moscow, the country's capital and largest city. Although not well-endowed with natural resources, the central industrial district produces one-fourth of Soviet industrial output, primarily because it is situated near the country's largest market. Products manufactured in the region tend to be of high value relative to their bulk and require a large pool of skilled labor. Some 30 percent of Moscow's industrial work force is em-

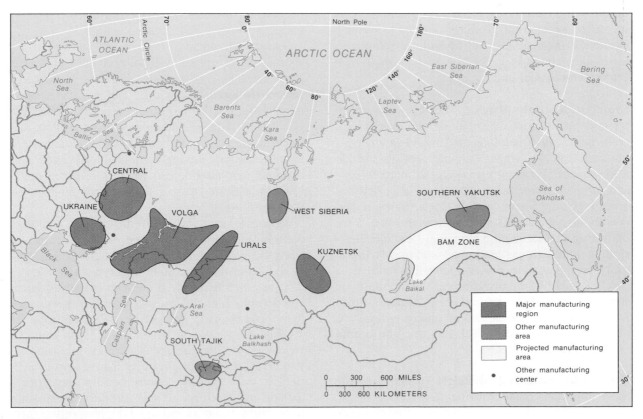

FIGURE 10–6
Manufacturing in the Soviet Union is clustered in the western or European portion of the country, though the government has encouraged growth of manufacturing regions in the center of the country east of the Ural Mountains.

ployed in making linen, cotton, wool, and silk fabrics. Moscow factories also specialize in chemicals and light industrial goods.

Ukraine industrial district. The Donets coalfield in the Ukraine industrial district is the country's leading region in the production of coal and the second leading region in the quantity of coal reserves. The Ukraine district also has large deposits of iron ore, manganese, and natural gas. As a result of these assets, the region produces nearly half of the country's pig iron and steel. The largest plants are located at Krivoy Rog, near iron ore fields, and Donetsk, near coalfields.

Volga industrial district. Situated along the Volga and Kama rivers, the district grew rapidly during World War II, when many plants in the central and Ukraine districts were occupied by the invading German army. The Volga district contains the largest petroleum and natural gas fields in the Soviet Union. Within the district, individual communities specialize in different products. The motor-vehicle industry is concentrated in Togliatti, oil refining in Kuybyshev, chemical in Saratov, metallurgy in Volgograd, and leather and fur in Kazan'.

Urals industrial district. The Ural mountain range contains more than a thousand types of minerals, the most varied collection found in any mining region in the world. Valuable deposits include iron, copper, potassium, manganese, bauxite, salt, and tungsten. Proximity to these raw materials has encouraged the Soviet Union to locate in the region new industrial activities such as iron and steel manufacturing, chemicals, and machinery and metal fabricating. Although well endowed with metals, industrial development in the district is hindered by a lack of nearby energy sources. Coal must be shipped nearly 1,500 kilometers (900 miles) from Karaganda and Kuznetsk; and oil and natural gas are piped in from the Volga-Ural, Bukhara, and central Siberian fields.

Kuznetsk industrial district. Kuznetsk is the most important manufacturing district east of the Ural Mountains. The region contains the country's largest reserves of coal and an abundant supply of iron ore. Soviet planners have taken advantage of these natural assets to invest considerable capital in constructing iron, steel, and other factories in the region.

Japan

The most important industrial region outside Europe and North America, Japan is one of the world's three leading industrial states. Despite heavy destruction in the country during World War II, Japan now ranks industrially behind only the United States and the Soviet Union. How did the Japanese accomplish this economic growth?

Japan may appear to have few geographic assets. Because it lacks many natural resources, the country must import nearly all of its energy and raw materials. For example, Japan possesses only 0.2 percent of the world's iron ore, yet it is one of the world's leading steel producers. Also, the country is far from the major concentrations of wealthy consumers in North America and Western Europe, yet it has become the world's leading exporter of consumer goods.

Faced with isolation from world markets and a shortage of nearly all essential resources, Japan has taken advantage of its one abundant resource: a large labor force. During the 1950s and 1960s, Japan initially became an industrial power by producing goods that could be sold in large quantity at cut-rate prices to consumers in other countries. Prices were kept low despite the high cost of shipping goods to overseas markets because workers received much lower wages in Japan than in North America or Western Europe.

Japanese planners, aware that other countries were building industries based on even lower-cost labor, began to train workers for highly skilled jobs. At the same time, because wages remained lower than in other relatively developed countries, Japan could build high-quality products at a lower cost than those in North America or Western Europe. As a result, during the 1970s and 1980s Japan gained a reputation for high-quality electronics, precision instruments, and other products that required well-trained workers. The country became the world's leading manufacturer of such products as automobiles, ships, cameras, radios, and televisions.

As in other countries, industry is not distributed uniformly within Japan. Manufacturing is concentrated in the central region between Tokyo and Nagasaki, especially the two large urban areas of Tokyo-Yokohama and Osaka-Kobe-Kyoto.

Although industry is located elsewhere in the world, the four industrial regions of North America, Europe, the Soviet Union, and Japan account for most of the world's industrial production. Having looked at the "where" question for industrial location, we can next consider the "why" question: Why are industries located where they are?

K E Y   I S S U E

What Factors Influence the Choice of Location for a Factory?

Industry seeks to maximize profits by minimizing production costs. Geographers try to explain why one location may prove more profitable for the location of a factory than other places.

A company ordinarily faces two kinds of geographical costs: situation and site. **Situation factors** are those related to the transportation of materials into and from a factory. A firm seeks a location that minimizes the costs of transporting inputs to the factory and finished goods to the consumers. **Site factors** are those related to the costs of production inside the plant resulting from the unique characteristics of a particular location. Land, labor, and capital are the three traditional production factors that may vary among locations. While a variety of situation and site costs explain the location of factories, the particular combination of critical factors varies among firms.

Situation Factors

All manufacturers have buyers and sellers—companies and individuals who buy the product, and companies and individuals who supply the firm with inputs needed to manufacture it. One of the objectives of every company is to minimize the total cost of transporting inputs to its factory plus the cost of transporting finished products from its plant to consumers. The farther something is transported, the higher the cost; therefore, a manufacturer prefers to locate its factory as close as possible to its buyers and sellers.

A company that obtains all of its needed inputs from one source and sells all of its products to one customer can easily compute the optimal location for its factory. If the cost of transporting the product to the customer is greater than the cost of bringing in the necessary inputs, the optimal plant location is as close as possible to the customer. Conversely, if the inputs were relatively expensive to transport, the preferred location for the factory would be near the source of inputs.

Location near inputs. Every industry utilizes some inputs. For some firms, these inputs include minerals and other raw materials found in the physical environment. For others, the most important inputs may be parts or materials that other companies manufactured. If the weight and volume of one particular input is sufficiently great, the firm may locate near the source of that input to minimize transportation costs.

The North American copper industry provides a good example of economic activities that locate near the sources of inputs to minimize transportation costs. The first step in the production of copper products is the mining of copper ore. Much of the copper mined in North America is low-grade, with less than 1 percent of the ore being copper. The rest constitutes waste, known as gangue.

The next step in the production process is to concentrate the copper. This step, which removes 98 percent of the waste from the ore, takes place in concentration mills. These mills are located near the copper mines because the process of concentration transforms a relatively bulky raw material, copper ore, into a product of higher value per weight. Copper concentration is an example of a **bulk-reducing industry,** that is, an industry that produces a product that has a lower volume or a lighter weight after production than before.

The concentrated copper then becomes the main input for smelters, which separate the copper found in the concentrated ore from other metals. Smelting plants further reduce the weight of copper by about 60 percent. As a bulk-reducing industry, smelters are also located close to their main source of inputs—the concentration mills—in order to minimize transportation costs.

The purified copper produced by smelting plants, known as blister copper, is further treated at

Copper is being mined at this site in Arizona. Copper concentration and smelting plants are located near the mine because these industries are bulk-reducing.

refineries. Although there is no further weight reduction in the copper, the refineries still consider proximity to the mines, mills, and smelters a critical factor in the location decision.

A U.S. map demonstrates the locational needs for the various steps in copper processing. The most important location for copper mining—the Southwest—is also the center for concentration mills, smelting plants, and refineries. But one of the largest refineries is near Baltimore, 1,000 kilometers (600 miles) from the nearest copper mine (Figure 10–7). The Baltimore refinery imports most of its material from other countries.

Steel-making is another bulk-reducing industry that traditionally has been located primarily to minimize the cost of transporting inputs. The U.S. steel industry also demonstrates how the location can

change if the source and cost of raw materials change.

The main inputs in the production of steel are normally iron ore and coal. Both raw materials are extremely bulky, contain a high percentage of impurities, and must be used in large quantities. These characteristics have traditionally meant that steel factories must be located where the cost of transporting inputs is minimized.

The U.S. steel industry originally concentrated in the mid-nineteenth century in southwestern Pennsylvania, where iron ore and coal were both mined. Later in the nineteenth century, steel mills were more likely to be built in Cleveland, Youngstown, and Toledo, Ohio, in Detroit, and in other communities near Lake Erie (Figure 10–8). The shift to locations near Lake Erie was largely influenced by the discovery of iron ore in the Mesabi range of Minnesota. The Mesabi range soon became the source of virtually all iron ore used in the U.S. steel industry. Iron was transported to the new steel mills by way of Lake Superior, Lake Huron, and Lake Erie, while coal was shipped from Appalachia by train.

In the late nineteenth century, new steel mills began to be located farther west, in Gary, Indiana, Chicago, and other communities near the southern end of Lake Michigan. The main raw materials continued to be iron ore and coal, but changes in the steel-production process meant that relatively more iron ore was needed compared to coal. As a result, new steel mills were pulled closer to the Mesabi

range in order to minimize the costs of transporting the two types of raw materials. Coal was available from nearby southern Illinois as well as from Appalachia.

Most steel mills built in the United States during the first half of the twentieth century were located in communities near the West and East coasts, such as Los Angeles, Baltimore, and Trenton, New Jersey. These coastal locations were partly a reflection of further changes in the cost of transporting raw materials. Iron ore increasingly came from other countries, especially Canada and Venezuela, and locations near the Atlantic and Pacific oceans were more accessible to those foreign sources than locations

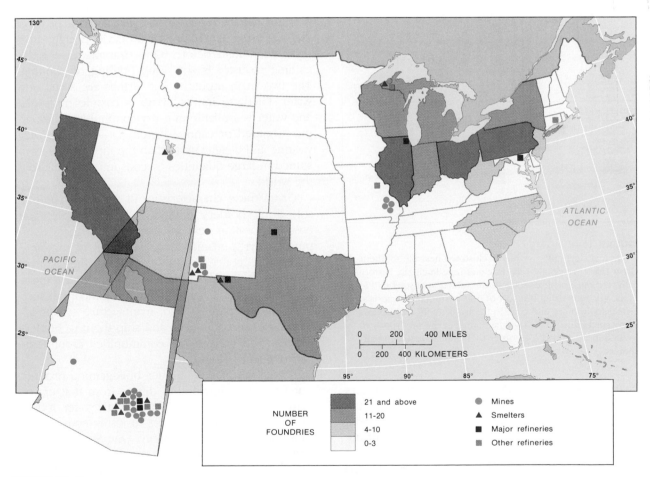

FIGURE 10–7
Examples of bulk-reducing industries. Most copper concentration, milling, and refining plants in the United States are concentrated in southwestern states, especially Arizona, to take advantage of proximity to copper mines. A few copper refining plants in coastal locations utilize imported material.

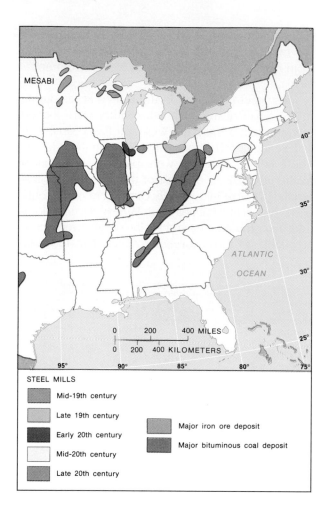

FIGURE 10–8
Integrated steel mills are highly clustered near the southern
Great Lakes, especially Lake Erie and Lake Michigan. Historically, the most critical factor in the selection of steel mill locations was minimizing the cost of transporting raw materials,
especially iron ore and coal, to the factories. In recent years,
many steel mills have closed, and most of the survivors are
located in the Midwest in order to maximize access to consumers.

near the Great Lakes. Furthermore, steel producers
make great use of scrap metal as an input in the
production process. Large quantities of scrap metal
are available in the large metropolitan areas of the
East and West coasts.

Recently, more steel plants have been closed
than opened in the United States. But the share of
national production concentrated in the southern
Lake Michigan area has significantly increased, while
the plants on the East Coast have also captured an

increasing percentage of national steel production.
The success of these regions derives from their accessibility to markets. In contrast with historical locational factors, successful steel mills are increasingly located near major markets. The coastal plants
can provide steel to customers in the large East
Coast population centers, while the southern Lake
Michigan plants are centrally located to distribute
their products throughout country.

Location near markets. For many firms, the optimal location is near the market—the place where
the product is sold. The cost of transporting goods
to consumers is a critical locational factor for three
types of industries: bulk-gaining, communications-
oriented, and single-market.

A **bulk-gaining industry** produces a product
that has a higher volume or a heavier weight after
production than before. One example of a bulk-
gaining industry is soft-drink bottling or canning.
The two main inputs in soft drinks are syrup and
water. Of these inputs, syrup is easy to transport,
and water is available in every community. The output—bottled or canned beverages—has a greater
volume and weighs more than the input and is consumed in large quantities by consumers throughout
the world.

Given these characteristics of input and output,
soft drink bottlers minimize their transportation
costs by locating near markets rather than near inputs, the syrup manufacturers. Locating near a large
population concentration minimizes the cost of
shipping the relatively bulky output to customers.
Consequently, the major soft-drink companies, such
as Coca-Cola and Pepsico, manufacture syrups according to secret recipes and ship them to bottlers
located in thousands of communities around the
world (Figure 10–9).

Scotch whiskey is another bulk-gaining product,
but its spatial distribution differs from that of soft
drinks. Although the product is mostly water, it does
not have enough consumers to justify construction
of a bottling plant in each city. One Scotch distiller
will have to serve more than one market and charge
higher prices to cover the delivery costs to the dispersed consumers.

More commonly, bulk-gaining industries manufacture products that gain volume but not weight.
One of the most prominent examples is the fabri-

cated metals industry. A fabricated metals factory brings together a number of previously manufactured parts as the main inputs and assembles them into a more complex product. Many commonly used products are so fabricated, including television sets, refrigerators, and automobiles. If the fabricated product occupies a much larger volume than the individual parts, then the cost of shipping the final product to the consumers is likely to be a critical factor. A fabricated industry seeks a location that minimizes the cost of shipping the relatively bulky product to the market.

Communications-oriented industries. Communications-oriented industries must be located near their markets in order to deliver their products to consumers as rapidly as possible. Several types of products must be sold quickly. An ex-

ample is fresh food. Bakeries and dairies must locate near their customers in order to assure rapid delivery, because no one wants stale bread or sour milk.

Many food producers are located far from their customers, especially those engaged in processing fresh food into frozen, canned, or preserved products. Cheese and butter, for example, are manufactured in Wisconsin because rapid delivery to the urban markets is not critical for products with a long shelf life. On the other hand, milk and cream, which must be used within several days, are produced near the places where they are consumed.

Products other than food can also be highly perishable and therefore require locations near markets to minimize transportation costs. The daily newspaper is a notable example. People demand delivery of their newspaper as soon after its produc-

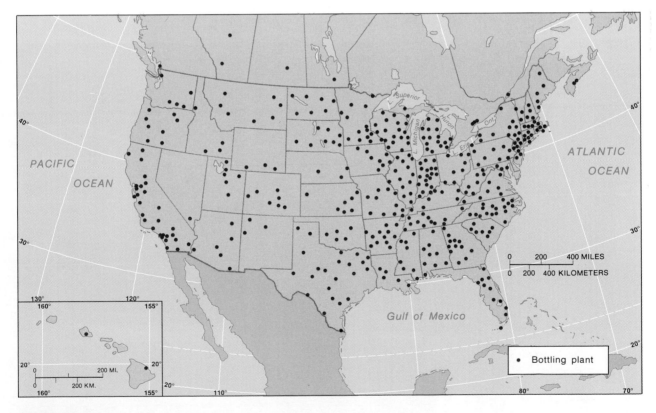

FIGURE 10–9
Distribution of U.S. and Canadian Coca-Cola bottling plants. A soft-drink bottling plant is a good example of a bulk-gaining industry, which needs to be located near consumers. Consequently, there are more than a thousand soft drink bottlers in the United States, situated near all major population concentrations.

tion as possible. Hence, the newspaper must be printed in a location that minimizes transportation time to consumers.

Difficulty with timely delivery is one of the main factors in the demise of afternoon newspapers. Morning newspapers are printed between 9 P.M. and 6 A.M. and delivered during the night, when traffic is light. Afternoon newspapers, printed between 9 A.M. and 5 P.M., must be delivered in heavy daytime traffic, which slows delivery and thereby raises production costs.

In European countries, national newspapers are printed in the largest city during the evening and delivered by train throughout the country overnight. In the past, the United States was too large to make a national newspaper feasible. With satellite technology, however, the *New York Times, Wall Street Journal,* and *USA Today* have moved in the direction of national delivery. These newspapers are composed in New York or Washington and the page images sent by satellite to other locations, such as Atlanta and Chicago, where the papers are printed. The papers are then delivered by air and surface transport to consumers around the country.

Specialized manufacturers. Specialized component manufacturers also cluster near the market. Single-market manufacturers make products that are designed to be sold primarily in one location. For example, several times a year, buyers from individ-

New York City's Garment District, near Seventh Avenue and 34th Street, is a center for production of fashionable knitwear. Manufacturers of specialized products, such as zippers and buttons, also cluster in the Garment District to be near their customers, the clothing makers.

ual clothing stores and department-store chains come to New York from all over the United States to select the high-style clothing they will sell in the coming season. As a result of decisions by these store buyers, manufacturers of fashion clothing receive orders for the production of a large quantity of certain garments in a short time. Consequently, high-style clothing manufacturers concentrate in New York.

The New York–based high-style clothing manufacturers in turn demand rapid delivery of large quantities of specialized components, such as clasps, clips, pins, and zippers. The specialized component manufacturers therefore also concentrate in New York.

Automobile production. The location of automobile production within the United States and Canada reflects the importance of situation factors. The industry also demonstrates that market changes can alter the optimal plant locations.

The automotive industry comprises two types of factories. Several thousand components plants manufacture one or more of the parts that go into vehicles. These parts are then combined into finished vehicles at about seventy assembly plants across the United States and Canada.

For a fabricated product, such as an assembled automobile, the critical factor in locating the factory is to minimize transportation of the finished products to customers throughout North America. Manufacturers of automotive components also try to minimize the cost of transporting their products to the customers; however, most are specialized manufacturers that sell to only one or two customers—automobile producers, such as General Motors and Ford.

Historically, General Motors and Ford divided North America into regions and located an assembly plant in or near a large metropolitan area within each region. For example, during the 1950s, GM operated eleven Chevrolet assembly plants, located in or near New York City; Baltimore, Maryland; Atlanta, Georgia; Flint, Michigan; Cincinnati, Ohio; Janesville, Wisconsin (80 kilometers northwest of Chicago); St. Louis and Kansas City, Missouri; Los Angeles and Oakland, California; and Oshawa, Ontario (50 kilometers northeast of Toronto). These eleven plants assembled the identical Chevrolet automo-

bile model for distribution within a designated region (Figure 10–10). Ford had a similar geographic arrangement for production of its low-priced model. Luxury cars, such as Cadillac and Lincoln, were assembled at only one plant, in both cases located in Detroit.

During the past fifteen years, the long-time distribution of automobile assembly plants changed. Factories located near major East and West Coast population centers have closed, while new ones have been built in the interior of the country, especially near interstate highways 65, 70, and 75 (Figure 10–11).

Interior locations have resulted from an increase in the variety of automobile models produced in North America. In the past, all models produced under one nameplate, such as Chevrolet, were substantially the same and differed mainly in minor details, such as body trim and seat covers. Beginning in the 1960s, the models of a particular nameplate began to vary in size, ranging from subcompacts less than 150 inches long to full-sized vehicles more than 210 inches long. The diversity of products sold in North America further increased by the expansion of sales of foreign vehicles, especially Japanese.

Instead of producing the same model for regional distribution at several assembly plants, automobile companies now operate assembly plants that specialize in production of one of their many models for distribution throughout the United States and Canada. In geographic terms, if a company has a product made at only one plant and the critical locational factor is to minimize the cost of distributing the product to consumers throughout the United States and Canada, then the optimal location for the factory is in the interior of the United States.

When assembly plants were located around the country, most components plants clustered in Michigan and adjacent states. These parts manufacturers typically sent their products to the automobile companies' warehouses and distribution centers in Michigan. Parts producers also clustered near the southern Great Lakes, because the region was the center for production of the industry's most important input, steel. Today, many parts are produced in factories near the assembly plant where they will be attached to the automobiles.

Proximity to the assembly plant is increasingly important for parts producers because of the diffu-

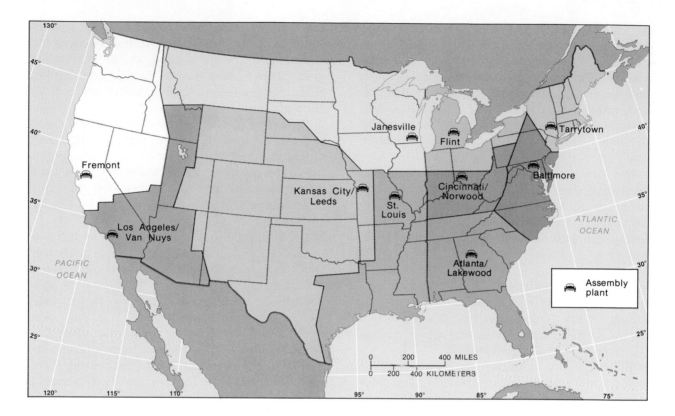

FIGURE 10–10

In 1955, General Motors assembled identical Chevrolets at ten final assembly plants located near major population centers. This distribution enabled GM to minimize the cost of distributing its relatively bulky products to consumers.

sion of "just-in-time" delivery. Under "just-in-time," parts are delivered to the assembly plant within minutes of actually being used, rather than weeks or months in advance. The clustering of parts manufacturers around their customers—such as around the new Japanese-operated assembly plants in the United States—clearly illustrates the influence of "just-in-time" (Figure 10–12).

Alternative modes of transportation. Inputs and products are transported in one of four ways: ship, rail, truck, and airplane. Firms seek the lowest-cost mode of transport, but the cheapest of the four alternatives changes depending on the distance that the goods are being sent.

The farther something is transported, the lower the costs per kilometer (or mile). Longer-distance transportation is cheaper per kilometer in part be-

cause firms must pay workers to load goods onto a vehicle and unload them at their destination regardless of the distance the vehicle travels. But the costs per kilometer decrease at different rates for each of the four modes, because the loading and unloading expenses differ for each mode.

The lowest-cost form of land transport is generally by truck for relatively short distances and by train for longer distances, because trucks can be loaded and unloaded more quickly and cheaply than trains. Therefore, trucks are most often used for short-distance delivery and trains for long-distance delivery. If a water route is available, transporting by ship is attractive for very long distances, because the cost per kilometer is even lower than for a train.

The airplane is normally the most expensive alternative for all distances, but an increasing number of firms transport by air to ensure speedy delivery of small-bulk, high-value packages. Air transport companies promise overnight delivery for most packages. They pick up packages in the afternoon and transport them by truck to the nearest airport. Late at night, an airplane filled with packages is flown to an airport located in the interior of the country, such as Memphis, Tennessee, or Dayton, Ohio. The packages are then transferred to other planes, flown to another airport, transferred to trucks, and delivered the next morning to the desired destination.

Break-of-bulk points. Regardless of the form of transportation, costs rise each time the inputs or products are transferred from one mode of transport to another. For example, workers must unload the goods from a truck and then reload them onto an airplane. The company may need to build or rent a warehouse to store the goods after unloading from one mode and before loading to another mode. Some companies may calculate that the cost of one mode is lower for some inputs and products, while another mode may be cheaper for other goods.

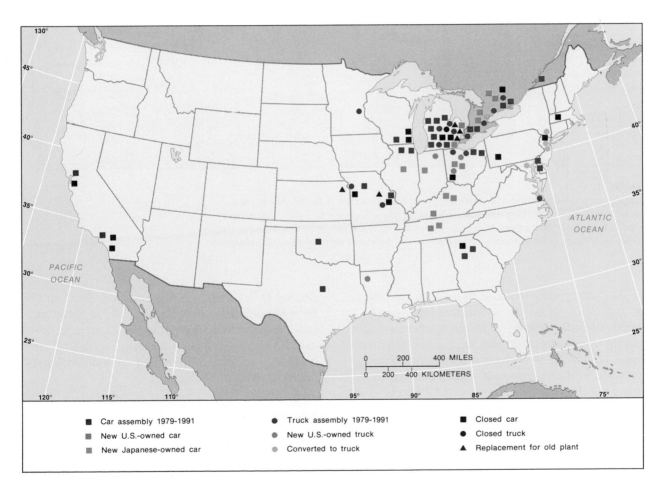

FIGURE 10–11
Distribution of U.S. automobile assembly plants. Producers of fabricated products, such as automobiles, select locations that minimize the cost of transporting the products to consumers. During the 1980s and early 1990s, motor vehicle producers selected locations for new assembly plants in the interior of the United States rather than near East and West Coast population concentrations, as was the case for fifty years. Most coastal plants were closed during the period.

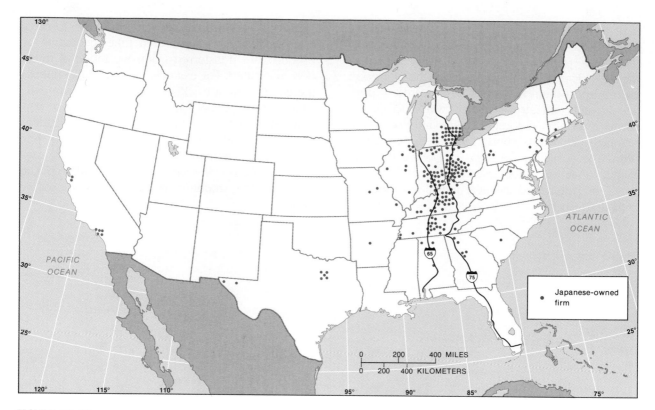

FIGURE 10–12

Japanese-owned manufacturers of automotive parts have clustered in the interior of the
United States, especially along interstates 65 and 75. These locations facilitate rapid delivery
of parts to final assembly plants, which are also clustered in the two corridors. Japanese companies avoid large cities, especially those traditionally associated with automotive production.

Many companies that use more than one mode
of transport locate at a break-of-bulk point. A
break-of-bulk point is a location where transfer
among transportation modes is possible. Important
break-of-bulk points include seaports and airports.

Situation factors remain important for many
firms, but the relative importance of different situation factors has changed. Locations near markets or
break-of-bulk points have become more important
than locations near raw materials for firms in relatively developed countries. Consumers concentrated in large urban areas have greater wealth with
which to buy products. Communications improvements have increased demand for rapid access to
products.

Situation factors, however, do not explain the
growing importance of Japanese and other Asian
manufacturers. Japan lacks important raw materials

needed by industries and is relatively far from the
most important North American and European markets. Manufacturing has grown in Japan and other
Asian countries primarily because site factors have
become increasingly important in industrial location decisions.

Site Factors

The cost of conducting business varies among locations depending on the price of a firm's factors of
production. The three main production factors are
land, labor, and capital.

Land. Modern factories are more likely to be located in suburban or rural locations rather than
near the center of a city. Contemporary factories
tend to require large tracts of land, because they

usually operate more efficiently when laid out in one-story buildings. The land needed to build one-story factories is more likely to be available in suburban or rural locations.

Firms also tend to select suburban or rural locations because land is much less costly there than near the center of the city. A hectare or an acre of land in the United States may cost only a few thousand dollars in a rural area, tens of thousands of dollars in a suburban location, and hundreds of thousands of dollars near the center of a city.

Specific parcels of land may attract industries for other reasons. Some firms seek locations that are accessible to energy sources. Prior to the industrial revolution, many economic activities were located near rivers and close to forests because water and wood were the two most important sources of energy. When coal became the predominant form of industrial energy in the late eighteenth century, location near coalfields became more important. Because coalfields are less common than streams or forests, industry began to be concentrated in a relatively few locations.

In the twentieth century, electricity has become an important source of energy for industry. Electricity is generated in a variety of ways, using coal, oil, natural gas, hydroelectric plants, and nuclear fuel. In the United States, firms normally purchase electricity from a utility company, a privately owned monopoly regulated by the state government.

Like home consumers, industries are charged a certain rate per kilowatt hour of electricity consumed, though large industrial users may pay a lower rate than home consumers. Each utility company sets its own rate schedule, subject to approval by the state regulatory commission. Industries with a particularly high demand for energy may select a location with lower electrical rates.

The aluminum industry, for example, requires a large amount of electricity to remove pure aluminum from aluminum oxide. The first aluminum plant was located near Niagara Falls to take advantage of the large amount of cheap hydroelectric power generated there. Aluminum plants have been built near other sources of inexpensive hydroelectric power, including the Tennessee Valley and the Pacific Northwest.

Industry may also be attracted to a particular location because of the amenities available at the site.

Not every location has the same climate, topography, recreational opportunities, cultural facilities, and living costs. Some executives select locations in the U.S. South and West because they are attracted to the relatively mild climates and opportunities for year-round outdoor recreation activities. Others prefer locations that are accessible to cultural facilities or major-league sports franchises.

Labor. The cost of labor varies considerably, not only from one country to another but within regions of one country. Types of industries for which labor costs comprise a high percentage of expenses are known as **labor-intensive industries.** Some labor-intensive industries require less-skilled, inexpensive labor to maximize profits, while others may need skilled labor.

The textile industry is a prominent example of a labor-intensive industry that generally requires less

Silicon Valley, south of San Francisco, California, is an important center for the production and repair of computer chips.

Low-cost labor has attracted cotton textile manufacturing to Asian centers, such as Hong Kong.

skilled low-cost workers. In the United States, textile firms have sometimes changed locations in order to be near sources of low-cost employees.

During most of the nineteenth century, U.S. textile firms were concentrated in the Northeast. The region's major attraction was a large supply of European immigrants willing to work long hours sewing in so-called sweatshops for low pay. In the late nineteenth and early twentieth centuries, clothing workers began to demand better working conditions and higher wages, and they formed unions to represent their interests. Their cause was furthered by tragic events, such as the 1911 Triangle Shirtwaist Company fire in New York, when 146 workers—mostly women—died because the owners locked the doors to the eighth-floor workroom (where the fire originated) to prevent them from taking breaks and stealing company property.

Employers argued that they could not afford to pay high wages and still make a profit. Because so many workers were needed in the industry, the

wages of each individual worker had to be kept low. Faced with union demands for higher wages in the Northeast, cotton textile manufacturers moved to the Southeast, where people were willing to work longer hours for lower wages. Although the workers earned less than their northeastern counterparts, they were eager to work in the clothing factories because wages were higher than in other types of work in the Southeast.

For their part, clothing manufacturers learned from their experience in the Northeast and maintained safer factories. With better working conditions and higher wages than previously found in the region, workers were less likely to vote for the union representation, thus keeping costs to industry low.

Cotton textile manufacturing in the United States is now located in the Appalachian and Piedmont mountains of the Southeast, especially the western parts of North and South Carolina and the northern parts of Georgia and Alabama (Figure 10–13).

Firms are dispersed among a large number of communities rather than concentrated in a few cities. They are in the same general region to take advantage of lower labor costs and consequently do not need to be located in the same city.

The clothing industry has not completely abandoned the Northeast. The wool industry has remained there because its labor demands are different from those of the cotton textile industry. The manufacture of wool clothing requires more skill to cut and assemble the material, and skilled textile workers are more plentiful in the Northeast.

An increasing number of firms require workers to perform highly skilled tasks, such as working with complex equipment or performing precise cutting and drilling operations. Companies may make more profit by paying higher wages for skilled labor than by producing an inferior product made with lower-paid, less-skilled workers.

One industry that demands highly skilled workers is electronics. Computer manufacturers have concentrated in the highest wage regions in the United States, especially New York, Massachusetts, and California. These regions have a large concentration of skilled workers because of proximity to major university centers (Figure 10–14).

Capital. Manufacturers typically need to borrow funds in order to establish new factories or expand existing ones. The U.S. motor vehicle industry concentrated in Michigan in the early part of the twentieth century in part because financial institutions there were more willing than those in the East to lend money to the industry's pioneers.

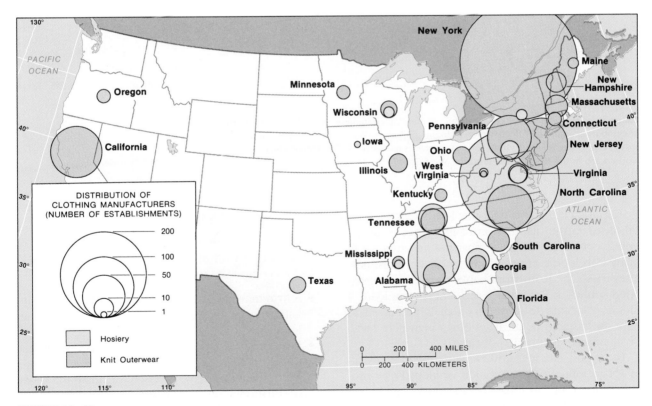

FIGURE 10–13
Distribution of manufacturers of hosiery (SIC 2252) and knit outerwear (SIC 2253). As a labor-intensive industry, manufacturers of hosiery select locations where they can obtain relatively low-cost workers. In the United States, the lowest-cost labor is concentrated in the Southeast. Products that require more skilled workers, such as knit outerwear, are still produced primarily near New York City.

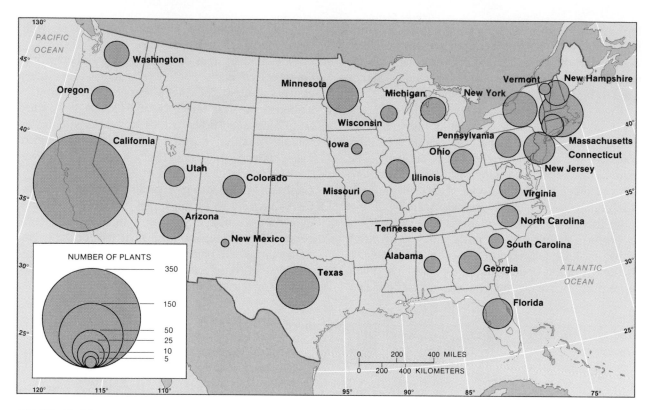

FIGURE 10–14

Distribution of manufacturers of electronic computing equipment (SIC 3571). Manufacturers of computing equipment need access to highly skilled workers to perform precise tasks and are willing to pay relatively high wages to attract such workers. The largest clusters of skilled workers are in the Northeast and on the West Coast.

The ability to borrow money has become a critical factor in the distribution of industries in developing countries. Because financial institutions in many developing countries are short of funds, new industries seek loans from banks in relatively developed countries. Enterprises may not receive loans if they are located in a country that is perceived to have an unstable political system, a high debt level, or ill-advised economic policies.

Local and national governments increasingly attempt to influence the location of industry by providing a variety of financial incentives, including grants, low-cost loans, and tax breaks. Communities compete with one another to offer new factories the most attractive financial package. Generally, the cost of the financial package is less than the additional revenues the new firm will generate in taxes and employment.

Obstacles to Optimum Location

The location chosen by a firm cannot always be explained by situation and site factors. Several other factors complicate location decisions:

◆ A firm may have more than one critical site or situation factor, each of which suggests a different location.
◆ Even if a firm has clearly identified its critical factor, more than one suitable location may emerge.
◆ A firm cannot always precisely calculate the costs of situation and site factors within the company or at various locations.
◆ The firm may select its location on the basis of inertia and history. Once a firm is located in a particular community, expansion in the same place is likely to be cheaper than moving operations to a new one.

• The calculations concerning optimal location can be altered by government grants, loans, or tax breaks.

As a result of these uncertainties, a firm may select a location for reasons other than site or situation factors. Nonetheless, awareness of these location factors is useful for government policymakers who seek to increase industrial development in their countries.

What Industrial Problems Do Countries Face?

Leaders of countries throughout the world consider the stimulation of industrial development to be one of their most fundamental problems. Government officials define the problems of industrial development from the perspective of their particular country, but geographers point out that problems of industrial growth faced by one country are related to conditions elsewhere in the world.

Industrial Problems from a Global Perspective

From a global perspective, the fundamental industrial problem is a gap between the demand for industrial products and the capacity of the world's factories to produce the goods. Global industrial capacity has increased more rapidly than demand for many products.

Stagnant demand. Except during periods of major wars or economic depressions, demand for a wide variety of industrial goods generally increased from the beginning of the industrial revolution in the late eighteenth century until the mid-1970s. Industrial growth in relatively developed countries was fueled by long-term increases in population and wealth. More people with more wealth demanded more industrial goods.

Since the mid-1970s, demand for many industrial goods has not continued to expand at the same rate in the relatively developed countries. Most relatively developed countries have little, if any, population growth. Because salaries have not risen as fast as prices during the past twenty years, the average person has not been increasing his or her level of spending (when adjusted for inflation).

Demand has also been flat for many consumer goods in the relatively developed countries because of market saturation. Nearly every household that desires a color television, a refrigerator, and an automobile has already purchased them. Most purchasers of these products now replace older models rather than buy for the first time.

Industrial output is also stagnant because of increased demand for high-quality goods. Consumers in the relatively developed societies increasingly select specific models on the basis of quality and reliability rather than low price, and they replace those models less frequently.

Japanese automobile companies first penetrated the U.S. and Canadian markets by selling models that were relatively inexpensive to purchase and operate. But those Japanese companies eventually expanded their share to more than one-fourth of the North American automobile market despite raising their prices substantially by selling products that were widely acknowledged to be built better than American models. In recent years, U.S. automobile manufacturers have made higher quality a major goal, but American consumers still generally perceive that Japanese models are superior.

Changing technology has resulted in declining demand for some industrial products. For example, global demand for steel now is lower than in the mid-1970s. Today's typical automobile uses one-fourth less steel than those manufactured twenty years ago. Automobile manufacturers now build smaller and lighter vehicles, having replaced steel with plastic and ceramic products in the body, chassis, passenger compartment, and trim.

Increased capacity. While demand for products such as steel has stagnated since the 1970s, global capacity to produce them has increased. Higher industrial capacity is primarily a result of two trends: the global diffusion of the industrial revolution and the desire by individual countries to maintain or initiate production despite a global overcapacity.

Historically, manufacturing was concentrated in a few locations. From the beginning of the industrial revolution until recently, demand for products manufactured in the relatively developed countries increased in part through sales to countries that lacked competing industries. Industrial growth through increased international sales was feasible when most of the world was organized into colonies and territories controlled by the relatively developed countries.

For much of the nineteenth century, output in some industrial sectors was higher in the United Kingdom than in the rest of the world combined. From the late nineteenth century until recent years, the United States, the Soviet Union (previously Russia), Germany, and several other countries in Europe and North America joined the British in dominating global industrial production. Then, Asian countries, such as Japan and South Korea, became major industrial producers. Now, few colonies remain in the world, and nearly every independent country wants to establish its own industrial base.

The steel industry illustrates the changing distribution of the global economy. In the mid-1970s, the relatively developed countries of North America, Western Europe, and Japan accounted for nearly 67 percent of the world's steel production, compared with approximately 25 percent in Eastern Europe and the Soviet Union and less than 10 percent in developing countries.

Global steel production in the early 1990s was virtually the same as it was in the mid-1970s, but production levels changed significantly in various regions. During the period, production declined by nearly one-fourth in North America and Western Europe, increased slightly in Eastern Europe and the Soviet Union, and more than doubled in the developing countries. In just fifteen years, the share of the world's steel production in North America and Western Europe declined from nearly 67 percent to less than 50 percent, while the developing countries increased from less than 10 percent to more than 20 percent of the world's output. Developing countries such as Brazil, South Korea, Taiwan, India, and China have substantially increased steel production, while the relatively developed countries—including even Japan—have reduced production (Figure 10–15).

As a result of the global diffusion of steel mills, capacity exceeds demand by a wide margin. Many companies have been unable to sell enough steel to make a profit and have gone out of business. But the governments of many relatively developed countries have been reluctant to let their steel mills close. Consequently, the problem of excess capacity and unprofitable operations persists.

Steel mills in many countries receive substantial government financial support in order to remain open. Many European governments heavily subsidize the continued operation of their steel mills because, if the mills closed, governments would have to pay unemployment compensation to the laid-off workers and deal with the social problems caused by increased unemployment. Maintaining a steel industry also ensures countries of a domestic steel source in times of crisis.

The steel industry has declined more rapidly in the United States than in other relatively developed countries in part because of the government's reluctance to provide substantial subsidies. Since the mid-1970s, production has declined by one-third and employment by two-thirds in the U.S. steel industry. Communities where the steel industry originally concentrated have suffered severely from the decline. For example, Youngstown, Ohio, had more than 26,000 steel-industry jobs in the mid-1970s but has lost 80 percent of them since then. Some of the unemployed steel workers have taken lower-paying jobs in other businesses, some have migrated to other parts of the country in search of jobs, and some have retired or remained unemployed. The steel industry's problems has affected the economic well-being and morale of the entire community.

Industrial Problems in Relatively Developed Countries

Countries at all levels of economic development face a similar challenge: to make their industries competitive in an increasingly integrated global economy. Despite sharing the same overall goal, though, countries face distinctive geographical issues in ensuring that their industries compete effectively. Industries in relatively developed countries must protect their markets from new competitors. Countries once governed or still governed by communist parties must prepare their industries to compete in a global market-driven economy. Developing countries of Africa, Asia, and Latin America must identify new markets and sources of revenue to generate industrial growth.

Competition among blocs. Industrial competition in the relatively developed world increasingly takes place among blocs of countries. Countries within three groups —North America, Western Europe, and East Asia—cooperate more extensively with each other but compete against the other two regions to promote industrial growth.

In North America, the United States and Canada have eliminated virtually all trade barriers, while similar efforts have been made among the members of the European Community. Cooperation is less extensive in East Asia, where Japanese industries tend to set the lead in exporting industrial goods to other countries.

The free movement of most products across the borders has led to closer integration of industries within North America and Western Europe. For example, traditionally most automobiles sold in Canada were manufactured in Canada, but now most automobiles sold in Canada are assembled in the United States. On balance, however, Canada exports twice as many automobiles to its southern neighbor as it imports. Every Chevrolet Caprice and Ford Taurus sold in Canada is actually assembled in the United States, but every Chevrolet Lumina and Ford Crown Victoria sold in the United States is actually assembled in Canada.

At the same time they have promoted internal cooperation, the three trading blocs have erected barriers to restrict the ability of industries from other regions to compete effectively. European Community members slap a tax on goods that were produced in other countries. Japan has lengthy permit procedures that effectively hinder foreign companies from selling there. The Japanese government maintains quotas on the number of automobiles its companies can export to the United States in order to counter charges of unfair competition.

Transnational corporations. Industries within relatively developed countries are increasingly controlled by large transnational corporations, some-

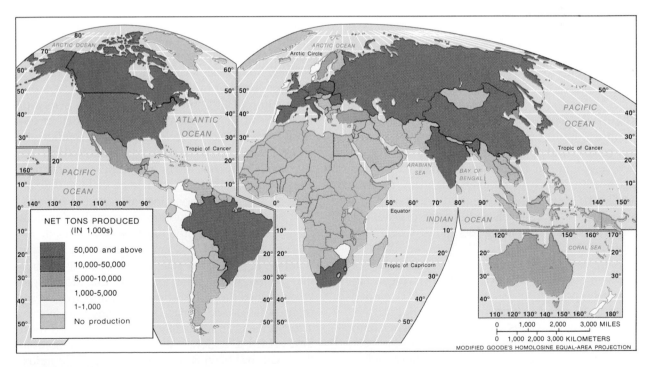

FIGURE 10–15
World production of steel. Steel production has diffused from Western Europe and North America to other regions. The Soviet Union has been the world's largest producer of steel for a number of years, while Japan has replaced the United States as the second largest. China has surpassed several European countries to become the world's fourth-largest producer.

times called multinational corporations. A transnational corporation operates factories in countries other than the one in which its headquarters is located. Initially, transnational corporations were primarily American-owned, but in recent years Japanese, German, and other European companies have been active as well.

Some transnational corporations locate factories in other countries to expand their markets. Manufacturing the product where it is to be sold overcomes the restrictions that many countries place on imports. Furthermore, given the lack of economic growth in many relatively developed countries, a corporation may find that the only way it can increase sales is to move into another country. Transnational corporations also open factories in countries with lower-cost site factors, in order to reduce production costs. The site factor that varies among countries most dramatically is labor.

Japanese transnational corporations have been especially active in the United States in recent years. Several hundred Japanese-owned corporations have built factories in the United States, primarily to develop new markets for electronics, automotive components, and metal products. Most of these plants have been located in a handful of interior states, including Ohio, Indiana, Kentucky, Michigan, Tennessee, and Illinois.

Regional disparities. Within relatively developed countries, industries are often concentrated in certain regions with almost no presence in others. The lack of a uniform internal distribution of industry has been a source of difficulty for many relatively developed countries. One region of a country may have lower income levels and other economic indicators as a result of having less industry than other regions.

For example, the United Kingdom has a disparity between the relatively poor north and west and the relatively prosperous south and east. Unemployment is 50 percent higher in the north and west, while average incomes are 25 percent higher in the south and east. Other European countries have similar regional differences arising from industrial location patterns. French industry and wealth are concentrated in the Paris region, whereas the south and west suffer. Per capita income is three times higher in the north of Italy than the south, while Sweden's

south is much more developed than its north. In each case, industry is concentrated in the regions most accessible to the large concentrations of population and wealth found in western and central Europe.

Germany has had a particularly difficult problem with regional disparities. The eastern portion of the country has required massive financial assistance to modernize its industries, a legacy of the forty-year period when the region comprised the separate, communist-run German Democratic Republic.

A number of relatively developed countries have adopted policies to lure industries to poorer regions and discourage growth in the richer regions. In the United Kingdom, for example, the south and east are much wealthier than the north and west. To aid development in the less-prosperous regions, the government has designated several Development Areas and Intermediate Areas (Figure 10–16). Industries that locate in one of these areas may be entitled to receive loans, grants, tax reductions, and other government aid. On the other hand, industries may be required to obtain government permission to locate in an Unassisted Area. Other European countries also have regional policies that employ financial incentives and regulations to encourage industrial location in peripheral regions and discourage it in the congested cores.

The European Community provides assistance to regions that suffer from lack of industrial investment, such as Greece, Ireland, Portugal, southern Italy, and most of Spain. Funds are also available for declining industrial areas, including the northern areas of Denmark, England, France, Italy, and Spain (Figure 10–17). Regions that are eligible for support are required to submit five-year development plans explaining how the funds would be used.

The problem of regional disparity is somewhat different in the United States. The South, historically the poorest U.S. region, has had the most rapid growth since the 1930s, stimulated partly by government policies and partly by changing site factors. The Northeast, traditionally the wealthiest and most industrialized region, claims that development in the South has been at the expense of the old industrialized communities of New England and the Great Lakes states.

Regional development policies in relatively developed countries were reasonably successful as long as the national economy as a whole was expanding, because the lagging regions could share in some of the national growth. In the 1990s—an era of limited economic growth for relatively developed countries—governments increasingly began questioning the wisdom of policies that strongly encourage industrial location in poorer regions. Excessive controls on industrial location could harm the overall national economy. Relatively developed countries have not completely abandoned policies that aid poorer regions, but the level of financial commitment has been severely reduced.

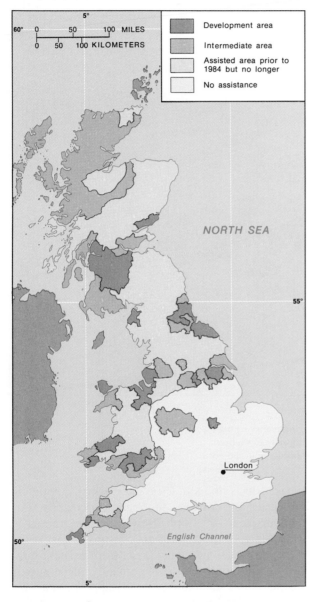

FIGURE 10–16
Assisted areas in the United Kingdom. Several European governments have adopted policies to assist the poorer regions within their countries. In the United Kingdom, for example, firms willing to locate in the north and west receive government subsidies. During the 1980s, however, the level of subsidies available for poorer regions declined in several countries, including the United Kingdom.

Industrial Problems in Developing Countries

The poorer countries of Africa, Asia, and Latin America seek to reduce the disparity in wealth between themselves and the European and North American countries. Because the extent to which economic growth can be built on agriculture is limited, the leaders of virtually every developing state encourage the construction of new industries. Industrial development not only could raise the value of exports—which these countries need to generate the funds to buy other products—but also could supply local people with goods that are currently obtained from imports. If Western countries built their wealth on industrial modernization, why can't other countries do it?

In some respects, developing countries face industrial problems that are similar to the past experiences of today's relatively developed countries. In a similar way that countries industrialized in the past, developing countries in the contemporary world must overcome two obstacles.

First, as in the past, today's newly industrializing countries are relatively distant from the main markets—the wealthy consumers in the relatively developed countries. In the early nineteenth century, factories in the United States and central Europe were far from England, then the world's most important concentration of wealthy consumers. In the twentieth century, the major concentrations of wealthy consumers are in North America and Western Europe, distant from the developing countries of Africa, Asia, and Latin America. To minimize the obstacle of geographic isolation, countries that wish to develop their industries must invest scarce resources in constructing and subsidizing transportation facilities.

Second, as in the past, today's developing countries lack support services critical for industrial de-

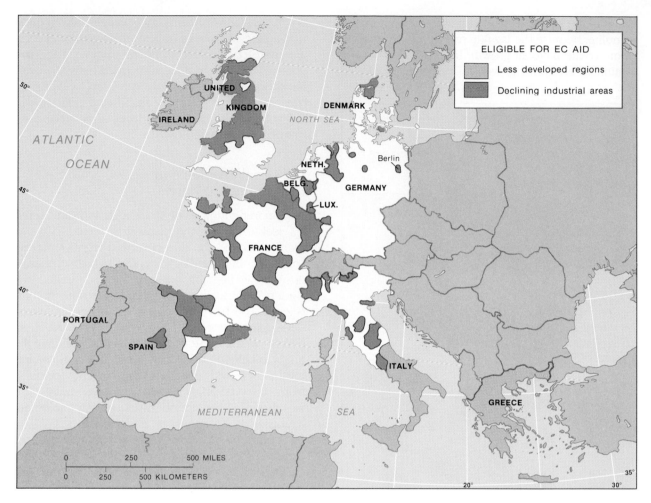

FIGURE 10–17
The European Community assists regions that have either relatively few industries or high
concentrations of declining industries. Less industrialized regions are primarily in southern
European countries, while regions suffering from industrial decline are primarily in the north.

velopment, including adequate transportation and
communications systems and domestic sources of
equipment, tools, and machines needed to build
and operate new factories. Developing countries
also lack universities capable of training the large
number of factory managers, accountants, and other
experts needed for industrial development. Support
services are obtained either by importing advisers
and materials from other countries or by borrowing
money to develop domestic sources.

Countries currently industrializing also face a
new obstacle. Traditionally, newly established factories in Europe, then North America, and more recently Asia have depended to some degree on sell

ing products in countries that lacked competing
industries. But currently there are few untapped foreign markets to exploit. New industries therefore
must either sell primarily to consumers inside the
country or take away customers from existing businesses in other countries. Frequently, the domestic
market is too small and poor to support large-scale
industrial development.

In view of the obstacles in launching new industries for which access to markets is a critical locational factor, what kind of factories can developing
countries attract? According to principles of economic geography, two other critical locational factors remain: access to raw materials and site costs.

In fact, new factories in Africa generally have been those for which either access to raw materials or a site factor is critical. Some African countries take advantage of proximity to raw materials. Mineral resources, such as bauxite in Guinea, uranium in Niger, iron ore in Liberia, and copper in Zambia, are processed for industrial uses elsewhere in the world. African countries also process food and agricultural products, such as palm and peanut oil, flour, and beer. Fertilizer is produced from phosphate in Morocco and Tunisia and from nitrogen in the Ivory Coast, Zambia, and Zimbabwe.

Also attracted to locations in developing countries are industries for which the most critical site factor is access to abundant, low-cost labor. For example, the textile industry still considers low-cost labor to be its most critical site selection factor. Consequently, textile manufacturers that migrated within the United States from New England to the Southeast earlier in the twentieth century because of lower-cost labor have migrated again in recent years to Asia, Latin America, and Africa. Workers in developing countries are willing to work in textile mills for a fraction of the wages paid in any region of the United States, including the Southeast. The Bata Company, for example, has shoe factories in the Sudan, Zambia, Nigeria, the Ivory Coast, and Cameroon.

Transnational corporations have been especially aggressive at taking advantage of low-cost labor in developing countries. To remain competitive in the global economy, transnational corporations carefully review all steps in their production and identify those processes that can be performed by low-paying, low-skilled workers in developing countries. Given the substantial difference in the level of wages paid to workers in relatively developed and developing countries, transnational corporations find it advantageous to transfer some work to developing countries despite higher transportation costs. At the same time, operations that require highly skilled workers are still performed in factories in relatively developed countries. The transfer of some types of jobs to developing countries is known as the international division of labor.

Many African countries possess iron ore; but steel, perhaps the most important industry for a developing country, has had difficulty getting started in Africa. The only large, integrated steel mill in Africa south of the Sahara and north of South Africa is in Zimbabwe, though small plants have been established in Nigeria, Ghana, Uganda, Zaire, and Ethiopia, using scrap metal as the input. Without cooperation among several small states, steel manufacturing is not likely to develop further in Africa.

Communist and Former Communist Countries

Early communist theorists, such as Karl Marx and Friedrich Engels, believed that communism would triumph in relatively developed countries, where exploited factory workers would lead the revolution. Their social and economic programs were based on conditions in advanced industrial societies.

But when communist parties gained control of Russia in 1917, Eastern Europe after World War II, and other countries more recently, few were advanced industrial powers. Instead, the communists had to promote socialism in poor, agricultural societies.

As a centrally planned society, the Soviet Union had an economy directed by government officials rather than private entrepreneurs. The country's state planning commission, known as Gosplan, developed a series of five-year plans to guide industrial development. The plans prescribed the production goals for the whole country by economic sector and region. They specified the type and quantity of minerals, manufactured goods, and agricultural commodities to be produced and the factories, railways, roads, canals, and houses to be built in each part of the country.

The five-year plans featured three main industrial policies. First, Soviet planners placed emphasis on so-called heavy industries, such as iron and steel, machine tools, petrochemicals, mining equipment, locomotives, and armaments. To allow industrial growth, the country also promoted development of mining, electric power, and transportation facilities.

Second, Soviet planners sought dispersal of industrial production facilities from the European portion of the Soviet Union. Soviet leaders considered the concentration of industry in the west to be a liability, because the country had been invaded from the west by Napoleon in the nineteenth century and Hitler in the twentieth century. Planners also wished to promote more nearly equal levels of economic development throughout the country and believed that dispersal of industries would accomplish this goal.

Third, Soviet planners preferred to locate manufacturing facilities as close as possible to sources of raw materials rather than near markets. This policy reflected in part the needs of the particular industries emphasized in the Soviet plans and in part the lack of effective consumer demand. By emphasizing heavy industry located near sources of raw materials, Soviet planners gave lower priority to the production of consumer goods, such as telephones, washing machines, shoes, and dishes.

In recent years, the Soviet Union and other Eastern European countries have recognized that their centrally planned industrial policies were inefficient. Because demand for consumer goods exceeded production levels, shortages developed. Soviet citizens have been forced to spend hours standing in line to obtain some goods, and they utilized private networks of communication to learn when some goods would be available. State-run industries were burdened with too many bureaucrats as well as workers who lacked incentives to work hard. After years of inadequate levels of government investment, aging factories were outdated. Telephone lines and other communications systems could not serve the needs of modern industries.

As a result of a generation of inefficient management, industries in the former communist states of Eastern Europe have been unable to compete against those in Western Europe. Once heavy government subsidies were lifted from the Eastern European industries, a large percentage of them went bankrupt, throwing millions of workers out of jobs.

The challenge for Eastern Europe's industries is to define a new role in the global economy. The restructuring of the Soviet Union's economy in order to encourage modernization and more efficient use of assets is known as *perestroika*. Eastern Europe possesses important economic assets: labor costs are lower than in other relatively developed countries, and the region is closer to Western European markets than other low-cost labor areas, such as Asia, Latin America, and Africa. Western industries may transfer to Eastern Europe production operations that can be performed by lower-paid less-skilled workers.

Summary

These again are the key issues concerning the geography of industry:

1. **What were the origin and process of diffusion of industrialization?** The industrial revolution dates from the late eighteenth century in Great Britain, when a series of inventions transformed industrial production. By 1900, only four other countries could be classified as industrial: Belgium, France, Germany, and the United States. During the twentieth century industrialization has diffused to several dozen other countries in Europe, Asia, and the Western Hemisphere.

2. **How is industry distributed?** In contrast to agriculture, which covers a large percentage of the earth's land area, industry is highly concentrated. Approximately three-fourths of the world's industrial output is concentrated in four regions—the North American manufacturing belt, northwest Europe, the west-central part of the Soviet Union, and Japan.

3. **What factors influence the choice of location for a factory?** Factories try to identify the location where production costs are minimized. Critical industrial location costs are situation factors for some firms and site factors for others. Situation factors involve the cost of transporting inputs into the factory and products from the factory to consumers. Site factors involve the cost of doing business at a particular location because of the characteristics of different production factors, especially land, labor, and capital.

4. **What industrial problems do countries face?** The world faces a problem with industry because global capacity to produce many goods exceeds the demand. Relatively developed countries in North America and Western Europe have a distinctive problem which results from an uneven internal distribution of industry and wealth. Communist countries are increasingly challenged by their citizens to produce consumer goods rather than continuing to concentrate on heavy industry. Developing countries, located further from markets, must attract industries for which access to inputs or low-cost labor are critical.

Free Trade in North America

The governments of Canada, Mexico, and the United States are attempting to eliminate tariffs and other barriers to free trade among the three countries. The agreement would be similar to one in effect since 1989 between the United States and Canada.

As competition increases among regional blocs of countries, U.S. and Canadian business and government leaders see substantial benefits to including Mexico in a free trade zone. With the addition of Mexico, the North American free trade area would rival the European Community as the world's most populous and wealthy market.

Creating an integrated North American economy would be a formidable task, given the substantially lower standard of living in Mexico than in the United States and Canada. U.S. and Canadian labor-union leaders are concerned that if barriers were removed, more manufacturers would relocate production to Mexico to take advantage of lower wage rates. Such labor-intensive industries as food processing and textile manufacturing would be especially attracted to a region where prevailing wage rates are lower.

Environmentalists fear that under a free trade agreement, firms would move production to Mexico, where laws governing air and water quality standards are less stringent than in the United States and Canada. Mexico has adopted regulations to reduce air pollution in Mexico City; catalytic converters were required on Mexican automobiles beginning in 1991.

According to industrial location theory, firms select locations for a variety of situation and site factors. Wage rates and environmental controls constitute two of the important site factors, but such factors as access to markets and to skilled workers are also critical.

Geography's global perspective in analyzing industrial location reinforces the fact that the problems of an unemployed steel worker in Youngstown, Ohio, are related to worldwide characteristics of the steel industry. The future health of industry in the U.S. depends on a national commitment to a combination of competition and cooperation in a global economy.

To recapture competitiveness with other nations' industries, North American business leaders must learn more about other nations' culture, politics, and economy. The success enjoyed by Japanese and Korean businesses in North America derives to a considerable extent from the fact that executives in those countries know more about U.S. society than Americans know about Asia. Asian officials are likely to speak English and are familiar with the tastes and preferences of American consumers, whereas few American officials speak Japanese or Korean and have relatively little knowledge of Asian buying habits.

At the same time, global industrial development depends on increased cooperation among different nations. As a result of lower transportation costs, more people in the world have access to more goods at lower prices than in the past. Given this trend, consumers in industrialized countries are increasingly challenged to choose between the purchase of the highest-quality, lowest-cost goods regardless of where they were made and the support for local industries against foreign competitors at any price.

Key Terms

Blast furnace A furnace in which burning is forced by a current of air under pressure, used to produce iron.

Bleaching To whiten or remove color or stains.

Break-of-bulk point A location where transfer is possible from one mode of transportation to another.

Bulk-gaining industry An industry in which the final product weighs more or comprises a greater volume than the inputs.

Bulk-reducing industry An industry in which the final product weighs less or comprises a lower volume than the inputs.

Carding A process of cleansing, disentangling, and collecting together fibers prepatory to spinning.

Cast iron A mix of iron, carbon, and silicon that is cast in a mold and is hard, brittle, and nonmalleable.

Coke A substance remaining from coal after it is heated and turned into a liquid; used as a fuel.

Communications-oriented industry An industry for which rapid delivery of the product to consumers is a critical factor.

Cottage industry Manufacturing based in homes rather than in a factory, commonly found before the industrial revolution.

Dross The scum or impurities that form on the surface of melted metal.

Forge A furnace in which metal is heated and wrought.

Labor-intensive industry An industry for which labor costs comprise a high percentage of total expenses.

Ore A mineral mined for its valuable contents, frequently a metal, such as iron.

Pig A crude mold or casting of a metal, such as iron.

Puddling The process of converting pig iron into a tough, commercial form of iron, known as wrought iron, by subjecting it to heat until it is pasty and frequently stirring it in a furnace.

Rollers A revolving cylinder used to untwist cotton.

Rolling The process of passing pig iron between iron rollers to remove impurities.

Site factors Location factors related to the costs of factors of production inside the plant, such as land, labor, and capital.

Situation factors Location factors related to the transportation of materials into and from a factory.

Smelt To melt an ore, such as iron ore.

Spindle A long slender pin around which thread is twisted in a spinning wheel.

Spinning frame A machine that stretches, twists, and winds yarn.

Textile A fabric made by weaving, used in making clothing.

Weaving The process of forming cloth by lacing together strands of yarn.

Wrought iron A form of iron that is tough, malleable, and relatively soft.

Thinking Geographically

1. What have been the benefits and costs to Canada of its free trade agreement with the United States?
2. To induce Toyota to build its U.S. production facilities in Kentucky, the state spent $49 million to buy the 1,500 acre site, $40 million to construct roads and sewers, and $68 million to train the new workers. Kentucky also agreed to spend up to $168 million to pay the interest on loans should Toyota decide to borrow money to finance the project. Did Kentucky overpay for Toyota?
3. Foreign cars account for one-fourth of the sales in the midwestern United States, compared to half in California and other west-coast states. What factors might account for this regional difference?
4. Draw a large triangle on a map of the Soviet Union, with one point near Moscow, one point in the Ural Mountains, and one point in Central Asia. What are the principal economic assets of the three regions at each side of the triangle? How do the distributions of markets, resources, and surplus labor vary within the Soviet Union?
5. What are the principal manufacturers in your community? How have they been affected by increasing global competition?

Further Readings

Amin, Ash, and John Goddard, eds. *Technological Change, Industrial Restructuring, and Regional Development*. London: Allen and Unwin, 1986.

Ashton, Thomas S. *The Industrial Revolution*. New York: Oxford University Press, 1964.

Behrman, Jack N. *Industrial Policies: International Restructuring and Transnationals*. Lexington, MA: Lexington Books, 1984.

Bell, Michael E., and Paul S. Lande, eds. *Regional Dimensions of Industrial Policy*. Lexington, MA: Lexington Books, 1982.

Birdsall, Stephen S., and John W. Florin. *Regional Landscape of the United States and Canada*. 2d ed. New York: Wiley, 1981.

Blackbourn, Anthony, and Robert G. Putnam. *The Industrial Geography of Canada*. New York: St. Martin's Press, 1984.

Bluestone, Barry, and Bennett Harrison. *The Deindustrialization of America: Plant Closings, Community Abandonment, and the Dismantling of Basic Industry*. New York: Basic Books, 1982.

Brotchie, John F., Peter Hall, and Peter W. Newton, eds. *The Spatial Impact of Technological Change*. London: Croom Helm, 1987.

Casetti, Emilio, and John Paul Jones III. "Spatial Aspects of the Productivity Slowdown: An Analysis of U.S. Manufacturing Data." *Annals of the Association of American Geographers* 77 (March 1987): 76–88.

Caves, Richard E. *Multinational Enterprise and Economic Analysis*. Cambridge, U.K.: Cambridge University Press, 1982.

Dicken, Peter. *Global Shift: Industrial Change in a Turbulent World*. 2d ed. London: Harper & Row, 1990.

Earney, F. C. F. "The Geopolitics of Minerals." *Focus* 31 (May–June 1981): 1–16.

Gillespie, A. E., ed. *Technological Change and Regional Development*. London: Pion Ltd., 1983.

Gould, Peter. *Spatial Diffusion*. Washington, D.C.: Association of American Geographers, 1969.

Habakkuk, H. J., and M. M. Postan, eds. *The Cambridge Economic History of Europe*. Vol. 6. Cambridge, England: Cambridge University Press, 1965.

Hamilton, F. E. Ian, ed. *Contemporary Industrialization.* London and New York: Longman, 1978.

Hamilton, F. E. Ian, and G. J. R. Linge, eds. *Spatial Analysis, Industry and the Industrial Environment: Progress in Research and Applications. Volume I: Industrial Systems* (1979); *Volume II: International Industrial Systems* (1981); *Volume 3: Regional Economies and Industrial Systems* (1983). Chichester: Wiley.

Harris, C. D. "The Market as a Factor in the Localization of Industry in the United States." *Annals of the Association of American Geographers* 44 (December 1954): 315–48.

Hoare, Anthony G. "What Do They Make, Where, and Does It Matter Any More? Regional Industrial Structures in Britain Since the Great War." *Geography* 7 (October 1986): 289–304.

————. *The Location of Industry in Britain.* New York: Cambridge University Press, 1983.

Hoffman, George W., ed. *Eastern Europe: Essays in Geographical Problems.* London: Methuen, 1971.

Langton, John. "The Industrial Revolution and the Regional Geography of England." *Transactions of the Institute of British Geographers,* New Series 9 (no. 2, 1984): 145–67.

Langton, John, and R. J. Morris, eds. *Atlas of Industrializing Britain, 1780–1914.* London: Methuen, 1986.

Law, Christopher M., ed. *Restructuring the Global Automobile Industry.* London: Routledge, 1991.

Massey, Doreen, and Richard Meegan, eds. *Politics and Method: Contrasting Studies in Industrial Geography.* New York: Methuen, 1986.

Oakey, Raymond P. *High Technology Small Firms: Innovation and Regional Development in Britain and the United States.* New York: St. Martin's Press, 1984.

Oxford University Cartographic Department. *Oxford Economic Atlas: The United States and Canada.* London: Oxford University Press, 1975.

Pattie, Charles J., and R. J. Johnston. "One Nation or Two? The Changing Geography of Unemployment in Great Britain, 1983–1988." *Professional Geographer* 42 (August 1990): 288–298.

Peet, Richard, ed. *International Capitalism and Industrial Restructuring.* Boston: Allen & Unwin, 1987.

Rubenstein, James M. "Changing Distribution of the American Automobile Industry." *The Geographical Review* 76 (July 1986): 288–300.

Schmenner, Roger W. *Making Business Location Decisions.* Englewood Cliffs, NJ: Prentice-Hall, 1982.

Scott, Allen J., and Michael Storper, eds. *Production, Work, Territory.* Boston: Allen and Unwin, 1986.

Smith, David M. *Industrial Location: An Economic Geographical Analysis.* 2d ed. New York: Wiley, 1981.

————. "A Theoretical Framework for Geographical Studies of Industrial Location." *Economic Geography* 42 (April 1966): 95–113.

South, Robert B. "Transnational 'Maquiladora' Location." *Annals of the Association of American Geographers* 80 (December 1990): 529–570.

Stafford, Howard A. "Manufacturing Plant Closure Selections within Firms." *Annals of the Association of American Geographers* 81 (March 1991): 51–65.

Storper, Michael, and Richard Walker. *The Capitalist Imperative: Territory, Technology, and Industrial Growth.* New York: Basil Blackwell, 1989.

Toyne, Brian, Jeffrey S. Arpan, David A. Ricks, Terence A. Shimp, and Andy Barnett. *The Global Textile Industry*. London: Allen and Unwin, 1984.

Warren, Kenneth. "World Steel: Change and Crisis." *Geography* 70 (March 1985): 106–17.

Webber, Michael J. *Industrial Location*. Beverly Hills: Sage, 1984.

ZumBrunnen, Craig, and Jeffrey Osleeb. *The Soviet Iron and Steel Industry*. Totowa, NJ: Rowmand and Allanheld, 1986.

Also consult these journals: *Journal of Industrial Economics; Journal of International Economics; Journal of Marketing; Journal of Transport Economics and Policy; Journal of Transport History; Journal of Urban Economics.*

11
Settlements

I f you fly across the United States on a clear night, you can look down on a pattern of lights. Unless you are flying over mountains or deserts, you will see different-sized clusters of lights. If you kept a tally, you would see more small than large clusters. The small clusters of light come from villages and towns, the large ones from cities and metropolitan areas.

Geographers observe that the distribution of settlements has a regular pattern in the United States and other relatively developed countries. Geographers document these regularities and apply economic geography concepts to understanding why this pattern exists.

The regular distribution observed in North America, however, is not found in developing countries. Geographers explain the reasons for this difference and why the absence of a regular pattern is significant for developing countries.

Obtaining Goods in Romania

The Preda family lives in Comena, a Romanian village of 800 inhabitants. The Predas are farmers, working outside the village in government-owned fields. The family has enough food and income to survive without difficulty, but some goods are hard to obtain. Because the village has only a few shops, Elena Preda must travel for an hour by bus to a larger town to buy everything she needs.

The problem in Romania is that there are two large gaps in the sizes of settlements. The first gap is between the largest settlement, Bucharest, with 2.4 million inhabitants, and the second largest, Braşov, with 350,000. The second gap is between towns of 10,000 people and rural villages of 1,000.

These two gaps constitute a hardship for residents of small villages, who must travel long distances to reach an urban settlement with shops and such services as hospitals. Because most Romanians do not have cars, the government must provide expensive rural bus service so that people can reach the towns. A trip to a shop or a doctor that takes a few minutes in the United States could take several hours in Romania.

A comparable distribution of settlements in New York state would be if the Albany, Buffalo, Rochester, Syracuse, and Utica metropolitan areas were all wiped off the map. Other than New York City, the state's largest settlements would be Binghamton, Poughkeepsie, and Niagara Falls. Residents of New York State would then be forced to choose between shopping in Binghamton or traveling several hours to New York City.

Few people live in isolation. Most people reside in some form of **settlement,** which is a permanent collection of buildings and inhabitants. Settlements occupy a very small percentage of the earth's surface but exert a profound influence on the world's culture and economy. The most important economic role for settlements is a place to obtain goods and services. Beyond that, though, settlements are both storage centers of the world's cultural and economic wealth and points of origin for the dissemination of innovative economic and cultural ideas.

We can observe two kinds of settlements, urban and rural, each with distinctive characteristics. Geographers are concerned with the distribution of these settlements—where they are located and why.

KEY ISSUE

Where Are Goods and Services Located?

In some respects, the selection of a location for distributing a good or service is much simpler than choosing the location of a factory. A manufacturer has to balance a variety of situation and site factors to determine the optimal location, but retailers and service providers generally consider only one geographic factor to be important: access to markets.

While access to markets is clearly the most important geographic factor for locating goods and services, the process of selecting the optimal site is in many ways more challenging than for a factory. Retailers and service providers must make precise calculations to find a profitable location. Increasingly, geographers are hired by large banks, department stores, supermarkets, and other service providers to calculate whether a particular site has the potential to be sufficiently profitable to justify corporate investment.

To select a suitable location for a new store or service establishment, a retail or service provider asks two geographic questions:

- Are enough customers located nearby to justify the shop or service?
- Assuming enough customers are nearby, where is the best location for the shop or service?

Geographers turn these intuitive questions into scientific studies that can mean the difference between profit and loss.

Are Enough Customers Nearby?

A potential retailer needs two pieces of geographic information about the good or service that will be provided at a new establishment: the range and the threshold. The **range** is the maximum distance people are willing to travel to obtain a good or use a service. The **threshold** is the minimum number of people needed to support the good or service.

Range. Every good or service has a unique range. People are willing to go only a short distance for some goods and services, such as those provided by a grocery store or a laundromat, but they will travel a long distance for other goods and services, such as a major league baseball game or symphony orchestra concert. A convenience grocery store has a small range, whereas a supermarket has a large range. If a circle is drawn on a map around the location of a good or service, the radius of the circle is the range of the good or service.

The range must be modified to take into account that firms at other locations may already be providing the good or service. As a rule, people tend to go to the nearest available service. If you are in the mood for a McDonald's hamburger you are likely to go to the nearest McDonald's. Therefore, the range of a good or service must be determined from the radius of a circle that is irregularly shaped rather than perfectly round. The irregularly shaped circle takes in the territory for which the proposed site is closer than the existing competitors.

For example, on a map of Dayton, Ohio, we can indicate the location of all of the Kroger supermarkets and draw irregularly shaped circles around each of them. The radii of these circles represent the range for each store. The median radius for Kroger supermarkets in Dayton is approximately 2 kilometers (1.3 miles). The range of Stop-N-Go convenience shops is only approximately 1 kilometer (0.6 miles) (Figure 11–1).

The range must also be modified because most people think about distance in terms of time rather than linear measure. If you ask people how far they are willing to travel to go to a fast-food restaurant or

FIGURE 11–1
A supermarket, such as Kroger, has a larger threshold and a larger range than a convenience store, such as Stop-N-Go. As a result, Krogers are fewer in number and farther from one another than is the case for the Stop-N-Gos. Note that the stores are not distributed uniformly through the Dayton metropolitan area. Relatively few stores are located in the southwest and northeast, which are predominantly industrial areas, and in the west, which contains relatively low-income residents.

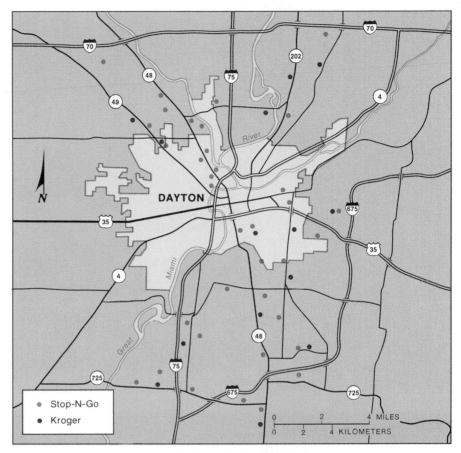

a baseball game, they are more likely to answer in terms of minutes or hours rather than miles or kilometers. If the range of a good is expressed in travel time, then the irregularly shaped circle should be drawn to reflect the fact that travel time varies depending on road conditions. One hour may translate into 90 kilometers (55 miles) on an expressway but only 50 kilometers (30 miles) on a narrow road.

To determine the range of a good or service, geographers observe consumer behavior. We can ask people in a laundromat, supermarket, or stadium where they came from; we can ask people at home where they normally go to buy food, have their clothes cleaned, or attend a sporting event. The results give a picture of how far the typical customer is willing to travel to use various services.

Threshold. The threshold is the second piece of geographic information needed to determine if a good or service has enough customers nearby. Ev-

ery enterprise needs a minimum number of customers in order to generate enough sales to make a profit. Once the range has been determined, a retailer or service provider can determine if a particular location is suitable by counting the number of potential customers inside the irregularly shaped circle. Geographers can determine, for example, that the median threshold for a Kroger supermarket in Dayton is approximately 30,000 people. Census data will help in counting the number of people within a community.

The method of counting potential consumers inside the range depends on the product. Some goods and services—such as convenience grocery stores and fast-food restaurants—appeal to nearly everyone. But many goods and services appeal primarily to certain groups of consumers. A movie theater tends to attract younger people, whereas a chiropractor tends to attract older people. Poorer people are more likely to go to a pawn shop,

Convenience stores, such as 7-11, have small thresholds and small ranges. Shopping malls, such as Stanford Shopping Center in Palo Alto, California, contain department stores that have large thresholds and large ranges. Large parking lots typically surround these malls.

whereas wealthier people are more likely to shop at a jewelry store. An amusement park attracts primarily families with children, whereas a nightclub is more appealing to single persons. If a good or service is designed to appeal primarily to certain customers, then only that sort of person should be counted inside the range.

Developers of shopping malls, department stores, and large supermarkets typically count only higher-income people, perhaps those whose annual incomes exceed $50,000. Even though the stores may attract people of all incomes, higher-income people are likely to spend more and purchase items that carry higher profit margins for the retailer. Hence, in the Dayton area, Kroger operates more supermarkets in the south, where higher-income people are clustered, and fewer in the west, a lower-income area.

The range and threshold together can determine whether a good or service should be established in a particular community. Suppose you want to know if a convenience store should locate in your community or neighborhood. First you need to compute the range—the maximum distance people are willing to travel for that product. You might survey local residents and determine that people are generally willing to travel up to fifteen minutes to reach a convenience store.

The second step is to compute the threshold. Suppose a convenience store must sell at least $10,000 worth of goods per week to make a profit, and the average customer spends $2. The store needs at least 5,000 customers per week, spending $2 each, to achieve the break-even sales level of $10,000. If the average American goes to a convenience store once a week, the threshold in this example would be 5,000.

Should a convenience store locate in your community? Draw a fifteen-minute radius around the community, adjusting the boundaries to account for any nearby competitors, and count the number of people within the irregularly shaped circle. If more than 5,000 people are within the radius, then the threshold may be high enough to justify locating the convenience store in your community.

Where Is the Best Location?

Having determined that the threshold and range justify providing a particular good or service, the next geographic question is where the firm should be located to maximize profits. According to geographers, the most profitable location is the closest to the largest number of potential customers.

Best location along a straight line. Suppose that you want to establish a pizza delivery business in your community. Where is the best place to locate it? Assume for a moment that you are seeking the optimal location for your business in an elongated community—such as Miami Beach, Florida, Atlantic City, New Jersey, or Ocean City, Maryland—that has only one important north-south street and a number of short east-west streets that are numbered consecutively.

The best location is the one that minimizes the distance that the store's van must travel to deliver pizzas to all of the potential customers. That location can be determined precisely rather than through a trial-and-error technique: it corresponds to the median, which mathematically is the middle point in any series of observations. In a linear community, such as an Atlantic Ocean resort, the service should be located where half of the customers are located to the north and half to the south (Figure 11–2).

Best location in a two-dimensional settlement. Most communities have more than just one main street. In these cases, computing the best location is a bit more complicated. The basic principle, though, remains the same: the best location is the one that minimizes the distance to the service for the largest number of people. To compute the best location for a service, geographers have adopted the gravity model from physics.

According to the geographic **gravity model,** consumers have two habits. First, the greater the number of people living in a particular place, the greater the number of potential customers for a service. A community that contains 10,000 people will generate more customers than a community of only 1,000 people. Second, the farther people are from a particular service, the less likely they are to use it. People who live 1 kilometer from a store are more likely to patronize it than people who live 10 kilometers away.

The best location for a service can be calculated by combining these two pieces of information (Figure 11–3). Geographers follow these steps:

FIGURE 11–2

To determine the optimal location for a good or service in a linear community, find the median. Assume that you have seven potential customers, labeled A through G, distributed in the community as shown in A. If the shop were located at 5th Street, the van would have to travel eleven blocks to deliver a pizza to Family A at 16th Street, ten blocks to reach Family B at 15th Street, two blocks to reach Family C at 7th Street, zero blocks to reach Family D at 5th Street, two blocks to reach Family E at 3rd Street, three blocks to reach Family F at 2nd Street, and four blocks to reach Family G at 1st Street. The van would have to travel a total of 11 + 10 + 2 + 0 + 2 + 3 + 4 blocks, or 32 blocks, to deliver pizza to all of the seven customers.

Compare this location to any other possibility. For example, if the shop were located at 7th Street, then the van would have to travel nine blocks to reach Family A, eight blocks to reach Family B, zero blocks to reach Family C, two blocks to reach Family D, four blocks to reach Family E, five blocks to reach Family F, and six blocks to reach Family G. The van would have to travel a total of 9 + 8 + 0 + 2 + 4 + 5 + 6 blocks, or 34 blocks, to deliver pizza to each of the seven customers. This is a greater distance than if the shop were located at 5th Street. In fact, no other location results in a lower aggregate set of distances than 5th Street. In this example, 5th Street is the median observation, because at that street an equal number of customers are located on either side. Three customers—A, B, and C—are located to the north, and three customers—E, F, and G—are located to the south.

Suppose that the settlement has eleven potential customers rather than seven, as shown in B. Families A and B live at 16th Street, Families C, D, and E at 15th Street, Family F at 7th Street, Family G at 5th Street, Family H at 3rd Street, Family I and J at 2nd Street, and Family K at 1st Street. The median location is the middle observation among these eleven families, the place where five families live to the north and five families live to the south. The pizza delivery service should be located at 7th Street, because A, B, C, D, and E live to the north; G, H, I, J, and K live to the south.

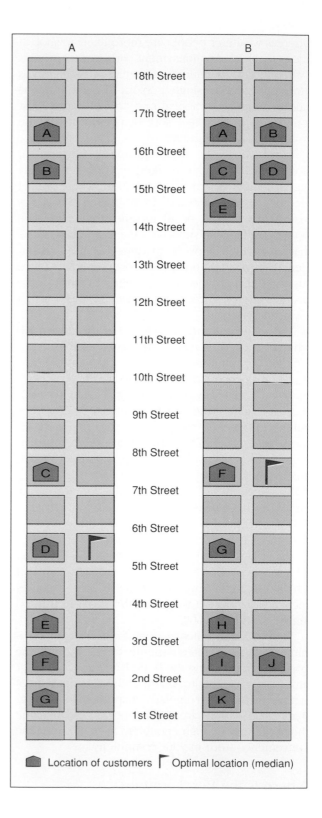

🔷 Location of customers ⌐ Optimal location (median)

1. Identify a possible location for a new service.
2. Determine the population for each community containing people who might use the service.
3. Measure the distance from the selected location to each of the surrounding communities within the range.
4. Divide the population in each community by the distance from that community to the location being considered for the new service.
5. Add the figures from step 4 together, that is, find the sum of all the populations divided by distances.
6. Select a second possible location for the new service and follow steps 2 through 5 again.
7. Compare the sum from step 5 of the first location with the sum from step 5 of the second lo-

cation. The location with the highest sum has the highest potential number of users and is therefore the best location for the service.

KEY ISSUE

Why Are Goods and Services Concentrated in Settlements?

Geographers see a strong relationship between the best location for a good or service and the location of settlements. Because a good or service seeks proximity to a large number of people, the best locations tend to be where people concentrate together in a small area. The population concentra-

FIGURE 11–3
Geographers can compute the relative potential for a service at various locations. For example, to determine whether a service should be located in Tract 7.01 or Tract 11 in Hamilton, Ohio, follow these steps: (1) Determine the potential population of patrons in each of the other neighborhoods; these figures are shown in italics. (2) Measure the distance from each neighborhood to one of the alternative locations; for example, the distance from Tract 1 to Tract 7.01 (location B) is approximately 4.5 kilometers (2.8 miles). (3) Divide the population in each neighborhood by the distance from that neighborhood to the proposed location of the service. (4) Sum up all of the populations divided by distances; this figure is the relative potential of a service at a particular location. (5) Repeat steps 2 through 4 for alternative location A. The optimal location for a service is the tract with the highest relative potential.

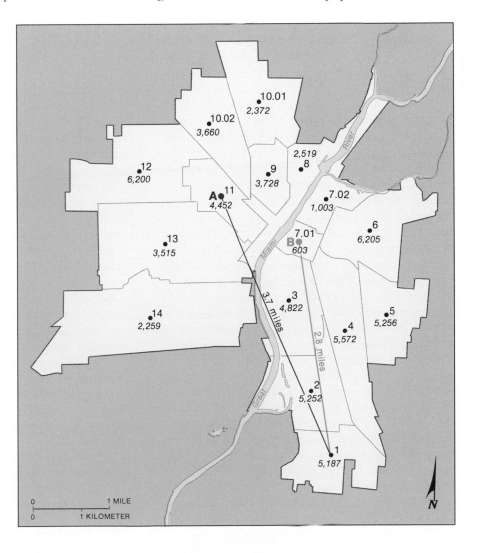

tions needed to support most goods and services are found in settlements.

Central Place Theory

The geographic concept of central place theory helps to describe the regular distribution of settlements and to explain why the regular distribution exists. Central place theory was first proposed in the 1930s by a German geographer, Walter Christaller, based on his studies of southern Germany. August Lösch in Germany and Brian Berry and others in the United States further developed the concept during the 1950s. The theory applies most clearly in regions that are not heavily industrialized or interrupted by major rivers and mountain ranges, such as the Great Plains regions of Canada and the United States.

According to **central place theory,** a central place is a market center for the exchange of goods and services by people who are attracted from the surrounding area. The central place, as the name indicates, is centrally located to maximize accessibility for people from the surrounding region. Central places compete against each other to serve as markets for the provision of goods and services. This competition, according to central place theory, creates a regular pattern of settlements.

Small settlements provide goods and services that have small thresholds and ranges. They are limited to goods and services with small thresholds and ranges because the number of people living within the range of a small community is too small to support most types of goods and services. A large department store will not survive in a small settlement because the minimum number of people needed to support the service is greater than the number actually living within the range of the small community.

Larger settlements provide goods and services with larger thresholds and ranges. At the same time, individual neighborhoods within larger settlements also provide goods and services with small thresholds and ranges. Shops patronized by a small number of nearby people can survive in a neighborhood, along with large stores patronized by a large number of people from all over the settlement.

People buy some things at shops in smaller settlements or neighborhoods and other things in large settlements. Because consumers wish to spend as little time and effort as possible in obtaining goods and services, they go to the nearest shops that fulfill their needs. There is no point in travelling to a distant Woolworth or Sears if the same merchandise is available at a closer branch.

Consumers tend to travel to a more distant shop to buy something only if the price is much lower than at a nearby shop. The additional time and effort involved in shopping at a more distant location is usually justified only for very expensive products, such as automobiles and furniture.

Market area. The area surrounding a shop from which customers are attracted is known as the **market area** or hinterland. The territory inside a circle drawn around the shop is the market area. Remember, the radius of the circle is the range of the good or service.

A market area is a good example of a nodal region—a region with a core where the characteristic is most intense. Most consumers located near the center of the circle purchase goods and services from the local shops. The closer to the periphery of the circle, the greater the percentage of consumers who shop at other locations. People located on the circumference of the market area are as likely to shop for goods and services elsewhere.

Circles can be drawn to designate market areas around settlements, not just individual shops. Small settlements with small ranges and thresholds have small market areas, whereas larger settlements have larger market areas. Several small circles can be drawn within a large market area to represent the market area of neighborhood shops.

Because everyone must go somewhere for goods and services, no territory should be excluded from the circles delineating the market areas. But the use of circles causes a geometrical problem. When a number of circles are placed next to one another to represent adjacent market areas, one of two arrangements results: either circles overlap or gaps are left between them. Neither pattern is consistent with the theory that people tend to go to the nearest shops.

An arrangement of circles that leaves gaps would mean that people living in the gaps were outside the market area of any shop. But if people do not get goods and services from somewhere they will not survive. Therefore, they must live within the

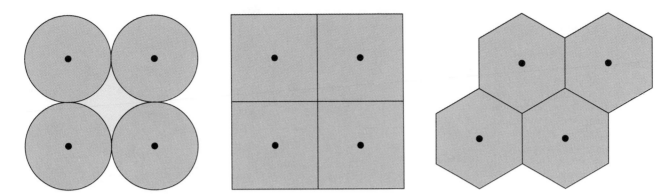

FIGURE 11–4
Geographers use hexagons to depict the market area of a good or service to obtain a compromise between the geometric properties of circles (equidistant from the center to the edge) and squares (nesting together without a gap).

market area of some shops. A pattern of overlapping circles is also unsatisfactory. One or another shop must be the closer, and this will be the one people tend to patronize. Therefore, the market areas of the two shops must be separated by a line that does not overlap territories.

Consequently, the theory requires a geometric shape that has no gaps or overlaps such as those left by circles. Squares fit together without gaps but do not satisfactorily depict the range of a good. If the market area is a circle, the range—which is the radius or distance from the center to the circumference—can be measured, because every point along a circle is the same distance from the center. In contrast, the range cannot be measured on a square because the distance from the center varies along the perimeter of a square.

To represent a market area, the hexagon is the best compromise between the square and circle (Figure 11–4). Like squares, hexagons nestle together without leaving gaps. Although all points along the perimeter of a hexagon are not the same distance from the center, the variation is less than with a square. Consequently, hexagons can be drawn around every settlement to indicate market areas. Small settlements with small thresholds and ranges have smaller hexagons.

Hierarchy of settlements. Small settlements with small thresholds and ranges are numerous and close together, whereas larger settlements are rarer

and farther apart. This hierarchical pattern can be illustrated with a series of overlapping hexagons of different sizes. Small settlements with small market areas are represented by a series of smaller, contiguous hexagons. Larger hexagons, representing the market areas of larger settlements, are overlaid on the smaller hexagons, because consumers tend to shop in smaller settlements for some goods and services and in larger settlements for other things (Figure 11–5).

In his original study, Christaller showed that settlements in southern Germany were arranged according to a regular hierarchy. He identified seven sizes of settlements, which he called market hamlet, township center, county seat, district city, small state capital, provincial head capital, and regional capital city. The average market hamlet in southern Germany, for example, had a population of 800, a market area of 45 square kilometers (17 square miles), a range of 3.8 kilometers (2.4 miles), and a threshold of 2,700 people. The average distance between market hamlets was 7 kilometers (4.4 miles). The figures were higher for the average settlement at each increasing level in the hierarchy. Brian Berry has documented a similar hierarchy of settlements in parts of the U.S. Midwest.

Every settlement can be ranked in order from the largest to the smallest population. Geographers observe that in many relatively developed societies the ranking of settlements tends to produce a regular pattern, known as the **rank-size rule.** Accord-

FIGURE 11−5
According to central place theory, settlements are arranged in a regular pattern. Larger settlements, with larger ranges and thresholds, are fewer in number and farther apart from one another than are smaller settlements. Yet larger settlements also provide goods and services with smaller ranges and thresholds; consequently, larger settlements have both larger and smaller market areas drawn around them.

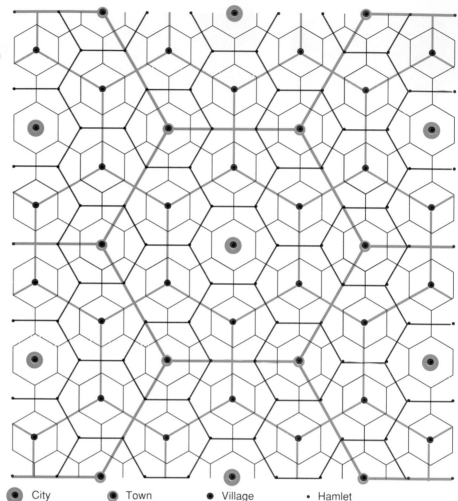

● City   ● Town   ● Village   · Hamlet

ing to the rank-size rule, the nth largest settlement in the country is $1/n$ the population of the largest settlement. Thus, the second-largest city is 1/2 the size of the largest, the third-largest city is 1/3 the size of the largest, and so forth. When plotted on logarithmic paper, the rank-size distribution becomes a straight line. If the hierarchy of settlements does not look like a straight line on logarithmic paper, then the society does not have a rank-size distribution of settlements (Figure 11−6).

The distribution of settlements closely follows the rank-size rule in the United States and in a handful of other countries. Several of the relatively developed countries in Europe follow the rank-size distribution among the smaller settlements but not

among the largest ones. Instead, the largest settlement in these countries is called a **primate city,** which is a settlement of a country that has more than twice as many people as the second-ranking settlement (Figure 11−6).

In France, for example, Paris has around 10 million inhabitants, but the second largest settlement, Marseille, has only around 2 million, instead of the 5 million that the rank-size rule predicts. London, the largest settlement in the United Kingdom, has around 11 million, while Birmingham, the second-largest, has only around 2.6 million.

Many developing countries also have a primate city. But in these countries the rank-size rule tends to fail at other levels in the hierarchy as well. As previously noted, Romania has no settlement between 350,000 and 2.4 million inhabitants and too few settlements between 10,000 and 1,000 inhabitants.

The existence of a rank-size distribution of settlements is not merely a mathematical curiosity but has a real impact on the quality of life for a country's inhabitants. A regular hierarchy indicates that the society is sufficiently wealthy to justify provision of goods and services to consumers throughout the country.

Economic Base of Settlements

Although the market areas of settlements may vary in size, every settlement serves as a center for the provision of goods and services to people living in a surrounding hinterland. At the same time, a settlement may specialize in a particular economic activity. Detroit, Michigan, specializes in motor vehicle production; Gary, Indiana, in steel manufacturing; Las Vegas, Nevada, in providing entertainment; Ann Arbor, Michigan, in university activities; and Washington, D.C., in government services.

Every settlement has a certain number of shops and offices, depending on its size, but not every city has a steel mill, university, or casino. These specialized economic activities are not distributed uniformly across the landscape but are concentrated in particular locations. A community's distinctive economic structure derives from its **basic industries,** which are firms that sell their products primarily to consumers outside the settlement. Enterprises whose customers live in the same community are known as **nonbasic industries** or sometimes as local service industries.

A community's collection of basic industries is known as the **economic base.** The significance of an economic base is that products sold outside the settlement bring money into the local economy, thus stimulating the provision of more nonbasic industries. New basic industries attract new workers to a community; the new workers in turn bring their families with them. The community must provide additional goods and services to meet the needs of the new families. Thus, a new basic industry, such as a steel mill, stimulates the establishment of new shops, such as supermarkets and laundromats, but a new nonbasic business, such as a super-

market, will not induce construction of new factories.

Geographers can identify a community's basic industries by computing the percentage of the community's workers employed in different types of businesses. The percentage of workers employed in a particular industry in a settlement is then compared to the percentage of all workers in the country employed in that industry. If the percentage is much higher in the local community, then that type of business is a basic economic activity.

Geographers can classify U.S. settlements according to the type of basic activity. Compared to the na-

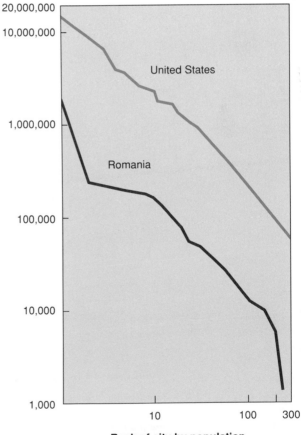

FIGURE 11–6
Settlements in the United States generally follow the rank-size distribution, as reflected by the nearly straight line on logarithmic paper. In contrast, Romania has a shortage of settlements whose population is between 350,000 and 2.4 million and of those with fewer than 10,000 inhabitants.

tional average, some communities have a very high percentage of workers employed in the production of durable manufacturing goods, such as steel and automobiles. The economic bases of other communities are classified as nondurable manufactured goods, mining, construction, communications, public administration, finance, service, wholesale, and retail (Figure 11–7).

Each type of basic activity has a different spatial distribution in the United States. Most of the com-

munities whose economic base is the manufacturing of a durable good are clustered between northern Ohio and southeastern Wisconsin, near the southern Great Lakes. Nondurable manufacturing industries, such as textiles, are clustered in the Southeast, especially in the Carolinas. Public administration centers are dispersed around the country, because these communities typically contain a state capital, large university, or military base. Service communities include such entertainment and recre-

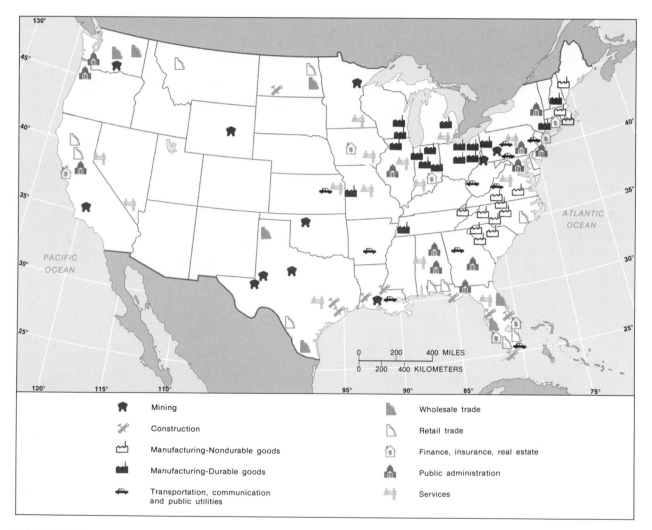

🐾	Mining	🏔️	Wholesale trade
⚒️	Construction	🏠	Retail trade
🏭	Manufacturing-Nondurable goods	💲	Finance, insurance, real estate
🏭	Manufacturing-Durable goods	🏛️	Public administration
🚗	Transportation, communication and public utilities	👥	Services

FIGURE 11–7
A city is shown on the map if it has a significantly high percentage of its labor force engaged in one type of economic activity (a city was included if the percentage of its labor force in one sector was more than two standard deviations above the mean for all cities in the United States). Cities that do not appear on the map specialize in more than one type of economic activity or are close to the national average for all sectors.

ation centers as Las Vegas and Reno, Nevada, as well as such medical centers as Rochester, Minnesota. Mining communities tend to be located in mountainous or coastal areas, where coal, petroleum, and other resources are located. Some settlements, especially larger ones, may specialize in more than one economic activity. New York and Chicago, for example, are both financial and wholesale centers.

Why Are Settlements Established?

Although most settlements exist primarily to serve economic functions, the earliest settlements probably were established for other reasons. The precise reasons for the formation of the first settlements are shrouded in mystery, because they occurred before recorded history. The most important economic distinction is between rural and urban settlements.

Origin of Settlements

To understand the possible reasons for the creation of permanent settlements, picture the situation before they existed. Human beings were nomads, migrating in small groups across the landscape in search of food and water. They obtained food through gathering wild berries and roots or killing wild animals.

Why would the nomadic groups require permanent settlements? No one knows the precise sequence of events through which settlements were established, though analysts offer several explanations, including religious, cultural, military, political, and economic reasons.

Religious reasons. The first permanent settlements may have served religious purposes, specifically as places to bury the dead. After all, what could be more permanent than a grave? Nomadic groups may have had rituals honoring the dead, perhaps memorial services on the anniversary of a death. Having established a permanent resting place for the dead, the group might install priests at the site to perform the appropriate rituals.

Settlements continue to play an important role as religious centers. By the time recorded history be-

gan, one of the most prominent features of many settlements was the temple. Until the invention of skyscrapers in the late nineteenth century, religious buildings were normally the tallest structures in the community.

Cultural reasons. The settlement may also have served as a place to house women and children, permitting the men to travel farther in their search for food. Women created objects for the household, and children were educated in the settlement.

Making pots and educating children may have originated for practical reasons, but over thousands of years these activities provided the basis for the creation and transmittal of a group's heritage and values. Today, settlements contain society's schools, libraries, museums, and archives—the permanent repository for passing on knowledge from one generation to the next.

Political and military reasons. The group's political leaders also chose to live permanently in the settlement, which may have been chosen for its strategic location to protect the group's land claims. Elaborate structures were built in the settlement to house the leaders. The group's priests, teachers, women, children, and political leaders living in these settlements were vulnerable to attacks from other groups, so for protection soldiers stayed in the settlement. The settlement probably was also a good base from which the group could defend nearby food sources against competitors.

To provide adequate defense for the military and religious leaders, the group would surround the settlement with a wall, strong enough to withstand attack. Defenders could be placed at windows or on top of the wall, holding a strategic advantage over the attackers. Thus, settlements became citadels—centers of military power. Walls proved an extremely effective defense for thousands of years, until the introduction of gunpowder in Europe in the fourteenth century revolutionized warfare. Even after cannonballs could destroy walls, they were still being built around cities. Paris, for example, built a new set of fortifications surrounding the city as recently as the 1840s and did not completely remove them until 1932 (Figure 11–8).

Although settlements no longer have walls, their military and political functions continue to be im-

FIGURE 11–8
Paris was surrounded by a wall, originally for protection. Periodically, a new wall would be constructed to encompass new neighborhoods on the periphery.

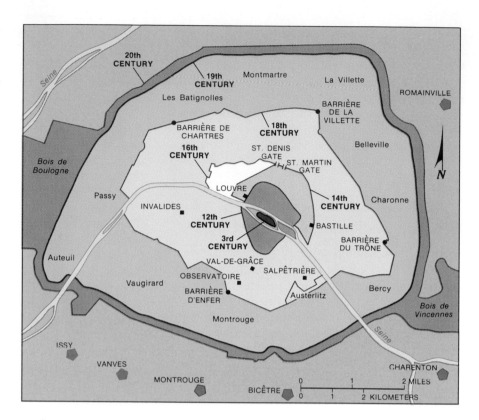

portant. The largest structure in the Washington, D.C., area—the Pentagon—houses the U.S. Department of Defense. Similarly, the military leaders of the Soviet Union work in the Kremlin, the medieval walled area of central Moscow.

Economic reasons. The religious, military, and political leaders and their dependents needed food, which was supplied by the group through hunting or gathering. As long as the group was gathering surplus food for the people in the settlement, someone probably wondered, why not bring in a bit extra in case of hard times, such as drought or war? The settlement thus acquired an economic role, as a warehouse to permanently store an extra supply of food.

Through centuries of experiments and accidents, people realized that some of the wild vegetation they had gathered could produce food if deliberately placed on the ground and nursed to maturity. The settlement might then become an agricultural center, as discussed in Chapter 9. Eventually, people were able to produce most of their food through deliberate agricultural practices and no longer had to survive by hunting and gathering.

In addition to food, people needed tools, clothing, shelter, and other objects. Settlements therefore became manufacturing centers. Men gathered the materials needed to make a variety of objects, including stones for tools and weapons, grass for containers and matting, animal hair for clothing, and wood for shelter and heat. Women used the materials men gathered to make many of the needed household objects.

Not every group had access to the same resources, because the vegetation and animals varied across the landscape. The settlement therefore was likely to become a trading center. People brought objects they had collected into the settlement and exchanged them for objects others had gathered. The settlement served as neutral ground where several groups could safely come together to trade goods. To facilitate trade, officials in the settlement regulated the terms of transactions, set fair prices, kept records, and created a currency system.

Although the reasons for the initial creation of settlements are not clear, their development can be documented. Settlements evolved primarily for two types of economic reasons. Some became centers for agriculture, while others became centers for manufacturing, warehousing, and trading. Agriculture is the predominant economic activity in communities that are now called **rural settlements,** while manufacturing, warehousing, and trading are the main economic activities in **urban settlements.**

Clustered Rural Settlements

Most settlements of the world are rural rather than urban, because most people survive by farming rather than by manufacturing or trading. Even in relatively developed societies, where most people work in manufacturing or service industries, rural settlements remain numerous, though the percentage of the total population living in them is small. A number of families may live in a clustered rural settlement and work in the surrounding fields. Such a **clustered rural settlement** typically includes barns, tool sheds, and other farm structures, as well as homes, religious structures, schools, and supporting services. In common English, this type of clustered rural settlement is called a hamlet or village.

Each person living in a clustered rural settlement is allocated strips of land in the surrounding fields. The fields must be accessible to the farmers and are thus generally limited to a radius of one or two kilometers from the buildings. The strips of land are allocated in different ways. In some places, individ-

Most rural settlements in Africa are clustered. Houses and other farm structures are built close to each other, and the fields surround the settlement.

ual farmers own or rent the land; in other places, the land is owned collectively by the settlement or by a lord, and farmers do not control the choice of crops or use of the output.

Parcels of land surrounding the settlement may be allocated to specific agricultural activities either because of the characteristics of the land or because of decisions by the inhabitants of the settlement. Consequently, farmers typically own or have responsibility for a collection of scattered parcels in several fields. This pattern of controlling several fragmented parcels of land has tended to encourage living in a clustered rural settlement in order to minimize travel time to the various fields.

Traditionally, when the population of a settlement grew too large for the capacity of the surrounding fields, new settlements were established nearby. This was possible because not all land was under cultivation. The establishment of satellite settlements in the past is reflected in contemporary place names. For example, the parish of Offley, in Hertfordshire, England, contains the following rural settlements: Great Offley (the largest), Little Offley, Offley Grange (barn), Offley Cross, Offley Bottom, Offley Place, Offleyhoo (house), and Offley Hole (Figure 11–9). All are within a few kilometers of one another.

Patterns of clustered rural settlements. Homes, public buildings, and fields in a clustered rural settlement are arranged according to local cultural and physical characteristics. There are two general types of patterns: circular and linear.

The circular pattern consists of a central open space surrounded by structures. The central space is used as a common grazing land, protective enclosure, or site for public buildings, such as the church. Fields surround the settlement. Examples of circular settlement patterns include the Kraal villages of Africa and the Rundling settlements of south Germany (Figure 11–10).

Linear rural settlements feature buildings clustered along a road, river, or dike, to facilitate communications. The fields extend behind the buildings in long, narrow strips. Linear rural settlements can be found in the portions of North America settled by the French. The so-called French long-lot, or seigneurial, settlement pattern, was commonly used along the St. Lawrence River in Quebec and the lower Mississippi River.

In the French long-lot system, houses were erected close to the river, the principal means of communications. Lots as much as 100 kilometers (60 miles) deep were established perpendicular to the river, so that each original settler had access to the river. Eventually, the long, narrow lots were divided into a system of ranges. Because French law required that each son inherit an equal portion of an estate, the heirs established separate farms in each range. Roads were constructed parallel to the

FIGURE 11–9
The rural landscape reflects the historical pattern of growth through establishment of satellite settlements. This map shows some of the settlements in the parish of Offley, England.

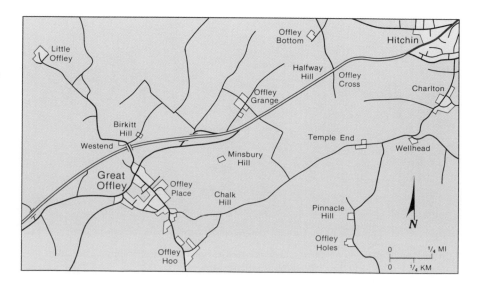

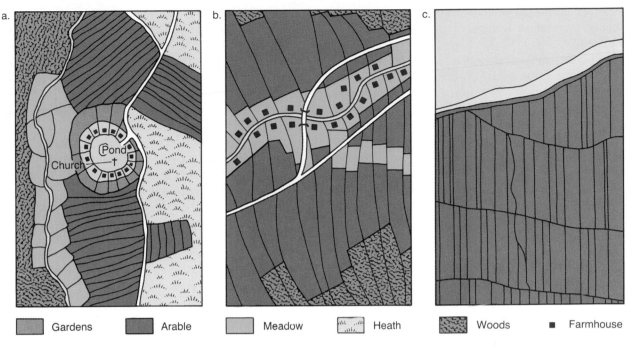

| ▦ Gardens | ■ Arable | ▨ Meadow | ⋰ Heath | ▦ Woods | ■ Farmhouse |

FIGURE 11–10
Distinctive clustered rural settlement patterns include circular arrangements in Germany (A)
and linear arrangements in France (B). Areas of North America settled by the French also display a type of linear arrangement known as the long-lot system (C).

river to provide access to inland farms. In this way, a new clustered linear settlement emerged along the road parallel to the original riverfront one.

Dispersed Rural Settlements

In the past 200 years, dispersed rural settlements have become more common, especially in North America and the United Kingdom, because in relatively developed societies they are generally considered more efficient than clustered settlements. **Dispersed rural settlements** are characterized by farmers living on isolated farms rather than in villages.

A number of European countries converted their rural landscapes from clustered to dispersed patterns to improve agricultural production. A prominent example of this conversion process was the **enclosure movement** in Great Britain between 1750 and 1850. The British government transformed the rural landscape by consolidating the individually owned strips of land surrounding a village into a large farm owned by a single person. If necessary, the government forced people to give up their former holdings.

The benefit of enclosure was greater agricultural efficiency, because a farmer did not have to waste time scurrying between discontinuous fields. With the introduction of mechanical devices, farms operated more efficiently at a larger scale. Because the enclosure movement coincided with the industrial revolution, the villagers who were no longer able to farm moved to urban settlements and became factory and service workers.

Although the enclosure movement brought greater agricultural efficiency, the cost was the destruction of the traditional self-contained world of village life. Population declined drastically in villages, as displaced farmers moved to urban settlements. Some became the centers of the new, large farms, but villages that were not centrally located to the new farm's extensive land holdings were abandoned and replaced with entirely new farmsteads at more strategic locations. As a result, the isolated, dispersed farmstead, unknown in medieval England, is now a common feature of that country's rural landscape.

Dispersed settlements became the predominant rural pattern in the American colonies, though clustered settlements were important in some places. The first European colonists established settlements along the East Coast in three regions: New England, the Middle Atlantic, and the Southeast. The colonists of these three areas came from different places in Europe and for various reasons. Along with their distinctive religions, languages, and political views, the colonists brought unique farming experiences. These backgrounds resulted in a variety of colonial rural settlement patterns.

New England rural settlements. The rural landscape in New England reflects the fact that it was originally settled primarily by groups who left England for religious freedom or other cultural reasons. Typically, durng the seventeenth century, a group received a grant of 4 to 10 square miles (10 to 25 square kilometers) of land from the English government and then traveled together to America to settle the land. Most members of the group came from the same English village and belonged to the same church. Once in the colony, members of the group wished to live near each other to reinforce their common cultural and religious values.

The group, therefore, established a clustered settlement near the center of the land grant. The center of the village usually consisted of open space known as the common. Settlers grouped their homes and public buildings, such as the church and school, around the common. In addition to their houses, each of the settlers in the village had a home lot of ½ to 2 hectares (1 to 5 acres), which contained a barn, garden, and enclosures for feeding livestock.

The diversity of topography, soil, and drainage in the New England landscape led to the need for a complex division of land ownership among the colonists. Each villager owned several discontinuous parcels of land outside the village in order to be able to farm a variety of land types. Beyond the fields, the town held pastures and woodland for the common use of all residents.

The clustered pattern was encouraged by the close relationship between the church and daily activities. The leader of the settlement was often an official of the Puritan church. Land was not sold but was awarded after the town's residents were assured that the recipient would work hard. Outsiders could not obtain land in the settlement without permission of the town's existing residents. Another reason colonists favored clustered settlements was for defense against Indian attacks.

By the eighteenth century a more dispersed distribution began to replace the clustered settlements in New England. Two factors were particularly responsible: population increase and economic development.

The village system was most appropriate for a small, stable population. As the population increased through births and immigration, the villages could not provide newcomers with an opportunity to own land in the village. When no additional farmland was available around the village, a new village had to be established nearby. As in the older settlements, the new village contained a central common surrounded by houses and public buildings, home lots, and outer fields. But, the shortage of land eventually forced new arrivals to strike out alone to claim farmland on the frontier.

At the same time, demand for more efficient agricultural practices led to a redistribution of farmland. People bought, sold, and exchanged land to create large, continuous holdings instead of several isolated pieces. The old system of several discontinuous fields had a number of disadvantages. To prevent the planting of incompatible crops in different strips of the same field, villages had to restrict what farmers could plant. Farmers lost time moving between fields, and the village had to build more roads to connect the small lots.

The descendents of the original settlers were less interested in the religious and cultural values that had unified the original immigrants, and they permitted people to buy land regardless of religious affiliation. The cultural bonds that had encouraged the original settlers to live near each other were no longer strong.

The New England landscape today contains the remnants of the old clustered rural settlement pattern. Many New England towns still have a central common surrounded by the church, the school, and various houses. But the modern New England town is little more than a picturesque shell of a clustered rural settlement, because the residents work in factories, shops, and offices, rather than on farms (Figure 11–11).

Southeast rural settlements. In contrast with the New England distribution, the typical form of rural settlement in the Southeast became a dispersed pattern known as the plantation. The plantation was a large farm that produced crops such as tobacco and cotton for sale in Europe and the northern colonies.

The successful functioning of a plantation required a large number of workers. The two main sources of labor were indentured whites, who were legally bound to work for the plantation for a period of time, or black slaves forcibly transported from Africa and sold to the plantation owner.

Small, dispersed farms were more important than plantations when the southeastern colonies were first settled in the seventeenth century. Plantations became more profitable in the eighteenth century after a large supply of labor was identified and markets for tobacco and cotton expanded.

The plantation's wealthy owner lived in a large mansion, which frequently fronted on a body of water. Surrounding the mansion were buildings to serve the owner's needs, including the laundry, kitchen, dairy, and bakery. Other buildings on the estate included a flour mill, carpenter shop, stables, coach house, and living quarters for the slaves (Figure 11–12).

Middle Atlantic rural settlements. The Middle Atlantic colonies were settled by a more heterogeneous group of people than in New England or the Southeast. Early settlers came from Germany, Hol-

FIGURE 11–11
The center of New Haven, Connecticut, retains its colonial pattern. Churches and public buildings were arranged around a centrally located common open space.

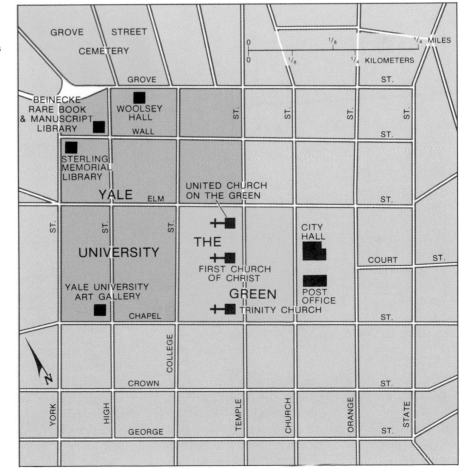

FIGURE 11–12
George Washington's restored home at Mouth Vernon, Virginia, illustrates the arrangement of buildings in a southern U.S. plantation. Flanking the main house are other structures, including kitchens, slave quarters, and storehouses.

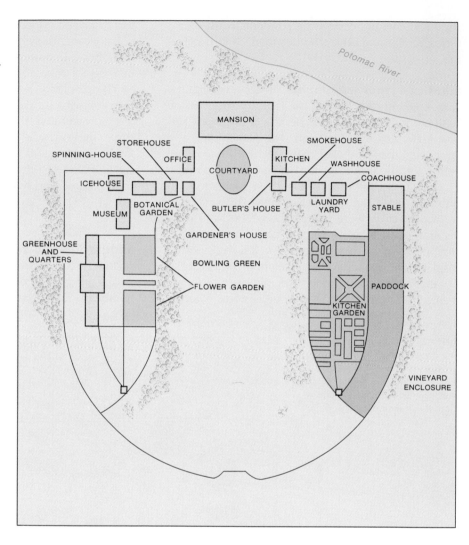

land, Ireland, Scotland, and Sweden, as well as from England.

Most Middle Atlantic colonists came as individuals rather than as members of a cohesive religious or cultural group. They bought tracts of land from speculators or directly from those such as William Penn, Lord Baltimore, and Sir George Carteret who had been given large land grants by the British government.

Inhabitants of the Middle Atlantic colonies were the main source of pioneers to the American West. The pioneers crossed the Appalachian Mountains and established dispersed farms on the frontier. Land was plentiful and cheap, and people bought as much land as they could manage. As new agricultural practices came to favor larger farms, the settle-

ment pattern in the American Midwest became even more dispersed.

KEY ISSUE

Why Do Settlements Grow?

Although a majority of the world's people still reside in rural settlements, the percentage living in urban settlements is rapidly increasing and, at current growth rates, will constitute a majority within a few years. This movement from rural to urban settlements reflects a shift in the way people earn a living, from agriculture to manufacturing and services.

Before modern times, virtually all settlements were rural rather than urban, because the economy was based on the agriculture of the surrounding fields. Shops and services met the needs of the farmers living in the village. Some urban settlements, however, have existed for thousands of years, primarily as trading, administrative, or military centers. The following section examines some of these premodern urban settlements.

Development of Urban Settlements

The oldest well-documented urban settlement is Ur, in Mesopotamia (present-day Iraq). Ur, which means fire, was the settlement that Abraham inhabited prior to his journey to Canaan, in about 1900 B.C.

Archaeological expeditions have unearthed ruins in Ur that date from about 3000 B.C. The settlement was compact—perhaps covering 100 hectares (250 acres)—and was surrounded by a wall. A dense network of narrow winding streets and courtyards ran through the city. The center included a temple, royal palace, and cemetery and was surrounded by residential areas, each of which also had a temple (Figure 11–13).

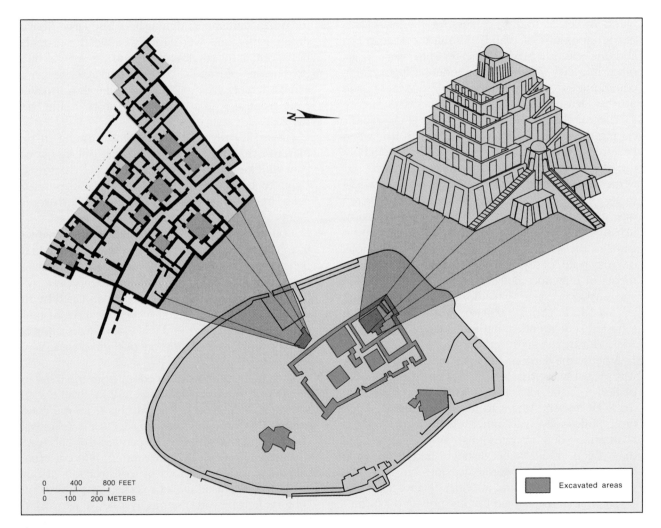

FIGURE 11–13
The remains of Ur, in present-day Iraq, provide evidence of early urban civilization. The most prominent building was a palace; surrounding the palace was a dense network of small residences built around courtyards and opening onto narrow passageways. The excavation site was damaged during the 1991 war in the Persian Gulf.

Settlements also date from the beginning of documented history in Egypt, the Indus Valley, and China, as well as elsewhere in Mesopotamia. Settlements may have developed independently in each of the four areas, or they may have originated in Mesopotamia. From these four centers, the concept of urban settlements diffused to the rest of the world.

Urban settlements in Europe. Settlements were first established in the Eastern Mediterranean region around 2500 B.C. The oldest settlements in this region include Knossos on the island of Crete, Troy in Asia Minor, and Mycenae in Greece. These settlements served as trading centers for the inhabitants of the thousands of islands dotting the Aegean Sea and the eastern Mediterranean. They were organized into **city-states**—independent self-governing communities that included the settlement and nearby surrounding countryside.

The number of urban settlements grew rapidly during the eighth and seventh centuries B.C., when hundreds of new towns were founded throughout the Mediterranean lands. The residents of one settlement would establish a new settlement elsewhere in the region to fill a gap in trading routes and open new markets for goods. The process of diffusion of urban settlements from the eastern Mediterranean lands to the west is well-documented. For example, the city-state of Syracuse established new settlements in Italy and Sicily between 750 and 700 B.C. and further west at Marseille, France (then known as Massilia), about 600 B.C. Massilians in turn founded settlements along the coast of present-day Spain during the sixth century B.C.

Athens, the largest city-state in ancient Greece, was probably the first city in history to attain a population of 100,000. The substantial contribution made by ancient Athens to the development of culture, philosophy, and other elements of Western civilization demonstrates that urban settlements have been traditionally distinguished from rural ones not only by economic activities but also by a concentration of cultural activities (Figure 11–14).

The rise of the Roman Empire provided a further boon to urban settlement. With much of Europe, North Africa, and Southwest Asia under Roman rule, settlements were established as administrative, military and trading centers. Trade was encouraged by the construction of new roads and the security the Roman army provided. The city of Rome—the empire's administrative, commercial, and cultural center—grew to at least 250,000 inhabitants, though some claim that the population may have reached as high as 1 million. The city's centrality in the empire's communications network was reflected in the old saying, "All roads lead to Rome."

The fall of the Roman Empire in the fifth century brought a decline in urban settlements in Europe. The prosperity of the majority of urban settlements had rested on the ability to conduct trade in a secure environment provided by the empire's armies. With the empire fragmented into the control of hundreds of rulers, trade decreased, and the need for urban settlements diminished. The large Roman urban settlements were greatly reduced in population or abandoned altogether, and for several hundred years, Europe's cultural heritage was preserved largely in monasteries and other isolated rural areas, as well as outside of Europe in the Middle East.

Urban life revived in Europe beginning in the eleventh century. Feudal lords established new urban settlements and gave the residents charters of rights to establish the settlements as independent cities. In exchange for a charter of rights, urban residents agreed to fight for the lord.

Both the lord and the urban residents benefited from the arrangement. The lord obtained people to defend his territory for less cost than the maintenance of a standing army. Urban residents preferred periodic military service to the burden faced by rural serfs, who were forced to devote most of their efforts to farming the lord's land and were allowed to keep only a small portion of their own agricultural output.

With their newly won freedom from the constant burden of rural serfdom, the urban dwellers set about expanding trade. The surplus from the countryside was brought into the city for sale or exchange, and markets were expanded through trade with other free cities. Trade among different urban settlements was enhanced by construction of new roads and increased use of rivers. By the fourteenth century, Europe was covered by a dense network of small market towns serving the needs of particular lords.

The typical medieval European urban settlement was a dense, compact town, frequently surrounded by a wall. Important public buildings, palaces, and

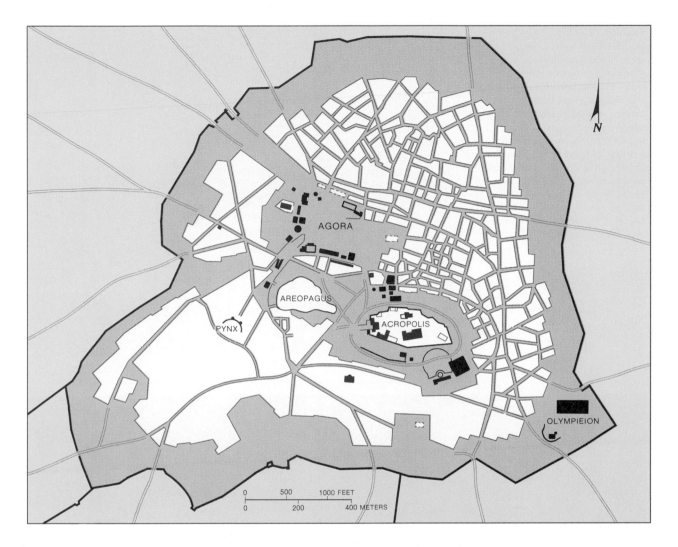

FIGURE 11–14
Dominating the skyline of modern Athens is the original hilltop site of the city, called the Acropolis. Ancient Greeks selected this site to facilitate defense of the city and to erect shrines to their gods. The most prominent structure on the Acropolis is the Parthenon, built in the fifth century B.C. to honor the goddess Athena. The structure in the foreground, the Propylaea, also dates from the fifth century B.C. The Erechtheum, built on the site of an older temple to Athena, stands to the left of the Parthenon.

FIGURE 11–15

Modern Zierikzee is a town of about 9,000 inhabitants in the southwestern part of the Netherlands. The medieval core of the city was protected by heavy fortifications; although a stone wall has been removed, a canal still surrounds the area, and three gates from the old wall remain. Several churches, the city hall, and a market square are prominently located in the center of Zierikzee. The photo below, of the far south east corner of the area shown on the map, shows one of the old gates.

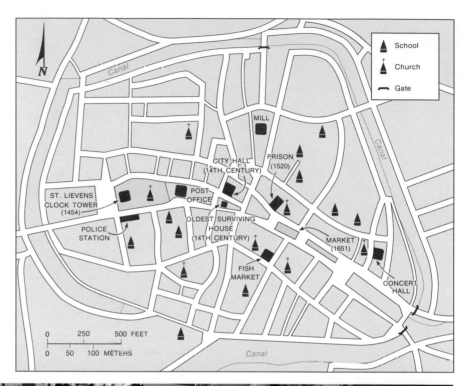

churches were arranged around a central market square (Figure 11–15). The tallest and most elaborate structure was usually the church, many of which still dominate the landscape of smaller European towns. Because of the lack of space for construction within the settlement, ordinary shops and houses were nestled into the side of the church and the surrounding walls. In modern times, these modest buildings have generally been demolished, and only the more substantial medieval structures remain. Contemporary tourists can appreciate the architectural beauty of the large medieval churches and palaces but do not receive an accurate image of the densely built medieval town.

Rapid Urban Growth

While urban settlements have existed for thousands of years, rapid urban growth is very recent. Until modern times, urban settlements attracted only a small percentage of the total population and rarely reached a population of more than a few thousand inhabitants.

In the past two centuries, the world has experienced rapid urbanization. Relatively developed countries have been transformed from predominantly rural to predominantly urban societies. The process of **urbanization** involves two changes in the distribution of population in a country: an increase in the *number* of people living in urban settlements and an increase in the *percentage* of people living in urban settlements. These two types of increases occur for different reasons.

The increase in the *number* of urban residents is a function of the total population increase in the society. As the population of the country grows, some of those additional people inevitably will live in urban settlements.

Rome, the largest urban settlement of the ancient world, probably was no larger in population than the modern Des Moines, Iowa. Most urban historians estimate that the first settlement to exceed 1 million inhabitants was London in approximately 1810. Today, more than 100 cities exceed 2 million (Figure 11–16).

At the same time, urbanization means an increase in the *percentage* of urban dwellers and a corresponding decrease in the percentage of rural residents. The increase in the percentage of urban resi-

TABLE 11–1
Percent of world's population living in urban areas.

Year	Percent
1800	3
1850	6
1900	14
1950	30
1991	43

dents is a function of the society's changing economic structure. A high percentage of urban residents reflects the fact that most of the jobs are in factories, offices, and services rather than on farms.

In 1800, only 3 percent of the world's population lived in urban settlements, compared with more than 40 percent today (Table 11–1). If current trends continue, by the end of the twentieth century, the population of urban settlements may exceed that of rural settlements for the first time in human history.

Traditionally, the process of urbanization has been one of the central elements in a society's economic development. Urban settlements grew in part because a country's overall population increased and in part because people moved from the countryside to work in the factories and services that had concentrated in the urban settlements.

To some extent, the traditional relationship between urbanization and economic development is still true, because the percentage of the population living in urban settlements is higher in relatively developed societies. Nearly three-fourths of the population in relatively developed countries live in urban settlements, compared with only one-third in developing countries. The difference in the level of urbanization is caused by economic conditions. The majority of people in developing countries are agricultural workers, who live in rural settlements. In relatively developed countries, factory, office, and service jobs are concentrated in urban settlements.

While the percentage of urban residents is higher in relatively developed countries, developing countries have an increasing number of very large urban settlements. In 1950, only three of the ten largest urban areas in the world were in developing countries, compared with six in the 1990s (Table 11–2).

FIGURE 11–16
Cities with a population of 2 million or more. Although the percentage of people living in urban areas is greater in relatively developed countries, most of the world's largest urban areas are now located in developing countries. The rapid growth of cities in developing countries reflects an increase in the overall national population, as well as migration from rural areas.

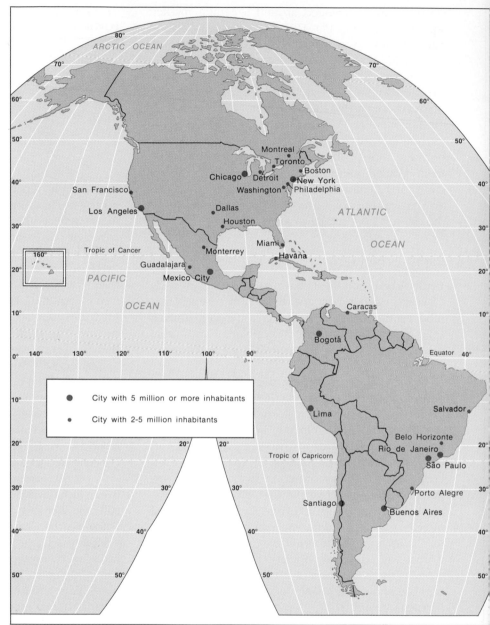

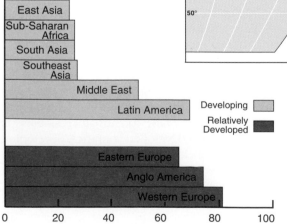

PERCENT URBAN

It is difficult to rank the world's cities in order of population, because the definition of what constitutes an urban area differs from one country to another and because up-to-date figures are rarely available, even in relatively developed countries. By utilizing different methods of delineating boundaries, London, Mexico City, New York, and Tokyo have all claimed in recent years to be the world's

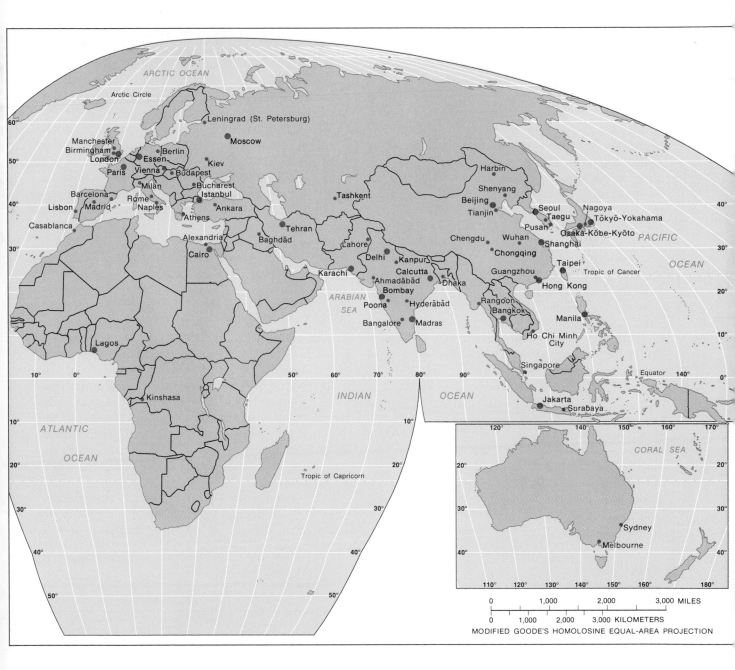

MODIFIED GOODE'S HOMOLOSINE EQUAL-AREA PROJECTION

largest urban area. In 1991, the Population Crisis Committee applied a consistent definition to estimate the population of cities around the world and concluded that the Tokyo-Yokohama region in Japan was the world's largest urban area, followed by Mexico City and New York.

That places in developing countries dominate the list of largest urban areas is a remarkable event, since urban growth has been historically associated with relatively developed economies. Urban settlements grew because newly created jobs in factories, shops, and offices attracted migrants from the countryside. But urban settlements in today's developing countries do not have rapidly expanding employment opportunities. People are migrating from rural to urban areas because of very poor economic conditions in rural settlements rather than realistic prospects for jobs in the cities. The rapid growth of urban areas in developing countries is also partly a reflection of an overall increase in population.

The new residents in the rapidly growing urban areas of the developing world generally live in poor conditions, with as many as half the people residing in squatter settlements consisting of illegally erected shacks and tents. These people lack urban services, such as running water, electricity, paved streets, transportation, schools, and shops. Thus, the rapid growth of cities in the developing countries is not a measure of an improved level of economic development, as was the case historically in North America and Western Europe.

Immigrants to New York and London may have lived in squalid conditions, but an expanding economy at least provided them with jobs, even if rather menial and poorly paid. An adequate supply of jobs is simply not available in Mexico City, São Paulo, and the other large urban settlements of today's developing countries.

Problems in Defining Urban Settlements

When you are standing at the corner of Fifth Avenue and 34th Street in New York, staring up at the Empire State Building, you know that you are in a city. When you are standing in an Iowa cornfield, you know that you are in the country. But defining where the city ends and the countryside begins is increasingly difficult in both relatively developed and developing societies. Social and physical definitions attempt to distinguish urban and rural settlements, but none fully captures the differences.

Social differences. During the first part of the twentieth century, a number of social scientists observed striking differences between urban and rural residents. During the 1930s, Louis Wirth argued that an urban dweller followed a different way of life than someone living in a rural area. Wirth defined a city as a relatively large, dense, and permanent settlement of socially heterogeneous people. The three characteristics of an urban settlement—large size, higher population density, and greater social heterogeneity—produced differences in the social behavior of urban and rural residents.

The large size of an urban settlement influences social relationships. If you live in a rural settlement you know most of the other inhabitants and may even be related to many of them. The people with whom you relax are probably the same ones you see in local shops and at church. In contrast, if you live in a city you will know only a small percentage of the other residents. You meet most people in specific roles: your supervisor, your lawyer, your supermarket cashier, your electrician. Most of these relationships are contractual: you are paid wages according to a contract, and you pay others for goods and services.

High density also produces social consequences for urban residents. The only way that a large number of people can be supported in a small area is

TABLE 11–2
World's most populous urban areas.

1991 Rank	Urban Area	Country	Population (millions)	1950 Rank
1	Tokyo-Yokohama	Japan	28.7	4
2	Mexico City	Mexico	19.4	17
3	New York	U.S.A.	17.4	1
4	São Paulo	Brazil	17.2	23
5	Osaka-Kobe-Kyoto	Japan	16.8	12
6	Seoul	S. Korea	15.8	50
7	Moscow	U.S.S.R.	13.2	5
8	Bombay	India	12.9	15
9	Calcutta	India	12.8	10
10	Buenos Aires	Argentina	12.4	9

Source: Population Crisis Committee. *Cities: Life in the World's 100 Largest Metropolitan Areas*, 1991.

The population of São Paulo, Brazil, has increased from less than five million inhabitants in 1960 to 17.2 million in 1991, and it is currently the world's fourth most populous city, behind Tokyo, Mexico City, and New York.

through specialization. Each person in an urban settlement plays a special role or performs a specific task to allow the complex urban system to function smoothly. At the same time, high density can also encourage people to be competitive in order to survive in a limited amount of space. Social groups compete to occupy the same territory, and the stronger group dominates.

The larger the settlement, the greater the variety of people. A person has greater freedom in a city than in a rural settlement to pursue an unusual profession, sexual preference, or cultural interest. In a small town, your peculiar behavior might be noticed and scorned, but urban residents are more tolerant of diverse social attitudes. No matter what your values and preferences, in a big city you can find people with similar interests. Yet, though you

may have freedom and independence in a city, you may also feel lonely and isolated. Residents of a crowded city often feel that they are surrounded by people who are indifferent and reserved.

Wirth's definition of a city may still apply to developing countries, but in relatively developed societies the social distinctions between urban and rural residents have blurred. According to Wirth's definition, more than 90 percent of the population in relatively developed societies now is urban. More than 95 percent of workers in relatively developed societies hold "urban" types of jobs. Nearly universal ownership of automobiles, telephones, televisions, and other modern communications and transportation systems has also reduced the differences between urban and rural lifestyles in relatively developed societies. Almost regardless of where you live

459

in the United States, you have access to urban jobs, services, culture, and recreation.

Physical differences. Historically, physical differences between urban and rural settlements were easy to define, because cities were surrounded by walls. The removal of walls and the rapid territorial expansion of cities have blurred the traditional physical differences. In the absence of walls, urban settlements can be physically defined in three ways: the legal boundary, the continuously built-up area, and the functional area.

The term *city* is normally used to define an urban settlement that has been legally incorporated into an independent, self-governing unit. Virtually all countries have a local government system that recognizes the legal boundaries of cities. A city has locally elected officials, the ability to raise taxes, and responsibility for providing a variety of services. The boundaries of the city define the geographic area within which the local government has legal authority. *Town* can refer to an urban settlement that is not legally incorporated, especially in England, while in the United States the term is commonly used to indicate a relatively small urban settlement.

In the United States, cities are the legal creatures of the states. The Constitution enumerates the powers allocated to the federal government. All powers not given to the federal government are reserved for the states, with the exception of those rights reserved for the people, with which no government may interfere. Nowhere in the Constitution are cities mentioned. Each state may establish any form of local government it chooses.

Most U.S. states are divided into counties, though counties have considerable power in some states and little authority in others. A county in turn may contain a variety of local governments, including independent cities and townships. The state decides the precise powers held by each government unit. Some states give the local governments home rule, that is, permission to perform a wide variety of activities and raise tax revenue. Others require that the local government apply to the state legislature each time it needs something.

Until recently in the United States, as cities grew, their legal boundaries were changed to include the new territory. The process of legally adding land area to a city is known as **annexation.** Rules con-

cerning annexation vary among states. Normally, land can be annexed into a city only if a majority of residents in the affected area vote in favor of it. In the nineteenth century, peripheral residents generally desired annexation because the city offered better services, such as fresh water, sewage disposal, trash pickup, paved streets, public transportation, and police and fire protection. Thus, while U.S. cities grew rapidly in the nineteenth century, few definition problems arose, because the legal boundaries frequently changed to accommodate the newly developed areas.

Cities now, however, are less likely to annex peripheral land because the residents prefer to organize their own services rather than pay city taxes for them. As a result, U.S. cities in the twentieth century are surrounded by a collection of suburban jurisdictions, whose residents prefer to remain legally independent of the large city. Originally, some of these peripheral jurisdictions were small, isolated towns that had a tradition of independent local government before being swallowed up by urban growth. Others are newly created communities whose residents wish to live close to the large city but not be legally part of it.

The number of local governments exceeds 1,400 in the New York area, 1,100 in the Chicago area, and 20,000 throughout the United States. Approximately 40 percent of these 20,000 local governments are general units of local governments and the remainder serve special purposes, such as schools, sanitation, transportation, water, and fire districts.

Long Island, which extends for 150 kilometers (90 miles) east of New York City and is approximately 25 kilometers (15 miles) wide, contains nearly 800 local governments. The island includes 2 counties, 2 cities, 13 towns, 95 villages, 127 school districts, and more than 500 special districts, such as for garbage collection.

The multiplicity of local governments on Long Island leads to problems. When police or fire fighters are summoned to the State University of New York at Old Westbury, two or three departments sometimes respond, because the campus is located in five districts. The boundary between Mineola and Garden City runs down the center of Old Country Road, a busy, four-lane route. Mineola set a 40-mile-per-hour speed limit for the eastbound lanes, while Garden City set a 30-mile-per-hour speed limit for the westbound lanes.

The fragmentation of local government in the United States, which makes such regional problems as traffic, solid-waste disposal, and building affordable housing difficult to solve, has led to calls for metropolitan government. Most U.S. metropolitan areas have a **council of government,** which is a cooperative agency consisting of representatives of the various local governments in the region. The council of government may be empowered to do some planning for the area that local governments cannot logically do.

Strong metropolitan-wide governments have been established in a few places in North America. Two kinds of metropolitan governments exist, federations and consolidations. Toronto, Ontario, has a federation system, while several U.S. urban areas have consolidated metropolitan governments.

Toronto's local government has two tiers. The region's six local governments, which range in size from 100,000 to 600,000 inhabitants, are responsible for police, fire, and tax-collection services. A regional government, known as the Metropolitan Council, or Metro, sets the tax rate for the region as a whole, assesses the value of property, and borrows money for new projects. Metro shares responsibility with local governments for public services, such as transportation, planning, parks, water, sewage, and welfare.

Indianapolis, Indiana, and Miami, Florida, are examples of U.S. urban areas that have consolidated city and county governments. The boundaries of Indianapolis were changed to match those of Marion County. Government functions that were previously handled separately by the city and county are now combined into one joint operation located in the same office building. Miami and Dade County have combined some services, though the city boundaries have not been changed to match the county.

The creation of metropolitan governments has been somewhat easier in other countries, where the national government has more authority. In the United Kingdom, for example, the national government can change local government boundaries if it wishes. During the 1970s, the British government redrew the country's local government boundaries and created six new metropolitan governments, including Greater London, Greater Manchester, West Midlands around the city of Birmingham, West Yorkshire around Leeds, Merseyside around Liverpool, and Tyneside around Newcastle.

Then, in the 1980s, the British government decided to eliminate the Greater London Council, which had been created only a few years earlier to govern the London region. The national government decided that the 1,580-square-kilometer (610-square-mile) London metropolitan area would be better governed by thirty-two local boroughs than by one regional government.

Derek Senior, a geographer and a member of the royal commission that restructured British local government, filed a minority report calling for a more radical local government restructuring in England. He identified the important cities in England and allocated the surrounding countryside to each, so that local government would truly be based on a series of urban regions. Senior's plan was rejected because the government wished to change the traditional counties as little as possible.

The combination of rapid growth and political fragmentation has led to the need for new urban definitions. One definition now used in the United States is the **urbanized area,** which consists of the largest city in the area—known as the **central city**—plus its contiguous built-up suburbs where population density exceeds 1,000 persons per square mile (400 persons per square kilometer). Approximately 60 percent of the U.S. population live in urban areas, divided approximately equally between central cities and surrounding jurisdictions.

The concept of urbanized areas has been of limited usefulness in the United States because few statistics are available about them. Information about urbanized areas is difficult to obtain because most data in the United States (as in other countries) are published at the level of local government units, and urbanized areas do not correspond to local government boundaries.

The urbanized area also has limited applicability because it does not accurately reflect the full extent of influence an urban settlement has in contemporary society. The area of influence of a city extends beyond the legal boundaries and adjacent built-up jurisdictions. Commuters may travel a long distance to work and shop in the city or built-up suburbs. People in a wide area watch the city's television stations, read the city's newspapers, and support the city's sports teams. Therefore, another definition of an urban settlement is needed to account for the more extensive zone of influence.

The U.S. Bureau of the Census has created a method of measuring the functional area of a city known as the **metropolitan statistical area (MSA).** An MSA includes the following:

1. A central city with a population of at least 50,000
2. The county within which the city is located
3. Adjacent counties in which at least 15 percent of the county residents work in the county containing the central city and at least two of the following four tests apply:
   a. A residential density in the county of at least 60 persons per square mile
   b. At least 65 percent of the residents working in nonfarm jobs
   c. A population growth rate during the 1970s of at least 20 percent
   d. At least 10 percent or 5,000 persons living in an urbanized area

Studies concerning metropolitan areas in the United States are usually based on information about MSAs. MSAs are widely used because many statistics are published for counties—the basic building block for MSAs (Figure 11–17). Older studies may refer to standard metropolitan statistical areas (SMSAs), which the census used before 1980 to designate metropolitan areas in a manner fairly similar to MSAs.

MSAs have two geographical problems. First, they include a considerable amount of land that is not urban by most other definitions. For example, the Great Smokies National Park is located partly in the MSA of Knoxville, Tennessee, and Sequoia National Park is located partly in the MSA of Visalia-Tulare-Porterville, California. The territorial extent of MSAs is illustrated by the fact that they comprise approximately 20 percent of the total U.S. land area, compared with only 2 percent for urbanized areas. The urbanized area typically occupies only 10 percent of the MSA's land area but contains over 75 percent of its population.

The second geographical problem is the overlapping of adjacent MSAs. A county located between two central cities may send a large number of commuters to jobs in each. If two adjacent metropolitan statistical areas have overlapping commuting patterns, they may be combined into a consolidated metropolitan statistical area (CMSA). CMSAs include New York–Northern New Jersey–Long Island, Los Angeles–Anaheim–Riverside, and Chicago–Gary–Lake County.

If part of a CMSA exceeds 1 million, then it may be classified as a primary metropolitan statistical area (PMSA). Again, the building block is the county. A PMSA consists of at least one county that has all of the following characteristics:

1. A population of more than 100,000
2. At least 60 percent of the residents working in nonfarm jobs
3. Less than 50 percent of the county's workers commuting to jobs outside the county

Difficulties involved in designating MSAs, CMSAs, and PMSAs can be seen in the southeastern corner of Wisconsin. Kenosha and Racine counties each have a city with more than 50,000 people and therefore qualify as separate MSAs. But these two metropolitan counties are sandwiched between the much larger Chicago and Milwaukee metropolitan areas. The northern part of Racine County is within a half hour of downtown Milwaukee, and the southern part of Kenosha County is within an hour of downtown Chicago. The Bureau of the Census decided to call Kenosha County a separate MSA and to designate Racine County as a PMSA within the Milwaukee-Racine MSA.

Why do officials in Kenosha and Racine counties care whether they are a separate MSA or merely part of Milwaukee or Chicago's CMSA? First, several types of federal assistance are allocated to MSAs. The separate designation may bring more funds to be used at the discretion of the county rather than shared with other counties in the Milwaukee or Chicago region.

Local officials also wish to preserve their separate MSA designation because it increases the county's visibility. The Bureau of the Census publishes a considerable amount of information at the level of the MSA. Many private companies also compile information and make initial investment decisions at the level of the MSA. Advertising agencies select MSAs as test markets, and developers choose MSAs for new sites for shopping centers. As a separate MSA, a county like Kenosha increases its likelihood of being selected by an investor.

FIGURE 11–17
Surrounding the city of Washington (coextensive with the District of Columbia) is an urbanized area that spreads into the states of Maryland and Virginia. The Washington Metropolitan Statistical Area includes five counties each in Maryland and Virginia, as well as the District of Columbia. The Baltimore Metropolitan Statistical Area lies immediately to the northeast of Washington.

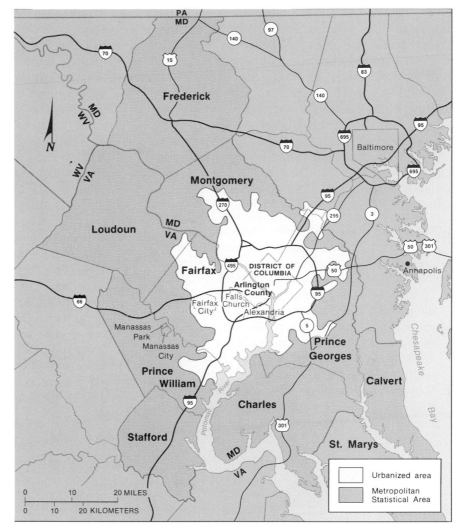

Summary

Urbanization is a process with a beginning, middle, and end. The United Kingdom and the United States are urbanized countries, where the percentage of urban dwellers has remained fairly constant in recent decades. Using a social definition of urban settlement, virtually all residents of relatively developed countries can be considered urban. According to a physical definition, such as the MSA designation by the census, approximately three-fourths of the U.S. population live in metropolitan areas. The traditional advantage of a settlement was its centrality, which provided accessibility to goods and services.

When people traveled by horse or on foot, the relative communications advantage of a particular location was extremely important.

Now that virtually all people in relatively developed countries have access to modern communications, the importance of centrality may have diminished. The overwhelming majority of people are able to communicate instantly with anyone else in the country by means of telephone. The car, which nearly all U.S. families own, links all settlements in the region, while the airplane ties together settlements around the world. Future technological advances, such as home computers and cable television, will further improve communications.

The diffusion of rapid communications systems in relatively developed countries—and presumably in developing countries in the future—poses a challenge to the geographic analysis of the current system of settlements. Possessing instant communications tools, people are less restricted to living in a particular settlement because of their employment. As discussed in the next chapter, Americans freed from the old locational constraints are moving out of cities across the landscape in a more uniform distribution.

These again are the key questions concerning settlements:

1. **Where are goods and services located?** Retailers and service providers first determine if there are enough nearby customers to justify locating in the community. To answer this concern, two characteristics of a good or service are needed: the range and the threshold. Once a decision is made that enough customers are located nearby, retailers and service providers select locations within the community that minimize the aggregate travel time for all potential customers.
2. **Why are goods and services concentrated in settlements?** The concentrations of population needed to support most goods and services are found in settlements. Geographers have developed a concept called central place theory to help describe why settlements tend to occur in a regular pattern in relatively developed societies.
3. **Why are settlements established?** Although settlements exist today primarily as market centers, they were originally established for noneconomic reasons, including religious, cultural, military, and political factors. Ultimately, settlements developed for two types of economic reasons. Rural settlements evolved as places to live for farmers, while urban settlements provided goods and services to factory, office, and service workers.
4. **Why do settlements grow?** Since 1800, the percentage of the world's population living in urban settlements has increased from 3 percent to more than 40 percent. Until recently, urban growth was associated with economic development, but in the past two decades, the world's largest cities have increasingly been located in developing countries. Although urban and rural areas present different visual images, in reality, the distinction between the two is increasingly difficult to determine.

Romanian Policy

C A S E S T U D Y
R E V I S I T E D

The Romanian government has implemented a policy to improve the rank-size distribution of settlements. Restrictions have been placed on the growth of Bucharest, and people need a permit to move there. The government has built new apartments and shops in cities such as Braşov.

At the other end of the spectrum, rural settlements have been designated for upgrading to small urban settlements. Their populations will grow from a few hundred to several thousand inhabitants. New apartments, schools, hospitals, and shops are being provided, as well as electricity, paved roads, and sanitation. In this way, families living in rural areas can have greater access to the goods and services essential for achieving a higher standard of living.

Nicolae Ceaucescu, Romania's long-time leader, launched a policy of completing wiping out small villages because he believed that rural residents did not wholeheartedly support him. Eastern Orthodox churches and homes were demolished and replaced with monuments honoring Ceaucescu and his family. After Ceaucescu was overthrown in late 1989, the new Romanian government faced the challenge of reviving a popular program of bringing electricity, paved roads, and other improvements to rural settlements, while disavowing the previous policy of indiscriminate demolition.

Key Terms

Annexation The process of legally adding land area to a city in the United States.

Basic industries Industries that sell their products primarily to consumers outside the settlement.

Central city The largest city in a metropolitan area.

Central place theory A theory that explains the distribution of settlements, based on settlements serving as market centers for people living in the surrounding area; larger settlements are fewer and further apart than smaller settlements and serve a larger number of people who are willing to travel further for goods and services.

City-state An independent state comprising a city and its immediate hinterland.

Clustered rural settlement A rural settlement in which the houses and farm buildings of each family are situated close to one another and fields surround the settlement.

Council of government A cooperative agency consisting of representatives of local governments in a metropolitan area in the United States.

Dispersed rural settlements A rural settlement pattern characterized by isolated farms rather than clustered villages.

Economic base A community's collection of basic industries.

Enclosure movement The process of consolidating small land holdings into a smaller number of larger farms in England during the eighteenth century.

Gravity model A model that holds that the potential use of a good or service at a particular location is directly related to the number of people in a location and inversely related to the distance people must travel to reach the good or service.

Market area Also known as hinterland, the area surrounding a central place, from which people are attracted to use the place's goods and services.

Metropolitan statistical area (MSA) A central city of at least 50,000 population, the county within which the city is located, and adjacent counties meeting one of several tests indicating a functional connection to the central city.

Nonbasic industries Industries that sell their products primarily to consumers in the community.

Primate city The largest settlement in a country, if it has more than twice as many people as the second-ranking settlement.

Range The maximum distance people are willing to travel to obtain a good or use a service.

Rank-size rule A pattern of settlements in a country, such that the nth largest settlement is 1/n the population of the largest settlement.

Rural settlement A settlement in which the principal occupation of the residents is agriculture.

Settlement A permanent collection of buildings and inhabitants.

Threshold The minimum number of people needed to support a good or service.

Urban settlement A settlement in which the main economic activities are manufacturing, warehousing, and trading.

Urbanization An increase in the percentage and in the number of people residing in urban settlements.

Urbanized area A central city and its contiguous built-up suburbs.

Thinking Geographically

1. Determine the economic base of your community. Consult the *U.S. Census of Manufacturing* or *County Business Patterns*. To make a rough approximation of a community's basic industries, compute the percentage of the nation's population living in the community. It will be a small number, such as 0.0005. Find the total number of firms or employees in the United States in each industrial sector. Multiply the national figures by the local population percentage. Subtract the result from the community's actual number of firms or employees for that type of industry. If the difference is positive, one of the community's basic industries has been identified.

2. Your community's economy is expanding or contracting as a result of the performance of its basic industries. Two factors can explain the performance of your community's basic industries. One is that the sector is expanding or contracting nationally. The second is that the industry is performing much better or worse in the community than in the nation as a whole. Which of the two factors better explains the performance of your community's basic industries?

3. Rural settlement patterns along the U.S. East Coast were influenced by migration during the colonial era. To what extent do distinctive rural settlement patterns elsewhere in the United States result from international or internal migration?

4. Where are the major shopping malls located in your community? How does the distribution relate to the location of major highways? What physical and social factors help to explain irregularities in the distribution?

5. Does Louis Wirth's definition of urbanism as a way of life apply to contemporary cities in developing countries?

Further Readings

Archer, Clark J., and Ellen R. White. "A Service Classification of American Metropolitan Areas." *Urban Geography* 6 (1985): 122–51.

Benevolo, Leonardo. *The History of the City,* 2d ed. Cambridge, MA: MIT Press, 1991.

Berry, Brian J. L. *The Geography of Market Centers and Retail Distribution.* Englewood Cliffs, NJ: Prentice-Hall, 1967.

———. *The Human Consequences of Urbanization.* New York: St. Martin's Press, 1973.

Bourne, L. S., and J. W. Simmons. *System of Cities.* New York: Oxford University Press, 1978.

Bourne, L. S., R. Sinclair, and K. Dziewonski, eds. *Urbanization and Settlement Systems, International Perspectives.* New York: Oxford University Press, 1984.

Carter, Harold. *An Introduction to Urban Historical Geography.* London: Edward Arnold, 1983.

Chisholm, Michael. *Rural Settlement and Land Use.* 3d ed. London: Hutchinson, 1979.

Christaller, Walter. *The Central Places of Southern Germany.* Englewood Cliffs, NJ: Prentice-Hall, 1966.

Daniels, P. W. *Service Industries: A Geographical Appraisal.* London: Methuen, 1986.

Davis, Kingsley. *Cities: Their Origin, Growth, and Human Impact.* San Francisco: W. H. Freeman, 1973.

Demangeon, Albert. "The Origins and Causes of Settlement Types." in *Readings in Cultural Geography,* edited by P. L. Wagner and M. W. Mikesell. Chicago: University of Chicago Press, 1962.

Detwyler, Thomas, and Melvin Marcus, eds. *Urbanization and Environment.* Belmont, CA: Duxbury Press, 1972.

Dickinson, Robert E. "Rural Settlements in the German Lands." *Annals of the Association of American Geographers* 39 (December 1949): 239–63.

Furuseth, Owen J., and John T. Pierce. *Agricultural Land in an Urban Society.* Washington, D.C.: Association of American Geographers, 1982.

Gottmann, Jean. *Megalopolis.* New York: Twentieth Century Fund, 1961.

Harris, Chauncey D. "A Functional Classification of Cities in the United States." *Geographical Review* 33 (January 1943): 86–99.

Hauser, Philip M., and Leo F. Schnore, eds. *The Study of Urbanization.* New York: Wiley, 1965.

Jacobs, Jane. *The Economy of Cities.* New York: Vintage Books, 1970.

King, Leslie J. *Central Place Theory.* Beverly Hills: Sage Publications, 1984.

Kirn, Thomas J. "Growth and Change in the Service Sector of the U.S.: A Spatial Perspective." *Annals of the Association of American Geographers* 77 (September 1987): 353–72.

Longley, Paul A., Michael Batty, and John Shepherd. "The Size, Shape, and Dimensions of Urban Settlements." *Transactions of the Institute of British Geographers,* New Series 16 (1991): 75–94.

Lösch, August. *The Economics of Location.* New Haven: Yale University Press, 1954.

Marshall, J.N. "Services in a Postindustrial Economy." *Environment and Planning A* 17 (1985): 1155–67.

Morrill, Richard. "The Structure of Shopping in a Metropolis," *Urban Geography* 8 (1987): 97–128.

Mumford, Lewis. *The City in History.* New York: Harcourt, Brace, and World, 1961.

O'Kelly, M. E. "Multipurpose Shopping Trips and the Size of Retail Facilities." *Annals of the Association of American Geographers* 73 (June 1983): 231–39.

Scofield, Edna. "The Origin of Settlement Patterns in Rural New England." *Geographical Review* 28 (October 1938): 652–63.

Scott, Peter. *Geography and Retailing.* London: Hutchinson University Press, 1970.

Trewartha, Glen T. "Types of Rural Settlements in North America." *Geographical Review* 36 (October 1946): 568–96.

Wheeler, James O., and Ronald L. Mitchelson. "Information Flows among Major Metropolitan Areas in the United States," *Annals of the Association of American Geographers* 79 (December 1989): 523–543.

Wirth, Louis. *On Cities and Social Life.* Chicago: University of Chicago Press, 1964.

Also consult these journals: *Journal of Historical Geography; Journal of Regional Science; Journal of Rural Studies; Urban Geography.*

12
Urban Patterns

If you are a football fan, you know that the Detroit Lions actually play their home games in a stadium located in Pontiac, Michigan, 50 kilometers (30 miles) from downtown Detroit. The Los Angeles Rams play in Anaheim, California, and the Dallas Cowboys in Irving, Texas. The New York Giants and New York Jets play their home games in another state altogether, at the New Jersey Meadowlands.

The movement of football clubs is simply one element in a general trend towards suburbanization of people and activities in the United States and Canada. More people in these two countries live in suburbs than in central cities. The changing structure of our cities is a response to conflicting desires. We wish to spread out across the landscape to avoid the problems of the city, but at the same time we want access to the city's jobs, shops, culture, and recreation.

This chapter examines the causes and consequences of the evolving urban patterns. For example, how do fans reach the football stadium located in Irving or New Jersey? The only way to get there may be by car. What happens to people who don't have cars? In the old days—when the Cowboys played at the Cotton Bowl in downtown Dallas and the Giants played at Yankee Stadium in the Bronx—people could use public transportation to reach the stadiums. Today, it is inconvenient, if not impossible, for people without cars to attend games. Although attendance at a football game may not be a central part of everyone's life, think about daily activities, such as working and shopping. Where are jobs and shops now located? Increasingly, they are in the suburbs.

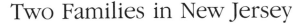

Two Families in New Jersey

Ruth Merritt lives in the city of Camden, New Jersey. At twenty-four, she is a single parent with three children, ages seven, two, and one. Her income, derived from the community's program of aid to families with dependent children, is $235 per month.

The Merritt family lives in a four-room apartment in a row house that was divided some years ago into six dwelling units. The apartment has generally adequate plumbing and kitchen facilities, but the residents sometimes see rats in the building. The rent is $75 per month, plus an average of $50 per month for electricity and other utilities. Although Ruth Merritt receives food stamps, her monthly expenses for food, clothing, and shelter exceed her income. In cold weather, she must sometimes reduce the food budget to pay for heat.

The Aquino family lives in Cherry Hill, New Jersey, 10 kilometers east of Camden. William Aquino is a lawyer who commutes to downtown Philadelphia, across the Delaware River from Camden. Diane Aquino works for a nonprofit organization with offices in the suburban community in which they live. Their two children attend a recently built school in the community.

The Aquino family's dwelling consists of a detached house with three bedrooms, a living room, a dining room, a family room, and a kitchen. The attached garage contains two cars, one for each parent to get to work. The half-acre lawn surrounding the house provides ample space for the children to play. The Aquinos bought their house five years ago for $150,000. The monthly payments for mortgage and utilities are nearly $2,000, but the family's combined annual income of $100,000 is more than adequate to pay the housing costs.

The Merritt and Aquino households illustrate the contrasts that can be found in U.S. urban areas. As we have seen throughout this book, dramatic differences in material standards exist around the world. But the picture drawn here is based on families living in the same urban area, only a few kilometers from one another.

Were these examples taken from an urban area elsewhere in the world, the spatial patterns might be reversed. In most of the world, the higher-status Aquinos would live near the center of the city, while the lower-status Merritts would live in the suburbs.

This chapter examines the patterns and problems observed in the modern city. Although significant differences exist between the internal structure of urban areas in the United States and elsewhere in the world, problems arising from current spatial trends are nonetheless quite similar.

The modern city is a complex mosaic of people and activities. Geographers are concerned with describing where different types of activities are located in a city and where different types of people live. Geographers also try to explain the reasons for the location of particular activities and people within the city.

As discussed in Chapter 11, the urbanized area includes the central city and the surrounding suburbs. This chapter is organized around the activities found in these two distinctive areas. The central city includes a central commercial core and inner residential neighborhoods. Suburbs include manufacturing and commercial districts as well as residences.

KEY ISSUE

What Activities Are Found in the Central City?

The center is the best-known and most visually distinctive area of most cities. It is usually one of the oldest districts in a city and is often located on or near the original site of the settlement. The precise boundary of the central area is not always easily defined but in common usage corresponds roughly to the area built up at the time of construction of railroad tracks and terminals in the mid-nineteenth century, especially in Europe.

The Central Business District

The center of U.S. cities—sometimes called the **central business district** (CBD)—is the area of the city where retail and office activities are concentrated. Similar definitions exist to define the center of cities in other countries. The CBD is relatively small and compact—less than 1 percent of the urban land area—but contains a large percentage of the urbanized area's shops, offices, and public institutions (Figure 12–1).

Retail and office activities are attracted to the CBD because of its accessibility. The center is the easiest part of the city to reach from the rest of the region and is the focal point of the region's transportation network.

Importance of the CBD for retailing. Three types of retail activities tend to concentrate in the center of the city because of a need to be accessible to everyone in the region. First, a shop may be located in the center if it has a high threshold, that is, a large minimum number of customers needed to support the service. This type of shop has traditionally preferred a central location to be accessible to a large number of customers. Examples include large furniture or department stores.

Frequently, large department stores in the central business district clustered across the street from each other. Retailers referred to the intersection nearest the clustering of department stores as the "100 percent corner." Rents were the highest at the 100 percent corner, because it was the location in the city that had the highest accessibility for the largest number of potential customers.

In recent years, many shops that have high thresholds have closed their downtown branches, especially large department stores. Central areas that once contained three or four large department stores may now have none at all or perhaps one struggling survivor. The customers for downtown department stores comprise downtown office workers, inner-city residents, and tourists. Department stores with high thresholds are now more likely to be located in suburban malls.

The second type of shop that tends to be located in the center has a high range, that is, a great maxi-

FIGURE 12–1
The central business district of Minneapolis, Minnesota, is dominated by retail and office buildings. Also clustered in the downtown area are a number of public and semipublic buildings, including the city hall, government office buildings, and the central post office.

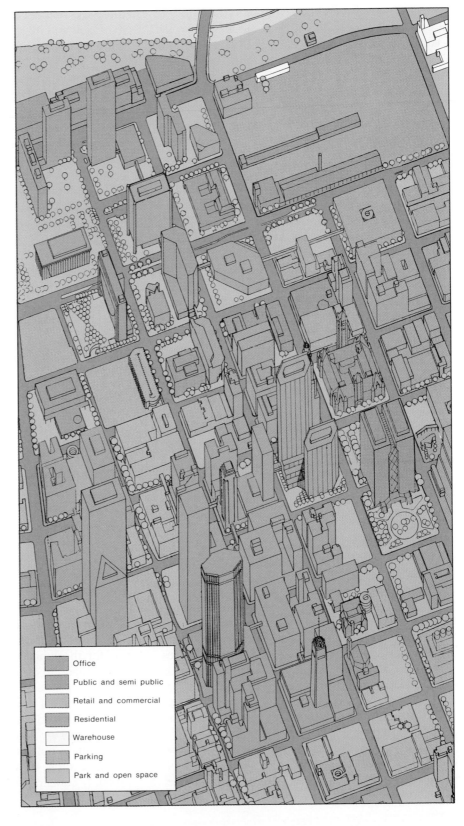

Office

Public and semi public

Retail and commercial

Residential

Warehouse

Parking

Park and open space

mum distance customers are willing to travel to use the service. A shop with a high range is likely to be a very specialized store whose customers are not likely to patronize it frequently. Highly specialized stores are placed in central locations because their customers are scattered over a wide area. An expensive jewelry or fur shop, for example, attracts shoppers from all over the urban area, though each individual customer is not likely to visit the store frequently.

A number of cities have preserved their old downtown markets that feature a large number of stalls, each operated by individual merchants. These markets may have a high range, because they attract customers willing to travel relatively far to find products that are more exotic or of higher quality than those in their neighborhood supermarkets. At the same time, inner-city residents may utilize these markets for their weekly grocery shopping.

Many shops with high ranges have joined department stores in moving to suburban shopping malls. But shops with high ranges can thrive in a number of central business districts if they combine retailing with recreational activities. People are willing to travel a long distance to a downtown shopping area that offers unusual shops in a dramatic setting, perhaps a central atrium with a fountain or a view of the harbor.

A third type of retail activity located in the center serves the large number of people who work in the center and shop during lunch or working hours. These shops provide office supplies, computers, and clothing. Services such as rapid photocopying, restaurants, shoe repairers, film processors, and dry cleaners also concentrate in the center to serve office workers.

Central business districts in cities outside of North America are more likely to contain supermarkets, bakeries, butchers, and other stores that sell food. Many of the customers have difficulty buying groceries closer to their homes because such stores may have limited opening hours in the evenings or on weekends. The 24-hour supermarket is rare outside of North America, because of government regulations, preferences of shopkeepers, and long-time shopping habits.

In contrast to the other two types of retailers, shops that appeal to nearby office workers are expanding in the central business district, in part because the number of downtown office workers has increased and in part because downtown offices require more services.

Importance of the CBD for offices. Offices cluster in the center because of accessibility. Officials in the advertising, banking, finance, journalism, and legal professions particularly depend on proximity to professional colleagues. Lawyers, for example, locate downtown to be near government offices and courts. Services such as temporary secretarial agencies and instant printers locate downtown to be near lawyers, forming a sort of chain of interdependency that continues to draw offices to the center of the city.

Despite the diffusion of modern telecommunications, many professionals still exchange information primarily through face-to-face contact with others in the same line of work. Financial analysts exchange information about attractive stocks or impending corporate takeover attempts. Lawyers meet with one another to settle their clients' disputes out-of-court. Offices are centrally located to facilitate rapid communication of fast-breaking news through spatial proximity. Face-to-face contact also helps to establish a relationship of trust based on shared professional values.

A central location is also helpful for offices that employ workers who live in a variety of neighborhoods. The top executives may live in one neighborhood, the junior executives in another, the secretaries in another, and the custodians in another. Only a central location is readily accessible to all groups. Firms that need highly specialized employees are more likely to find new talent in the central area, perhaps currently working for another company located downtown.

High land costs in the center. The accessibility of the center produces extremely strong competition for the limited sites available. As a result, the value of land in the center is very high. A hectare of land may cost several thousand dollars in a rural area and tens of thousands of dollars in a suburb. If a hectare of land were available in a large CBD such as New York or London, it would cost several hundred million dollars.

The central business district of Tokyo, Japan, probably contains the world's most expensive land.

Transactions there have exceeded $250,000 per square meter ($1,000,000,000 per acre). If this page were a parcel of land in Tokyo, it would sell for more than $12,000.

Tokyo's high prices result from a severe shortage of buildable land. Buildings are legally restricted to a height of less than 10 meters—normally three stories—because of fear of earthquakes, even though recent earthquakes have demonstrated that modern, well-built skyscrapers are safer than older three-story structures. Japanese tax laws favor retention of agricultural land; although it is the world's most populous urban area, Tokyo contains 36,000 hectares (90,000 acres) of farmland.

Two distinctive characteristics of the central city follow from the very high land costs. First, land is used more intensively in the center than elsewhere in the city. Second, some activities are excluded from the center because of the high cost of space.

Intensive land use. The demand for space has given the central city a three-dimensional character. Compared with other parts of the city, the central area makes more extensive use of space below and above ground level.

A vast underground network exists beneath most central cities. The typical "underground city" includes multistory parking garages, loading docks for deliveries to offices and shops, and water and sewer lines. Subways run under the streets of larger central cities. Minneapolis, Montreal, Toronto, and other cities have built extensive systems of pedestrian passages and shops beneath the center. These underground areas help to segregate pedestrians from motor vehicles and provide protection from harsh winter weather.

Typically, telephone, electric, and cable television wires run beneath the surface in central areas. Not enough space is available in the center for the large number of telephone poles that would be needed for such a dense network, and the wires would be unsightly and hazardous.

Skyscrapers. The demand for space in the central city has also made high-rise structures economically feasible. A collection of downtown skyscrapers provides a city with one of its most important visual images and unifying symbols. Suburban houses, shop-

ping malls, and factories look much the same from one city to another, but every city has a unique downtown skyline as a result of the particular arrangement and architectural styles of its high-rise buildings.

The first skyscrapers, built in Chicago in the 1880s, were made possible by two inventions: the elevator and iron-frame building construction. The first high-rises caused great inconvenience to neighboring structures, because they blocked out light and air. The invention of artificial sources of lighting, ventilation, central heating, and airconditioning have helped to relieve these problems. Most North American and European cities enacted zoning ordinances early in the twentieth century in part to control the location and height of skyscrapers.

More new office space has been built in the CBDs of Boston, Los Angeles, New York, and many other North American cities during the past decade than in any other previous decade. Banks, insurance companies, and other financial institutions have built new offices to house their expanding workforce. Private developers have erected skyscrapers as speculative ventures. As a result of recent downtown building booms, skyscrapers are again causing problems.

When too many skyscrapers are built near each other, people are unable to get to and from them without suffering delays. Streets become congested because the skyscrapers generate a considerable amount of traffic. Sunlight rarely penetrates to the sidewalks and the small parcels of open space that remain.

Construction of high rises may also be affected in the future by the need to conserve energy. As the sun and natural air are increasingly relied upon again for light and ventilation, the old complaints about high rises may return.

The nature of an activity influences which floor in a typical high rise it occupies. Some shop owners may demand street-level locations to entice the most customers and thus are willing to pay relatively high rents for space. Professional offices are less dependent on walk-in trade and thus can occupy the higher levels at lower rents. Hotel rooms and apartments may be included in the upper floors of a skyscraper to take advantage of the lower noise levels and the panoramic views. The residents of the world's tallest apartment building, the ninety-seven-

The skyline of downtown Zurich, Switzerland, as in many European cities, is dominated by medieval churches and public buildings rather than by office buildings, as is typical in American cities. The twin-spired building to the left is the Grossmünster (Large Cathedral), erected between the eleventh and thirteenth centuries. In the right foreground is the nineteenth century Swiss National Museum; behind it is the main train station. The thin, green spire in the background is the twelfth century Das Fraumünster (Lady Cathedral); immediately to its right is St. Peter's Church, which has the largest clock dial in Europe, a diameter of 8.66 meters (28 feet 5 inches).

story John Hancock Center in Chicago, sometimes are above the clouds and telephone the doorman to find out about the weather at street level.

The one large U.S. city without skyscrapers is Washington, D.C., where no building is allowed to be higher than the U.S. Capitol dome. Consequently, offices in downtown Washington rise no more than thirteen stories. As a result, the typical office building in Washington uses more land than in

other cities, and the city's central office district spreads out over a much wider area than those in other cities of comparable size.

European CBDs. The central area is less dominated by commercial considerations in Europe than in the United States. In addition to retail and office functions, many European cities contain a legacy of low-rise structures and narrow streets built as long ago as medieval times that today are protected from the intrusion of contemporary development. The most prominent structures may be churches and former royal palaces, situated on the most important public squares, at road junctions, or on hilltops. Many parks in the center of European cities were first laid out as private gardens for aristocratic families and only later were opened to the public.

Some European cities have tried to preserve their historic core by limiting the number of cars and high-rise buildings. During the early 1970s, several high-rise offices were built in Paris, including Europe's tallest office building, the 210-meter (688-foot) Tour Montparnasse. The public outcry over the damage done to the city's historic skyline was so great that officials had to reenact lower maximum height restrictions. Officials in Rome periodically try to ban all private automobiles from the center of the city, because they cause pollution and congestion and damage ancient monuments.

The central area of Warsaw, Poland, represents an extreme example of preservation. The Nazis completely destroyed Warsaw's medieval core during World War II, but Poland rebuilt the area exactly as it had appeared, using old photographs and drawings for guidance. The reconstruction of central Warsaw served as a powerful symbol of cultural tradition for the Polish people after the upheavels of World War II and the postwar communist takeover.

Although constructing large new buildings is difficult, many shops and offices still wish to be in the center of European cities. The alternative to new construction is renovation of older buildings. But renovation is more expensive and does not always produce enough space to meet the demand. As a result, rents are much higher in the center of European cities than in U.S. cities of comparable size.

Land uses excluded from the CBD. High rents and the shortage of land discourage two principal types of activities from concentrating in the central area: manufacturing and residential. The typical modern industrial plant requires a large parcel of land in order to spread out operations in one-story buildings. Suitable land is more likely found in the suburbs.

The number of manufacturing jobs in the central part of Paris declined from more than 500,000 in the late 1960s to 400,000 around 1980 and 200,000

in the early 1990s. The Citroen automobile factory, situated along the River Seine barely one kilometer from the Eiffel Tower, has been replaced by high-rise offices and apartments. Warehouses on the southeast edge of the central area have also been replaced by office and apartment towers. Slaughterhouses in the northeastern part of central Paris have been replaced by a park and museum complex.

Port cities in North America and Europe have transformed their harbors from industrial to commercial and recreational activities. Once ships docked at piers that jutted out into the water, and warehouses lined the waterfront to facilitate the loading and unloading of goods. Because today's large ocean-going ships are unable to maneuver in the tight, shallow waters of the old inner-city harbors, port facilities have moved to more modern facilities downstream. Cities have demolished derelict warehouses and rotting piers along their waterfronts and replaced them with new offices, shops, parks, and museums.

Once-rotting downtown waterfronts have become major tourist attractions in a number of North American cities, including Boston, Toronto, Baltimore, and San Francisco, as well as in European cities such as Barcelona and London. The cities took the lead in clearing the sites and constructing new parks, docks, walkways, museums, and parking lots; large convention centers have been built to house professional meetings and trade shows. Private developers have added hotels, restaurants, boutiques, and entertainment centers to accommodate the tourists and conventioneers.

Few people live in the central area, because offices and shops can afford to pay higher rents for the scarce space. Annual rents in downtown high-rise office buildings range from $10 to $40 per square foot depending on the city. At $20 per square foot annually, the rent for a typical two-bedroom apartment would exceed $800 per month.

The shortage of affordable space is especially critical in Europe, because Europeans are more likely than Americans to prefer living near the center of the city. Prohibitions on constructing new high-rises induce developers to convert older houses into offices.

Abandoned warehouses have also been converted into residences in a number of central business districts. City officials welcome the additional

Faneuil Hall, in downtown Boston, was constructed in 1742 and rebuilt two years after a fire in 1761. In colonial times, a market occupied the first floor, and the second floor was a meeting hall. The building, along with the adjacent Quincy Market, has been renovated as a marketplace.

People have migrated from central cities for a combination of pull and push factors. First, people have been lured to suburbs, which offer larger homes with private yards and modern schools. Second, people have sought to escape from the dirt, crime, congestion, and poverty of the central city.

Commuting. Because relatively few people live in the center of many North American cities, urban areas are characterized by high levels of commuting into the CBD in the morning and out in the evening. The intense concentration of people in the center during the working hours strains the transportation system, because a large number of people must reach a small area of land at the same time in the morning and disperse at the same time in the afternoon. As much as 40 percent of all trips made into or out of a central business district may occur during four hours of the day, two each in the morning and afternoon. The four consecutive 15-minute periods that have the heaviest traffic are called the **rush** or **peak hours.**

In larger cities, public transportation may carry a substantial number of people during peak travel hours. Such transportation is better suited than cars to the movement of large numbers of people, because each traveler takes up far less space. But most American commuters prefer to travel by car. One-third of the high-priced central land is devoted to streets and parking lots, though multistory and underground garages also are constructed.

The Zone in Transition

Surrounding the CBD is an area that has been given many names, including the zone in transition, the gray area, and the twilight zone. The **zone in transition** comprises older industries and warehouses, as well as residential areas. In U.S. cities, the zone contains three predominant types of residential areas: older low-quality housing, public housing, and renovated housing.

Low-quality housing. Most occupants of inner residential areas in U.S. cities are low-income nonwhites, a pattern that is largely a product of poor race relations. Many neighborhoods in the United States are racially segregated, with blacks or Hispanics concentrated in one or two large continuous ar-

downtown residents but are reluctant to see the permanent loss of industrial space, even though realistically, new manufacturers are highly unlikely to move into multistory downtown lofts. The warehouses may require expensive alterations to meet local code standards with regard to emergency exits and ventilation.

Large numbers of people used to live in central cities. For example, the City of London—the region's one-square mile financial center and the site of its earliest settlement—contained 128,000 residents in 1851. The population declined to about 72,000 in 1871, 13,000 in 1921, and 5,000 today. The central business districts of North American cities have witnessed comparable population losses.

eas of the inner city and whites living in the sub-urbs.

As the number of low-income and minority families continues to increase in the city, the territory they occupy expands. Neighborhoods can shift from predominantly white middle-class occupants to low-income nonwhites within a few years. Middle-class white families move out of a neighborhood to newer housing farther away from the center and sell or rent their houses to lower-income nonwhite families. Large houses built in the nineteenth century by wealthy families are subdivided by absentee landlords into a number of smaller dwellings for occupancy by low-income families. This process of subdivision of houses and occupancy by successive waves of lower-income people is known as **filtering.** The ultimate result of filtering may be abandonment of the dwelling.

Like a car, a tape player, or any other object, the better a house is maintained, the longer it will last. Landlords stop spending money to maintain houses when the rents they can collect are less than the maintenance costs. In such a case, the building soon deteriorates and is no longer fit for occupancy. Not even the poorest families are willing to rent the dwelling. This is the point in the filtering process at which the owner may abandon the property, because the value of the structure is less than the cost of taxes. Thousands of vacant and abandoned houses stand in the inner areas of American cities.

A century ago, low-income inner-city areas in the United States were teaming with throngs of recent immigrants from Europe. Today, these areas house barely 10 percent of the population of 1900 and less than half of the population of 1960. Schools and shops close because they are no longer needed in inner-city neighborhoods with rapidly declining populations. Through the filtering process, many poor families have moved to less-deteriorated houses farther from the center.

The process of deterioration in American urban neighborhoods is aggravated by blockbusting and redlining. Real estate agents who practice **block-busting** start by convincing white property owners to sell their houses at low prices, preying on their fear that nonwhite families will soon move into the neighborhood. The agent then sells or rents the houses to nonwhite families at a considerable profit. Some banks engage in **redlining,** so named be-cause the banks draw lines on a map and refuse to loan money for property within the boundaries. Families who try to fix up houses in the inner city therefore have difficulty borrowing money. Although both these practices are illegal in the United States, enforcement of laws against them is frequently difficult.

North American and European cities demolished much of the substandard inner-city housing between the 1950s and 1970s through urban renewal programs. Under urban renewal, cities designated blighted inner-city neighborhoods, acquired the properties from private owners, relocated the residents and businesses, cleared the site, and built new roads and utilities. The cities then turned the land over to private developers or to public agencies, such as the board of education or parks department, to construct new buildings. National government grants helped cities pay for urban renewal.

Urban renewal has been criticized for destroying the social cohesion of older neighborhoods and reducing the supply of low-cost housing. Because blacks comprised a large percentage of the displaced population in U.S. cities, urban renewal was often derisively labelled "Negro Removal" during the 1960s. Most North American and European cities have turned away from urban renewal since the 1970s, and national governments, including the United States, have stopped funding it.

Public housing. Many old, substandard houses in the zone in transition of European and North American cities have been demolished and replaced with public housing. In the United States, **public housing** is reserved for low-income households, who must pay 30 percent of their income for rent. A housing authority, established by the local government, manages the buildings, while the federal government pays for construction and the maintenance, repair, and management costs not covered by rents.

Public housing accounts for only 2 percent of all dwellings in the United States, though it may total more than 10 percent in the zone in transition of many cities. More than 33 percent of all housing is publicly owned in the United Kingdom, for example, and the percentage is even higher in northern cities, such as Liverpool, Manchester, and Glasgow. Private landlords control only a small percentage of housing in the United Kingdom, for the most part confined to central London and resort communities.

Elsewhere in Western Europe, governments typically do not own the housing, but they subsidize construction costs and rents for a large percentage of the privately built housing. Developers of low-cost housing may be either nonprofit organizations, such as church groups and labor unions, or profit-making corporations that agree to build some low-cost housing in exchange for permission to build higher-cost housing elsewhere. The U.S. government has also provided subsidies to private developers, but on a much smaller scale than in Europe.

A number of the high-rise public-housing projects built in the United States and Europe during the 1950s and early 1960s are now considered unsatisfactory environments for families with children. The elevators are frequently broken, juveniles terrorize other people in the hallways, and drug use and crime rates are high. Some observers claim that the high-rise buildings caused the problem, because too many low-income families are concentrated into a high-density environment. The public-housing authorities in Dallas, Texas, Newark, New Jersey, St. Louis, Missouri, Liverpool (England), Glasgow (Scotland), and other cities in the United States and Europe have demolished high-rise public housing projects in recent years because of poor conditions.

More recently constructed public housing projects have consisted primarily of walk-up buildings and row houses, with high-rise apartments reserved for elderly people. Cities have also experimented with so-called scattered-site public housing, in which dwellings are dispersed through the city rather than clustered in a large project.

In recent years, the U.S. government has stopped providing funds for construction of new public housing projects. Some federal support is available to renovate older buildings and to help low-income households pay their rent, but the overall level of funding is much lower today than in the late 1970s. As a result, the supply of public housing and other government-subsidized housing diminished by approximately 1 million units between the early 1980s and the early 1990s. During the same period, the number of households needing low-rent dwellings increased by more than 2 million.

In Britain, the supply of public housing, known as council estates, has also declined, because the na-

tional government has forced local authorities to sell some of the dwellings to the residents. The British, however, have expanded subsidies to nonprofit housing associations, which build housing for groups with special needs, including single mothers, immigrants, the disabled, and the elderly, as well as the poor, by providing subsidies to nonprofit housing associations.

Renovated housing. In addition to areas of older low-quality housing and public housing, the third type of residential area found in the zone in transition is the high-class neighborhood. In some cases, older neighborhoods never went through a process of decline. They contained some of the city's socially elite citizens, who maintained an enclave of expensive property near the center of the city. In other cases, inner-city neighborhoods have only recently achieved high status as a result of renovation by the city and private investors. Some middle-class families are moving back to the zone in transition, a process known as **gentrification.**

Gentrification occurs for a number of reasons. Some middle-class families are attracted by housing prices, which are lower in the zone in transition than in suburbs. Houses in the zone in transition may not only be less expensive, but they may also be larger and more substantially constructed than suburban homes. They may contain attractive architectural features, such as ornate fireplaces, cornices, high ceilings, and leaded-glass windows.

Renovated homes in the zone in transition also attract middle-class persons who work downtown. Proximity to work places spares people the strain of commuting on crowded freeways or public transit systems. Others wish to take advantage of the cultural and recreational opportunities increasingly available in many central areas. Renovated housing in the zone in transition is more likely to appeal to those who do not have children, because they are less likely to be concerned with the quality of nearby schools.

Renovation of an old house near the center of the city can be nearly as expensive as buying a new suburban home. Cities encourage young middle-class families to renovate homes in the zone in transition by providing low-cost loans and tax breaks. Public expenditures for renovation have been criticized as subsidies for the middle class at the expense of poor people, who are forced to move out of the revitalized neighborhoods because the rents in the area are suddenly too high for them.

Cities try to reduce the hardship on poor families in two ways. First, since 1970 U.S. law has required that families forced to relocate as a result of public action receive reimbursement for moving expenses as well as payments for rent increases over a four-year period; Western European countries have similar laws. Second, cities renovate old houses specifically for lower-income families, either through the public housing or other housing programs. By renting renovated houses, the city can also help to disperse low-income families throughout the city instead of concentrating them in large public-housing projects in the zone in transition.

KEY ISSUE

What Are the Causes and Consequences of Suburbanization?

Although inner-city neighborhoods attract an increasing number of middle-class families, the movement is quite small compared to the process of suburbanization. The modern Northern American city is surrounded by increasingly extensive residential suburbs, made possible by transportation improvements. The suburbs are inhabited by families who wish to live at a lower density than is possible near the central area. To serve these suburban residents, commercial activities have expanded as well.

Attraction of Suburbs

Every public opinion poll taken in the United States and Western Europe shows people's strong desire to live in a suburban setting. In most polls, more than 90 percent of the respondents prefer the suburbs to the zone in transition.

Suburbs in those regions of the world offer a variety of attractions: a detached single-family dwelling rather than a row house or apartment, private land surrounding the house, space to park cars, and a greater opportunity for home ownership. The suburban house provides space and privacy, a daily retreat from the stress of urban living. Families with children are especially attracted to suburbs, which

offer more space for play and protection from the high crime rates and heavy traffic that characterize inner-city life. As incomes have risen in the twentieth century, first in the United States and more recently in Western Europe, more families can afford to buy suburban homes.

The suburban population has grown much faster than the overall population, especially in the United States. According to the Bureau of the Census, the U.S. population classified as suburban has increased from 20 percent in 1950 to 60 percent today. To put it another way, since 1950 the U.S. population has increased by about 100 million people. During that time, population has increased by about 135 million in suburbs and declined by about 35 million in central cities and rural areas.

U.S. suburbs are characterized by **sprawl**, a consequence of the process of building new housing. Private developers, who are responsible for selecting new housing sites, look for cheap land that can be readily prepared for construction—that is, land frequently not close to the existing built-up area. Sprawl is also fostered by the desire of many families to own large tracts of land.

Sprawl is costly and inefficient. Roads and utilities, such as water and sewer lines, must be built to connect isolated new developments with the rest of the built-up area. The cost of these new roads and utilities is either funded by taxes or installed by the developer, who passes on the cost to the new residents through higher house prices. Sprawl also wastes land. Some prime agricultural land may be lost through construction of isolated housing developments, while other sites, held by speculators, may lie fallow even though new houses have not been built on them.

Changes in Transportation Systems

Sprawl makes people more dependent on transportation systems for access to work, shopping, and leisure activities. People do not travel aimlessly: their trips have a precise point of origin, destination, and purpose. More than half of all trips are work-related, either commuting between work and home or business trips such as deliveries. Shopping or other personal business and social journeys each account for approximately one-fourth of all trips.

The suburbs of European cities, such as Genoa, Italy (below), are more likely to consist of apartment buildings accommodating lower income households. In contrast, U.S. suburbs, such as Staten Island, New York (right), are more likely to contain detached, single-family houses surrounded by private yards.

Historically, the growth of suburbs was constrained by transportation problems. People lived in crowded cities because they had to be within walking distance of shops and places of employment. The invention of the railroad in the nineteenth century enabled people to live in suburbs and work in the central city. Cities then built street railways—frequently known as trolleys, streetcars, or trams—and underground railways (subways) to accommodate commuters.

Many of the so-called streetcar suburbs built in the nineteenth century still exist and retain unique visual identities. They consist of houses and shops clustered near a station or former streetcar stop at a much higher density than is found in newer suburbs.

The automobile. The suburban explosion in the twentieth century has relied on automobiles rather than railroads, especially in the United States. In the nineteenth century, rail and trolley lines had restricted suburban development to narrow ribbons within walking distance of the stations. Automobiles have permitted large-scale development of suburbs at greater distances from the center, in the gaps between the rail lines. Automobile drivers have much greater flexibility in the choice of residence than was ever before possible.

Automobile ownership is nearly universal among American households, with the exception of some poor families, older individuals, and people living in the center of big cities, such as New York. More than 95 percent of all trips within U.S. cities are made by car, compared to fewer than 5 percent by bus or rail. Outside the big cities, public transportation service is extremely rare or nonexistent.

The U.S. government has encouraged the use of cars by paying 90 percent of the cost of 70,000 kilometers (44,000 miles) of limited-access high-speed interstate highways. The use of cars is also supported by policies that limit the price of fuel to less than one-half the level found in Western Europe. A few years ago, Senator Daniel Patrick Moynihan, a former Harvard professor, quipped that the United States has a national urban growth policy—the interstate highway system. He was referring to the dominant role of new expressway construction in fostering decentralization of U.S. cities.

Public transit. In North America, public transportation has been the major casualty of the commitment to the automobile. Ridership on public transportaton declined in the United States from 23 billion per year in the late 1940s to 7 billion in the early 1990s. At the end of World War I, U.S. cities had 50,000 kilometers (30,000 miles) of street railways and trolleys that carried 14 billion passengers a year, but only a few hundred kilometers of track remain. The number of U.S. and Canadian cities with trolley service declined from about fifty in 1950 to eight in the 1960s: Boston, Cleveland, Newark, New Orleans, Philadelphia, Pittsburgh, San Francisco, and Toronto.

Buses offered a more flexible service than trolleys, because they were not restricted to operating only on fixed tracks. General Motors acquired many of the privately owned streetcar companies and replaced the trolleys with buses that the company made. But bus ridership has declined from a peak of 11 billion riders per year in the late 1940s to 5 million in the 1990s. Commuter railroad service, like trolleys and buses, has also been drastically reduced in most U.S. cities.

The one exception to the downward trend in public transportation in the United States is the subway, now known to transportation planners as fixed heavy rail. Cities such as Boston and Chicago have attracted new passengers through construction of new lines and modernization of existing service. Chicago has been a pioneer in the construction of heavy-rail rapid transit lines in the median strip of expressways. Entirely new subway systems have been built in recent years in a number of U.S. cities, including Atlanta, Baltimore, Miami, San Francisco, and Washington, D.C.

The federal government has permitted Boston, New York, and other cities to use funds originally allocated for interstate highways to modernize rapid transit service instead. New York's subway cars, once covered with graffiti sprayed by gang members, have been cleaned so that passengers can ride in a more hospitable environment. As a result of these improvements, subway ridership in the United States has increased 2 percent per year since 1980.

The trolley—now known by the more elegant term of fixed-light rail transit—is making a modest comeback in North America. Once relegated almost exclusively to the role of tourist attraction in New Orleans and San Francisco, new trolley lines have been built or are under construction in several cities, including Baltimore, Maryland; Buffalo, New York; Portland, Oregon; Los Angeles, Sacramento, San Diego, and San Jose, California; St. Louis, Missouri; and Edmonton and Calgary, Alberta. But new construction in all these ten cities amounted to only approximately 200 kilometers (130 miles) during the 1980s and early 1990s.

California, the state that most symbolizes the automobile-oriented American culture, leads in the construction of new fixed-light rail transit lines. San Diego has added more kilometers than any other city, although Los Angeles will have the most extensive new system, once it is completed. Los Angeles had a rail network of more than 1,600 kilometers (1,000 miles) as recently as the late 1940s, but the lines were abandoned when freeways were constructed to accommodate rising automobile use. In San Diego, one line that runs from the center south to the Mexican border has been irreverently dubbed the "Tijuana trolley," because it is heavily used by residents of nearby Tijuana, Mexico.

Public transportation is particularly suited to bringing a large number of people into a small area in a short period of time. Consequently, its use is increasingly confined in the United States to rush-hour commuting by workers in the CBD. A bus can accommodate thirty people in the amount of space occupied by one automobile, while a double-track rapid transit line can transport the same number of people as sixteen lanes of urban freeway.

Ironically, people who are too poor to own an automobile may still not be able to reach places of employment by public transportation. Low-income people in the United States tend to live in inner-city neighborhoods, but the job opportunities—especially those requiring minimal training and skill—are often located in suburban areas not well-served by public transportation. Inner-city neighborhoods have high unemployment rates at the same time that suburban firms have difficulty attracting workers. In some cities, governments and employers subsidize vans that take low-income inner-city residents to suburban jobs.

Public transportation is cheaper, less polluting, and more energy-efficient than the automobile. People generally do not consider all of the costs in-

The competition for space in the central area of large cities creates problems of congestion throughout the world. Commuters in Tokyo, like most major cities in the world outside the United States and Canada, depend on trains and other forms of public transportation. This photograph has not been reversed; approximately one-third of the countries in the world, including Japan, require motorists to drive on the left-hand side of the street.

volved in using automobiles—delays imposed on others, increased need for highway maintenance, construction of new highways, and pollution. Most people overlook these important costs, because the car offers privacy and flexibility of schedule.

Despite modest recent sucesses, most public transportation systems are caught in a vicious circle, because fares do not cover operating costs. As patronage declines and expenses rise, the fares are increased, which drives away passengers and leads to service reductions and still higher fares. Public expenditures to subsidize construction and operating costs have increased, but public officials in the United States do not consider that public transportation is a vital utility deserving of subsidy to the degree long assumed by European governments.

In contrast, even in the relatively developed Western European countries and Japan, where automobile ownership rates are high, extensive networks of bus, tram, and subway lines have been maintained, and funds for new construction have been provided in recent years. Since the late 1960s, London has opened 27 kilometers (17 miles) of subways, including two new lines, plus 18 kilometers (11 miles) in light rail transit lines to serve the docklands area. During the same period, Paris has built 65 kilometers (40 miles) of new subway lines, including a new system, known as the *Réseau Express Régional* (R.E.R.) to serve outer suburbs (Figure 12–2).

Smaller cities have shared the construction boom. In France alone, new subway lines have been built since the 1970s in Lille, Lyon, and Marseille, and hundreds of kilometers of entirely new tracks have been laid between the country's major cities to operate a high-speed train known as the TGV *(train à grande vitesse)*.

The automobile is an important user of land in the city. An average city allocates about one-fourth of its land to roads and parking lots. Valuable land in the central city is devoted to parking automobiles, though expensive underground and multistory parking structures can reduce the amount of ground-level space needed. Modern six-lane freeways cut a 25-meter (75-foot) path through the heart of cities, and elaborate interchanges consume even more space. European and Japanese cities have been especially disrupted by attempts to insert new roads and parking areas in or near to the medieval central areas.

Technological improvements may help motorists elude congested traffic areas. At the beginning of the journey, the driver enters into a computer the starting and destination points, and a screen mounted on the dashboard of the car displays a map, stored on a compact disk, showing the best route to avoid traffic tie-ups. The computer is alerted about traffic conditions by sensors in the wheels or by radio signals. When the automobile enters a high-speed freeway, computers control both its speed and the spacing between it and other vehicles. The potential diffusion of this type of technology reflects the strong preference on the part of most people in relatively developed countries to continue using private automobiles rather than switch to public transportation.

Commercial Activities in the Suburbs

In the United States, growth in the number of people living in suburbs has stimulated nonresidential construction as well. Suburban shops have been built to serve the needs of nearby residents. Industry has moved to the suburbs to find space for expansion. Many offices have also located in suburbs to take advantage of lower land costs.

Suburban shopping malls. Suburban residental growth has led to changes in the traditional retailing patterns. Historically, urban residents bought food and other daily necessities at small neighborhood shops located in the midst of housing areas and then shopped in the CBD for other products. Since the end of World War II, however, sales in downtown shops in the United States have not increased, while sales in suburban areas have risen at an annual rate of 5 percent.

Downtown sales have stagnated because suburban residents who live far from the CBD are increasingly unwilling to make the long journey there. At the same time, small corner shops are no longer found in the midst of newer residential suburbs. The low density of residential construction prevents people from walking to stores, and restrictive zoning practices often exclude shops from residential areas.

Instead, retailing has been increasingly concentrated in planned suburban shopping malls of varying sizes. Corner shops have been replaced by supermarkets located in small shopping centers.

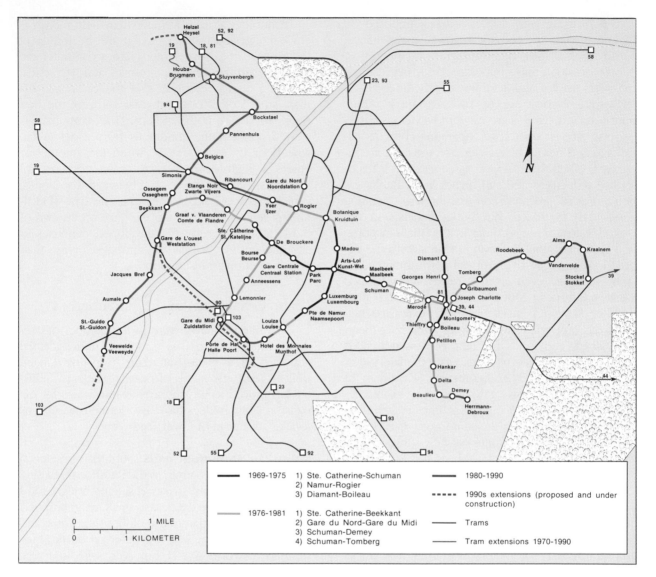

FIGURE 12–2

European cities, including Brussels, have made substantial financial investments to improve their public transport systems in recent years. Brussels provides a good example of a public transport system that integrates light rail (tram) and heavy rail (subway or metro). Trams initially utilized most of Brussels' metro tunnels, which were called "pre-metro" lines. But the tunnels were large enough to convert to heavy rail lines as funds became available.

Larger malls contain department stores and specialty shops traditionally reserved for the CBD. Generous parking lots surround the stores. Shopping malls require as many as 40 hectares (100 acres) of land and are frequently located near key road junctions, such as the interchange of two interstate highways (Figure 12–3).

Some shopping malls are elaborate structures: multilevel structures with more than 100 stores arranged along covered walkways. Shoppings malls have become centers for a variety of activities in suburban areas that lack other types of community facilities. Retired people sit on the benches to watch the passing scene, while teenagers arrive after school to meet their friends. Concerts and exhibitions are frequently set up in the malls.

A shopping mall is built by a developer, who buys the land, builds the structures, and leases space to individual merchants. Rents are typically set as a percentage of sales revenues. The key to a successful large shopping mall is the inclusion of one or more "anchors," which are usually large department stores. Typically, consumers drive to a mall to shop at an anchor and, while there, patronize the smaller stores. In smaller shopping centers, the anchor is frequently a supermarket or discount store.

While retail activities expand in the suburbs, CBDs fight for survival. The total volume of sales in downtown areas has been stable, but the pattern of demand has changed. Large department stores have difficulty attracting their old customers, whereas smaller shops that cater to the special needs of the downtown labor force are surviving. Patrons of downtown shops tend increasingly to be downtown employees who shop during the lunch hour.

Many cities have attempted to revitalize retailing activities in the CBD and older neighborhoods. One popular method is to ban motor vehicles from busy

FIGURE 12–3
Most shopping malls in the Atlanta metropolitan area, as elsewhere in North America, are located in the suburbs rather than the inner city. The optimal location for a large shopping mall is near the junction of two interstate highways.

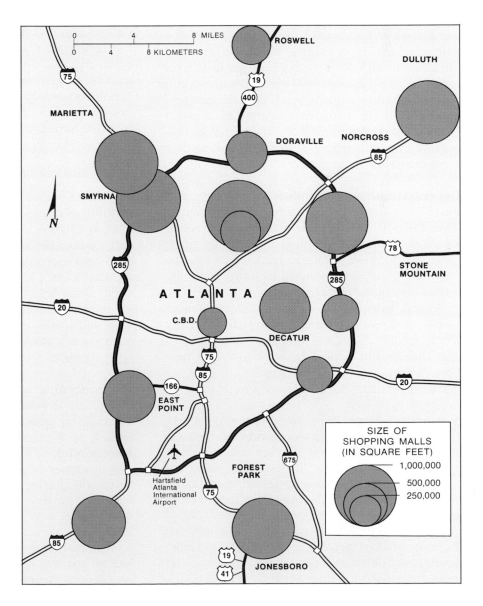

shopping streets. By converting streets to pedestrian-only walkways, cities emulate one of the most attractive attributes of large shopping malls. Shopping streets reserved for pedestrians are widespread in northern Europe, including the Netherlands, Germany, and the Scandinavian countries.

Entirely new large shopping malls have been built in several downtown areas in North America in recent years. In Boston, the eighteenth-century market known as Faneuil Hall was transformed from a derelict area to a modern shopping center. Philadelphia's Market Square East—a downtown four-level shopping center of 185,000 square meters (2 million square feet)—is anchored by two large department stores and provides direct access to a subway station and multistory parking garage. Harbor Place in Baltimore includes two shopping pavilions integrated into a collection of waterfront museums, tourist attractions, hotels, and cultural facilities. These downtown malls have successfully attracted suburban shoppers as well as out-of-town tourists because they offer unique recreation and entertainment experiences, not merely shops.

Decentralization of industry. Factories and warehouses have moved to suburban locations for several reasons. First, industries increasingly receive inputs and distribute finished products by truck. Suburban locations facilitate truck shipments by providing good access to main highways and minimizing central-city traffic congestion.

Second, factories and warehouses demand more land for efficient operation. Conveyor belts, forklift trucks, loading docks, and machinery are spread out over one level in modern factories. Industries have been attracted to suburban locations because of availability of large tracts of lower priced land.

Suburban offices. Firms are attracted to suburbs because rents are much lower than in the CBD. Offices that do not require face-to-face contact increasingly consider locating in lower-cost suburban space. Employees can drive to suburban offices on uncongested roads and park their cars without charge.

Suburban office locations can pose a hardship for some workers. Secretaries, custodians, and other lower-status office workers may not have cars, yet public transportation does not serve the site. Other office workers may miss the stimulation and animation of a central location, particularly at lunch time.

While geographers observe inner-city changes and suburban sprawl, they have searched for general models to explain the internal spatial patterns of urban areas as a whole. Three models, presented in the next section, have been developed.

How Are Different Social Groups Distributed Within an Urban Area?

Geographers and other social scientists understand that people are not distributed randomly within an urban area but, depending on their characteristics, tend to concentrate in particular neighborhoods. Three models help to explain where different types of people tend to live in an urban area: the concentric zone, sector, and multiple nuclei models.

Three Models of Urban Structure

The three models describing the internal social structure of cities were all developed with Chicago in mind. Chicago is located on a flat prairie, and except for Lake Michigan to the east few physical features have interrupted the region's growth. Chicago includes a CBD, known as the Loop, because elevated railway lines form a loop around it. Surrounding the Loop are residential suburbs to the south, west, and north. The three models were later applied to cities elsewhere in the United States and in other countries.

The concentric zone model. The first model to explain the distribution of different social groups within urban areas was created in 1923 by a sociologist, E. W. Burgess. According to his **concentric zone model,** a city grows outward from a central area in a series of concentric rings, like the rings of a tree. The precise size and width of the rings vary from one city to another, but the same basic types of rings appear in all cities in the same order (Figure 12–4).

The first of five zones is the CBD, where nonresidential activities are concentrated. The CBD is surrounded by the next ring, the zone in transition,

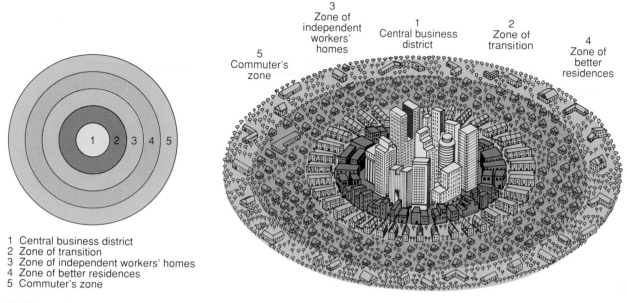

5
Commuter's
zone

3
Zone of
independent
workers'
homes

1
Central business
district

2
Zone of
transition

4
Zone of
better
residences

1 Central business district
2 Zone of transition
3 Zone of independent workers' homes
4 Zone of better residences
5 Commuter's zone

FIGURE 12–4
According to the concentric zone model, a city grows in a series of rings surrounding the central business district.

which contains industry and poorer-quality housing. Immigrants to the city first live in this zone in small dwelling units, frequently created by subdividing larger houses into apartments. The zone also contains rooming houses for single persons.

The next ring—the zone of working-class homes—contains modest older houses occupied by stable, working-class families. The fourth zone has newer and more spacious houses for middle-class families. Finally, Burgess identified a commuters' zone, beyond the continuous built-up area of the city. Some people who work in the center nonetheless choose to live in small villages that have become bedroom communities for commuters.

The sector model. A second model of urban structure, the **sector model,** was developed in 1939 by a land economist, Homer Hoyt. According to Hoyt, the city develops in a series of sectors, not rings (Figure 12–5). Certain areas of the city are more attractive for various activities, originally because of an environmental factor or even by mere chance. As a city grows, activities expand outward in a wedge or sector from the center. Once a district with high-class housing is established, the most ex-

pensive new housing is built on the outer edge of that district, further out from the center. The best housing is therefore found in a corridor extending from downtown to the outer edge of the city. Industrial and retailing activities develop in other sectors, usually along good transportation lines.

To some extent, the sector model is a refinement of the concentric zone model rather than a radical restatement. Hoyt mapped the highest-rent areas for a number of U.S. cities at different times and showed that the highest social-class district usually remained in the same sector, though it moved farther out along that sector over time.

Hoyt and Burgess both claimed that social patterns in Chicago supported their model. According to Burgess, Chicago's CBD was surrounded by a series of rings, broken only by Lake Michigan on the east. Hoyt argued that the best housing in Chicago developed north from the CBD along Lake Michigan, while industry located along major rail lines and roads to the south, southwest, and northwest.

The multiple nuclei model. Geographers C. D. Harris and E. L. Ullman developed the multiple nuclei model in 1945. According to the **multiple nu-**

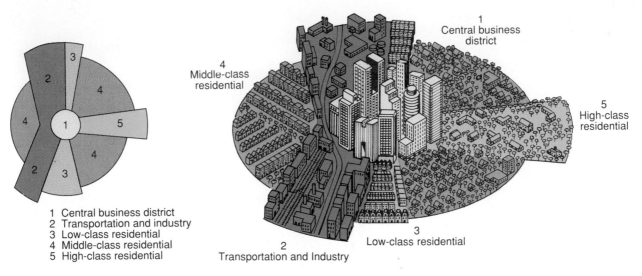

1 Central business district
2 Transportation and industry
3 Low-class residential
4 Middle-class residential
5 High-class residential

FIGURE 12–5
According to the sector model, a city grows in a series of sectors, wedges, or corridors,
which extend out from the central business district.

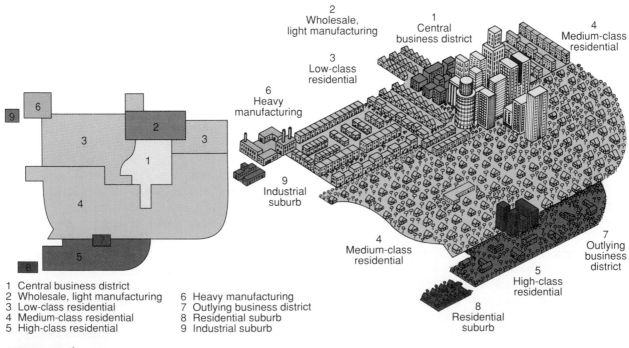

1 Central business district
2 Wholesale, light manufacturing
3 Low-class residential
4 Medium-class residential
5 High-class residential
6 Heavy manufacturing
7 Outlying business district
8 Residential suburb
9 Industrial suburb

FIGURE 12–6
According to the multiple nuclei theory, a city consists of a collection of individual nodes or
centers, around which different types of people and activities cluster.

clei model, a city is a complex structure that includes a collection of nodes or centers, around which activities revolve (Figure 12–6). Examples of these nodes include a port, neighborhood business center, university, airport, and park.

The multiple nuclei model holds that some activities are attracted to particular nodes while others try to avoid them. For example, a university node may attract well-educated residents, pizzerias, and bookstores, whereas an airport may attract hotels and warehouses. On the other hand, incompatible land-use activities will avoid clustering in the same locations. Heavy industry and high-class housing, for example, rarely exist in the same neighborhood.

Geographic Applications of the Models

The three models help to explain where people with different social characteristics tend to live within an urban area. They can also help to explain why certain types of people tend to live in particular places.

Effective use of the models depends on the availability of data at the scale of individual neighborhoods. In the United States and many other countries, that information comes from a national census. U.S. urban areas are divided into **census tracts,** which contain approximately 5,000 residents and correspond if possible to neighborhood boundaries. Every decade, the U.S. Bureau of the Census publishes data summarizing the characteristics of the residents living in each tract. Examples of information the bureau publishes include the number of nonwhites, the median income of all families, and the percentage of adults who finished high school.

The spatial distribution of any of these social characteristics can be plotted on a map of the community's census tracts. Computers have become invaluable in this area of study, because they permit the rapid creation of maps and the storage of a large amount of information about each census tract. Social scientists can compare the distributions of characteristics and create an overall picture of where various types of people tend to live. This kind of study is known as social area analysis.

None of the three models by itself completely explains why different types of people live in distinctive parts of the city. Critics point out that the theories are too simple and fail to consider the variety of reasons that lead people to select particular residential locations. Because the three models are all based on conditions that existed in U.S. cities between the two world wars, critics also question their relevance to modern urban patterns in the United States and elsewhere in the world.

In reality, if the models are combined rather than considered independently of one another, they do help geographers explain where different types of people live in a city. People tend to live in certain locations within a city depending on their particular personal characteristics. This does not mean that everyone with the same characteristics must live in the same neighborhood, but the models say that most people tend to prefer residing near other people who have similar characteristics.

Consider two families with the same income and ethnic background but one a married couple with young children and the other an unmarried pair with no children. The concentric zone model suggests that the married household will live in an outer ring and the unmarried one in an inner ring (Figure 12–7). The sector theory suggests that given two families the same age with the same number of children, the family with the higher income will live in a different sector of the city than the poorer one (Figure 12–8). The multiple nuclei theory suggests that people with the same ethnic or racial background are likely to want to live near one another (Figure 12–9). Putting the three models together, the geographer can identify, for example, the neighborhood in which a childless, rich, Asian-American family is most likely to live.

The dozens of social characteristics mapped for an urban area can be combined into a generalized drawing showing the city's main social areas. The three models complement rather than compete against one another in explaining where people live, because elements of all three models are present in an urban area. For example, the distribution of blacks in the Baltimore urbanized area combines the concentric zone, sector, and multiple nuclei theories (Figure 12–10). Consistent with the concentric zone model, blacks are clustered in the inner city, surrounded by a zone that is racially mixed and a large outer ring that is virtually all-white. The sector model also helps to explain the

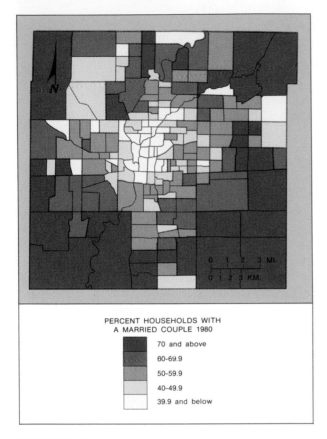

PERCENT HOUSEHOLDS WITH
A MARRIED COUPLE 1980

70 and above

60-69.9

50-59.9

40-49.9

39.9 and below

FIGURE 12–7
The distribution of married couples follows the concentric zone model in Indianapolis. The percentage of households with a married couple is lower near the central business district and higher in the outer rings of the city.

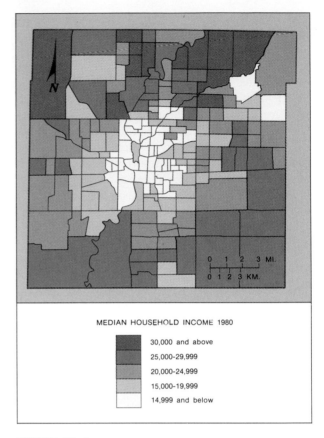

MEDIAN HOUSEHOLD INCOME 1980

30,000 and above

25,000-29,999

20,000-24,999

15,000-19,999

14,999 and below

FIGURE 12–8
The distribution of high-income households follows the sector model in Indianapolis. The median household income is the highest in a sector that extends to the north of the central business district.

racial patterns of the city, because a comparison of the current pattern with the past would show that black neighborhoods are expanding in sectors to the northwest and north along several radial roads.

The multiple nuclei is also useful in explaining the racial patterns. The black population in Baltimore is concentrated in three neighborhoods, one each located to the east, west, and south of the CBD. Historically, two independent centers of black culture developed in Baltimore on the east and west sides, and, even today, few blacks move between the two sides. The south side concentration dates from the 1940s, when the city began to build several thousand public housing units on formerly vacant land.

Use of the Models Outside North America

The three models may describe the spatial distribution of social classes in the United States, but what about cities elsewhere in the world? The spatial distribution of social characteristics in American urban areas differs from that found elsewhere in the world. These differences do not invalidate the models, but they do point out that social groups in other countries may not have the same reasons for selecting particular neighborhoods within their cities.

Europe. In European cities wealthier people tend to live in townhouses and apartments near the cen-

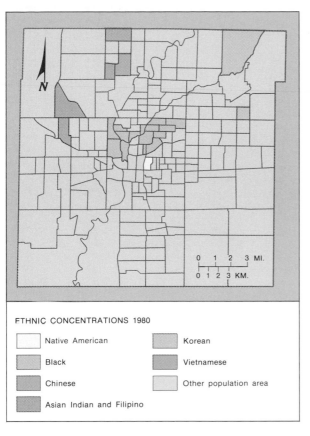

ETHNIC CONCENTRATIONS 1980

- [ ] Native American
- [ ] Black
- [ ] Chinese
- [ ] Asian Indian and Filipino
- [ ] Korean
- [ ] Vietnamese
- [ ] Other population area

FIGURE 12–9
The distribution of minorities follows the multiple nuclei model in Indianapolis. The black concentration consists of census tracts that are 90 percent or more black. The other groups are clustered in tracts that contain at least five percent of the total population in Indianapolis of that ethnic group.

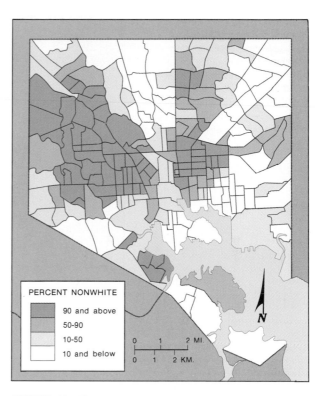

PERCENT NONWHITE

- [ ] 90 and above
- [ ] 50-90
- [ ] 10-50
- [ ] 10 and below

FIGURE 12–10
Concentric zone, sector, or multiple nuclei? The distribution of blacks in the city of Baltimore shows elements of all three models of the internal structure of cities.

ter, while poorer people are relegated to the outskirts of town (Figure 12–11). A central location provides proximity to the region's best shops, restaurants, cafes, and cultural facilities. Wealthy people are also attracted by the opportunity to occupy elegant residences in carefully restored, beautiful old buildings.

By living in high-density, centrally located residences, wealthy people in Europe do not have large private yards and must go to public parks for open space. To meet the desire for large tracts of privately owned land, some wealthy people in Europe purchase abandoned farm buildings in clustered rural settlements for use as second homes on week-

ends and holidays. Some of the worst traffic jams in Paris occur on summer Sunday nights, when families return from their weekend homes. A trip from the weekend home to the city that normally takes one hour can take four hours on Sunday night.

Poorer people are housed in high-rise apartment buildings in the suburbs and face the prospect of long commutes by public transportation to reach jobs and other urban amenities. High-density apartment buildings for poorer people are less expensive to build in Europe than in the United States and help to preserve the countryside from development.

Developing countries. The rich also live in the center of cities in developing countries, for some of the same reasons as in Europe. In addition, a central location is attractive because services such as water and electricity are more readily available and reliable. As in Europe, the poor are currently accom-

FIGURE 12–11
Neighborhoods in Glasgow, Scotland, classified as deprived are located primarily in outer areas, rather than in inner areas, as would be the case in U.S. cities. Areas of social deprivation contain high concentrations of unemployed people receiving public assistance. Most of the areas of high social deprivation consist of massive housing projects built after World War II.

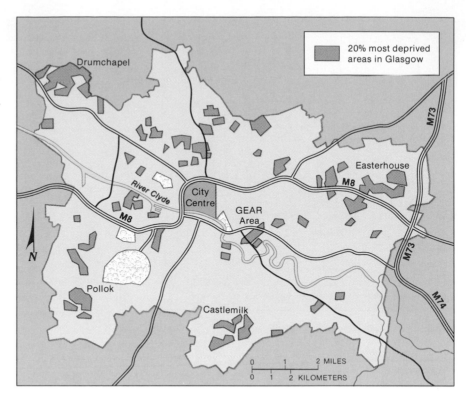

modated in the suburbs. But developing countries are unable to provide enough housing to meet the demands of a rapidly growing number of poorer people. Their cities are growing because of both the overall population increase and migration from rural areas for job opportunities.

In view of the shortage of housing, a large percentage of poor immigrants to urban areas in developing countries live in **squatter settlements.** Squatter settlements are known by a variety of names, including *barrios, barriadas,* and *favellas* in Latin America, *bidonvilles* in North Africa, *bustees* in India, *gecekondu* in Turkey, *kampongs* in Malaysia, and *barung-barong* in the Philippines. Typically, a squatter settlement is initiated by a group of people who move together literally overnight onto land outside the city, owned either by a private individual or (more frequently) by the government. People move with all their possessions, which usually are so few that they can be easily carried. The leaders of the invasion allocate small parcels of the seized land to each participating family.

At first, squatters do little more than camp on the land or sleep in the street; in severe weather, they may take shelter in markets and warehouses. Families then erect primitive shelters with scavenged cardboard, wood boxes, sackcloth, and crushed beverage cans. As they find new bits of material, they add them to their shacks. After a few years, they may build a tin roof and partition the space into rooms, and the structure acquires a more permanent appearance.

Squatter settlements have few services because neither the city nor the residents can afford them. Latrines are usually designated by the settlement's leaders, and water is carried from a central well or dispensed from a truck. The settlements generally lack schools, paved roads, electricity, telephones, or sewers. In the absence of bus service or available private cars, a resident may have to walk two hours to reach a place of employment.

To improve their housing conditions, squatters have two basic choices. One alternative is to move illegally into better-quality, vacant housing closer to the center of the city. The second alternative is to rent slum housing legally from a landlord. Squatters rarely have the financial means to move directly from a squatter settlement into decent housing on legally owned land.

The percentage of people living in squatter settlements, slums, and other illegal housing ranges from 33 percent in São Paulo, Brazil, to 85 percent in Addis Ababa, Ethiopia. The United Nations estimates that more than half of the residents in Lusaka (Zambia), Ankara (Turkey), Bogotá (Colombia), Dar es Salaam (Tanzania), and Luanda (Angola), also live in some form of illegal housing (Table 12–1).

Governments in developing countries face a difficult choice with regard to squatter settlements. If the government sends in the police or army to raze the settlement, it risks sparking a violent confrontation with the displaced people. On the other hand, if the government decides that improving and legalizing squatter settlements is cheaper than building the necessary new apartment buildings, it may encourage other poor rural people to migrate to the city to live as squatters.

Studies conducted in developing countries show the applicability of the three models of internal structure of cities, though the location of particular social groups may vary. For example, in Rio de Janeiro, Brazil, high-income people are clustered in the center of the city and to the south, while low-income people are located in the northern suburbs (Figure 12–12). The distribution of income groups coincides with other social characteristics, such as the percent of households with a telephone, automobile, or television. High-income groups are clustered near the center in part because of greater access to services, such as electricity and sewer hookups (Figure 12–13).

Physical geography also influences the distribution of social classes within Rio. The original site of the city was along the west shore of Guanabara Bay, a protected harbor. Residents were attracted to the neighborhoods immediately south of the central area, such as Copacabana and Ipanema, in order to enjoy spectacular views of the Atlantic Ocean and access to beaches. On the other hand, squatters and other low-income households have clustered along

TABLE 12–1

Population residing in squatter settlements.

City	Population (in 1000s)	Population in Squatter Settlements (in 1000s)	Percent in Squatter Settlements (%)
Addis Ababa, Ethiopia	1668	1418	85
Luanda, Angola	959	671	70
Dar es Salaam, Tanzania	1075	645	60
Bogotá, Colombia	5493	3241	59
Ankara, Turkey	2164	1104	51
Lusaka, Zambia	791	396	50
Tunis, Tunisia	1046	471	45
Manila, Philippines	5664	2266	40
Mexico City, Mexico	15032	6013	40
Karachi, Pakistan	5005	1852	37
Caracas, Venezuela	3093	1052	34
Nairobi, Kenya	1275	421	33
Lima, Peru	4682	1545	33
São Paulo, Brazil	13541	4333	32

Source: United Nations Center for Human Settlements, *Land for human settlements* (Nairobi, Kenya: UN CHS, 1984), p. 9; quoted in Gill-Chin Lim, "Housing Policy for the Urban Poor in Developing Countries," *Journal of the American Planning Association* (Spring 1987), pp. 176–185, at p. 178.

FIGURE 12–12
The highest income areas in Rio de Janeiro, Brazil, are located near the central business district, while low income people are more likely to live in peripheral areas.

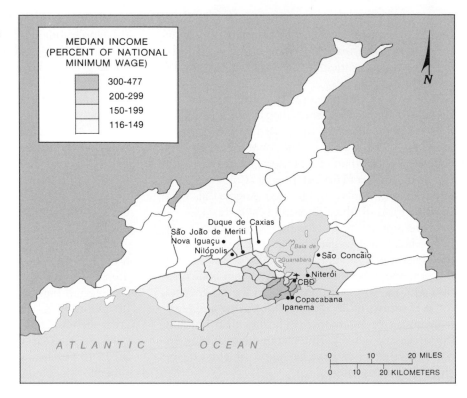

FIGURE 12–13
High income people are attracted to central areas in developing cities like Rio because services, such as municipal sewers, are more widely available than in peripheral areas.

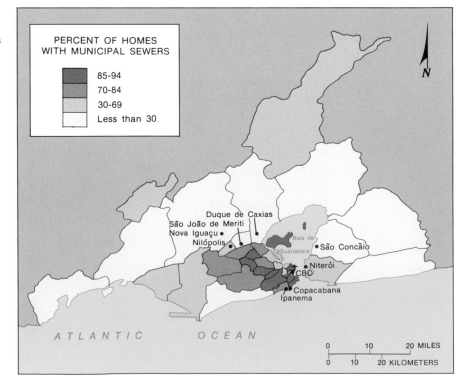

A large percentage of people in the rapidly growing cities of developing countries live in squatter settlements, such as this *favella,* known as Santa Marta, in Rio de Janeiro, Brazil (left). Rio's wealthier neighborhoods (right) are nestled between the hills and the Atlantic Ocean, while the favellas are built on the hillsides, where services are difficult to provide.

the northern edge of the city, where steep mountains have restricted construction of other types of buildings. Development on the east side of Guanabara Bay was restricted until a bridge was constructed in the 1970s.

KEY ISSUE

What Problems Arise from Urban Spatial Patterns?

The spatial distribution of social groups within urban areas produces problems. Despite the fact that certain types of people in one society tend to live in different parts of the urban area than people in another society, emerging urban problems are increasingly universal.

Central Cities

Economic conditions have improved during the past decade in many North American and European CBDs, primarily because of an unprecedented pace of office construction. Downtowns that were generally considered dead and beyond help as recently as the 1970s are now filled with both local residents and tourists, even during evenings and weekends when offices are closed. The new downtown offices, shops, and recreation facilities provide cities with additional tax revenues that can be used to maintain essential services.

The underclass. The atmosphere of animation and prosperity found in many CBDs does not extend to the surrounding residential areas. With the exception of a handful of renovated neighborhoods, the zone in transition is inhabited by large numbers of persons who are frequently referred to as a permanent **underclass.** These inner-city residents are increasingly trapped in an unending cycle of economic and social problems and are not able to share in the revival of the CBDs.

The underclass suffers from relatively high rates of unemployment, alcoholism, drug addiction, illiteracy, juvenile delinquency, and crime. For them, schools have deteriorated, and affordable housing is increasingly difficult to find. Neighborhoods lack adequate police protection, fire services, and shops, as well as hospitals, clinics, and other health-care facilities.

Future prospects are especially bleak for the underclass because they are increasingly unable to compete for jobs. Inner-city residents lack the technical skills needed to obtain most jobs, because fewer than half complete high school. The gap between the skills typically demanded by employers and the training of inner-city residents is getting much larger. In the past, people with limited education could become factory workers or filing clerks, but today these jobs require knowledge of computing and handling electronics. Meanwhile, inner-city residents don't even have access to the remaining low-skilled jobs, such as janitors and fast-food servers, which are increasingly located in the suburbs.

Despite the importance of education in obtaining jobs, many people in the underclass do not live in an atmosphere that emphasizes the value of good study habits, such as regular school attendance and completion of homework assignments. The household may consist of only one parent, who may be forced to choose between working to generate sufficient income and staying at home to provide child care.

Trapped in a hopeless environment, some inner-city residents turn to drugs. While drug-taking is a problem in many suburbs and rural areas as well, rates of use in recent years have increased most rapidly in the inner-cities. Some users turn to crime in order to obtain the money they need to buy drugs. Gangs form in inner-city neighborhoods to control the lucrative distribution of drugs. Violence erupts when two gangs fight over the boundaries between their drug distribution areas.

An increasing number of the underclass are homeless. Several million Americans sleep in doorways, on heated street grates, and in bus and subway stations. Los Angeles County alone has an estimated 35,000 homeless persons, attracted by the area's relatively mild climate. Homelessness is an even more serious problem in developing countries. An estimated 300,000 people in Calcutta sleep, bathe, and eat on sidewalks and traffic islands.

Roughly a third of the homeless in the United States are individuals who are unable to cope in society after being released from hospitals or other institutions. But most people are homeless because they are unable to afford housing and have no regular source of income. Homelessness may have been sparked by family problems or loss of job.

Segregation. The city contains a large number of submarkets, with the residential choice for most people realistically limited to a relatively small number of locations. Even small cities display strong social distinctions among neighborhoods. A frequently noticed division is between the east and west side of a city, with one attracting the higher-income residents and the other left to lower-status and minority families. A family looking for a new residence is likely to consider only a handful of districts, whose residents' social characteristics and financial resources are similar to their own. Residential areas designed for wealthy families developed in scenic, attractive areas, possibly on a hillside or near a waterfront, while the flat, physically uninteresting land closer to industry was built up with cheaper housing.

In the late 1960s, the National Advisory Commission on Civil Disorders, known as the Kerner Commission, concluded that U.S. cities were divided into two separate and unequal societies—one black and one white. More than two decades later, segregation and inequality persist.

Blacks comprise two-thirds of the population in Atlanta, Detroit, Gary (Indiana), and Washington, D.C., and a majority in a number of other large U.S. central cities, including Baltimore, Birmingham (Alabama), New Orleans, Newark (New Jersey), and Oakland (California). Within U.S. metropolitan areas, two-thirds of whites live in suburbs and one-third in central cities, while two-thirds of blacks live in central cities and one-third in suburbs. Blacks comprise more than 25 percent of the U.S. central-city population but 7 percent of the suburbs.

Other U.S. metropolitan areas contain large concentrations of Hispanic residents. Over one-third of the population are Hispanic in the MSAs or CMSAs of Albuquerque (New Mexico), Los Angeles, Miami, and several Texas cities, including Corpus Christi, El Paso, and San Antonio. Hispanics also constitute over one-sixth of the population of the New York City and San Francisco metropolitan areas. Overall, two-thirds of Hispanics live in central cities.

Fiscal problems. The concentration of low-income minority residents in the central cities has produced financial problems. Despite higher taxes generated by new CBD projects, central cities face a growing gap between the cost of needed services and the availability of funds to pay for them. The percentage of people below the poverty level living in U.S. central cities increased during the 1980s and is more than twice as high as in the suburbs. Since 1950, overall population has declined by more than 40 percent in the central cities of Buffalo, Cleveland, Detroit, and St. Louis, and by more than one-fourth in a number of other cities, including Boston, Cincinnati, Dayton, Jersey City, Louisville, Minneapolis, Newark, and Rochester. The number of tax-paying middle-class families and industries has invariably declined by higher percentages in these cities.

A city has two choices to close the gap between the cost of services and the amount of available taxes. One alternative is to raise taxes, a move that could drive remaining wealthier people and industries from the city. The other alternative is to reduce services by closing libraries, eliminating some public-transit routes, collecting trash less frequently, and delaying replacement of outdated school equipment. Aside from the hardship imposed on those laid off from work, cutbacks in public services could also encourage middle-class residents and industries to move from the city.

To avoid this dilemma, cities have increasingly sought funds from the state and federal governments. The federal government increased its share of contribution to city budgets from 1 percent in the 1950s to 25 percent in the early 1980s. Since early 1980s, though, the federal government has substantially reduced its contributions to local governments. State governments and private corporations have increased financial assistance to cities to offset partially the loss of federal funds. The high

level of outside financial support has obscured the intensity of the fiscal crisis faced by cities as a result of shifting patterns of land use.

Suburbs

As you travel outward from the center of a city, you see a declining density at which people live. In the central city, people live in apartments or row houses, with as many as 250 dwellings on a hectare of land (100 dwellings per acre). The inner suburbs have larger row houses, semidetached houses, and individual houses on small lots, at a density of about ten houses per hectare (four houses per acre). A detached house typically sits on a lot of ¼ to ½ hectare (0.6 to 1.2 acres) in new suburbs and a lot of 1 hectare (2.5 acres) or more on the fringe of the built-up area.

The change in density in an urban area is called the **density gradient.** According to the density gradient, the number of houses per unit of land diminishes as distance from the center of the city increases.

Two changes have affected the density gradient in recent years. First, the number of people living in the center itself has decreased. The density gradient thus has a gap in the center, where few people live. Second, the trend has been for fewer differences in density within urban areas. The number of people living on a hectare of land has decreased in the central residential areas through population decline and abandonment of old housing. At the same time, density has increased on the periphery through construction of apartment and row house projects and diffusion of suburbs across a larger area (Figure 12–14).

In European cities, the density gradient has also been affected by the construction of low-income high-rise apartments in the suburbs and by stricter controls over the construction of detached houses on large lots. The result of the two changes is to flatten the density gradient and reduce the extremes of inner and outer areas traditionally found within cities.

Suburban segregation. One significant characteristic of the modern residential suburb is the high degree of two types of segregation. First, residents are separated from commercial and manufacturing

FIGURE 12–14

The density gradient has changed in Cleveland during the twentieth century. In 1910, population was highly clustered in and near the central business district. By 1970, population was distributed over a much larger area, the variation in the density among rings was much smaller, and the area's lowest densities were found in the rings near the central business district. The map shows the current boundaries of the city of Cleveland. (Data from Avery M. Guest, "Population Suburbanization in American Metropolitan Areas, 1940–1970," in *Geographical Analysis,* Vol. VII (July 1975): 267–83, Table 4. Used by permission of the publisher.)

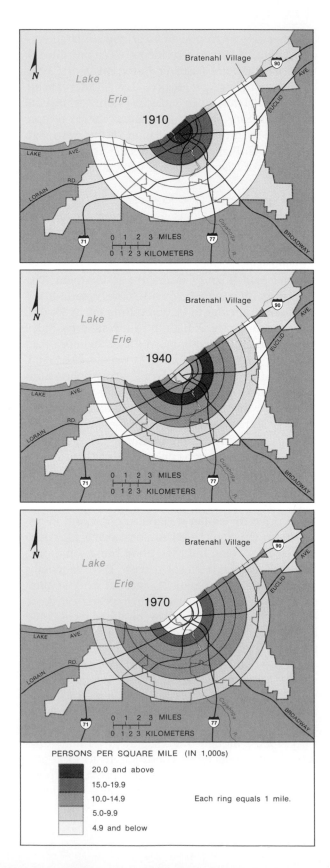

activities, which are confined to compact, distinct areas. Second, housing in a given suburban community is usually built for people of a single social class, with others excluded by virtue of the cost, size, or location of the housing.

The homogeneous suburb is a twentieth-century phenomenon. In older cities, activities and classes were more likely to be separated vertically rather than horizontally. In a typical urban building, shops were located on the street level, with the shop owner or another well-to-do family living on one or two floors above the shop. Poorer people would live on the higher levels or in the basement, the least attractive parts of the building. The basement was dark and damp, and before the elevator was invented the higher levels could be reached only by climbing many flights of stairs. Rich families lived in houses with space available in the basement or attic to accommodate servants.

Once cities spread out over much larger areas the old pattern of vertical separation was replaced by territorial segregation. Large sections of the city were developed with houses of similar interior dimension, lot size, and cost, appealing to people with similar incomes and lifestyles.

Zoning ordinances, developed in Europe and North America in the early decades of the twentieth century, encouraged the process of spatial separation. Such ordinances prevented the mixing of various land-use activities within the same district. In particular, single-family houses, apartments, industry, and commerce were kept apart, because the location of one activity near another was considered unhealthy and inefficient.

The strongest criticism of U.S. residential suburbs is that low-income and minority people are unable to live in them because of the high cost of the housing and the unfriendliness of already settled residents. Suburban communities discourage the entry of lower-income and minority people because of fear that property values will decline if the high-status composition of the neighborhood is altered. Legal devices, such as requiring each house to sit on a large lot as well as prohibiting apartments, prevent low-income families from living in many suburbs.

Busing. The segregation of residential communities according to race has led to a difficult situation in many school systems. Since 1954, when the U.S.

Supreme Court ruled that racially segregated school systems are inherently unequal, cities have been faced with the need to improve the racial balance in their schools. The goal of integration has conflicted with the strong desire of many parents and educators that children should live within walking distance of school. As long as neighborhoods have a homogeneous population, the two goals are mutually exclusive.

Some school districts have tried to promote integration by busing students from their homes to schools elsewhere in the city. Busing has been unpopular, but in some communities no other system has been found to integrate schools. In many communities, white parents have chosen to send their children to private schools rather than have them attend integrated public schools. Ironically, because the private school is frequently further away than the public school, children are bused anyway.

Inefficient use of land in suburbs. While cities cope with the problems of decline, many suburbs have the opposite difficulty—managing growth. As long as demand for single-family detached houses remains high, land on the fringe of urbanized areas must be converted from open space to residential land use.

The current system for developing land on urban fringes is inefficient, especially in the United States. Land is not transformed immediately from farms to housing developments. Instead, developers buy farms for future construction of houses by individual builders. Developers frequently reject land adjacent to built-up areas in favor of detached isolated sites, depending on the price and physical attributes of the alternatives. The rural-urban fringe in U.S. cities therefore looks like Swiss cheese, with pockets of development and gaps of open space.

The supply of land for construction of new housing is more severely restricted in European urban areas. Officials attack sprawl through designating areas of mandatory open space. London, Birmingham, and several other British cities are surrounded by **greenbelts,** rings of open space. New housing is built either in older suburbs inside the greenbelts or in planned extensions to small towns and new towns beyond the greenbelts (Figure 12–15).

The U.S. low-density suburb also depletes farmland. In reality, sprawl has little impact on the total farmland in the United States. But sprawl does make

FIGURE 12–15
Patterns of suburban development. The United States is characterized by much more sprawl than the United Kingdom. New housing is more likely to be concentrated in new towns or planned extensions of existing small towns in the United Kingdom, whereas in the United States, growth occurs in discontinuous projects.

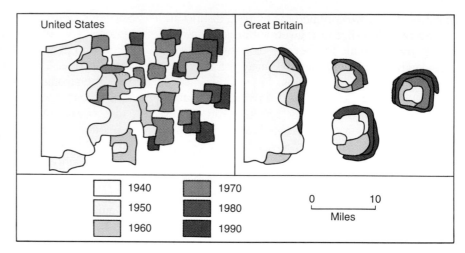

1940	1970
1950	1980
1960	1990

0   10
Miles

it harder for city dwellers to get to the country for recreation, and it can affect the supply of local dairy products and vegetables. The low-density suburb requires more energy, especially because the automobile is required for most trips. On the other hand, restriction of the supply of land on the urban periphery has driven up house prices in Europe. Restrictions on new building sites could further decrease the ability of low-income families to find affordable housing in U.S. suburbs.

Summary

Here is a review of the key issues raised at the beginning of the chapter:

1. **What activities are found in the central city?** The North American central city is dominated by retailing, offices, and other commercial activities. Surrounding the CBD is an inner residential area containing older low-quality housing and public housing as well as pockets of high-status renovated housing.
2. **What are the causes and consequences of suburbanization?** The suburban lifestyle—as exemplified by the detached, single-family house with surrounding yard—attracts most people. With land scarce and expensive in the center, housing is provided in suburbs. Transportation improve-

ments—most notably the railroad in the nineteenth century and the automobile in the twentieth century—have facilitated the sprawl of urban areas. Among the negative consequences of large-scale sprawl are segregation and inefficiency.

3. **How are different social groups distributed within an urban area?** Three models have been developed to explain where various types of people live in urban areas: the concentric zone, sector, and multiple nuclei. None fully explains the internal structure of the city, but the three combined present a useful framework for understanding the distribution of social and economic groups within an urban area. Although each city has a unique structure, any city can provide a useful case study of the application of the three models.
4. **What problems arise from urban spatial patterns?** The suburbanization of the population has led to problems for both central cities and suburbs. Central cities face an increasing gap between tax revenues and demands for services. Tax-paying middle-class households and industries have moved out of the cities, while more assistance is needed for low-income minority households in the central cities—a group increasingly considered a permanent underclass. Suburbs face problems of coping with growth rather than decline.

Contrasts in the City

What is the future for cities? As this chapter shows, contradictory trends are at work simultaneously. Why does one inner-city neighborhood become a slum and another a high-class district? Why does one city attract new shoppers and visitors while another languishes?

Camden, New Jersey, displays the strong contrasts that characterize American urban areas. The central city of Camden houses an isolated underclass, while suburban Camden County prospers. The population of the city of Camden has declined from 117,000 in 1960 to less than 80,000 today. Nearly 85 percent of the city's residents are black and Hispanic, while the white population has declined from 90,000 in 1960 to 10,000 today. Only 1 percent of the households remaining have annual incomes of more than $50,000, compared with 20 percent in the rest of the country and 10 percent among all black households.

More than 40 percent of Camden's residents are under eighteen, closer to the level found in developing countries than to the rest of the United States. Job prospects are not promising for these young people, because more than half have left school without obtaining a high-school diploma. In the past, Camden's youths could find jobs in factories that produced Campbell's soups, Esterbrook pens, and RCA Victor records, radios, and televisions, but the city has lost 90 percent of its industrial jobs. The Esterbrook and Campbell factories in Camden are closed, though Campbell's corporate offices remain; General Electric now operates the former RCA factory but with a labor force at only 15 percent of the level during the 1960s. Camden's unemployment rate is more than twice the national average.

As Camden's population and industries decline, few shops have enough customers to remain open. The city once had thirteen movie theaters, but none are left. The murder rate soared after gangs carved up the city into districts during the mid-1980s to control cocaine trafficking.

Meanwhile, Camden County—excluding the city—has grown from 275,000 in 1960 to more than 400,000 today. Cherry Hill has more than 75,000 residents today, compared to less than 10,000 in 1960, and will surpass Camden as the largest city in the county before the end of the decade. About 85 percent of Cherry Hill's high-school graduates go on to college. Yet, despite its rapid population growth and trained labor force, Cherry Hill has attracted so many new jobs that the major obstacle to further economic growth is a shortage of qualified workers.

Camden's mismatch between the locations of people, jobs, resources, and services exemplifies the urban crisis throughout the United States, as well as in other countries. Geographers help us to understand why these patterns arise, and what can be done about them.

Key Terms

Blockbusting A process in which real estate agents convince white property owners to sell their houses at low prices because of fear that black families will soon move into the neighborhood.

Census tract An area delineated by the U.S. Bureau of the Census for which statistics are published; in urbanized areas, census tracts correspond roughly to neighborhoods.

Central business district (CBD) The area of the city where retail and office activities are clustered.

Concentric zone model A model of the internal structure of cities in which social groups are spatially arranged in a series of rings.

Density gradient The change in density in an urban area from the center to the periphery.

Filtering A process of change in the use of a house, from single-family owner occupancy to abandonment.

Gentrification A process of converting an urban neighborhood from a predominantly low-income renter-occupied area to a predominantly middle-class owner-occupied area.

Greenbelt A ring of land maintained as parks, agriculture, or other types of open space in order to limit the sprawl of an urban area.

Multiple nuclei model A model of the internal structure of cities in which activities revolve around a collection of nodes or centers.

Public housing Housing owned by the government; in the United States, it is rented to low-income residents, and the rents are set at 30 percent of the families' incomes.

Redlining A process by which banks draw lines on a map and refuse to lend money to purchase or improve property within the boundaries.

Rush (or peak) hour The four consecutive 15-minute periods in the morning and evening with the heaviest volumes of traffic.

Sector model A model of the internal structure of cities in which social groups are arranged around a series of sectors or wedges radiating out from the central business district.

Sprawl Development of new housing sites at relatively low density and at locations that are not contiguous to the existing built-up area.

Squatter settlement An area within a city in a developing country in which people illegally establish residences on land they do not own or rent and erect home-made structures.

Underclass A group in society prevented from participating in the material benefits of a relatively developed society because of a variety of social and economic characteristics.

Zone in transition An area surrounding the central business district containing primarily older industries, warehouses, and low-rent housing.

Zoning ordinance A law that limits the permitted uses of land and maximum density of development in a community.

Thinking Geographically

1. What impact will hosting the 1996 Olympics have on the urban structure of Atlanta?
2. Compare Toronto and Detroit. How do the central business districts and the inner residential areas compare in the two cities? What might account for these differences?
3. Draw a sketch of your community or neighborhood. In accordance with Kevin Lynch's *The Image of the City,* place five types of information on the map: districts (homogeneous areas), edges (boundaries that separate districts), paths (lines of communication), nodes (central points of interaction), and landmarks (prominent

objects on the landscape). How clear an image does your community have to you?

4. To Jane Jacobs, an attractive urban environment is one that is animated with an intermingling of a variety of people and activities, such as can be found in many New York City neighborhoods. What are the attractions and drawbacks to living in such environments?

5. In socialist cities, urban land-use activities are allocated by government rather than private market decisions. To what extent would the absence of an urban land market affect the form and structure of socialist cities? What impacts may Eastern European cities experience with the switch to market economies?

Further Readings

Berry, Brian J. L., and John D. Kasarda. *Contemporary Urban Ecology.* New York: Macmillan, 1977.

Bourne, Larry S., ed. *Internal Structure of the City.* 2d ed. New York: Oxford University Press, 1982.

Bratt, Rachel G. *Rebuilding a Low-Income Housing Policy.* Philadelphia: Temple University Press, 1990.

Brunn, Stanley D., and Jack L. Williams, eds. *Cities of the World: World Regional Urban Development.* New York: Harper and Row, 1983.

Cervero, Robert. *America's Suburban Centers: The Land Use–Transportation Link.* Boston: Unwin and Hyman, 1989.

Clawson, Marion, and Peter Hall. *Planning and Urban Growth.* Baltimore: The Johns Hopkins University Press, 1973.

Frieden, Bernard J., and Lynne B. Sagalyn. *Downtown Inc.: How America Rebuilds Cities.* Cambridge: MIT Press, 1989.

Golany, Gideon, ed. *International Urban Growth Policies: New-Town Contributions.* New York: Wiley, 1978.

Guest, Avery M. "Population Suburbanization in American Metropolitan Areas, 1940–1970." *Geographical Analysis* 7 (July 1976): 267–83.

Harris, Chauncey D., and Edward L. Ullman. "The Nature of Cities." *Annals of the American Academy of Political and Social Science* 143 (1945): 7–17.

Hoyt, Homer. *The Structure and Growth of Residential Neighborhoods.* Washington, D.C.: Federal Housing Administration, 1939.

Johnston, R. J. *City and Society: An Outline for Urban Geography.* London: Hutchinson Education, 1984.

Ley, David. *A Social Geography of the City.* New York: Harper & Row, 1983.

Lowder, Stella. *The Geography of Third World Cities.* New Jersey: Barnes and Noble Books, 1986.

Lynch, Kevin. *The Image of the City.* Cambridge: MIT Press, 1960.

Mayer, Harold M., and Charles R. Hayes. *Land Uses in American Cities.* Champaign: Park Press, 1983.

Park, Robert E., Ernest W. Burgess, and Roderick D. McKenzie, eds. *The City.* Chicago: University of Chicago Press, 1925.

United States National Advisory Commission on Civil Disorders, Otto Kerner, chairman. *Report.* New York: Dutton, 1968.

White, Paul. *The West European City, A Social Geography.* London and New York: Longman, 1984.

Whyte, William H. *City: Rediscovering the Center.* New York: Doubleday, 1988.

Also consult these journals: *Environment and Planning; Journal of Housing; Journal of Urban Economics; Journal of the American Planning Association; Land Economics; Planning; Urban Land; Urban Studies.*

13
Resource
Problems

I magine what the future will bring:

THE SCENE: A typical American city, Christmas 1999.

TAKE 1: The streets are deserted because gas costs $10 a gallon and is hard to find. Food prices have skyrocketed because of a lack of low-cost petroleum to operate farm equipment and to manufacture fertilizers. Consequently, families can afford no more than a few vegetables for Christmas dinner. With the local economy depressed, the city has no money to treat the sewage being dumped in the nearby lake. As a result, ice skating on the lake is prohibited, and the water is unsafe to drink. Bottled water is served at Christmas instead of eggnog and champagne, which are too expensive. Family members huddle into one room of the house to keep warm. The hard-to-obtain tree is used for firewood rather than Christmas decoration. The extra stockings are worn, not hung by the chimney.

TAKE 2: The streets are buzzing with small, silent, electric-powered cars, as people bring home Christmas presents. Turkeys and hams are more plentiful and cheaper than ever because of new breeding techniques. Houses are snug and warm because of airtight construction and solar heating panels. Because the lake was cleaned up, it is safe for skating, swimming, and fishing. Christmas presents include computerized work-saving devices operated by solar electricity chips.

We cannot predict the future. We do not know whether current world problems will get better or worse. As geographers, we can understand that many of the world's problems are interrelated. Understanding the complexity of activities on the earth's surface is the first step towards solving the problems.

A Self-Sufficient Family

The Chang family lives in a house in Berkeley, California. They generate heat and hot water from rooftop solar panels. The family's diet consists of food grown in the backyard, including crops planted in the garden and fish raised in a pond. Waste is stored and treated with grass and leaves to produce an odorless fertilizer for use on the backyard crops. Human waste is added to the compost rather than flushed with water into the municipal sewer system.

The Chang family members lead lives that are sensitive to conditions in the physical environment. They avoid using nonrenewable resources, such as petroleum, that threaten to become more expensive and scarce. They minimize adverse impacts on the physical environment by recycling their waste products. They consume foods that they grow themselves rather than obtain food from processors.

In contrast with the Chang family, most people in relatively developed societies contribute to the depletion of the world's scarce resources and adversely affect the quality of the physical environment. Why do these practices occur? They are a product of the industrial revolution, which has brought unprecedented wealth to people living in the world's relatively developed countries. But much of that wealth rests on a combination of ignorance and disregard of processes in the natural environment. Misuse of the environment, through ignorance or greed, has produced pollution and shortage of resources.

Fortunately, the technical advances that degrade the environment also produce increased knowledge about the workings of the environment. We are paying more attention to the environmental consequences of our actions and to ecologically sound solutions to our problems.

Geographers are concerned with understanding the relationship between human actions and the physical environment. From a human perspective, the physical environment comprises a large collection of resources available for people to use. A **resource** is a substance in the physical environment that has value or usefulness to human beings and is economically feasible and socially acceptable to use. A substance is a resource if people know about it and possess the technological means to obtain and use it.

Human beings sometimes use resources without considering their limits or constraints. Geographers study the uses and abuses of resources. They also help develop strategies that maximize the uses and minimize the abuses of resources.

We observe three important misuses of resources. First, human beings deplete the supply of scarce resources, especially for energy production. Second, human beings destroy resources through pollution. Third, human beings fail to make full use of needed resources, especially to increase the global food supply.

As discussed in Chapter 1, human geography explains the arrangement of people and activities across the earth's surface through two approaches: the human-environment approach and the regional studies approach. According to the first approach, geographers argue that the physical environment influences and sets limits on human actions, though people can choose a variety of actions. According to the regional studies landscape approach, geographers explain why human actions produce distinctive regions on the earth's surface.

We depend on both geographic approaches to study resource problems. As geographers, we understand that the energy crisis derives both from depletion of resources and from differences in the way energy resources and consumers are distributed across the earth's surface. We see that the pollution problem comes from the concentration of substances that harm the physical environment in particular regions. We find that the food-supply problem relates in part to identifying the limits of a region's physical environment and in part to the regional distributions of food production and need.

KEY ISSUE

What Is the Energy Crisis?

We depend on an abundant supply of low-cost energy to run our industries, transport us, and keep our homes comfortable. But we are depleting the global supply of some energy resources, and we must develop alternative sources to preserve our current standard of living.

In general, the term **energy** refers to the capacity to do work. Every living thing, whether plant or animal, possesses the capacity to do work and is consequently a storehouse of potential energy. The rate at which work is actually performed in a given period of time is known as **power.**

To perform most tasks, human beings historically relied on power supplied by people or animals, known as **animate power.** Energy generated from burning wood or diverting the flow of water supple-

FIGURE 13–1
Petroleum, natural gas, and coal are the three principal sources of energy.

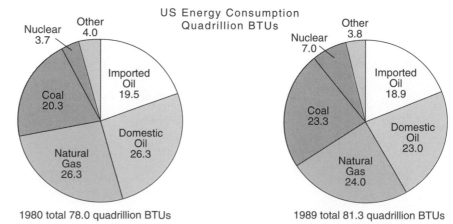

US Energy Consumption
Quadrillion BTUs

1980 total 78.0 quadrillion BTUs

1989 total 81.3 quadrillion BTUs

mented animate power. Since the industrial revolution, human beings have expanded their use of **inanimate power** by creating machines that harness the large amount of potential energy stored in the physical environment.

Fossil Fuels

Three substances provide more than 80 percent of the world's energy and over 90 percent of North America's energy: petroleum, natural gas, and coal. In relatively developed countries, the remainder comes primarily from nuclear, solar, hydroelectric, and geothermal power (Figure 13–1). Wood provides much of the remaining energy in developing societies.

Historically, wood was the most important energy source throughout the world. As a consequence of the industrial revolution, coal supplanted wood as the leading energy source in the late nineteenth century in North America and Western Europe. Petroleum was first pumped in 1859 but was a relatively unimportant resource until the diffusion of automobiles in the twentieth century. Natural gas was originally burned off as a waste product of oil drilling but has become a major energy source in recent years.

Energy is used in three principal places: businesses, homes, and transportation systems. The most important energy source for businesses is coal, followed by natural gas and petroleum. Some businesses use coal directly in an industrial operation, while others rely on electricity, generated primarily at coal-burning power stations.

At home, energy primarily is used to generate heat and hot water. Natural gas is the most common source of home heat and hot water, followed by petroleum. Like businesses, homes also use electricity supplied from coal-burning power plants. Petroleum products operate virtually all transportation systems, including automobiles, trucks, buses, airplanes, and some trains. Only subways, streetcars, and some trains run on coal-generated electricity.

Petroleum, natural gas, and coal are known as fossil fuels. A **fossil fuel** comes from the residue of plants and animals buried beneath the earth's surface millions of years ago. As the earth's crust moved, these buried plants and animals were subject to intense changes in pressure and temperature.

Two characteristics of fossil fuels are responsible for the global energy problem. First, the supply of fossil fuels is finite. These substances were created at one time in geologic history, and when they are used, they are gone forever as energy sources. Second, fossil fuels are not distributed uniformly beneath the earth's surface. Some regions enjoy a large supply of one or more fossil fuels, while others have little.

Finiteness. The three main fossil fuels are examples of **nonrenewable sources of energy,** that is, once burned, they are used up for all time. The global energy crisis arose in part because human beings are rapidly depleting the remaining supply of the three fossil fuels, especially petroleum.

How much of the fossil fuels remains? Despite the critical importance of the question for the future, no one can answer that question precisely. Petroleum, natural gas, and coal are found in fields beneath the earth's surface. For fields that have been discovered, scientists can estimate the amount of remaining energy, which is known as a **proven reserve.** Although scientists can measure the amount of proven reserves with reasonable accuracy, no one knows how many fields in the world have not yet been discovered. The amount of energy in fields not yet identified but thought to exist is a **potential reserve.** When a potential reserve is actually discovered, it is reclassified as a proven reserve.

Even with estimates of the proven and potential reserves of an energy source, no one can determine when the remaining reserves will be depleted. How much energy is consumed in a year must be known to make that determination. If the rate of use declines, the date an energy source is depleted is postponed.

At current rates of use, proven reserves of petroleum and natural gas will last for only a few decades. Unless scientists actually discover large fields of potential reserves and convert them to proven reserves, the world's petroleum and natural gas reserves will be depleted in the twenty-first century. Scientists disagree sharply on the amount of potential reserves. Estimates at current rates of use range from as low as zero to as high as a couple of hundred years. Estimates for proven coal reserves are higher, perhaps several hundred years, at current rates of use.

Countries in the Middle East possess two-thirds of the world's proven petroleum reserves.

Scientists do agree that the process of extracting proven reserves will become increasingly difficult. The most easily identifiable fields have already been discovered and exploited. Potential reserves converted in the future to proven reserves are likely to be located in remote places, such as beneath the oceans or polar regions. And the cost of discovering new fields has increased, because of more elaborate exploration procedures and a lower probability that exploration will lead to identification of a potential field.

To extract the remaining reserves from currently identified proven fields, industry must employ expensive techniques, such as pumping water or gas into the wells to push out the remaining supply. The problem of removing the last reserves from a proven field is comparable to drinking cola from a glass with a straw. Most of the liquid flows smoothly through the straw, but the last amount is relatively hard to extract.

Petroleum and natural gas are also found in so-called unconventional sources, such as shale rock, light sands, and off-shore aquifers. Scientists regard sources as unconventional if there are no financially or ecologically sound ways to extract energy from those sources. No one has good estimates of the potential reserves in unconventional sources. The cost of other energy resources must increase dramatically before unconventional sources would be profitable to exploit. Even then, the adverse environmental impacts of using these sources is likely to be high.

Distribution of fossil fuels. The global distribution of fossil fuels raises two problems. First, some regions have relatively abundant reserves of one or more fossil fuels, while other regions have little. Second, fossil fuel reserves are not located in the same regions as their consumers.

In general, the relatively developed countries of North America, Europe, and the Soviet Union possess a disproportionately large share of fossil fuel reserves. They contain approximately one-fourth of the world's population but possess more than half of the world's proven reserves of the three major fossil fuels. By far the largest proven reserves of fossil fuels are located in the Soviet Union. The Soviet Union possesses more than one-third of the world's proven natural gas reserves and more than one-fourth of the proven coal reserves; it also ranks sixth in the world in proven petroleum reserves. The United States, like the Soviet Union, has more than one-fourth of the world's proven coal reserves, but its proven petroleum and natural gas reserves are relatively small.

European countries possess one-sixth of the world's proven coal reserves, for the most part in Germany and Poland, but less than 5 percent of the petroleum reserves and less than 10 percent of the natural gas reserves. The region's major sources of petroleum and natural gas lie beneath the North Sea. Japan has virtually no proven fossil fuel reserves.

Overall, the developing regions do not have a fair share of energy reserves, but the situation varies by type of fossil fuel. Developing countries possess only one-tenth of the world's proven coal reserves, but nearly one-half of the natural gas and nine-tenths of the petroleum.

Energy reserves are not distributed uniformly within the developing world. A handful of the developing countries are well endowed with one of the fossil fuels, but most countries in Africa, Asia, and Latin America have relatively little. China accounts for most of the proven coal reserves in developing countries. Approximately 60 percent of the world's proven petroleum reserves are concentrated in the five Middle Eastern states of Saudi Arabia, Kuwait, Iran, Iraq, and the United Arab Emirates (Figure 13–2).

Although relatively developed countries account for more than their fair share of fossil fuel reserves, they consume an even higher percentage, more than three-fourths of the world's total. The United States alone consumes nearly one-fourth of the world's production of energy, while the Soviet Union is the world's second largest energy consumer (Figure 13–3).

Because relatively developed countries consume more energy than they produce, they must import energy, especially petroleum, from developing countries. The United States imports nearly half of its petroleum, Western European countries more than half, and Japan more than 90 percent. U.S. dependency on foreign petroleum began in the 1950s, when oil companies determined that the cost of extracting domestic petroleum reserves had become higher than foreign sources. Imported oil in the United States increased from 14 percent of total consumption in 1954, to 22 percent in 1965, and to 40 percent by 1974. European countries and Japan increasingly depend on foreign petroleum because of limited domestic supplies.

The largest percentage of petroleum imported by relatively developed countries comes from the Middle East, where most of the world's proven reserves are concentrated. U.S. and European companies originally exploited and controlled Middle Eastern petroleum fields. The companies sold the petroleum at a low price to consumers in relatively developed countries and provided the Middle Eastern governments with only a small percentage of the profits.

Government policies changed in countries with large petroleum reserves, especially during the 1970s. The foreign-owned petroleum fields were either nationalized or more tightly controlled, and prices were set by governments rather than by petroleum companies.

Several petroleum-producing countries formed an organization in 1960 called the Organization of Petroleum Exporting Countries (OPEC). OPEC includes eight Middle East countries (Algeria, Iran, Iraq, Kuwait, Libya, Qatar, Saudi Arabia, and United Arab Emirates) and five others (Ecuador, Gabon, Indonesia, Nigeria, and Venezuela). Beginning in the 1970s, OPEC became a major force in controlling the world price and supply of petroleum.

One of OPEC's first major acts was to organize a boycott during the winter of 1973–74. Most member states refused to sell petroleum to North Amer-

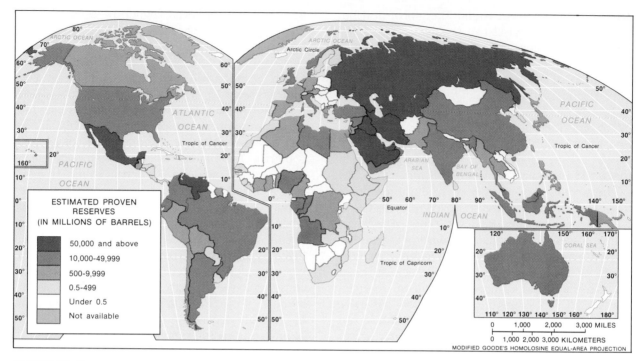

FIGURE 13–2
Petroleum is produced in more than fifty countries, but the Soviet Union and the United States together account for more than one-third of global production. The distribution of current production does not match the distribution of proven reserves or the likely distribution of potnetial reserves. The countries bordering the Persian Gulf have a higher percentage of proven reserves compared to current production, while the United Kingdom and the United States have relatively low levels of proven reserves.

ican and Western European countries to protest their support for Israel in its 1973 war against Egypt, Jordan, and Syria. As a result, motorists in relatively developed countries had difficulty obtaining fuel.

Each service station in the United States was allocated a small quantity of fuel, which usually ran out early in the day. People could buy gas on odd-numbered days of the month only if their license plates ended in an odd number, or on even-numbered days only if their license plates ended in an even number. Some motorists waited in lines all night for fuel. To prevent "topping-off," the fuel gauge had to register below one-half to legally buy gas. Some Western European countries took more drastic action. The Netherlands, for example, banned all motor-vehicle travel on Sundays, except for emergencies.

OPEC lifted the boycott in 1974 and instead began to raise the price of petroleum. The price of a barrel of oil rose from $3 before the boycott to $12 immediately after. During the 1970s, OPEC countries continued to raise the price, until a barrel cost more than $35 in 1981. OPEC members met periodically to set new prices and production levels for each country.

The policies of OPEC states caused a massive increase in the cost of petroleum for Western countries. To import petroleum, U.S. consumers spent $3 billion in 1970, $42 billion in 1978, $60 billion in 1979, and $80 billion in 1980. The rapidly escalating cost of petroleum was a major cause of severe economic problems in relatively developed countries during the 1970s.

The massive price increases hurt people in developing countries even more. Developing coun-

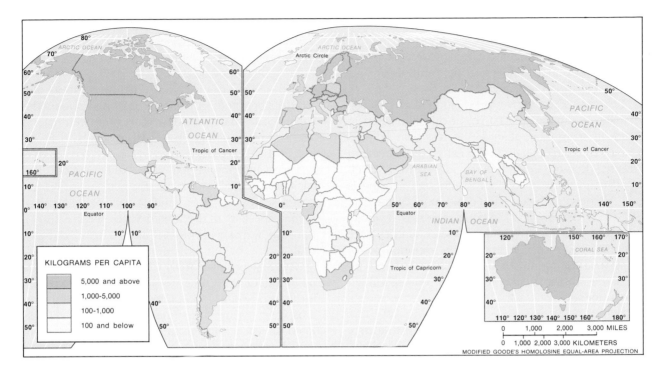

FIGURE 13–3

World per capita energy consumption. As was the case with petroleum production, the United States and the Soviet Union rank at the top of the list; together they account for nearly 45 percent of the world's consumption of energy. By comparing this map with Figure 13–2, we can see the extent of global interdependence in the production and consumption of energy. Countries in the Middle East are important exporters of energy, because they are major producers of petroleum, but they are relatively low users of energy. On the other hand, European countries and Japan must import large amounts of energy, because they are relatively low producers but large consumers.

tries depended on low-cost imported petroleum to spur industrial growth. Agriculture in developing countries also suffered, because many fertilizers contain petroleum products. In contrast to North American and Western European states, developing countries could not reduce the overall financial burden by providing opportunities for OPEC petroleum revenues to return in the form of investments in real estate, banks, and other assets.

OPEC's influence lessened in the 1980s and 1990s in part because member states could no longer reach agreement among themselves. Iraq fought a long war with a fellow OPEC member— Iran—and invaded another member—Kuwait. Yet another member, Libya, pursued more radical policies, including support for terrorists. As a result of

internal disagreements, OPEC countries began to produce a surplus of petroleum. Relatively developed countries also began to stockpile several month's worth of petroleum to minimize the adverse effects of a sudden cutoff in the flow from the Middle East.

In the early 1980s, the large consuming states of North America and Western Europe reduced petroleum consumption by 15 to 25 percent. Saudi Arabia remained the only major U.S. petroleum supplier in the Middle East, though Japan and Europe depended on other states in the region. The other major U.S. suppliers—Venezuela, Canada, and Mexico—were all firm allies located in the Western Hemisphere. Europeans benefited from discovery of petroleum in the North Sea, while the United

States exploited fields in Alaska. As a result of these relations, the portion of total consumption accounted for by Middle East petroleum fell to approximately one-half in Japan, one-fourth in Europe, and one-sixth in the United States.

Because of excessive production and reduced demand, the price of a barrel of oil plummeted in 1986–87 from more than $30 to less than $10, before rising sharply again in the early 1990s after Iraq invaded Kuwait. Consumption in relatively developed countries has also risen, although demand is still 10 percent below the peak level of the late 1970s. As proven and potential reserves dwindle, however, many relatively developed countries have become even more dependent on imported petroleum than during the 1970s, and they are more vulnerable to disruptive cutoffs at the whims of foreign governments.

Short-term solutions. It is unlikely that society will literally "run out" of petroleum and natural gas. Instead, some time in the twenty-first century,

proven reserves will shrink, and potential reserves will be prohibitively expensive to explore. As a result, human beings will be compelled to convert to other sources of energy.

Natural gas offers limited relief, because its global distribution is similar to that of petroluem. The United States has only a few years of proven natural gas reserves, though potential reserves may be higher than for petroleum.

Direct burning of coal and coal-generated electricity can partially substitute for petroleum. Proven coal reserves are more much extensive than petroleum, especially in the United States (Figure 13–4). But several major problems hinder expanded use of coal.

The first problem from expanded use of coal is pollution. Coal burning results in the release of sulfur, hydrocarbons, and other pollutants into the atmosphere. Many communities suffered from polluted air earlier in this century largely because of coal burning and encouraged their industries to switch to cleaner energy sources.

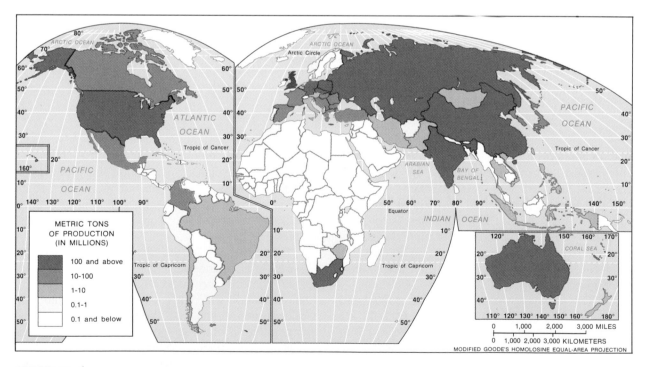

FIGURE 13–4
Coal production is more highly clustered than petroleum production. Three countries—China, the United States, and the Soviet Union— account for more than one-half of all coal production.

The second problem associated with coal is mine safety. Hundreds of U.S. miners are killed or injured each year, especially in underground mines. The miners are also prone to black lung disease, for which the U.S. government must pay several billion dollars per year in compensation. More elaborate safety precautions make underground mining somewhat safer but raise the cost of obtaining coal.

Third, coal mining causes environmental damage, including the destruction of forests and other surface vegetation. After the coal mine is abandoned, some operators make little or no effort to restore the land for other uses. Soil erosion can harm nearby farmers and other residents. Many communities now require mining companies to undertake reclamation projects after closing the mine, but adverse environmental impacts can persist. Because of mine safety problems, surface strip mining has increasingly replaced underground mining, but strip mining is more environmentally destructive.

The fourth problem with coal consumption in the United States and several other countries is difficulty in transporting it from the mines. Coal is generally transported from the mines by railroad, but the U.S. rail system cannot handle additional shipments without major investments in new tracks and cars.

The final problem related to coal is its suitability as a fuel for transportation. The rapid and inexpensive movement of people and goods is a fundamental requirement of an economically developed society. Since the invention of the automobile in the late nineteenth century, inexpensive and abundant petroleum has been the basis for modern transportation systems. To be a useful substitute for petroleum products, coal must be adapted to motor vehicles.

Our children and grandchildren may be amazed to learn that in the twentieth century we routinely drove automobiles that weighed several thousand pounds and burned gasoline at a rate of a gallon every 20 miles. Within decades, these large gasoline-powered automobiles likely will become dinosaurs consigned to museums, and instead we will probably drive small, lightweight electric-powered vehicles. Like other appliances, we may plug the vehicles into electric outlets to recharge the batteries. Service stations may offer battery rechargers rather than petroleum products. General Motors and other manufacturers have built prototypes of electric-powered cars, and those are likely to be offered for sale soon, especially if petroleum prices increase.

Alternative Energy Sources

Coal-generated electricity can reduce the impact of depleted petroleum reserves over the next century or two, but coal, like petroleum, is a nonrenewable fossil fuel that will eventually be depleted, and it offers little hope to countries that lack substantial reserves. In the long run, human beings can solve the energy crisis only by converting to renewable resources. A **renewable source of energy** has a theoretically unlimited supply and is not depleted when used by people. Two types of renewable energy sources, nuclear and solar, figure most prominently in current energy planning. Other alternatives to fossil fuels may become more important in the future.

Nuclear energy. The big advantage of nuclear power is the large amount of energy released from a relatively small amount of material. One kilogram of enriched nuclear fuel contains more than 2 million times more energy than 1 kilogram of coal.

Nuclear power has become an important source of energy in several countries, especially in Europe and Japan. Nuclear power supplies one-third of all electricity in Europe, including two-thirds in Belgium and France, one-half in Hungary and Sweden, and one-third in Finland, Germany, Spain, and Switzerland. Outside of Europe, Japan, South Korea, and Taiwan also rely on nuclear power for much of their electricity (Figure 13–5).

The United States and Canada are less dependent than Europeans on nuclear energy, in part because of more abundant coal reserves. Nuclear power generates approximately 20 percent of the electricity in North America as a whole, with New England drawing most of its electricity from nuclear power (Figure 13–6).

Five interrelated problems severely restrict the use of nuclear power instead of coal to generate electricity. The first problem associated with nuclear power is the danger of an accident. A nuclear power plant produces electricity from energy released by splitting uranium atoms in a controlled environment, a process known as **fission.** One of the prod-

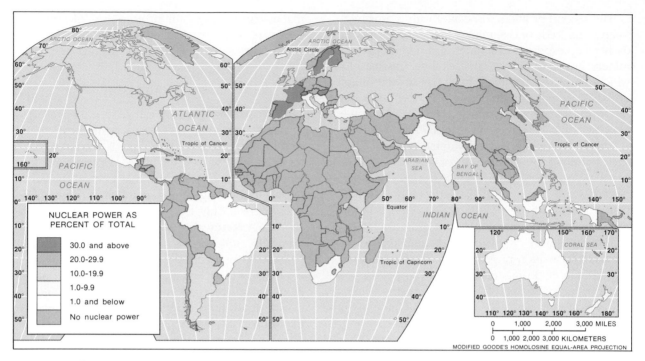

FIGURE 13–5
Nuclear power plants are clustered in the relatively developed regions, including North America, Europe, and Japan. Nuclear power has been especially attractive to relatively developed countries that lack abundant reserves of either petroleum or coal.

ucts in a nuclear reaction is **radioactive waste,** which is lethal to people exposed to it. Elaborate safety precautions must be taken to prevent the fuel from leaking out of the power plant.

The Soviet Union reported that a 1986 accident at its Chernobyl nuclear power plant caused thirty-one deaths, including two at the accident site itself and twenty-nine elsewhere who were exposed to severe radiation and burns. But experts have not been able to measure the total health damage from exposure to radiation leakage at Chernobyl. Estimates of additional cancer victims range from several thousand to more than a million. An unknown number of birth defects will also result from the accident.

The negative impacts of the Chernobyl accident extend beyond the borders of the Soviet Union. Half of the eventual victims may be residents of other European countries. Because of the contamination threat from radiation, most European governments temporarily banned the sale of milk and fresh vegetables, though some Europeans joked about lettuce that glowed in the dark.

In recent years, nuclear power plants constructed by the Soviet Union in Eastern Europe, especially during the 1960s, have reported problems as a result of defective parts and secrecy about operations. At a Soviet-built nuclear power plant in East Germany, eleven of the twelve cooling pumps were knocked out by a fire and a power failure. Had the twelfth pump failed, the reactor core would have begun an unstoppable process of meltdown. At the very least, the 50,000 inhabitants of the nearby city of Greifswald would likely have perished from the radioactivity. This accident took place in 1975, but the Soviet Union and East Germany kept it secret for fifteen years.

The second problem with nuclear power is the need to store waste products following the reaction. The spent fuel and other radioactive waste products must be stored for several thousand years, until they are no longer lethal. But no country has devised an effective storage system for the radioactive waste products. Localities oppose the construction of storage facilities, because if they leak, radioactive waste

FIGURE 13–6
Percentage of net electric energy generation produced by nuclear reactors, by state. Nuclear power is a relatively important source of electricity in the Northeast and the Midwest. At a number of locations, more than one nuclear plant have been built.

can contaminate the local water supply and cause other severe environmental problems. Even if an effective long-term storage system were built, an important question remains: What government, army, or other human institution will survive for several thousand years to assure that no leakage or theft occurs?

Despite being the world's fourth largest country in land area, the United States has failed to find a suitable underground storage site. Yucca Mountain, 110 kilometers (70 miles) northwest of Las Vegas, Nevada, was selected as a nuclear waste storage site in 1987, but subsequent studies determined that the site was unsuitable. The area had a risk of volcanic activity, raising fear that radioactive material might seep into the ground water. A second strategy, to store waste in salt beds 650 meters (2,150 feet) beneath the New Mexico desert, 40 kilometers (26 miles) east of Carlsbad, was also postponed because

of the possibility of leakage of waste into the ground water.

The third problem with nuclear power is that a bomb can be made from the material. Nuclear power has been used in warfare twice. On August 6, 1945, the United States dropped an atomic bomb on Hiroshima, Japan, and three days later it bombed Nagasaki, Japan. Since then, several other countries have developed nuclear weapons, but no one has dared to use them, because most government leaders recognize that the world's next nuclear war could destroy all human life on earth.

Even if we are confident that governments will not use nuclear weapons, can we be as confident about terrorist organizations? Terrorists could steal a small amount of nuclear fuel and construct their own nuclear weapons. A few years ago, a Princeton undergraduate wrote a term paper that outlined how to make a nuclear weapon. He was accused at first of leaking government secrets, but the student showed that most of his information came from the encyclopedia and a few unclassified government documents. Following publicity about the term paper, several organizations and foreign governments contacted the student for technical assistance in making a bomb. Incidentally, the student received only a C for the paper.

A fourth problem with nuclear power is the scarcity of uranium. Like the fossil fuels, uranium ore is a nonrenewable resource, and proven reserves will be depleted in less than a century at the current rate of use. Proven uranium reserves are not distributed uniformly across the earth's surface. The United States, Canada, South Africa, Australia, and the Soviet Union rank among the world's leaders. One-fifth of the world's proven reserves are concentrated in South Africa, but access to that supply is uncertain because of the country's racial problems.

The chemical composition of natural uranium further aggravates the scarcity problem. Uranium ore naturally contains 99.3 percent uranium-238 and only 0.7 percent uranium-235. To start a nuclear chain reaction, a higher percentage of uranium-235 must be present. Consequently, uranium fuel, known as enriched uranium, containing 3 percent uranium-235, must be prepared.

Scientists have addressed the problem of scarce uranium reserves by developing a different kind of nuclear power plant, known as a **breeder reactor.** A breeder reactor uses plutonium, which can be created from the more common form of uranium, and produces a chain reaction that results in more plutonium at the end of the process than at the beginning. By producing more fuel than they use, breeder reactors turn uranium into a renewable energy resource.

While the breeder reactor solves the resource supply problem, the risks associated with using plutonium are greater than those already described for uranium. Plutonium is more lethal than uranium and would cause many more deaths and injuries following an accident. Plutonium is also easier to fashion into a bomb. Like uranium, plutonium remains radioactive for thousands of years. Because of the high risks associated with its use, few breeder reactors exist.

The final problem with using nuclear power is its high cost. Nuclear power plants cost several billion dollars to build, primarily because of elaborate safety measures. Without double- and triple-backup systems, nuclear energy would be too dangerous to use. As a result, the cost of generating electricity is much higher from nuclear plants than from coal plants.

The future of nuclear power has been seriously hurt by the combination of high risks and costs. Most countries in North America and Western Europe have curtailed construction of new plants. Sweden, which received nearly half of its electricity from nuclear power in the 1980s, plans to begin shutting plants by 1995 and to abandon its nuclear power plants completely by the year 2010.

Solar energy. Solar-generated electricity does not carry the health or environmental risks of nuclear energy. We can never run out of solar energy, because the sun is a renewable energy source.

Two kinds of systems generate solar energy: passive and active. A **passive solar energy** system generates energy from fixed glass plates built into the structure, without the use of mechanical devices. A greenhouse is a good example of a building heated by passive solar energy. The sun's rays penetrate the glass panels to heat the interior of the greenhouse, and the heat is retained through tight construction. The same principle can be applied to heating homes and other buildings on sunny days.

An **active solar energy** system makes use of mechanical devices and moving parts to maximize the amount of energy collected. For example, solar energy can be generated with **photovoltaic cells,** which are made from silicon, an abundant element. A bank of photovoltaic cells can be encased in glass and wired together to produce electricity. The bank of cells can be mounted on the roof at an angle that maximizes exposure to direct sunlight.

Another device to generate solar energy is a flat-plate collector, which is an insulated glass box, typically placed on the sun-facing roof. Inside the box are pipes filled with air or water. The heat that builds up in the pipes can be used for home heating and hot-water supplies.

Two questions persist about solar energy:

◆ How can solar energy be used in colder climates?
◆ How can solar energy be used on cloudy days?

Scientists have the technological means to overcome both problems, but the solutions may make

Active solar energy, such as photo-voltaic cells in roof-top panels, can provide most of a home's hot water and electricity needs. This Vermont house relies on solar energy, even though it is located in a relatively harsh climate.

solar energy more expensive for many people than other alternatives.

The energy released from the sun is about 10,000°F, but by the time the rays reach the earth the temperature is considerably lower, because the sun's energy has diffused over a large area during its long journey. To be useful energy in colder climates, the sun's diffused rays must be concentrated.

The process of concentrating the sun's rays is not difficult. Scouts learn that sunlight focused with a lens at the proper angle can burn a piece of paper. In warmer climates, the sun's rays can provide heat and hot water with little concentration. In colder climates, compensation is made simply by collecting more of the sun's rays by building a larger collecting device and rotating the lenses as the sun's position in the sky changes. In cloudy weather, another system can store the energy generated from the sun. For example, water heated by the sun can be retained in protected storage containers.

Because of high installation costs, solar energy is more expensive than other sources of energy for most consumers. At this time, electricity provided by a solar power plant costs two or three times the amount of a coal-fired plant. But solar equipment is generally installed on the consumer's roof rather than at a central power plant, as is the case with other energy sources. A family must pay several thousand dollars to construct a solar energy system capable of providing virtually all household heat and electricity. The family is also responsible for maintenance and repair of the system.

While initial construction costs are much higher, monthly heating and electricity bills are much lower once the system begins operation. Users of solar energy do not face rising monthly electricity bills from a power company, which passes to its consumers the increasing costs of purchasing fossil fuels and constructing new facilities. Solar energy is economical for consumers who remain in the same house for many years and can benefit from low monthly operating costs. For most families, solar energy will become more attractive when other energy sources become more expensive. One indication of solar energy's bright future is that petroleum companies have bought the major U.S. manufacturers of photovoltaic cells.

Hydroelectric power. Water has served as a source of power since before recorded history, but in the last hundred years it has been used to generate electricity, known as **hydroelectric power.** To generate hydroelectric power, falling water rotates turbines housed in a power plant. The falling water is often created by building a dam across a river. Behind the dam, a lake or reservoir stores water. A hydroelectric power plant produces inexpensive electricity and may help a community to provide flood control, drinking water, and recreation opportunities. The United States obtains 3 percent of its energy from hydroelectric power.

Further expansion of hydroelectric power is limited by the lack of acceptable sites to build new dams. Construction of a hydroelectric plant can cause severe damage to aquatic life and adjacent land areas. Turkey's recently built dam on the Euphrates River has been strongly opposed by Syria and Iraq, the two other countries through which the river passes. Turkey's neighbors fear that the new dam diverts too much water from the river and increases its salinity (saltiness).

Geothermal energy. The interior of the earth may contain a mass of very hot, sometimes molten rock. The hot rocks may encounter water beneath the earth's surface and produce steam or hot water that can be tapped by drilling wells. Energy from the steam or hot water produced from hot underground rocks is called **geothermal energy.**

Geothermal energy is most feasible at the rifts along the earth's surface where different plates of the earth's crust meet. These rifts are also the sites of many earthquakes and volcanoes. Geothermal energy is being tapped in several locations, including California, Italy, and Japan, and other rift sites are being explored. Iceland and Indonesia make extensive use of this resource to meet their energy needs.

Fusion. A potential form of renewable energy is **fusion,** which is the joining of the nuclei of two forms of hydrogen, deuterium and tritium. At very high temperatures, the fusion results in a loss of mass and the release of a very large amount of energy in the form of a gas that can turn turbines and generate electricity.

Alternatives such as fusion do not offer immediate solutions to the energy crisis but may become more practical if the prices of current energy sources substantially rise. Human beings are not "running out" of energy on earth, but the era of dependency on nonrenewable fossil fuels for energy will probably constitute a remarkably short period of human history.

K E Y I S S U E
What Are the Main Types of Pollution?

Human actions can destroy resources as well as deplete them. When we produce goods and services that are supposed to improve our health and well-being, we may destroy resources. We misuse resources such as air and water by regarding them as unlimited, unchanging, and freely available for use

in the production of goods and services. In the long run, the destruction of resources for the production of goods and services can harm our health and economic prosperity.

Not all human actions harm the physical environment. Every resource has the capacity to accept some human abuse. When we wash chemicals into a river, we may or may not damage the water, because a river has the capacity to accept some discharges. Adverse impacts result when human actions generate more waste than the capacity of the resource to accommodate it. Human action that adversely affects a resource is known as **pollution.**

Geographers observe that one resource may have a higher capacity to withstand pollution than another, and the capacity of a particular resource may vary by location. To study the causes and consequences of pollution, we must understand the characteristics of different resources.

Pollution also varies among regions according to types of human actions. In general, we find higher levels of pollution in regions of population concentrations than in sparsely inhabited regions. When a large number of people live in a small area, their actions are more likely to exceed the capacity of the environment. Pollution also varies according to levels of economic development. Human actions in developing countries can adversely affect the environment, but most pollution is an unwanted by-product of production in relatively developed economies.

Pollution Sources

To better understand the causes of pollution, Blair Bower at Resources for the Future, a nonprofit research organization, asks us to consider a dairy cow as an analogy to a factory. We can think of a dairy cow as a factory that uses two main inputs—feed and water—to produce a desired output or product—milk (Figure 13–7).

Pollution results because a cow, like a factory, generates undesired outputs as well as the product. In the case of a cow, the undesired output is manure. An undesired by-product produced along with the principal purpose of an enterprise is called a **nonproduct output.** However, a nonproduct output may or may not constitute pollution. To be pollution, a nonproduct output must be a **residual,** which is a nonproduct output that is discharged into the environment. A residual in turn becomes pollution if the level discharged into the environment exceeds the capacity of the environment to accept it.

The manure from the dairy cow is a nonproduct output. If that manure is discharged into the environment, it becomes a residual. In some societies, manure is not a residual, because it is reused rather than discharged. In South Asia, for example, manure is dried and used for fuel, while in many other societies it is used for fertilizer.

In relatively developed countries, farmers "throw away" manure rather than reuse it, because purchasing commercial fertilizer is cheaper than collecting and treating manure. But manure is not precisely "thrown away." More properly speaking, manure constitutes a residual, because it is allowed to collect on the ground.

If the manure discharged into the environment in relatively developed countries is causing pollution, several strategies exist for reducing the adverse impact. By changing the feed (the types of inputs), the production of manure may be reduced. Alternatively, instead of reducing the production of the residual, farmers can disperse the manure, perhaps by spreading the manure over a larger area, converting it from a solid to a gas by burning it, or washing it into a nearby stream. These alternatives may not be practical, but they illustrate the variety of strategies available to deal with pollution problems.

When we throw something away, we do not perceive that we are converting a nonproduct output to a residual by discharging it into the environment. But the laws of conservation of mass and energy dictate that matter is not destroyed. The same quantity of material going into the production of a product is always present after production. Therefore, when we throw something away, we have not eliminated that product. Instead, we may have caused pollution, depending on where we "threw away" the nonproduct output. Humans contribute to one of five kinds of pollution when they discharge residuals into the environment: air, water, land, heat, and noise.

Air pollution. So-called normal air comprises 78.09 percent nitrogen, 20.94 percent oxygen, and 0.93 percent argon. The remaining 0.04 percent includes at least 13 other elements. Air pollution is a concentration of one or more of the rare elements at a greater level than found in normal air.

The most common air pollutants include carbon monoxide, sulfur dioxide, nitrogen oxide, hydrocarbons, and solid particulates. Concentrations of these pollutants in the air can damage property and adversely affect the health of people, other animals, and plants.

Three types of activities generate most of the air pollution: motor vehicles, industries, and power plants. In all three cases, most of the pollution re-

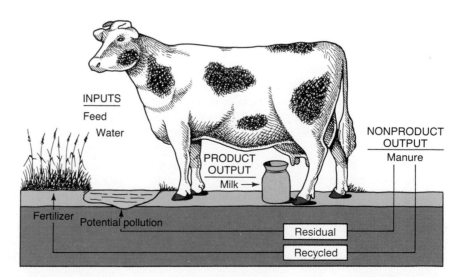

FIGURE 13–7
A dairy cow serves as a model for understanding pollution. The cow has a set of inputs (feed and water) and a product (milk). Manure is a nonproduct output; if it is discharged into the environment, it becomes a residual. Instead of becoming a residual, a nonproduct output can be recycled, in this case perhaps as fertilizer. If it washes into a stream, it may become pollution.

sults from the burning of fossil fuels. The combustion of fuel in car, truck, and motor cycle engines produces carbon monoxide, hydrocarbons, nitrogen oxides, and other pollutants. Factories and power plants produce sulfur dioxides and solid particulates, primarily from burning coal. Catalytic converters, which have been attached to U.S. cars since the 1970s, have reduced carbon monoxide emissions by more than 75 percent and nitrogen oxide and hydrocarbon emissions by more than 95 percent.

Many urban areas suffer from **photochemical smog,** an atmospheric condition formed from a combination of weather patterns and air pollution, primarily from motor-vehicle emissions. People in Denver refer to their smog as the brown cloud. The U.S. Environmental Protection Agency (EPA) ranks Denver as the worst city for concentrations of carbon monoxide and the second for particulates. The Rocky Mountains trap the gases and help to produce a permanent temperature inversion. Ironically, these mountains, which attracted a large number of migrants to Denver, are obscured by smog on many days and aggravate the smog problem.

The problem is not confined to relatively developed societies. Santiago, Chile, nestled between the Andes Mountains and the Coastal Range, suffers from severe smog problems. Motor vehicles are also responsible for much of the pollution in Santiago, especially particulates from burning diesel fuel, combined with dust kicked up from driving on unpaved streets. Mexico City, which is situated in a valley surrounded by mountains, is one of the world's smoggiest cities, especially in the winter, when thermal inversions each morning trap the polluted air and prevent it from rising. To reduce emissions, the Mexican government has prohibited motorists from driving one day a week, depending on the last number of their license plate. Pemex, the government-owned oil company, has introduced additives that reduce carbon monoxide and hydrocarbon emissions.

Scientists worry that human actions are destroying the **ozone,** the layer of the atmosphere that protects life from harmful ultraviolet radiation. Damage to the ozone is being inflicted primarily by **chlorofluorocarbons (CFCs),** which are gaseous compounds used as solvents, propellants in aerosols, and refrigerants, as well as in plastic foams and fire extinguishers.

When introduced in 1930, CFCs revolutionized refrigeration because they were safer than refrigerants then in use, such as ammonia and sulfur dioxide. Until CFCs were invented, many people refused to buy refrigerators because of fear that they leaked poisonous gases. CFCs became popular in the 1950s as a propellant for aerosol products such as hair sprays and deodorants.

The United States and Canada banned the use of CFCs as aerosol propellants in 1978, but they are still used to make other products in North America and elsewhere. Representatives of ninety-three countries have agreed to phase out the production of use of CFCs by the end of the century.

Burning of fossil fuels results in discharge of sulfur dioxide and nitrogen oxides into the atmosphere. These emissions react with sunlight, water, and other chemicals to produce forms of sulfuric and nitric acids that return to the earth as rain, snow, sleet, mist, fog, or clouds. This kind of pollution, now generally known as **acid rain,** is responsible for destruction of some plant and aquatic life and may adversely affect human health.

Acid rain has completely eliminated aquatic life from 4 percent of the lakes in the eastern United States and Canada; another 5 per cent in the eastern United States and 20 percent in eastern Canada have acidity levels that threaten some species. Acid rain has contributed to the decline of the red spruce tree at higher elevations. Buildings, monuments, and other structures made of marble and limestone have suffered corrosion from acid rain.

Geographers are particularly interested in the effects of acid rain because the worst damage is not experienced at the same location as the emission of the pollutants. Within the United States, the adverse effects of acid rain are most severe in 6 areas: Appalachia, the southwestern one-third of the Adirondack Mountains of New York State, Michigan's Upper Peninsula and northern Wisconsin, the highlands of northwestern Florida, and the coastal lowlands of both New England and the Mid-Atlantic states (Figure 13–8). Yet the biggest source of emissions that produce acid rain is Ohio, followed by other industrial states along the southern Great Lakes.

The problem of acid rain is compounded by the fact that pollutants emitted in one country cause adverse impacts in another. The acid rain falling in Ontario, Canada, can be traced to the burning of

FIGURE 13–8
The most severe adverse effects from acid rain do not occur where the pollutants are emitted into the air. As a result of prevailing wind patterns across North America, damage is generally found to the east of the emissions.

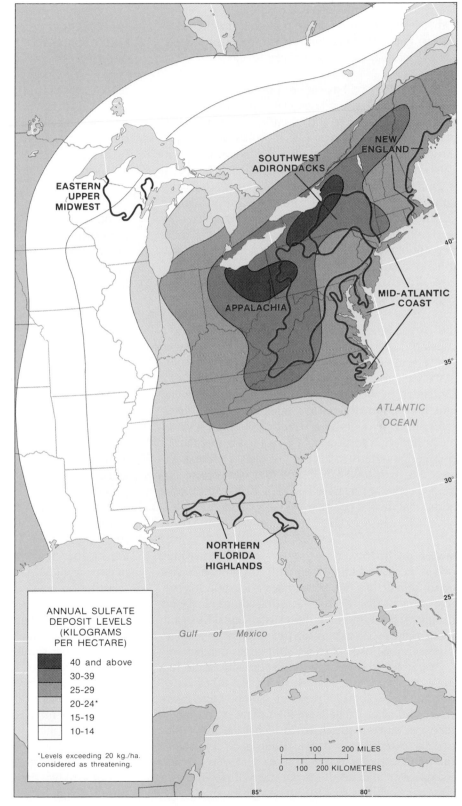

EASTERN UPPER MIDWEST

SOUTHWEST ADIRONDACKS

NEW ENGLAND

APPALACHIA

MID-ATLANTIC COAST

NORTHERN FLORIDA HIGHLANDS

ATLANTIC OCEAN

Gulf of Mexico

ANNUAL SULFATE DEPOSIT LEVELS (KILOGRAMS PER HECTARE)

40 and above
30-39
25-29
20-24*
15-19
10-14

*Levels exceeding 20 kg./ha. considered as threatening.

0   100   200 MILES
0   100   200 KILOMETERS

fossil fuels at plants in the U.S. Great Lakes region. Officials at the source of the pollution may be reluctant to impose strong controls on the offending factories because they fear damaging the local economy.

Eastern Europe has suffered especially severe effects from acid rain, a legacy of communist policies that encouraged the construction of factories and power plants without pollution-control devices. Destruction of forests is widespread because of acid rain emitted from Eastern Europe's major industrial region, which includes southeastern Germany, southern Poland, and northern Czechoslovakia. Czechoslovakia, the European state most affected by acid rain, has found severe damage in more than 80 percent of the Bohemian Forest and more than one-third of its other forests.

The destruction of trees has harmed Eastern Europe's seasonal water flow. In dense forests, snow used to melt slowly and trickle into rivers; now, on the barren sites, it melts and rushes down quickly, causing flooding in the spring and water shortages in the summer.

Perhaps the most severe impact is on human life. One-third of the residents of Leningrad, the Soviet Union's second largest city, suffer from upper respiratory-tract ailments as a result of the high level of air pollution. A forty-year-old man living in Poland's polluted southern industrial area has a life expectancy ten years lower than his father had at forty. Poland is estimated to have between 20,000 and 50,000 additional deaths per year due to pollution.

Water pollution. Water serves many human purposes. People drink water and consume fish and other aquatic life. Water provides a location for recreation activities, such as boating, swimming, and fishing. At the same time, water is essential for many industrial processes and for the disposal of sewage. These various uses of water sometimes conflict.

Water has the capacity to decompose some human wastes without adverse impact on other activities. But the volume of residuals dumped into many rivers and lakes exceeds their capacity to accommodate the wastes without harm to marine life. Pollution is extensive, because water is a convenient dumping area for waste; it is easy to dump waste into a river and let the water carry it downstream where it becomes someone else's problem.

Industries such as steel, chemicals, paper products, and food processing are major water polluters. Each requires a large amount of water in the manufacturing process and generates a large amount of wastewater. Food processors, for example, use water to rid fruits and vegetables of the pesticides and chemicals that were used in the growing process as well as to remove skins, stems, and other parts of the fruits and vegetables that are not included in the final packaging.

A second major source of water pollution is municipal sewage. Sewers carry the wastewater from sinks, bathtubs, and toilets to a muncipal treatment plant, where most, but not all, of the pollutants are removed. The treated wastewater is then typically dumped back into a river or lake.

A third major water polluter is agriculture. Fertilizers and pesticides spread on fields to increase agricultural productivity are carried into rivers and lakes by the irrigation system or natural runoff. Ironically, expanded use of these products may both help avoid a global food crisis and destroy aquatic life by polluting rivers.

Polluted water threatens the survival of aquatic plants and animals in two ways. First, pollution can lower the water's level of **biological oxygen demand (BOD),** which is the amount of oxygen required by aquatic bacteria to decompose a given load of organic waste. Bacteria can decompose organic residuals dumped into the water, but the process requires the use of some of the water's oxygen. The more oxygen from the water needed to break down the wastes, the less there is available for the survival of aquatic life. The lower the level of BOD, the cleaner the water is, because less oxygen is needed to fight pollution.

Pollution can also produce **eutrophication,** which is a process of enriching the water with excessive levels of nutrients. Residuals discharged into water may contain nitrogen, phosphorus, or other elements that stimulate aquatic life and produce an overabundance of certain organisms, especially algae. If the algae are not suitable food for other organisms in the body of water, the algae will compete for an increasing percentage of the available oxygen. Drinking-water systems suffering from excessive concentrations of algae may require expensive additional treatment.

Consuming contaminated fish may harm people's health. Even if only small amounts of poisonous

The Exxon Valdez oil spill, cleaning oil from the beach at Naked Island, Alaska, (right). Oil is put in bags to be collected and burned. The Exxon Valdez was towed to dry-dock in California (below).

chemicals are dumped into a body of water, they may settle in fish. Some fish may accumulate an excessive concentration of these residuals by consuming other species. Salmon from the Great Lakes became unfit to eat because of high concentrations of DDT, which washed into streams after farmers used it as a pesticide.

Perhaps the world's most extreme instance of water pollution is the Aral Sea, in the Soviet Union. Once the world's fourth-largest lake, the Aral has lost nearly half of its water since 1960. Carp, sturgeon, and other species of fish have disappeared, and the last fish died in 1983. Large ships lie aground in salt flats that were once the seabed, outside of fishing villages that have been abandoned because they lie tens of kilometers from the rapidly receding shore (Figure 13–9).

The Aral Sea died after its tributaries, the Amu Dar'ya and the Syr Dar'ya rivers, were diverted to irrigate cotton fields in the late 1950s and early 1960s. Chemicals sprayed on the field flowed into the sea. Ironically, the cotton is withering because winds deposit salt from the exposed lakebed on the cottonfields. Because most households in the surrounding Kara-kalpak Autonomous Region obtain their water directly from ditches rather than through pipes from treatment plants, two-thirds of them suffer

from liver disorders, typhoid, or cancer of the esophagus.

Many Western European and North American communities have successfully cleaned up their bodies of water. One dramatic example is the River Thames, which passes through London, England. Prior to the industrial revolution, the Thames had been a major source of food for Londoners. Some apprentice workers even went on strike in the early 1800s because their masters fed them too much fish. But during the industrial revolution, the Thames became the principal location for the dumping of waste. The fish were all killed, and the water was unsafe to drink. The river looked dark and murky and smelled bad. Dickens called the Thames "London's Styx," after the river of the underworld in ancient Greek mythology that the dead had to cross.

In the late 1960s, the British government began a massive cleanup effort to restore the Thames to health. Regulations prevented industrial dumping in the river, and sewer systems were modernized to reduce the discharge of inadequately treated sewage.

On July 28, 1982, a salmon was caught in River Thames near Hampton Court, just upstream from London. The event was remarkable, because it was

FIGURE 13–9
Once the world's fourth largest fresh water lake, the Aral Sea has declined in area by nearly one-half since 1960. The principal cause was diversion of the Amu Dar'ya and the Syr Dar'ya rivers to irrigate cotton fields.

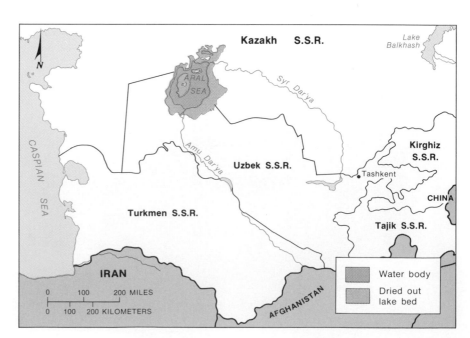

FIGURE 13–10
Paper products account for the largest percentage of solid waste in the United States, followed by food products and yard rubbish.

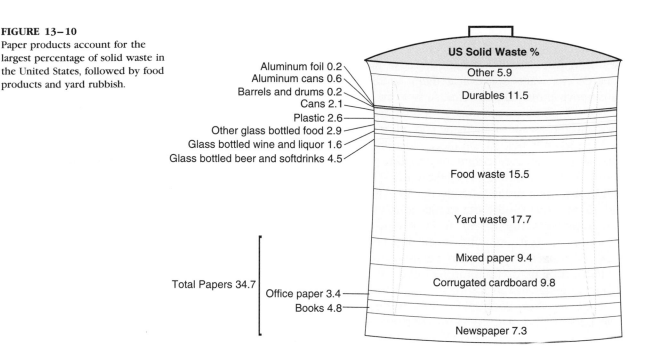

US Solid Waste %

Aluminum foil 0.2
Aluminum cans 0.6
Barrels and drums 0.2
Cans 2.1
Plastic 2.6
Other glass bottled food 2.9
Glass bottled wine and liquor 1.6
Glass bottled beer and softdrinks 4.5

Other 5.9
Durables 11.5

Food waste 15.5

Yard waste 17.7

Mixed paper 9.4

Total Papers 34.7
Office paper 3.4
Books 4.8

Corrugated cardboard 9.8

Newspaper 7.3

the first salmon caught in the river since 1833. Salmon are particularly sensitive to pollution, and for nearly 150 years the Thames was too polluted for salmon to survive.

To demonstrate the success of the cleanup operation, the Thames Water Authority has released 50,000 young salmon (known as parr) into the river each year since 1979. When they are approximately two years old the salmon (then known as smolts) migrate from the river to the sea, where they spend one to three years. The salmon then return to the river to seek spawning grounds upstream. Several dozen of the 50,000 salmon released into the river in 1979 were the first to be caught in July 1982.

Actually, the first salmon may have been caught several days earlier. An Englishman produced a salmon allegedly taken from the Thames and claimed the prize offered to the person who caught the first one. The government authorities who tested his salmon, however, ruled that it had come from the man's freezer, not from the Thames.

Land. The third alternative available to people for the disposal of residuals is land. As a side effect of consuming products, people accumulate large quantities of unwanted nonproduct outputs, such as packages, wrappers, and containers made of paper, plastic, and glass. The average person throws away

approximately 2 kilograms (4 pounds) of solid waste per day in the United States, nearly twice as much per capita as in 1960. Paper products, especially corrugated cardboard and newspapers, account for more than one-third of all solid waste in the United States. Discarded food products and grass clippings, leaves, and other rubbish cleaned up from yards each account for one-third of the waste (Figure 13–10).

Some people demonstrate their lack of concern for the appearance of the physical environment by tossing their unwanted nonproduct outputs on the side of the road, where they cause visual pollution for others. But even consumers who carefully dispose of their solid waste in proper trash containers unknowingly contribute to an increasing pollution problem.

Most households in relatively developed societies and many in developing societies fill trash cans or plastic bags with their solid waste and place them near the street for collection at designated times. The garbage hauler then takes the solid waste to a nearby landfill. Contrary to how both air and water pollution are normally reduced (by dispersing residuals), solid waste pollution is minimized by concentrating the residuals at a few landfills.

Disposing solid waste by hauling it to a landfill is no longer an option for many communities. Half of the states in the United States will run out of space in their landfills during the 1990s (Figure 13–11). Few new ones are being built, because most citizens do not want to live near them. Landfills also cause environmental problems, such as the contamination of underground water supplies from leakages and the escape of methane and other gases.

A community that has no more space in its landfill may pay another community to take its solid waste. Some communities regularly transport their solid waste long distances. San Francisco, for example, disposes its solid waste in Altamont, California, 100 kilometers (60 miles) away. Passaic County, New Jersey, hauls its solid waste 400 kilometers (250 miles) west to Johnstown, Pennsylvania.

The problem of transporting solid waste long distances generated an absurd situation in 1987. The town of Islip, New York, sold its solid waste to a private person who planned to transport the waste to Morehead City, North Carolina, and convert it to methane gas. The 3.1 million kilograms (3,100 tons) of refuse were trucked to Long Island City and transferred to a barge named the Mobro for the journey to North Carolina. But officials in Morehead City obtained a court injunction prohibiting the unloading of refuse there.

The Mobro then continued farther south in search of a home, but communities in Alabama, Mississippi, Louisiana, Texas, and Florida all refused to accept it. After Mexico, Belize, and the Bahamas also turned it away, the barge returned to New York, after nearly two months and a 9,000-kilometer (5,500-mile) journey. Four months later, the trash was burned in New York City, and the ashes were trucked back to Islip, where the trash had started its journey six months earlier (Figure 13–12).

Communities address the lack of landfill space in two ways. First, many places require citizens to sep-

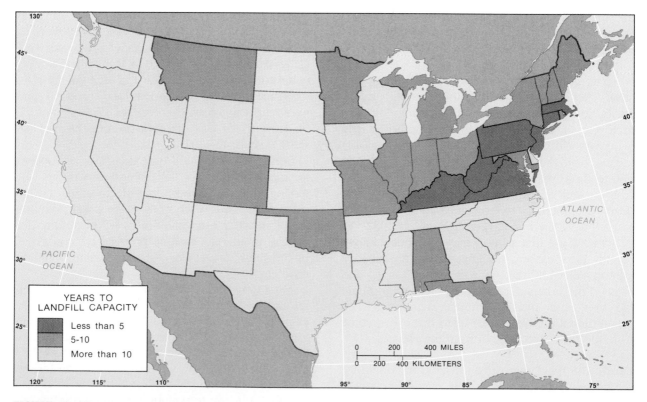

FIGURE 13–11
Many communities in the United States are running out of space to deposit solid waste. By the end of the 1990s, landfills in nearly half of the states will have no additional capacity.

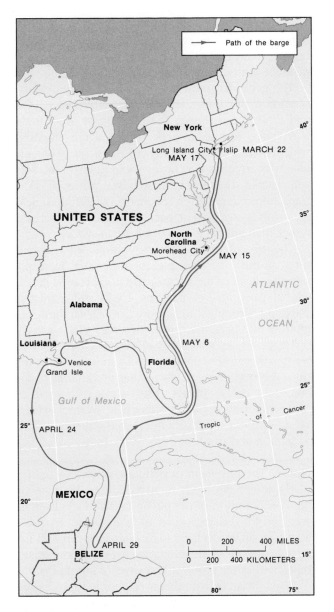

FIGURE 13–12
The problem of solid-waste disposal was graphically illustrated by the 1987 journey of the barge Mobro. The city of Islip, New York, faced with no room in its local landfill, hired a company to remove its waste by barge. The waste was supposed to be disposed in a landfill near Morehead City, North Carolina, but the state prohibited the Mobro from landing there. The barge was towed into the Gulf of Mexico but was refused landing rights by the states of Alabama, Florida, Louisiana, and Texas, as well as by Belize and Mexico. Finally, following a two-month, 9,000-kilometer (5,500-mile) journey, the Mobro returned to the New York area, where four months later the waste was unloaded and burned.

arate their trash by types, such as newspaper, glass, plastic, and aluminum. Each type of rubbish may be collected on different days or in separate trucks or at separate times on the same day. The trash collector sends paper to mills, cans to tin recycling companies, and glass to bottlers. To encourage recycling, some communities charge high fees to pick up nonrecyclables but take away recyclables for a small fee or for free. In other places, citizens are fined for failing to comply.

Second, many communities burn solid waste. Within a decade, most solid waste in the United States may be incinerated. In addition to reducing the need for landfills, incineration can produce electricity, because the fire's heat can boil water, which produces steam that can be used to run a turbine. Yet burning solid waste may increase air pollution. Thus, solving one pollution problem may increase another pollution problem.

Toxic wastes are especially difficult to dispose. If poisonous industrial residuals are not carefully placed in protective containers, the chemicals may leach into the soil and contaminate groundwater or escape into the atmosphere. Nuclear wastes that remain radioactive for thousands of years represent a particularly difficult toxic-waste disposal issue.

A serious problem resulting from improper toxic-waste disposal occurred in Niagara Falls, New York, where several hundred families living near the Love Canal were exposed to chemicals released from a waste disposal used by Hooker Chemicals and Plastic Company. During the 1930s, the company had placed toxic wastes in metal drums and buried them at a dump site. In 1953, the site was given to the Niagara Falls Board of Education, which built a school on part of the site and permitted developers to construct several hundred homes on the remainder.

Over the years, heavy rainfalls eroded the dump site and exposed the metal drums. In 1976, residents started to notice a strong stench and oozing slime from the drums. They also began to experience a high incidence of liver ailments, nervous disorders, and other health problems. After four babies were born with birth defects on the same block, New York State officials relocated most of the families from their homes and began an expensive effort to clean up the site.

Consolidated Edison workers removing asbestos from a Grammercy Park building in New York City. Asbestos, once widely used in insulation, readily separates into long flexible fibers that lodge in the lungs, increasing the risk of cancer.

The Love Canal incident is not unique—toxic wastes have been improperly disposed of at thousands of dumps. The U.S. Environmental Protection Agency has created a list of the worst toxic waste sites throughout the country. The effort required to clean up so many sites will be long and expensive (Figure 13–13).

As toxic-waste disposal sites become increasingly hard to find, some European and North American firms have tried to transport their waste to West Africa. Some firms have signed contracts with West African countries, while others have found isolated locations to dump waste without official consent.

Heat. Some discharges of residuals into the environment produce heat that may damage the planet.

The burning of fossil fuels contributes to higher temperatures in two ways: the burning itself directly heats the air, and the products of that burning can produce a greenhouse effect.

The **greenhouse effect** results from the release of carbon dioxide, methane, nitrous oxides, CFCs, and other gases during the burning of fossil fuels and other industrial processes. Carbon dioxide, which is responsible for half of the greenhouse effect, is nearly transparent in visible light, so the sun still reaches the earth's surface. But carbon dioxide traps infrared radiation given off by the land, sea, and clouds, sending it back to the earth's surface rather than allowing it to dissipate in space.

The greenhouse effect may increase temperatures on the earth's surface, melt the polar ice caps, raise the level of the oceans, and flood coastal cities. Global precipitation patterns could shift, causing crippling droughts in productive agricultural regions, while bringing rain to deserts.

Heat pollutes water as well as air. Discharges of warm water into rivers or lakes by industrics can reduce the oxygen content of water and therefore increase the BOD. Species of fish adapted to a particular temperature cannot survive in warmer water. Heat pollution especially hurts cold-water fish such as salmon and trout.

Noise. The fifth form of pollution is noise, a particularly severe problem in urban areas, because of the concentration of people and activities in a small area. Prolonged exposure to high noise levels—above 85 or 90 decibels—can impair sleep and induce hearing loss, heart attacks, hypertension, irritability, and other physical and psychological effects.

Many urban activities expose people to excessive noise levels. The decibel reading is 85 in a discotheque, 88 near a jackhammer, 92 on the back seat of a bus above the engine, and 98 when a New York subway train pulls into a station. To place these numbers in context, the chirping of the alarm on a battery-operated clock registers 44 decibels.

A major generator of noise pollution in many urban areas is the airport. Some of the world's busiest airports are situated close to population concentrations, such as La Guardia Airport in New York, National Airport in Washington, D.C., Logan Airport in Boston, and Heathrow Airport in London. A jet taking off produces 140 decibels nearby; although the

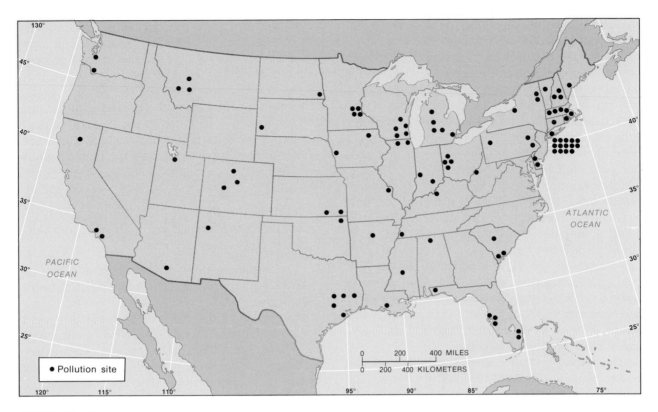

FIGURE 13–13
The U.S. Environmental Protection Agency maintains a national priorities list of hazardous waste sites, ranked according to the severity of the hazard. This map shows only the 100 worst sites.

level diminishes away from the runway, hundreds of thousands of people who live near airports are disturbed by excessive noise. Late-night flights are banned from inner-city airports to allow people to get some sleep. Newer airports are built farther from residential concentrations to minimize noise problems, although additional air pollution is generated by motorists forced to drive farther to reach them.

Pollution Reduction Alternatives

Given the five choices for disposing residuals—air, water, land, heat, and noise—there are only two basic alternatives for reducing pollution. One alternative is to reduce the amount of residuals discharged into the environment. The second is to increase the capacity of the environment to accept the discharge of residuals.

Reduce discharges. The amount of residuals discharged into the environment can be reduced in two ways:

- Reduce the amount of nonproduct output created.
- Recycle the nonproduct output rather than discharge it into the environment.

There are two ways of reducing the generation of nonproduct output: change the mix of inputs or reduce the demand for the input. Returning to the example of the dairy cow in Figure 13–7, to reduce the generation of nonproduct output (manure), a change can be made in the mix of inputs (the amount or type of feed). This alternative also applies to a major source of air pollution, motor vehicle emissions. To reduce the generation of lead—once a significant nonproduct output—society has changed one of the inputs into motor vehicle engines from leaded to unleaded gasoline.

The second way to reduce the generation of nonproduct output is to reduce consumer demand for the input. If the cow receives less food and water, it may produce less manure. A similar alternative has been used to reduce motor-vehicle pollution. Motor vehicles now generate less pollution (the nonproduct output) in part because they consume less gasoline per mile (the input) than in the past.

Once a nonproduct output is discharged into the environment, it is a residual. At that point, the only alternative for reducing the amount of residuals discharged into the environment is recycling. Recycling can take two forms. One is to reuse the residual directly in the same production process. The cow's manure can be used as fertilizer to grow the cow's food, which results in the production of more milk and manure. Rather than discharge wastewater into a river, a food processor can use the water again in the production process.

The second recycling alternative is to reuse the residuals in a different production process. The cow's manure can be used for other purposes, such as cooking fuel or heat. The vegetable pulp produced as an unwanted by-product of food processing can be used to make pet food.

Increase environmental capacity. The second way to handle pollution is to increase the capacity of the physical environment to accept discharges. There are two ways to increase the capacity of the environment:

◆ Make more efficient use of the resource currently receiving the discharge.
◆ Transform the residual and discharge it into a different part of the environment.

The first alternative can be accomplished in a variety of ways, depending on distinctive characteristics of the resource. The pollution caused by the concentration of the cow's manure can be spread over a larger area. This alternative may seem absurd at first, but remember that the capacity of a resource to accept the discharge of residuals is not fixed but varies among places and at different times.

Garbage being compacted in Tokyo Bay to reduce the volume of solid waste.

The identical amount of wastewater discharged into a river may or may not constitute pollution, because the volume of water flowing in a river varies by place and time. A relatively deep and fast-flowing river has a higher capacity to absorb the waste water than a shallow and slow-moving one. To minimize pollution, a community can store wastewater at a treatment plant when the river level is low and release it when the river is high.

A community may be able to reduce air pollution by building a higher smokestack, which increases the capacity of the atmosphere to accept discharges, because gaseous residuals are dispersed more if they are discharged at a greater height. A community may also be able to reduce air pollution by reducing the number of trips during the morning and evening rush hours and spreading the use of motor vehicles more evenly through the day. This dispersion can be accomplished by staggering working hours rather than requiring everyone to arrive and leave work at the same time.

The other way to increase environmental capacity is to transform a residual so that it is discharged into a resource that has the capacity to assimilate it. The laws of conservation of mass and energy dictate that while matter cannot be destroyed, it can be transformed among the five alternatives: gas (the air), land (solids), water (liquids), heat, and noise.

For example, a coal-burning power plant could discharge gases into the atmosphere, causing air pollution. To reduce air pollution, the power plant can install a wet scrubber to wash the particulates out of the gas. This process transforms the gaseous residual into a liquid one—water containing suspended solids. That water can be discharged into a stream. If the stream is polluted by the discharge, then the wastewater can be cleaned by using a settling basin to remove the suspended solids. In this way, the residual is transformed into a solid waste for disposal on land.

All four of the principal pollution-reduction alternatives apply to the example of a coking plant. The main input to a coking plant is a mix of types of coal, and the product output is coke, which becomes an input in steel production. The coal is placed in a blast furnace and cooked at very high temperatures to form the coke. Four nonproducts result: gases, tars, oils, and heat. The first three nonproducts are captured and sold to other companies for recycling in other production processes. Heat is discharged into the environment and becomes a residual.

The hot coke is taken to a quench station and doused with water to cool it. This process transforms heat into a liquid residual—dirty water—and a gaseous residual—steam. The water is recycled in the same production process, while the steam is discharged into the environment. To minimize the level of pollution, the steam is discharged from a tall smokestack. The fourth alternative for reducing pollution—changing the mix of coal used as inputs—is also employed, because the amount of gases emitted by the burning of coke varies depending on the mix of coal (Figure 13–14).

Pollution is a consequence of the demand for many products in an industrial society. But when consumers discard unwanted nonproduct outputs that accompany the desired products, they are not literally throwing away anything; they are merely discharging the unwanted by-product into the environment.

Fortunately, the environment has the capacity to accept some of these discharges. Consumers must learn to use this environmental capacity most efficiently. At the same time, consumers must learn to waste less, either by reducing the consumption of products that result in unwanted by-products or by recycling more. With careful management, we can enjoy the benefits of both industrial development and a cleaner, safer environment.

KEY ISSUE

How Can We Expand Global Food Supply?

Human actions may result in more efficient use of some resources, rather than their depletion or destruction. One dramatic example of human efforts to make more efficient use of available resources is the increasing capacity of the earth's surface to provide food.

By examining strategies for expanding the world's food supply, we return to the problem of overpopulation raised near the beginning of the book. We concluded that we can meet the overpopulation problem in part by reducing population

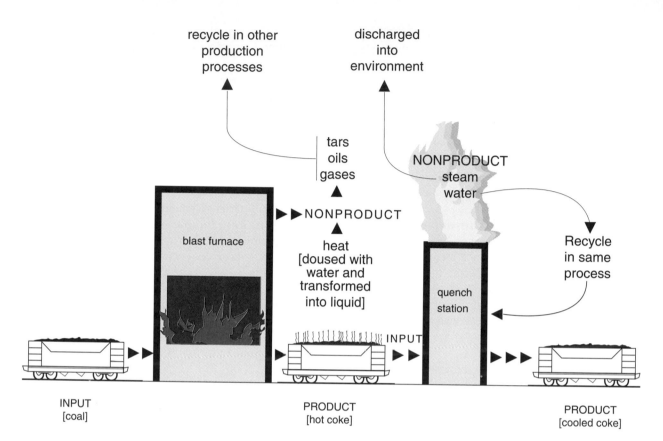

FIGURE 13–14

A coking plant illustrates the application of the principal pollution-reduction alternatives:

1. Reduce discharges of residuals
   a. Reduce the amount of nonproduct output (change mix of coal)
   b. Recycle the nonproduct output (reuse quenching water)
2. Increase environmental capacity
   a. Make more efficient use of the currently used resources (tall smokestack for discharging steam)
   b. Discharge into a different part of the environment (transform heat into liquid and gaseous residuals)

growth. The other way to avoid overpopulation is to expand the capacity of the earth to support life.

The ratio of population to food supply has become more favorable in many regions, especially in Asia, where population growth has slowed, while food supply has grown. The challenge in these regions is to continue recent progress by further expanding food resources. In other regions, especially Sub-Saharan Africa, the problem is getting worse. Food supply must be quickly expanded to meet the needs of Africa's rapidly expanding population.

We can identify four alternatives for increasing the food supply:

- Expand the land area used for agriculture.
- Increase the productivity of land now used for agriculture.
- Identify new food sources.
- Increase exports from other countries.

Expand Agricultural Land

Historically, world food production has increased primarily from expansion of the land area used for agriculture. When the world's population began to increase more rapidly in the late eighteenth and nineteenth centuries, pioneers could migrate to uninhabited territory and convert the land to agricultural use. Sparsely inhabited land suitable for agriculture was available for migrants in areas such as western North America, central Russia, and the pampas of Argentina. People believed that good agricultural land would always be available for pioneers willing to migrate.

Today, few scientists believe that further expansion of agricultural land can feed the growing world population. Since approximately 1950, the world's population has increased more rapidly than the expansion of agricultural land.

At first glance, the traditional alternative should still be available, because only approximately 11 percent of the world's land is currently cultivated. Growth is possible in North America, where some arable land is not cultivated for economic reasons, and the tropics of Africa and South America offer some hope for developing new agricultural land.

Desertification is a particularly severe problem in the Sahel region of Africa. Sand is threatening to overtake the village of Oursi.

But prospects for expanding the percentage of cultivated land are not good in much of Europe, Asia, and Africa.

In some regions, the amount of available agricultural land is actually declining rather than increasing. Farmland is frequently abandoned because of an excess or shortage of water. Human actions are causing many of the world's largest deserts to expand, a process known as **desertification.**

Desert lands that can support a handful of pastoral nomads are overutilized because of rapid population growth. Excessive crop planting, animal grazing, and tree cutting exhaust the soil's nutrients and preclude any agricultural activity. The United Nations estimates that desertification removes 27 million hectares (104,000 square miles) of land from agricultural production each year, an area roughly equivalent to the size of the state of Colorado (Figure 13–15).

Excessive water threatens other agricultural areas, especially drier lands that receive water from human-built irrigation systems. If the irrigated land has inadequate drainage, the underground water level rises to the point where roots become waterlogged. The United Nations estimates that 10 percent of all irrigated land is waterlogged, mostly in Asia and South America. If the water is salty, the plants may also be damaged by excessive salinity. The ancient civilization of Mesopotamia may have collapsed in part because of waterlogging and excessive salinity in the agricultural lands near the Tigris and Euphrates rivers.

Urbanization may also contribute to reducing the amount of agricultural land. As urban areas grow in population and land area, farms on the periphery are replaced by homes, roads, shops, and other urban land uses. In North America, farms outside urban areas are left idle until the speculators who own them can sell them at a profit to builders and developers, who actually convert the land to urban uses.

Increase Productivity

During the 1960s, population began to grow more rapidly than the expansion of agricultural land, especially in developing countries. At the time, many experts issued grim forecasts of massive global famine within a decade. However, these dire predic-

FIGURE 13–15
Degree of desertification hazard within the arid lands. In 1977, the United Nations held an international conference on desertification. As part of the conference, the organization issued a map showing the places in the world where the threat of desertification is greatest. The most severe problems occur in Africa's Sahel region, located south of the Sahara near 15° north latitude. Other areas at risk include central Australia and the southwestern parts of Africa, Asia, North America and South America.

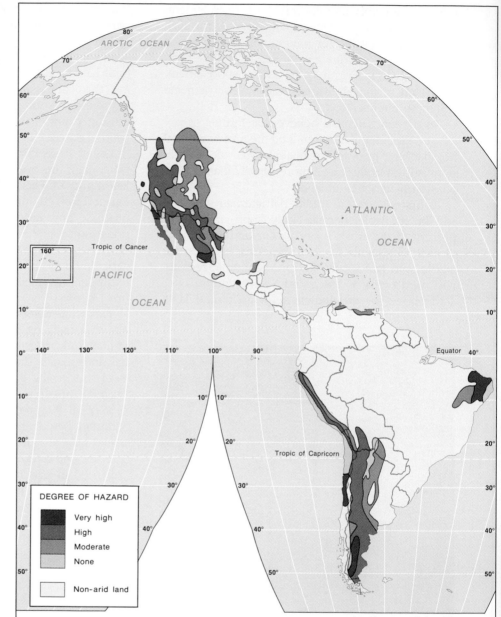

ARTIFICIAL FERTILIZER USAGE (kg/ha)

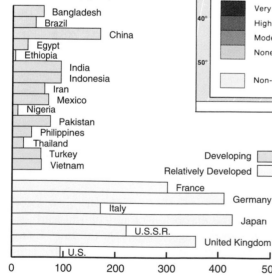

tions have not come true, because new agricultural practices have permitted farmers throughout the world to achieve much higher yields from the same amount of land.

The invention and rapid diffusion of more productive agricultural techniques between the 1960s and 1980s is known as the **green revolution.** The green revolution involves two main practices: the introduction of new higher-yield seeds and the

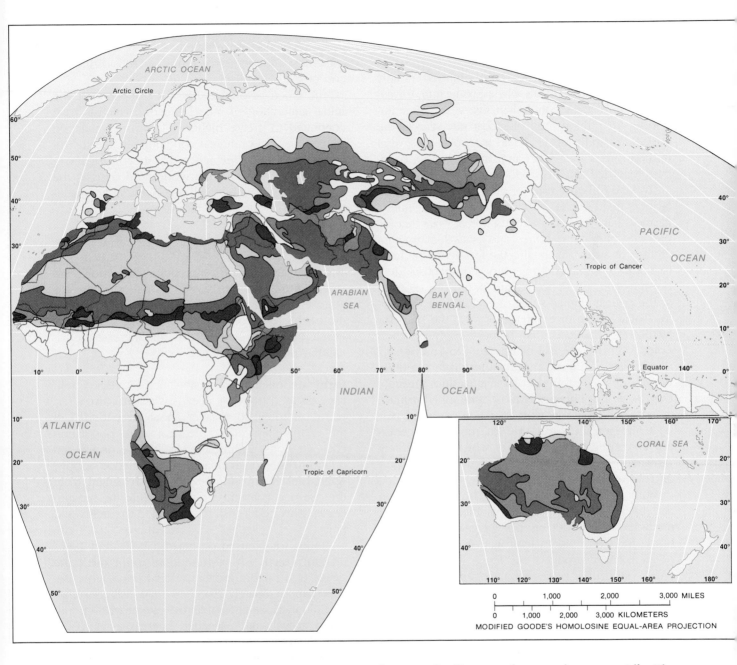

MODIFIED GOODE'S HOMOLOSINE EQUAL-AREA PROJECTION

greater use of fertilizers. Because of the green revolution, agricultural productivity has increased at a global scale faster than population growth.

During the 1950s, scientists began an intensive series of experiments to develop a higher-yield form of wheat. A decade later, the new so-called miracle wheat seed was ready. Shorter and stiffer than traditional breeds, the new wheat was less sensitive to variations in the length of days, responded

better to fertilizers, and matured more rapidly. The Rockefeller and Ford foundations sponsored many of the studies, and the program's director, Dr. Norman Borlaug, won the Nobel Peace Prize in 1970.

The International Rice Research Institute, established in the Philippines by the Rockefeller and Ford foundations, concentrated on creating a miracle rice seed. During the 1960s, scientists introduced a hybrid between Indonesian rice and Taiwan dwarf rice that was hardier and increased yields. More recently, scientists have developed new high-yield maize (corn).

The new miracle seeds were diffused rapidly around the world. India's wheat production, for example, more than doubled in five years. After importing 10 million tons of wheat per year in the mid-1960s, India by 1971 had a surplus of several million tons. Other Asian and Latin American countries recorded similar productivity increases.

To take full advantage of the new miracle seeds, farmers need to use more fertilizer and machinery. Farmers have known for thousands of years that application of manure, bones, and ashes somehow increases or at least maintains the fertility of the land. Not until the nineteenth century did scientists identify nitrogen, phosphorus, and potassium (potash) as the critical elements that caused the rise in fertility. Today, these three elements form the basis for fertilizers—products that farmers apply on their fields to enrich the soil by restoring lost nutrients.

Nitrogen, the most important fertilizer, is a ubiquitous substance found in large quantities throughout the world. Europeans most commonly produce a fertilizer known as urea, which contains 46 percent nitrogen. In North America, nitrogen is generally converted to ammonia gas, which is 82 percent nitrogen but more awkward than urea to transport and store.

Both urea and ammonia gas combine nitrogen and hydrogen. The problem is that the cheapest methods for producing both types of nitrogen-based fertilizers obtain hydrogen from natural gas or petroleum products. As fossil fuel prices increase, so do the prices for nitrogen-based fertilizers, which then become too expensive for many farmers in developing countries.

In contrast with nitrogen, phosphorous and potash reserves are not distributed uniformly across the earth's surface. Two-thirds of the world's proven phosphate rock reserves are clustered in Morocco and the United States. Proven potash reserves are concentrated in three countries: Canada, the Soviet Union, and Germany.

To make most effective use of the new miracle seeds, farmers need tractors, irrigation pumps, and other machinery. But many farmers in developing countries cannot afford to buy this equipment, nor in view of rising energy costs, can they pay for the fuel to operate the equipment. To maintain the green revolution, governments in developing countries must allocate scarce funds for subsidizing the cost of seeds, fertilizers, and machinery.

The green revolution has not stopped after the initial generation of miracle seeds. Scientists have continued to create higher-yield hybrids that are adapted to environmental conditions in specific regions. The green revolution has been largely responsible for preventing a world food crisis in the 1970s and 1980s, but will these scientific breakthroughs continue in the future?

Identify New Food Sources

The third alternative for increasing the world's food supply is to develop new sources of food. There are at least three ways to promote more effective use of the earth's resources for food: cultivate the oceans, develop higher-protein cereals, and increase the palatibility of rarely consumed foods.

Cultivate oceans. At first glance, increased reliance on food from the oceans is an attractive alternative. Although they cover about three-fourths of the earth's surface and lie near most population concentrations, oceans historically have provided a relatively small percentage of world food supply. Approximately two-thirds of the fish caught from the ocean is consumed directly, while the remainder is converted to fish meal and fed to poultry and hogs.

Hopes were raised during the 1950s and 1960s that increased fish consumption could meet the needs of a rapidly growing global population. Between approximately 1945 and 1970, fish consumption did increase faster than the rate of world population growth and exceeded beef as a source of animal protein. But since 1970 the world fish catch has increased more slowly and in some years has actually declined.

Overfishing has caused the lack of growth in the number of fish caught. The population of some fish species has declined because they have been caught at a more rapid rate than they can reproduce. Overfishing has been particularly acute in the North Atlantic and Pacific oceans.

To protect fishing areas, several countries have claimed control of the oceans beyond the longacepted 3 nautical miles. Peru and Ecuador have declared a 200-mile off-shore limit in the Pacific, while Iceland has established a 50-mile jurisdiction in the North Atlantic. These countries seize foreign fishing boats that ignore the extended boundary claims.

Peru has been especially sensitive to the overfishing problem after the country's catch of anchovies, its most important fish, declined by more than 75 percent between 1970 and 1973. To prevent further overfishing, the government nationalized its fish meal production industry, but the Peruvian experience demonstrates that the ocean is not a limitless source of fish.

Increased use of fish for food may depend on the development of fish farming, rather than fishing in the ocean. Fish farming accounts for approximately 6 percent of the world's total fish catch, but 40 percent of China's fish is raised on farms. India and the Soviet Union rank behind China as the second and third leading countries for fish farming. In the United States, only catfish and trout are produced in any quantity on farms.

Higher-protein cereals. A second possible new source of food is the development of higher-protein crops. People in relatively developed countries obtain proteins by consuming meat, but people in developing countries generally rely on wheat, corn, and rice, which lack certain proteins. Scientists are experimenting with hybrids of the world's major cereals that have higher protein content.

People can also obtain needed nutrition by consuming foods that are fortified during processing with vitamins, minerals, and protein-carrying amino acids. This approach achieves better nutrition without changing food consumption habits. But fortification has limited application in developing countries, where most people grow their own food rather than buy processed food.

Increase palatibility of foods. To fulfill basic nutritional needs, people consume types of food adapted to their community's climate, soil, and other physical characteristics. People also select foods on the basis of religious values, taboos, and other social customs that are unrelated to nutritional or environmental factors. One way to make more effective use of existing global resources is to encourage consumption of foods avoided for social reasons.

A prominent example of an underused food resource in North America is the soybean. Although soybean is one of the region's leading crops, most of the output is processed into animal feed, in part because many North Americans avoid consuming tofu, sprouts, and other recognizable soy bean products. However, burgers, franks, oils, and other products that don't look like soybeans are more widely accepted in North America. New food products have been created in developing countries as well. In Asia, for example, high-protein beverages made from oil seed meats resemble popular soft drinks.

Increase Exports From Other Countries

The fourth alternative for increasing the world's food supply is to export more food from countries that produce surpluses to places that have shortages. The three most important export grains are wheat, maize (corn), and rice. Few countries are major exporters of food, but increased production in these countries could cover the gap elsewhere.

Prior to World War II, Western Europe was the only region in the world that imported a large quantity of grain. Prior to independence, colonies supplied food to the European population concentrations. Asia became a net grain importer in the 1950s, Africa and Eastern Europe in the 1960s, and Latin America in the 1970s. Population increases in these regions largely accounted for the need to import grain. By 1980, North America was the only major exporting region in the world.

In response to the increasing global demand for food imports, the United States passed the Agricultural, Trade, and Assistance Act of 1954, frequently referred to as P.L. 480. Title I of the act provided for the sale of grain at low interest rates, and Title II gave grants to needy groups of people.

The largest beneficiary of U.S. food aid has been India. In 1966 and 1967, when the monsoon rains failed, 60 million Indians were fed entirely by U.S. grain. At the height of the rescue, 600 ships filled with grain sailed to India, the largest maritime maneuver since the Allied invasion of Normandy on D-Day, June 6, 1944. The United States allocated 20 percent of its wheat crop those years to feed India's population.

The United States remains the largest exporter of grain and accounts for nearly two-thirds of all corn and soybean exports, one-third of wheat, and one-fifth of rice. Since 1980, however, the United States has decreased its grain exports while other countries have increased theirs. Thailand replaced the United States as the leading rice exporter, and other Asian countries, such as Pakistan, Vietnam, and India, account for most of the remaining rice exports. Australia and France have joined the United States and Canada as major wheat exporters (Figure 13–16).

The Soviet Union is by far the leading grain importer and ranks at or near the top in wheat, corn, and rice. The Soviet Union and Japan together account for one-half of the world's corn imports, while the Soviet Union and China together account for one-fourth of the wheat imports. Asian countries account for nearly all of the rice imports.

Africa's Food Supply Crisis

Some countries that previously depended on imported grain have become self-sufficient in recent years. Higher productivity generated by the green revolution is primarily responsible for reducing dependency on imports, especially in Asia. India no longer ranks as a major wheat importer, and China no longer imports rice. As long as population

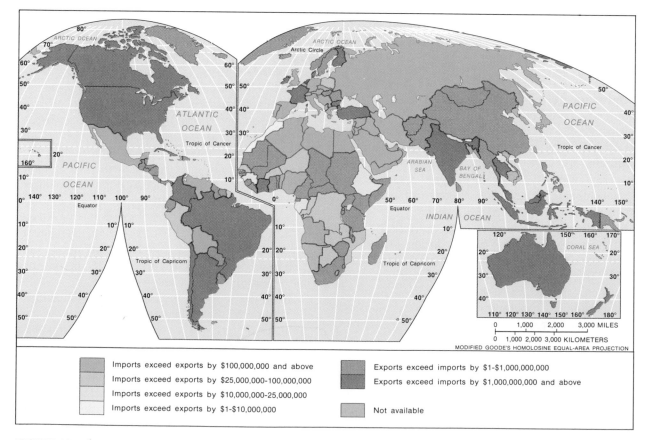

FIGURE 13–16
Most countries in the world must import more food than they export. The United States exports more food by far than any other country, compared to the amount it imports. Argentina, Australia, Canada, and France are the other leading food exporters.

North American and Western European countries send food to Ethiopia to reduce the threat of starvation. However, rapid population growth (see Chapter 2) and large-scale forced political migration (see Chapter 3) hinder relief efforts.

growth continues to decline and agricultural productivity continues to increase, the large population concentrations of Asia should be able to maintain a delicate balance between population and resources.

In contrast, Sub-Saharan Africa is losing the race to keep food production ahead of population growth. The United Nations Food and Agricultural Organization estimates that 70 percent of the African people do not have enough to eat and widespread famine exists in half of the African countries. By all estimates, the problems will get worse in the coming years.

Production of most food crops is lower today in Africa than in the 1960s. At the same time, population is increasing more rapidly than any other world region. As a result, production of food per person declined during the 1970s and 1980s in all but a handful of the region's countries—in several cases by more than 20 percent. At current population growth rates, by the end of the century, agriculture in Sub-Saharan Africa will be able to feed little more than half of the region's population.

The problem is particularly severe in the Sahel region, a 400- to 550-kilometer-wide (250- to 350-

mile-wide) belt in West Africa which marks the southern border of the Sahara. The most severely affected countries in the Sahel region include Gambia, Senegal, Mali, Mauritania, Burkina Faso, Niger, and Chad.

Traditionally, the region supported a limited amount of agriculture. Pastoral nomads moved their herds frequently, permitting vegetation to regenerate. Farmers grew groundnuts for export and used the receipts to import rice.

With rapid population growth, however, the size of herds increased beyond the capacity of the land to support animal life. Animals destroyed the limited vegetation through overgrazing and clustered at the scarce water sources. Many died of hunger. Farmers exhausted the nutrients in the soil by overplanting and reducing the amount of time the land remained fallow. Soil erosion increased after most of the remaining trees were cut down to provide urban residents with wood and charcoal for cooking and heating. Productivity declined further following several unusually dry years in the 1970s and 1980s.

Government policies have aggravated the food shortage crisis. To make food affordable for urban residents, governments keep agricultural prices low. Constrained by price controls, farmers are unable to sell their commodities at a profit and therefore have little incentive to increase productivity.

Summary

We have examined three contemporary problems concerning the use of the earth's resources. The two approaches geographers emphasize in analyzing problems—the human-environment approach and the regional studies approach—help us to understand the distinctive sets of issues and characteristics of different resource problems.

These again are the key issues in Chapter 13:

1. **What is the energy crisis?** Human beings are depleting the earth's scarce supply of fossil fuel resources for the production of energy. Fossil fuels are finite resources that are not distributed uniformly beneath the earth's surface. In the long run, we must turn to renewable energy sources, but they remain more expensive and difficult to use at this time.

2. **What are the main types of pollution?** Human beings are destroying some of the earth's resources through pollution. Pollution is the discharge into the environment of a residual—the unwanted and valueless by-products of production. Residuals are discharged into one of five environmental systems—air, water, land, heat, and noise. We can reduce pollution only by decreasing the amount of residuals we generate or by modifying the residuals after their creation.

3. **How can we expand global food supply?** Human beings fail to make full use of the earth's resources to feed the rapidly growing population. Four alternatives exist to increasing the food supply: expand the amount of cultivated land, increase productivity of land now used for agriculture, develop new food sources, and expand exports from productive countries. Because of increased productivity, most regions of the world are generating enough food to meet the needs of their population. The exception is Sub-Saharan Africa, where the gap between food supply and population size is growing wider.

Future Directions

Some scientists believe that further depletion and destruction of the earth's resources will lead to disaster in the near future. A group of scientists known as the Club of Rome presented a particularly influential statement of this position a few years ago in a report titled *The Limits to Growth.* According to these scientists, many of whom were professors at the Massachusetts Institute of Technology, the combination of population growth, resource depletion, and unrestricted use of industrial technology will disrupt the world's ecology and economy and lead to mass starvation, widespread suffering, and destruction of the physical environment.

Most geographers recognize that unrestricted industrial and demographic growth will have negative consequences, but they do not believe that the dire predictions of *The Limits to Growth* are inevitable. Although human actions have depleted some resources, substitutes may be available. Although pollution degrades the physical environment, industrial growth can be compatible with environmental protection. Demand for food is increasing, but human actions are also expanding the capacity of the earth to provide food.

Geographers emphasize that each resource in the physical environment has a distinctive capacity for accommodating human activities. Just as a good farmer knows how many animals can be fed on a parcel of land, a scientist can pinpoint the constraints that resources place on population density or economic development in a particular region. This type of study is called **carrying capacity analysis.**

Geographers recognize that people make locational decisions for a variety of political, social, and economic reasons that ignore physical environmental factors. Many geographers argue that decisions concerning new projects should include consideration of critical factors in the physical environment which could constrain development. A region's water, topography, climate, soil, and other physical characteristics may pose problems for a proposed project unless measured in advance. Government policies throughout the world increasingly accept this position.

Consistent with this increasing global awareness of environmental issues, the U.S. government enacted the National Environmental Policy Act in 1969. According to the act, whenever a federal agency proposes a project that may significantly affect the environment it must prepare an **environmental impact statement.** The environmental impact statement must consider unavoidable adverse environmental impacts of the proposed project, alternatives to the proposal, and irreversible commitments of resources that would be required.

Geographers analyze the causes of the energy, pollution, and food supply problems in part by understanding the relationship between human actions and the physical environment. Geographers also explain these problems in part by studying differences in the regional distributions of producers and consumers of various resources. Like other issues discussed in this book, the problems of energy, pollution, and food supply are interrelated. Actions to solve one problem in one location will produce impacts on other problems in other regions.

The Chang family described at the beginning of the chapter is trying to lead an environmentally sensitive and self-sufficient life, but they are not typical in the modern world. Whether we like it or not, our well-being depends on the actions of people throughout the world.

Key Terms

Acid rain Pollution formed by conversion of sulfur and nitrogen oxides to acids that return to the earth as rain or snow.

Active solar energy Solar energy system that collects energy through the use of mechanical devices, such as photovoltaic cells or flat-plate collectors.

Animate power Power supplied by people or animals.

Biological oxygen demand (BOD) The amount of oxygen required by aquatic bacteria to decompose a given load of organic waste; a measure of water pollution.

Breeder reactor A nuclear reactor that produces a chain reaction that results in more plutonium at the end of the process than at the beginning.

Carrying capacity analysis A study which measures a region's natural resources in order to identify constraints on the maximum level of population density or development.

Chlorofluorocarbon (CFC) A gas used as a solvent, a propellant in aerosols, and a refrigerant, as well as in plastic foams and fire extinguishers.

Desertification Expansion of deserts due to human actions.

Energy The capacity to do work.

Environmental impact statement A report required in the United States whenever a project that is likely to significantly affect the environment is proposed to be built with federal funds.

Eutrophication A process of enriching water with nutrients that can stimulate aquatic life and cause an overabundance of plant life.

Fission The splitting of an atomic nucleus to release energy.

Fossil fuel Energy source formed from the residue of plants and animals buried beneath the earth's surface millions of years ago. As the earth's crust moved, these buried plants and animals were subject to intense changes in pressure and temperature.

Fusion The joining of the nuclei of two hydrogen atoms to release energy.

Geothermal energy Energy from steam or hot water produced from hot or molten underground rocks.

Green revolution Rapid diffusion of new agricultural technology, especially new high-yield seeds and fertilizers.

Greenhouse effect An increase in the temperature of the earth's surface caused by trapping infrared radiation in carbon dioxide, which is produced by burning fossil fuels.

Hydroelectric power Power generated from falling water.

Inanimate power Power supplied by machines.

Nonproduct output An undesired by-product produced along with the principal purpose of the enterprise.

Nonrenewable source of energy A source of energy that is a finite supply capable of being exhausted.

Ozone A gas that absorbs ultraviolet solar radiation, found in a layer of the atmosphere located between 16 and 40 kilometers (10 and 25 miles) above the earth's surface.

Passive solar energy Solar energy system that collects energy without the use of mechanical devices.

Photochemical smog An atmospheric condition formed through a combination of weather conditions and pollution, especially from motor-vehicle emissions.

Photovoltaic cell Solar energy cell, usually made from silicon, that collects solar rays to generate electricity.

Pollution Human action that adversely affects a resource.

Potential reserve The amount of a resource thought to exist but not yet discovered.

Power The rate at which work is performed in a given time period.

Proven reserve The amount of a resource remaining in a discovered field.

Radioactive waste Particles from a nuclear reaction that emit radiation; contact with such particles may be harmful or lethal to people, and waste must therefore be safely stored for thousands of years.

Renewable source of energy A resource that has a theoretically unlimited supply and is not depleted when used by people.

Residual A nonproduct output that is discharged into the environment; a residual constitutes pollution if the level discharged into the environment exceeds the capacity of the environment to accept discharges at that location.

Resource A substance in the physical environment considered to have value or usefulness.

Thinking Geographically

1. What steps has your community taken to recycle solid waste and conserve resources?
2. Companies that produce cars in the United States must meet a Corporate Average Fuel Efficiency (CAFE). If the average miles per gallon achieved by all of the company's American-made cars do not achieve a government-mandated level, then the company must pay a stiff fine. Should the U.S. increase the CAFE standards in order to conserve fuel and reduce air pollution, even if the result is a loss of American jobs?
3. A recent study compared paper and polystyrene foam drinking cups. Conventional wisdom is that foam cups are bad for the environment because they don't degrade in landfills. However, the manufacture of a paper cup consumes 36 times as much electricity and generates 580 times as much waste water. Further, as they degrade in landfills, paper cups release methane gas, a contributor to the greenhouse effect. Which type of cup should companies like McDonald's be encouraged to use?
4. Pollution is a byproduct of the production process. How can relatively developed countries, which historically have been responsible for generating the most pollution, encourage developing countries to minimize the adverse effects of pollution as they improve their levels of development?
5. Malthus argued two hundred years ago that overpopulation was inevitable because population increased geometrically, while food supply increased arithmetically. Was Malthus correct?

Further Readings

Bower, Blair T., and Daniel J. Basta. *Residuals-Environmental Quality Management: Applying the Concept.* Baltimore: The Johns Hopkins University Center for Metropolitan Planning and Research, 1973.

Brown, Lester R., et al. *State of the World.* New York and London: Norton, annually since 1984.

Brown, Lester R., and Edward C. Wolf. *Reversing Africa's Decline.* Worldwatch Paper 65. Washington, D.C.: Worldwatch Institute, 1985.

Brown, Lester R., and Pamela Shaw. *Six Steps to a Sustainable Society.* Worldwatch Paper 48. Washington, D.C.: Worldwatch Institute, 1982.

Bugliarello, George, Ariel Alexandre, John Barnes, and Charles Wakstein. *The Impact of Noise Pollution.* New York: Pergamon Press, 1976.

Calzonetti, Frank J., and Barry D. Solomon. *Geographical Dimensions of Energy.* Dordrecht, The Netherlands: D. Reidel, 1985.

Chakravarti, A. K. "Green Revolution in India." *Annals of the Association of American Geographers* 63 (September 1973): 319–30.

Clements, Donald W. "Recent Trends in the Geography of Coal." *Annals of the Association of American Geographers* 67 (March 1977): 109–25.

Cole, H. S. D., Christopher Freeman, Marie Jahoda, and K. L. R. Pavitt. *Models of Doom: A Critique of the Limits To Growth.* New York: University Books, 1972.

Commoner, Barry. *The Poverty of Power.* New York: Knopf, 1976.

Cuff, David, and William J. Young. *The United States Energy Atlas.* 2d ed. New York: Free Press, 1984.

Cusack, David F., ed. *Agroclimate Information for Development: Reviving the Green Revolution.* Boulder, CO: Westview Press, 1983.

Cutter, Susan L, Hilary Lambert Renwick, and William H. Renwick. *Exploitation, Conservation, Preservation: A Geographic Perspective on Natural Resource Use,* 2d ed. New York: Wiley, 1991.

Ehrlich, Anne H., and Paul R. Ehrlich. *Earth.* New York: Franklin Watts, 1987.

Flavin, Christopher. *World Oil: Coping with the Dangers of Success.* Worldwatch Paper 66. Washington, D.C.: Worldwatch Institute, 1985.

———. *Electricity's Future: The Shift to Efficiency and Small-Scale Power.* Worldwatch Paper 61. Washington, D.C.: Worldwatch Institute, 1984.

———. *Nuclear Power: The Market Test.* Worldwatch Paper 57. Washington, D.C.: Worldwatch Institute, 1983.

Greenberg, M. R., R. Anderson, and G. W. Page. *Environmental Impact Statements.* Washington, D.C.: Association of American Geographers, 1978.

Griff, David. *The World Food Problem 1950–1980.* New York: Basil Blackwell, 1985.

James, Peter. *The Future of Coal.* 2d ed. London: Macmillan, 1984.

Kates, Robert W., Christoph Hohenemser, and Jeanne X. Kasperson, eds. *Perilous Progress: Technology as Hazard.* Boulder, CO: Westview, 1984.

Knight, C. G., and P. Wilcox. *Triumph or Triage? The World Food Problem in Geographical Perspective.* Washington, D.C.: Association of American Geographers, 1975.

Meadows, Donnela H., Dennis L. Meadows, Jorgen Randers, and William W. Behrens III. *The Limits To Growth.* 2d ed. New York: Universe Books, 1973.

Mounfield, P. R. "Nuclear Power in Western Europe: Geographical Patterns and Political Problems." *Geography* 70 (October 1985): 315–27.

Murdock, Steve H., F. Larry Leistritz, and Rita R. Hamm, eds. *Nuclear Waste: Socioeconomic Dimensions of Long-Term Storage.* Boulder, CO: Westview Press, 1983.

National Geographic. *Energy: Special Report.* Washington, D.C.: National Geographic Society, 1981.

National Research Council, Board on Radioactive Waste Management, Panel on Social and Economic Aspects of Radioactive Waste Management. *Social and Economic Aspects of Radioactive Waste Disposal: Considerations for Institutional Management*. Washington, D.C.: National Academy Press, 1984.

Openshaw, Stan. *Nuclear Power: Siting and Safety*. London: Routledge and Kegan Paul, 1986.

Pasqualetti, Martin J., and K. David Pijawka, eds. *Nuclear Power: Assessing and Managing Hazardous Technology*. Boulder, CO: Westview Press, 1984.

Pollack, Cynthia. *Decommissioning: Nuclear Power's Missing Link*. Worldwatch Paper 69. Washington, D.C.: Worldwatch Institute, 1986.

Postel, Sandra. *Conserving Water: The Untapped Alternative*. Worldwatch Paper 67. Washington, D.C.: Worldwatch Institute, 1985.

————. *Air Pollution, Acid Rain, and the Future of Forests*. Worldwatch Paper 58. Washington, D.C.: Worldwatch Institute, 1984.

Schmandt, Jurgen, and Hilliard Roderick, eds. *Acid Rain and Friendly Neighbors: The Policy Dispute between Canada and the U.S.* Durham, NC: Duke University Press, 1985.

Sills, David L., C. P. Wolf, and Vivien B. Shelanski, eds. *Accident at Three Mile Island: The Human Dimensions*. Boulder, CO: Westview Press, 1982.

U.S. Congress, Office of Technology Assessment. *Acid Rain and Transported Air Pollutants: Implications for Public Policy*. Washington, D.C.: U.S. Government Printing Office, 1984.

Also consult these journals: *Ecologist; Energy journal; Energy policy; Environment.*

Conclusion

Careers in Geography

An increasing number of students recognize that geographic education is practical as well as stimulating. Employment opportunities are expanding for students trained in geography, especially in teaching, government service, and business.

Teaching. As of 1990, a Ph.D. in geography was offered at fifty-one U.S. and twenty Canadian universities, while the Master's was the highest available degree at ninety-eight U.S. and seven Canadian universities. Traditionally, the majority of trained geographers have become teachers in high schools, colleges, or universities.

A career as a geography teacher is promising, because schools throughout North America are expanding the amount of geography in the curriculum. Educators increasingly recognize geography's role in teaching students about global diversity.

While a number of university geography departments have emphasized good teaching over research, others are increasingly concerned with research. The Association of American Geographers includes several dozen specialty groups organized around research themes, including agricultural, industrial, medical, and transportation geography.

Government. Some geographers find employment with cities, states, provinces, and other units of local government. Typically, these opportunities are found in departments of planning, transportation, parks and recreation, economic development, housing, or other similarly titled government agencies. Geographers may be hired to conduct studies of local economic, social, and physical patterns; to prepare information through maps and reports; and to help to plan the community's future.

Many national government agencies also employ geographers. In the United States, the Bureau of the Census in the Department of Commerce has a geography division that studies and reports on changing national population trends. Other U.S. government agencies that employ geographers include the Department of Defense Mapping Agency, the Soil Conservation Service and Geological Survey in the Department of Interior, and the National Aeronautics and Space Administration.

Geographers contribute their knowledge of the location of activities, the patterns underlying the distribution of various activities, and the interpretation of information from maps. For example, in the 1940s the British government hired the geographer L. Dudley Stamp to conduct a land-use study of the entire country. Stamp identified the country's best agricultural land and contributed to the development of laws that strictly protected valuable land from urban development.

In recent years, geographers have been hired by government agencies because of their ability to interpret data generated from satellite imagery. Geographers also increasingly display information and interpret information through computer-generated maps.

Another career area for geographers is government foreign service, especially if they have expertise about other parts of the world. The tradition of geographic service in foreign affairs strengthened after World War I. The American geographer Isaiah Bowman advised President Woodrow Wilson on redrawing the map of Europe after the war, so that national boundaries more closely conformed to cultural patterns. At approximately the same time, the British geographer Halford J. Mackinder advised the British government on military strategy. He argued that the world's heartland, Eastern Europe, was surrounded by a rim of maritime powers. The key to Mackinder's international military strategy was in understanding the relationship of the location of countries to their opportunity to exercise either land or naval power.

Business. An increasing number of American geographers are finding jobs with private companies. The list of possibilities is long, but here are some common examples:

◆ Developers hire geographers to find the best locations for new shopping centers.
◆ Real-estate firms hire geographers to assess the value of properties.
◆ Supermarket chains, department stores, and other retailers hire geographers to determine the potential market for new stores.
◆ Banks hire geographers to assess the probability that a loan applicant has planned a successful development.
◆ Distributors and wholesalers hire geographers to find ways to minimize transportation costs.

◆ Multinational corporations hire geographers to predict the behavior of consumers and officials in other countries.
◆ Manufacturers hire geographers to identify new sources of raw materials and markets.
◆ Utility companies hire geographers to determine future demands at different locations for gas, electricity, and other services.

For more information on careers in geography, contact the Association of American Geographers or the National Council for Geographic Education, both in Washington, D.C.

Woody Allen's Final Word to the Graduates

This book perhaps should end with a word about the future to the graduates of the course. Woody Allen is not a geographer, but his "Speech to Graduates" effectively captures some of the interrelationships among various human actions and the physical environment that form the core of human geography:

> More than any other time in history, mankind faces a crossroads. One path leads to despair and utter hopelessness. The other, to total extinction. Let us pray we have the wisdom to choose correctly. . . .
>
> Science is something we depend on all the time. If I develop a pain in the chest I must take an X ray. But what if the radiation from the X ray causes me deeper problems? Before I know it, I'm going in for surgery. Naturally, while they're giving me oxygen an intern decides to light up a cigarette. The next thing you know I'm rocketing over the World Trade Center in bed clothes. . . .
>
> At no other time in history has man been so afraid to cut into his veal chop for fear that it will explode. Violence breeds more violence and it is predicted that . . . kidnapping will be the dominant mode of social interaction. Overpopulation will exacerbate problems to the breaking point. Figures tell us that there are already more people on earth than we need to move even the heaviest piano. If we do not call a halt to breeding, by the year 2000 there will be no room to serve dinner unless one is willing to set the table on the heads of strangers. Then they must not move for an hour while we eat. Of course energy will be in short supply and each car owner will be

allowed only enough gasoline to back up a few inches. . . .

Summing up, it is clear the future holds great opportunities. It also holds pitfalls. The trick will be to avoid the pitfalls, seize the opportunities, and get back home by six o'clock.[1]

Human geographers do not know how to solve all of the world's problems of population growth,

---

[1]Reprinted with the permission of the author and the publisher. Reprinted from "My Speech to the Graduates," *Side Effects,* by Woody Allen. Copyright © Random House, Inc., and Woody Allen.

cultural and political conflict, economic development, and abuse of resources. This course has tried to expose you to the need to understand differences among human actions in different regions, the interdependencies between people and the environment, and other geographic perspectives on world problems. Above all, it is this book's aim to have heightened your sense of global awareness, that is, an understanding that our comfort—if not survival—necessitates a greater understanding of the human and physical processes that take place on earth's surface.

Appendix
Map Scale and Projections

Phillip C. Muehrcke

Unaided, our human senses provide a limited view of our surroundings. To overcome these limitations, humankind has developed powerful vehicles of thought and communication, such as language, mathematics, and graphics. Each of these tools is based on elaborate rules, each has an information bias, and each may distort its message, often in subtle ways. Consequently, to use these aids effectively, we must understand their rules, biases, and distortions. The same is true for the special form of graphics we call maps: we must master the logic behind the mapping process before we can use maps effectively. A fundamental issue in cartography, the science and art of making maps, is the vast difference between the size and geometry of what is being mapped—the real world, we will call it—and that of the map itself. Scale and projection are the basic cartographic concepts that help us understand this difference and its effects.

Map Scale

Our senses are dwarfed by the immensity of our planet; we can sense directly only our local surroundings. Thus, we cannot possibly look at our whole state or country at one time, even though we may be able to see the entire street where we live.

Cartography helps us expand what we can see at one time by letting us view the scene from some distant vantage point. The greater the imaginary distance between that position and what we are looking at, the larger the area the map can cover but the smaller the features on the map will appear. This reduction is defined by the *map scale,* the ratio of the distance on the map to the distance on the earth. Map users need to know about map scale for two reasons: (1) so they can convert measurements on a map into meaningful real-world measures and (2) so they can know how abstract the cartographic representation is.

Real-world measures. A map can provide a useful substitute for the real world for many analytical purposes. With the scale of a map, for instance, we can compute the actual size of mapped features (length, area, or volume). These calculations are helped by three expressions of map scale: a word statement, a graphic scale, and a representative fraction.

A *word statement* of a map scale compares X units on the map to Y units on the earth, often abbreviated "X units to Y units." For example, the expression "one inch to ten miles" means that one inch on the map represents ten miles on the earth (Figure A–1). Because the map is always smaller than the area that

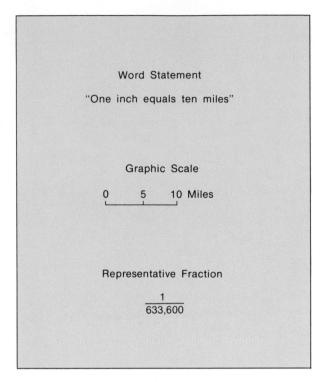

Word Statement

"One inch equals ten miles"

Graphic Scale

0   5   10 Miles

Representative Fraction

$\dfrac{1}{633,600}$

FIGURE A–1
Common expressions of map scale.

The third form of map scale is the *representative fraction* (RF). An RF defines the ratio between the distance on the map and the distance on the earth in fractional terms, such as $\frac{1}{633,600}$ (also written 1/633,600 or 1 : 633,600). The numerator of the fraction always refers to the distance on the map, and the denominator always refers to the distance on the earth. No units of measurement are given, but both numbers must be expressed in the same units. Because map distances are extremely small relative to the size of the earth, it makes sense to use small units, such as inches or centimeters. Thus, the RF 1 : 633,600 might be read as "1 inch on the map to 633,600 inches on the earth."

Herein lies a problem with the RF. Meaningful map-distance units imply a denominator so large that it is impossible to visualize. Thus, in practice, reading the map scale involves an additional step of converting the denominator to a meaningful ground measure, such as miles or kilometers. The unwieldy 633,600 becomes the more manageable 10 miles when divided by the number of inches in a mile (63,360).

On the plus side, the RF is good for calculations. In particular, the ground distance between points can be easily determined from a map with an RF. One simply multiplies the distance between the points on the map by the denominator of the RF. Thus, a distance of five inches on a map with an RF of 1/126,720 would signify a ground distance of 5 × 126,720, which equals 633,600. Because all units are inches and there are 63,360 inches in a mile, the ground distance is 633,600 ÷ 63,360, or 10 miles. Computation of area is equally straightforward with an RF. Computer manipulation and analysis of maps is based on the RF form of map scale.

has been mapped, the ground unit is always the larger number. Both units are expressed in meaningful terms, such as inches and miles or centimeters and kilometers. Word statements are not intended for precise calculations but give the map user a rough idea of size and distance.

A *graphic scale,* such as a bar graph, is concrete and therefore overcomes the need to visualize inches and miles that is associated with use of a word statement of scale (see Figure A–1). A graphic scale permits direct visual comparison of feature sizes and the distances between features. No ruler is required; any measuring aid will do. It needs only to be compared with the scaled bar: if the length of one toothpick is equal to two miles on the ground and the map distance equals the length of four toothpicks, then the ground distance is four times two or eight miles. Graphic scales are especially convenient in this age of copying machines, when we are more likely to be working with a copy than with the original map. If a map is reduced or enlarged as it is copied, the graphic scale will change in proportion to the change in the size of the map and thus will remain accurate.

Guides to generalization. Scales also help map users visualize the nature of the symbolic relation between the map and the real world. It is convenient here to think of maps as falling into three broad scale categories (Figure A–2). (Do not be confused by the use of the words *large* and *small* in this context: just remember that the larger the denominator, the smaller the scale ratio and the larger the area that is shown on the map.) Scale ratios greater than 1:100,000, such as the 1:24,000 scale of U.S. Geological Survey topographic quadrangles, are large-scale

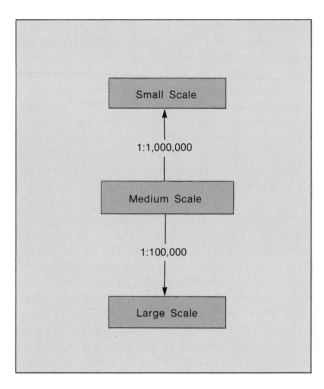

FIGURE A–2
The scale gradient can be divided into three broad categories.

maps. Although these maps can cover only a local area, they can be drawn to rather rigid standards of accuracy. Thus, they are useful for a wide range of applications that require detailed and accurate maps, including zoning, navigation, and construction.

At the other extreme are maps with scale ratios of less than 1:1,000,000, such as maps of the world that are found in atlases. These are small-scale maps. Because they cover large areas, the symbols on them must be highly abstract. They are therefore best suited to general reference or planning, when detail is not important. Medium- or intermediate-scale maps have scales between 1:100,000 and 1:1,000,000. They are good for regional reference and planning purposes.

Another important aspect of map scale is to give us some notion of geometric accuracy; the greater the expanse of the real world shown on a map, the less accurate is the geometry of that map. Figure A–3 shows why. If a curve is represented by straight line segments, short segments (*X*) are more similar to the curve than are long segments (*Y*). Similarly, if a plane is placed in contact with a sphere, the difference

between the two surfaces is slight where they touch (*A*) but grows rapidly with increasing distance (*B*) from the point of contact. In view of the large diameter and slight local curvature of the earth, distances will be well represented on large-scale maps (those with small denominators) but will be increasingly poorly represented at smaller scales. This close relationship between map scale and map geometry brings us to the topic of map projections.

Map Projections

The spherical surface of the earth is shown on flat maps by means of map projections. The process of "flattening" the earth is essentially a problem in geometry that has captured the attention of the best mathematical minds for centuries. Yet no one has ever found a perfect solution: there is no known way to avoid spatial distortion of one kind or another. Many map projections have been devised, but only a few have become standard. Because a single flat map cannot preserve all aspects of the earth's surface geometry, a mapmaker must be careful to match the

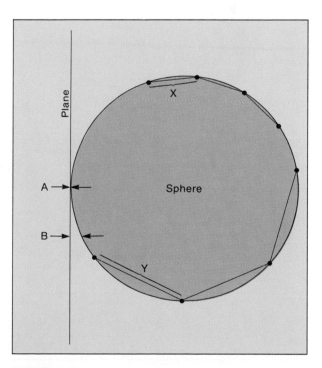

FIGURE A–3
Relationships between surfaces on the round earth and a flat map.

projection with the task at hand. To map something that involves distance, for example, a projection should be used in which distance is not distorted. In addition, a map user should be able to recognize which aspects of a map's geometry are accurate and which are distortions caused by a particular projection process. Fortunately, this is not too difficult.

It is helpful to think of the creation of a projection as a two-step process (Figure A–4). First, the immense earth is reduced to a small globe with a scale equal to that of the desired flat map. All spatial properties on the globe are true to those on the earth. Second, the globe is flattened. Since this cannot be done without distortion, it is accomplished in such a way that the resulting map exhibits certain desirable spatial properties.

Perspective models. Early map projections were sometimes created with the aid of perspective methods, but this has changed. In the modern electronic age, projections are normally developed by strictly mathematical means and are plotted out or displayed on computer-driven graphics devices. The concept of perspective is still useful, however, in visualizing what map projections do. Thus, projection methods are often illustrated by using strategically located light sources to cast shadows on a projection surface from a latitude/longitude net inscribed on a transparent globe.

The success of the perspective approach depends on finding a projection surface that is flat or that can be flattened without distortion. The cone, cylinder, and plane possess these attributes and serve as models for three general classes of map projections: *conic, cylindrical,* and *planar* (or azimuthal). Figure A–5 shows these three classes, as well as a fourth, a false cylindrical class with an oval shape. Although the *oval* class is not of perspective origin, it appears to combine properties of the cylindrical and planar classes (Figure A–6).

The relationship between the projection surface and the model at the point or line of contact is critical because distortion of spatial properties on the projection is symmetrical about, and increases with distance from, that point or line. This condition is illustrated for the cylindrical and planar classes of projections in Figure A–7. If the point or line of contact is changed to some other position on the globe, the distortion pattern will be recentered on the new position but will retain the same symmetrical form. Thus, centering a projection on the area of interest on the earth's surface can minimize the ef-

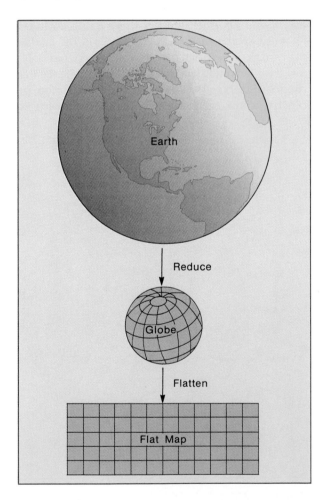

FIGURE A–4
The two-step process of creating a projection.

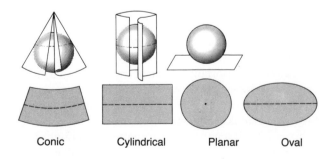

FIGURE A–5
General classes of map projections. (Courtesy of ACSM)

FIGURE A–6
The visual properties of cylindrical and planar projections combined in oval projections. (Courtesy of ACSM)

Cylindrical

Planar

Oval

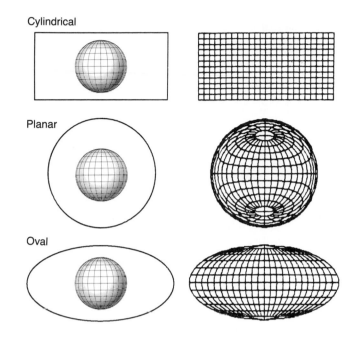

fects of projection distortion. And recognizing the general projection shape, associating it with a perspective model, and recalling the characteristic distortion pattern will provide the information necessary to compensate for projection distortion.

Preserved properties. For a map projection to truthfully depict the geometry of the earth's surface, it would have to preserve the spatial attributes of *distance, direction, area, shape,* and *proximity*. This task can be readily accomplished on a globe, but it is not possible on a flat map. To preserve area, for example, a mapmaker must stretch or shear shapes; thus, area and shape cannot be preserved on the same map. To depict both direction and distance from a point, area must be distorted. Similarly, to preserve area as well as direction from a point, distance has to be distorted. Because the earth's surface is continuous in all directions from every point, discontinuities that violate proximity relationships must occur on all map projections. The trick is to place these discontinuities where they will have the least impact on the spatial relationships in which the map user is interested.

We must be careful when we use spatial terms because the properties they refer to can be confusing. The geometry of the familiar plane is very dif-

ferent from that of a sphere; yet when we refer to a flat map, we are in fact making reference to the spherical earth that was mapped. A shape-preserving projection, for example, is truthful to local shapes—such as the right-angle crossing of latitude and longitude lines—but does not preserve shapes at continental or global levels. A distance-preserving

Cylindrical

Planar

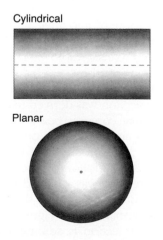

FIGURE A–7
Characteristic patterns of distortion for the cylindrical and planar projection classes. Here, darker shading implies greater distortion. (Courtesy of ACSM)

FIGURE A−8
The useful Mercator projection, showing extreme area distortion in the higher latitudes. (Courtesy of ACSM)

projection can preserve this property from one point on the map in all directions or from a number of points in several directions, but distance cannot be preserved in the general sense that area can be preserved. Direction can also be generally preserved from a single point or in several directions from a number of points but not from all points simultaneously. Thus, a shape-, distance-, or direction-preserving projection is truthful to these properties only in part.

Partial truths are not the only consequence of transforming a sphere into a flat surface. Some projections exploit this transformation by expressing traits that are of considerable value for specific applications. One of these is the famous shape-preserving *Mercator projection* (Figure A−8). This cylindrical projection was derived mathematically in the 1500s so that compass bearings (called *rhumb* lines) between any two points on the earth would plot as straight lines on the map. This trait let navigators plan, plot, and follow courses between origin and destination, but it was achieved at the expense of extreme areal distortion toward the margins of the projection (see Antarctica in Figure A−8). Although the Mercator projection is admirably suited for its intended purpose, its widespread but inappropriate use for nonnavigational purposes has drawn a great deal of criticism.

The *gnomonic projection* is also useful for navigation. It is a planar projection with the valuable characteristic of showing the shortest (or great circle) route between any two points on the earth as straight lines. Long-distance navigators first plot the great circle course between origin and destination on a gnomonic projection (Figure A−9, top). Next they transfer the straight line to a Mercator projec-

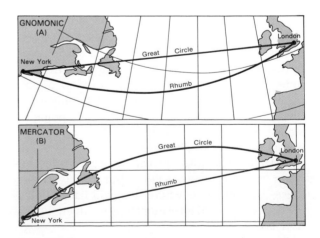

FIGURE A−9
A gnomonic projection (A) and a Mercator projection (B), both of value to long-distance navigators.

tion, where it normally appears as a curve (Figure A–9, bottom). Finally, using straight-line segments, they construct an approximation of this course on the Mercator projection. Navigating the shortest course between origin and destination then involves following the straight segments of the course and making directional corrections between segments. Like the Mercator projection, the specialized gnomonic projection distorts other spatial properties so severely that it should not be used for any purpose other than navigation or communications.

Projections used in textbooks. Although a map projection cannot be free of distortion, it can represent one or several spatial properties of the earth's surface accurately if other properties are sacrificed. The two projections used for world maps throughout this text illustrate this point well. *Goode's homolosine projection,* shown in Figure A–10, belongs to the oval category and shows area accurately, although it gives the impression that the earth's surface has been torn, peeled, and flattened. The interruptions in Figure A–10 have been placed in the major oceans, giving continuity to the land masses. Ocean areas could be featured instead by placing the interruptions in the continents. Obviously, this type of interrupted projection severely distorts proximity relationships. Consequently, in different locations the

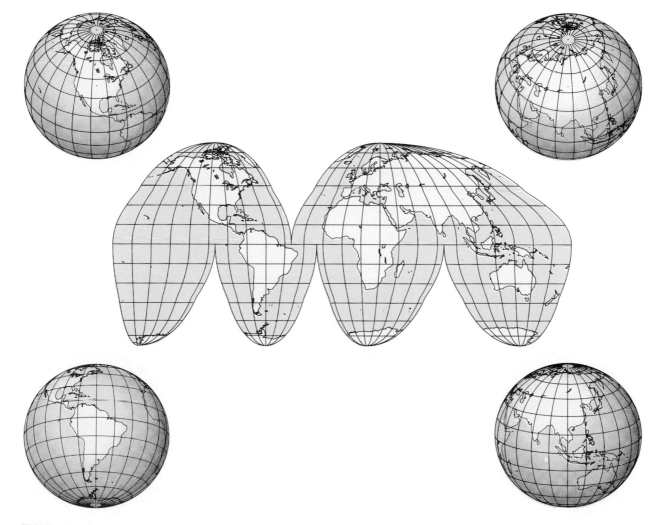

FIGURE A–10
An interrupted Goode's homolosine, an equal-area projection. (Courtesy of ACSM)

properties of distance, direction, and shape are also distorted to varying degrees. The distortion pattern mimics that of cylindrical projections, with the equatorial zone the most faithfully represented (Figure A–11).

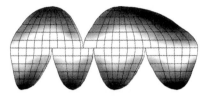

FIGURE A–11
The distortion pattern of the interrupted Goode's homolosine projection, which mimics that of cylindrical projections. (Courtesy of ACSM)

An alternative to special-property projections such as the equal-area Goode's homolosine is the compromise projection. In this case no special property is achieved at the expense of others, and distortion is rather evenly distributed among the various properties, instead of being focused on one or several properties. The *Robinson projection,* which is also used in this text, falls into this category (Figure A–12). This oval projection has a global feel, somewhat like that of Goode's homolosine. But the Robinson projection shows the North Pole and the South Pole as lines that are slightly more than half the length of the equator, thus exaggerating distances and areas near the poles. Areas look larger than they really are in the high latitudes (near the poles) and smaller than they really

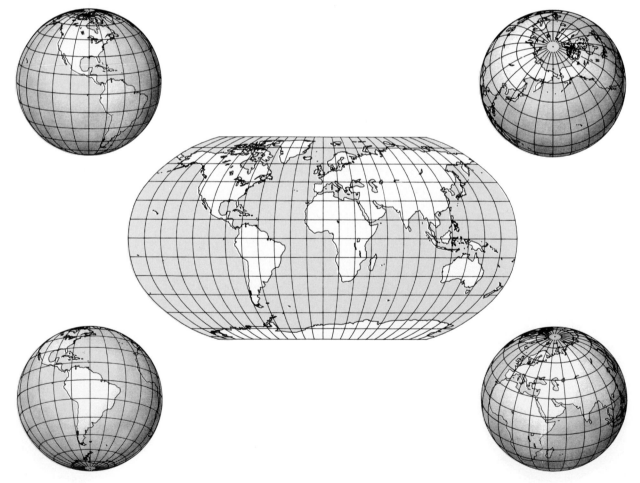

FIGURE A–12
The compromise Robinson projection, which avoids the interruptions of Goode's homolosine but preserves no special properties. (Courtesy of ACSM)

are in the low latitudes (near the equator). In addition, not all latitude and longitude lines intersect at right angles, as they do on the earth, so we know that the Robinson projection does not preserve direction or shape either. However, it has fewer interruptions than Goode's homolosine does, so it preserves proximity better. Overall, the Robinson projection does a good job of representing spatial relationships, especially in the low to middle latitudes and along the central meridian.

Scale and Projections in Modern Geography

Computers have drastically changed the way in which maps are made and used. In the preelectronic age, maps were so laborious, time-consuming, and expensive to make that relatively few were created. Frustrated, geographers and other scientists often found themselves trying to use maps for purposes not intended by the map designers. But today anyone with access to computer mapping facilities can create projections in a flash. Thus, projections will be increasingly tailored to specific needs, and more and more scientists will do their own mapping rather than have someone else guess what they want in a map.

Computer mapping creates opportunities that go far beyond the construction of projections, of course. Once maps and related geographical data are entered into computers, many types of analyses can be carried out involving map scales and projections. Distances, areas, and volumes can be computed; searches can be conducted; information from different maps can be combined; optimal routes can be selected; facilities can be allocated to the most suitable sites; and so forth. The term used to describe these processes is *geographical information system,* or GIS (Figure A–13). Within a GIS, projections provide the mechanism for linking data from different sources, and scale provides the basis for size calculations of all sorts. Mastery of both projection and scale becomes the user's responsibility because the map user is also the map maker. Now more than ever, effective geography depends on knowledge of the close association between scale and projection.

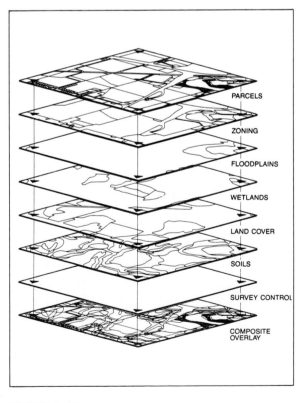

FIGURE A–13
Within a GIS, environmental data attached to a common terrestrial reference system, such as latitude/longitude, can be stacked in layers for spatial comparison and analysis.

Credits

FIGURE 1–15 Adapted from Stanley D. Brunn, "Sunbelt USA," *Focus* 36 (Spring 1986): 35. Used by permission of The American Geographical Society.

FIGURE 3–9 Copyright © 1980 by The New York Times Company. Adapted by permission.

FIGURE 3–15 Adapted from Barbara E. Fredrich, "Family Migration History: A Project in Introductory Cultural Geography," *Journal of Geography* (November 1977): 222. Reprinted with the permission of the Journal of Geography and The National Council for Geographic Education.

FIGURE 4–2 Adapted from *Encyclopaedia Britannica,* 15th edition (1987), 22: 660.

FIGURE 4–3 and **4–4** Adapted from Antoine Meillet and Marcel Cohen, *Les langues du monde* (Paris: Centre National de la Recherche Scientifique), 1952.

FIGURE 4–5 Adapted from *Encyclopaedia Britannica,* 15th edition (1987), 28: 358.

FIGURE 4–6 Adapted from *Encyclopaedia Britannica,* 15th edition (1987), 23: 346.

FIGURE 4–7 Adapted from A. K. Ramanujan and Colin Masica, "A Phonological Typology of the Indian Linguistic Area" *Current Trends in Linguistics* 5 (1969): 561, with permission of Mouton de Gruyter, a division of Walter de Gruyter & Co.

FIGURE 4–8 Reprinted from George Cardona, Henry M. Hoenigswald, and Alfred Senn, "Indo-European and Indo-Europeans," in *Proto-Indo-European Culture* by Marija Gimbutas, University of Pennsylvania Press, Philadelphia, 1970.

FIGURE 4–9 Adapted from A. Meillet and M. Cohen, *Les langues du monde,* 1952, carte XIB.

FIGURE 4–11 Adapted from *Encyclopaedia Britannica,* 15th edition, 1987, 22: 766 and 769.

FIGURE 4–12 Adapted from *Encyclopaedia Britannica,* 15th edition, 1987, 29: 907.

FIGURE 4–15 Adapted from *Children's Games in Street and Playground* by Iona and Peter Opie. © Iona and Peter Opie 1969. Published by Oxford University Press 1969.

FIGURE 4–16 Adapted from Hans Kurath, *A Word Geography of the Eastern United States* (Ann Arbor: University of Michigan Press), 1949, Figure 3.

FIGURE 4–17 Adapted from F. A. Barrett, "The Relative Decline of the French Language in Canada," *Geography* 60 (2), 1975, p. 128, by permission of the Geographical Association.

FIGURE 5–1 Adapted from D. Sopher, *Geography of Religions* (Englewood Cliffs, N.J.: Prentice Hall), 1967.

FIGURE 5–2 From W. Shepherd, *Historical Atlas,* by permission of Barnes & Noble Books.

FIGURE 5–3 Adapted from Jan and Mel Thompson, *The R. E. Atlas: World Religions in Maps and Notes* (London: Edward Arnold), 1986, p. 44; by permission of the publisher.

FIGURE 5–5 Adapted from Douglas W. Johnson, Paul R. Picard, and Bernard Quinn, *Churches and Church Membership in the United States* (Bethesda, MD; Glenmary Research Center), 1971.

FIGURE 5–6, 5–7, 5–8, 5–9, 5–10 From Ismail Ragi al Faruqi and David E. Sopher, *Historical Atlas of the Religions of the World* (New York: Macmillan), 1974.

FIGURE 5–15 Adapted from *Encylopaedia Britannica,* 15th edition (1987), 28: 181.

FIGURE 6–1 Adapted from John F. Rooney, Jr., Wilbur Zelinsky, and Dean R. Louder, eds., *This Remarkable Continent: An Atlas of United States and Canadian Society and Culture* (College Station, TX: Texas A&M University Press), 1982, page 244, figure 11–13, George O. Carney.

FIGURE 6–3 Reproduced by permission from the *Annals* of the Association of American Geographers, Volume 68, 1978, p. 262, figure 11, W. K. Crowley.

FIGURE 6–5 Reproduced by permission from the *Annals* of the Association of American Geographers, Volume 66, 1976, p. 490, figure 2; P. P. Karan and E. C. Mather.

FIGURE 6–6 Reproduced by permission from the *Annals* of the Association of American Geographers, Volume 55, 1965, p. 559, figure 10; F. B. Kniffen.

FIGURE 6–7 Reproduced by permission from the *Annals* of the Association of American Geographers, Volume 55, 1965, p. 560, figure 11; F. B. Kniffen.

FIGURE 6–11 Adapted from John F. Rooney, Jr., and Paul L. Butt, "Beer, Bourbon, and Boone's Farm: A Geographical Examination of Alcoholic Drink in the United States," in *Journal of Popular Culture,* Vol. 11 (1968) 4: 842–48. Reprinted with the permission of the editor.

FIGURE 6–12 Adapted from Barbara A. Shortridge and James R. Shortridge, "Consumption of Fresh Produce in the Metropolitan United States, *Geographical Review,* Vol. 79 (1989) 1: p. 86, Table IV. Used by permission of the American Geographical Society.

FIGURE 6–13 Adapted from John F. Rooney, Jr., "American Golf Courses: A Regional Analysis of Supply," *Sport Place International,* Vol. 3 (1989) 1/2: pp. 6–8, figures 3, 4, and 6.

FIGURE 8–15 Adapted from "Panel on Nationalism in the USSR: Environmental and Territorial Aspects," *Soviet Geography,* Vol. XXX (1989), 6: p. 451, figures 2 and 3.

FIGURE 8–16 Adapted from Paul E. Lydolph, "Recent Population Characteristics and Growth in the USSR," *Soviet Geography,* Vol. XXX (1989), 10: p. 714, figure 4.

FIGURE 9–3 Reproduced by permission from the *Annals* of the Association of American Geographers, Vol. 26, 1936, p. 241, figure 1; D. Whittlesey.

FIGURE 10–2 From Peter A. Gould, "Spatial Diffusion" (Washington, D.C.: Association of American Geographers) Resource Publication in Geography, No. 4, 1969, page 52 (including figure 57). Reprinted by permission.

FIGURE 11–5 From Walter Christaller, *Die Zentralen Orte in Südeutschland* as found in *The Central Places in Southern Germany,* a translation by Carlisle W. Baskin (Englewood Cliffs, N.J.: Prentice-Hall, 1966). Used by permission.

FIGURE 11–7 Adapted from J. Clark Archer and Ellen R. White, "Service Classification of American Cities," *Urban Geography,* Vol 5 (1985): 122–151.

FIGURE 11–13 Adapted from Leonardo Benevolo, *The History of the City* (Cambridge, MA: MIT Press), 1980, figures 31, 33, and 36.

FIGURE 12–1 Adapted from University of Minnesota, Cartography Laboratory, Department of Geography, 1986.

FIGURE 12–15 From Marion Clawson and Peter Hall, *Planning and Urban Growth* (Baltimore: The Johns Hopkins University Press), 1973, p. 131. Published for Resources for the Future, Inc. by the Johns Hopkins University Press.

FIGURE 13–7 From Blair T. Bower and Daniel J. Basta, *Residuals—Environmental Quality Management: Applying the Concept* (Baltimore: The Johns Hopkins University Center for Metropolitan Planning and Research), 1973, p. 3.

FIGURE 13–8 Adapted from William K. Stevens, "Study of Acid Rain Uncovers a Threat to Far Wider Area," *The New York Times,* January 16, 1990, p. 21, map. Copyright © 1980/87/90 by the New York Times Company. Reprinted by permission.

FIGURE 13–11 Adapted from "How Much Time Do We Have?" *Newsweek,* November 27, 1989, p. 68, map.

FIGURE 13–12 Copyright © 1987 by the New York Times Company. Reprinted by permission.

FIGURES A–5, A–6, A–7, A–8, and A–11 Reprinted by permission from *Choosing a World Map* (Falls Church, VA: American Congress on Surveying and Mapping, 1988).

FIGURES A–9 and A–13 Reprinted by permission from Phillip C. Muehrcke, *Map Use: Reading, Analysis and Interpretation,* 2nd ed. (Madison, WI: JP Publications, 1986).

FIGURES A–10 and A–12 Reprinted by permission from *Which Map Is Best?* (Falls Church, VA: American Congress on Surveying and Mapping, 1987).

Photo Credits

All photos copyrighted by the company or individual listed.

P. vii: Maryland Cartographics.

CHAPTER 1 Opener: Banaue rice terrace, Luzon, Philippines; Steve Vidler/Leo de Wys Inc. P. 6: Historical Picture Service. P. 10: Michael Melford/The Image Bank. P. 11: Steve Vidler/Leo de Wys Inc. P. 21: Georg Gerster/Comstock. P. 26: Larry Hamill. P. 31: (l) Tony Stone Worldwide/Barbara Van Cleve; (r) Tony Stone Worldwide/Jim Pickerell. P. 37: Rick Gerharter/Impact Visuals.

CHAPTER 2 Opener: Highland village on market day, Ambositra, Madagascar; Tony Stone Worldwide/Brian Parsley. P. 57: McNeely/Sipa Press. P. 75: Steve McCurry/ Magnum Photos Inc. P. 76: Danny Lehman. P. 80 Betty Crowell.

CHAPTER 3 Opener: Vietnamese boat people; McMillan/Sipa Press. P. 92: Alfred/Sipa Press. P. 100: Michael S. Yamashita. P. 109: Danny Lehman. P. 111: Donna Binder/Impact Visuals. P. 123: Lewis Hime/ Bettmann Archives.

CHAPTER 4 Opener: An American in the Himalayas: Barbara Rowell. P. 143: Laski/Sipa Press. P. 145: Kenneth Rapalee/Root Resources. P. 160: Steve Vidler/ Four by Five. P. 166: Nina Berman/Sipa Press.

CHAPTER 5 Opener: Rainbow over the Potala Palace, Lhasa, Tibet; Galen Rowell. P. 187: Wolfgang Kaehler. P. 192: Tony Stone Worldwide/Jean-Marie Truchet. P. 193: Ric Ergenbright. P. 194: Aral/Sipa. P. 205: Tony Stone Worldwide/Sarah Stone. P. 208: Torregano/Sipa Press.

CHAPTER 6 Opener: Preparing tea, Zansgar, India; W. Hille/Leo de Wys Inc. P. 221: Blair Seitz/Photo Researchers Inc. P. 235: Kuus/Sipa Press. P. 240: Kentucky Fried Chicken. P. 241: Souleye Cisse.

CHAPTER 7 Opener: Earth from space; Richard Gorbun/Leo de Wys Inc. P. 268: Chris Cartter/Impact Visuals. P. 269: John Heaton/After Images. P. 273: Mark Peters/Black Star. P. 277: Laski/Sipa Press. P. 291: J. Witt/Sipa Press.

CHAPTER 8 Opener: School session, South Cotabato, Philippines; Eric L. Wheater/The Image Bank. P. 304: (t) Steve Vidler/Leo de Wys Inc.; (b) Tony Stone Worldwide/Pete Seaward. P. 310: (t) Steve McCurry/ Leo de Wys Inc.; (b) Tony Stone Worldwide/Andrew Sacks. P. 313: (t) Kevin Rose/The Image Bank; (b) Wim Van Cappellen/Impact Visuals. P. 331: (t) Roger Ball/Picturesque; (b) Guido Alberto Rossi/The Image Bank.

CHAPTER 9 Opener: Rice terrace, Bali; Barbara Traub. P. 357: David Hiser Photographers/Aspen. P. 361: Tony Stone Worldwide/Dan Smetzer. P. 362: Michael Yamashita. P. 364: John Deere. P. 365: Craig Hammell/ Stock Market. P. 380: Steve McCurry/Leo de Wys Inc.

CHAPTER 10 Opener: Mazda plant, Hiroshima, Japan; Brian Brake/Photo Researchers Inc. P. 393: Victoria and Albert Museum. P. 402: Betty Crowell. P. 406: Van Bucher/Photo Researchers Inc. P. 411: Jim Pickerell/ Comstock. P. 412: Martha Vega.

CHAPTER 11 Opener: Walls of the old city, St. Paul de Vence, France; Kenneth Rapalee/Root Resources. P. 434: (t) Larry Hamill; (b) Steve Proehl/The Image Bank. P. 445: Nicholas De Vore III, Photographers/ Aspen. P. 453: Amos Schliak/Viesti Associates. P. 454: Netherlands Board of Tourism. P. 459: Nicholas De Vore III, Photographers/Aspen.

CHAPTER 12 Opener: Madison Avenue, New York, N.Y.; David Pollack/The Stock Market. P. 476: Tony Stone Worldwide/Siegfrie Eigstler. P. 478: David R. Frazier/Photo Researchers Inc. P. 482: (t) Leo de Wys/ Leo de Wys Inc.; (b) Larry Hamill. P. 484: PHOTRI/ ORION. P. 497: (l) J. C. Lozovet/The Image Bank; (r) Tony Stone Worldwide/Sue Cunningham.

CHAPTER 13 Opener: Manhattan skyline; Danilo Boschung/Leo de Wys Inc. P. 512: Bernard Gerard/ Viesti Assoc. P. 521: George Glod/Four by Five. P. 527: (t) Paul Fusco/Magnum Photos, Inc.; (b) Richard Sambrook. P. 532: Townsend P. Dickinson/Comstock. P. 534: Michael Yamashita. P. 537: Georg Gerster/ Comstock. P. 543: Chris Rainier, Photographers/Aspen.

Selected Map Index

Index

571